924 GILMAN

THE STORY SO FAR...

COMPILED, EDITED, & DESIGNED BY BRIAN EDGE

iv

INSPIRATION BY: 924 GILMAN, POB 1058, BERKELEY, CA 94701
SHOWINFO: (510) 525-9926, BOOKING: (510) 524-8180
www.924gilman.org

PUBLISHED BY: MAXIMUMROCKNROLL, POB 460760, SAN FRANCISCO, CA 94146
www.maximumrocknroll.com

PRINTED BY: 1984PRINTING, 674 23RD ST., OAKLAND, CA 94612, (510) 435-8338
www.1984printing.com

DISTRIBUTED BY: AK PRESS, 674-A 23RD ST., OAKLAND, CA 94612, (510) 208-1700
www.akpress.org

PREPRESS BY: H & H IMAGING, SAN FRANCISCO, CA
www.hhimaging.com

PHOTOS THIS PAGE AND PREVIOUS BY LAUREN L.
PHOTO ON PAGE VI BY AYUMI N.
FRONT COVER PHOTO BY EMILIE V.
BACK COVER PHOTO BY KAROLINE C.

2004 MAXIMUM ROCKNROLL

CONTENTS

Aaron Cometbus
Adrienne D.
Athena K.
Ben De La T.
Ben Ditch
Ben S.
Branwyn B.
Brian Edge
Cammie T.
Celia S.
Charles L.
Chloe
Chris A.
Chris S.
Chris D. & Lydia P.
Chris H.
Clayton M.
Dan W.
Dave EC
Dave Scattered
Dean D.
Devon M.
Eggplant
Emilie V.
Ernst
Fraggle
George S. (via Susan S.)
Hawk
Jake Kelly
Jake Filth
Jane G.
Janelle Hessig
Jemuel Gardner
Jerme S.
Jesse Townley
Jessica S.
Jim Widess
Joe G.
John H.
Jonathan D.
Josh Levine
Julie R.
Kamala P.
Katja G.
Ken S.
Kerith Pickett
Larry W.
Lauren L.
Leigh Vega
Marcus P.
Marcus Da Anarchist
Marshall S.
Martin Sprouse
Matt F.
Megan March
Michael D.
Mike Goodbar
Mike K.
Mike Stand
Mike H.
Murray B.
Orlando X.
Pat Wright
Rachel Siebert
Rebecca W.
Richard
Robyn M.
Russell
Sammy G.
Sean M.
Sita R.
Steve List
Steve S.
Susan S.
Tim Yohannan (via Hawk)
Tyler Hutton
Vivian S.
Zarah

CONTRIBUTORS

INTRODUCTION: BRIAN W. aka BRIAN EDGE

Gilman changes people's lives. It gives them inspiration; it gives them hope. It's what holds some people together when life is tearing them apart. It shows them that there are things in the world to care about, to take responsibility for. It instills in them the sense that some things do matter, and perhaps most importantly, that they themselves matter, especially those who've been told they would never amount to anything. How does Gilman do this? Simply by providing an opportunity that people can run with, or not, as they choose to. It is, after all, only a building. But it's the people that take advantage of this opportunity that have made Gilman special, magical. These people are what this book is about.

Not everyone was in favor of doing a book. These stickers appeared around Gilman during one of the book attempts.

I started putting this material together two other times (mid-late '90s) before this attempt. Both times, I was to be the editor/compiler for "someone else's" book. Both times, it didn't feel completely right and didn't go very far. In voicing this frustration to a friend, the response was simply, "why not do it yourself?" So here it is. This final version was given approval at a Gilman membership meeting in April 1999. Each succeeding year I'd do a few more interviews, coax a few more written pieces out of folks, collect a few more photos, etc. At first I was afraid that I wouldn't be able to get exactly what I wanted from people, which was to show just how much Gilman meant to them. My fears were quickly extinguished, though, as piece after piece captured everything I wanted and more. The heartfelt responses I received made it easier (somewhat) to be patient. What started out as a one-year project became two, then three, four, and finally, five. But I purposely set no hard deadline because I wanted it to be as thorough as I could make it. And if that meant waiting on a key person or two, then so be it. I figured I'd only realistically be able to do this once.

Putting this together has also allowed me to stay in touch with (and be reinspired by) a community that has meant so much to me, and has been the biggest part of my life, for the last twenty-six years. A community that's creative, constructive, and caring. Yes it's punk rock, but it's the side of punk that most people don't know about or hear about in the media. It's where people are putting things together instead of tearing them apart, and helping others out instead of curs-

Brian Wehmeyer
General Partner
Blacklist Mailorder
475 Valencia St
San Fran., CA 94103

To Whom It May Concern,

Since its inception in Jan. 1987, the Gilman Street Project has been a major asset to the disaffected young people both in the immediate area and worldwide. Media coverage of its policies and successes has inspired others to attempt similar projects of their own, contributing greatly to constructive, positive methods of dealing with their differences with society rather than in destructive, negative ways. This can only benefit everyone, as we all have seen the disasters that result from taking away all of a person's options to try and improve the world around them.

The Gilman Street Project is unique in that it tries very hard to provide a pleasant, safe atmosphere for people with common beliefs/values to gather and meet. The all-volunteer staff actually care about the patrons and artists alike, the all-consuming money aspect that adversely affects so many other similar endeavors is not a factor here. Also, the opportunities the Gilman Street Project provides for young people to obtain valuable skills that will help them later on in life can't be found elsewhere. Where else would a teenager be allowed to run a sound system, book bands to play, or be in charge of a whole show? The confidence and experience this gives in dealing with others and being responsible cannot be measured. To attempt to take away this important outlet because of a few easily rectified complaints would be an irreparable loss. The benefits the Gilman Street Project provides far outweigh the occasional difficulties it causes.

Having been deeply involved in the first two years of its construction and operation I strongly believe in the ideas behind the Gilman Street Project and have witnessed first hand the sincerity of those currently involved to continue with those ideas.

Sincerely,
Brian Wehmeyer

Support letter I wrote during the first attempt by the city to shut Gilman down (1991/1992)

ing them out. It's ordinary people doing extraordinary things, for no fanfare or fame, no praise, no recognition. Why, then? To share in, and be a part of, those magical moments, to feel like you belong, to matter, to make a difference. I've found that it's all too easy to drift away from a culture/community if you're no longer directly involved, and, after the extinction of the last project I worked on prior to this, I found myself way out on the edges, about to lose touch completely. That still might happen down the road, but at least now it'll be on a positive note rather than a negative one. Reading the pieces in this book has removed the cynicism and disappointment I felt after we gave up and pulled out of Gilman in Sept. 1988. It's now obvious to me that it was worth it, that the people who have come along, kicked ass, sacrificed, and perservered, are exactly the kind of people the place was built for. It's the people in this book that make me proud of our community. I wanted to do this book as a way of saying thanks to these people, to give them a memento that they could show others and say, "This is what I've done to help make the world a better place."

Hey- does anybody know what ontological dualism is? Me either. I do know how it feels when somebody treats me like shit for no reason though. I've been reading this newspaper called Anarchy lately. Most of the paper is about rationally discussing "the unshackling of desire and it's relation to ontological dualism, that is, dialectically speaking, of course." But then the same newspaper spends alot of space belittling people who believe in religion, spirituality, ecology, or anything else that doesn't coincide with the "mainstream anarchist anti-ideology."

So, why am I wasting time and space in Absolutely Zippo, right? Because Zippo has real words in it, like shit and happy and even helluv. Why should you need a dictionary to dissect what you know you feel? And at the risk of getting unbearably sappy- regarding "the unshackling of desire", I don't think it has anything to do with rationality. It's learning how to play "Louie, Louie" on the bass, or an (enter rad band's name) show, or a helluv intense discussion with somebody you'd never imagined talking to before. And I suppose the reason I'm doing this in Zippo is because I don't feel like I need a PhD to write in here. Or a rationale for feeling how I feel at any given time. Many of the people who will read this are those who make me glad to exist and relieved to know I'm not alone all the time.

Ugh- well I truly have rambled myself into some confused corner, now haven't I? Well, maybe I was trying to make a point somewhere in here. Probably not. I guess what it comes down to is changing things. Changing this world, dirty air water, changing people's minds who are out to hurt you. Changing my attitude. It doesn't help if you start off belittling people. Especially people who are trying. People who care. Pointing out to me where my ideology is politically incorrect doesn't really make me want to listen, telling me you care about something in this world, does. Changing this world is not about correct terminology, proper grammar, or putting people down. Smiling at somebody and asking how they are if they look a little lost, that's a beginning. —ONE OF THE P.P.—

A piece that Becca wrote for the Bay Area fanzine *Absolutely Zippo*. I think it captures where a lot of people at Gilman are coming from.

At how many other clubs would security take the time to sit with a messed-up patron and try to take care of him?

Both photos by Larry W.

I also really wanted to give something back to the community at large. Finding other people who shared my dissatisfaction with bland, sterile music contrived by office executives after a marketing survey determines that it'll sell, my disenchantment with the blind trust in the media, government, and schools, and my disconnection with the insecure, misguided hyperpatriotism of the masses, was what allowed me to keep my sanity. I wasn't alone—I had friendship, a sense of belonging/fitting in somewhere, and incredibly powerful music and lyrics that still affect me like nothing else I've heard.

> *"Music is an indirect force for change, because it provides an anchor against human tragedy. In this sense, it works towards a reconciled world. It can also be the direct experience of change. At certain points during some shows, the reconciled world is already here, at least in that second, at that place. Operation Ivy was very lucky to have experienced this. Those seconds reveal that the momentum that drives a subculture is more important than any particular band. The momentum is made of all the people who stay interested, and keep their sense of urgency and hope."*
> *— Jesse M., Operation Ivy*

Because I couldn't coax everyone to write something on their own (which I would have preferred), I had to do interviews (about half the pieces ended up being interviews). I didn't include the questions from the interviews, I just structured the responses into an essay form as best I could. If some of the pieces are choppy, then it was probably an interview. Then again... Also, some people that were asked chose not to contribute to this book (David H., Radley H., George S., Nando, Tall Tim, to name a few), but the work, sweat, blood, and sometimes money, they put in hasn't been forgotten or overlooked. Neither has the multitude of people who have worked there that I wasn't able to find and/or wasn't able to ask. Respect and thanks to all of you.

One thing I really wanted to avoid was painting a picture of Gilman as Disneyland—one step through the doors and your life is instantly better. Sorry, it doesn't work that way. The people who got the most out of the place put an awful lot in, too. I would have liked to have had more pieces that were critical of Gilman, but very few people chose that route. The only editing I did with the pieces that people wrote themselves was to use initials instead of whole last names (for privacy reasons), and to remove specific names of people/bands being slagged (I didn't want the book to turn into a slagfest). For the inteviews, I tried to just keep the parts that I thought were interesting, good reading. Everyone I did an interview with was sent a copy to change as they saw fit. Very few people responded with any changes. My initial goal was to have 100 pieces. I ended up with 78. I'm mostly satisfied that this is a pretty fair representation of the first 17 years of Gilman. 17 years of Friday/Saturday night shows every week (and a fair amount of Sunday shows), with only two periods of closure: for about a month and a half in late 1988 after the *Maximum RocknRoll* group pulled out and before the new group was ready, and for about a month in early 1995 for earthquake retrofitting. Also, only two shows have been shut down by police (that I've been able to find out about): once in Oct. 1989 and once in March in the late nineties, 1997, I believe. And the shows are still only $5.

The impact of Gilman on the Bay Area community in general has also been quite substantial, as evidenced not only by the thousands of signatures on petitions and the many letters of support by patrons, parents, and local businesses gathered during various crises (police/zoning board, brewpub, DiCon), but also by the financial assistance rendered to numerous organizations and individuals in need through benefit shows, and of course, by being a place for tens of thousands of people to go and get away from the rest of the world for a while.

> *"That's a big problem when people try to form these alliances with political groups from within punk. It's really hard to have a common goal. There are, however, exceptions that I'm really proud of, such as Gilman Street. It has worthy and yet modest goals. They're not trying to change the world, but rather just change the world for themselves. To have a place to play; to have a place to meet; to provide a space for their own community. I think those are really good objectives, despite how difficult it is to form and run co-ops."*
> *— Penelope Houston, Avengers/solo artist, Punk Planet interview, May 1999*

> *"A lot of the ideas Tim Y. and others experimented with here did challenge the general inertia of the audience with rather limited success. It is hard to implement change from the top down. However, a lot of our consumerist capitalism is justified by the idea that 'we' are just giving the public what they want. Through advertising, and other means, from an early age our mostly young public out there has been programmed to want things that do not truly fulfill, but leave them with an alienated sense of emptiness, that they have been sold a bill of goods shall we say. The ones more happy with that bill of goods probably wouldn't come near a place like Gilman St. All in all, the kids that come to Gilman St. are a discontent lot, particularly with the status quo. The word 'educate' originally meant to draw what is inside out. As a former teacher, I think Gilman St. can educate but not indoctrinate. It can help open eyes that have been blinded by programmed bullshit, but we can't control what those eyes will then see. In each person there is a star, a spark of genius, that all too few let out. I think Gilman St.'s most important work is to help at least some of those that come to realize their own stardom, whether on stage or off. All too often we see this syndrome of 'you're on the stage so entertain me' type of passivity. Too many clubs are content with this. We've always sought to be different. If we give up this differ- ence, as I feel we have come close to doing, then in my opinion we might as well close the club. The dream that started Gilman St., and distinguished it from other clubs, would then be dead."*
> *— excerpt from Michael D.'s open letter to Gilman membership 1990/1991*

Almost everyone comes here initially because of the music, but the ones who work the hardest and longest are the ones who find that "rockin' out" just isn't enough—there has to be more. Gilman becomes a part of you, provides options on how to live your life, and shows that it doesn't have to be a competitive world, it can be a cooperative one. As Chris S. said in his interview, "It was set up for the patrons and bands, but it mattered most to the workers."

Photos by Larry W.

DEDICATIONS

Tim Yohannan (the Dad), without whom Gilman never would have existed.

Jim Widess (the Patron Saint), without whom Gilman wouldn't have existed very long.

Everyone who's ever worked there (the Kids), without whom Gilman would be just another club.

Respect   photos by Susan S.

THANKS

Pat W., Susan S., Murray B., Larry W., Lauren L., Jesse T., Cammie T., Branwyn B., Eggplant, Emilie V., and Paul C., for letting me go through all their Gilman stuff that they've collected over the years, especially Pat and Jesse, who have been involved there the longest, and who really helped me out with information. Sita R. for help with photo editing. Steve List for the "Gilman Show List." Gilman for allowing me to do this book "officially." MRR for publishing it. And you, if you ever worked there or went to a show there.

NOTES

First print run, May/June 2004: 5,000 copies, on 100 lb. Utopia dull paper, 12 pt. coated cover. Printing costs: $6.60 per book. Printed by 1984Printing, an independent printer offering small-run, sheet-fed offset printing. All archive material collected donated to Gilman. All profits from the sales of this book split equally between MRR and Gilman. Retail outlets take 40% of the cover price, distributor takes 20% of the cover price, so we're clearing $.60 per book sold through our primary distributor. Primary distributor: AK Press (akpress.org), a workers' co-operative that publishes and distributes titles published by independent presses. Visit MRR's website at www.maximumrocknroll.com, for contact, distribution (non-store), and mailorder info for both this book and their monthly magazine covering the DIY punk scene around the world.

CHAPTER ONE

THE BEGINNING

TIM Y. / MRR

1986-1988

"...MOMENTARILY ERADICATING THE LAWS OF COOL".

-STEVE S.

Bathrooms, 1986   photo by Murray B.

Tim Yohannan - (INTERVIEWED BY HAWK, APRIL 1996)

At one point, there was an attempt by a group of us to get an all ages club open in Berkeley. This was a number of years before we went into Gilman. We had gotten a number of people together, and Bill Graham had said he would help fund the thing. He had come on our (MRR) radio show, and we had criticized him for being at all involved with the punk scene. He had said that he wasn't out to exploit the punk scene, and to prove it, he said that he would put up the money if we would find a place, get the people to run it, do all the legwork. So we did all of that and then he said "fuck you." It was just a typical publicity stunt for him. But that was many years before Gilman, that wasn't the start of Gilman.

So what's so radical about punk/hardcore, what sets it apart from other music forms? "Well, the lyrics are radical" say some, but hell, lots of musical forms are just as lyrically rad. "It's the super fast music" say others, but even that's become generic and predictable.

It's not uncommon to hear punks speculating about what the "next" phase will be, an understandable undertaking, but when wondering about what might make punk vital again, I think most people are looking in the wrong direction.

It seems that most hardcore and speedmetal bands are having a very predictable affect on their audiences these days, eliciting very similar responses (moshing, circles, pit action, and often stupid violence), and most bands seem willing to leave it at that. It doesn't matter how well-intentioned the band is as individuals, how sharp their lyrics are--as long as they play at a certain speed or with a certain level of power, they will be unable to evoke anything resembling an intelligent response, will not be able to spur imagination or creative juices, will not inspire the crowd to constructiveness. It is here, in the performance, that most all punk/hardcore bands have proven themselves to be.....very traditional and boring.

From my point of view, bands have a responsibility in what reactions they bring on. If the velocity of the music puts people in rages that cause violence, or if their music deadens senses, bands (especially supposed hardcore bands that say they "care") need to think about how they can deal with that. Sure, they're intent on playing well, and can't really see beyond the second row of heads to know what's really going on--how can they possibly have the presence of mind and energy to deal with all the bullshit that erupts, from general violence to the now-normal state of idiocy and passive consumerism on the audience's part.

Well, I think that's a cop out. If punk bands are truly "alternative", they would put as much effort into their responsibility as into learning to play well or writing good lyrics or saying all the right things in interviews. Maybe, if they gave a shit, punk bands could add a member or two to the band whose sole purpose would be to determine what was happening and then construct approaches for dealing with that--sort of directors of the performance, someone who has some theatrical abilities, a spotter for the band, but a bone fide member nonetheless. Bands write about violence, apathy, idiocy, etc., all the time, but lyrics are one-dimensional, and what better way to really bring home the point but to use the audience as the living laboratory that exemplify those lyrics.

Punk was once a satirical mirror of society, but today those mainstream values have permeated punk. The metal or rock attitude has influenced both lyrics, music and attitudes. And the business aspect of rock has invaded the "alternative" scene as well. We are now the same as mainstream society.

So, bands that really feel they are "punk", really "alternative", should take advantage of their opportunity now, use their audience as a way to make points, a way to educate, a way to make shows lively and fun, and a way to add a whole new meaning to punk.

Can you imagine shows where some band members walked into the audience and played, or where these new proposed band members were as accepted a part of the groups as are drummers, where spontaneity and dealing with trouble or the crowd's sheep-like mentality were as common as metal guitar solos? Can you envision clubs where promoters actually encouraged bands to create an intelligent or artistic confrontation with "normal" values, or can you picture bands who decided that maybe less time spent on learning to be tight/hot shot musicians might leave more time to be more creative, communicative, and interesting performers?

Obviously, this is too much of a responsibility for bands alone. But at our warehouse project, this is something we're going to encourage in bands, a new dimension that can be added to shows to really make them "punk" and radical. At a time when more and more hardcore bands might as well be playing at arena shows, I'd like to see a return to the roots, an addition of creativity on the communication scale, a simpler form of punk and a more challenging aspect of performance--democratization again, with less solos, egos and posing, and more attention to values, eye-opening concepts, awakening the audience and themselves.

When I leave a show, I want my brain and imagination to be as exercised as my body. THAT would be really radical. Lyrics and good intentions aren't enough. It's time for a whole new front, a humorous, biting, multi-dimensional and imaginative way to confront our society--right there at the show. If gigs are boring and staid, redefine them and it'll rejuvenate punk. It's the dimension we've all been wanting--not a whole new form of music, but a whole new way of delivering it.

Tim's MRR column, Dec. 1986

But then, sometime during 1985, I decided to get serious about putting a club together, and started looking for a location. Then I ran into this lunatic named Victor Hayden, who had a similar idea as well, so we were both looking. He was the one who actually found the space at 924 Gilman. I was hesitant, but everyone who looked at it thought it was great, and said "we gotta do it." So, we did it. We talked to the landlord, got the lease, that was April 1986. Then we started trying to pull together the people who could make things happen.

We put up flyers, talked about it on the MRR radio show, and ran ads in MRR magazine. We started having meetings there and put a plan together about what we wanted to do. We were completely oblivious about what we were about to go through, however, which was eight months of paying rent on the place before we could even open, and investing over $40,000 in the place for rent, construction, etc., also before we could open. Also, there was a huge amount of red tape, hearings with the city, inspections by health, fire, police, etc. I had done a lot of precinct organizing for Berkeley Citizen's Action

Group, and they were in power at the time in Berkeley, so I called on friends who were now on different boards with the city, and asked them to help by voting for the existence of this place. Overall, the city was pretty supportive. The mayor at the time, Gus Newport, was totally supportive. Part of us getting the permit for the place was "politicking" the neighborhood, both business and residential, convincing them that we were "okay" and wouldn't ruin the neighborhood. Wonder what they think now!

Early meetings, 1986   photos by Murray B.

The most amazing part was the landlord, who I thought was a bit of a "Nervous Nellie," and I thought that there was no way that this would work out. We were honest about what we were doing, but we knew he had no idea what he was getting into. I was amazed he never had a heart attack about the way the place ended up looking and what went on there. I guess he just got used to it! But he's been totally great all along, completely supportive. Lots of people helped us. We didn't know shit about construction, and people were coming out of the woodwork, just showing up and helping, people who had the skills we needed, carpenters, plumbers, electricians. We had to change the plumbing, build new bathrooms, etc., and pass the inspections. So we learned in a hurry. We got our final approval from the city the afternoon of our first show, which was New Year's Eve, Dec. 1986.

One of our first policies was that we weren't going to announce who was playing. I loved that policy. All we would announce is that an event would happen at the space on Friday and Saturday nights. We wanted people to support the space rather than just a particular band. The membership policy was instituted primarily as a way to try and control the violence that was happening at shows at the time. And it also turned out that the additional revenue generated by the membership fees made the difference between survival and not. Originally it was a lifetime membership. But it was a short lifetime! We had it where Friday nights were experimental/alternative shows, and Saturday nights were the hardcore shows. We usually had Sunday "matinee" shows as well. We really wanted to get away from the predictability that punk shows had acquired. We had the "mind fuck" committee, who tried to mess with people's heads at shows. We had an open mic policy, where we'd leave the mic on after each band played and anyone could get up on stage and rant, call bands on their lyrical content or attitude, etc. Very few people utilized this, unfor-

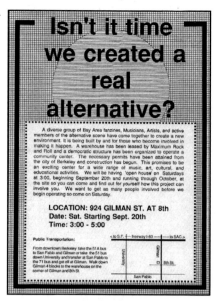

Isn't it time we created a real alternative?

A diverse group of Bay Area fanzines, Musicians, Artists, and active members of the alternative scene have come together to create a new environment. It is being built by and for those who become involved in making it happen. A warehouse has been leased by Maximum Rock and Roll and a democratic structure has been organized to operate a community center. The necessary permits have been attained from the city of Berkeley and construction has begun. This promises to be an exciting center for a wide range of music, art, cultural, and educational activities. We will be having 'open house' on Saturdays at 3:00, beginning September 20th and running through October, at the site so you can come and find out for yourself how this project can involve you. We want to get as many people involved before we begin operating so come on Saturday.

LOCATION: 924 GILMAN ST. AT 8th
Date: Sat. Starting Sept. 20th
Time: 3:00 - 5:00

Public Transportation:

From downtown Berkeley take the 51A bus to San Pablo and Gilman or take the 51 bus down University and transfer at San Pablo to the 71 bus and get off at Gilman. Walk down Gilman 4 blocks to the warehouse on the corner of Gilman and 8th St.

tunately. A couple of times I remember the show being stopped and us having a meeting with everyone, right then and there to deal with some shit that was going on. To me, that was what a punk club, and shows, should be about. We were trying a lot of different and/or new concepts. We had bands help work the shows in order to play there. The whole point of the place was to try and create, or further, an alliance between participants and bands to run the place together. Ultimately, most of these concepts didn't work out. If we didn't announce who was playing, people didn't come. Bands didn't want to work, and did so only grudging-ly. The "mind fuck" committee didn't really work. The open mic didn't really work. We had some potlucks, some benefits, some self-defense classes. We would drop the prices as the show went on, but I thought it should be the opposite, the prices should start low and go up!

I remember one show where Stikky brought milk and cookies for everyone, to prove that they were more straight edge than the straight edgers. Another time they played bingo or something like that with the crowd. There was a Ramones "cover night" where all the bands just did Ramones songs. I remember Isocracy ver-sus The Naked Lady Wrestlers. The stage was decked out like a boxing ring. First one band would play one song and then the other band would play a song, and then an "applause meter" would indicate who won each "round." Of course the bands

would hurl much "abuse" at one another as well. Isocracy would always bring tons of junk, and try to fill Gilman with it, it was like a carnival. We had giveaway nights, where we'd give away a bike, or bike parts. We had a show where, if you brought a Big Wheel, you got in free. I wanted to have everyone in the pit on Big Wheels, kinda like bumper cars, instead of beating the shit out of each other. I remember an attempted robbery, where some local street person (not a punk) grabbed the cash box during a show and tried to make a run for it. He didn't get very far before he was tackled. The cash box and all the money went flying. People were picking it up and giving it back. Soon after that we got a cash box that bolt-ed to the table!

Big guys on tiny bikes, 1987
photo by Murray B.

At first we tried doing our own security, but that took too much out of us, dealing with the same drunken assholes every show. Then we hired an off-duty Berkeley cop (maybe a reserve cop) to do security. And that actually worked pretty good because he was in police uniform, and the assholes would see that guy out front and split. But he ended up not being able to do it anymore, so we hired a uniformed security guard from a company. And that worked out reasonably well too. The police were, for the most part, supportive. They didn't harass us, they basically just dealt with what we asked them to. Eventually we went back to doing our own security.

And eventually I burned out. I felt like the place had not lived up to its potential. There were certain amazingly high moments, but overall it wasn't doing what I thought it could. People's brains should be "on" when they leave a show, not "off." But that rarely happened. So we decided to pull out and shut it down. My feeling was, this scene didn't deserve a place this cool, and if people weren't really going to make it "theirs," and they're just going to act like consumers, then I didn't want to be killing myself for that. Financially, the first year it lost money, and the second year it did a little better than break even. The finances were all run through MRR, we were the leaseholder. So it was shut for a month or two, and then some of the folks that were there with us, along with some new folks, felt that they wanted to reopen it and give it a try, so they did. The landlord said okay, so we passed the lease on to them, gave them the sound system, and gave them money as well, matching the money they had raised to help reopen. We called it the Gilman Street Project, they renamed it the Alternative Music Foundation. I don't think anybody ever thought of

Since I started going off in last month's column, I might as well continue. Being involved with the running of the warehouse has added a whole new set of insights, many of which are not that pleasant, but the exceptions are pretty wonderful.

Bands: So few bands support each other it's sad. When younger bands play, they do so in half empty houses. How many bands show up and pay to see other lesser-knowns? There could be such a good scene if the hundreds of local bands attended each other's shows, offering encouragement and advice. One notable exception is Isocracy, who go to just about every gig at the warehouse, pay to get in, and really support all the bands. Not only that, when they play, they really make it a memorable experience.

Older Scenesters: A lot of people really urged us to finance and help organize the Gilman St. Project, the idea being that we'd help get it off the ground, and others would essentially run the place. In reality, most of them have faded away, their reasons varying from "We don't like some of the decisions voted on" or "It isn't exactly what we envisioned", etc. Hell, it isn't exactly what I envisioned either, but it's a starting place. These are excuses, not reasons. The bottom line

is that few people are really willing to roll up their sleeves and dedicate themselves to the hard work entailed in building something. Sure, many peopole have their own projects (bands, zines, relationships, etc), but so do those of us working hard on this. Dealing with the democratic structure is cumbersome and trying, but if people can't struggle to make that work, can't adjust to the give and take of compromise, then how are they going to deal with changing anything in society? Laziness too takes its toll, the "Well if I don't do it, I know someone else will." Lame. There are many positive exceptions to this mentality though, like Aaron Cometbus, Tom and Nicole, Darren, Delores, Lisa, Seth, George, Katja, Brian, Cammie, Orin, etc., fully dedicated people.

Excerpt from Tim's MRR column May '87

One of Tim's favorite bands, The Rolling Scabs   photo by Murray B.

Tim's classic grin, circa 1987   photo by Murray B.

it as that, it's always just been Gilman.

I'm glad it's lasted this long and I'm glad that someplace like this exists. I think we ended up alienating a lot of people, the second group was much more lax, which had its good and bad points. For us though, what people should understand, is that if you give birth to the thing, your attitude is gonna be different. We were so protective of the space, having seen it go from an idea to a reality, and then to have assholes come in and try to fuck it up. I was really harsh on people. We were killing ourselves trying to make the space work, and had no patience for fuckheads.

Gilman's first graffiti!
photographer unknown

Caught drinking
photographer unknown

Now, on to something that's coming a bit more into focus: an update on the Gilman St. Project. First, finances: This July, the warehouse broke even for the first time, a welcome statistic. I think it's mainly due to all the bands on the road as well as kids being able to hang out more. For those months where we don't make ends meet (costs run about $2500 a month), MRR picks up the tab.

Several months ago we began doing flyers, after 3 months of just word-of-mouth advertising. This has helped to some small degree, and was a compromise that the majority of the members wanted. Speaking of members, the whole membership idea has worked pretty well. People regularly volunteer for all the chores, though we wish more would get directly involved, if only to help clean up after shows. But, largely because of the membership concept, we have been able to maintain the type of environment that we want: one that's non-violent, largely fun-loving, but also serious when necessary. There has yet to be a real fight inside, and we've even been able to collectively set the tone for making intimidation itself seem absurd. This has been done non-violently and word has gotten around that people who come to shows looking to hurt, bother or intimidate others aren't welcome.

Bands who've passed through almost always mention that Gilman was one of their few bright spots, that the atmosphere was an inspiration to them, and they wish there was a similar club in their city. So do we, and we hope that visitors will spread the word that it is possible for punks to create a place of their own and maintain the environment they want. That is an important victory.

We've had our share of controversies and dissent, too. Recently, The Feederz played, and Frank Discussion brought in a dead dog and cat and threw them on stage. The fur was flying, and many people that night were outraged, some even going to the press, SPCA, etc. We held many meetings to discuss the issues raised: animal rights, the role of art, health issues, etc. The process was democratic, and despite the wide range of reactions to the Feederz, people dealt with it all intelligently and diligently. For me, this too was a great victory, that punk can still incite argument, ferment, discussion, and that reality and music can meet.

All in all, the project is much more heartening than I had expected by this point, spawning lots of local bands and a regional feeling of solidarity amongst many people who care. The drinkers sometimes hang out nearby and bring down heat on us, but the police have been very cooperative, and I think we've been able to convince most of the problem causers to leave the area.

There are still many aspects that need more development, especially in the realm of intellectual stimulation, but hopefully people will begin to do some planning there too. We have had some plays, a few exhibitions, movies, etc, but a lot more of these kinds of events need to be regularly integrated into the schedule. A surprisingly big hit was the installation of a basketball hoop, causing a vegan-vegetarian-smoker-carnivore-druggie tournament on the 4th of July. Everyone seems to shoot a few hoops at one point or another throughout shows, a sort of zen/spastic therapy.

While the punk scenes in many areas seem under assault by greedy promoters and parasitic violent assholes, at least there is one place where punks are truly "uniting" to reclaim their scene. I'm sure there are a few other good examples here in the States, but I hope that the message we're sending out gets received and implemented everywhere else. At a time when attendance is down at shows, violence and racism is up, and record sales decline across the board, it's important to begin the rebuilding process. Fight back!

Excerpt from Tim's column, Oct. '87

'Bout time for a Gilman update. It's been an interesting few months recently, and we're now celebrating being open 1 year. This year has taken an incredible amount of energy, but it's largely been rewarding. We've been able to get the place on solid financial footing (have done

break-even or better for the last 7 months), and have been able to prove that a truly alternative, non-violent self-run club can exist here in the heart of capitalist America. But, as with most idealistic experiments, things do degenerate. There is always the tendency to take something for granted after a period of time, to assume it will always be there. When that happens, people get lazy. They start making other assumptions as well—and soon decision-making and implementation of policy gets left to fewer and fewer, which evolves into a bureaucracy, an elitist clique.

I recently saw this happening on some subtle levels at Gilman—it wasn't that people stopped caring or stopped volunteering, but because they knew that if they didn't show up or take a particular action then someone else would, they relieved themselves of some aspect of responsibility. With that in mind, and with my own growing personal exhaustion, I warned folks that unless the situation changed and people were willing to rethink their commitment and put aside the time and energy to shake things up, I would be withdrawing from the project as I sensed imminent burnout. The unfair part of that statement was that because the venture is in MRR's name, I would have to withdraw our wholehearted legal and financial support. I was hoping that most people wouldn't take this as a threat, but as a challenge to further implement the community control ideas at the heart of the project. There was a lot of discussion among individuals and at the next monthly meeting, about 150 people showed up and took part in a discussion of how to get the place more democratized. It was decided to set up a large training session for those interested in learning how to run the shows from A to Z, and over the next month those people will be creating their own schedules for work. With everybody shouldering a little more, it will lessen the weight from the 10 or so people who've been at it the most (Many, many people volunteer at shows, but it's a bit different to really coordinate the proceedings).

Personally, this will give me more time to work on special shows. Recently, we had a celebration of women in music (lately, there's been a resurgence of women in punk bands in the Bay Area), one of the most wonderful nights we've ever had. There was a free food spread (prepared by a friend of Frightwig, who were awesome that evening). The Yeastie Girlz put on a show that amazed everyone (and which is available on their tape—educational and fun as hell!). Phantom Creeps and Vomit Launch were impressive, and people really had traumatic experiences walking through the doorway that had been built into a giant vagina. Another special event is the Jan 1 "Battle of the Big Mouths", Naked Lady Wrestlers vs Isocracy. We've built the stage into a boxing ring, with each band taking turns playing a song and with a live mike for the band offstage to belittle the one onstage. We have scoring cards for all everybody entering to decide who wins what rounds, with Walter being the ref. It's these kinds of events, plus the integration of movies, speakers, etc, into shows that I want to concentrate on.

On the security front, it seems that every time a group of skins showed up at Gilman, we had lots of damage to the bathrooms and a lot less enjoyable show due to macho behavior on the dance floor. Some skins arrived a couple of nights to just harass and beat up people outside, so we decided to make the law work for us instead of against us. We approached the Berkeley Police Reserves who normally send police to special events at $11 an hour. But when they heard that none of us get paid, they volunteered their time for free to do outside security. After a few confrontations, the skins in question no longer found it in their interest to come all the way over to Gilman to get "welcomed" by the police. We do let in individual skins who've shown that they are into the whole idea of Gilman and can respect others, but those who display contempt (skins or otherwise, we feel under no obligation to allow entry to people looking to abuse others) will have to find some other locale for their kicks. Some anarchists initially raised their eyebrows about utilizing the police, but I feel that if the cops are willing to work with us, can distinguish between those people who are cool and those who are thugs, then we should request their services. We pay taxes and are doing nothing illegal. And 98% of the time, the police have been extremely cooperative, have not cast any kind of attitude towards us, and just help out with the situation. I'm sure this is a rarity, as Berkeley is still a strange place.

All in all, Gilman is doing well, and I hope to see it really begin to hit new levels of creativity next year. And I'd like to congratulate all the people who've worked at making it happen, both individuals and bands. Many of the bands refuse to take money and kick it back to the club, which is amazing. One word to bands though: we seem to be booking local bands (of which there are hundreds!) 2-3 months in advance, so—when you get your show, please try to do something extra unusual, thought-provoking or creative—make it memorable.

Tim's MRR column, Feb. 1988

Dear Gilmoids,

Too much of the work and responsibility here at Gilman is falling on too few shoulders. Yes, there are a regular amount of people who volunteer for various tasks, but they can show up or not as they please, and ultimately the main burdens are falling on about 10 of us, myself mainly.

This is a very unhealthy situation, one which I won't allow to continue much longer since it will only get worse. Too many experiments start out idealistic and gradually evolve into another bureaucracy, a leadership of just a few. It's all too easy for people to let that happen, and most so-called "leaders" thrive on that situation, but I won't. There are too many signs of this decay—not just the lack of people willing to take true responsibility for the decision-making—and the time and energy to implement those decisions. How can it be that a week or two after our most dangerous crisis with security, almost none of the "regulars" show up on a Saturday night to deal with the potential problem? Yes, everyone had a reason, but again the burden fell on a few—that's scary, as well as bullshit. Another sign of taking it all for granted is that many of the "regulars" hang outside during the opening bands nowadays, not bothering to check out/support the new groups. Too cool, or too secure?

What I'm trying to get at is that unless there is a qualitative change of direction being made clear to me, a strong indication that many of the people who come here frequently are organizing to alter this situation and come forward with new plans for the operation of the club, there will be no club after January 1. It's too easy to assume this will go on as is, believing in the back of your mind that Tim, Brian, David, Paul, Jane, Martin, Radley, etc will take care of it all if you don't. Not so: Brian is leaving for a few months again, Jane is moving away, Tim is burning out under the stress of responsibility, and the others don't want to be caught dead (no pun intended) in the same situation I'm in now.

At the next meeting, Saturday December 5 at 8 PM, I will formally announce this. I hope you all take this seriously. Because I am the person who is legally and financially responsible, I can't walk away and hope that a few others will fill my shoes. It's either everyone gets together with their friends and, recognizing that Gilman will be gone soon, starts coming forward with plans and the time and commitment to implement them, or it's over. (One suggestion is that bands themselves—since they are already "organizations"—start meeting with each other to discuss how to get further involved in the operation of Gilman). I will gladly stay on to help with your "revolution", but a lot of you need to grow up, and maybe that's not too fair, but if you want this place, and want it healthy, _you're_ going to have to demonstrate that its strength and power comes from you all, and not from a few fools who are doing most of the work.

Feel free to talk with me about this any time, because I don't want to "pick up my marbles and leave." I'd much rather help you all assume direct administration of this experiment.

Thanks,

Open letter to membership from Tim Y., late Nov. 1987. Our first "crisis." This led to several large meetings (see photo below) but no sustained change.

Gilman "crisis" meeting, Dec. 1987 (?)   photo by Cammie T.

OK, now on to a Gilman St. update. Any experiment that relies on ideals and volunteerism has a tendency to get watered down, taken for granted, and ends up with most of the work falling upon relatively few shoulders. Such was the case at Gilman, and while we tried to do something about that unequal distribution of responsibility 3 months ago, our attempts at awakening people had not worked. So, a month and a half ago, we put forward the proposal that Gilman either close immediately for good or else close for a month and then hold one final meeting to see if the will was there as well as a regained perspective (after 3 shows a week for a year, it gets blurry). We'd rather close it down than have it become "just another rock club".

The problems are not financial (it is breaking even now), but emotional (burn out). Over the last 5 weeks, it's become apparent that most people do not want it to die, and many proposals have been put forward on how to reorganize the place. The meetings are long and a strain (the democratic process really exhausts people), but the commitment is there. So, we won't close, at least for now. We do have to re-new our lease for 3 more years in Sept., and if we can't pull off the necessary changes by then, we won't be masochists and ink it.

Let me fill you in on some of the main concepts being advanced (they are in the formative stages, but by the time you read this, should be fairly well defined and initially implemented). First, our labor pool needs to be supplied by more people, and bands members are the immediate choice. They are the only people who get paid at Gilman, and do get to have fun and a creative outlet when they play, so it's been agreed upon that for every show a local band gets, they will also work one night as security or clean up. Band members have been meeting as a group, and most strongly support this idea. Out-of-town bands too will have some form of responsibility, though that's not yet been defined. Bands are not being forced to work; they have a choice of whether or not they want to play a community-run club, and to decide if they are part of that community. Hopefully, these band meetings will evolve a way for bands to take a more active and creative role in booking, putting on more special and memorable shows.

Those people not in bands have been meeting too, and are now attempting to organize themselves into groups with special interests—their creative outlets. While they too need to help with the daily work of running a show, they've got to develop a more creative outlet, be it through a regular newsletter, guerilla theater, poetry, car pool coordinating, welcoming committees, running the store or zine library, putting on art shows, redecorating the place, holding swap meets, pot lucks, etc, etc. This group is the most disorganized body, but the one who can make or break the place. Ultimately, the idea of a membership-run club falls on them to develop, a way to make that a living reality that smacks anyone in the face when they first walk in the door, to give it heart and really communicate that to others so that they too can get involved.

A third group who are meeting seperately are the "coordinators", that group of masochists who have already put in the most time and have the best over-all idea on how to run the club's diverse functions. They are creating a training program for those other sickies who want to get involved in that aspect of organization, and who have the responsibility of seeing to it that all groups interlock effectively.

We'll know fairly soon if it will work, but at the moment the enthusiasm is rising, the weekly meetings (Sundays at 5 PM) are well attended, and despite the strains, I think we've re-awakened the ideals behind the club. I'll give you further updates on this rather insane experiment, but regardless of the outcome, I think an awful lot of people will never again be able to slink back into just being "punk rock consumers".

Tim's MRR column, May 1988

MARTIN SPROUSE

Tim Yohannan first told me about his idea for a punk club in 1984. He wanted to start a place operated entirely by its participants, with no division between bands and audience. The shows would be based on ideas as well as music. Basically, Tim wanted to start a punk rock clubhouse.

I moved to San Francisco the following year to help coordinate *MaximumRocknRoll*, giving Tim more time to organize this new project. Tim was an amazing recruiter. Even before a space had been found he had assembled an impressive group of people who would eventually build and open Gilman.

Victor Hayden found the actual building in the summer of 1986. *MaximumRocknRoll* covered the startup costs, the lease was signed, and a fledging group of volunteers started work. Construction began, committees were formed, and club policies were drafted. After a battle with the city of Berkeley and a couple of near-death experiences with jackhammers, Gilman opened the following New Year's Eve.

Flyer by Martin S.

In trying to create a new type of punk club, we experimented with unusual policies and organizational strategies. Some of these ideas were quickly voted into oblivion while others became the foundation of Gilman. One of the more memorable policies was that every asshole was confronted and every fight was stopped, no matter how complicated or confusing it made the show. This held true for every show for the two years that we ran Gilman. This was a rare or even unheard-of approach for a club to be based on, especially coming from a scene where fighting was normal and assholes ran the show (sometimes literally).

There was nothing heroic about our tactics. In the early meetings, a heated argument evolved about the merits of stockpiling an arsenal of baseball bats as a method of dealing with trouble. Needless to say, that proposal got voted down. Soon after, the membership policy was developed which gave us full justification to remove anyone who violated it. We didn't have to explain much, we just had to get the assholes out or better yet, keep them from coming in.

What developed at each show was a spontaneous group determined not to let things get out of control. This was part policy (in case of trouble, everything stops and everyone helps), and part protective ownership by the members. None of us were good fighters and no one remotely resembled a bouncer, but as a group we wouldn't back down. We dealt with trouble in numbers: the bigger the problem, the bigger the numbers. There were huge confrontations, sometimes involving the entire crowd blocking the front door, keeping the bad guys out. It was great to see 15-year-old girls yelling at some asshole to get the fuck out of their club.

Some people put their asses on the line more than others. There were always two or three of us who were in front of the crowd who would catch more shit than the others. At times, these confrontations were as frequent as the shows and five times as draining. Often, those of us coordinating never saw the bands because we were too busy dealing with the shit. To be honest, I remember the assholes and problems more than the shows. For me, this lead to frustration, resentment, and a bad case of pneumonia.

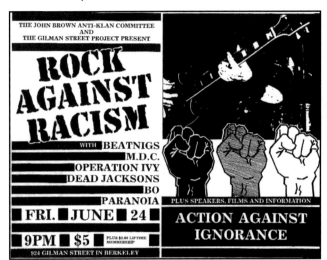

Poster by Martin S.

Sign at Gilman's front door, 1987. Tim Y.'s viewpoint was that if we didn't challenge it (racism), it meant we accepted it. photo by Murray B.

In late 1988, Gilman went through its first transition. Our group had become frustrated at the dwindling number of volunteers and high level of apathy in running the club. After a bitter custody battle, a new group of coordinators took over. Policies were "loosened up" and Gilman started to suffer from growing pains. Things were going to get ugly before they got better. For example, nazi skinheads were now welcomed at Gilman. At one show, there was a group of skinheads, one of them proudly wearing a KKK shirt. No one seemed to notice or care. With no particular plan or back up in mind, I confronted the group by myself. Words were exchanged and the situation quickly turned into a standoff. No one was going to back down and the majority of the crowd just wanted the band to start. I was actually told by a couple of people that I was the one fucking up the show. I remember thinking "I'm about to get my ass kicked by the Klan, then get my Gilman membership revoked for starting a fight." For me, Gilman had turned into something worse than just another typical punk club. This was one of the last shows that I saw at Gilman.

Ultimately, Gilman recovered, and once again set a precedent for other punk clubs. What started as a conversation has evolved into a club whose continuing influence remains impossible to measure and whose longevity no one could have guessed. More importantly, the countless generations who have been, or are, a part of Gilman continue to be an example of how an independent community can start, grow, and exist.

MAXIMUMROCKNROLL **PRESENTS**

The Gilman Street Project Double 7" Compilation

12 S.F. Bay Area Bands

TURN IT AROUND!

SIDE ONE
CORRUPTED MORALS - WHERE IS HE? - 1:43
SWEET BABY JESUS - SHE'S FROM SALINAS - 2:01
ISOCRACY - CONFEDERATE FLAGS - 2:07
NO USE FOR A NAME - GANG WAY - 2:00

SIDE TWO
CRIMPSHRINE - ANOTHER DAY - 2:40
OPERATION IVY - I GOT NO - 1:15
STIKKY - FUN ON THE FREEWAY - 1:49
NASAL SEX - FREEZER BURN - 1:48

SIDE THREE
YEASTIE GIRLZ - YEAST POWER - :35
RABID LASSIE - CONTRAGATE - 1:42
SEWER TROUT - WALLY & THE BEAVER GO TO NICARAGUA - 2:11
ISOCRACY - ZBHR - :56
OPERATION IVY - OFFICER - 1:55

SIDE FOUR
SWEET BABY JESUS - PATHETIC - 1:49
CRIMPSHRINE - REARRANGED - 1:58
STIKKY - MOSHOMETER - 1:23
BUGGERALL - TWO TAPS - 2:25

File under: GEEKCORE
MRR 002

Engineered by Kevin Army at Dangerous Rhythm, Oakland
except Corrupted Morals at An Ol' Ear, San Francisco
Nasal Sex by Dirk Dize at Creative Sound, San Jose
Yeastie Girlz by Radley at Gilman

Mastered by George Horn at Fantasy, Berkeley
Pressed at Alberti, Monterey Park
Cover & Booklet printed at Positive Press, Oakland
Layout by David Hayes
Flyer by Chris Wilder
2000 copies
October 1987

Photo Credits:
Cover, Corrupted Morals & Nasal Sex by Cammie
Crimpshrine, Operation Ivy & Rabid Lassie by Murray
Labels & Sweet Baby Jesus by Murray & Cammie
Isocracy by Murray, Cammie & Joel
Sewer Trout by Anne Marie & Mark
Stikky by Wayne

Coverboy: Waller

MAXIMUMROCKNROLL

Front and back cover of the double 7" Gilman comp, released in Nov. 1987

Turn it around... and by that we're referring to the punk scene. At a time when the scene is plagued by mindless violence, intimidation, vandalism, and general stupidity, at a time when bands and promoters are getting "professional" (meaning greedy, selfish and cut throat) and, at a time when it's all becoming more like the mainstream than an alternative, there are groups of dedicated people who are determined to fight back and revitalize things. One such group is the ever-growing crew at the Gilman Street Project. Both old scenesters, young scenesters, and non-scenesters have banded together to implement their ideals, to create an example of how things can be, and then try to spread this practical message to others who feel the same elsewhere.

Gilman Street has but a few guiding principles: no alcohol or drugs in or around the warehouse, and no violence or vandalism in or around the warehouse--dealing directly with the causes of many a club's downfall. It's a membership clubhouse, one where all decisions get determined by those who attend shows, where people come to see Gilman as their refuge, where people come to shows and events because they like the feelings as much as they like the bands.

In a nutshell, we're reestablishing a sense of community in the scene. Our feeling has been that if the majority of those going to shows don't like the stupidity, that they, along with those organizing events, and the bands themselves, can control their environment. We don't have much in this hideous world, but we can at least care for/about each other, can engender an inspiring, creative space, and can, non-violently, kick ass on those mainstream, parasitic values which have nothing to do with punk whatsoever.

This record is dedicated to those who care, bands and fans alike, a testimony to the fact that if enough people try, that scene unity can be realized and it's not just a hollow slogan. And to those who live elsewhere, we send a simple, realistic message to you: Turn It Around ! - Tim Y.

As in the general punk scene, the music and ideas expressed through this record only represent half of what Gilman Street has come to be. The remainder is equally as catchy but a lot harder to document. This half is made up of the people who actually make the shows happen, from beginning to end. They volunteer their time to set up the shows, make and post the flyers, sign up new members, take money at the door, coordinate the events on the stage, do the sound, operate the store, create and enforce the club policies inside and out, clean up, fix up and just keep the place in one piece. This slowly growing group of people are much more than fans, they are participants.

Gilman Street has had some great effects on the local scene. It's a place where old and young bands can communicate with an equally diverse audience who in turn can do the same with the bands. It's a place where assholes are dealt with non-violently by a force comprised of club members who stand their ground. It's a place where paying and working members will stick around til 3:00 am, after an exhausting six hour show to join in a meeting to voice their opinion concerning a club problem. It's a place where people can be themselves.

Although the project (at the time of this release) is nearing it's one year anniversary, in many ways it still has a lot to accomplish. The first step of establishing a friendly (at times completely silly; hence the tag "Geekcore") atmosphere has been achieved. Now, the club should gain a stronger hold on a serious political side and the 'Mind Fuck' department deserves a lot more attention. The participation level is high enough to keep the club going without everyone burning out, but participation in key decision-making is always in the need of more input. Gilman Street is not Utopia and it never will be, but it does have a lot of the neccesary ingredients for something very close.

The ideas behind this record are an accurate reflection of just some of the goals that the bands, participants and members of Gilman want to fulfill through it's existance. Hopefully the inspiration here will spread, moving all of us who care one more step forward and creating a need for another compilation who's title should be "Turn It Inside Out." - Martin Sprouse

Why these bands? These bands were chosen because of their support of the Project. Only one of these bands has appeared on vinyl before (two songs on another compilation.) The people in these bands can be found at Gilman on any given night. There's always some of them there, to the point of it seeming strange if one of them is absent. They come to the meetings, work the shows, play the benefits and put just as much, if not more, into the club than they get out of it. It's definitely a family. Not that you have to be in a band to be a part of it, not at all. People who are visiting for the first time often remark how quickly they fit in. So it's the people in these bands that make the difference, and that's why they are on this record, which by now you may have noticed, is a double 7"...

Why a double 7"? Most distributors won't even take 7"s to begin with, so we're obviously not in it for the money. It's more of a statement, maybe we're trying to set an example, to get people off of their asses and create something. It's time for a rebirth of the D.I.Y. attitude. Avoid the big distributors, Boycott the big promoters, Fuck the major labels, Wake up and DO IT YOURSELF ! - David

Text from the inside of the *Turn It Around* comp. It was rereleased a few years later as a 12". Long out of print.

JANE G.

In the summer of 1986, I was living in the San Francisco Bay Area, playing bass in a "post-punk" band (Ten Tall Men) that played in regular clubs. I had no real job at the time—I was making ends meet by putting up flyers for a Berkeley club—and somehow I ended up taking over the booking (unpaid) at a bar in San Francisco called the V.I.S. Club, on Divisadero Street. It turned out to be a mostly unpleasant learning experience, but it did lead to my involvement at Gilman.

Mitzie W. contacted me about booking a show at the V.I.S. for a band from DC called Beefeater. At the time I had no idea there was such a thing as an independent do-it-yourself (DIY) hardcore/punk scene. The Beefeater show at the V.I.S. was my first introduction to that scene.

I had to check IDs at the door, since the V.I.S. was a bar, and the drinking age in California was 21. Being underage myself—I was 20—I knew what it felt like to get turned away at the door, so I really hated checking IDs. Still, I had to do it—I had been yelled at by the bar's owners for letting in people without checking ID (I tried to make up for it by telling people quietly that they could show me any kind of ID—even if it showed they were underage—and I would let them in, and as long as the owner saw me checking IDs, it would be okay). But it made feel bad.

So when Brian Edge introduced himself and started telling me about a new all ages not-for-profit collective space that was being set up in Berkeley, I was definitely interested (there was already one all ages not-for-profit space in the Bay Area—the Farm, in San Francisco. It was a cool place in many ways, but it had begun to get a reputation for drawing violent skinheads).

The new space was on Gilman Street in the northwest corner of Berkeley, just a few blocks from where I was living at the time. I learned from Brian that it was being financed by *Maximum RocknRoll* (MRR), a DIY punk magazine that I had never heard of. Brian arranged for me to come check out the space, and meet Tim Yohannan and Martin Sprouse from MRR. It was just a space, but I liked their ideas for how it would function, run by volunteers who would make the decisions collectively. Brian mentioned to me that Tim and Martin were looking for someone to live in the MRR house in San Francisco and work on the magazine in exchange for low rent. I had never seen MRR magazine, and Tim was clearly skeptical, but he gave me copies of the magazine so I could get an idea of what it was like. I liked the letters section best, because it was such an open democratic forum.

So I ended up moving into the MRR house and working as a shitworker for the magazine, and getting involved in a serious way at what came to be called the Gilman Street Project.

If MRR was a discovery for me, Gilman was a revelation. I was coming into the DIY hardcore punk scene with no prior knowledge, so most of the bands people talked about I had never heard of. But I loved how we were taking responsibility for an alternative space and making it function, setting our own rules, making collective decisions.

In the Gilman Street Project's first year of existence, I think most of us there were swept up in the energy of creation. It was brand new, wide open, anything was possible. Those of us involved since before the first show (Dec. 31, 1986) felt a definite sense of collective ownership over the space. But the energy was contagious, and the membership structure made it clear to everyone who came in that this was not an ordinary club (in order to get in you had to become a member by paying $2 and signing a lifetime membership card, promising to abide by certain rules). Some people hated it, of course, because they didn't want to have a collective experience, they just wanted to go to a show. But a lot of people were drawn in by the dynamic of the experiment, and ended up getting involved, coming to meetings, volunteering, etc.

1987   photo by Murray B.

Apart from the membership cards, one thing that set Gilman apart from other clubs was the basketball hoop (Tim Y.'s idea, since he loved playing basketball). No real basketballs were allowed because they might hurt someone—instead we used red foursquare balls, about the size of a basketball but much, *much* bouncier. The bounciness meant you couldn't play "real" basketball. Sometimes we did silly, unsportsmanlike things like tackling and tickling people when they got the ball, or grabbing it and running around the room with it. But even when we stuck to the basic rules, playing with a ball that bouncy made it hard to take anything seriously. It was a mind-fuck and an equalizer: when jock punks came in who thought they knew the sport, their perfect shots just bounced off the backboard and they discovered that they had to adust to a new environment.

There was actually a mind-fuck committee in Gilman's early days—it was supposed to come up with ways to keep things from becoming too predictable, too much like other clubs—but it soon became clear that mind-fuck situations didn't really have to be concocted; Gilman was so wide open, so full of creative energy, that it sparked unconventional behavior. People invented new and silly ways to dance and stagedive, and bands like Isocracy—made up of Gilman volunteers—came up with numerous stunts to keep themselves and the audience entertained at their shows (this usually involved a lot of throwing stuff back and forth).

At some point I started buying bags of organic carrots at the health food store down the road and handing them out at the shows. When new people came who didn't know anyone, they would sometimes stand there looking insecure and shy, and I would hand them a carrot. They were surprised and thought I was weird, but it helped break down the idea of acting cool and aloof. Gilman was the anti-cool, a goofball paradise.

When Gilman first opened, the hardcore punk shows were on Friday nights, plus Saturday nights and Sunday matinees. That quickly became too much for everyone, and at one of the meetings Tim Y. suggested dropping the Friday night shows. A small group of us proposed an alternative: doing non-hardcore shows on

Friday nights, which we would organize as a separate crew so the hardcore show volunteers wouldn't get burned out. Tim and others resisted initially—they didn't like the idea of having non-punk music, and they thought it would end up being the same people running the show anyway—but we voted at the meeting to give it a try.

The Friday night crew was a small but tight unit, made up of me, the mem-

Friday night, 1987   photo by Murray B.

bers of a local band called Thinking Fellers Union Local 182 (Paul, Mark, Hugh, Anne, and Brian—who at the time had recently arrived in the Bay Area from Iowa), plus some folks whose names I've forgotten, and of course Radley, the sound guy, who never missed a show.

The Friday night shows were not always spectacular, and sometimes the crowd was sparse, but it was a good way to show people coming from outside the hardcore punk scene that this DIY world existed, that there was an alternative to the kind of mainstream bars and clubs where non-hardcore bands usually played. For me, it was also a way to link the new DIY scene at Gilman with some of the old friends I had met through my booking experiences and through my first band (that band, Ten Tall Men, broke up early in 1987 —shortly after playing a show at Gilman—maybe partly because my bandmates didn't share my newfound attachment to the DIY scene).

I also kept volunteering at the Saturday hardcore shows. I had a great time at the shows, although most of the time I didn't pay much attention to the bands. One exception was when Angry Red Planet was on tour from Detroit. I had never heard of them before, but they crashed at the MRR house, so we stayed up talking all night (among other things, they told me all about racial segregation and environmental disasters in Detroit). They loved Gilman and ended up playing two days in a row there. Neither show had a big crowd, but they didn't seem to care. We all had a blast, jumping around and playing basketball.

At Gilman I also met Cammie T. and Joyce, and we started the Yeastie Girlz. Cammie and I had been talking a bit about gender issues at Gilman, about how the atmosphere was sometimes overwhelmingly dominated by boy energy. Macho hardcore attitudes weren't entirely absent from Gilman, but they were definitely discouraged. So the energy that dominated that first year was more about being nerdy ("geekcore" reigned supreme). Girls can be nerdy too, of course, and most of us were. But the fact that boys greatly outnumbered girls (just as in the punk/hardcore scene in general) meant Gilman was overwhelmed by boyish nerd energy. That frustrated adolescent male sexuality, pumped up on six-packs of Jolt cola ("all the sugar, twice the caffeine"), often turned the shows into a boyfest, in which the existence of girls was not really acknowledged.

The Yeastie Girlz came together at a BBQ festival and basketball tournament at Gilman, where everyone ate a lot of food and formed vegan and straight-edge basketball teams to fight it out against meat-eating and alcohol-drinking teams for the championship. It was a lot of fun, but I was cranky because I was fasting at the time for health reasons (bad time to fast, during a BBQ). At some point,

Cammie, Joyce, and I got together and decided to form the Yeastie Girlz. Because I was too hungry and cranky to do anything else, I sat around and came up with what would become the first Yeastie Girlz rap. The three of us worked on it and practiced it. Because it was Gilman, and because we were a part of it, we could just get up on stage and do it.

The Yeastie Girlz came out of a punk attitude, and we called our style "live vaginacore a capella rap," but it was really more of an educational comedy performance with audience participation. We used a lot of raw language, talked openly about bodily functions, threw tampons around, and splattered the audience with yogurt (while explaining that it's a good home cure for yeast infections). Cammie played a tampon applicator as a musical instrument. We tried to demystify all that "girl" stuff that no one—girls or boys—ever talks about.

The Yeastie Girlz ended up playing a few shows at Gilman that year (1987). In the fall we organized a Sunday show of women's bands. We wanted to make the show special, so we created a special entrance across the doorway—a giant vulva made from foam, covered with fabric and fake fur, which you had to push your way through to get into the show. The Yeastie Girlz performed, along with Frightwig, Vomit Launch, Bitch Fight, and others (Bitch Fight was one of the few female Gilman punk/hardcore bands that emerged that first year; another was Kamala and the Karnivores. These female bands didn't get nearly as much attention or encouragement as their counterpart boy bands, like Crimpshrine, Operation Ivy, Isocracy, etc.)

Yeastie Girlz, 1987   photo by Murray B.

The Yeastie Girlz handed out dozens of free speculums that I got from the Berkeley Free Clinic. The Clinic gave us the speculums to distribute on the condition that we explain to people how to use them —which we did, on stage, using "Vagina May," a lifesize stuffed doll (we had to cut a hole on her to give her a vagina). We also performed the Sesame Street song "Rubber Ducky," which Joyce sang while dressed in a giant vagina costume (donated to us by a City College professor who had used it to teach sex education during the women's self-exam movement of the 1970s). Cammie and I accompanied the song by pretending to hump a couple of yellow rubber ducks in a masturbation frenzy, a stunt which really pushed the limits of audience comprehension.

I honestly don't think the Yeastie Girlz could have emerged anywhere else but Gilman during its first year of existence. The Yeasties were a product of Gilman's openness, its appreciation of mind-fuck and creativity, of challenging ourselves and others, and of just blowing up the boundaries of the normal and the acceptable. To me, the Yeastie Girlz belong in that time and place.

At the end of 1987, I left on a trip to Mexico and Central America. I spent two and a half months in Nicaragua, where I saw how a sort of Gilman-style revolution had taken place—except this one was for real. I saw reflected in Nicaragua my experience at Gilman—the opening of a whole new space where the old rules don't apply, a process of group decision-making instead of top-down power, and the way in which everyone pitched in together, volunteering their time and energy, to make the project work. And I saw just how threatening this all is to those who seek to maintain their grip on power. So threatening that the US sent guns and "trainers" to create a proxy army (the "Contras") to kill ordinary Nicaraguans who had dared to embrace the extraordinary experiment of revolution (at Gilman we had our own "Contras": a group of violent rightwing skinheads who came one night in late 1987 to attack us—because we were "wimps" who didn't like to fight, because we had dared to try something different, because we didn't recognize their power).

Those who weren't part of it can say that Gilman was really all about Tim Y. and MRR, because they held the economic power over it. Just as some might say that Nicaragua in the 1980s was really about Daniel Ortega and the FSLN, because they held the political power. But revolutions are about the power of the people, not the leaders.

Gilman could also be criticized for failing to effectively challenge the lack of gender and ethnic diversity of the punk scene in general. Gilman was certainly flawed—no process is perfect—and much of the intial energy was lost over the subsequent years. And it wasn't unique: here in New York City, where I've lived since 1989, volunteers were creating a similar revolution at a space called ABC No Rio, which still thrives.

Of course, a revolution of punk rock kids creating a space to see music is not on the same scale as an entire people reclaiming their land and their country. But that doesn't make our experience any less valid. We came together, empowered ourselves and each other, and unleashed our ideas and creativity. We saw what was possible and we made it happen. Wherever our separate paths led afterwards, no one could take that away from us.

Above: 1986   photo by Murray B.
Below: 1986   photographer unknown

Above: 1987   photo by Murray B.
Below: 1987   photo by Cammie T.

KATJA G.

I moved to Berkeley in the summer of 1986 from a small town in Northern California. I met a guy while I was working handing out flyers on Telegraph Avenue who told me about a group that was trying to put together a punk club in Berkeley. I thought it sounded great. Coming from a small town where you were lucky to go to a show at all, to be involved in helping put on shows sounded really exciting.

I started going to some of the early meetings where we would make plans and go to look at some proposed locations for the club. I was 16 or 17 and just happy to be a part of all of it. I didn't have any specific goals going in; I was young and shy and just wanted to help however I could.

I mainly worked the door at first after the club opened, then eventually started helping with coordinating shows as well. It was a big deal for me, to meet the *Maximum RocknRoll* folks, meet the people in bands, things like that. I never dreamed I would be a part of something like that. For the first time I was part of what was going on, not just a fan or consumer. I got to see what really went on behind the scenes, what it really takes to put on a show, and how much responsibility was involved. That was the great thing about it, too—it was a bunch of kids/friends running the club, putting on shows, and playing in bands.

Planning meeting, '86. Was Gilman really ever this clean?
photographer unknown

My move to start coordinating shows came after encouragement from some of the older people there. I think if you're a little nervous or shy about doing something, a little nudge in a certain direction is probably a good thing. I didn't end up doing it all the time, but it was good to have done it. It seemed natural at the time when I began; it didn't seem like a real big deal. After I left Gilman, I took what I learned there and put on a few shows myself at other locations.

I also really liked the safe environment at Gilman—you didn't have to watch your back constantly. I've seen the apathy at other places where I've gone to shows towards people getting beat up, and the total lack of concern or anyone taking responsibility for what goes on. Another good thing at Gilman was that there was so much creativity there—people doing all kinds of great things, everyone not being afraid to be goofy.

In order to not be closed down by local police we had to have rules, such as no drinking in or around the club, no fighting, things like that. You'd sometimes be ridiculed by the "real punks" if they recognized you as someone who worked at Gilman when you were walking down the street. That didn't surprise me. It was a little intimidating at the time, but it was definitely worth it to be able to see, and be a part of, all the great things that happened there. I didn't see it at the time, mainly because I was as young as I was, but now, reflecting, I can see the value of having to stand up for something I believed in, even in the face of threats or ridicule. I can see now just how much we did accomplish and how important it was to have a place like that for kids to go. Certainly danger has always been an element of punk and I don't think you could ever escape that, or would want to, but stupid fights aren't part of that. Punk has also always had a feeling of lawlessness as part of its appeal, and trying to run a club, with rules and such that are necessary for its long-term survival, runs counter to that. I can understand why many people rejected the place, although the biggest deterrent for most was that you couldn't drink there.

Toward the end, though, I think we all felt really burned out on having to deal with some of the assholes who came to the shows and politics of running a club as a collective. I think us leaving was inevitable. It didn't seem like anyone wanted the place to close, just that we didn't want to be the ones having to run it. We were consistently doing Sunday shows each week, as well as the Friday and Saturday ones, and it started becoming not very fun. In all honesty, there was a certain amount of pressure on us to work as well. Anyone who has worked with Tim Yohannan knows that he drove himself really hard and expected others to do the same, which is not always humanly possible for most people. I did try working less there toward the end, but it didn't seem to matter. I think for most things, even if they're really exciting at first, they just run their course and you move on. Fresh blood is what keeps Gilman going.

The greatest thing about being there for me was learning how to stand up for myself and for what I believed in. I can look back now and see how strong we really were to be able to deal with all that crap we got. It makes me really proud. I learned how to stand up for myself at meetings too. At my work now, during meetings, I sometimes get flashbacks of those Gilman meetings, and how you could easily get steamrolled if you didn't stand your ground. Gilman made me a lot more confident in dealing with those situations. I'm glad it hasn't closed. I still love going to shows there and seeing younger people with the same level of enthusiasm as we had when we were there. I think that's great.

I didn't work there again after it reopened in late 1988. I've attended shows there occasionally since those first two years it was open. I can't really compare how it is now with how it was for us, other than the atmosphere of the shows, which seems about the same. For us, it was such a big part of our lives; everybody knew everybody else and hung out together. I don't know how similar that part is for the people working there now.

I also wanted to mention how important the bands were that played there. If it wasn't for them, Gilman wouldn't have existed very long!

Above: 1987   photo by Cammie T.

Left: 1987   photo by Murray B.

JIM WIDESS

The Caning Shop moved to Gilman in 1979. I first came in here as a tenant, in the back where we are now. The building was a distribution center/warehouse for Blaupunkt auto stereos, and I rented our space from them. They were the ones who put the offices in the front, and the main space was used as a warehouse. We ended up buying the whole building from them in 1984. The only tenant we really had before the club was Warm Things—they used it as a retail outlet shop before they moved. They made down quilts/bedding. They were here twice, from Christmas season 1984 till Feb. 1985, and from Christmas season 1985 till early 1986. The rest of the time we used it for our classes and workshops. Other people came to check the space out. One person wanted to open a small home brewery there, some automotive repair places were interested, Outback (a clothing manufacturer) checked it out, and a few others, including Tim Yohannan, but only the club idea sounded appealing.

924 and 926 Gilman (The Caning Shop), 1991   photo by Susan S.

From the beginning, his proposal sounded terrific. I liked what he was doing, I liked him, and he seemed easy to work with. I was enthusiastic about his enthusiasm. My employees were all enthusiastic about it as well. My father owned the building at the time, and he had no problems at all with the delays and red tape that were encountered with the city once MRR and Co. came into the space and tried to open the club. He was a very generous person—he surprised me with his generosity towards the club, like reduced rent before it actually opened, things like that. I felt confident that the club would eventually clear the hurdles and open up. I've been in Berkeley for a long time, and I knew how things worked, and I felt it actually went surprisingly smoothly.

Once it did open and start running, it's been nice since our times of use have always been complementary and don't conflict. And I've been able to rent the space back for my classes and such when the club isn't using it. Most of the people taking the classes have heard of the club already and don't have that much of a problem with how the space looks inside. Most of the problems are with the residual smoke, so we run the fans for an hour or so before the class, and if it's still bothersome to them, I'll refund their money, or have them come to class when it's scheduled to be held in my shop. I always go in before every class and tell the people who haven't been here before about the place. That it's the only all ages music club in the Bay Area, it's been open since New Year's, 1987, it's all run by the volunteers and the kids, it's a good space, the graffiti is all inside, and they're responsive to the community. But a few people, especially when I get a teacher from out of the area, do have a problem with it, and I try to book them only for classes in my shop, because the inside of the club is just so foreign to where they come from. I try to be sensitive to that, but this is Berkeley. I just try to emphasize that this is a good space, but I do recommend that they come over to my shop to use the bathroom! And, if anybody does complain, it's okay, I'll give them their money back. Most are okay with it, and I get lots of repeats. The kids are usually pretty good about cleaning it up well if they know there's a class the next day.

Caning shop class, 1995   photo by Pat W.   photo by Larry W.

It's gone pretty well over the years, with the various people running the space. The only really shaky times were at the beginning, with the violence and the broken windows, but that was ultimately dealt with. I've enjoyed working with the different people over the years—they've been responsible and concerned. After the earthquake in 1989, we had to retrofit the building, so the shop moved into the club area for a few weeks and we compensated them for that, as well as an additional month or two's rent to get back up to speed. If they've ever fallen behind on rent, and I don't remember that they have, it hasn't gotten to the point where it's been a concern to me. The trash inside the club caught on fire once. I smelled the smoke and came over. It was out already by the time I got over there. I was worried, and I was going to write a letter to the club saying that this can't happen again, but I showed it to my father first, and he said not to send it, so I didn't.

Only one neighbor has been a problem (DiCon), and the club has really worked at dealing with them. From what I gather, the representative that DiCon sent to the meetings thought that the club was cool, so I don't know how long she stayed the representative of DiCon! From my understanding, the problem was that DiCon wanted to put on a Friday night shift and that their employees were afraid of, or intimidated by, the patrons of the club.

I've always been impressed by the responsiveness of the kids when dealing with the community. I thought their response to the brewery across the street, when it was first proposed, was pretty cool. And now the brewery's a supporter of the club. But beyond their physical appearance being different, they're good kids. I love having them in the neighborhood—they're polite, they're just regular old kids. There used to be a local merchant's association (that's no longer around) and the club was very involved with that. There was one other landlord that was complaining about the graffiti on his building. People from the club have been taking care of it and painting it over, even though most of it wasn't generated by patrons of the club. There's been other sporadic complaints around the neighborhood, but the club always takes care of it. Some of these businesses have then written letters of support for the club during the club's dealings with DiCon.

I have a notable number of customers whose kids have gone to the club. I've never attended one of the music events—it's too smoky for me. I've been serenaded frequently on Saturday and Sunday nights when I've been working late in the shop. I've gone to the art shows. We had a book-signing party in the shop one Sunday, relevant to making musical instruments out of gourds, and some of the kids came over to check it out. We had drums and flutes, some stringed instruments, they liked it.

I couldn't think of a more perfect use that benefits us both as well as making a very important social impact. Parents will come during the day to check the space out, because their kids are interested in going there, and I'll show them around and tell them about the club. I have no problem recommending it. They have AA meetings there, there were mask-making workshops for a while, art shows. During the day my only stipulation is no loud music, which impacts my business.

My dad passed away last year (1998) and passed on the building to me.

The kids have changed over the years, but the way the space has been used, and the kinds of things that have been happening there, are still consistent. I have my own druthers: I wish there was more creativity in the music, it seems pretty monotonous. I worry about all the anger that this generation has, and I also understand why that is. I think that society has failed kids in many, many ways. I certainly wouldn't be sad to see some happy music, not from a childish standpoint, but something that's celebrating a little bit different feelings. It's a place for the kids to go, where they can deal with a supportive family. The need for this kind of a space is even stronger now than when it first opened. I think they learn things from each other here. And hopefully there's some influences here to get them to take in a larger picture than just their own misery, or their own happiness, or their own focus, to try and get some expanding. I fantasize that they're in better shape going to a club meeting here on a Saturday night than they are going to an AA meeting. Why shouldn't a 16 or 21-year-old be able to run a business? I would be surprised if they couldn't do it. There has been the factor of the fatherly figure overlooking things there over the years, and I worry that if that figure wasn't there, to help with things, hold a hand or give a kick when necessary, how the space would do. I don't think there's anything wrong with that either, they are only 16 or 21-year-olds, they're not expected to be CEOs, they're in training, so I think you need a mentor in the picture. It was a wonderful vision that Tim had, and a wonderful legacy that he left. It's giving a lot of kids a start, a chance to try something out. As far as I'm concerned, it's their space, and they can stay here as long as they want it.

ADRIENNE D.

I was 17 and growing up in a small town called Pleasanton, in California, and I was one of only a handful of punks. I thought that being a vegetarian meant peeling the pepperonis off of a pizza and then, presto, it's instantly a vegetarian pizza! I had a mohawk, but the sides were around an inch long and it was bleached blond with an orange streak in it that I had to constantly hide from my mom. She told me that she wasn't going to be seen in public with me if I looked like a freak. I bought all my "punk" clothes at a local thrift store, which meant buying brown work-men boots and spraypainting them black. Buying old-man golf pants and making them tight and fitted with safety pins. Stealing one of my dad's white t-shirts and writing "society fucked me so fuck you!" on it really big on the back with a felt-tip pen. I went to a high school where there was only one other person who was into punk and she was the one that got me into it in the first place!

I would walk around the streets of my small town and get yelled at con-stantly. Told I was a freak, that I was ugly, that I was fucked up. And you know what? Those people were right. I was an ugly, fucked up freak. I was a punk rocker when not a lot of people even knew what punk was about. The pressure to conform and be "normal" was immense. Punk wasn't cool. Punk wasn't in the pages of *Vogue*. There were no punk bands signed to major labels with corporate videos being played on television. If you were a punk, most people thought that there was some-thing really fucking wrong with you and treated you like shit.

I remember feeling a lot of confusion back then. On one hand, I was so happy and so excited to have discovered and been introduced into the punk scene. It made me feel as if I was actually slipping into my own skin, and as if the restraints and binds that had held my soul in before were finally setting me free. As if I could breathe again. But I also felt a little lost in the punk scene. I had bought some records by Crass and the Subhumans. I understood the lyrics and really took them to heart, but I felt as if I wasn't doing my part to help bring about change. Sure, I looked like a freak and that was challenging society in some ways. Making people realize that it wasn't how you looked on the outside that mattered, but what kind of person you are on the inside that really counts. But I knew I wanted to be doing something with the intensity and energy and passion that the punk scene inspired in me. As I skateboarded around Pleasanton, I felt as if I was burning up with ideas and energy that couldn't be contained by the small town I was trapped in.

I began to escape to Berkeley. I would take the local bus to the BART sta-tion and then into Berkeley. I didn't quite know where to go to meet punks, but Telegraph Avenue seemed to have its fair share of freaks. I remember going there and seeing a group of older, cooler, much-more-sophisticated-than-me punk rock-ers that I knew I really wanted to be friends with. I was starving for contact with peo-ple involved in the punk scene. I would walk over to this group of total strangers and say "Hey, you guys are punk rock and I'm punk rock, so we should be friends." You'd expect that I'd get laughed out of the city, but every single time I said that, I'd find myself surrounded by people who were willing to hang out and get to know me. It was during one of those trips into Berkeley that I met a fellow named Aaron, and it's through him that I got involved with Gilman Street. Gilman hadn't even started yet. No shows, no stage, no sound system...nothing. But there was a space that people had finally found and that space was 924 Gilman Street.

When I went to my first meeting, I was so intimidated that I could barely make it through the door. The place seemed to be filled with people who knew what they were doing and why they were there, and who had known each other for years. Plus I was meeting people that I'd only read about in the pages of *Maximum RocknRoll*. I don't know about you, but being 17 and growing up in a small cow town and finally meeting Tim Yohannan was a total mindfuck! Now there was a person who had been involved in the punk scene since day one and had really accomplished some amazing and tangible things. Done things that had changed the viewpoints and altered the way that people perceived their world. Even though I felt intimidated, I knew that Gilman was the right place to be. Eventually, everyone sat down on the floor and Tim started talking about the space, and most of the people in the room began to discuss what their ideas were and what they hoped to accomplish by opening a place for punk bands to play that was completely run and organized by punks. I remember at one point someone began to talk about what kind of "manpower" they would need to build the stage and finish the walls. Someone else interrupted and said it wasn't manpower they needed, but people power. I had to smile. It felt awesome to be around people who would actually protest the use of the word "manpower!" Even something that small made me feel thrilled inside. This is what I had hungered for. This was what I had been searching for in the punk scene and had never found. I found it at Gilman. A place to express myself. An environment that encouraged ideas and needed my youthful energy and my willing exuberance. I was giddy! I was elated! I had found a home.

I wasn't closely involved with Gilman for years and years. I was one of the initial people who helped to get the club open and who dedicated a lot of time and energy into it, but other parts of my life pulled me away, and eventually, I was only going to Gilman for the occasional show. It wasn't until a few years after Gilman had opened that I began to be more involved on a different level. I had just started singing in a band with some people I had just met. There was a girl named Todd, her friend Paula, and Paula's friend Karin. None of us really knew each other very well. Todd had played in a couple of other bands, but nothing too big. Paula was just learning how to play bass, and Karin was an enigma! We were basically strangers to each other and we decided to do a band and call it Spitboy. Through Spitboy, Gilman was once again a place that felt as comfortable to me as my own home. I remember our first show at Gilman and feeling just as terrified as I did the first time I walked into that space so many years ago. Come to think of it, I always feel terrified before I play, so I guess that wasn't Gilman's fault. Stepping onto the stage at Gilman began to feel like walking around in my own living room. An environment that was nurturing and caring. A place where I could laugh and tell stories and bad jokes (What do you call a ghost in a chicken coop? Poultrygeist!) or stand on stage and discuss issues of rape and sexual abuse and cry openly without feeling vulnerable. It was home, and I have never felt as safe and at ease on any stage as I did within the walls of Gilman.

I moved away from the Bay Area in 1995 and I only go back once or twice a year. Most of my time in the Bay Area is now spent hanging out with family or with my best friend Wendy. But around a year ago, I did get a chance to go to a show at Gilman Street to sing a song with the band Aus Rotten. And once I stepped onto that stage, I felt like I was coming home.

JOSH LEVINE

I started going to punk shows around 1977, mostly in San Francisco, because that's where they were. When I moved to the East Bay from Marin around 1981, there wasn't much going on there. Just Ruthie's Inn and the occasional show at Barrington Hall (a student co-op) and various other small clubs that came and went.

I had known Tim Yohannan from shows and from just being around the scene, and always looked at him as "one of those older super-achievers" or whatever, and never really talked to him much. By the time Gilman started getting organized, I was "married with a kid when I should be having fun," as the song goes. I had had plenty of fun already, and was locked down into the 40-hour work week and the baby-having life. Alesha (my wife) and I got in on Gilman as soon as the building was intially rented. We had heard about it from friends and seen flyers at shows. Some of our good friends were very enthusiastic about a volunteer-run club, and I was curious. I remember the first organizational meetings at the club—we used to all sit around on the floor, and then Tim would start the meeting and we would all get to say whatever we thought would be good as far as how the club would be built and run. We would drive down there with the baby, unpack the stroller, and we'd sit there and try to make decisions about this and that. At least Alex got to sit in his stroller.

During one of those early meetings, I remember Tim told me, "that hippie bullshit attitude doesn't belong here," or something to that effect, after some comment I had made, and that was about the point where I really felt like a part of Gilman and felt like I had something to contribute. People I met there became friends, friends I worked with there became bandmates. As the walls were being soundproofed, and the stage was being built, I was also practicing two nights a week with my new band, So What.

It was at one of the first meetings that my friend Vince and I met George, an older guy who ran a machine shop down the street. George had heard about the club forming and come to take part. We got to talking after that meeting, and found out that he played drums (Vince played guitar and sang, and I still play bass) and that he had a garage to practice in, even though it was out in El Sobrante.

There was something in the air, you could say, back then. A good feeling, or a sense of pulling together, and unity among people who just wanted a place to see bands that was free of sexism, homophobia, racism, and especially violence. Shows were not as safe then—there were shows I went to before Gilman where I got beat up. Shows where I was lucky not to get beat up. Shows where I went to jail, just for being a punk rock kid out after curfew. And worse, shows where I saw people getting beat up by skinheads, or jocks, and there was not a damn thing I could do about it if I wanted to stay healthy. Those were the kind of things that motivated us to get involved.

I was not very good at construction, and dropped a hammer in a wall at one point that had to be extricated, but that was not important. There were people who knew what they were doing working side by side with inexperienced 22-year-olds like myself, and together we got it done. My memory is a bit hazy, but I'm pretty sure I can't take credit for very much at all as far as actually building the place was concerned, but I didn't care. We still came to the vegan potluck dinners, work parties, and parties at various people's houses we had worked with at the club.

Prior to the first actual show, we were forming committees to handle all the different aspects of running the club. Everybody was on one, and they were all important, so I made up my own committee, and was delighted when about five people wanted to join it. I think Tim asked me what committee I wanted to be on during a meeting, and I said "the mindfuck committee," and explained that we would be concerned mainly with entertainment and anti-entertainment, making people think, and causing general and random mayhem during shows. The mindfuck committee pulled some good stunts during the first few shows. There were water balloons, a fire drill, lots of random fake fights with blood, and of course, having security throw someone out very dramatically, only to walk back in immediately afterward all smiles (a custom still practiced to this day).

It was after the first few shows that I pretty much fucked off for a few years. I got kicked out of the club for drinking, asked to go home a few times for being drunk, and then moved away. I lived in Chico, CA and Olympia, WA from 1989 to about 1992, and started going back to Gilman soon after I moved back.

For me, it was when I quit drinking that I appreciated the club even more. It's an environment for music and social interaction that doesn't revolve around booze. I believe that kids love booze. God knows I do, but that's not the most important thing there. If you go to a party at someone's house, it's usually all about beer. Not at the club. Not for me, at least... It was funny working security there after I got sober, knowing where all the places were to hide out and drink in a two block radius of the club.

For a while after I moved back, I went to shows and enjoyed them. Then I started volunteering more and more, and then started coordinating, stage managing, counting money, and having keys. I still do when they let me. Now I'm in my thirties. My son Alex likes to go to shows there now, especially to play basketball and play computer games. It's really cool that he likes the club, because we built it for the kids anyway...

GILMAN

KIDS

Clockwise from above: photos by Larry W., Murray B., Murray B., Cammie T., Larry W.

STEVE S.

Fuck you!! I got to see all the good shows, with all the old legendary bands, and you didn't, and everything now is not nearly as cool or as fun as the things you missed out on, nyaah, nyaah, nyaah. I was seeing all the cool bands like Green Ivy Shrine or Operation Crimp Day when you were still wanting to make out with **Jordan** because he was your favorite New Kid. **Neener neener!** Sure, I'm not young and cute like you, and sometimes I don't wear pants, but you still must bow before my **awesome scenester cred**: I personally built the stairway leading to the *now defunct sound booth*. I was there when a young Ice-T opened up for MDC, and knew Lint back when he played bass for No Doubt. **I am the shit!** Everything that happened after I sold out is just crap, and you kids wouldn't have lasted three seconds back in my day, where you couldn't just slam in the pit, you had to *leap-frog* over each other, and dodge life-size Don Johnson cutouts while you were doing it, as you smoked your "Swisher Sweets" Isocra-cigar. Now that was **entertainment!** But it occurs to me maybe I'm being too hard on you little young'uns. Maybe you're not intentionally *trying* to be lame... maybe you're just satisfied with bands like the Hellbillies and Spazz and Drive Like Jehu because you never saw how punk rock should be done. Let me take you back in time so you can see the difference for yourselves...

It was 1987. Jon Bon Jovi ruled the airwaves, and baggy pants were only seen on *rodeo clowns*. Reagan had his finger on the button and **his colon on nationwide TV.** Needless to say, the time was ripe for shit to get torn up. But nobody could have predicted that the serious business of overthrowing the crappy Bay Area music scene would result in a wacky Romper Room the way it did. (Note to *zit-faced newcomers*: the "Romper Room" quote originally came from the gym-teacher-lookin' singer of an East Coast HC band. He was expecting a million goons moshing and punching each other, and got a platoon of geeks having fun and laughing at his hockey stick...hence his legendary quote: "What is this? *Fuckin' Romper Room??"* But you missed it. Wait, I missed it too. But it was still rad because I COULD'VE seen it, I wasn't too busy collecting *Pogs* like you kids. Morons.)

Here's something else you didn't know: at the time, when people referred to the "Gilman scene," they meant geek-core bands like Isocracy, Boo Hiss Pfft, Stikky, and Naked Lady Wrestlers as much as OPIV, MTX, ELO and the like. Only *later* did people make a distinction between the geek bands and the "Legendary East Bay" melodic bands. Back in '87 people weren't going around saying, "Dude, I'm trying to decide if my band should be legendary or geeky... do you think we sound *legendary*?" Sure, I saw all the damn bands *you* wanted to see and then fellate in the well-lit backstage area *next to the deli trays*, but the shows that stick in my mind were the geek bands. Sure, OPIV could play a song all the way through, and have a catchy chorus, *but where's the fun in that?* A good show wasn't about music, it was about **chaos**. And since this was Gilman, the chaos wasn't like a **skinhead stabbing you in the eye** with a screwdriver, the chaos was massive amounts of pop culture trash, styrofoam Isocra-peanuts, bureaucratic forms, pinecones (!), **Isocra-pieces-o-cardboard**, moviestar cutouts, and *nonstop insults* that Isocracy would bring to hurl at the audience, who would hurl them back, while unplugging the musicians and tackling them afterwards, with songs culminating in ritual de-pantsing as often as not.

Sure, every generation considers the styles of its teen years to be "the best", but I have _actual scientific proof_ that early Gilman was way better than you could have dreamed... the Second Law of Thermodynamics, to be precise. That's right... **entropy**. Even if you love shitty emo hardcore or power violence, you can't dispute the fact that Gilman started in '87, and entropy says that everything decays over time, going from a higher-ordered state to a lower-ordered state, gradually losing energy. And when shit was as disorderly as early Gilman to begin with, it's not going to take a long time for it to start _sucking_. Vintage Gilman had energy... the pent-up enthusiasm of a bunch of kids who had been bored shitless for years on end, all simultaneously going, **"Oh fuck!! We have an outlet now"!!**... and all saying, "Hey, these guys just built a club up from nothing, imagine what me and my friends could do if we set our minds to it..." Gilman didn't succeed in driving other clubs out of business, but it did succeed in momentarily eradicating the laws of "cool." Everyone was too curious to see what they could get away with in this new environment. They were so curious they forgot to constantly check over their shoulder to see if it was hip, they forgot to act all bored and blasé, because that would have interfered with the _fun_.

Then entropy sets in, and people start to take the club for granted. The bands are afraid to experiment because they want to imitate their idols note for note, and don't want to do anything silly because they're serious about gaining social status. Nobody bothers to put on a real show because, "If we try really hard we won't look cool, we'll look dorky. We might play a wrong note..." In turn, the audiences come to expect less from the bands and just want to passively watch, and later, buy a t-shirt. The following chart shows exactly how lame everything has become as a result of entropy:

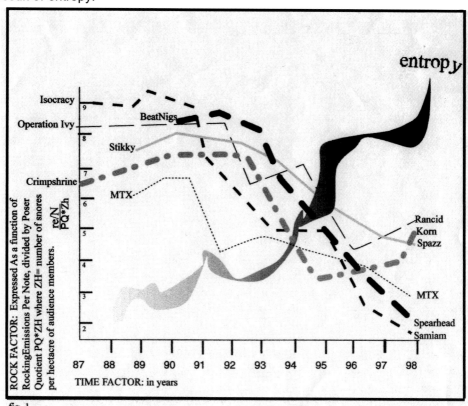

fig. 1

Perhaps all this scientific physics talk is going over your head... let me dumb it down by giving you actual examples of amazing shit that I saw, that *you totally missed, and will never get to see*, because it would never ever happen nowadays, but I don't care 'cuz I was there, **haw haw:**

You missed Frank Moore and the Cabaret of Chaos... basically a half-dozen naked women dancing and rubbing up against this quadriplegic guy who is "lip synching" to old showtunes: "URRREHHHH... EHHHH (gurgle...) oo**EEEEEuhhhhhh**..." I thought I was hard, listening to Slayer and Black Flag and shit, but Frank Moore made me cry real tears.

You missed the Yeastie Girlz, who, it's been noted, have big ovaries. Darryl Hannah and Bikini Kill aren't shit compared to the **mighty "a capella vaginacore rap"** of the Yeastie Girlz. You don't understand girl power until you've been sprayed with yogurt from Cam Master Clit's homemade anti-yeast infection remedy concocted live onstage between songs about *spermbrains and runny shit*, and the yogurt splashed on your fashionable, complimentary bowtie made from a pinched Maxipad: ("It's got FLOWERS on it!! That's so CUTE!!") And may I just say at this point: **fuck the Lilith Fair**. When they get the Yeastie Girlz, the Great Kat, Phranc, and Gaia, then I'll go and "kick up ass." I bet you missed the <u>Yeastie Girls vs. the Mentors</u> concert as well. I'm not kidding.

You missed the whole culture: it would be a common sight to see some Mohican pedaling a <u>Big Wheel</u> around the pit. Or a bunch of kids in **hideous polyester suits** moshing in slow-motion. No giant-size Hessians would stagedive on you and break your arm, but an acne-spotted bald girl with Coke-bottle glasses might bop you in the head with a Nerf ball. We had limbo pits, and "Neanderthal pits" where we'd mock would-be tough guys with our knuckledragging pantomimes. If you came on a bad night, you might have seen me with a skinhead-girl's haircut, making annoying sounds with a Flexatone.

You missed one of the **worst shows ever**, on January 10, 1987. While you were begging your mom to let you stay up and watch that handsome hunk *Magnum PI*, Short Dogs Grow were inviting the *entire audience* on stage to spruce up the rock music with a friendly game of Twister. Then, between bands, we'd have an "open mic" deal: if you had something to say, you could get up and tell everyone, "Hey the bass player isn't vegetarian—I saw him eating a <u>big thing</u> of bacon off the deli trays backstage! *That band sucks!!*" If nobody had shit to say, the sound person would fuck with the crowd by playing non-punk music: Chuck Berry, Madonna, Glen Miller, whatever. On this night, some pretentious poet guy got on the open mic and was boring everyone until a wise-acre got on the other microphone and started beatboxing really loud, thus forcing the poet-guy to try to rap, and it was funny, **too bad you missed it.** Plus you missed the Feederz coming on stage with a pre-op transsexual crucified to this 8-foot cross later that night. And keep in mind this was one of the most boring shows ever. *<u>All the other shows were much more entertaining.</u>*

You missed the Beatnigs putting on some of the best shows in the entire Reagan era: *every person in the building packed shoulder to shoulder, pogoing in unison, doing these gigantic, yard-high, aerobic pogo leaps that made it look like the entire floor was rising and falling, while getting showered with sparks from the skillsaw and screaming "the CIA, the CIA!!" at the top of our lungs.* Not only did you miss it, but their shitty studio album gives you no idea how cool they were, so that won't help you a bit, even if you bought it for fifty cents in the bulk bin like I did.

You missed the very first show of a bunch of gangly 15-year-olds, who would later kick out Aaron Cometbus and change their name to **Korn**.

You missed the virtuostic, bombastic, Rush-like instrumentals of the Naked Lady Wrestlers: a trio of middle-aged men led by the vainglorious Max Volume, they lost no time in yelling at the kids how they were **much more talented** than all the other bands on the bill **put together**, and it was a shame they had to play such a shitty small hall instead of the Cow Palace, and play to a bunch of snot-nosed little kids who **couldn't begin to comprehend their magnificence**. Then they'd do a five minute drum solo just to irritate the <u>fuck</u> out of everyone.

You missed Sweet Baby Jesus, not to be confused with the Big Baby Jesus, the Wu-Tang guy. If there's rap metaphors to be had, Sweet Baby is more like the *Melle Mel of pop-punk*. Or maybe the *Cold Crush Brothers of pop-punk*: they started it and never got paid crazy loot when it took off years later, 'cuz you kids heard Green Day on fuckin' Live 105 and, oh, what's the use...

I could provide hundreds more examples, but there's one event that totally sums up <u>*Gilman's relentless deterioration*</u>: the punk prom. The first prom was in the Spring of 1988, and it was a truly tasteless, savage satire of high school's obsession with social status. The entire auditorium was done up like a cheesy high school gym, complete with sloppy banners and crepe paper. The banners read **"Welcome to John Wayne Gacy Junior High, Home of the 'Fightin' Clowns'"!!** There were two MCs that would introduce the bands. One was the school librarian, wearing a butt-nuzzler moustache and a cardigan, saying things like, *"Thanks Mister house music man and we'd like to thank the junior class for putting this on for us and thank the Isocracy Club for doing security, aren't they wonderful"?* The other MC was this Vegas has-been crooner called **Vic Vapo**, who looked resplendent in his greased back hair, fake gold chain, maroon leisure suit, and <u>skintight see-thru socks</u>. He'd weave on stage, popping pills, and ramble on about John Wayne Gacy, and then give this pathetic, drunken Vegas-style showbiz intro to the next punk band. He was a hard act to follow. The climax was the crowning of the prom king and queen, who were also in on the gag, showing up in a nice tuxedo and big dress. They were made to wear these **humiliating construction-paper "crowns" that were awkwardly huge, and had balloons imprisoned in them**. Then they had to slowdance to a recording of some <u>Cinderella power ballad</u>, while a third actor, playing a jilted quarterback, ran in, screaming "I SHOULDA BEEN PROM KING!! I'M HER BOYFRIEND!! YOU FUCKIN' FAGGOT!" and the Isocracy Club had to hustle him out the side door. Then Thinkin' Fellers Union played, and they didn't sound like the Grateful Dead back then either. In other words, the old Gilman treated prom as the butt of a joke.

Compare to the new Gilman punk prom of 1998: *Gevalt!!* No tasteless decorations. No sense of humor. The only ones in costume were me and my crazy French bulldagger pal Forsman. We show up at the end of a line of 100 conservatively attired college dorks here to see *Rolling Stone* favorites Sleater-Kinney, all staring at me in my slutty, bright red strapless gown, and Forsman's midget cowboy ensemble. I started yelling, "None of you people know how to fuckin' PARTY"!! *What else could I do?* The bands were uniformly wretched, but the worst thing was, some dumb Greek shows up to the prom **wearing the same dress as me**. Forsman and I had fun by ignoring the bands and playing the parts of drunk-slutty-bimbo and misogynist-cowboy. I'd be talking to some punker dude and Forsman would try to start a fight with the guy: "Are you talking to mah bitch??" And I'd be like, all, "This is my *special night* and I can dance with anyone I fuckin' want to! I'd rather dance with anyone else, 'cuz *you don't know how to fuckin'* **party!!** I'm so wasted!!" And Forsman would start yanking me around, screaming and yelling sexist epithets...

Then it was time for the "prom queen and king" contest. Naturally I entered, hoping to lend some class to the proceedings, but despite acting drunk, knocking over the Greek, grabbing the mic, and informing everyone present that they **didn't know how to fuckin' party**, I lost. It turns out, the contestants weren't being judged on how well they mocked prom, but on how many friends they had. Slowly it dawned on us that there was <u>no satire to be had at this particular prom</u>. We were attending a legit prom, which just happened to be at a punk club. **These morons were FUCKING SERIOUS.** I guess nobody that night ever felt like a loser or an outcast in high school, *they were all there to relive their glorious prom night one more time.* Since this isn't a letter to *Maximum RocknRoll*, I'm not going to argue that celebrating a prom isn't punk. I'm just going to state it's <u>**quite possibly the lamest fucking idea Gilman had ever had until they let the Amino Assholes stink up the stage**</u>.

Gilman used to be funny, and enthusiastic, and geeky, now it's serious, jaded, boring, and status-obsessed. If you're not a *has-been scenester* who is basically sick of the music, and *just shows up to see if anyone important is in the audience*, you're a <u>little trendy kid</u> who gets all hype on weak bands 'cuz you don't know that those bands are like a *fifth generation ripoff of a good band I saw.* Gilman is like an **obese and co-dependent uncle** who always gives you $5 and a place to sleep when you come home off a <u>three-day crack binge</u>: It tries to be nice, but just ends up encouraging lame behavior. A really cool uncle would lock his doors and force you to either die or go into rehab. **Gilman should just fold and force the kids to actually dream up something new that they can get excited about.** But that would probably mean they'd all jump on the techno bandwagon, and lord knows that's not an improvement. SO, maybe Gilman isn't like **an obese and co-dependent uncle**, maybe it's more like a **long-suffering, crippled grandmother** who gives you $20 every week for crack just so you don't start mugging pregnant women at Lamaze class. She knows you're fucking up, but wants you to keep from sinking lower. *Clearly she hasn't heard of entropy.* Speaking of entropy, *maybe I'm being too harsh on you kids.* Since I've clearly proven that the Second Law of Thermodynamics is making Gilman suck, really you had *no choice* about becoming lame. You're just caught up in the entropy and it's *not your fault.*

That's right. Just forget everything I said... don't pay attention to this old sellout. Enjoy your emo, and your large pants. *Go ahead.* I'm sure it'll be kinda fun. I mean, it'll do.

fig. 2: the Flexatone

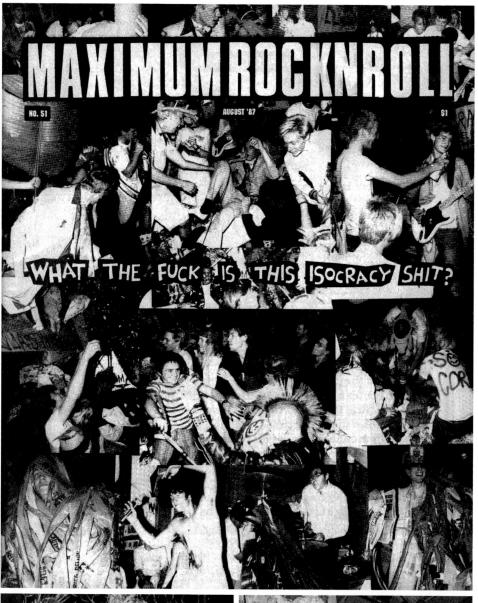

MAXIMUMROCKNROLL

NO. 51   AUGUST '87 $1

WHAT THE FUCK IS THIS ISOCRACY SHIT?

Isocracy, 1987   photos by Murray B.

MURRAY B.

I first heard about Gilman through Tim Yohannan and *Maximum RocknRoll* in 1986, when the first planning stages were being made public. I don't think I went to any of the meetings at Gilman before it opened, but I did help with some of the construction. I thought it had promise, it was about the right size.

1986   photo by Murray B.

I remember going to one of those City of Berkeley planning meetings discussing Gilman. I remember Tim Y.'s insistence on setting up a place that would actually stay in existence a long time, unlike other places like Ruthie's Inn or Barrington Hall, places that came and went. I thought that was a good thing.

The membership aspect was interesting. At first they weren't announcing who was playing at the shows, just that you should just come and support the place and see what happened. That seemed strange to me.

Eventually Gilman got more amenities and got more club-like—the store got more reliably run, things like that. It became a better place to go to, I think. The sound quality was pretty bad in the beginning, and that got better over the years.

The "no alcohol" policy was annoying, since you had to drink outside or go to a nearby restaurant or something. Also, there's not many seats or tables inside, so it's limiting socially—you can't sit around a table and talk.

It's a different experience than the other clubs that I'm used to going to. I went to one or two of the membership meetings at Gilman after it opened, but it reminded me a little too much of student radical meetings, so I wasn't too interested in working there. There was always going to be two or three people with a strong agenda and an urge to ramrod everything down other people's throats. It doesn't make for a very enjoyable experience. What were the people coming together to do? Because really, most of the time, what it amounts to is that there are a couple of people that are actually organizing everything, and everybody else is just sort of following them along. Things are only going to happen in meetings when something is going wrong, and then they're not going to be very pleasant to attend.

1991   photo by Murray B.

The impression I got over the years that I went there regularly (1987 to 1996) was that things at Gilman stayed pretty much the same, it just seemed like there were fewer "regulars" and more new people. The best thing about Gilman for me was that it was reliable, it was open, and it had shows every weekend. The whole early "geek-core" trash-fests with Stikky, Isocracy, etc., were pretty memorable and fun.

All photos by Murray B., 1988-1994

KAMALA P.

Victor H. rushed to my coffee warehouse job that day in 1986 and proclaimed that he had found the place. Victor was quite the eccentric. He and I had been working together for over a year putting on illegal punk shows in illegal locations all over the East Bay and San Francisco: New Method Warehouse, Own's Pizza Parlor, the Seventh Street Warehouse, and many other places whose names I cannot remember. Always we were under the threat of having the shows shut down by cops or by any of the other forces that be.

When Victor and I started doing shows at Own's Pizza Parlor, a hole-in-the-wall place with unbelievably crappy pizza, we thought that we had found our place. The owner, Own, was willing to let us have shows and was even going to legalize it by getting an entertainment permit. Our first show was, by our standards, a great success. It was Nomeansno's first appearance in the Bay Area, and joining them on the bill was Victim's Family, the Lookouts, The Mr. T Experience, and Complete Disorder. All the bands were great and fifty people came. We were ecstatic that we were able to pay Nomeansno $100 and give Own $125. He, however, didn't seem to concur. He asked us to raise our door price and get more people in. It turns out he was expecting to get rich off the scheme. Deflated, Victor and I finished off the shows we already had booked there and went back to dreaming about a place for us.

Victor was an eccentric. As closely as he and I worked together on organizing shows, I never saw where he lived, nor did I know how he earned his income. He was an artist, but I never saw any of his work. He had an amazing amount of energy, and was about 45 years old when I met him. An ex-hippie who had sworn off drugs a long time ago, a mutual friend of ours, later revealed to me that Victor was, in fact, a pill-popper of amphetamines. Victor always wore black jeans, black boots, a black windbreaker, and black horn-rimmed glasses. This mutual friend also elbowed his way into Victor's house once, looked in his closet, and found seven identical sets of this costume (minus the horn-rimmed glasses). Victor worked tirelessly at promoting our shows. He found spaces for our shows, flyered all over the place, and was a whirlwind during the shows, being everywhere at once, until the wee hours of the morning. To be quite honest, I don't remember how Victor and I met.

Summertime in 1986, he drags me away from work. We go out to get a hot fudge sundae for lunch and he tells me about this warehouse on Gilman Street in Berkeley. He had met with the landlord earlier and it sounded promising. Victor had been honest with him. We wanted to make a punk club there. The landlord was nonplussed, even pleased. "That would be perfect, because I run weaving classes behind the warehouse during the day, so I really don't want anything going on here during those hours," quoted Victor of the landlord.

"You mean, he would actually want us there?" I asked unbelievingly.

Victor nodded, and we headed down there. At the time, Gilman Street below San Pablo Avenue was a very industrial area, so most everything shut down after 6:00 PM. Our closest residential neighbors were a block away and the only two businesses open after 6:00 PM were an independent movie theater and a burrito place. It was a perfect location, we would not offend anyone here with our looks or noise. Additionally, at $2,000 per month for a 2,000 square foot location, it wasn't a bad deal.

I couldn't sleep that night. It was a dream, this place. Victor and I could put shows together and not worry about the cops or rely on the whims of an owner wanting to make a buck. Though it was attainable, Victor and I didn't have the money. We had just started saving our money, and neither one of us expected to find the ideal place so soon. I spent all night thinking. I couldn't get my brain to stop.

The next week Victor and I met everyday and tried to concoct schemes for getting money. But every scheme was just that. "Tim from MRR is looking for a place as well," Victor said to me one day. "He's been saving for a while."

"I already asked him. He's dead set on getting something in San Francisco. He has something against the East Bay ever since his house over here was robbed!" I joked.

Now, for me, that would signal the end of the issue. Not for Victor. He harassed Tim every day, called him and insisted Tim come and look at this place on Gilman. Finally, out of frustration, Tim climbed into Victor's Volvo station wagon and headed over to the East Bay. And Tim fell for the place.

Soon, however, Victor and I felt pushed out. Tim had a very different idea about the space than we did. He wanted it to be a collective effort, whereas Victor and I had thought of the thing as our baby. In the end, Tim's ideas, generally, made the most sense, but at the time, we were chagrined. One meeting in particular disturbed us. Tim and company had this idea of not advertising the shows. "We want people to come here regardless of who's playing and make it into a kind of community center." Victor and I were appalled. At the time, the punk scene was so tiny that we felt it was unfair, especially to the touring bands, to limit advertising. Victor, our friend Ryan, and I walked into another room and shut the door to gripe about this idea, when suddenly we heard pounding on the door. It was Lawrence L., and he was yelling, "What are you guys talking about in there that you can't share with the group?" Victor and I decided to step back from the developments at 924 Gilman and lick our wounds. For us, our dream almost came true, and we came very close to having our own space.

Gilman opened New Year's Eve, 1986. I was driving up University Avenue when I saw a dirty white van with a Washington license plate. I signaled to the van to pull over and I asked, "Are you guys Subvert?" Indeed they were, so I invited them to stay at my house. They were grateful and came over. We joked about the non-advertising policy at Gilman. "Where are you guys playing?" I'd jokingly ask. "Oh, we can't tell you that!" They all decided to do something for New Year's and they ended up forgetting where I lived and my phone number. The singer of Subvert got separated from his band and ended up at a Grateful Dead concert dropping acid. By morning, he had completely forgotten everything except for my name. He called MRR and said to Tim, "Hi, my name is Eric and I sing for Subvert. I've lost my band and for some reason the word Kamala keeps coming up in my mind as being linked to my band. Is Kamala a person, place, or thing?" Tim laughed and gave him my number. I found the rest of his band six blocks away, sleeping in their van in front of a motel.

As frustratingly usual, Tim had a better idea about running a show space than we did. I soon found myself back in the fold of the Project. He had an amazing capacity to galvanize people, and he had very creative ideas for doing shows. For Victor and me, just having a space for us punks was a novelty in and of itself. Tim, however, was determined to not just have shows, but to have shows with themes, to have eclectic bills, and to really create a community center for the freaks and run by the freaks. Some of Gilman Street's ideas I didn't like. For example, there was a Goddess Night show, in which only female bands played. I found this concept condescending and refused to be involved in any part of it. There was also a night which the Feederz played and the singer, up on stage with live cockroaches glued to his bald head, threw a dead dog into the crowd, splattering many with blood.

However, many of the early shows are etched positively in my memory. One show in particular was New Year's Eve, 1987, one year after Gilman opened. Max was the guitar player in a band called The Naked Lady Wrestlers, and he was very full of himself. He challenged Gilman's house band, Isocracy, to a competition. Tim made it into a "fight match," with referees, the stage transformed into a boxing ring, and chances for the crowd to vote for their preferred band of the night. Isocracy and The Naked Lady Wrestlers took turns of three-song sets. When the bands had finished, we found Max and his cohorts stuffing the ballot box. Despite the attempt at political corruption, Isocracy won the "fight" and were crowned the winners.

The development of Isocracy happened because of Gilman. Isocracy turned Gilman into a playground. Every time they played, Gilman's floors would be covered by junk by the end of their set, be it stuffed animals, dirty diapers, or candy. I pitied the bands who were forced to play after them. No other space in the world, besides Gilman, would've put up with their antics. One particular Isocracy set I remember was when a young man by the name of Slither (so named for his missing two front teeth), brought huge bags of kitty litter to the show and poured it into the crowd during Isocracy's set. The subsequent kitty litter dust forced everyone to evacuate after the show, and caused weeklong respiratory problems for every patron there.

I remember Operation Ivy's first show, which took place at Gilman. We all liked their music. Jesse M., the singer, had an interesting stage presence at the time, which he thankfully grew out of. His arm traversed his stomach as if he had appendicitis.

At the time of Gilman's opening, we had a lot of trouble with skinheads coming in and causing many fights and problems. We all argued how best to deal with them. The pacifist camp said that we shouldn't fight with them because we then would be reducing ourselves down to their level. The other camp said, "Fuck it, let's beat the shit out of them." One night, frustrated by so many years of skinhead rowdiness, the two camps came together. MDC was playing at Gilman and it was rumored that skinheads were going to come to the show and beat up Dave, the singer for MDC, because of their new song "Skinhead." A gang of about twenty skinheads showed up and tried to rush the door, but we were all fed up by then. A huge fight, complete with baseball bats, chains, and chairs, erupted in front of Gilman. The gang rushed to their cars and we were on top of the cars, banging in windshields, knocking off rear-view mirrors, and riddling their cars with dents. They drove away and never came back. I guess they were shocked by our new-found unity. So ended that argument.

When Tim decided to hand over Gilman to another group, I was disappointed. Despite the fact that he "took Gilman away from Victor and me," Tim and his crew had succeeded in creating more than a punk-show space and many of us, as humans and as bands, grew together as a result. The space has suffered, in my opinion, in recent years, because people who had the same vision as myself now run the space. I don't know what's happened to Victor. Last I heard, he had moved to L.A. Gilman is still a unique place, and I feel lucky to have had the space with me throughout my twenties. While I have many ideas for making Gilman into the place it once was (including bringing back the "no advertising" policy), I would feel hypocritical in doing so. I don't have the energy for going in and dealing with a collective. I consider myself an autonomous person and I would blow up many blood vessels trying to accomplish anything under the elephantine weight of the collective process. So I shall keep my opinions to myself until the time comes, if it ever does, when I am willing to put aside my personality traits and agree to compromise.

At a time when just about the whole scene seems to be heading pell mell away from some of punk's original ideas (do-it-yourself attitudes, anti-commercialism, cooperation, grassroots communities, etc.), a good-sized chunk of the Bay Area scene has decided to run headlong against the grain. As you may have read in previous issues, MRR has been trying to save enough money to finance a community-run cultural center (We've tried for 3 years, but either never found the right place or had enough money to do it right), but this dream was by no means our's alone. A cluster of people who used to put on shows at New Method warehouse, and later at Own's Pizza, had the same hopes.

So, we combined our energies, and recently (five months ago), Victor (madman that he is) located a sire in Berkeley (after looking almost daily for a year) and convinced me (actually, it was more like dragged me kicking and screaming) to go for it. We then rented the warehouse, all 3000 square feet of it, and started plowing through the red tape. We had to wait 4 months for a hearing before the Board of Adjustment, and finally got our day on Sept. 8. In preparation, we held meetings every Thursday night for about 3 months, and through word-of-mouth built up a core of 60 people who broke into four committees: security, booking, membership, and construction. These committees democratically formulated the proposals for the governing of the clubhouse (not a club) which were then discussed and altered by consensus of the whole membership, and when we went in for our hearing we had done all our homework. Not only were we able to be specific about our intentions, but we also did parking studies, neighborhood petitions, etc., etc., and even got the support of Berkeley's socialist mayor, Gus Newport.

Anyway, the Board approved our proposal by an 8-1 vote, and now we've entered the construction phase, which should be completed by the end of October. We are building a stage, soundproof some walls, build 2 wheelchair-accessible bathrooms, etc. Some of our expenses are running like this: sound system $6000, lighting $1000, electrical work $1000, construction materials $3000, insurance $2500, monthly rent $2000---by the time we open we'll have spent approximately $26,000 on this project.

But now, let me tell you about some of our ideas/ideals. This joint is gonna be a clubhouse for the scene. Events in the place will take place on weekend nights (see the following article on how we'd like them to bring a whole new definition to what a "show" is, harkening back to the wild, unpredictable mix of the early days of punk. Nowadays, you can pretty well tell what a show will be like before you ever go to it). We'll rent out rehearsal space for cheap, as well as have "community meetings" and other forums, films, etc. We want to create an environment that fosters communication, not only between performers and members, but also between members themselves.

Did I say members? Right, this will be a membership clubhouse, and anyone can join--for a mere $2 and a commitment to participate in a violence-free, vandalism-free environment. Because of the danger of getting busted, no alcohol will be allowed inside either. It's the responsibility of members to not only abide by these few guidelines, but to encourage others to abide as well. It's the only way we'll be able to stay open, and the best way to have an honest, creative situation. Security is being governed by the security committee, who in turn must answer (as do all committees) to the membership at large--but we all realize that ultimately we are all security people--it is our place together to create and preserve.

The success of this experiment will depend on our imagination and our commitment. Right now we've got lots of both, and have begun an outreach program to get as many people as possible to our open houses (every Saturday from 3-5 PM throughout the construction period) to get acquainted with each other. One of the main problems at the "commercial" punk shows now is that most people don't know each other anymore. We want to re-establish that sense of community, of common purpose, and feel that's the best way to insure a healthy, non-violent scene.

As you can see, our hopes are pretty high and only time will tell whether this experiment can serve as an example that people can still create, don't have to "sell out" to commercialism, and even some of the hardened cynics around here are starting to get excited. I'll keep you appraised as to how it goes. Meanwhile, if you want to help out and live in the area, come visit. If you live far away but would like to join (in case you ever visit here), all you need to do is send in $2 (and 25¢ postage) for a membership card. And if you'd just like to help out financially, you're more than welcome to send in a donation. Thanks,   Tim

SOME FEATURES OF THIS CLUBHOUSE:

An open mike for people to question bands on opinions, lyrics, attitudes, etc

A membership requirement of commitment to non-violence and creative effort--the reestablishment of "community"

No advertising of specific bands--only that shows will take place on given days, hopefully exposing people to more experiences

A library, as well as zine and record sales

A new definition of what a show is: tons of surprises from the stage--not just bands, but also speakers, movies, performance.

Non-stage weirdness from the Mindfuck Committee, a 3-ring circus as well as educational fun

Cooperation not competition: guaranteed minimum payments to performers, as well as fair splits determined by the artists themselves

Taken from an article written by Tim Y. in MRR, Nov. 1986

VIVIAN S.

Being a jazz musician didn't exactly prepare me to work in a punk club. But, at the age of 45, I was ready to try something new in my life.

Jake, my son, and singer with the soon-to-become-band named Filth, asked me to go with him to a meeting at the newly formed Gilman Street Project. The club was at its beginning stages and I was there to help mold its foundation. It was a wonderful sight to behold—all ages, all races of young adults working together to create a music club that was a safe place to congregate.

After the club opened, I went, at first, just to hear the music. It was a new experience for me as I didn't know much about the music. I began to really like the sounds and to understand what the musicians were trying to say to the audience. I became friends with most everyone, and consequently, I became known as Ma Sob, being from El Sobrante.

After a short length of time, I started working in the club store with my daughter, Nina. It was there that I really got to know a lot of the musicians and their friends. At times, outside of Gilman, we would hang out together in cafes.

For a period of time, while working at the store, I also became one of the bouncers at Gilman. I stopped several fights, threw out quite a few guests, and mended some bloody noses. The bouncer job was not for me, as my purpose of being at Gilman was to have fun, not to get beat up.

After two years of working there, I decided to move on and develop other things in my life.

I now look back at my years at Gilman with wonderful memories. It was there that I started writing music. I now have two released CDs out in the world. I can very happily say that working and hanging out at the Gilman Street Project was a very needed experience at that time in my life.

Thank you Gilman!

West County Times **March 15, 1988**

Project club a place to listen, stomp and celebrate

WEAR SOME sturdy shoes. And a helmet. It's Friday night, and you're going to The Gilman Street Project in Berkeley, one of the Bay Area's most exciting punk rock clubs.

But first you have to find it. Located in Berkeley's industrial area, The Project, like a '20s speakeasy, is a word-of-mouth operation. No signs will guide you. Start at the Rialto Theater and cross Gilman to number 924, a dimly lighted doorway sandwiched between a caning shop and Allied Radiator Co.

If in doubt, just check out the foot traffic. If it looks like Hollywood sent over actors from "The Night of the Living Dead," and "Rumble on the Docks," then you've arrived at The Project.

Inside, you'll be greeted by whey-faced girls with kohl-circled eyes, their hair a combination of butched sidewalls and spiked pompadours tinted iridescent magenta, royal blue or chartreuse. Or they may sport rooster cuts, skunk strips or skin heads. The total effect is that of a junkie hair stylist run amok.

Not to worry though. That's just punk. But does the word "punk" put you off? Does it still connote a street-smart kid with a bad attitude?

In the 1970s, "punk" took on new meanings. For some it defined the new young rebel with a cause. For others, it became a cause for alarm when the Sex Pistol's Sid Vicious introduced an ideology that embraced violence, graphic lyrics and sadomasochism.

"Even though punk has originally been involved with negativity and darkness, it's becoming brighter. The scene (at The Project) reminds me of the Fillmore — the zany hippy places. To me, what's going on at Gilman is the next logical step (for punk)," said Lawrence Livermore, a columnist for Maximum Rock and Roll, an underground punk rock magazine.

When The Gilman Street Project opened on New Year's Eve 1986, the founders of Maximum Rock and Roll, who advanced $40,000 in start-up funds, hoped to create a new kind of non-profit club where people could meet for music and communication.

Their goal was a new alternative "where punk, mod, radical, conservative, hippie or just plain Joe would be acceptable," according to the club brochure.

Members pay a one-time $2 fee and are asked to sign a pledge to remain sober, drug-free and reasonably non-violent on and about the club premises. Open Friday, Saturday and Sunday nights from 7 until the last band packs up, The Project charges $4 at the door. Alcoholic beverages are not allowed. All ages are allowed.

Tonight, Vivian Sayles is riding shotgun for the security crew. Positioned by the entry, the striking green-

Please see **PROJECT,** Page 2D

PROJECT

From Page 1D

eyed blonde with a modified punk haircut pleasantly greets and instructs newcomers to the club.

A 13-year resident of El Sobrante, the vivacious mother of four composes and performs classical and jazz piano. She's also in a choir at St. Joseph's Church in Pinole.

But at The Project, she's just another volunteer, a coordinator of bands, personnel, sound equipment and lighting.

And occasionally she's a bouncer. Sometimes revelers come to the club who think it's, y'know, fascist to charge entry fees.

Like tonight. Enter the studded Hulk, a gate-crasher with bolts in his earlobes, a leather jacket with so many studs that it glows in the dark, a body the size of a small condo. Bald head, mean eyes, green teeth and no entry fee in his wallet.

Sayles gripped the hulk's wrist as he lumbered by her and spun him around. Smiling sweetly, she showed him the door.

Was she frightened? "Nah," Sayles shrugged. Even when they look that mean, she said, they're just youngsters and don't mean any harm.

"I like being around these kids. They're honest and fun to talk to. And even when I don't like some of the music, I enjoy its newness," she said.

Sayles first came to The Project in early 1986. Impressed with the club's pacifist, anti-drug philosophy, she became a volunteer along with her daughter, Nina, 21, and son, Jake, 18. Nina studies broadcast communications at San Francisco State, and Jake is a warehouseman for Peet's Coffee in Berkeley.

Jake — who helped build the stage, walls and sound system — calls The Project a "unique experience in the Bay Area, a punk Disneyland," where bands, fans and promoters have an equal stake in maintaining the club.

Periodically, The Project has threatened to shut down, due to a shortage of funds or of volunteers. Several hundred volunteers met earlier this month to discuss "restructuring." The club plans to remain open, for the moment at least.

Vivian Sayles said the majority of people who come to the club are pleasant and well-behaved.

Unless we're talking thrash. This is where the heavy shoes and helmet come in handy. When a fast, aggressive song gets rolling, people form a rough circle and begin to move around rapidly, flinging their bodies wildly in a game of human bumper cars called "thrashing." It's like a conga line gone berserk.

"It looks a whole lot more violent than it is," Jake said.

On a good night, the 3,000-square-foot warehouse — every inch spray-painted with slogans, cartoons and murals — fills to its 270-person capacity, with another 100 fans turned away at the door.

The Project features underground art, theater and comedy, but it's music that packs in the crowds. They come for bands like Nasal Sex, Crimpshrine, and Rabid Lassie.

Besides various forms of punk, Gilman bands also include heavy metal and "noise." Instruments for the latter are kitchen implements such as electric mixers and egg beaters that produce, shall we say, a scrambled sound.

To a first-time visitor, the music may sound like a mixture of electronic feedback, an ear-splitting bass line and unintelligible lyrics.

But punk enthusiasts say it's the lyrics that tell all. Like 1960s folk protesters, punks protest everything from conformity to wars, pollution and Mom's apple pie.

"They're deeply interested in political causes, and even though they don't actively protest like the hippies, they think and feel as deeply about today's problems," Vivian Sayles said.

Is she a punk rocker? In a way, she said pensively. She likes its spirit of protest.

— Carol Percy

JAKE FILTH

Fuckkkkk... It was a little scary going to shows back then. You would have to watch your back. No one else would. The Mab, Ruthie's Inn, the Farm, in 1983, 1984, 1985. Shit. You could be dancing, having fun, next thing you know, twenty skinheads are mobbing you! Fuck, some of the punks were as bad as the skins! Fights at every show, and rarely would anyone jump in and help you out. Punks regularly got beat down by jocks and skins and rednecks. This created for a scene with a lot of hard motherfuckers. Even if you didn't get in a brawl at the show, you would come out of the pit bruised and bleeding. At the least. Uh! Scary and beautiful in its intensity.

As two decades pass, remembrance can get a little hazy. I was 13 or 14 years old when Jeff and Aaron first dragged me to KPFA. They brought me to MRR radio (on the walk there, two blocks, a skin broke my little finger with his boot). Tim Yohannan was immediately and genuinely friendly. Beer and cigarettes for all! Shit, I had a good time and continued going in the years ahead. Tim had an idea about punk. Surprisingly unarticulated, considering *Maximum RocknRoll* gave him an outlet to express anything he could say. I decided to be involved in this vision of a unified punk scene, of which the Gilman Street Project would be the third article. The venue section, one could say.

Martin and Kamala invited me to come on down and help build this thang. Me and my mother went down and got our first membership cards! Before the place even opened! Cool!

We built the stage, painted, nailed in soundproofing. We held meetings that decided club policy on alcohol, membership, band lyrical standards, security, etc. Crazy that these original doctrines have stuck with Gilman through the years, while audience and core committee members change frequently. The ideals stuck.

One of the more radical decisions we made was to have zero hired security. No fuck bouncers. The kids would be on guard. This was an important step 'cuz when the bouncers at other previous punk spots saw the kids dancing, they would get "confused" and try to fuck us up. And when a real fight did break out, the bouncers wouldn't do shit to stop it. At the Gilman, we, the punx, would put an end to the drinking and the violence so inherent in the punk world. And so 924 tore punk apart.

Not everyone wanted a "happy pit." Not all the punks want a sober, safe environment. Many of these people thrived on the intense violence and bitter emotional release dark stinky punk venues gave up. Hence, when told by their own folk they couldn't get drunk and thrash anymore, a schism borned. Gilman vs. them.

These punks of the early eighties were not spawned from a society that felt any love for its self-rejected. No cheerleaders with dyed pink hair were present then. No jocks with noserings paving a clear path for tattooed freaks. Hot Topic? No. Fat Wreck Chords? No. Average society fucks had not yet (at least not since the middle late 1970s) stolen our fashion thereby making it okay for *us* to wear what we always have worn. In that era, AMERICA FUCKING HATED PUNKS. Cops would come to shows and fuck punks up. Our parents wouldn't look at us, groups were formed to "deprogram" punks, our teachers refused to have us sit in their classes. This rejection created for a certain being in these kids. A certain breed of hardcore kid. We hated back. Shit, we knew the bomb was gonna be dropped. We knew we had no time to remake this world. Angry, angry in a razor-to-the-skin kind of way. And the reason any of us survived this literal, potential fleshing was by going to the gig and thrashing out our frustration. This did lead to violence. This led to a raging, unstoppable boundless enthusiasm.

Gilman's idea of a united punk scene could not encompass this fierce energy. So the 924 Gilman killed this energy. Screamer, Angus, Johnny Puke, Scab and their ilk were first ostracized by the Gilman punks, then eventually banned altogether.

If your brain works in historical, dramatic waves like mine, then one could notice two things happening around this happy punk venue: one, 924 Gilman had created a new punk, or two, Gilman was just a harbinger of punk creation and punk future.

The whole Gilman crew stuck together. Security, membership, booking along with concerned audience members fought until the last generation of punks born under the bomb got tired and drifted away. Not much actual fistfighting. We just locked the doors to them, and ignored them on the street. Imagine. They drifted away, these "mad punks." We invisibled them.

Fighting has always been what led Gilman to be a safe place. Friends getting together to whup down another group of friends. It happened again in the early '90s when the Grimples and Filth and the Econo boys, along with all the Oakland punks *not* directly involved in The Project that is Gilman, kicked the living shit outta the local skins enough times that they all left town. That made the spot safe for years, sure.

I left membership, and all direct involvement, in the Gilman in 1988 or 1989, before the second round of violence.

Something in the heart, if not the soul itself, of punk was killed.

Above: front door, 1987   photographer unknown
Right: 1987   photo by Cammie T.

MATT F.

Being the garbageman at Gilman will be something I will always remember. From the summer of 1987 to the summer of 1988 I handled my trash duty with pride.

So, it being my neighborhood, where me and my best friend Tim Armstrong grew up, it was obvious to me that being part of something as special as Gilman, I would take my trash duty seriously. Gilman Street was always more than just a place to play music for me. Tim Yohannan did all kinds of odd jobs there, and at one meeting he went on a tirade about all the things he did for the place, and one of them was that every Monday he would take out the garbage and haul it to the dump. Well, in the middle of all this commotion I raised my hand and said, "I'll do the trash." Tim just looked at me and said, "Fine, meet me after the meeting." So of course I was really stoked because I was gonna be the garbageman. I was then handed a key for the door and also an alarm key, and my eagerness for Monday morning consumed me.

Monday morning came and Yohannan came down and showed me what I needed to do. Basically, I would pick up all the bags that everyone put together, throw them in the back of the Operation Ivy car—because the thing had the hugest trunk—and I would run it to the Berkeley dump and pay my six bucks to toss it. In between a cup of coffee and a Winston, I would fling the bags outta the trunk into a big pile and congratulate myself on a job well done.

The first time I ran solo on trash detail, I went outside to put the last bag in the trunk and this little fucker was going through it. I said, "What the hell are you doing?" He answered back, "Man, there's cans in there." So with that knowledge, we went through the garbage and separated the cans from the other shit. From then on I put the cans aside for my new little friend.

I took this job seriously like I would take any job. Anybody who knows me would tell you the same thing. I had this job for a long time and I loved it. I fucking loved being the garbageman. Sometimes I would tell the people cleaning with me to separate the cans or whatever. I was serious, and no recyclable would be wasted on my watch. You see, the way it worked is, I would pick up the trash every Monday on my own time, and on my own money, and my reward for being the trash man was that I would get into one show a week free. But it was not always like that. At the time, I would get reimbursed the six bucks, but that was it. So I knew what I had to do.

About a month into my new job, I went to the next meeting with a plan in my head. All I really wanted was the same privilege that everyone else got. One show a week free. If you worked the door that's what you got and I wanted the same thing. To be honest, I felt a little nervous about asking for this because I felt I was being a little ostentatious about it, but it worked out well and one show a week was granted. Then Isocracy played.

You have to realize that these guys would get every piece of trash from every dumpster in North America, it seemed, months before they would play. Everything imaginable: old shredded phone books, toys, shoes, you get the picture. Anyway, they would bring it to the show and throw it around inside while they were playing. I mean, don't get me wrong, it was a great show, but a nightmare in the aftermath. One Monday I came in and it appeared as if the cleanup crew had just given up. There was stuff everywhere. I don't know how many bags I filled, but I had to make two or three trips to the dump. This got to me. I must have been in a bad mood or something. Fine! I'm gonna go back to the next meeting and relay my grievance. My speech went a little like this, "I'm not gonna name any names, but Isocracy played and obviously the cleanup crew gave up and that's fine and all, but if I'm gonna do this trash detail I want one show a week free and two if Isocracy plays." No one gave me any flack, so on with my Monday morning cleanups I went.

I would imagine, at times, of having my own garbage truck, that's how into this job I was. Then one day the phone rang and my services were no longer needed. Out went the dreams of the garbage truck, but no one could take away my garbage credentials...

A message to the guy who has my old job now, plain and simple. The black Hefty bags are the best, and remember to separate the cans, and maybe your garbage truck dreams will come true.

Above: Matt wanted to use this graphic of him. I believe Murray B. took the original photo.

Below: Isocracy at work, 1988   photo by Murray B.   Garbagemen pre-Matt   photo by Cammie T.

DEVON M.

I worked there a little bit during the first couple of years it was open (1987 and 1988) and booked shows there for a couple months in the late 1980s/early 1990s—I don't remember exactly when. Mostly I just attended shows there.

I first heard about Gilman through *Maximum RocknRoll* magazine in 1986. I first went to a show there in early 1987. There were only about twelve people there and it was a bit of a shock at first, because I was used to going to other clubs where it was usually really crowded and violent. Gilman shows were generally smaller and mostly goofy, driving around on Big Wheels, etc. But I really liked it that way, it was much more fun. It felt like you were just going and hanging out with your friends and "playing" rather than going to a show. We would go every weekend, it didn't matter what bands were playing. Everyone knew each other's names—it was kinda like *Cheers*. Every time you went there, you'd meet somebody new, and it just got bigger and bigger like that. It became known as "Romper Room" to the thuggy types, who couldn't deal with the silliness.

Eventually the shows got bigger, more people started coming, and the feeling started to change from just a bunch of friends, all equal, to "fans" and hero worship—that typical rock shit. We wouldn't just go to the shows; my friends and I would plan crazy shit, whether our band was playing that night or not. Like bringing a card-table and playing cards in the middle of the pit, with people complaining, "How are we supposed to mosh?" We had them mosh around us, with one or two occasionally dashing in to get dealt a hand. Or another time, one of my friends, Sir Davey Augustus Sillysauce G-String the 3rd, a.k.a "the Love Bandit," climbed a ladder with a Big Wheel in each hand and struck a Christ pose for a band's entire set. Another time we made a "square" pit when a band called Thrashing Hectic Circle played. The band didn't think it was very funny. Sometimes we would bring ridiculous cos-

1987   photo by Murray B.

tume changes and change our clothes during each song of a band's set and do different dances as well. Some of the more "serious" bands didn't seem to appreciate it very much, but eventually it seemed that they got used to it, or just seemed to tolerate it better. Tim Y. actually would ask us sometimes to go in and "goof up" tense, heavy pits, kinda like sending in the clowns at a rodeo if the bull gets loose. It didn't always work, and we kinda felt like "mosh police" sometimes, not spontaneous.

We got a band together, Boo! Hiss! Plffpt! Why Don't We Throw Some Tomatoes At Those Guys?, and it was a perfect outlet for our ridiculousness. I had no aversion to being an idiot, and I don't think anyone else in the band did either. It annoyed most people except those in the audience who knew us. Gilman was the real inspiration for us to be like we were. I think we probably would have been killed if we played at most other venues. It actually didn't feel any different being on stage versus being in the audience. I was doing the same stupid things regardless.

The last time I went during the "MRR years" was the Final Conflict show in late 1988. I was so disheartened by that show and all the carnage and violence and blood. That really showed me how far Gilman had fallen. And then, a week or so later, the club closed down. When the next group reopened the place, I was skeptical. I thought, "how can they possibly recreate what had existed there?" It seemed kinda sacrilegious, to a degree. But I went to a show there a little while after it opened, saw all these kids having fun, and my negativity lessened. I still felt a little old and jaded, but thought it was pretty cool. Hearing the creepy stories about some of the people involved in this second group now running the space, though, made me a little ill.

During those first couple years when I was there a lot, I didn't participate that much in the actual workings of the club—mostly just cleaned up after shows or helped at the door—but I was aware of the structure, how it worked, and what everyone's role was. With so few people attending those early shows, you got to meet all the people working the shows as well, and see what was involved with their jobs. I got to see what went in to putting on a show and how it all worked. To me, if punks don't run the place, there shouldn't be a punk show there.

I still go there fairly regularly, once or twice a month, when my band isn't on tour. But now I just go to see certain bands play there, as opposed to just hanging out there. It does have more of a "club" feel now to me than it used to, but it also has the feeling of a bazaar sometimes, with all the different vendors there selling their wares.

There was a brief period of time where I had some conflicts with some individuals running the place, and thought that if it did get shut down, new venues would rise phoenix-like out of the ashes. However, as city ordinances, neighbors, businesses, and authoritarians make it harder and harder to open all-ages venues, I see Gilman as a vital place despite any ups and downs I may have felt towards it in the past.

I think the relatively frequent worker turnover at Gilman is good. It keeps the jaded, bitter, angry folks at a minimum and brings in the enthusiastic, motivated folks.

Gilman gave me lots of confidence in dealing with others, better social skills, etc. It also gave me an opportunity to meet way more people than I would have otherwise. It was where I first met openly gay punks, vegans, and true anarchists. It expanded my world on a lot of things. It was where I could be myself. I never had to think about if I looked cool enough or if people would accept me.

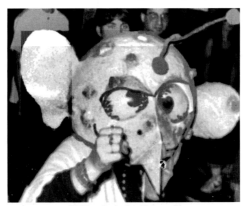

1987   photo by Murray B.

KERITH PICKETT

I heard about Gilman through a friend that I was dating at the time. I remember the first time I went (fall, 1987). I was 16, and it was our mission to get in without paying, which was pretty funny since I ended up being a regular volunteer there, making sure everyone else paid to get in and followed the rules. We hid behind one of the couches in the "community" room (now the office) when they were kicking everyone out to clear the club before the show started. Everyone knew we were there, we were laughing and being so ridiculous. I guess they just chose to let us slide that time.

My first impression of the place was, "Why haven't I been here before?" It was like I had found something that I had been looking for, but hadn't known was missing. It was my first encounter with live punk rock. It was amazing to me, and absolutely what I needed at that time in my life. I remember being enthralled by the community that I didn't know had coordinated itself into something greater than just rebellion. Here was something that was focused, somewhat refined, and made into a community center. It was exhilarating and exciting. After a couple months of going there, I started volunteering. I felt like I was getting so much from everyone there, the way people helped each other work together and try to make it a good experience for everyone, that I felt I needed to contribute something.

The Crew, 1987   photo by Cammie T.

I worked the door a lot, and did security sometimes, although that was really hard, being a little girl and trying to deal with skinheads. There was a group of us working there from the same high school: Stacey, Kim, Marsha, and me. We all knew each other and supported each other, especially when doing security, because it seemed like there were a lot of fights going on at the time. There was a lot of tension with certain groups that would consistently come and harass us. We always had each other's backs, and that was an important part of being there, knowing that my girlfriends were there with me. I remember a particularly big fight out front with skinheads, after we had decided we weren't going to let them in the club at all anymore. I learned, from that night, that we have the power in numbers, and that if we need to fight an "enemy," then we can get it together and we can make it happen. I felt so victorious, because things changed after that. The skinhead threat didn't loom so large anymore and what had once seemed unattainable (getting rid of the skinheads), now was reality.

It wasn't easy for me to start working there—it was very intimidating. Getting shot down on a point or issue at meetings made it hard to keep coming back and voicing opinions. But after I did, I was really glad that I had, but there were definitely some barriers there. For instance, I remember having democratic voting, and the outcome might be in one direction, and then having Tim Yohannan overrule the decision. I was flabbergasted. It was like, "Why did we bother having a vote?" I have a lot of respect for Tim. I think he really went out on a limb putting that place together. It's just that if he had been up-front and been willing to say, "Look, when it comes down to it, I'm the one paying for this thing, so, I'm sorry, but that's just not how it's gonna be," it would have made it easier to deal with. There was hypocrisy there, because for me, it was a community center, and that was my inspiration for working

Meeting, 1987   photo by Cammie T.

there. It was always a little bit of a struggle on that level.

Gilman wasn't my first experience with volunteering and community groups, but I had always felt alienation in other groups, like I was always the freak at the honorary clubs. Gilman was a place where I could be myself and fit in at the same time, to be accepted as the weirdo that I was, to accept my contribution regardless of how I looked. That's what made having the barriers at Gilman more of a challenge to me, and made me try and succeed within that framework. I realized that you're only going to get out as much as you put into a thing. I invested myself into Gilman pretty heavily, maybe too much sometimes, like getting down on someone hard if they tried to scam or something. I was wearing it like a badge or something, like I was one of the bricks in the building's walls. I started to see Gilman as something of my own. I saw it more as a place for me to hang out at rather than just go there to see bands. I ended up working there till the latter part of 1988, when the MRR group left. I didn't continue volunteering with the next group that came in after MRR. I kept coming back as a member and punkaholic and continued to find ways to fulfill that community need.

While attending SF State, I volunteered for MRR magazine doing layout and getting school credit. I used to resent the term "shit worker" for the contributors on the zine, but I loved doing graphics and being active, so I even worked at Epicenter for a while. Eventually I realized that I needed to move on. I didn't want to work at "Tim's place," on his terms. I wanted to be involved in something that I could give more direction to. I didn't feel like it could have changed very much the way that it was with Tim running it. I felt like I needed to do something a little more important with my life than helping put on punk rock shows and being a shitworker. I started working at the campus volunteer center and for a local child assault prevention group producing public relations materials. College marked an ending point for me working with Tim. I wanted to contribute in places where I felt people appreciated the work I did and took me seriously. Gilman was pretty thankless in a lot of ways, and it became tedious, and it became scary. Some nights were really scary, so I wanted to do something safer. I wanted to do something with a more tangible community effect, outside of my punk rock "family."

I think Gilman, MRR, and Epicenter helped prepare me for my later volunteer efforts. Going to meetings, learning about the group dynamic, the structure of a nonprofit-type group, decision-making, all definitely applied to work I did later with other groups. It allowed me to be more of a leader, because I had a vision of how I could make things different, and maybe better. I still go to Gilman occasionally. I am glad that it's still around, because there'll always be kids who need what I needed when I started working there—who maybe need a place that they can run to and take refuge in. I think a lot of young punk rockers have something to run away from, and part of what we are is an expression of that angst, and I think that's a vital part of what our community is about.

I love it when I go to Gilman and see an awesome show where the kids are really enjoying each other and feeling the music, and learning about being part of an alternative culture. You can see the sense of comfort and ease in them that maybe they can't find at home or at school. I think Gilman is most attractive to the younger generation of punks. The truth is, most of my friends don't go there much anymore—they like to go to places where they can drink while watching a band. I still like going there, though, and getting caught up in the contagious spirit of the people and the music. Sometimes I have to laugh at myself when I'm there, because I'll go two blocks away and have a beer behind a bush, and I feel so fucking ridiculous—I'm thirty years old and doing this! But Gilman is the heartbeat of the Bay Area punk scene, still. The music coming out of there is like a geyser that will not be stopped, and that's beautiful to me.

One experience that really encapsulates what Gilman is to me was the first time I saw Neurosis there. It was very spiritual for me, spiritual in the sense of my spirit seeing itself reflected in something else. The power they had, the anger and the political frustration that they expressed in their music rang so true to a note that was playing in me. I felt a sense of recognition of, "They get it too! I'm not alone!" Gilman gave me a sense of being able to share my burden with other people. We were punks struggling through it together, and coming up dancing. So angry, yet we're dancing and enjoying it, despite it all.

"Their (club members) education matters tremendously to me. We're doing something here that should be done in school, but that gets missed. Civics is a joke to most kids. The club is not entertainment as far as I'm concerned. The punk scene involves a sense of community, and values like responsibility for each other and building something. The bottom line criteria is whether these kids adopt responsibility and take care of it. For ten years the punk scene has been weaving the fabric. This club exemplifies the values of doing it yourself and staying non-commercial."
—Tim Y., from an article in The Voice (Bay Area newspaper), Sept. 1987

1986: We built something   photo by Murray B.

REBECCA W.

I first heard of the Gilman Street Project before it was even a physical entity. It was partly through MRR magazine and through friends. I actually even stopped by once during one of the planning meetings when they finally had the space and were planning construction, etc. Little did I know how large a part this place would play in my future.

As my friends and I hung out in Berkeley (Telegraph Avenue, more specifically) a lot at that time, it was a pretty natural progression for me to end up going to Gilman. The Berkeley Square and the Omni were the options for the under-21 crowd, but the idea of having to buy drink tickets really didn't appeal to me. Besides, Gilman was encouraging people to participate and have input in their whole process. What a 15-year-old, non-musically talented, quasi-punkette could have to contribute was yet to be seen, but of course, just the idea of being able to go to shows for free in trade for work was very appealing.

Some of what Gilman was about was really intriguing to me. The idea of giving teenagers control in their lives, what a concept! It seemed like if it wasn't your family telling you what to do, it was school. If it wasn't them, it was the police. I was pretty damn tired of the whole mess, and was mostly trying my hardest to keep the hell away from it all while having as much fun and as many adventures as I could find. Just like most teenagers I suppose.

I had been pretty politically active for a year or so, but was pulling away from the group I was working with. So I was used to working hard for a cause. Hell, I was used to working all my life. Gilman was a very attractive proposition and it seemed like I could actually have some fucking fun for a change. So after attending a few shows as a "customer," I volunteered as soon as I could. I believe I started out with door duties and membership-sales duties. When people realized I could count and wouldn't run off with the cash, I also worked the cash box and the store. After a while it didn't really matter where I was, it just depended on whether I got there early enough to pick out what I felt like doing—if not, oh well. On occasion I would do side door security or regular security. While I didn't mind helping clean up after a show, I often couldn't, as I would inevitably get stranded in Berkeley overnight (our bus system is ridiculously inadequate). It always felt a little more fulfilling to be participating in some event rather than merely attending. I felt like I would actually help the shows happen rather than feeling like it was up to the band or whatever to amuse or entertain me. After a time, you could say that it pretty much was my life every weekend for a couple of years.

Through Gilman, I was able to get to know and meet a lot of people. I assume that even now there are people from around the world that come to check it out. Nowadays, I'm not really in contact with most of my old friends from the club. However, I don't think that really matters. I think that getting to know them and exchange ideas and opinions, and learning from each other, was the most important part of the place for me. It's nothing personal that we don't see each other anymore. I like to think that we all are busily involved in fascinating projects that take up all our time. I did see some great shows, great bands (and found new favorite bands), but getting to know the people behind those bands and befriending newcomers was the most interesting part of the place for me. Hell, to be perfectly honest, on some nights I had no idea who was playing—it was just such a good place to hang out and talk to people.

1987   photos by Murray B.

I know Gilman's got this rep for being overly serious, uptight, and having this in-crowd phenomenon happening with all the folks that work there a lot. But you know, most of the people that I remember hearing this from were either over 21 or were often caught drinking outside too close to the club. It didn't matter if they didn't like it then and it still doesn't matter now. There were, and are still today, very few places a 14-year-old kid can go to see a show, and even work it if they wanted. So screw all those grouchy, cynical old folks who don't like it. Gilman was partially created to be a specifically all ages venue. As for the accusations about unprofessional business practices, I think that people often forget that this is a volunteer-run organization. What do you honestly expect? People will indubitably fuck up every once in a while. Everyone learns on the job. We are very sorry if it screwed someone over somehow. As you can see, I'm still pretty protective about Gilman. This was the place where I had a chance to grow up on my own terms. Besides that, this was an East Bay pride kind of thing too. We struggled to put this thing together from scratch and it was the only thing of its kind in California.

It was a fun environment, where I rarely ran into nazis/boneheads. That was a much more common occurrence in San Francisco at the time. When I would go to shows at the Farm, which was my other favorite place to go (RIP), I always felt like I had to watch out for the inevitable roaming idiots that came. Whereas at Gilman, if trouble came a-knocking, the show would stop and people would actually come together as a group to break up fights. At one point, we collectively decided to be outspoken about being a nazi-free zone at the club. Now that was unusual. I really think it's a bizarre thing that so many people and businesses won't blink twice if an obvious nazi walked into their work, and would unthinkingly serve them or take their money. I mean, I'm not suprised that stuff like that happens elsewhere in the U.S., but here, in the oh-so-multicultural San Francisco Bay Area?

Gilman was also my first experience with collective decision-making. It's a good feeling to know that if you had a problem with the way things were happening, you could talk about it with others at the meetings, and if you could get enough folks to agree with you, you all could change things around. While I didn't feel like I did contribute much to the discussions (I was just a little shy), I did try to be there for the meetings anyway. This helped me out a lot in the dojo (which I'll get to in a second), as we try to run things collectively also. While no money changes hands for most of the volunteers, most people gave a lot of time and energy to the Gilman Street Project.

The head directors definitely gave a lot of themselves. Now that was a grueling job. We went through a lot of folks, almost bleeding them dry. It's very difficult to try to guide a group into working collectively and not hierarchically. Unless you've been in those shoes, or been pretty damn close to the person in those shoes, you really have no idea how hard that is. It seems to me that people would often end up letting the head person make the "ultimate" decisions. Looking back now, I notice that a lot of "head honchos" got a lot of the blame and not much glory. They all seemed to suffer from massive burnout before abdicating their positions. Luckily for the club, there was always someone there to pick up the reins when it was time.

While I rarely go to Gilman these days, the place still holds a lot of links to my life. Gilman was where I first met Mike E., who was teaching a self-defense workshop while I smoked cigarettes in the background. Again, little did I know that I'd get sucked into martial arts (big time) and that Mike would become one of my closest friends. A few years later, I ran into him again and started doing Jujitsu and Shinkendo when he started his martial arts school in Berkeley (Suigetsukan—AKA the dojo—as in, "Yeah, I'm doing Jujitsu at the dojo.") We get a lot of Gilman folks filtering through our school, which I think is really cool because I get to still feel a little connected to the place, though there's always been a kind of give and take between the two groups anyway: we've done security trainings and self-defense workshops there, and at one point in time, there were three or four martial art geeks masquerading as security for the club. Being that we both are non-profit, volunteer-run collectives, I often see a lot of similarities: we both try to cater to the alternative communities in the area, as well as trying to give support to newer groups trying to do similar things. As with Gilman, the dojo folks could really take part in the planning of the school via meetings, and while the head instructors (just like the head director at Gilman) invariably hold a lot of sway as to what happens, regular student-people can still make changes happen. For me, this is where going to all those Gilman meetings comes in handy; I cut my teeth on collective process at Gilman. Now that I have more to say, it's really great that I feel like I can voice my opinions and be heard and get things accomplished. And once again, I found another place where I can live my life on my own terms.

At Gilman Street

Seems like it was only yesterday
nothing to do and nowhere to play
but then we could go down
to Gilman Street
and see Op IV every week
no violence, drugs or alcohol
just maximum rock and roll
at Gilman Street, it's the place to be
it's the seat of the punk rock scene
'cause we got the beat
and we don't eat meat
it's a club, it's a place, it's a thing
and if the band is hell-of-rad
then Tim will start to bounce his head
all the kids will jump up on the stage
and they'll hit the microphone in your face
and you will get a fat lip
you will get a fat lip from the pit
at Gilman Street, it's a safe retreat
for a zillion punk rock bands
'cause they've got the club,
and it's not enough
but at least it's not Bill Graham
it's Gilman Street
Radley does the sound
Honey watches the door
and James McKinney
sweeps the floor
Isocracy made a mess
we demand nothing less
and if you've got nothing better to do
there's a meeting every Sunday afternoon
you can talk about skinheads at the shows
and you can vote
on whether you're gonna vote
and you can make a speech
you can rant, you can rave, you can preach
at Gilman Street
it's democracy, it's just one big family
it's a bunch of geeks, it's a lot of freaks
it's a club, it's a place, it's a thing
it's Gilman Street

Taken from the Mr. T Experience's *Big Black Bugs Bleed Blue Blood* 12", 1989

CAMMIE T.

I had just graduated from high school, summer of 1986, and was just getting into punk. Before that I had been more of a radical hippie girl from the suburbs. I was very political throughout high school. I lived in a terrible suburb and rebelled against everything. Punk seemed like a natural extension of the way I was feeling. I started listening to the *Maximum RocknRoll* radio show and heard about Gilman being put together, and how everyone should come down and help. There was no question that I was going to do it. So I went down there, and it was so much fun. None of the construction had started yet, and there were a lot of people there, with a lot of ideas. We broke up into committees. I was a member of the "mindfuck" committee. We wanted to make something weird and loony happen during the shows. After a while, it became evident that we weren't needed, because that kind of stuff just happened anyway. I think it just lasted for about the first month after Gilman opened before it became obsolete.

Up until going to Gilman, I was an outcast in my peer group at school. I never felt like I had a family of friends. While listening to the MRR show and hearing them talk about Gilman, I just knew that that would be the place for me, and those people would become my family, and that's what started to happen. I finally started to feel comfortable, like I was among "my people." It was run somewhat collectively. We would vote, or try to reach a consensus. We had a "facilitator." But there were always problems because there were one or two people who had extremely strong opinions, and in the end, it didn't matter what we decided in the meeting, because those certain people had the "veto" power, because they had the "bank." Ultimately they made the final decisions for everyone. So it was kind of a false structure—we all pretended to be a part of a collective, and we did get our say, but it was like having parents. They'd let you "play" to a certain extent, and then, when you went over the line, they'd say "hell no!" In retrospect, I think that was good, because it was so chaotic there, I don't think we could have gotten anything done another way. Some of those meetings would go on for hours, it was painful, sometimes terrible screaming at each other. I still always went, though, no matter how painful. These were the meetings after it had opened. Before it opened, the meetings were fun, it was kind of like, "What should we make next?"

Tearing it up, 1987   photo by Murray B.

I remember the mysterious "Men in Black." Three guys who wore all black showed up one day, didn't say anything, and did tons of construction. No one knew who they were. The place had its own momentum and there was room for almost every kind of person. I remember there were some people who didn't like it there, and they didn't come back. But for the most part, almost everybody was touched by that place. I didn't really have any expectations of the place because I hadn't been part of the punk scene before that. It became way more silly than I could ever have imagined, though. It was wild and great. It was like preschool, but we were kind of adults. We had the "happy pits." I remember Aaron

Cometbus dumpster-diving for photos from one of the developing places and bringing tons of them to Gilman, and throwing them into the audience, and littering the whole place with these photos of people you didn't know but were strangely fascinated by.

I wanted the space to be more politically active—more benefits, more change, more information put out on various topics. One thing that I did notice, and that struck me after a while, was that it was just a lot of boys. I would go there and just see boys on stage, and boys in the pit, boys everywhere, except for a few of us girls who were working at the place, and a few in the audience. It started to kind of get to me. I really wanted there to be more females in bands. I got tired of the whole gender imbalance, not just Gilman, but the punk scene in general. At the big July Fourth picnic/BBQ show that first year, me and two friends, Jane and Joyce, were there and talking about the "boy thing." We were half jokingly saying that we should do some kind of "girl band" to counteract the overly male atmosphere. We were throwing out names, and one of us came up with the "Yeastie Girlz," because the "Beastie Boys" were so big at the time. It was an all-day show, lots of bands, and as the day wore on, Jane was outside writing something, and she came up to me and said, "Hey, I wrote a Yeastie Girlz rap song." So we worked on it a little bit and decided to perform it right then and there. That, in a nutshell, is what made Gilman so great, because we could. We could just write a song and then jump up on stage and do it. It didn't matter that we sucked, because it was in the spirit of the place. We just thought it was all a joke, but Tim Yohannan decided to put us on the *Turn It Around* Gilman compilation record because there were no other women on it. That was the beginning of the Yeastie Girlz. Tim was the first person to take us seriously. Our message was so female—we sang about yeast infections, getting your period, tampons, and we had these really elaborate between-song things that we would do, show-and-tell (with props) sex-education type stuff, and yet we were doing it for mostly boys. So sometimes we would get harassed. It wasn't like we were always surrounded by loving friends. A lot of times we felt kind of embattled, like we were standing up for all women in fighting the fight. It was intense sometimes. But if that was a real problem, then we shouldn't have performed at a Mentors gig—ha! We opened for Gwar once too.

I think that sense of family was true for us inside the clique, and it definitely was a clique, and there were people who would come to Gilman who weren't part of the clique who I'm sure didn't feel that same feeling. I was there for just two years, but every weekend for those two years. There were the bad nights as well as the good, working security and having to deal with assholes, being tired and smoking too many cigarettes and feeling like shit, or the nights when no one came. But all those great nights really made up for it. I think Gilman made a huge difference for a lot of people, exposing them to new ideas, new information, and new attitudes. Gilman totally changed my life. If I hadn't had Gilman Street after high school, I would have felt like there wasn't a place for me. I probably would have just continued to feel isolated and like I didn't have any kinship with anyone. It opened up huge doors for me. Same with my meeting Tim Y. and getting involved with MRR magazine. That got me really started on my photography (which is my profession today). I was going to college and taking photography during my Gilman years, and that was a natural place to be shooting. It was the beginning of my learning to go out into the world and document things that were happening around me. It changed a lot of other people's lives too, and instead of having a lot of angry and alienated teenagers with nothing to do, you had a place where those teenagers could go and be creative and constructive.

My involvement at Gilman ended when the MRR group left. I was pretty burned out and I was ready to move on to something else. I guess I kind of outgrew it. I got what I needed from it, I experienced all these great things, and eventually it stopped being great for me. The music was never really the main draw for me. Sure, there were bands that I really liked, but the people and the atmosphere were it for me. I hold those two years at Gilman dear, it was one of the best parts of my life. I'd like there to be a place like that for my son to go to when he gets older. Gilman opened up other avenues for me as well. I went to Russia and met punks there and did photo-stories there, and ended up living in Moscow for a time. Gilman gave me a lot of confidence, and inspired my creativity, gave me a better sense of myself. No one had really trusted me before my going to Gilman. To be entrusted with responsibility really helped me, and I know it helped a lot of others as well. Everything I am now, mom, photojournalist, teacher, was shaped out of that experience at Gilman.

1987   PHOTOS BY CAMMIE T.

LYDIA PAWESKI & CHRIS DODGE

A CONVERSATION ABOUT GILMAN

Lydia: I first heard of Gilman through Brian Edge. We were at a club and he told me about Gilman opening. I decided that it would be something good to get involved with, because I had just moved to San Francisco and didn't know many people. I took the opportunity and started going to some planning meetings. I also worked on Gilman when it was still in the construction process, as far as redoing the interior, even helped with spackling. I was there on opening night, at the show that first New Year's Eve, and it was really exhilarating to be there even though I had only been in on it for a few months. It was very cool to see it all come together.

1986   photo by Murray B.

Chris: I found out about Gilman when I was living in the South Bay. Chris and Todd Wilder and Big Wayne and I would usually go to shows together in those days and we heard that *Maximum RocknRoll* was starting up a club in Berkeley. We saw flyers for meetings that were being held on Sundays to talk about organizing it, doing construction work and such. We always intended to go; it seemed like the punk rock "thing" to do to volunteer our time, but when it came time to do it, we decided we'd...rather not.

Lydia: "Don't" It Yourself.

Chris: Very "Don't" It Yourself. It was a different kind of "DIY." We heard about the club opening, we'd seen flyers for it, and they'd have shows but not list who the bands were. We really wanted to go, but since it was an hour away, we didn't want to drive all the way up there and take our chances on a bunch of bands that we might not like at all. We ended up not going until we heard through the grapevine that Youth of Today was playing about a month or two after Gilman opened. That was the first Gilman show the four of us went to: Youth of Today, MDC, the Lookouts, and Justice League. Immediately Gilman struck me as a very different type of club than anywhere we had been to before. Even though we didn't know anybody, there was already a definite sense of community and interaction; everybody there could be involved in what was happening instead of just being a spectator. After that first show, I looked forward to going to Gilman as often as possible. Eventually, automatically, going up to Gilman became part of the weekend ritual.

Lydia: At some juncture, I met Chris. We met at a Sweet Baby Jesus show, during which they had a contest to "Win a Dream Date." They had one brown paper bag with the word "Guys" on it, and another one with the word "Gals" on it. They invited everyone to put their names in the appropriate bag and said at the end of their set they would draw one name from each bag and send the winners on a "Dream Date." I was at Gilman that night alone, as usual, because that was my hangout where I was making friends and meeting people, and that night was no exception. Without giving it a lot of thought, I figured, "what the hell?" and put my name in the bag and went on to enjoy the rest of the show. Chris was there with Chris Wilder and Todd and probably Wayne, along with some other friends. That whole group of friends were putting their names in the "Guys" bag a whole bunch of times as a joke. The set came to an end and Sweet Baby drew my name and then drew the name Chris. I hadn't met any of those guys before, so I was wondering about this Mystery Chris. Chris Wilder ended up joining me onstage next to Sweet Baby. We actually ended up liking each other a lot, for a while, and that was the night I met Chris Dodge, too, since he was there with Chris Wilder and all his buddies.

Chris: When Chris Wilder's name was chosen, all of our crowd was laughing at him because our objective was to get anyone other than ourselves chosen for the Dream Date. Then, when I got a look at Lydia, I thought she was cute! I thought, "Hey, this wouldn't be so bad after all..." But, through her going out with Chris Wilder, Lydia and I got to know each other and decided that we'd make a pretty good match together, although that happened a lot later, and there was no scandal involved, thankfully.

Lydia: Chris Wilder stood up to our wedding, along with Gilman veterans Walter Glaser and Wayne. Gilman played a large role in the legend of Chris and Lydia.

Chris: The first time I played Gilman was with Stikky around April of 1987, after it had been open for just a few months. We played with MDC, Gang Green, and it was Operation Ivy's first club show. It was amazing; the crowd didn't know who we were but everyone was really into it. It was the first time I'd ever played in a punk band somewhere and people actually danced and applauded and responded positively to any band I was in. Of course I was thrilled about that. But the whole feeling of com-

munity was what drew us in to Gilman even closer, because immediately, other regulars from the club and other bands befriended us. Gilman turned into this unique scene where everyone grew up and learned a lot together as a community, almost like a big punk rock high school. With Stikky, we were able to get away with goofy stuff that went over well with the regulars there, who were

1987   photo by Murray B.

dubbed the "Gilman Geeks." Much of the time, the Gilman crowd went against the grain of typical punk stereotypes in the interest of having fun. The first show I played with Stikky in April of 1987, we handed out milk and cookies to the whole crowd just as a joke on all the overly positive youth crew bands of the time. They all had tons

1988   photo by Murray B.

of songs about being positive, and we thought, "What could be more positive than milk and cookies?" We got the crowd to stand in line and had volunteers pouring milk and handing out cookies to everybody. I think that night was what endeared us to people like Tim Yohannan and people in the other bands who had no idea who we were up until that point. Another notable Gilman moment for us was playing with Slapshot from Boston, who were known as being a militant tough guy straight edge band. We did our own little straight edge tribute, of sorts. We did a variation of the children's game Pin The Tail On The Donkey, except it was "Pin The X On Ray's Hand." We drew an enormous poster-sized picture of Ray Cappo from Youth of Today holding a microphone. We then had audience members come up onstage between songs. We blindfolded them, gave them a large "X" with tape on it, and then they tried getting it on Ray's hand. I don't remember who won, but we did give out prizes. On New Year's Eve, 1987 into 1988, we had a show with Isocracy and Operation Ivy. It was really huge and all the bands were arguing a little—not too much so as not to seem unpunk or selfish about the order, but we definitely haggled our way into playing last because we drove the farthest. But by doing this, we unknowingly doomed ourselves by playing after Isocracy, who were known for throwing tons of garbage out during their set. It was usually stuff they would find in dumpsters or on the side of the road or something. One time they gave away a bicycle they found; they had other stuff they found, I can't remember...

Lydia: Bagels...

Chris: Yeah, huge bags of bagels and just about anything they stumbled across. I remember on New Year's Eve they had these trash bags full of shredded paper and garbage like that; they threw it around the room and it generated all kinds of dust and dirt, which I couldn't help breathing in. There were insane piles of trash all over the stage when we were playing. I felt like we were Oscar The Grouch's Muppet Punk Band. I had a real hard time breathing. I was coughing and blowing my nose, and it was just solid black, very unhealthy. Since we were going into New Year's of 1988, Stikky did a New Year's 1978 show with a roller disco theme. Well, at least we thought it was sort of funny at the time. We played a disco intro, and Chris Wilder even wore roller skates

1987   photo by Murray B.

while he was playing. Another fun one was the Valentine's Day show. Todd and I had just been dumped by our girlfriends, so it was our time to vent and be bitter high school youth. We made it our Anti-Valentine's Day show, where we played such notable anthems as "Girls Suck," "Girls Still Suck," and "Boy, Do Girls Ever Suck." In between songs, we were lighting many things on fire that epitomized love and happiness, like a Carpenters album and an ABBA album. Chris Wilder even lit one of his old guitars on fire, and Radley, the house soundman, came running down in a panic from the sound booth with a fire extinguisher. It was pretty ironic that we lit the ABBA record on fire, because about eight years later, Chris Wilder and Lydia and I were in an ABBA tribute band together called Bjorn Baby Bjorn, but that's another story...

Lydia: One of my favorite Gilman people was Clawd. He was always sweet—so weird, yet so endearing. He seemed just a little bit deeper than a lot of the people there. There was one time I went to Gilman and Clawd was there; it was a pretty decent-sized show. As usual, Clawd came bounding up to say hello. But the difference this time was, he was not wearing one thread of clothing. I was trying not to laugh as best I could, and I gave him a big hug as I usually would, and said, "Hi Clawd, how's it going?" and he just said, "Oh, pretty good," and at that point I just burst out laughing because he was naked. Finally, when I regained my composure, I asked, "Clawd, what gives?" He said, "Well, I kind of did this as an experiment, and interestingly, you are the only person who has not gone out of your way to avoid speaking to me all night. Everybody here says they don't judge people by how they dress, but it seems like I might be getting judged about not dressing at all." I had to agree with Clawd that the Gilman crowd could at times be

Clawd, 1987   photo by Cammie T.

a bit punker-than-thou, and I guess they didn't know how to react to him that night. I always found Clawd to be one of Gilman's more interesting characters. I ended up enjoying my own fashion freedom at Gilman, though. There was one time I had just rolled out of bed and didn't feel like changing to go to the Sunday meeting because it was too early. I drove from San Fran to Gilman still in my pajamas, bathrobe, and slippers, and no one batted an eye. Gilman has meant a lot to me over the years, especially those early years when I was most active there. I think a big part of the Gilman Street Project is the word "project"—it was a lot about how individuals related to each other, other than just being a group of people watching a show. People invested their time in it, so there was more leverage behind individual expression. The "arts" theme never really took off there; I think it was mostly all about punk rock shows, but it just seemed to be very fertile ground creatively for relating to other people (like Clawd). One time I got too close to the pit and a couple of skinheads threw me on my back. I had the wind knocked out of me, and a bunch of Gilman folks brought me to the back room where they counted out the money. They put me on one of the mattresses back there so I could catch my breath. I remember thinking how everybody was really concerned, which was a unique situation in any club.

That exemplifies why Gilman really took off; there was a genuine camaraderie there. I'm pleasantly surprised that it's still around.

Chris: Well, Brian Edge's big question for this book was "Why Gilman?" I'll tell you why... because something like that had never been done before, and the punk scene was more than overdue for a place like Gilman. The rest of the Bay Area either had a lot of really bad pay-to-play clubs like the Stone, or a lot of crummy little hole-in-the-wall places where bands didn't know if they'd get paid at all or if they'd get beaten up by nazi skinheads. Gilman totally changed all that because everyone was treated fairly; it was fertile ground and there was a general acceptance of new ideas. They were open to doing new things and doing things differently, which basically meant things were more "real" and more honest than what the standard was up until that time. That included the policies of dealing with people who were into creating problems, like being too violent. In that case, a group of Gilman regulars would basically surround that person, tell him to calm down, and if he didn't, he'd be escorted out. It was as simple as that. Or, if a bunch of nazi skinheads showed up at the front door, the show would stop, and someone would say, "OK, we need help up front;" the band would stop playing and everyone would go to the lobby area and stand around the entrance to let these people know they weren't welcome. Stuff like that was really encouraging, because it showed that a difference could be made, and that a handful of troublemakers couldn't ruin a good time for a room full of cool people who were just there to enjoy the show. Despite all its years of ups and downs and changing hands, Gilman is equally as vital today as it was then. At the risk of sounding like an old man, I think the punk rock scene is a lot easier now, though. It seems like it's a lot easier to get involved, and there are a lot more resources available, and there are a lot more standards in place now for doing things the right way. It wasn't necessarily like that in the '80s, and Gilman helped build a sense of community among the people who went there, especially those who went there regularly. The success of Gilman spawned the inspiration for a lot of other places, like ABC No Rio in New York and various venues around the world. It's definitely been a positive influence and positive stronghold for expressing creativity and new ideas and exercising artistic freedom in general. Gilman still maintains its original integrity. Even though I played there in bands thirteen years ago, I'm still playing there these days, because it's a great place to play, plain and simple. I know I'll be treated fairly and it'll be a good time and that the people who work there and everyone who attends the show will be treated with respect and treat each other with respect. I've felt good about dealing with Gilman all these years, despite who's in charge. There's no other club I can just call up and they'd let me take over for a weekend every year, letting me book a showcase for my record label—the Slap A Ham Fiesta Grande shows that happened for seven consecutive years. All Gilman shows are five bands, but they'd let me get away with booking up to seven. They understood where I was coming from and they were accommodating in every way. I don't really know how to wrap this up because I could ramble on with stories and praises forever. I guess it's best summed up in two words: "Viva Gilman!"

BRIAN EDGE

We had concocted the grand scheme. We were going to have the coolest, funnest place around. Who wouldn't want to help out and hang out there? Everyone would think it was the best place ever, right? We were fools—naive, idealistic fools.

It's hard to say who came up with the idea for making our own club first, but Tim Y. certainly had a way of making things happen, turning ideas into reality. Tim/MRR started auctioning off complete sets of MRRs, placing an ad in the Feb. 1986 issue, to help raise money for the place and to get the word out. He also had been setting aside money from sales of MRR over the past year or two. Early planning meetings were held in the basement at the MRR house in San Francisco (maybe other places too, but I don't remember them) in early 1986. I don't know how many different people were looking for spaces, but I remember going with Tim to look at a couple places in Oakland, including what used to be the White Horse on Shattuck Avenue. The White Horse was palatial and gigantic; multiple rooms, awesome, but rather expensive. Tim actually got into discussions with Gary Tovar (who did Goldenvoice Productions, big Los Angeles promoter) to go in together on the place, but I don't think it ever got that serious.

Then the space at 924 Gilman was found by Victor H. A lease was signed in April 1986, and the flyering and advertising started up in earnest, letting everyone know that a space had been found, and to come down and help make it a community project. Lots of meetings, committees (membership, security, booking, etc.), construction, and city bureaucracy. We had no clue about construction (minor renovations were needed—new bathrooms and a stage), but people who did would miraculously appear and build what was needed. Tim was pretty familiar with city politics from his KPFA (local Pacifica network radio station) dealings (MRR radio show) and could work that angle pretty well. We all joined various committees. Making the club "members only" (membership was to be $2 and for "life") was decided on fairly early as a tactic that would help us get the necessary permits from the city. We thought it would sound "safer" (In actuality it probably didn't make a bit of difference to the city, they more or less had approved us before our final permit hearing even began, but the extra money generated from selling membership cards really was a lifesaver).

We also came up with things like: not announcing who was playing, twenty-minute sets max, dividing up the night's receipts in front of the bands, having an open mic between bands to make announcements or question lyrics, things like that—ideas that seemed good or interesting at the time but didn't really work out (except for the money division, which is still done the same way to this day). It was all pretty exciting and we were all enthusiastic. The days of fighting, violence, and having to watch your back at shows were going to be history.

We planned and schemed, did our homework on the zoning board (including attending some of their meetings to get a sense of the people on the board), lined up "responsible adults" to speak at our hearing, basically we way over prepared. After all the work and money we put in, we definitely didn't want to blow it. Sept. 8, 1986, we had our hearing before the Berkeley Zoning Board. We had about fifty or so people show up in support, and about five or six people spoke. One was Kamala P.'s (see her piece earlier in this chapter) dad, who concluded with this brilliant dagger, "The people involved in this project are responsible and dedicated— keep them from becoming alienated and cynical, show them that there are instances where following the rules can end in a successful conclusion." We were approved unanimously (with one abstention, from the person whose district Gilman was located in).

Board of Adjustments   September 8, 1986
RE: 924 GILMAN STREET   Tim Yohannon

REQUIRED CONDITIONS:

1. Prior to the issuance of Building Permits, the applicant shall bond for the installation of street lights. The bond shall include all the cost on Ninth and Tenth from Camelia to Harrison and on Gilman and Camelia from Ninth to Tenth Streets if improvements are necessary to a maximum of $1000.

2. The building shall be upgraded and improved as required by Codes and Inspection.

3. The facility shall operate as described in the application as a membership facility, not as a commercial dance facility.

4. The hours of operation are limited to 8 AM to 2 AM Friday and Saturday, Sunday from 2 PM to 10 PM. Weeknight, evening use for rehearsals and organizational meeting may occur between 6 PM and 10 PM. Performances or shows are prohibited except during the specified weekend evenings. Changes in hours must be approve by the Board.

5. Security shall be provided for all performances, and shall include at least two people at the entrance, two inside the hall, and two on the exterior. These personnel shall be easily identifiable by means of clothing or badges, and can be members of the organization. Hired security personell is not necessary.

6. No alcohol shall be provided on the premises nor shall it be brought into the facility by members.

7. No advertising of the events by means of newspapers, radio or posters shall be permitted. Leaflets on the Berkeley High School Campus or Public Service announcements on KPFA are allowed.

8. Transfers of this Permit to other operators or owners shall be subject to review by the Board of Adjustments.

9. This use permit shall be reviewed by the Board of Adjustments six months after start of operation for compliance to conditions and possible imposition of additional conditions or changes to existing conditions. The permit may also be subject to review by the Board upon receipt by the Current Planning Section of verifiable complaint of detriment or non compliance with conditions.

Conditions passed by the Berkeley Zoning Board

We had passed what we thought was the biggest hurdle, and that it would be all downhill from there. Actually, we still had three and a half months of chasing and pacifying city inspectors and fire marshalls to get final approval to hold our first event. Needless to say, it was frantic and stressful those last couple months before we finally opened. The finances were getting strained and we were unsure of when we would be allowed to open. We held a benefit show at the Farm in San Francisco (a place we felt a kinship towards and that was staffed by very nice folks) Dec. 27. It was an all-day affair with seventeen (!) bands and raised a fair bit of money. With all the delays, we finally had our first show Dec. 31, 1986. We received

final approval from the fire marshall that same afternoon (the soundboard on the walls needed to be sprayed with fire retardant). One of the more exasperating requirements was that the front door couldn't open onto city property. Given that there was about twenty feet of sidewalk between our front door and the street, this seemed a bit much. So, we had to build a whole new doorframe/entryway (recessed), and it's still that way today.

Opening night went well (except for some lame idiots that climbed up on the roof and tried to sneak in through the skylight— good luck getting down!) but attendance dropped off fairly rapidly after that. People just weren't interested in coming unless they knew who was playing, and if it was a band that they particularly wanted to see. We couldn't change

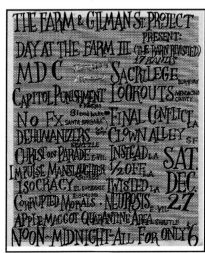

The big Farm show

people's attitudes about that (although there was a core group of staff and "regulars" that would show up most every show just to be there, but they weren't enough to keep the club afloat financially). So we started flyering and using free listings in the local papers (the List didn't exist yet!) That helped somewhat, but still didn't allow us to break even on a consistent basis. Also, we were receiving a good bit of positive press from the local media, and in particular from University of California Berkeley radio station KALX.

BEAT NIGS — FUGAZI
CRIMPSHRINE   YEASTIE
GILMAN ST PROJECT   GIRLZ
924 gilman st berkeley
Friday May 20 9pm
(ex- Minor Threat /Embrace & Rites of Spring)

Flyer by Brian E.

The atmosphere and mood at Gilman were great from the beginning. The element of danger was missing, but not particularly missed. Anytime there was a scuffle/fight, the house lights would be turned on and everyone would surround the disturbance and help out. Fifty small people found that together we could be big, particularly after some scary, but successful, standoffs against assholes. We were basing our security on communication rather than intimidation. We were hoping to foster a respect for the place and the people in it. In a sense, along with our designated security people, we expected everyone who agreed to be a member to also be "security" while at Gilman, helping watch out for the place. Through our construction and building process, where people got to know each other, we were hoping to alleviate people's lack of self-confidence, so that if a problem occurred they wouldn't feel that it was themselves alone against a gang, it would be all of us standing up with each other. And, to a certain extent, that's basically what happened. It was very inspiring to know that we wouldn't have to put up with stupid shit and intimidation any more.

That first year was pretty magical, a renaissance, reminding me a lot of the atmosphere of the punk scene in the late '70s, lots of creativity, spontaneity, excitement, enthusiasm, and anticipation. It got me excited about music again. It changed the way people thought about punk. It showed them it could be fun again, it didn't have to always be hard and violent. It could be anything they wanted it to be. It all seemed to be working out the way we wanted and hoped. But not quite...

Towards the end of the first year it became apparent that too much work was falling on too few shoulders. It was a struggle trying to get a community with "no rules" to support a place with rules. We tried to get the word out for folks to take on more responsibility, but that didn't really end up happening

SUN. SEPT. 20. 6 PM.   924 GILMAN.
GILMAN STREET PROJECT   BERKELEY

MDC
DAG NASTY
BEaT NIGS
SOULSIDE
NO USE FOR A
NamE   lc Hopkins

Flyer by Brian E.

to the extent we wanted. In retrospect, I think we held on to the reins a little too tightly, and didn't trust people enough, but with Tim/MRR bearing the financial responsibility, being cautious was understandable for the most part. On the other hand, that caution/control kept many people on the fringes, if they didn't bail out completely. Some of the meetings during that time, while packed (100-plus), got pretty ugly, with yelling, shouting, fingerpointing, etc. I can imagine people's reactions if it was their introduction to the place and its workings—probably lost a lot of people right there. So we had our first crisis. We were gonna close if more people didn't share the load.

Flyer by Brian E.

We got enough of a response to last into Sept. of the following year (1988), but the writing was on the wall. At the end we tried various restructuring proposals, including a group of four people who were going to take the place over. Nothing seemed solid enough though, so we closed the doors and left. The last "official" show was Sept. 11, 1988. We had a "private party" there sometime in Oct. with Ignition, a final farewell with just the workers and close supporters. It was sad and it was a relief. Sad because of the loss of our hangout, and the inevitable erosion of friendships linked with it. Relief because the babysitting of assholes (only a relative few, but persistent) was over, and the stress of having to make ends meet financially ("be successful") was gone.

Some of the things I remember (trying to avoid repeating others' memories):
• Having someone emcee the shows, introducing the bands and talking about the club
• Having a suggestion box at the front door, and having someone read them on stage during the show
• Me having to do sound opening night when the person we thought was going to do sound didn't show up. I

Flyer by Brian E.

was "elected" because I had watched the people who installed our system do a test the previous evening. I got through it (vocals only) and gradually learned how to run the equipment, eventually recording cheap demos for local bands there. After a short while, we were able to get a "real" sound person to work there

• Tues. nights being "art nights," where Gilman was open for people to come in and paint on the walls

• Frank Moore's "performance art" shows, with naked people, baked beans, and raw chicken pieces, and Frank caterwauling along to Top 40 songs. Luckily, they put plastic down on the stage first. Lots of teenagers standing transfixed with their mouths open

Isocracy, 1988   photo by Murray B.

• Isocracy, the house band. Their goal seemed to be to fill Gilman with garbage. One night they brought in a huge roll of plastic wrap, and, after it had been unrolled and crumpled up, they almost succeeded

• The "new band nights" becoming some of the biggest draws because so many great new bands were forming

• The singer of one band breaking up a fight by going into the audience and "interviewing" the two protagonists over the PA. When they heard how stupid they sounded, they sheepishly calmed down

• Early spring 1988, when so many people were coming to the shows that we actually stopped "advertising" again for a little while

• Late spring 1988, when we decided to have local bands work a show before they could play there (and have touring bands help out the night of their show). It wasn't particularly well received

• Having one band cry about there being no backstage after they were harassed before they played by audience members who thought their "new sound" sucked

• Having a band smoke pot on stage because they thought the club shouldn't have rules and that they didn't have to follow them. They were booted

• The phone booth in the store. It always had pirated access codes posted so you could make free long distance calls. Some people also tried to have sex in it

• The sideroom (now the office) being open as a lounge for all

• Some moron throwing a can of military/crowd control mace (not tear gas) into the club during a show. We managed to get it in a plastic bag before too much got out, but it still messed some people up and stopped the show for a little while

• Coming to the sad realization that the people who made things the hardest for us, and were the most antagonistic, were members of our own community

What are they doing in there?
1987   photo by Murray B.

68

• Lots of new people coming out of the woodwork, including what seemed to be a lot of people that were discovering punk for the first time and who had no preconceived ideas about what punk was supposed to be

• Never even considering being anywhere else. My weekends were Gilman

• People could be kids again, they could be silly and not feel self-conscious

• The Rock Against Racism show, June 1988, packed house, all sitting down and actually paying attention to the speakers and films. I thought it was the single best show we did. It was how I wanted every show to be. That night, to paraphrase Tim Y., "People left with their brains switched on, not off."

Hangin' out in the side room, 1987   photo by Murray B.

Flyer by Brian E.

But out of all the things that Gilman gave me, two stand out the most. I learned how not to be a passive bystander when shit's going down. And I learned the strength of the bonds that are formed when you go through triumph, joy, accomplishment, sadness, frustration, exhaustion, and violence together. Gilman ended up being much more than just a place to me, it became a state of mind.

After we left in 1988, I went to Gilman only occasionally as the years went by. In the late '90s I started selling books there for AK Press on a regular basis, and I was able to reacquaint myself with the place. New friendships were formed, and, along with them, the old comfortability resurfaced. The link, the connection, was still there, and always will be.

CONDITIONS AND POLICIES OF MEMBERSHIP

ADMISSION

1. GUEST LISTS ARE RESTRICTED TO BAND MEMBERS AND CREW ONLY.
2. ACTIVE MEMBERS WILL RECEIVE DISCOUNTS AND FREE ADMISSIONS IN ACCORDENCE WITH RULES GOVERNING ACTIVE MEMBERSHIP.
3. EVERYONE ELSE WILL PAY ADMISSION FEE AND RECEIVE A TICKET TO DETERMINE CLUB ATTENDANCE.

MEMBERSHIP CARD

1. MEMBERSHIP CARDS WILL BE ISSUED IN DUPLICATE, ONE IN THE POSSESION OF THE MEMBER,AND ON KEPT ON FILE AT THE DOOR. SIGNATURE WILL BE ON BOTH CARDS SO IDENTIFICATION CAN BE DETERMINED IF NECESSARY.
2. CARDS WILL BE DESIGNED TO PREVENT DUPLICATION.
3. CARDS WILL BE OBTAINED AT THE DOOR FOR A ONE TIME MEMBERSHIP FEE.
4. CARDS WILL BE REQUIRED AT THE DOOR FOR ADMITTANCE. IF MEMBER DOES NOT HAVE CARD, SIGNATURE MAY BE USED FOR IDENTIFICATION BY CHECKING AGAINST CARD ON FILE. THIS IS AT THE DISCRETION OF THE DOOR AND SHOULD BE DISCOURAGED.
5. CARD ON FILE WILL HAVE A PLACE FOR RECORDING ALL OFFENSES OF THE MEMBER.
6. ACTIVE MEMBERSHIP DISCOUNT IS AVAILABLE FOR THOSE WISHING TO CONTRIBUTE TIME TO THE RUNNING AND MAINTENANCE OF THE CLUB. AN ADDITIONAL CARD WILL BE ATTACHED TO CLUB FILE CARD TO RECORD ALL TIME WORKED
7. ADMITTANCE CAN BE DENIED TO ANYONE UPON THE ADVICE OF SECURITY

RULES OF MEMBERSHIP

1. ABSOLUTELY NO FIGHTING IN OR AROUND PREMISES
2. ABSOLUTELY NO ALCOHOL OR DRUGS IN OR AROUND PREMISES
3. ABSOLUTELY NO VANDALISM IN OR AROUND PREMISES

CONSEQUENCES OF VIOLATION

1. FIGHTING IN THE CLUB WILL RESULT IN SUSPENSION OF ADMITTANCE FOR TWO CONSECUITIVE WEEKS BEGINNING, FOLLOWING WEEKEND FROM DATE OF OFFENSE.
2. FOR NEIGHBORHOOD VIOLENCE, VANDALISM, AND DRUNKENESS FOUR WEEKS SUSPENSION.
3. FOR ALCOHOL OR DRUGS IN OR AROUND THE PREMISES , FOUR WEEKS SUSPENSION. THERE WILL BE NO PENILITY IF ALCOHOL IS SURRENDERED AT THE DOOR.
4. FOR CLUB VANDALISM AND SECOND OFFENSE FIGHTING MEMBER WILL BE REFUSED ENTERANCE FOR TEN WEEKS. REPAIR OF DAMAGE WILL BE REQUIRED. FAILURE OF RESTITUTION MAY RESULT IN PERMANENT SUSPENSION OF MEMBERSHIP.
5. HABITUAL VIOLATIONS WILL RESULT IN PERMANENT SUSPENSION OF MEMBERSHIP.

OFFENSES MAY BE BROUGHT BEFORE THE GROUP MEETING TO CONTEST THE JUDGEMENT OF MEMBERSHIP COMMITTEE.

SECURITY

ORGANIZATION-- 6 persons total per night
   Inside-- 3: stage manager and 2 on roving patrol
   Door --1: in conjunction with person from membership committee assisting in handling money and checking membership ID
   Outside-2: in immediate vicinity of venue
DURATION-- Entire show
ROTATION-- Outside group switches with inside group after half the show, specifics flexible
IDENTIFICATION-- undetermined at this time, but will be readily apparent
PROBLEMS/SOLUTIONS
   Inside-- graffiti: allowed if of a non-malicious nature
      vandalism: perpetrator turned over to membership committee for applicable disciplinary action
      alcohol/drugs: person responsible must immediately get rid of illicit materials or leave show (no return); repeated violations will lead to person being turned over membership committe for applicable disciplinary action.
      fighting: if person(s) responsible are not able to be immediately calmed down or are repeatedly causing trouble, they will be turned over to membership committee for applicable disciplinary action
   Outside-- graffiti: if obviously a result of our show, all attempts will be made to immediately rectify the problem and perpetrator will be turned over to membership committee for applicable disciplinary action
      vandalism: if obviously a result of our show, all attempts will be made to immediately rectify the problem and perpetrator will be turned over to police or membership committee for applicable disciplinary action
      trash: immediately clean up
      loitering: heavily/actively encourage person(s) to come into venue or leave area

Notes: 1) persons working security that night do not have to pay admission
    2) persons working security that night will assist with, but are not entirely responsible for, after-show clean-up
    3) persons within the security pool will have the option of mace or self-defense training available to them

GUIDELINES FOR ARTISTS WISHING TO PERFORM AT THE WAREHOUSE

The warehouse is not just for music; we intend to provide a forum for all kinds of creative efforts. These could include, but are by no means limited to: theater, poetry, dance, film and video, painting, and whatever else you can imagine. The key word here is alternative. We're not out to operate just another night club or gallery, and so preference will be given to artists working outside "normal" channels, i.e., those who don't have the backing of major record labels or academic or foundation funding.

Equally important is the artists' willingness to abide by the same conditions that all members of the club agree to. This specifically includes refraining from violence, vandalism, and the use of drugs or alcohol on club premises. In addition, performers must share responsibility with members of the audience for ensuring that these conditions are maintained.

Another unique feature of the warehouse is that members of the audience will not only be allowed, but encouraged, to take the stage following a performance to offer comments or criticism. For example, if someone feels that a band's lyrics or attitudes carry racist or sexist overtones, he or she would be given an opportunity to say so. One member of the band would then be allowed equal time (probably limited to five minutes for each side) to rebut the criticism.

The most controversial policy, even among our own membership, governs advertising: there won't be any. That means no flyers and no newspaper or radio announcements about what specific artists will be performing. The only publicity, by way of MAXIMUM ROCKNROLL radio and magazine and other alternative media, will be to the effect that the warehouse exists, that events will be happening every Friday and Saturday nights, and that people are welcome to become members and participate in those events.

Why are we insisting on this, to put it mildly, unusual approach? Mainly to avoid becoming, as stated before, just another night club or gallery. We want to build a membership whose first loyalty is to the warehouse, not to specific artists who perform there. We plan on putting together diverse and interesting bills and expect that word of mouth will result in shows being consistently well attended. This is an experiment, and therefore subject to change, if, after a certain amount of time, it doesn't appear to be working out. But for now, we expect all performers to abide by the no-advertising policy; those who deliberately violate it risk losing their opportunity to play at the warehouse. There is, by the way, at least one advantage to this policy: touring bands who have signed a contract to play only one Bay Area venue (a condition frequently being imposed on bands by some of the bigger promoters) could play an unadvertised warehouse show without violating the spirit of their contract. The advantages to unknown bands who don't have enough drawing power to get booked into commercial rock clubs should be obvious.

This brings us to perhaps the touchiest subject, that of money. First of all, it's important to bear in mind that the warehouse is not being operated for profit. Nobody involved with it is being paid for his or her efforts, and we're prepared, if necessary, to lose money during the first few months. Second, it's our belief that all performers should be paid at least enough to cover their expenses, as well as a percentage of whatever we take in at the door. We therefore offer these guarantees, payable regardless of how many people attend a given show: artists from the greater Bay Area (bounded by Santa Rosa, Santa Cruz, and Sacramento) will receive a minimum of $20. Artists from farther away than that will receive a minimum of $50. We realize that this is not a lot of money (though the majority of commercially operated "alternative" venues in the Bay Area consistently pay even less), but at least it will ensure that it will not be costing artists money out of their own pockets to perform for us.

Money taken in at the door will be divided in this way: 50% will go for the operation of the warehouse (rent, insurance, utilities, etc.; we expect expenses to run from $2500 to $3000 a month, and we have already laid out $26,000 before the doors have even opened) and the other 50% will be divided among the performers. To give you an idea of how much money we are talking about here, the warehouse has a capacity of approximately 300, depending on how strict the fire marshal is with us, and door prices will usually range from $3 to $5. Therefore, a full house could generate between $900 and $1500, half of which would go to the performers. Needless to say, if shows were consistently attended by capacity crowds, the warehouse could cover its expenses with considerably less than 50% of the door receipts, and thus the percentage paid to the artists could then be increased.

How will the money be divided among the different performers at a given show? Here again our approach differs considerably from "business as usual." For one thing, the artists themselves will have a say in how much they think each group should be paid, and for another, criteria normally used, such as how famous a group is or how many people a given act might draw, will not be particularly relevant because of our no-advertising policy. More attention will be given to the specific needs of the artists; for example, if a band has come all the way from Europe, or has just had its van broken into and its equipment stolen, they might be given an unusually large share of that evening's take. The final decision on payment will be made by whichever representative of the booking committee is present at a given show, but if performers feel they have been treated unfairly, they can always appeal to a meeting of the general membership.

We've laid down some pretty stringent conditions for performing at the warehouse, and it obviously won't be for everyone, especially those who are interested in music, art, theater, or whatever, primarily as a business. But those of you who like the idea of what we're trying to do are welcome to get in touch with us. The person to contact is Victor, and we recommend that you write to him, including as much information about yourselves as possible (obviously things like demo tapes would be helpful, but even more helpful would be a simple statement of purpose, in your own words, explaining who you are and what you're trying to accomplish through your art). Write to Victor at PO Box , Berkeley CA . You can also call (415) , but in most cases you'll get an answering machine; your calls will be returned much faster if we already have your written material in hand.

Lawrence Livermore, for the Booking Committee

Committee info, 1986

MAXIMUMROCKNROLL

P.O. Box   Berkeley, CA
(415)

To whom it may concern,

The space at 924 Gilman St. is the site of a proposed multi-cultural, multi-media center. It will be run under the aegis of Maximum Rock'n'Roll, an organization that has been active in Berkeley and the Bay Area for nine years. We have been doing a weekly 2-hour radio program on KPFA since 1977, have published a monthly 72-page magazine since 1982, have released several record albums on our own label, and have presented various musical/cultural events in many venues in the area--all with the aim of providing a positive forum for communication, an alternative for local musicians and artists to make their works/ideas known, and for creating better understanding among people. All our work is a labor of love, in that none of the participants or owners receive any remuneration for time donated.

Specifically, the site at 924 Gilman would be used for several purposes:

1) A showroom for fledgling artists, a place for them to display their works. The main room is 45' x 51', where public events will take place. There are two smaller room, about 15' square, which will be reading rooms/offices/rehearsal space. We are aware that the building will require certain changes as required by city codes. Our landlord also plans to improve the exterior of the building (painting and awning), and we feel that this project will be an improvement to the somewhat drab and nebulous nature of the existing buildings in the area.

2) A meeting hall for artists/participants to discuss issues/ideas of import to the creative community. These will be like "town hall" meetings, a way to focus ideas into action, a catalyzing point for the progressive side of the underground art movement. We feel that the need for an alternative center for the arts is long overdue and very important for the City of Berkeley, which has long been known as being an attractive and supportive city for creative people.

3) A place for bands/musicians/poets/performance artists to present themselves. It is our objective to have the artists themselves meet once a month to plan events, directly involving them in the organization of the club. This also helps bring together the energy and idealism of youth with the resources and maturity of older people--breaking down another needless gap among people with much in common.

4) It is our intention to have this venue be a membership club, meaning that it is open to anyone, as long as they agree to a "no violence/no vandalism" principle. We feel this is the best way to insure a community feel to the venue, to get people directly involved instead of just being consumers, and to insure that many of the negative aspects of events (such as what occurs at Ruthies Inn, for example) will not happen. It will be incumbent upon members to not only not abide by this credo, but to actively deter such behavior in others, both within the walls and in the nearby neighborhood (outside patrolling of the nearby vicinity will occur on an hourly basis--or more frequently, if necessary) to insure both the patrons' safety and to maintain our responsibility to the environment.

We intend to instill _nls self-patroling sense of _mmunity within this "clubhouse", and feel this is the manner which will limit problems. Security, as such, will be a responsibility of all members, will be organized through our meetings, and will require the close coordination of members, management, and artists. If necessary, we are not adverse to hiring outside security, though the concept of self-government is preferable. We will also work closely with the Berkeley Police Department, so that a small minority of trouble-makers don't ruin this for the great majority, who are a positive group seeking a fun, creative outlet.

5) Our main public usage hours would be from 8 PM-2 AM Friday and Saturday evenings, and Sunday from 2 PM-10 PM. There would possibly be midweek evening usage of a very limited nature, involving renting rehearsal space and/or classes of various types, but not involving public attractions. There may be a need for an occasional weekday evening for meetings, more likely on a monthly basis. The site will be operated by the three partners of Maximum Rock'n'Roll, aided by the artists themselves. We expect our customers to largely come from the Berkeley area, with a minority coming from the surrounding area. We intend to attract people from many age groups (the majority being under 21) and cultural identities by displaying works (paintings, photos)/performance (agit-prop, comedy, poetry)/music (reggae, rock, blues, avant-garde, classical)/multi-media (video, film) of interest to all, with the hope of creating more understanding across cultural barriers through firsthand knowledge and direct participation.

6) As the area involved is designated as a manufacturing zone with no nearby residences, and as most all businesses (save the Rialto Theater) are daytime-oriented, we feel this proposed project will have no negative environmental impact. As to parking, we feel the majority of our patrons will be young adults coming via public transportation. (The nearby 72 line bus runs all night on San Pablo Ave., and easily connects with the 52 bus, again a 24-hour line, which runs up to downtown Berkeley and the Campus area). We are conscious that the Board of Adjustments and the Berkeley Police Department are worried both about parking overload of the area, and about the possible increase of auto break-ins. We have surveyed the adjoining area, counted all the possible neighboring legal parking spaces from 10th St. to 4th St. and Harrison to Camelia. As one can see from the attached parking diagram, there is no lack of spaces, even at prime usage weekend hours. On the contrary, there are more legal, relatively safe parking spaces than one could find in just about anywhere in the SF-Berkeley area. Combining this amount of spaces, along with our projected low expectation of self-motoring patrons, and with our commitment to an exterior patroling responsibility, we feel that this important concern of city officials will not become a major problem. Also, there will be no advertising of our events (either in newspapers or by fliers)--just word-of-mouth, organic growth that will insure no rapid expansion and will also not complicate the potential parking problem. We have made the neighboring businesses (and residences blocks away) aware of our intentions, and have engaged their support, verified by petitions (also attached). Both the Rialto Theater and Ashkenaz (the other area night spots) have expressed strong support for our efforts.

Our goals are high, but realistic, and would provide a much-needed outlet for the many-talented but largely unappreciated artists and patrons. Occupancy would, of course, vary depending on the artist and city codes, but as this venue is not commercially oriented and is in no way a "typical nightclub", we don't expect overcrowding problems. No alcohol will be sold on the premises, and as we are investing what precious little money we have in this venue, we will not tolerate any behavior by patrons that will jeopardize its existence.

It's been our longtime experience that the majority of youths involved in the underground arts scene are well-motivated, are sick of being typecast as do-nothings, are tired of being exploited by club promoters who mainly care about making a buck, and long for an opportunity to prove themselves, not just to a larger community, but to themselves. With a greater and greater number of youths active in the anti-war movement, and with more and more discriminatory laws being pushed upon them, we feel it most important that the City of Berkeley take a step to reverse this negativity and "anti-youth" drift. Youths see "government" somewhat monolithically, and as the larger governmental institutions drive onward to divide and conquer, attacking the rights of gays, women, minorities, and young people, we would like to demonstrate that there is a distinction in types of government, that "progressive" government, especially one that's on record as supporting youth centers, can make a difference and set an example. And, we'd like a chance to implement our ideals and prove ourselves.

Thank you,

Tim Yohannan

Tim Y.'s initial submittal to Berkeley Zoning Board

MRR ad, Feb. 1987

UnderStand, 1987   photo by Cammie T.

GILMAN ST PROJECT

924 Gilman St/Berkeley
~~~-~~~ warehouse/ ~~~~~~ office

Guidelines for Coordinators

General: The key to doing this job well is communication, and earning the respect of those who you work with. It's very important to maintain good communication with the other coordinators (with whom you should confer every half hour or so) and with volunteers, always staying on your toes yet keeping some extra reserve of patience and energy for crisis situations. If you feel stress, try to diffuse it within yourself or through humorous seriousness. Try to explain things without being condescending. It is mandatory to be diplomatic. Finally, you must work as hard or harder than anyone else in order to gain their respect. One of each group of three should be responsible for unlocking at the outset (usually though, Radley will be there before you, but you should arrive at least one hour prior to the starting time) and closing up at the end. Make sure the alarm is turned on (when the prong is at 12 o'clock) after you lock up. Double check to see that the door itself is locked (sometimes you can turn the key and pull it out, but the bolt didn't really go all the way shut).

Outside Coordinator: Your task wil be to make sure that people are doing their assignments, and to fill in the gaps when they aren't. Make sure people make the rounds, go down 8th St, as well as cover the tracks. You will also be the person to spot trouble before it happens. If a group of skins or rowdies arrive, it is your job to organize a welcoming party who can accompany you in a non-menacing way when you go talk to them. You should ask if they intend to enter, and if they are still being assholes, then it's your job to tell them they can't enter, that we have the right to refuse admission to those who don't relate to the place and its ideals. If you sense a potential for violence, then have someone standing by to go call the police. In some cases, you might want to call the police before you go have your talk, waiting until the police are within sight before asking them to leave. We have the right to ask them to not enter, and also to leave the area. You should also inform people who are too intoxicated that they can't enter that night. You should keep your eyes open at all times, watching for potential problems. If the police are called, it's a good idea to ask everyone hanging outside to get back inside. You can also tell the foyer coordinator to cut off ins-and-outs. If you need back-up, ask the foyer coordinator to get the word out to get a crowd for you. You will also be the person who will greet the police and explain the situation, round up witnesses, etc. Also, keep an ear out for scammers who are dealing dope, drinking, or giving their cards to others. Ask outside security to report to you on any problems. Also, make sure outside security people are picking up trash throughout the night. At the end of the show, make sure a few people will make a trip up and down the block with a trash bag to get the worst of it.

Foyer Coordinator: First job you have is to see that the poster for that night's show is made and posted outside. Then, once all the bands have arrived and it's time to get things under way, you should start the process of clearing the hall. Then, your job will be to make sure the cash box is brought down and opened, that the people doing membership are given their start-up money (it is kept in the cash box, but seperate from the $45 start-up money for the door), as well as given new membership cards and pens. You also should make sure that the Inside Coordinator has turned in the band guest list to you before the show. You will then ask the volunteerss to meet and to decide who's working outside, inside, etc. Then, once the workers are all stamped, ask for band members to enter and get stamped. After that, the crowd can come in. Once the show is under way, you should help out by making sure everyone has enough small bills (usually that means taking big bills from membership and trading them for small bills from the door). Every so often you should collect the bigger bills from both boxes. Make sure you keep membership money and door money seperate. Membership money goes straight to the club and door money gets paid to the bands and club. You are also responsible for keeping the entrance relatively free, making sure non-paying people don't hang out in the doorway, and for keeping the line flowing in at the beginning. This means ushering out every few minutes that members can enter on one side, and those who need cards should enter on the other. This helps. Also, unless you know for 100% sure that someone who doesn't have a card is a member, people must now buy a new card for $2. No one is to be admitted to use the restrooms unless they have paid to get in. From time to time, clean up the tabletop, straighening out flyers, etc. Make sure the membership people are giving out those slips of info to new members (a supply is under the long bench in a box). While the last band is on, count out $45 from the door box, and take the rest upstairs and count in into piles of $100. Get a payment sheet from the lower left desk drawer, and enter the date and total door. Then, calculate out 1/3 and enter that, and finally enter the remainder for the bands. Make out your suggested split, and once the show ends, ask one member from each band to come upstairs to get paid. Show them your suggested split, ask if it's ok with everybody, make any adjustments that are necessary, and pay them. Get them to sign next to their names and count their cut again. Then, rubber band the house cut, rubber band the membership money, tag them with their totals, and put them in the cash box after you bring the boxes back upstairs (once the show is over). Find the cash log book in the lower left desk drawer, and enter the same info into that book.

Inside Coordinator: Once jobs are signed up for, make sure the stage manager gets the names and guest list for each band (only 2 guests per band), and get that list to the Foyer coordinator. Make sure the bands know where to put their equipment (the headliner should put theirs in the back, behind the barrier, the 2nd band next to theirs behind the barrier, the 3rd band in front of the barrier, the 4th band also in front of the barrier, and the opening band goes directly on stage. There are no sound checks. Make sure the stage manager tells the bands how long their sets are. Check and make sure the stage manager is staying on top of their job, especially in terms of length of sets. Make sure that those security people assigned to watching side door and equipment are doing it, and ask if they need relief every so often. The side door person should only let people out that are carting equipment, and only they can re-enter. Hand stamps should be checked before letting people in. Side door person should not open the door to knocks from the outside. Your job also means watching for troublemakers in the pit. You should talk with them if you see their behavior as something that might lead to a fight. Tension is easy to spot. Let them know why you're requesting them to calm down or why they shouldn't be hitting people who aren't in the pit and don't want to be hit. Be familiar with who the "happy pit" people are, and ask their help in changing the mentality of a rough pit. If someone gives you lip when you ask them to cool off, ask them to go out into the foyer to talk, where you won't have to yell and where you can have a more sober talk. Make sure you have support. If someone needs to be ejected, get a group to help you out. Don't be physical unless necessary, and use peer pressuree to deal with it. Don't be afraid to ask the stage manager or the band on stage to stop until the problem ends. If outside security needs you to stop a show till a problem at the door gets settled, please act quickly, and explain it to the crowd. Your main job will be to avert interior problems before they explode, and keeping a show mood up. Work with Radley if you need house lights on (it helps cool off a crowd). Check out the bathrooms for destruction or flooding. Make sure they are supplied with toilet paper and paper towels (kept in the loft). At the end of the shows, help organize the clean up crews, hand out brooms, bring down garbage bags to replace the full bags (which should be dragged to left of the front door). Get the last band to clear their equipment in good time. Make sure the side door is shut (test it with a good push) before all the lights are killed.

Emergency numbers:
MRR- (general advice)
Radley- (sound)
Marshall- (sound)
Brian- (general advice)
Alarm company- (we are account #)
Oren- (repairs)
Police-911 (immediate help)
Police- (anything else)
Landlord (Jim)

SOME FINANCIAL INFORMATION ON THE GILMAN STREET PROJECT

Gilman began with $40,000 in start-up funds, and for its first 6 months of actual operation ran at a $1000-a-month loss. The next three months we were able to break even more or less on regular expenses, but does not include such things as improvements to the sound system or ventilation system, or the outrageous increase in our liability insurance (It was $1400 a year for the first year, but was just jerked up to $7000 for the next year—even though we have not had one claim!) No one at Gilman draws a salary, as all labor is donated. This includes people working the door, security, sound, maintenance, etc.

Here is a list of our regular monthly expenses:

Rent and utilities	$2260
Liability and fire insurance	$600
Phone	$150
Maintenance	$150
Publicity	$150
Garbage	$50

Our income is generated two ways. First, from your $2 lifetime membership fee. This averages to about $800 a month. The rest comes from our share of the door, which is 1/3 of whatever comes in. The other 2/3 goes to the bands. We have averaged about $2000 a month, about a loss of $600 per month average. All losses are paid for by MRR, as was the start-up money.

A note to bands: We try to pay you as well as we can, out of pocket if necessary. We hope to at least cover your expenses, if not more. But, if you ever find that you can afford to kick back any portion of your payment to the club, it will be highly appreciated. We don't expect this, and won't hold it against those who can't afford to do so, but as we have no reason to assume that our losses will cease, it's a gesture that would be in keeping with our whole ethic of all participants having a stake in seeing that this venture remains open.

1987/1988 info

BECOMING A MEMBER: WHAT IT ENTAILS

This whole Gilman Street Project is based on some general principles, reaching back to before we opened the doors. For months, meetings were held to develop the guidelines for how such a club would function, and committees were formed to come up with the best way to promote a situation where bands, fans and promoters would all have something in common—an equal stake in maintaining a clubhouse. We wanted an environment free from many of the problems that have plagued most previous venues—violence, vandalism, and police problems. So, the committees (Membership, Booking, Security, Contstruction) came up with their proposals, and after much discussion, the guidelines were enacted. The membership idea was foremost (more on that in a minute), but the criteria of membership won the most approval. So, in becoming a member, you are agreeing to respect the democratic process which developed (and constantly refines) the criteria, this being: no violence or vandalism in or around the warehouse; and, no drugs or alcohol in or around the warehouse. These two agreements form the basis of being able to keep the environment friendly, as well as keeping the law off our backs.

GENERAL PRINCIPLES OF MEMBERSHIP   6/88

The Gilman Street Project is an ALL VOLUNTEER operated ALL AGES club. Its goal is to provide an friendly environment for bands and fans that is free from many of the problems that have plagued most previous venues: violence, vandalism, and police problems. The purpose of making all customers into members of the club is to introduce you to the ideal atmosphere encouraged here and to get you to agree (with your signature) to abide by the rules of the club that were democratically agreed upon (and are constantly refined) by involved members. The key rules are: NO violence or vandalism, and NO drugs or alcohol in or around the clubhouse. Also the members have recently voted to take an active stance by banning expressions of racism at the club.

A word about each... Violence includes stage-diving and thoughtless slam-dancing and that doesn't respect the safety of others and their ability to also enjoy the show - especially those more fragilely built who are forced to the back (behind tall heads) to avoid bruises. This is not a ban on 'the pit', but it is a BAN on ALL STAGE-DIVING because of personal safety and because it presents Gilman St. with a serious INSURANCE problem that is a constant threat to the existence of the club... the ban on drugs and alcohol around the club, besides the fact that they can promote violence and vandalism, is to keep the law away. Gilman St. does not have a liquor license nor does it want one since key to this club is ALL AGES. By sitting in your car or van just outside the club and guzzling your beers and leaving the cans for litter, you violate the agreement on your membership card... the No Racism policy is a reaction to the existence of White Power / Nazi skinheads and like-minded people who are constant promoters of violence and have disrupted shows... Coordinators of a show have the right to remove assholes and/or revoke the membership of anyone not complying with these general principles.

EVERYONE IS WELCOME TO THE CLUB EXCEPT FOR THOSE WHO DO NOT ALSO WELCOME EVERYONE !

OPERATION OF GILMAN ST.

FINANCES. It costs about $3,600 a month to keep Gilman St. running, including $2,200 for rent & utilities and $800/mo. for liability & fire insurance. Income fluctuates quite a bit from month to month and averages about $2,800/mo. from 1/3 of the door money (2/3 goes to the bands) and about $800/mo. from your $2 lifetime membership fee. Hence Gilman St. presently runs at about break even.

DECISIONS. Club operation is decided by democratic membership meetings held every 2ND & 4TH SUNDAY of each month at 5 pm. Issues severely impacting workers here may be motioned to have voting restricted to those working members.

MUSIC SHOWS. Booking is presently done through Tim Yohannan. Ideas for shows and bands should be referenced to him at _____ for submitting demos and scheduling...Shows are run by a group of coordinators who meet after each general membership meeting to get organized. You can get trained if you wish to help coordinate shows...the actual jobs of taking money, security and clean-up are done by volunteers who sign up an hour before each show. You are welcome to get involved this way. In addition, a system has been set up where bands help with the work load in order to play here.

BAND DEMOS. Your band can record its demo at the club. Call _____ and ask Marshal for more info.

GILMAN ST. NEEDS YOUR INPUT, IDEAS & INVOLVEMENT to expand and develop new activities at the warehouse not necessarily related to music shows. Possibilities include theater, poetry, movies/videos, decor, painting, potlucks, trips, carpooling, theme shows, but they need inspired individuals to make them happen.

How to get involved
at The Gilman Street Project

Above and left: 1988 info

Come to meetings: Meetings are held every second and fourth Sunday of the month at 5 pm. Meetings are open to all members and run democratically by members. Everyone is welcome to come.

Work at Gilman: Come and sign up to work an hour before any show. You can choose a variety of things to do to help out such as clean up, general security, etc. When you show up at a show early to work, just find out who is coordinating the show and ask the coordinator to sign you up to work. He/she will explain what the various jobs entail.

If you already work at Gilman and would like to do more you can be trained to stage manage, coordinate shows, help with outreach to new members, etc. To learn how to do these things, come to a coordinators meeting and ask any coordinator to be trained. (Coordinator meetings are held after every general meeting.)

As a member I recognize that I am personally responsible for my actions and, that cooperation with others is in my own self interest. I agree to respect the rights of others to express themselves and recognize my own individual right to self-expression. I understand that the club has been established by and for the membership and that membership extends beyond the entertainment aspects, but also includes my right and responsibility to be involved in its operation, maintenance, and policy direction as I may see fit. I agree to observe the regulations established by the club membership and understand that those regulations have been established so that the club can function legally and independently. I agree to abstain from violence, vandalism and the possession of alcohol and drugs in or around the club.

Above: back of membership card, 1986

A LITTLE BACKGROUND OF THE GILMAN STREET WAREHOUSE PROJECT

With all the factionalism that has been going on in the alternative music scene over the last couple of years there is one overwhelming reality that seems to unify the diversity that now exists. The scene is stagnant and dying. It is in response to this that a wide range of people -- musicians, artists, writers, politicos, young and old -- have come together to create a new alternative. Each wearing a different uniform, be it punk, mod, radical, conservative, hippie, or just plain 'Joe', a new coalition is being forged which has no uniform at all. A new beginning is in the offing and anyone is welcome to become involved to create what is, at this point, a mere possibility. All that is tangible now is that a warehouse has been leased, a group of somewhere around 100 people have organized themselves into several committees, and within a month or so, a new and unique venue will open for music, art, and any other form of communication and interaction.

The Gilman St. Project is not some over-night fantasy, but the result of several years of work and thought by some of the people who have been involved in the Bay Area underground music scene. It has been the long time plan of S.F./Berkeley's Maximum Rock and Roll to establish a 'youth cultural center' in the Bay Area and toward this end they have put away thousands of dollars for the time when it could happen. Meanwhile, in the East Bay a group of people centered around the New Method Warehouse were putting on shows, gaining experience and keeping alive the idea of a 'people' oriented music scene. From the New Method experience, much was learned about the obstacles that had to be dealt with for such a project to truly succeed. The operation was underground and therefore, subject to continual harassment from the local police. The greatest hassles however seemed to come from the scene itself. People did not fully recognize that what was going on was something unique that desperately needed their support. The success of the shows was due to the commitment of the individuals involved in making it happen. The motivation was to keep music, the free expression of ideas and right of assembly, alive. Because of this the shows were always exciting and well worth the effort. What was learned from the experience was that by attempting to communicate with people about what was going on (and the need for them to be somewhat more responsible for the 'scene') a visibly positive effect was the result. With something as fragile as a *people-generated, not-for-profit music hall*, one negative event can destroy the work of many. For example, a trashed toilet resulted in hundreds of dollars of damage to the building and an ajoining business. As a result, the warehouse scene came to an end when the owner threatened complete eviction of all those who lived there if the shows continued. With that, a lot of bands lost a place to play and people lost something important.

At that time, another temporary location was found and shows began happening at a rather innocuous pizza parlor called, 'Owns Pizza'. The proprietor, Ali, was approached with the idea of having "private" parties. Since business was not so good (to the point of practically non-existent) he went for it. Shows at Owns Pizza raised eyebrows, as well as mohawks at first, but the shows all turned out great. There was no vandalism, no violence, just a lot of fun for everyone, and we all cleaned up the place afterwards. There were probably 8 to 10 shows there until the city got into it. Getting things legal had become a necessary step in the evolution towards establishing a (for lack of a better term) functioning facility. An attempt was made to get a permit but after some discussion, it was decided that this was not quite the right place to put effort into.

To keep the underground music scene alive, it was going to be necessary to find an adequate location, a broad base of support, the money, as well as the necessary permits for the plan to really work. This is where Maximum Rock and Roll came into the picture. After the Owns group came across an ideal site, knowing that MRR had intentions of doing something similar, they were approached with the idea. They had some other projects on the line at the time and didn't feel that they were ready to put their money and energy into such an ambitious venture, but after looking at the place, talking with the people involved and considering the energy that seemed to be so strong in the East Bay they decided to give it a shot.

The owner of the warehouse was sold on the idea of having something like a cultural music/art center coming into the space. It sounded like a good idea to him, but before a lease could be signed the City of Berkeley would have to approve the idea. The place was held with half the monthly rent for the first couple of months. Dealing with the city was no easy matter and didn't happen over night. Months passed before the hearing date set by the Berkeley Board of Adjustments came. During that time weekly meetings were held at the site where ideas were discussed by a diverse group of people interested in becoming involved. The meetings were generally attended by fifty to seventy-five people, sitting on the hard cement floor with Tim Yohannan (of MRR) acting as coordinator. The direction the club would take was discussed at the Thursday night meetings and decisions were made as democratically as possible. Eventually a cohesive framework emerged and the picture became clearer for everyone involved.

Meanwhile, contacts were made, support from the Berkeley establishment was sought - the Berkeley Arts Council, the Mayors Office, the neighborhood, other businesses in the area and individuals within the Berkeley political community. The support was very positive and encouraging. Several meetings were held with the Berkeley police to determine what problems they could anticipate. Their general attitude was "We don't want any more work" so if they don't have to be coming out on calls for trouble then things will be OK, other wise.... The group discussed the concerns and suggestions of the Berkeley police and developed a coherent approach to dealing with them. The past experiences of many of those involved produced some very concrete policies that were adopted by the group. Though compromise and cooperation with the 'establishment' were part of the general atmosphere, the project never lost sight of its original goals. There was a sense of determination that overpowered the self-doubts and useless ideological dogmas of defeat. When the hearing date finally came, the support of the board was unanimous, with one abstention.

All the hard work had paid off and the people got what they had wanted, a self-regulating, autonomous cultural center, open to all ages dedicated to the nurturing and re-generation of our culture. Potentially, that is. Now, there are no major external obstacles to creating a place where people can express themselves, interact. Where people can be exposed to new sounds, images, and ideas. Where age does not restrict but where youthful ideas and energy can coexist with the experience and ability of age to the mutual benifit of both. It can be just about anything people want and need. It's all in the doing and that takes a lot of work. In building something with 'people power' there is a much greater need for individual involvement. In a commercial enterprise all the individual is expected to do is pay. It creates a real dualistic situation, the individual gets entertained and the business makes money. That may be good to a point, but with that, you are in a position of only being able to take what is offered (if you can afford it), as well as having your culture determined solely on the merit of its profitability. The initial goal of the warehouse is to bring people together to build something, of, by, and for people. Perhaps these (admittedly idealistic) high goals and expectations are too unrealistic to be achieved, but just looking around at the world, it seems we're dead meat anyway, so what else is there to do? It remains to be seen just what people are really capable of - so some people are going to try to make something happen here in Berkeley.

Taken from a pamphlet put together by Mike M. (*Bravear* Fanzine), 1986

...ABOUT THE PROJECT

To this point one of the many experimental ideas that has been decided upon by the original group is a membership structure. This is primarily the result of the desire to have some basic understanding and commitment between everyone involved. Potentially this center belongs to everyone and it's intent is to create something more than just a place for entertainment but also something which will be the result of individual involvement. What in fact this project will be is beyond the scope of any one individual, it is a creative group activity in the art of survival. A delicate relationship exists between the individual and the group. When either becomes dominant all positive social interaction breaks down. The group must have an abiding respect for the individual, abstaining from any form of coercion or mandatory conformity. At the same time the individual has the responsibility for his/her own actions and the effect of those actions upon the group. It will require an acceptance of diversity, a tolerance to change and work. Though involvement by the individual is encouraged and essential in the operation of the center, it will be solely determined by the individual alone, as to what their involvement will be. To use the center you must be a member. The shows will be low cost to cover expenses, pay the bands fairly and, perhaps, sponser other projects that the membership may decide worthwhile. There is a one time membership fee of $3.00, for which the member will receive a membership card for admittance.

During the shows the Security Committee will have several members whose job it will be to see that problems don't get out of control, but all members are expected to be involved in keeping things running smoothly. It is definitely preferable to avoid having outside security imposed upon us; this is best accomplished by everyone being responsible for what is going on in the warehouse. Several rules have been established which are necessary to keep the center open. Those include no alcohol or drugs, no violence and no vandalism in or around the warehouse. Jepordizing the warehouse will not be tolerated by anyone. Simply by using some common sense coupled with the self-confidence to stand up in defense of what we have mutually created we can go a long way in maintaining an enviornment where positive social growth can take place. We must not be intimidated by violence or general stupidity while at the same time avoiding it within ourselves.

Some of the more experimental ideas of the club are concerned with the variety of events presented and the way they will be booked. The booking committee will concentrate on maintaining consistently good and interesting shows and hopefully with that, people will come for the total experience rather than to just come out for a particular band. The 'show' is just as much the people as what's on stage; the music is just what we share. The shows will not be advertised and just what will be happening will not be known until the show itself. The intention is to create an oppurtunity for surprise and introduce the element of the unexpected and to transfer the emphasis upon the project itself. If people come with a minimum of pre-judgment about whether or not they will have a good time, chances are it could be some of the best shows ever.

The main hours for music will be Friday and Saturday nights, from 8 to 12, though some shows may go as late as 2. Weekend days and weeknights will be used for other things such as Art and Photo exhibits, educational forums, or any other events the membership may create. Week nights will also be available. The only potential limitation is our own lack of imagination and the energy to make it happen.

One other thing about this project, it has no name.

Taken from a pamphlet put together by Mike M. (*Bravear* Fanzine), 1986

It's the end result of a dream so powerful that a bunch of hardcore punks and over-aged adolescents performed like student government types to make it come true. And they did it all without government money, foundation funding, or a single grant proposal.

Their determination meant cooperating with a system that many had serious doubts about. "If we're gonna put this kind of energy and money into a project, we want it to be in the best possible position vis-a-vis the law," said Tim Yohannan. And on the road to going aboveground, they learned some lessons about organizing — and about politics, Berkeley-style.

The group sent out "lobbyists" to members of the Board of Adjustments, the Berkeley Arts Council, and others with influence in the community. Their efforts paid off. Backing from the mayor's office and from more "respectable" members of the art community enhanced the center's image and helped them to cut through the red tape that faces all new businesses in the city.

Then-mayor Gus Newport let the Board of Adjustments know that the city was behind any creative solution to the problems of youth loitering on Telegraph Avenue and elsewhere in the city, and word trickled down to the city's corps of inspectors as well. They came to the warehouse armed with helpful suggestions, along with their measuring tapes and rule books, and made special efforts to expedite the required paperwork, helping the group to get the doors open in time for the first show on New Year's eve.

Club members express the hope that exposure to Gilman Street will inspire "outsiders" to go out and do the same sort of thing in their own communities. But, as Yohannan says, "It's rare to find a large group of people whose values are dramatically anti-commercial and who are willing to put so much into something mainly based on heart. Would you find that kind of belief backed up by action in many other spheres of culture? I doubt it".

Taken from an article written by Mitzi W. in the *East Bay Express*, April 1987

Anarchy on Gilman St.

Music and art can bring people together through expression and communication, but the structure of most nightclubs puts a wall between the audience and the expression — limiting them to the role of receptors, rarely providing opportunity for participation in the actual expression.

At the Gilman St. Project, a progressive all-ages nightclub in North Berkeley, the audience is becoming part of the expression by working within the club, helping to decide club policy and musical lineups, and working with bands to bring these ideas to fruition.

Can a nightclub that mixes the dynamic and aggressive punk subculture with a variety of other alternative music styles and performance arts avoid the violence characteristic of so many punk oriented establishments? Members of the Gilman St. Project say yes. More difficult, they say, is maintaining a sense of community among club patrons while still drawing enough of an audience to keep the club out of the red.

The Gilman St. Project formed in the summer of 1986, when Tim Yohannon — one of the godfathers of the Bay Area punk scene — and friends from *Maximum Rock and Roll Magazine* sought to establish an all-ages alternative to the present music scene.

To avoid the problems of violence and alcohol consumption by minors, club activists designed the Gilman as a membership club. First-time patrons pay a $2 lifetime membership fee, and sign an agreement promising to refrain from vandalism, drugs or alcohol in or around the club.

That's right, there's no booze at the Gilman. At the bar — the snack bar — the drink of choice is JOLT. But don't think the no-alcohol policy prohibits a good time: quite the contrary. The atmosphere is much more relaxed than at all-ages clubs that serve alcohol, where uptight security guards are constantly searching for juvenile offenders. Most Gilman club members know and respect the rules and have a blast without booze.

If you're wondering whether the vitality of high energy music can be sustained in such an atmosphere, or if self-expression is ailing for lack of a creative spark, just step inside.

The interior of the Gilman St. Project is a gallery of graffiti and explosive art work. Walls are covered with Nagel-esque creatures and scenes of social and sensual revolution. The artwork is political, it's

musical and it's critical or philosophical, but it's always uncensored. Before the shows, many an artist, or would-be artist, has contributed to the ambiance with murals and caricatures. Want to make a statement? Grab a marker.

Highlighting the decor is one of many ways for members to get involved at the Gilman. Anyone can help run the club. None of the staff, including management, get paid, but many members will work part of the night and then get to watch the rest of the show. While most of the regulars have a traditional task, flexibility makes the system work. What's important to the regulars is being there.

The Gilman nurtures a strong sense of community that Yohannon said evolved out of membership and member participation.

Joel, ex-bassist for *Corrupted Morals* and a frequent volunteer at the club, became a member when the Gilman first began memberships last summer.

"Every weekend we had people come in and help build the place. Here, it's a family attitude. Lots of people know each other. This is like a home away from home," Joel said with a hint of pride. "Some people come here with this attitude that they don't want to have fun. They look at us like we're weird. They call us the 'fluffy punks,'" he said.

"People have an attitude here. It's about letting loose. You can act like a fool and that's O.K.," said Jane Guskin, who arranges bookings for the Gilman. "A lot of that punk meanness isn't around here."

Guskin believes much of the Gilman St. character comes from the diversification of its format. By bringing a potpourri of music and culture under one roof, the Gilman gives exposure to much that conventional night clubs ignore.

The club opened its doors on New Year's Eve last year, but early on the popularity and energy of the punk scene began to overshadow the presence of other music and art forms at the Gilman. That's when the club split Friday and Saturday into different themes. Saturday nights are predominantly punk, while on Friday nights, as club regular Mark Davies puts it, "pretty much anything goes."

"We're giving people the opportunity to do anything they want. This place is yours," Guskin said as she extended her arms to the world. "I think people would just jump at the chance if they knew about it. If they can do something halfway interesting, we give them a try."

Recently the club celebrated the "Summer of Lust," with a lineup of

pseudo '60s bands, body painting, and a condom blowing contest. Another night featured the "Composers' Cafeteria," a small orchestra's performance of avant-garde flavored classical pieces written by local composers.

But the Gilman's diversity isn't limited to music. Performance art, plays and films have all appeared in the club, and Guskin said she would like it to become as much of an art gallery as a nightclub.

"The possibilities are endless. Right now it's just this much," Guskin said, peering through fingers that looked as if she were holding a pebble.

The night I ventured into the club, clusters of Gilman St. regulars mingled about the house for hours prior to show time. There's no charge for hanging out during preshow hours. People were rapping, playing cards, comparing fashions and getting ready for the show. One wall has a basketball hoop, where fierce matches are played with a bright, hard plastic beach ball.

That night's workers made ready with the evening's preparations, without a hint of interstaff tensions. The biggest staff problem that door and security supervisor Brian

Wehmeyer encountered was having too many workers for the positions he had to fill, but all was settled amicably.

Godfather Tim sat quietly at a wooden picnic table taking it all in. Everyone stops to say hello, and Yohannon's fervor shines through his boyish smile as he greets workers and club goers alike with a degree of deference unusual in a club manager. It's obvious even to the casual observer that Yohannon really enjoys working with and around young people.

Taken from an article by Dan L. in the *Daily Cal* (UC Berkeley newspaper) Sept. 1987, photos by Kevin R. It was one of the best articles done on the place while we we there.

Rocking With Peace Punks

By ROBERT GOLDBERG

Berkeley, Calif.

It's evening in the flatlands of Berkeley, down by the marina. In a run-down neighborhood of old factories, Officer B.R. Knox of the Berkeley Police points to a long, low warehouse. The sign on the building reads "The Caning Shop—chair caning . . . rawhide . . . wicker," but out in front, teenagers with shaved heads and mohawks are gathering. "That's where they play that funky punk music," Officer Knox says, "that bump-and-grind stuff." He shakes his head. "I'm sure they got drugs in there."

Inside is a blast of light and heat and noise. Up on stage, Operation Ivy has just replaced Screeching Weasel. Throbbing, pounding, its music comes crashing down on the crowd, a brick wall of sound. Guitar and bass and drums mount a blistering sonic attack as the band smashes through its song.

Jammed around the stage, an audience of 250 is screaming and shaking. Some of the kids thrash from side to side. Some pogo up and down. And some climb up on stage and dive, head first, into the crowd. It looks like mass psychosis. It looks like a riot.

But on the walls of this warehouse are inscribed messages such as "Frontiers Divide People" and "Check Racism at the Door." Scattered on chairs are fliers that describe benefits for AIDS victims and Greenpeace. And by the door is the membership credo: "I recognize that I am personally responsible for my actions and that cooperation with others is in my own personal self-interest. I agree to respect the rights of others to express themselves.
. . ."

This warehouse at the corner of Gilman and Eighth is not just any punker hangout. It's the Gilman Street Project, the mecca of straight-edge.

What is straight-edge? Where are these kids coming from? Out of the punk movement that started in the mid-1970s in England with disaffected kids and socially critical, nihilistic bands such as the Sex Pistols and the Clash. Soon it grew to include all sorts of folks: fashion fiends with shaved heads and leather jackets, artsy egghead New Wave types with angular guitars (Blondie, Television, Talking Heads)—and especially bored teens with big boots who liked to get tanked up on cheap beer and kick the stuffings out of people who didn't agree with their neo-Nazi views.

In the power struggle among the factions within the punk movement, straight-edge represents a very small, but very dedicated splinter group (based here in the Bay Area, with a tiny international following) that has popped up within the past five years.

Its tenets are simple. No fighting. These are peace punks. No drugs, no pot, no beer, no wine. Sober peace punks. No meat, no chicken, no fish, no dairy products, no sugar. Some kids have to go a long way to rebel against the previous generation. These kids are, in short, non-violent vegetarian punk rockers. Only in Berkeley. . . .

Leaning against the wall, as Operation Ivy blasts into its last number, "Healthy Body, Sick Mind," 19-year-old Chuck Goshert proudly points to his watch face, emblazoned with an X. "X—that's the symbol of straight-edge," he says. For Mr. Goshert, a lanky, fresh-faced teen with a broken arm he got skateboarding, straight-edge means more than just rad music. "It's about self-respect," he says. "It's about having a positive attitude. Up until I was 15, 16, I used to drink and smoke a lot of pot. I used to get stupid all the time."

"I'm 20," confesses Kamala Parks, a peroxide blond with a bandana. "Almost everyone here is younger than me. I feel kinda old." For Ms. Parks, it's the music that keeps her coming back to Gilman Street. The music and the attitude. "You get some skinheads in here. But if they get into that violent thing, they're ejected."

Of course, that doesn't mean that at Gilman Street they don't slam—the time-honored punk dance in which everyone crashes into everyone else at top speed. "Sure I slam," says Ms. Parks. "Everybody slams. It's a good way to get out your feelings. I know it's done me a lot of good."

The doors of the Gilman Street Project opened New Year's Day, 1987. Started with $40,000 out of the pocket of Tim Yohannan, publisher of the magazine Maximum Rock N Roll (circulation 13,000), the club runs at a consistent loss of about $600 a month. But every Friday, Saturday and Sunday night, four to five bands play 30-minute sets, and 100 to 300 fans come in.

Strangely enough, this punk rock club is a mini-experiment in democracy. All these slamming, yelling kids are expected to pitch in. "Here, you're a member," says Ms. Parks. "You help out. Everybody helps out. No one at the club draws a salary. There are no decision makers. Everything's put up to a vote. And there are no leaders."

The democracy extends to the stage. "Anyone who wants to play, can," says Radley Hirsch, who runs the sound board. "We've had Dixieland jazz. We've had Middle Eastern music, with 21 belly dancers."

Right now, there's something on stage that's a little bizarre, even by Gilman Street standards. Frank Moore, a quadriplegic in a wheelchair, is front and center, writhing and moaning along with Helen Reddy's "I Am Woman." Two men and two women, naked except for some cellophane wrap, are circling the wheelchair, hopping and dancing. Chuck Goshert raises his eyebrows. "I don't want to put anyone down," he says, "but I can't say I appreciate this as art."

Mostly, however, at the Gilman Street warehouse, the sound is good old-fashioned punk rock, cranked out by bands with names like Rabid Lassie, Corrupted Morals, Nasal Sex, Isocracy, Sewer Trout and Grandpa's Become a Fungus. "They play two speeds at Gilman," says San Francisco recording engineer Mark Brooks. "Fast and faster."

As 2 a.m. rolls around, the last band is tearing through its encore. In the crescendo of metal noise, the dancers are slamming around the pit and flipping off the stage. Suddenly, abruptly, the band finishes, the lights come up, and Gilman Street goes through its most bizarre ritual of all. Still glistening with the sweat of their thrashing around, the punks—slammers and band members alike—pick up wastebaskets and brooms. Then, sweeping and scrubbing, they clean up their club.

The infamous *Wall Street Journal* article, Aug. 1988

Humane officials probe band's dead-animal stunt

BERKELEY — A humane officer is investigating complaints that the leader of a "shock-rock" band threw dead animals into the audience during a performance, officials said yesterday.

The concert by the group Feederz was held last Sunday night at a club at 926 Gilman St., according to Tim Burr, a disc jockey at KALX, the University of California at Berkeley radio station. He did not know the name of the club.

"I got calls from rock fans themselves who were quite upset about this," said Cheryl Barnes, a state humane officer in Berkeley.

Feederz fans "stomped and squashed" the carcasses, "while other (members of the audience) screamed in objection," said Angela Lynn Douglas of Albany, who attended the concert and complained to police afterward.

The band's leader, who calls himself Frank Discussion, carried the carcasses of a dog and cat into the hall over his shoulders, threw them onto the stage, and then tossed them into an audience of about 100 people, according to witnesses who complained to Barnes. She did not release their names.

Several dozen people surrounded Discussion, demanding that he remove the animals, said Barnes. He refused, until several people collected plastic bags into which they planned to place the bodies.

Several people demanded to know where he obtained the bodies, and he reportedly answered: "I checked them out from the Berkeley SPCA, and now I've got to return them," which Barnes said was not true.

Discussion eventually removed the carcasses from the hall, according to Barnes.

Neither Discussion, other members of the Berkeley-based band, nor owners of the hall could be reached for comment.

Barnes said her investigation will be aimed at determining how the animals died, or if they were killed or otherwise subjected to violence.

The infamous Feederz' dog incident. This article was taken from the *Oakland Tribune*, 1987

Above: the first Gilman Street T-shirt, 1987/1988. Design by Richie B.

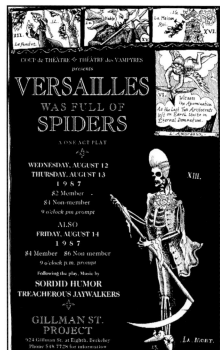

COUP de THÉÂTRE ✧ THÉÂTRE des VAMPYRES

presents

VERSAILLES

WAS FULL OF

SPIDERS

A ONE ACT PLAY

✧

WEDNESDAY, AUGUST 12
THURSDAY, AUGUST 13
1 9 8 7

$2 Member
$4 Non-member
9 o'clock pm prompt

ALSO

FRIDAY, AUGUST 14
1 9 8 7

$4 Member $6 Non member
9 o'clock p.m. prompt

Following the play, Music by

SORDID HUMOR
TREACHEROUS JAYWALKERS

✧

GILLMAN ST.
PROJECT

924 Gilman St. at Eighth, Berkeley
Phone 548-7728 for information

THE FIRST
ART SHOW
PANDEMONIUM

FEBRUARY 21 & 22

GILMAN ST. PRESENTS AN EXHIBIT OF VISUALS

SATURDAY AND SUNDAY   924 GILMAN ST.
12:00 TO 5:00 PM   IN BERKELEY   AT 8TH ST.

When Gilman was at its peak, maybe a year or more ago, I remember sometimes how I'd be out on the street or in the supermarket, or visiting my parents, and I'd find myself thinking, why can't I act the same way everywhere that I do at Gilman Street? Why can't I feel that same freedom to say or do just about anything that comes to mind, to bounce all over the gamut between sober, responsible organizer and total raving loon? And then sometimes I would slip into my Gilman mode for a minute or two, go riding up and down the aisles on a shopping cart making goony faces at all the little kids or step in between two strangers to tell them to stop fighting.

Then all of a sudden I'd remember, whoa, this ain't Gilman, dude, this is *reality* operating here, and I'd crawl back inside the guarded, cautious persona that I'm used to taking out on the street. Why can't the whole world be like one big Gilman? I guess in a lot of ways it really is; same kind of problems and same kind of joys, just on a way bigger and sometimes life and death scale. And even more than at Gilman, it's totally up to us to make it work, to make it fun, to make it happen, or to give up and let it die.

Excerpt from Larry L.'s column in MRR, Nov. 1988

MAXIMUMROCKNROLL

NO. 65   OCTOBER 1988 $2.00

ADVERTISEMENTS

THE GILMAN STREET PROJECT

Dec 31, 1986-Sept 11, 1988
R.I.P. -- The spirit lives!!!

As of September 11, the Gilman Street Project closed its doors. For the last 6-9 months, all of us involved in Gilman have been trying to deal with a series of problems in various ways. From time to time, the possibility of asshole troublemakers who couldn't gain access to the club tried to push the level of tensions up by their drinking in the area or by threats of violence, however thinly veiled. This did not really deter us from proceeding with Gilman, and we did hire a security guard to deal specifically with external problems. This alone was not the reason for closing, but certainly didn't make our job there any more enjoyable. We also had legal problems. A jock who came to Gilman fell while thrashing, broke his arm, and sued for $16,000. He won his case, which brought considerable heat down on us from our insurance company. They demanded we end "slam dancing", which we tried to do until we could get another insurance company. Our lease was also expiring, and we were prepared to enter into a new 3 year lease with our land-lord (who continued to be totally supportive right until the end), and to ink new insurance, as well as turn over the reigns to a fairly new crew of volunteers, but it became more and more apparent that we were dealing with a deteriorating situation.

If any one single cause could be cited for the membership decision to close, it could be said that burnout was it. Doing 2-3 shows a week for a year-and-a-half really takes its toll. Besides the physical and emotional exhaustion of those who do the bulk of the work, it renders most shows as routine. The spontaneity and specialness gradually dissipated. Gilman served a real function the first year, helping to galvanize a community, to demonstrate that alternative principles can work. We paid our bills, paid the bands well, and helped many new bands come into existence. We brought out a new spirit, or perhaps just an old punk spirit, that emphasized creativity as well as just having fun. The old macho bullshit got attacked, as well as creeping racist and fascist crap. But every new scene is but a fleeting moment, a spark that comes and then flickers out. Gilman's time came and went. One can't force spontaneity, and once people take a venue and idea for granted, it can no longer hold their imagination and effort. After trying to reverse that trend, it became apparent that this stage of Gilman's work was done.

The final meeting was pretty upbeat, with most people agreeing that it was time we did something for ourselves, and that closing was healthy and necessary. People did not feel de-feated or down. Quite the contrary, besides a feeling of relief, most of us felt that there were better ways for us to channel our energy and ideals, and that fighting a standing battle was a bad tactic. There are times when it is possible, when you have the numbers and possibility of winning such a struggle, but if those conditions do not exist, then a more guerilla approach is required, where you have more flexibility and mobility. The core group at Gilman will keep doing events, both through helping arrange special shows at other existing venues and through more word-of-mouth events. Fewer shows will make these gigs more exciting and spontaneous, less taken for granted. The membership felt it would be more creative to take a lower profile ap-proach and do shows only with bands that we really have a kinship with. MRR is committed to help fund these sporadic events, and everybody is actually pretty excited about this prospect (more news on this later!). We all feel that to keep Gilman open as "just another club" would be a disservice to the original ideals of Gilman, and that those values can be better served and im-plemented by a more underground approach.

While I'm sure most of us feel sad on some level, and there will always be a nostalgia trip happening, we also look forward to resurrecting the grassroots community approach that we headed for in the first place. To those bands and individuals who cared and worked their butts off, we salute you. To those who were merely consumers, I guess you'll have to do your gobbling elsewhere. It's amazing how little bitterness anybody involved feels, and so we hope to see those of you who care at some of these other events elsewhere. Thanks, Tim

P.S. At least as of now, it appears that there will still be a final....

RECORD SWAP MEET-Sunday October 30 Reservations for tables being accepted now ($10) Admission cost $1 -noon to 4 PM

MORE ON GILMAN CLOSING

By Tim Yo

Gilman Street Project was just that, a project, an experiment. It was an attempt to create a truly alternatively run space and to turn a violent scene around. It had its victories and its failures, and here are some of the possible reasons behind the closing and the lessons to learn.

BANDS: Gilman had hoped to bring together representatives of various bands to eventually lead to a band-run clubhouse. If enough bands had seen it in both their collective and selfish interest to have made that commitment, then it could have worked much better. Some bands (or members of bands) took it to heart, but most bands merely saw Gilman as a place to play and did only what was demanded of them.

AUDIENCE: It was up to the crowds to appreciate with respect what was rightfully theirs (a self-run club) and to put energy into making the place be special. Many did, many more did not. While most liked the idea, it was hard for them to translate that into constant involvement. Those people that like to drink at shows and get rowdy were alienated and frustrated from the start with Gilman's "no drinking" policy, which was necessary to keep an all-ages venue open. They either boycotted or outright fucked with Gilman. Many of those who liked the necessary policies and atmosphere took it for granted, leading to a consumerist outlook and stagnation. It was up to the crowds to challenge the bands to greater heights, less hypocrisy, and more creativity, but seldom did that happen.

STAFF: The people who volunteered to work regularly and bothered to attend decision-making meetings are the heros. They gave everything and then some. But a few cannot mke up for the majority who never got it. There was a toll-taking burnout factor. Most of the staffers, besides having regular jobs or school, had other important projects of their own: zines, bands, radio shows, labels, etc., and were spread pretty thin.

CONCLUSIONS: If Gilman was the only or main priority for most of the staff, then things might have been different. It took all they had to just cover the mandatory work, and left little or no time for many of the details, the subtle things that really lead to special outcomes. After all the energy was spent on booking, security, membership, and clean-up, there was precious little left for the outreach and communication that was necessary to create a more unique character for the place, a greater variety of experience, and for bringing new, excited blood into the stew. Most bands too failed to break out of their molds, to come up with innovating concepts for shows as well as more memorable individual performances. It remains to be seen if that shortsightedness will lead to the demise of most bands now that they have no other place to place publically besides parties. The audience, in general (and especially as time went on), were young, as were the bands. They had little to compare Gilman to, and it was easy for them to take a stable venue for granted. They also lacked the self-confidence and experience to assert themselves consistently. Some tried, but it was asking an awful lot of them. Here in the Bay Area, fans are pretty spoiled, and there's always been somewhere to go to shows. Weirdly enough though, when people call asking if Gilman is really shut, very few ask why when told "yes", and even fewer show any kind of anger or frustation at that.

WINS AND LOSSES: Many people got to make new friendships and shared a valuable growing experience. Many bands came into being because they now had an outlet to be heard as well as to be righteously paid. Some of these bands will last, most won't. There was a period of magic at Gilman, that undefinable time when a scene is born out of rubble, where creativity and friendship flourish. Something was created, but it didn't last forever. Maybe it can't. Maybe scenes must die before something fresh can come along again. Energy and creativity can't be forced, even if the right topsoil and fertilizer are applied. There was a time for Gilman's ideas to surface, and now perhaps a time for them to take a more underground outlet. Many of the Gilman people will keep working together on other projects. There is a sense of sadness and disappointment, but not a sense of defeat.

Going with the flow and learning to surface and strike at the right time, and then learning when to scale down and melt into the jungle at yet another right time are important lessons. Gilman accomplished only about 20% of its potential, but it was a fun and challenging 20% for most of its history. Most importantly, it provided a contrast for what can be done in the future. Onward.

LATE NEWS FLASH-

NEW CLUB TO OPEN AT GILMAN ST. SITE

It now appears a new group of people will be starting a new club at the location of 924 Gilman. Some of them were involved in the Gilman St Project, others are new. The principles appear to be somewhat along the lines of Gilman, though it will be somewhat more structured. They plan on beginning events in early November.

Taken from MRR news section, Nov. 1988

Classic Tim Y.: grab a piece of scrap paper, scribble "Gilman's closed forever, bye" on it, and tape it in the window at Gilman.

CHAPTER TWO

OPEN AGAIN

JONATHAN D./AMF

1988-1989

"...PERHAPS THE CLUB'S GREATEST SERVICE WAS TO INSPIRE PEOPLE AROUND THE WORLD TO TRY CREATING THEIR OWN."

— JONATHAN D.

Re-emerging from the depths, 1989   photo by Murray B.

JONATHAN D.

INITIAL INVOLVEMENT

My involvement in Gilman Street can be better understood with the following personal facts. I arrived in the Bay Area (Berkeley) in the fall of 1984, for physics graduate school, having had minimal contact with the punk rock genre (e.g. the Ramones' *Rock'n'Roll High School* movie, the Clash, and some new wave bands). My introduction to live music was primarily via local and traveling bands at the Berkeley Square (college radio fare) and the UC Berkeley radio station KALX, which I later volunteered at. I also got an introduction to punk via a fellow grad student familiar with the NYC scene (e.g. Richard Hell) and saw some of the last performances by the Dead Kennedys, Subhumans, etc. at the Mabuhay and the Farm. At the same time I sampled a number of Grateful Dead shows courtesy of a very mellow pothead housemate. In essence I took in a sampling of the plethora of Bay Area subcultures (music, politics, or otherwise) in my first few years, in part to explore if I fit into any of them.

Despite seeing some flyers or hearing about meetings to form a new club in Berkeley on Gilman St. in the fall of 1986, I did not actually attend a Gilman show until the summer of 1987—five months after the original Gilman Street Project had opened its doors and after initial 'glory' months of the collective coexistence of a community of artists, musicians, and politicos. My primary motivation for frequenting the club at the time was to increase my chances of meeting a certain girl who lived two blocks away from the club. I would also commonly see a movie at the nearby Rialto theater and see half a Gilman show. This period introduced me to the local East Bay scene of Isocracy, Stikky, Op Ivy, and Sweet Baby Jesus.

It wasn't until early the next year, in 1988, that I attended my first membership meeting, in part to learn about rumors that all was not well with the club and that Tim was demanding changes. It was my first experience of a "democratic" meeting in which trivial issues could go on forever due to the innumerable sidetracking stupid comments. It was also a strange sort of meeting in that despite the democratic structure with attempts to follow Robert's rules of order, it was obvious that one person had the most influential opinions and usually guided/strong-armed the ultimate decisions. Here I made the first connection to the person of Tim Yo whom I had heard ran MRR, a thick fine print zine that I had tried to penetrate a few times. Also, I learned the nature of the problems: violence at shows, burnout of too few volunteers having too much responsibility, and consumerism by audience and band members. This lead to the implementation of the infamous work-to-play policy in which local area band members were required to volunteer for working a show prior to their band being booked.

My next step of involvement was to take the challenge put forth to the membership by Tim Yo to take more responsibility. My one attempt to volunteer for security wasn't very pleasant—having to walk around outside the club including the unlit train tracks behind the club to tell scary-looking people to take their alcoholic drinks elsewhere. Hence I chose to participate in the subcommittee of show coordinators. The minutes of a meeting dated March 14, 1988, which I recorded, reveal that the coordinators were in need of structure in terms of scheduling, training, meetings, written job descriptions and standardization of forms for volunteer signup, guest lists, etc. Up to that point, the head coordinator was commonly decided just before the show from the pool of qualified persons (Tom, Cammie, Honey, Martin, Tim and

Paul), whomever was present. Signup sheets were impromptu, created on the back of flyers. I ended up creating some standardized forms, "Show Sheets" for volunteer signup, and job descriptions using my work Mac, and I worked a few shows that summer as an assistant show coordinator.

GILMAN STREET
PROJECT NEWSLETTER

August 19, '88   Issue No.0

Will there be an issue #1? A few months ago it was decided that a new partnership would take over the legal management of the Gilman St. Project. As the transition time of September comes nearer, the new partners as well as Tim Y. as well as the dozen or so 'active' members are still pondering if it is worth the effort to continue. Here are some of the thoughts expressed by individuals (not word for word) at the previous Sunday membership meeting (and for the last six months!):

-- "The club is fucking lame -- it has become stagnant creatively ... grafitti-wise, band names have replaced what used to be artwork."
-- "Shows are no fun to work . Shows aren't that special anymore -- only about one in ten shows do you come away with a real good feeling."
-- "Always the same small core of volunteers show up to work and coordinate, and bother to come membership meetings."
-- "We get little to no support from bands, who should be the strongest supporters of an all ages venue to play."
-- "Gilman has turned into just another rock club -- catering to the punk rock scenesters ... that's not acceptable."
-- "The ultimate reason for working should be for ourselves, TO HAVE FUN, rather than being martyrs for so many consumers, bands and audience alike, who don't give anything back."
-- "We have too small a pool of dedicated volunteers working too many shows leading to burnout, hence reducing the number of volunteers further."
-- "We are in a financial bind where we are pressured to always have so many shows to pay the rent and insurance -- it's a downwards whirlpool...a series of Catch-22s... a grind."
-- "Some bands are booked primarily because of the draw financially and not because they espouse any ideals of the club -- the result being headaches for workers from dealing with crowds who don't care one iota about the club."
-- "The $2 lifetime membership card serves a purpose (perhaps only symbolically) of informing newcomers of the rules and ideals of the club. Aside from the necessary income generated it is meaningless -- only to a small set of active volunteers does the concept of membership mean anything."

-- "Hardcore is our staple money-maker. We'd like to have the freedom to try other events without suffering financially."
-- "The largest contributors (timewise) to the club are so mired in just keeping the place operating adn don't get the chance to stand back and observe from a more distant perspective and organize new events."
-- "A few members put too much of their daily thoughts and emotions into the club, to the point of always worrying about the next crisis and feeling guilty about not coming one particular night ...and talking about Gilman as if it were some autonomous beast -- it's not healthy."
-- "There are too many NO's and restrictions at Gilman, whether initiated by the membership (alcohol, vandalism, violence, racism) or imposed in regard to insurance (stagediving, violent thoughtless slamming -- both of which there is no convincing support for anyway)."

Related (perhaps personal) questions:
-- Why do we get so little support from local bands for whom the club is their main outlet? Should they expect to get paid anyway for the opportunity to play here?
-- What exactly are the (many) reasons people are driven away from contributing to the workings of the club? Do opportunities need to spelled out more? Does the MRR circle and influence scare or alienate people?
-- Should the club operate as just another rock club? Are there enough active members willing to continue operating far below their aspirations of the place?
-- Will there be any opportunities in the near future to fill the void for people if there is no more Gilman?
-- What does it count that Gilman St. is famous via the MRR magazine; that touring bands temporarily reinspire individual workers by emoting how they wish their hometown had such a place? Or that other bands find Gilman to be the epitomy of the punk rock 'scene', an amplified version of the problems they've encountered everywhere else.
-- What about the large sums of money intially put into starting the club and developing the sound system?
-- What does it count that Gilman has a rather strong recording and demo-tape side activity?
-- Is it too late to reinspire any fun or creativity at Gilman?

END OF THE "PROJECT"

The next crisis was that despite any small improvements in organization from the coordinator, band and other subcommittees, Tim Yo wanted the ultimate responsibility of running the club out from under the umbrella of MRR. An important reason for this concerned the potential financial liability for someone getting hurt at the club. Up to that point, the club existed legally as part of *Maximum RocknRoll*, a "general partnership business," in which the partners could be individually liable for suits not covered by insurance. In particular, early in the year, an audience member (from Santa Rosa?) was injured slam-dancing and broke an arm (?) Despite his desire to not harm the club in any way, his parents sued, forbade any contact with their kid, and ultimately got awarded ~$14K from the Gilman $3K/year insurance policy (which of course was subsequently not renewed). This type of incident, which repeated itself a year later, has been the downfall for a number of all-ages clubs nationwide (another example is the OK Hotel in Seattle). At Gilman, this incident led to a strict ban on stagediving, with signs posted on the walls and meetings filled with critical analysis of the testosterone-high mosh pits and ideas for creative alternatives to make the dancing more female-friendly.

The solution to the MRR liability issue was that a core group of three to four volunteers would need to step forward to sign onto the legal responsibility for the Gilman Street Project. The people were to be approved by the membership and should have no significant personal assets that could be tied to the club. Finally, at least a half dozen people stuck their heads out, including the most passionate and vocal volunteers, Honey O. and Sharon T., a committed band member, Michael R. of Raskul, an old-timer DIY ex-hippie, Michael D., and a quiet newcomer, myself. Despite a passionate writeup of his vision and ideals, entitled "May a Thousand Flowers Bloom," Michael was not chosen. A new general partnership with four officers (myself, Honey, Michael, and Sharon) filed for an Alameda County fictitious business name of Gilman Street Project on August 22, 1988. Coincidentally, on that same date a *Wall Street Journal* article titled "Rocking With the Peace Punks" was published, in which the club was characterized as a mecca of straight edge.

At that time I also typed up Issue No. 1 (Sept. 1988) of the Gilman Street Project newsletter which reported recent changes enacted by the membership, including: fewer shows (five instead of eight per month) due to a limited workforce, increased door prices ($6 instead of $5) but with the start of a $20 monthly FastPass for all shows in a single month, hiring of a security guard (Richardson Security) to assist in outside patrol, and new booking personnel (Sian and Honey instead of Tim). In addition, it listed formal requests and contacts for volunteers for flyering, artwork, show coordinators, band demo recording, Blacklist Mailorder, and KALX radio.

However, show violence reared its ugly head again. The bad seeds of the punk scene, the drunken fighter and skinhead crowd who had been thrown out and banned from the club, had been targeting the club for harassment (with their infinite free time) by drinking and picking fights outside. In addition, Gilman volunteers were harassed at other clubs, including a particular incident involving a skinhead girlfriend attacking Katja, a close friend of Honey's and a super-volunteer, outside the Berkeley Square club. This particular incident, as well as some violence at a Saturday show headlined by the appropriately named band Final Conflict, caused Tim Yo to pull the plug the very next day (Sept. 12) at the Sunday membership meeting. The meeting was convened early and Tim had already halfway pushed and convinced everyone that closing was the best and only option by the normal 5:00 PM starting time. Officially, he convinced the membership that closing was the best/only option. The show that night, Savage Republic, became the last music show of the Project and bookings for the rest of the month were canceled. The Gilman Street Project general partnership filed for abandonment on Sept. 16, and the last official event was an MRR record swap at the end of the month.

The precise details of events leading up to the closure, the key incidents and feelings, are better explained by members of the MRR crowd. I am sure the feelings ranged from severe disappointment to relief (especially for Tim Yo). Personally, I felt both—the relief of not going through with such an unprecedented personal responsibility and the disappointment of being denied the chance to work as a team with Honey, Katja, and the other responsible volunteers.

THE AMF

After this abrupt change of plans, discussions were very soon started by the KALX volunteer contingent, i.e. Pat W., to seriously explore having a new organization of volunteers take over the lease if sufficient support and commitment existed. A key motivation was the simple appreciation of all the invested man hours and money ($40K), luck (supportive landlord), and timing that made the thought of the space reverting back to a car stereo store after only two years seem like such a waste. Another important concept was that a punk club primarily focused on putting on weekly all ages shows, while falling severely short of the orginal Gilman Street Project ideals of an all-encompassing community center for artists of all types, was still a very worthy endeavor, and filled a void in all ages shows. (In truth, the punk rock music scene came to dominate the Project early on and the idealistic artists fled after the first six months.) Hence the goal was to tone down the idealism and focus on trying to solve the music show problems encountered by the previous "management."

The first exploratory meeting advertised with flyers to test the level of interest in such a new organization was held at the club. Subsequent meetings were held elsewhere because Tim wanted it clear that the Gilman Street Project as such was over, and wouldn't let us meet at Gilman. Smaller planning meetings culminated in a larger meeting down the street at the Ashkenaz, courtesy of David Nadel, at

which new volunteers paid $5 to sign up as new founding members. On October 20, the new organization, the Alternative Music Foundation (or AMF), was officially created as a non-profit corporation in the State of California with the initial directors of Jonathan D., Lou E., and Pat W.

LOU

An important attendee of the first meeting was a black leather jackete~ business software consultant name Lou E. He became crucial to the reopening of the new club as well as immediately controversial. As an older person with knowledge of business, he lent a vital air of authority that boosted confidence taking this venture to the next level of organizing the sign-up of new volunteers, membership cards, booking of the first shows, etc. Many of the early details of writing the articles of incorporation were taken care of by Lou. During the preparatory month of October—the first two months of shows, meetings, booking, flyer coordination, etc. were all performed out of Lou's warehouse studio in Berkeley (behind the University Avenue Andronico's). In essence, the MRR apartment base of operations was supplanted by Lou's apartment.

Lou was immediately controversial, in part due to his non-punk "business" image that was close to the polar opposite of Tim Yohannan. The East Bay punk scene, as well as the MRR scene, was quickly suspicious of Lou and his motives. Indeed, Lou had not-so-secret grand plans for expanding the size and scope of shows, including ultimately moving to a larger, more centrally located venue, and at one point, he had an eye on a property in downtown Berkeley (near the Berkeley Repertory Theater). Part of the origin of these schemes lay in the harsh financial reality of the Gilman Street location: a $2K+ monthly rent and other expenses that required at least a few "big" shows per month to cover. Unknown at the time was whether the club could survive on punk shows alone. Among the myriad of non-ideal solutions (higher door prices, midweek rental of the space, etc.) was the concept of expanding the musical repertoire beyond punk to other revenue-generating, i.e. mainstream, all ages genres. Although a noble-sounding goal of servicing other community all ages music needs, it raised a very practical issue of whether the punk scene (volunteers or audience) could coexist with another, less radical, group of volunteers and shows.

SKA

Eventually Lou found a niche in courting the ska scene, by booking a few ska shows a month and recruiting volunteers from that scene to help with promotion and staffing of those shows. In essence he ran a ska operation out of his apartment that aggressively competed with other Bay Area ska promoters for name acts, including Bim Ska La Bim. The peak of Lou's ska promotions was booking a Gilman show for the English ska heavyweights Madness.

While the club did benefit financially from the number of successful ska shows, the operations did cause further tensions. It was clear that Lou's ska operations dealt with band guarantees, normal operations for that scene but anathema to the punk ethics and explicitly avoided for punk shows. The ska scene also brought its own set of minority troublemakers, i.e. the stereotypical macho, bomber-jacketed, moped-riding, Doc Marten-kicking, thugs whose uniform closely resembled the skinheads that the punk scene already had big problems with. Despite some overlap in the punk and ska scenes, e.g. the seminal ska-influenced Gilman punk band Operation Ivy and minimalist ska band with punk attitudes Skankin' Pickle, the two groups consisted of very different-thinking individuals going through the teenage experience. This coexistence conflict led to sort of a behind-the-scenes "war" for the "heart and soul" of the club between the East Bay punk scene and Lou that was a backdrop for the first year of the AMF operations. Frequent ska shows at Gilman, marked by a checkered border on club calenders, were a unique feature of that year. Ultimately ska did fade from the Gilman repertoire, but a few shows did continue in the second year (1990), even with the absence of Lou promotions.

CRISES

Even before the rise and peak of Gilman ska, significant crises in running the new club were encountered. The first crisis was the ongoing violence at shows, a carryover from the previous operation, and attempts to manage it. The skinhead phenomena was at its peak in those days and specific troublemakers that had beefs against the MRR folks for their strong anti-racist stance or creative energy in the scene, targeted the club most every weekend. Such human behavior (fights, etc.) by people in their mid-twenties was a shock to me personally, having never encountered it even in my own adolescence. Somehow I also missed the whole high school teenage drinking phenomenon as a kid.

Hence I did not personally have a clue as to the mentality of the situation or proper schemes to handle it. I think from day one of the new club, the concept was to sacrifice the all-volunteer ideal and institute paid security. It was a big step, because at issue was whether other jobs at Gilman would go the same route, leading to an all-paid staff, hierarchies of paid versus non-paid workers, etc. Financially this second step was not even practical at the time.

Our first paid security was Orlando (Special Forces), a long-time black punk rocker with a leather jacket and mohawk who could handle most every incident and was well known in the scene (and a teddy bear of a person). An early incident, involving a gang of San Jose skinheads jumping the front desk en masse at a small show and attempting to beat up the audience, led to an important reconfiguration of the front door and a trial at supplementing Orlando with a paid uniformed guard from a private agency.

FRONT DOOR

A longstanding weakness at the front door was that people could look over the front table (even from the outside sidewalk) and see all the action on the inside without paying to get in. Hence it was common for a troublemaker to hang out near the front door or periodically check out the inside action and look for opportunities, when security was preoccupied with an inside scuffle or momentary confusion, to sneak in and try to land a few of their own punches. On this particular night, an ill-advised booking of NYC industrial band Sink Manhattan drew a very small audience of KALX aficionados and surprisingly, a half-dozen skinheads, who were either extremely bored or had mistakenly drove all the way from San Jose thinking there would be a punk crowd to harass. Probably annoyed that there was absolutely no one outside to harass, they waited for an opportunity near the end of the show when the front desk was vacated to rush into the club and throw punches randomly at the audience, which barely outnumbered them.

This extreme violation of the club and threat to the safety of patrons made it painfully clear that a radical change was required at the front door. By the next weekend, a rush carpentry project, with primary design and construction help from George G. (7 Seconds), produced a sturdy two-walled crowd-flow barrier that blocked line-of-sight into the club and directed patrons immediately to the right for entry and hand-stamp checks. (Later, the wall to the left was removed to accommodate the purchase of a membership card—an entry requirement reinstated after the first year of the new operation).

The Sink Manhattan violence and potential for people to get seriously hurt also prompted Pat W. to temporarily withdraw support for the continued existence of the the club and he resigned as one of the three AMF board of directors. Soundman and KALX DJ Robin S. (aka Marshal Stax) replaced Pat as a signatory on the corporate documents. Pat, of course, soon continued to be deeply involved in the club and has done most all of the subsequent handyman and carpentry projects at the club to this date.

PROFESSIONAL SECURITY

The Sink Manhattan incident also led us to try out supplementing Orlando with a uniformed security guard. The first night of this experiment was an astounding fiasco—a tall black fellow, extremely drunk and without a uniform, came up to the club and claimed to be our security guard. No one believed him at first, but he kept insisting he was here to protect the little punk kiddies. Obviously we couldn't let him hang around, and he became more belligerent when we told him he couldn't work or get paid. Eventually we got him to leave, but it was probably clear that he would be reported back to the agency and lose his job. A half-hour later, this tall drunk guy charged down the street and attacked our own security, reportedly pulling out a knife. Orlando was able to ward off the attack without any cuts, but did receive a serious scare.

Hence trying out professional help became one of the worst possible security nightmares, introducing us to a whole new level of potential violence. After allowing a second uniformed security guard to work the next week with the personal guarantee of the agency owner, it was obvious that the professional security experiment was over. Even without the extraordinary bad luck of the previous week, each new guard would have to be educated as to what the whole punk scene was all about and how to handle various situations. Their immediate reaction to the smallest incident, to radio the police, was the surest way to shutdown the club in a few weeks. The appropriate security has always been people from, or knowledgeable about, the scene, sensitive to and respected by the kids, and capable of personally handling situations without requiring intervention of the police.

YOUNG SECURITY

After Orlando, we had a handful of new security with varying diplomatic skills, mostly drawn from the San Francisco music scene. Still, there were a number of security incidents every weekend that raised the question and criticisms of whether the club was really in control. By late summer (1989) this led to a special weeknight security meeting to discuss changes and strategies, especially for an upcoming final show of the band Christ On Parade. The Christ On Parade singer was very vocal against racism and the skinhead scene and it was expected to be a big show with a surplus of troublemakers. At this security meeting were a few new recruits, including Nando, who would play a crucial role that weekend.

At the show, security had its hands full as expected and the large crowds outside the club during and between bands drew the attention of the police, who cruised by more frequently on such nights to keep an eye out for drinking. Before, or shortly into, the Christ On Parade set, a scuffle inside the club was manhandled by Nando, who dragged the troublemaker out the side door and in the excitement (self-defense or enthusiasm) threw his own punch at the guy—unfortunately directly in front of a police officer. Naturally, this indicated to the police that things were out of control and they shut down the show—a first in the club's history.

This Christ On Parade incident turned out to be a mini-turning point in the club's security problems, but not as one might expect, i.e. that the ultra low point of having a show shut down by the police made us wake up to and address the problems. Rather, the key was that the new security, exemplified by Nando, was intimately linked to the Gilman scene in the sense that Nando threw his own parties and aspired to be in his own band. Nando became one of the best and longest lasting security personnel at the club (1990 to 1998, I believe).

Also decided at the pre-Christ On Parade security meeting was the implementation of T-shirts to identify and increase the visibility of the Gilman security staff. In later years this was extended to having the same T-shirts for volunteer security, which was restarted to supplement the paid security. The decline in the skinhead phenomenon and/or alcoholism of specific troublemakers in later years also helped remove violence as a central issue threatening the club's existence.

BOOKING

Another key development in the first few months of the new operation, and essential for the future of the club, was an overnight relocation of the main booking from Lou's apartment to the actual club. Courtesy of Pat W., a locked booking closet was constructed in the side room and a booking phone line installed. The move was in response to an impending crisis of weak or inappropriate shows in the upcoming schedule, no money to pay the bills, guarantees granted to some bands, and basically an inconsistent voice coming from the club to the outside world.

I personally took over booking, to the unfortunate alienation of two nice volunteers, Heather and Siobhan. Having had no prior booking experience myself, I also immediately planned some ill-advised evenings such as an all out-of-town Sunday bill (early Seattle grunge) in which no one came and all proceeds went to gas money. Another attendance flop (and favorite show of mine), ill-publicized and the night before Fugazi, was the first reformulation of a Flipper lineup (with female vocals). I also had a few accidental huge successes. One notable example was filling out a Beatnigs show (political/industrial), with MDC (punk) and Eskimo (hippie) on the same bill without appreciating ahead of time the large crossover audience that would come. A few times I also experimented with inserting (unannounced) the Dwarves or a short rap group set in the middle of an all straight edge show. In retrospect it wasn't very respectful to that (mostly jock) scene, but it made running those shows more interesting and tolerable for the non-straight-edge volunteers.

Another characteristic of the transitional year of AMF shows was the breakup and reformulation of bands in the East Bay scene. That year the club witnessed the last shows of Op Ivy (one of the biggest shows ever), Christ On Parade (shut down by the police), and Sweet Baby Jesus, and the formation and first shows of Green Day, Monsula, Seventeen, Skinflutes, Fuel, and others. Later years would see the Hellbillies, Rancid, and many more incestuous exchanges of band members and reincarnations of the original East Bay scene.

One of the least rewarding booking jobs was to screen demo tapes and try to give a fair appraisal of the many, many generic punk starting bands. Shows were never able to be reduced from five bands to a more manageable four bands, in part due to this crush of young bands wanting to play. One notable demo tape exception was a rough medium-slow melodic cassette by a SoCal band named Jawbreaker. Based on the demo cassette alone, I called them up and invited them to play Gilman —they did, the East Bay scene embraced them, they relocated to San Fran, etc.

VOLUNTEERS

With the exodus of the MRR and San Francisco volunteer crew, the new volunteer base for the AMF operation was immediately much younger (teens versus twenties), and hence less able to take on a high level of responsibility. For a good portion of my year at the club I became the head officer, the sole booker, head show coordinator (every show), 2:00 AM trash pickup duty, garbage dump coordinator, neighborhood liason, money drop-off person, financial officer, flyer coordinator—i.e., everything except sound. Nevertheless, despite this theme of a one-man behind-the-scenes operation, a (partial) list of key volunteers during the first year of the AMF includes: Jim A. (Fuel), Mike K., Bill and Skot of the Skinflutes, Stewart I. (real estate), Mike Stand (future head), Gar G. (ever-present), Dave EC (Vagrants), Paul (Monsula), and Jesse T. (fresh from Philly).

Burnout was inevitable for me, in doing everything, the repetition of shows and problems, shaky financial situation (always a month behind in rent), etc. While everything I did organizationally (booking closet, phone lists, bookkeeping, coordinator show sheets, job descriptions) was with the idea of others taking over or sharing responsibilities, I was not the inspirational motivator. Hence my biggest action towards getting some of the younger volunteers to take on responsibility was by stepping down after one year and creating a void. Afterwards, I did continued to provide some behind-the scenes support in bookkeeping for Michael D. and much later, for John H. with the store records.

REMINISCENCE

Looking back, I can suppress the memories of many bad incidents by looking at the continued existence of the club and being proud of having been part of the bridge from the closure of the MRR/Gilman Street Project to the current evolved state of 924 Gilman Street operations. Most interesting personally has been seeing the longevity of organizational tools and structures created during my term, and watching the young, marginally responsible twerps from that time take over running the club. Also fascinating is occasionally sitting in on (the very democratic) Saturday volunteer meetings, and seeing what new solutions and bylaws have been implemented, what past issues are still being rehashed over and over, and which grand failures of the earlier days are still remembered as examples of what not to do.

A long-lasting benefit from involvement with Gilman was the introduction to other music scenes such as the Beat Happening/K Records/Olympia community and the making of long-distance friendships such as David and Jean of Mecca Normal. More locally, I am particularly fond of my introduction to the wonderful East Bay household known as The Barn: Kim, Gina, Tracy, Jane, and Ethan.

1989   photo by Murray B.

WHY YOU SHOULD JOIN THE ALTERNATIVE MUSIC FOUNDATION

What is the Alternative Music Foundation?

The Alternative Music Foundation (AMF) is a member operated all volunteer organization dedicated to the operation of an all ages alternative music facility. To begin its operations the AMF has assumed the lease on the former Gilman Street Project building in Berkeley.

The AMF plans to offer music shows at least three days a week on Fridays, Saturdays, and Sundays. The entertainment consists of bands which perform alternative music formats which normally do not receive adequate exposure in the bay area. Dancing is encouraged. Who runs the AMF?

The members do through the directors of the AMF. There are basically two classes of membership:

o Regular Members

o Volunteers

The regular members elect the President, Vice-President, Secretary, and Treasurer of the AMF. The volunteers elect the remaining eight directors through the AMF committee system. What does it cost to be an AMF member?

Membership is $10.00 per year. However, during the initial sign up period between now and January 1 1989, members can join for $5.00. What do you get for being a member?

Members enjoy a number of benefits including:

o A $1.00 discount on all club sponsored activities. Basically if you attend 10 shows a year you pay for your membership.

o For certain very popular shows you get priority access to tickets to the show.

o You will be mailed the club's monthly magazine which contains the club calendar and articles of interest to members.

o You vote annually for the officers of the club.

o You get to attend quarterly membership meetings

How do I become an AMF member?

Just complete the attached membership application and mail it with your dues payment to:

Alternative Music Foundation
PO Box
Berkeley, CA

You should receive your membership card within two weeks. You can also join at any AMF activity. What does it take to become a volunteer?

First you must be a member in good standing of the AMF. Next you apply to be a member by doing one of the following:

o Attend one of the periodic open meetings the AMF conducts for those interested in being a volunteer. At this time you will receive presentations on volunteer activities. You will be given a chance to match your skills to the needs of the club.

o Signup to be a volunteer on one of the signup sheets posted at AMF activities.

o Call the AMF information number and indicate your desire to be a volunteer.

The AMF makes an effort to match your skills, aptitudes and availability to the needs of the AMF. This means sometimes you may have to wait for a volunteer opportunity to open up that matches your abilities. However, during the initial organizing period there are many vacancies and chances are very good you will be put to work right away. What does a volunteer do?

Volunteers are assigned to one of the committees which have responsibility for the operation of the AMF. To remain a volunteer you must work a minimum of 12 hours a month on AMF volunteer activities.

The actual work you do depends on which committee you are assigned to, and the current needs of that committee. For specific information you are encouraged to talk to other volunteers or check more detailed information on display at AMF activities. Do I get anything for being a volunteer?

Certain benefits also accrue to volunteers including:

o Volunteers receive free admission to each AMF sponsored activity.

o Volunteers attend monthly volunteer meetings where AMF operations and policies discussed.

o Volunteers vote for their particular committee chairperson. The chairperson of each committee serves on the AMF board of directors.

o Volunteers attend a monthly volunteer only event paid for by AMF.

What are some of the AMF committees?

AMF committees include:

Finance
Membership
Security
Show Operations
Booking
Facilities
Newsletter
Fund Raising
Repair and Maintenance

When will the AMF have its first show?

The AMF hopes to have its first show the weekend of November 4, 1988. Why should I join now?

The AMF is currently trying to raise the necessary $8,000 to $10,000, it will take to open the doors on the new facility. Membership dues are expected to pay at least half of this amount with contributions from the local community covering the rest. If you would like to see the AMF go into business, your support is needed now.

Also there are numerous volunteer activities which need to get done now. If you have the time, your efforts would be greatly appreciated. Where can I get more information?

Contact the AMF information number (415,   between 4:00 and 9:00 P.M. weekdays.

OPEN LETTER TO MEMBERS

This letter is being written to AMF members in order to insure that an number of issues concerning the club receive a proper presentation to all members. A reasonable attempt has been made to present all sides of each issue in this letter. The opinions expressed herein are not necessarily those of the author.

Resolution of these issues are vital to the continued operation of the club. There is a membership meeting scheduled for December 18, 1988. If you can not be here but feel that you have an opinion on any or all of these issues, make sure that your ideas are conveyed to the membership meeting on your behalf.

FINANCIAL CONDITION OF THE CLUB

The club lost over 500 dollars in the month of November. This number does not include long term debts that are due (sound system, loans, etc). This number is going to be even worse in December. The club is basically open now due to the good graces of its creditors. There have been a number of suggestions to improve the financial condition of the club. Some involve how shows are conducted and others involve getting money from other sources. Many of these are discussed in more detail in later sections.

Corporate Contributions

It has been suggested that contributions be solicited from large corporations to support the club. There are members who feel it is contrary to "the principles" of the club to have any thing to do with corporate contributions. Some members would argue that taking dollars from a company with unacceptable business practices at least prevents those dollars from being used for "evil" means. The compromise position might be to develop an "approved" list on contributors. There are several factors to consider in this decision:

o Most corporations make their giving decisions once a year in December for the coming year. The deadline has past for many companies already and it will almost certainly be too late for most by January. Arguing about the merits of particular companies could in fact be making the decision not take contributions due to the club's own inaction. ("To not decide is to decide").

o The club does not yet have a tax exempt status. This should happen in the next two months. Many corporations will make provisional contributions based on an organization obtaining a tax exempt status within a certain period.

Co-promotion

It has been suggested that more people might attend more shows if the club invested in paid advertising (on radio and in newspapers). With the limited resources of the club it would not be possible to pay for a truly effective advertising campaign. However, if companies could be found to co-sponsor shows (the advertisement would read "Company ABC and the AMF present") very effective campaigns could be waged. Once again the arguments about the evils of corporations rage around this topic. Also the additional argument is raised that corporate sponsorship of a show is inconsistent with the "scene".

As with out right donations corporation often set their advertising budgets for the coming year in December. A tax exempt status is not required to obtain co-sponsors.

Facilities Rentals

It has been suggested that the club be rented out to others when it is not in use for shows. This issue has raised a number of arguments. The issues discussed in the following sections do not deal with basic legalities of the situation.

Renting to Promoters

The club has been approached by at least three for profit show promoters who merely want to rent the club to put on their own shows. Arguments surrounding this issue include:

Arguments For:

o If the promoter uses the club on off-nights and does not do shows which compete for the "AMF audience" let them use the club.

Arguments Against:

o For profit shows are inconsistent with the "principles" of the club.

o The club should maintain "creative control" over any kind of performance oriented use of the club.

o The club could easily become financially dependent on a promoter who could then use his leverage to take over or at least dictate policy to the club.

o Before making any kind of a deal with any promoter, the club should solicit competitive proposals from all bay area promoters from Bill Graham on down.

Shows That Benefit Other organizations

The club has been approached to help stage shows on behalf of other organizations. The club would be paid some reasonable amount for the use of the club, but the remainder of the funds would go to benefit the using organization. Issues surrounding these type of shows include:

o The club should not mix in politics. If there is any controversy surrounding an organization they should not be able to use the club for a show.

o The club should actively support organizations with the "right" politics.

o The club should encourage diversity. If an organization can persuade enough qualified members to work at a benefit show for the organization, then the show should be held. Equal access for all.

Other Users of the Club

A search is underway to find non-show, off hours use of the club. Certain members have expressed concerns about the "correctness" of potential users. Arguments surrounding this issue include:

o If the user does not damage the space, why should we care what the user does with the space.

o The club must maintain its "scene" and "principals".

o The demo tape program may have to be sacrificed to accommodate renters able to pay more.

THEFT FROM THE CLUB

The club is being ripped off in a number of ways. The amount of money lost to these sources would have more than covered the November losses.

Missing Concessions Revenue

The store lost money during the month of November yet all of the merchandise purchased for the store was used during the month. This amounts to close to $500.00 unaccounted for.

Unpaid Admissions

Various members complain that large numbers of people are sneaking into shows. At the same time these people are unwilling to name names or point individuals out during shows. It only takes 10 people per show to cost the club between $400 and $500 a month. Much more stringent door procedures may have to be implemented including:

o Unduplicatable hand stamps.

o Actual ticket sales

o Ticket Audits

Unpaid Dues

There are many members attending committee meetings, being very vocal about club policy and yet they have never joined and paid dues. Also non-members are being given preference over members when it comes to working at shows. Many of these individuals plead poor and yet they always have money to buy booze or drugs. Steps which should be taken include:

o Barring non-members from the business portion of any club meeting (committee or full membership).

o Giving working at show preferences to members.

Penalties for Financial Transgressions

The club should adopt a policy of permanently banning members who commit or condone financial transgressions. Sneak into a show and your gone forever.

BOOKING POLICIES

There are a number of policy changes being considered which could have a major impact on the type of show that is seen at the club in future. Before discussing specific alternatives, it must be recognized that all shows to date have been financial failures. The club has yet to sell out a show (the Angry Samoans came close). The reason for low attendance can either be due to booking unpopular shows or due to failing to properly publicize a show. This section discusses booking issues only.

Guarantees

The club has been making guarantees to bands. This policy has resulted in at least one show taking a $400.00 loss. Arguments surrounding this issue include:

o You will not be able to get bands that draw good crowds without paying guarantees. Or to get the bands without a guarantee, the club will have to pay such high percentages of the door that the club will lose money anyway.

o Pay guarantees but get something in return from the bands (see further discussion under band support of shows).

o Many local or emerging bands would rather play with a big name band for nothing than play a poorly attended show where the band got paid.

Become a Benefit Only Club

Under this proposal the club would stop paying bands all together with the exception of possibly "gas money". The arguments include:

o The caliber of bands that would play for nothing regularly is such that shows might be so poorly attended, that the club would make less with 100% of the door than it would with a smaller percentage of a better attended show.

o The quality of shows would deteriorate to the point that the show would consist of bands practicing for bands.

Band Support of Shows

The issue has been raised as to whether the club gets what it paid for when it offers guarantees or high door percentages to bands. The club should become more aggressive in its negotiations with bands and require the following as conditions for playing the club:

o Exclusive engagements: Many bands play anywhere from 2 to 5 shows during a given weekend in the area. These same bands do not have enough draw to support the number of shows they book. There are an increasing number of clubs competing for the all ages punk attendance. The club can not afford to let bands divide up the draw as they do now.

o Band interviews: Bands and touring bands especially should be required to do a minimum of four radio interviews prior to the show.

o Promotional Items: Bands should be required to provide free copies of their records to local radio stations to be given away to listeners. Also limited numbers of tee shirts and demo tapes should be made available to the club to be used to promote the band.

Other Music Forms

It may be that other club owners learned from the example of the Gilman Street Project. There seem to be a lot of clubs booking punk shows and many of these shows are some form of all ages (18 and over). The market place may be so divided that the club can no longer support even two of its traditional shows a week. The club must consider whether it is willing to learn a new music format well enough to both book and promote another music form. Arguments surrounding this topic include:

o The club does not have the money to fund the "learning experiences" of the shows that bomb while learning how to book other kinds of bands.

o The club would be doing a disservice to the many bands that have already contacted the club and asked for an opportunity to play.

o When someone has promised to man phones a certain night and does not show up and the club misses the opportunity to book a band that would mean a major draw for the club.

o   Another music form would not fit the club's "scene".

THE FLAKE FACTOR

There seems to be a trend amongst many members to do less than a quality job when asked to help the club. The result is a number of small omissions that add up to reduced attendance all the way around.

o   If someone quits putting up fliers a few blocks early and that causes five people to not attend a show, the club has just lost $25.00.

o   If someone is late mailing press releases and the submission deadline is missed for two publications that might generate ten attendees, the club has lost $50.00.

o   The list could go on and on. Every member should review their activities to look at the quality of job they have done.

If members are not willing to apply themselves consistently then maybe they should not have a club.

PUBLICITY

Since day one the publicity committee has been undermanned and not done everything it could to publicize shows. Members seem to prefer the glamor of working at shows or booking bands to doing the behind the scenes work required to insure shows are well attended. Publicity issues include:

o   The value of flyers. Should there be any flyers at all? Are the flyers being distributed in the right places.

o   Paid advertising: Are the free listings that the club makes use of enough to adequately publicize a show. Can the club afford the money for an effective advertising campaign.

o   Public Relations: Several outside experts have informed the club that one hour of good public relations effort is better than hundreds of dollars of paid advertising. Are club members willing to undertake the tasks associated with a quality public relations effort.

DEMOCRACY AND THE CLUB

There is a growing disenchantment with the club on the part of many members. A number of criticism have been leveled which include:

o   "The booking committee runs the club".

o   "A select group of individuals runs the club without regard for the opinions or feelings of others".

o   "I have never been contacted or asked to do anything for the club in spite of asking on numerous occasions if there was anything I could do to help."

Each of these remarks points to the need to change the way the club deals with its members.

Decision Making

The club must strike a delicate compromise when it comes to making decisions. For the club to operate effectively on a day to day basis there are certain decisions which must be made right now. Other decisions are of policy nature and should involve the entire club. The trick is knowing when the a decision falls into which category.

Setting Policies

For example the entire club should not be assembled to decide whether a particular band should play or not. The club membership should set the general guidelines and the booking committee should decide which specific bands meet the guidelines. A topic at the next membership meeting will probably be whether certain bands should be allowed to play at the club. The club would do itself the greatest service if it could decide on a policy of who plays or not without mentioning any bands by name.

Respect for Decisions

Most club members are sophisticated enough that they recognize that they must allow others to make certain decisions on how the club is run. The current problem is that many members feel that they never had any say in picking the person who makes the decisions for them. The club should hold elections at the earliest date.

On the other hand those making decisions should realize that remarks like "those who do the most work should make the decisions" are an unacceptable attitude. Even if someone puts in less time than someone else at the club does not mean they have less say in what goes on. If this principle is not respected before long the person has no desire to work at all.

There must be a stricter adherence to democratic procedures at club meetings. Many decisions are made currently because a vocal minority manages to shout down or wear out a less vocal majority. There should be more formal vote taking on a number of issues.

<u>Including Other Members</u>

The club must recognize a need to include others in the activities that they perform. Effective use of this process begins with recognizing that there are different attitudes about the club and that all are acceptable:

o   There are members who are willing to commit hours of effort to club. However, these members do to their particular skills or personality, need to have direction as to what to do.

o   There are other members that do to the rest of the activities in their life can only commit limited hours to the club. Remember the club started on the premise that no one would spend over 20 hours a month working on club business. The club must be able to effective plan how to use the efforts of these individuals.

o   The smallest minority of members are those who know how to perform a particular club function and basically do what ever it takes to get the job done.

The biggest challenge is for those who know what needs to be done to effectively include other members in the process of getting the job done. Introductory management courses acknowledge that the biggest problem that confronts most individuals is being able to delegate work to others. The three factors that stand in the way of effective delegation are:

o   The individual is on a personal power trip that centers around doing all the work themselves.

o   The individual is unwilling to take the time to train someone how to do the task at hand.

o   The individual would rather do more "physical" work than undergo the psychological stress that accompanies getting someone else to do the work.

Most of the members showing early signs of burn out are doing it to themselves. The club has over 175 members most of whom did not join for the financial advantages of being a member. With that many people willing to work, operating the club should be a breeze.

It is hoped that this document provides food for thought and that all members are encouraged to attend the next meeting and make themselves heard. Want to talk about it before hand call Lou at   .

                                                                                    Lou E.

924 Gilman St./ Alternative Music Foundation

AGENDA   December 17, 1988

I. Statement of conflict among directors of the nonprofit corporation
        - personality and vision for the club incompatibilities
        - individual statements by the directors (membership discussion deferred)
        - (general) purpose of the AMF according to the articles of incorporation
        - need for a clear vision of the club and unity of 'the core' members

II. Structure of the organization (Alternative Music Foundation)
        - present status   - drafting of membership bylaws
        - alternative internal structures
        - the purpose that membership serves
            - the effect of the structure on the direction of the club
        - discussion of the appropriateness of a vote (versus deferrment)

PAT WRIGHT

i came to gilman via KALX fm, cal berkeley's student & community radio station. i ignored pop music in the 70s; i was nesting. by
1981, nesting was over, no dependents resulting. i was 39. i once again
noticed music around that time thanx to kalx. kalx was playing patti
smith piss factory & the dead boys & etc. after being a (passive) lis-
tener for a year or so i went over to the kalx studios in nov. 82 &
offered to help & thanks to getting plugged in by office mgr. synthia
sizer, became an active, helping kind of shitworker (a tim yohannan
term). the death of a friend thru suicide in 81 had made me look closer at the few cultural institutions around hot enough to keep us marginal people interested & engaged in life & people... & kalx was pretty hot at that time... in 86 when flyers showed up at kalx talking
about the idea of gilman & recruiting for help to put it together, i
thought another idealistic flash in the pan & thought i'd skip the
experience, but by spring of 88 i'd been to a few shows at gilman
(thanks to the kalx guest list) and thought it was a pretty cool place
for the kids to have, so when i heard gilman was in danger of closing
unless big changes took place, i thought what the heck is going on &
started going to meetings, & got caught up in the attempt to keep the
place alive by restructuring the existing maximum rock n roll club
gilman st project into a new, 4 person co-directorship.

this was going to be tim's way of getting out from under--the
gilman st project was his direct responsibility & liability. for various reasons including more in an ongoing series of security incidents,
coming to a head sat 11 sept of 88, tim lost interest in seeing the
club continue in any form. he lobbied heavily for the final vote to
abandon the attempt to continue the club. the vote (sun 12 sept 88)
among the 4 prospective new co-directors was 3 to 1 against continuing.
the one vote in favor of continuing gilman was cast by jonathan denlinger (also from kalx) who became a key figure in the new group. called
together by flyers, word of mouth, and kalx radio spots we met on the
sunday following the vote-to-close, at the 924 warehouse to discuss the
possibility of continuing.

when tim found out about us meeting at gilman, he was very upset
and said we couldn't meet at 924; he wanted the place to close; the
gilman st project was over. we talked to david nadel at ashkenaz, who
welcomed us to meet at his large dance practice studio in the back of
ashkenaz (a few blocks from 924).

i can understand tim's reaction (only in hindsight; it just made
me mad at the time) by comparing it with my own regularly recurring
gut sense of unease in those years over how easy it would have been for
gilman to become a shitty commercial venture; a place to raise frogs
for the snakes. jonathan expresses the same general angst about the
place in jan 89, saying in his open letter to members, I will feel
guilty and ashamed if the work put into this club so far becomes exploited and perverted into a stepping stone for a very commercial music
venue.

the initial group trying to restart a club at 924 included NO
members of the original mrr work group, except for tall tim. radley
came back after a short while. the rest of mrr stood back from the new
club.. jonathan , marshall, myself, mike k., jim a., bill s., lou,
matt (op ivy) , jennifer c., skot m., mike l.; you'd have to add many
others here to be fair.. were the primary shitworkers of the new club.
. i can't bring back all the names...the initial responsible parties
(corporate officers) wound up primarily thru default being jonathan,

myself (later marshall) and lou -- you had to be 21 to legally be a corporate officer and our new format was to become a non-profit corporation. lou came in because he wandered by the warehouse when marshall
from the kalx group was putting up a sign in the window of 924 gilman
about starting up a new club & got to talking with marshall. he had
a background in management, an interest in alternate musics and a computer. we stumbled thru the first few months with him in the dance of
opening a new club in the warm ashes of the old, but he was basically
way too commercially oriented for anything but conflict to emerge in the
relationship and he was eventually kind of pushed out of the helicop-
ter.

        in the interregnum between 11 sept 88, the gilman st proj-
ects last show and 4 nov, first show of 924 gilman, there was an intense
buzz of activity.   there was no club & no shows.   until the rent was
paid by the new group (mid october?),   there were no meetings at the
924 space.   lots of the activity involved lou's all important computer (remember this is 88!) . there were meetings at lou's,and at ashkenaz & at picante restaurant on 6th st .   the new crew had to really zero in on the job since there was not the financial backing that
gilman st project had from mrr, and little experience at running shows
since the most experienced workers had left in the mrr group.   the hat
was passed in the new group and enough money was raised/borrowed to cover
the first month's rent and 6 months insurance (by the way lou did not
bankroll the new club--thats an urban legend you can put in the com-
post. he put about the same amount of ¢ that 4 or 5 others put in the
collection pot). a bank account was opened. after it was clear to tim
yo that we really were going to do a club, he promised us the sound system for as long as we needed it (except for the monitors, which belonged
to someone else).   during the period when there was no gilman, (56
days) 12 sept to 3 nov 88, various committees formed and met, in addition to the regular weekly sunday meeting.   my calendar shows 26 meetings.

        it was pretty much all of us stumbling forward together, none of
us having ever done anything like this.   dirk dirksen, who had run the
mabuhay gardens punk club in the late 70s came to a couple of our meetings and was helpful and supportive, as was the sainted david nadel of
ashkenaz.

        i asked around & kalx dj patty sheehan suggested that we get
orlando (special forces) to do security.   he was willing & started,
if i remember correctly, with the first show of the new club 4 nov 88
(isocracy& etc) .   orlando & i both worked most shows for the first
year and burned out around the same time in late 89. Eliot (orlando's
pal) took over as head of security when orlando stopped doing it and
nando came on as paid security during eliot's watch..

        in my very active period i experienced several serious burnouts
and cut back my expectations and commitments in various ways, several
times, but each time, when i'd walked away (in my mind at least) i'd
look back and see the thing still muddling along, still seeming kind
of yes worth a shit, still needing a little of this or that, something or other i could provide without ruining my life... i've always
seen a value here that is pretty unique.. When gilman succeeds it's
because everyone's working without expectation of immediate direct positive strokes; the reward being the continued existence of the place....
this group of kids has always been pretty hard nosed, and stuck to how
you actually make it work, and keep your scene & space in the real
world, as opposed to the fun of being a righteous victim & having someone to blame "for taking away your scene & space". i mean the seduc-
tive blame that cripples progressive forces everywhere; you bask in

your (high) ideals; when these ideals fail you have someone other than
yourself to blame; and ultimately you don't have to DO any work at
all, since nothing actually happens, just the fun you have drama-
tizing your blame of some obvious target.

at gilman you don't get paid and you don't get the credit you
deserve, but you do get the company and (sometimes) recognition of
people you (mostly) respect (the other workers). you also get the fun
of helping to put on what is occasionally a pretty good party; and of
keeping your group's space.... when we're doing it right, we find some
way to make it a homey & comfortable place for the devoted shitworkers, as well as for the (helpless & passive) consumerist audience
that we cheerfully serve.

Proof that Gilman *does* occasionally get cleaned, 1992   photo by Pat W.

gilman is funny like this for me, often, the music is bad (i
mean, sounds bad to me that nite), you go in hating everyone, generally, but you come out feeling... oh well, they're just assholes like
me... -- that's not a bad experience.

i'm never really sure if it's worth a shit. my estimation of
the value of gilman goes thru wild fluctuations, week by week, show by
show. a bottom ring in this universe is when gilman functions as a
shrine of machoism, one of dante's circles of hell, a place replicat-
ed enough already all over human culture. blaag from the dwarves
pronounced gilman a pussy farm; far above these descending circles of
hell is blaag's pussy farm, where the women run everything... & close
to that, at its best, it's the elysian fields, where you meet everyone
you ever knew (& liked) and hang out all nite and talk up a storm and
have a great time... this does happen regularly on an irregular basis
over the months...

however, i also gotta add that in some respects, we have often
been quite ordinary & not above ditching those we feel we no longer have
a need for... or who don't pass somebody's litmus test... instead of

Painting over neighborhood graffiti, 1993   photo by Pat W.

chewing up the passive sheep-like audience that we serve -- (they deserve it , but they don't care enough to notice our disdain...) -- like alot of families, we often have found someone from among our own little group to string up.... occasionally one of those who've given the max or at least a lot...& that ain't good.. the sense of WE that has to come into it is very hard to hold on to .... as abstractly & hostile-ly as people treat each other....

-my summary view of the succession of head coordinators :
- in their own way , each saved the place & re-made the structure-
1. tim yo; the mom-dad. gave birth to the place in hope & pain... & then by the time it became an outta control 14 year old (sept 88), threw it outta the house, (closed the club), out of self preservation.
2. jonathan denlinger; re-started, with few assumptions and a strong sense of the value of the place.. oh, and a new name for the club, after getting the boot from dad...
3. michael d.; an idealist & a hard worker; held the fort at a tough time & tried to make a thousand flowers bloom... michael was a part of the original club in 87 and knew just what it was like to be on the outside..
4. george s.; staked out the wasteland of a floundering scene & held it..... & voila ! the skinheads lost interest ! was it magic? we'll never know...
5. mike stand; when george left there was still a piece of the founda-tion missing-- gilman had never been on a firm foundation financially. mike organized things so that it was possible, & then turned it around financially, from the red to the black (green day helped!!!)
6. branwyn & charles; expanded the core group exponentially
7. charles; empowered a ton o' people to get into the power spots (note: they used to be thought of as shit jobs, before chas) & the younger generation finally decided it could take over & run the place. charles also took alot of abuse from us. sorry charles.
8. chris; the most disinterested & thus possibly most effective; also longest serving, i believe... he truly drew everyone into helping..far more than ever before.
9. jemuel & sammy. they are serving now so i'll say nothing

- checklist for doing gilman anywhere -- could it be done elsewhere? obviously yes, but......this is for another book , or maybe this book will be enough...just remember, without john h. & others interfacing with the neighbors & the community & the police dur-ing the week & without security & the coordinator staying in close & constant contact with each other & the police during shows, it would be just like any other american city, any other american divorce....
also, without tim yo's precinct walking & local political bonafides, & john hart's insistence that we go & talk to the city zon-ing board etc. every time there's a problem.. there are a million ways for anything to fail. its amazing anything succeeds. 924 gilman's very much a created thing, and as such it's fragile & subject to breakage &

in fact must be re-created every week...

Also possibly essential for this gilman... just a couple of older-generation people to help who are: willing to do lots of shit-work; don't expect to be part of the scene, just a part of the community that is holding that scene together; don't be king control freak; don't hate the music.... & other things i'd discuss with you if you were here...

it's not a miracle that gilman exists; it's a tragedy that a gilman doesn't exist in every american city.. it only takes about 2 or 3 percent of a community to give that community a community center, but it doesn't happen on its own, the 2 or 3 percent have to be there, have to work hard at it, have to stay workin' at it..... the people who call it magic or a miracle mostly just don't want to get into the shit-work it takes to make it a go.... what we're doing at our best is mod-eling how not to replicate the american tragedy, by being a communi-ty, instead of being atomized units in front of tv sets.

gilman has worked because there's nothing to get. no money, especially. nothing to get but the fun of putting on a pretty good party ....no fight for somebody's gov't funding, no courting of finan-cial big daddies....no struggle to get funding ....just the relentless struggle to have enough big shows to pay the rent ... no struggle amongst us workers for some paid position.... there aren't any. we went thru that phase & it was a disaster.... we paid charles some-thing like 175$ a month as head coordinator which worked out to about 1.98 an hour. people resented it so much that he eventually refused to take it. there's no rift between the paid staff & unpaid staff because there's no paid staff... that is , except for the security job, and non-show cleanup job, which people don't tend to fight over.... the original mrr club stuck to the no paid security policy to the end. new club felt this was one of the downfalls of the original club, so always paid a volunteer -at least something- to take the responsibili-ty. there is a slight class difference between unpaid volunteers and paid security, but the unpaid volunteers know that paid security & cleanup are still essential-ly volunteers, since only someone who really cared about the club would do these jobs, whether paid or unpaid.

Earthquake retrofit (store), 1995   photo by Pat W.

items to be added: --- john h.'s endless, relentless struggle of paint-ing out graffitti & interact-ing with the neighbors on this & getting their under-standing of the limits we are able to put on this problem by riding herd on the details; keeping them from getting overwhelmed & instead help-ing them see it as a bunch of details that we are going to deal with it ....

....my primary usefulness to gilman over the years has been trash removal. without regular purging, the physical plant packs up steadi-ly with stuff, and people's precious memorabilia, and the useable inte-rior space gets used up by the irrelevant. it's best not to talk about it because it can't be done by committee. no-one is going to tell you

what to throw out. you've got to figure out what's truly irrelevant &
just get rid of it. if you fail , if you piss people off by throwing
out the wrong stuff , the job goes back to the meeting (effectively to
committee) and ultimately won't get done. of course, no-one has ever
said that i could or should do this job in this way. i've just gotten away with it because i mostly haven't pissed people off by throwing out the wrong stuff. occasionally there has to be some serious
arm twisting, when volunteers start squirrelling away personal stuff
at gilman.   this is predictable and will quickly choke out the community in the whole affair, when suddenly it becomes the gilman-stor-
age-lockers-for-the-in-group type thing. you usually can't just throw
this type stuff out. you have to figure out how to get the person
storing stuff irrelevant to gilman to remove the stuff, without a major
crisis, because it's the right thing to do for the club. personal
storage at the expense of the community removes the possibility of using
that space for some membership or community activity (and almost always
represents a fire hazard, as well.) it's an obvious argument anyone can
understand - -if it's hammered on-- and it usually has to be.   Oh, yes
and perks that don't subtract anything from the community's use of the
place are ok w' me... 3 may 03
      i wish i had a close, but i dont. bye pat wright .

        ..oops, one more thing.... can you see the bumpersticker on
my soul ? --it's the 70s bumpersticker - DON'T FOLLOW ME, IM LOST TOO
- have i made it clear? don't stick me in the adult box; I'm just a
lost child that's hung on.   i'll go with the buddha on this -- i dont
know what's going on here, work it out yourself ...   Bye -   pat w.
1 nov 03

What is Consumerism

its when you feel "well what are 'they' doing
to improve this crummy club"
when you know its no-ones club but the communitys;
that its wide open to good energy from anyone in
the community that can add to it.
      This is a community club. You are it -- it is
you. there is no capitalist at the head of it.
there is no Mr. Big at the head of it. Can you
deal with having your own scene with no bad guy
to blame all your problems on? I doubt it.

      Can you resist saying "what are 'they' doing
to improve this club?" ?
its not 'their' club, its yours.   the question
is not what 'they' are doing to make it continue as a
community focus-place, & pay the rent, but what
are you doing to make it something your own place.
   As long as you resist this reality,
you're a consumerist and youd be just as well off
at home in front of a T.V.

Written by Pat W. and posted at the club, 1988

MARSHALL S.

I lived in the area, and I remember walking by the space during the day occasionally and seeing the flyers for shows in the window. Also, I worked at KALX, the UC Berkeley college station, and heard about the shows at Gilman through that. I wasn't into punk that much, but I was curious about the place, and it was close by, so I ended up going to a show there. This was late 1987. Actually, I got there early and one of the regular membership meetings was going on, and I found out you could volunteer there. I had done sound at Berkeley Square before, so I had some experience in that, and Gilman was close to my house, so it was an easy choice to make.

I was there for every show for about a year, until the *Maximum RocknRoll* crew left, mostly setting up the sound equipment on stage and keeping an eye on it while the bands played. Occasionally I got to do sound for an opening band. I liked this whole new, fresh musical experience. I had been to lots of big rock shows and I liked that the bands at Gilman didn't take themselves so seriously. I had never seen anyone from the audience allowed to get up on stage and sing along with the band before, let alone twenty people! I had never seen stagediving before either. There were no dressing rooms or backstage at Gilman—the bands would be walking around in the audience with everyone else; everyone was equal. And the people at Gilman shows seemed much

Where's the stage? 1988   photo by Murray B.

friendlier than what I was used to. It turned me off rock shows completely. I also liked the relative smallness of the shows, and how you could recognize faces in the audience from previous shows, and start to get to know them a little. As it turned out, it seemed like almost all of these folks were in bands themselves. And that got me thinking that maybe I could do this too. I had always wanted to be in a band. I had been in a cover band years ago with my friends, but we never played out anywhere. I was inspired by the fact that even if you weren't very good, you might still get a good reaction from the audience. It all seemed really positive, get up there and have fun. I got a bass, learned how to play, and joined a band. After the MRR crew pulled out, I was part of the group that came in and reopened the place. That was the start of the Alternative Music Foundation, and incorporating and all that. I thought being a corporation, with a president, etc., was very un-Gilman, but I was willing to do whatever it took to reopen the place. I worked there consistently from 1988-1990 (then sporadically from 1990-1993, rarely since). Many of the people involved with that second group were very motivated. I started doing sound more and recording band demos there. It didn't seem the same to me as before, almost like we were the "B" team, and we were just trying to keep it open, knowing it wouldn't be like it was.

Once the band I joined started playing out more and touring, I had to do less at Gilman. Then after that band broke up, I came back to working at Gilman again, and worked occasionally there for another few years. My life certainly changed because of Gilman. Gilman inspired me to join a band, and by touring with them I got to see lots of places and do lots of things I never would have otherwise. When I was in high school in the late '60s, I used to record bands with a portable reel-to-reel tape recorder, and some local band had wanted me to be their roadie on tour. But my dad hated rock 'n' roll, and wouldn't let me go. That was the closest I had gotten until Gilman, many years later. I never thought I was a good enough musician to be in a band until Gilman came along.

The main thing I thought was good about Gilman was that it brought a lot of different people together—it was like the hub of a wheel. People who never would have met each other otherwise were brought together. It had a big impact on a lot of people. One big difference between the first group at Gilman and what went on since, was the belief in the place—and the desire to promote it to others, almost like a religion—that the first group had, getting up on stage and talking about the place during shows, stressing the importance of the meetings, the idea of it being a membership club, etc. That's something that should be reinforced or promoted more now, but maybe people don't believe in it like they used to. Also, I think the bills should be mixed, different types of bands together rather than separated into like genres each night. I hardly go there at all now, partly due to age, partly because I'm not seeing very much that's new there any more, it seems like a loop or something, over and over.

1987   photo by Cammie T.

MIKE K.

One day an old hippie teacher in my school invited a Vietnam vet to come and speak about Reagan's pro-fascist policies in Central America. The dude was fucking intense. After he was done speaking, my friend and I went up to talk with him. Noticing that we were into punk rock by our scruffy and scraggled appearance, he gave us a brochure about a new all ages punk club and community space opening up in Berkeley. He told us that this shit was for real, and that these folks had their stuff together. My friend and I decided to venture out one Saturday night to see a show. We were instantly hooked. I had gone to shows before, but never had felt the open feeling I experienced here. I saw a place built by the kids with their own blood and sweat, not the money-motivated greed of some fuck rock promoter.

The place blew my mind. My understanding for the potential of punk rock was expanded instantly. Beyond the loud music and crazy haircuts, I was suddenly able to see a new way of life, something I could live too. I had always subscribed to the radical politics fused deep into much of the music that I listened to, but somehow these politics, although crucial to giving me direction and purpose, always seemed disconnected from my actions. They lacked the connection that would give them "meaning," relevance in my day-to-day experience. Somewhere between the distanced slogans and abstract calls to arms, we had discovered through Gilman a way to give our politics some application in our actual lives. It opened up all kinds of possibilities. We had discovered punk's prime directive of DIY (do-it-yourself), to make all the talk real in the here and now, and, equally as important, to have fun doing it. The whole space stood as a "threat by example."

We returned to school on Monday quite changed. My friend Dan just looked at me and said, "Fuck this place, it can never be the same again." We hated our school, and now after being opened to new possibilities, it just seemed totally absurd. Our blind hatred for the place began to transform from an inarticulate reluctance to participate into a coherent and focused understanding of why we had to burn this fucking place to the ground, destroying everything that it stood for. This new revelation gave us the courage to believe that we might be able to make our most naive, unrealistic, and romantic ideals a reality. It would just take hard work. Gilman became our source of real education. We had never seen anything actually built by kids before. The punks there were different than the psycho macho fuckers that just wanted to beat the shit out of people. Punks that were so against the system, yet the only people they ever seemed to beat up were other punks. I'm sure a lot of these guys have gone on to be cops. These Gilman kids, though, were nerds—true, unabashed nerds. The place put me at ease. It was 1987 and I started going to shows more regularly. I learned that this punk was more participatory than the more accessible "consumer punk" I was weaned on. Eventually, I started volunteering—coordinating and stage managing shows from 1988 to 1991.

In thinking back about how the club changed the trajectory of my life, the one thing that comes to mind is my perception of history and how and who it is created by. I used to be resolved to the fact that history was a larger-than-life process. In fact, it was so much larger than life that my life and the lives of those around me had no possible way of impacting the larger course of events. I felt like a fucking microscopic bacterium drifting aimlessly. Before Gilman, my friends and I did not have much hope that we could seriously redirect the course of our lives, let alone larger events. There was a disconnection between the everyday reality we labored through and the mythical arena in which real change, real politics, and real life took place.

Again, my early exposure to punk music inevitably affirmed this perception. Whether it was Joe Strummer or Jello Biafra kicking down knowledge to the kids, the voices screaming through my torn up three-inch stereo speakers, although empowering, were still distant and other-worldly. There was something about the inherent makeup of the Gilman scene that was different. It was here that the kids in the audience were also the kids making the music and starting to put out records and zines. I think this is something that we take for granted now, almost to the extent to where it is shifting back to a hierarchy or isolation of different roles. As the nineties come to a close, punk has been so absorbed and incorporated into the popular culture that it's hard to find any sense of militancy and urgency left. Hip movie-stars and millionaires now sport punky hair and tattooed attitudes in the pages of *People* magazine. It's even gotten to the point where it's old hat to see punk friends popping up in the pages of these same magazines. Advertisers succeeded in cementing the identity of "Gen X" into the self-perception of young people. Cashing in on the old skepticism and disenfranchisement that punk had helped long ago to embed deep in the hearts of the youth. Now this same disillusionment is almost casually calculated and manipulated by capitalism to sell new, useless things to a new generation of up-and-coming big spenders. Things have changed quite a bit, and sadly the direct connect between band and audience seems, more often than not, to be missing. There used to be so much more power when the bands and the audiences were from the same scene, sharing community in addition to music. But the stages have since grown taller, and today the relationship between band and audience seems more one of product and consumption.

In thinking back about what to write about Gilman, I find myself having a difficult time trying to think of stories or defining moments that encapsulated the history of the club. When I think back, I am inundated with a spaghetti of tangled-up memories. It is difficult not to look back and pick out the obvious ones, the OP IVs, Green Days, MRRs, and Lookout Records as being somehow the definitive ones. When I really think back, I am struck by the multitude of experiences happening simultaneously that shaped that place. There are countless long-forgotten people that few remember, let alone know where they are now. All that is left is the reverberating echoes of memories and intangible contributions they left on the place. There was a stark contrast in being at Gilman Street when it was empty and being there during a crowded show. It was the freaks that gave Gilman its character and heart, a twisted-up mix of obnoxious crazies and hard-working quiet kids that pumped life into an otherwise cold and dirty cement warehouse. This eclectic bunch of people, that I might have only known by face or first name, were not the movie-star personalities or photogenic moments that will most likely be what gets documented, as Gilman fades from the memories of those who were actually there and is ultimately cemented into some iconic musical history by the army of hack rock-critic eulogizers that were off in college listening to Pet Shop Boys records while the youth were tearing shit up.

For me, the culmination of geek-freak pride was an Isocracy show. The anticipation would build prior to the show as Al Sobrante pulled his VW bus to the side door and started unloading bags upon bags of junk and eccentric trash. Their shows were a call to arms for all the nerd punks and freak outcasts that would gather to not only dance like crazy, but to shake, scream, lurch, and act like animals or airplanes, human ferris wheels or giant robot rats. These were the real kids having their say with a silly grin to back up their clenched fists. Whether it was Jason, the singer, calling out a bunch of scary asshole skins by dedicating the song "Rodeo" to those nazi shitheads, or the relevance of fending off the drunk, "fuck shit up" "Screamer punks" by putting Gilman's no-alcohol policy to music with the asskicking cut-to-the-chase of "Two Blocks Away"—"Get a brain, this ain't a pub, you jerks who drink to close our club." Their shows were a chaotic mess of goofy attitude, serious yet intelligent, caustic humor, and out-of-tune yet anthemic guitars and fucked-up costumes. They played while the youth danced the night away through four foot piles of plastic wrap, stuffed animals, and old shoes that engulfed the whole room. The kids of Gilman could bust out some bad-ass dance moves. They were often synchronized without any premeditation. It was the audience, not the bands, who most often improvised their reaction to the music with spontaneity that defied boring rituals.

My friends and I had what we called the CG (cool guy) mosh crew. It was meant as a partial parody of the tough guy straight edge crews that would turn up the macho "mosh-o-meter," clearing the floor of anyone who "couldn't take the pit." We were a less intense incarnation of the "Mindfuck Committee," who took it as their task to challenge the whole nature of show spaces, or as they saw it, "the paradigm of punk show reality." The CG mosh crew took it as our job to de-escalate tense and violent moments with utterly stupid and out-of-place dancing. Whether it was dog-piling, leap-frogging, or the super-sloth-powered Lurch, the tough guys were usually left standing there totally deflated and confused. The dance floor was filled with weirdos, rendering the idea of a slam pit meaningless. The outside world of macho punk posturing was somewhere between mortified and extremely confused by what those strange kids in Berkeley were up to. One East Coast HC band's singer even went so far as to call Gilman the "Romper Room" of punk rock. He meant it more as an insult, but we freaks wore it like a badge of honor.

Twelve years have passed and I still go to shows at Gilman. I still feel it has relevance and serves an important role in providing access and giving a space to young people to get involved with the DIY punk scene. There always seems to be new young people volunteering with the few old faces that persist. It is easy to forget that at different points the club was in really serious jeopardy of closing down permanently. I remember a time after the club reopened when there would be ten people and no volunteers at a show, and a crew of nazis would show up looking to fuck shit up. I remember an all-day fest of bands no one had heard of or wanted to see. Because no one was there to work, I had to run between coordinating, stage managing, doing sound, and both front and side doors. While I was away from the sound board, one of the lamer bands decided to do sound for themselves, turning the board up as loud as it could go, almost blasting out the sound system. The club was in some serious debt then and fortunately things are quite different now. Because Gilman has been around for so long, it has seen many generations come and go. At its best, I think it truly provided a springboard to other alternative political and lifestyle directions for many of these people. Without a space like Gilman, access would be left to cliques of insiders who happen to catch wind of exclusive word-of-mouth shows. Even though I can still appreciate what Gilman represents, it is still really hard to think back and remember the place. Things have changed so much for Gilman. Like a thousand scattered pieces, those who have left their imprint on the place have splintered in so many different directions. And though I think this is good, it sometimes makes me sad that the continuity and intimacy of the community is long gone for me and my peers. Even with the constant flood of new kids making that space theirs, the club is ultimately a very different place. I still consider myself a punk at age 30, but being a punk means something quite different in 1999 than it did in 1988 (I'm sure it meant something different in 1978 as well). Reminiscing about the "good old days" often makes me a bit depressed. It's like trying to remember details about an old friend long disappeared and forgotten. In its time and place, Gilman gave a buch of freaks and weirdos the ability to feel real with one another. Like some secret sect of an occult society, it provided the language for us to understand that being different and cast out from mainstream culture did not mean we had to feel marginalized and disempowered. We could create our own ideal world in the present.

For Gilman Street, as with punk rock, its larger role has changed. In the late '90s freakiness is a much safer thing. Gilman does not serve as quite the outpost it once did for the disenfranchised. This is not to say the kids who are doing stuff now are somehow fake. But just as I may have been seen as having it easier than the punks of 1977, the roles of punk rock have shifted. For freak culture has been stolen from the real freaks, regurgitated and retransmitted through the filters of mass media culture and consumer capitalism. How ironic is it that Green Day songs are played at high school proms? Investment bankers and hipster CEOs now speak the language once only known to us. Those of us that wanted to spread the punk message to the larger world got their wish, and now we're left dazed, wondering what the fuck happened. The real weirdos have had to hunker down, throwing their anchors deep and waiting for the storm of appropriation to pass. Even though the role of Gilman has changed, we can still take solace in knowing that we helped build something real, a space that, with the blood of new kids, still struggles to situate itself in resistance to the fucked up flow of things.

When I go to shows now, I sometimes drift off from the band, looking at and studying the walls. I think about all the graffiti piled on top of itself. The painted slo-

1998   photo by Pat W.

gans, band names, and sometimes unintelligible ramblings that were left there to mark the moment. I remember in 1988 when Ignition played one of the last shows, if not the last show, at the old club. They screenprinted a large Ignition logo just to the right of the stage. The show itself kind of sucked, but the band kicked ass, and I remember them today as being one of the best bands I've ever seen. For years that print managed to stay visible on that wall, and every time I'd see it, I'd instantly recall a flood of faces and old friends from that time that I had forgotten about. Even after most of it was covered by new generations of spraypaint, the "TION" part of it managed to stay visible for years. Like old graffiti left on the walls, sometimes obscuring what had come before, the memories of the countless people that made Gilman what it was, and what it is, persist.

I realize more and more that when you do stuff with integrity, when you do stuff because you believe in it, when you do stuff because you have to, you can't expect to be recognized, remembered, or thanked by the history books. For me, I have to trust that my actions have meaning, not by how many people end up knowing the specific stories and quaint amusing characters, but by the residual effects of action. That the work years ago, of a bunch of 17-year-old freaks, had impact. Whether it was making millionaires and rock stars out of our peers, or providing a safe space for future freaks to realize their own power, we created a momentum that carried through the years. There was no way for us to possibly conceive of the impact of the place back then, just how far this shit could eventually go. And the lesson I have taken is to continue pushing forward with no way of knowing where we might take this in another ten years.

GILMAN STREET CLOSES; CAN IT RISE AGAIN?

The Gilman Street Project, the greatest place in the history of rock and roll, closed its doors on September 11. The club was the victim of several factors, among them the high cost of rent and insurance, the growing difficulty of attracting enough volunteer labor to run the place, and the continual harassment of a couple gangs who felt affronted by the club's policies against violence, racism, vandalism, and on-premises consumption of alcohol or drugs.

The situation was further complicated when *Maximum Rocknroll*'s Tim Yohannan, who had put up the original $40,000 investment to get the club started (*Maximum Rocknroll*, a monthly magazine with a circulation of about 13,000, is produced by a staff of unpaid volunteers, and it has a long-standing policy of putting any profits back into similar community-oriented efforts) felt that he no longer wanted to be financially and legally responsible for Gilman Street.

Several other people stepped forward and agreed to put their names on the lease, but before the transfer of responsibility came about, members decided at the September 11 meeting that they weren't confident of enough support from the volunteer workers necessary to run the place, and that they feared Gilman was evolving into "just another rock club." They voted to close after that evening's show.

The loss of Gilman, while not entirely unexpected to those involved in its day-to-day operation, came as a shock and disappointment to many who might have only attended an occasional show there, and others in far off places who had never even seen the place, but saw it as a sort of punk rock mecca that perhaps they would some day be fortunate enough to visit. I myself have gotten questions or comments about its passing from correspondents in at least half a dozen other countries.

Ironically, only weeks before it closed, Gilman received official recognition of its being on the cutting edge of the new underground when no less an establishment organ than the *Wall Street Journal* did a substantial and relatively accurate feature on it (its main deviation from reality was characterizing the place as the headquarters of straight edge punk, a misrepresentation that a few days later got a lot of laughs at a beer party heavily peopled by Gilmoids).

In its year and a half existence, Gilman spawned at least a dozen bands, some of which are on their way to being very successful, and gave a reliable and well-paying venue to hundreds of other bands that otherwise might not have had one. It also had a big part in the birth of Lookout Records; oh well, let's admit it: Lookout Records would probably not exist if it weren't for Gilman. Most important, from a purely personal point of view, it gave yours truly some of the most fun times of my life, and gave me the opportunity to meet some of the coolest people on this planet (no, I'm not sure they were all natives). The void its demise has left in my social life is roughly akin to the void it's left in the world of northern California underground music.

Fortunately there is still some hope that a resurrected form of Gilman, probably under a different name, will emerge out of the ashes. A group of people, most of whom were Gilman regulars, is trying to establish a nonprofit foundation to run the place. Apparently they've been having regular meetings and things look at least possible. I'm sorry to say I haven't been able to be a part of it so far because I've been holed up in front of a computer in the Mendocino backwoods for about a month or more now trying to get this issue to you. Now that it's finally on the streets (or in them, as the case may be), I'll be able to spend more time in the Bay Area seeing what's what. But if you're not already part of it yourself, you'll have to wait till next issue to find out. You should know from experience how long that can be. So if you want Gilman or something like it to happen, you know what to do. Don't you?

Article written by Larry L., taken from *Lookout* zine, fall 1988

EGGPLANT (ROBERT B.)

I am not good at remembering everything, especially
things like dates. I do remember though that it was a
sunday and that it was a depressing and small show.
Atomic Gods from Las Vegas was playing and i never ①
heard them but saw an ad in Mr-r. I had school the
next day(9th grade) and under normal circumstances
i would go back to Pinole to my mom and my stepdad.
At around six thirty i went into the Gilman store,for
at that time the pay phone was there. Infact.The week
before b 4 was my dream weekend.Each night the bands
who were starting to affect the blood circulating in
me were playing.Friday was going to be the first gilman
benefit with op ivy and crimpshrine. Saturdays show was
corrupted morals and nerurosis. And sunday i could easily
watch every band,full attention.surrogate brains
isocracy christ on parade the beat nigs. As you can
see i was startin to spend more time at gilman,yet
weekends i offically was to spend with my dad. He was
way cool, and so i spent my new teenage moments at the
club. As my dream w eekend approached my mom and her
2nd husband insist i go camping with them and their
friends. I butted heads with them to keep my weekend.
I knew their trips and it wasn't new, Rock and Roll
on the way up, break out the dirt bikes,the food,the
pot and budweiser, the guns. They agreed to give me
the show on sunday. So iwaited the whole weekend eager
to get to gilman. Late on sunday afternoon they
decided to go jet skiing for the first time.I was so
angry of being lied to and cheated of a whole weekend i refused to ride it. And I2 years later when we
put on a week long Geekfest on a lake i refused to
even touch the things. So somewhere on the way back
from camping on The Property i decided to take up
the offer/threat that always grew and loomed above:
THATS THE WAY IT IS AND IF DONT LIKE IT YOU CAN MOVE
OUT. GO STAY WITH YOUR DAD. When i told her i had to
hang up the phone for i just heard my mom start to
cry. Stepping out of the phone booth i felt the groun
d move, the walls around me started to blurr. This
wasn't my first show but its when my week days and
weekends start to lose distinction. It was when i
learn to develop my love for pre dawn hours.When i
learn to stop showering.To stop eating meat. I cut
out more time watching tv. And i spent an enormous
amount of my childhood acquainted with television.My parents
grew pot and Party'd and were typical.I had to
stay home alot and couldnt bring friends over. But
i was fos tering a preface to spending time alone
and could spend

                all day in my room.

I often wondered about the outside world. The things
that happen at night,where people gather, while i sat
over the heat vent with a blanket.Years later at Gilm
when things got slow i would wonder what people did at
other places.I would think about being home on a frida
night. And there were times i dropped it all and danced
UUUUUUUUUUUUUUUU

Unfortunately as i became more engulfed into gilman st. and the many facets of punk, my dad went into
despairity. Into speed and instability.Into blind rage and death. So naturally i started to feel that my
involement with the scene was a parallel. Strange that
by moving in with my dad a nd relishing in the free-
doom of a cool parent then did i los e the good thing
good things i had when i only saw him on
weekends. I was glad to make this choice at first &
only w hen the gears were in motion,and everything
was moving forward did doubt start to set in. All of
a sudden its 1993.im out of high school,all my favorite people a re gone,or broken up,and my fa vorite
bands ,and no one knowss but wee are at war with Iraq,
And whatt people know is that they w ant to forget a-
bout Iraq and Armagedon,and forget Rodney King and
police not prosecuted for openly beating him.

I went to the blub becaus e i still dreamed of
playing there. And i valued observing the different
showss.I liked that people knew my face,but diddnt
know who i w as.The Bla tz 7" was out there and
people could use Robert Eggplant's name to sneak into showss.Dont stop writing always forward.And the
next two years i felt like i lived in a desert.

It was in the gilman store one non show nite
did i once engage in oral sex.Some friends were g-
athered watching City of The Los t Children.I was
cuddling with my partner.That lead into foddling then
masturbating,then sneaking off into the store.I think
the club brings out quite alot of attractive people.
Rarely did i get full blown s leazy with people i
diddn't know.A mixture of not w anting to contribute
to the myth of pushy man,along with the right amount
of confidence a t the right time. But i did lose my
virginity from someone i knew casually after a show.
I spent years horney, and longing to be in love,pro-
grammed into me from pop music/culture untill theo
growing pressure helped my choose. She called her mo
m afterwaards who insisted her return and thus my
first nite...alone.
                painting of man

painting gilman

One of thebiggest relifs over the past few years was
taking a day to paint the walls.I had been to several non show get togethers to clean up. Sweeping,
 mopping the floors,peeling gum.But putting stuff up
and making a messss is the buisnesss done in the play
room.And Gilman was often put down as being nursery.
little kids. So Lorrin and Stephanne whh always worked the store decided to paint it completely ora nge.
Even the microwave.It was smooth for a couple days,th-
en a few months la ter a new coat of tags came up.
The orange remain impressionable.I woke one day on the
 couch to Chriss Sparks with spray paint fumes in the
 air.When he was done and i drank some of the clubs
 fucked up w ater was there a prima tive skeleton.It
 was aweeome. In the Georgee and Nondo time the club
 gradully wass persuaded into hosting raves. NonALcoh
lic mind you.Once Nondo painted the walls black,every
wall in reaching distance.BREAk out the neon lites,the
dj and surround sound, and the non punk crowdd.I would
have to look outside myseaf on those weekends nites w/
nothing planned and no show. And I find gilman a good
habit for if i choosee to i could go with no money,i
 could still be there.
     I think graffitti as a good analgy.with the peopl
i diddnt fell at home with. You would feel kinda dumb
protesting aanew arrival, but w ith time it getss
covered up. There were delega tes from the Real World
thaat kept me on my toes and working compromisee.Worki
n a dissh was hing job,paying rent-barely,roaming jr.
 colleg es,going to martial arts class 2-4 times a wee
..And id go to the club to thrive only to be inunudated
with the samm thing...AFI,Lookout,obhc,gangs from down
south,persona l type fanzines,skinheads,Nation of
ulyes ss,Swwing Utters,Screw 32,black fork,charless,
mike staand,sita,zara dull dull unfriendly. A security
staff impatient and out numbered. A going thru the
motions.A tiny rock concert. Sla yer pits.Grimple Sp-
itboy.Suddenly the scene in responsse to greenday,
rancid,and offspring made everyone into assholes-me.
Asshole me.So like everyone elsse i take time to look
 for any w all s pace to write my name.
     I spent a couple yearss from 9I to 95 sober.Of
course mostthedrug i ever took or sold was there for
me the previous yea rs.But gra dua lly i'd be at a
punk hous e wwatching a band and drank water whhle a
full keg wwaaited.There were times i felt disdain top
wards my friends stories of seeking adventure with
huffing,pills ,and crack.

even though they were the ssubject matter of some
eally great songs.Amphetamine was a sure snub for me.
ronic since the East Bay and especial] segements of
.ts punk had a saturation of spped. Like as if our
overnment wass intent to make sure the war on drug s
which is a war on people,poor people, would specificly
claas h with the previous counter culture of berkeley
and its mellowwout open mind drugs.Pot.Acid.Drum circles..Punks now meant living in Oakland and dressi
ng in black,acting uptight & too cool, and playing
usic that is essentially heavy metal.Black Sabbath.
think the common punk rocker and i started on div-
ergent paths. One example of this was knowing more &
more people who would only come out to watch the headlining ba nd, i would sooner delight in the open-
ng,out of town, unknown acts. I think people forg et
they haven't seen it all.

One of the best things i felt gilma n hass tooff
er is that every weekend, every show ,would consist
of a different mix of people than previous showws.
It made doing a fanzinea great reward. Our words &
a rt would go all over the place. Every weekend the
ow er wouldd surge and folks would come out to un-
load. Oddly enough people from oakland,s.f.,or even
berkeley wouldn't be there every weekend. More often
only going to their friends bands or the cool ones.
Nevermind that the reason people don't like theclub
was tha t the people running the show we are so uptight,and they're that way because they are the only
onessrunning the shhw week after week. When i first
ent to the club late winter of '87 i believed the
propag anda its inha bitants created. There was was
little illusion stopping me from getting clos e to
he stage,I guess on the s urface Gilma n's sens e
of fun a nd pla y is intimidating. You gotta buy the
ard and try not to sneak beer inside. The whhle air
f goodwill and what not could feel forced. Though
hru time the atmosphere the club created would bec-
me a primary foundation i learn to start on. To kin-
der a certain happiness between huma ns with a str-
ng cornerstone of a room one could feel safe. Where
elsee whuld one feel oka y to patticipate in a dog
pile.

My dad never really went to the shows,even the
nes where bands would pla y our backya rd.I did ssm-
ke p ot with him and listen too cheaper than the beer
nd he diddnt say we sucked. After my mom went thru
er 2nd divorce she searched around to connect. For

(4)

awhile she became the wild child of the family.She
wwassborn in Germany then moved to berkely in the
50's. She spent her childhood looking over the you
nger children from her mother's 2nd marriage. By t
by the time she turned i8 s he married my dad,gave
birth to my s ister and justt to eventually piss me
off,moved to pinole. In her late 40's free of B.S.
she started to makk carefree decisions. Including
starting to get involved with Randy Savagg. Not only
was he younger thann she, he was a year behind me
back in highh school. And when i still lived wi th h
her baack in Jr high,his brother Kevin Savage and s
ssum other bigger kids fro m the High sschool got
me to let them in house and wee stole some pot. So
she was doing whatever the hell sshe w anted for a
change. And she came into a show. It was a small
Citizen Fish gig on a sunday afternoon. What people were there stood around stiff and uncomfortable
but s aafe. It was on mothers day and i snnck her
in. She was right up front dancing and she kept
telling the s inger to dedicate a song for the wol-
ves.(thatt w as a current fetish of hers for they
are ann endangered speices) And w hen he did as she
asked she sstarted to howl. I mys elf felt sulf con-
sciouss.

Written by Robert B., taken from the *Absolutely Zippo* anthology book.

ORLANDO X.

A friend and I went to some of the early meetings before Gilman opened. We went door to door in the neighborhood and talked to people about the club and what would be happening there, and also collected signatures on a petition in support of our opening the club in their area. We covered about a four to five block radius, business and residential. People would invite us in and ask us questions about the place—they seemed interested. Other than that, I didn't get very involved with the club during the first two years.

Gilman was never really accepted by the "established" Oakland/Berkeley punk scene, mainly because you couldn't drink there, and that whole scene was a big drinking/drug-taking scene. It wasn't that most of them had anything against Gilman—Gilman was putting on great shows, it's just that they wanted to drink. There were a few, though, that hated Gilman, and wanted to hassle the place every chance they could, simply because they couldn't get their way, and they weren't able to do whatever they wanted there. If you have valid, logical reasons, fine, but they didn't.

After the second group took over Gilman in late '88, Pat W. asked me to do security there. I was doing paid security jobs at bigger venues at the time and didn't want to work at Gilman for free, so they offered me a minimal amount, about twenty dollars a show. I believe I was the first paid security there. I only worked there about a year. I remember the show where I quit. My girlfriend at the time was up front and heckling the band on stage. One of the band members then kicked her in the face. I got up on stage and grabbed the guy, with people separating us before we fought. I then went to the show coordinators for the night and told them I didn't think the band should be allowed to continue. The band, the coordinators, and I all argued for about twenty minutes, with the end result being that the band was allowed to keep playing. I walked out and haven't worked there since. I've continued to go to shows there occasionally, the bands I've been in have played there, and I've helped break up fights if they occur, but I felt that since they didn't support me, I wasn't going to keep working there.

There's a lot of work involved in doing security properly—you not only have to keep an eye on everyone, but be able to spot things developing before they break out, keep in contact with those you're working with and let them know what's going on, and keep the show running smoothly.

I still feel a certain kinship towards the place, and I'm glad kids still have a place to go that's relatively safe. I'm a lot older than most everyone there now, and I like to drink, so I don't go there very much anymore. It has crossed my mind a few times, when I've heard that the current head coordinator was leaving, to maybe try my hand at running the place, but I don't know if I would have the time though, realistically. If I was running it, I'd get a better stage, more furniture, and a place for bands to store their equipment during the show. I'd try to get more bands shows there—I think it could be done. The booking policies there now seem really elitist. Some bands can get shows there very easily, play all the time, other bands send demo after demo, make call after call, and rarely get to play there at all. There's a lot of favoritism. I'd stock the snack bar better, clean the men's bathroom. I'd have more non-music events, films, readings, things like that—more Sunday events.

Gilman's a really important part of the community. If it got shut down, that would be it for the East Bay. There was Burnt Ramen, but that's gone now.

One thing that really sticks with me, and means a lot to me, is the people that have come up to me over the years and thanked me for helping them out with a bad situation there, a fight, injury, etc. That feels really good. Another time, my leather jacket got stolen there, and Gilman bought me another one. That was really cool. One of the funniest things I remember, was one night when my band, Special Forces, was playing there, and four or five people from the audience lifted me off the stage while we were playing, carried me into the women's bathroom, put me into one of the stalls, and wouldn't let me out.

ALTERNATE MUSIC SOCIETY BULLETIN

INSIDE:
Membership Meeting Announcement
Our Purpose / Three Key Areas
Stolen Cartoons / Calendar
ELVIS LIVES! Sid, too!
Committees / More All Ages shows
newnotgilmandamnitthing / Classifieds
mailing address page exclusive

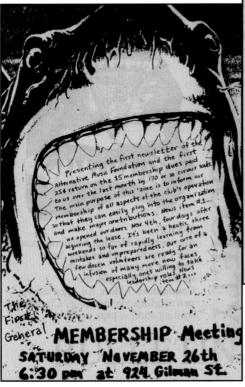

Presenting the first newsletter of the Alternative Music Foundation and the first 25¢ return on the $5 membership dues paid to us over the last month by 170 or so curious souls. The main purpose of this 'zine is to inform our membership of all aspects of the club's operation so that they can easily plug into the organization and make major contributions. News item #1... we opened our doors Nov. 4th, four days after acquiring the lease. It's been a hectic three weekends so far of rapidly learning from mistakes and unpreparedness. Our core of a few dozen volunteers are ready for an infusion of many more new faces, especially ones willing to take leadership roles. News item #2...

The First General MEMBERSHIP Meeting SATURDAY NOVEMBER 26th 6:30 pm at 924 Gilman St.

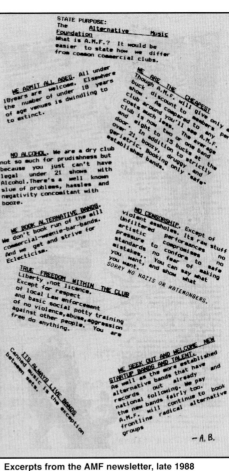

STATE PURPOSE:
The Alternative Music Foundation. What is A.M.F.? It would be easier to state how we differ from common commercial clubs.

WE ADMIT ALL AGES. All under 18 years are welcome. Elsewhere the number of under 18 years of age venues is dwindling to extinct.

NO ALCOHOL. We are a dry club not so much for prudishness but because you just can't have legal under 21 shows with Alcohol. There's a well known slue of problems, hassles and negativity concomitant with booze.

WE BOOK ALTERNATIVE BANDS. We don't book run of the mill commercial-weenie-bar-bands. And we get and strive for Eclecticism.

TRUE FREEDOM WITHIN THE CLUB. Liberty, not licence. Except for respect of local law enforcement and basic social potty training of no violence, abuse, aggression against other people. You are free do anything.

WE ARE THE CHEAPEST Though A.M.F. will give only a buck discount to members, show, As compared to any club around you'll see A.M.F. costs much less. The average club is now two or one band door. In addition to strictly over 21, boozy, druggy and geriatric, Booking only safe, established bands.

NO CENSORSHIP. Except of violent assholes. Its raw stuff Unfiltered artistic performances pressure to compromise standards to conform no mistakes, no fear of safe you want. You can say what you want, and show what SORRY NO NAZIS OR HATEMONGERS.

WE SEEK OUT AND WELCOME NEW STARTUP BANDS AND TALENT. As well as the more established alternative bands that have records out already national following. We pay the new bands fairly too. A.M.F. will continue to book frontline radical alternative groups

Canned music is the exception between sets. LIVE ALWAYS LIVE BANDS.

— A. B.

Excerpts from the AMF newsletter, late 1988

The ALTERNATE MUSIC FOUNDATION has assumed the stewardship of Once beleagured 924 Gilman street. Once known as the Maximimum Rock and Roll's 'Gilman Street Project.' This facility was well prepared and established as a regular billing for Alternative music. It is inherited complete with all necessary licences a stage, control loft, bathrooms, adequate floor space, and a corps of experienced volunteers. To lose it would be an unprecedented waste. It cannot easily be replaced.

SECURITY

Presently we are recruiting a pool of intelligent in-house security who are being paid for their profesional service. So far we are happy to introduce Orlando (of Special Forces) and Tom & Mark who happen to be licensed for such work.

We are also still experimenting with uniformed outside security as well as making contact with the Berkeley police to inform them all about our operation.

The door entrance has been modified (construction thanks to George G. and Malcolm C.) for easier policing by door security and better sidewalk illumination is in store.

MONEY

The A.M.F. has opened the doors on a shoestring budget with various outstanding debts and loans that will need attention soon as well as the $2,200 monthly rent for the warehouse.

For income, our first month of shows are benefits for the startup of the club agreed to by all the bands playing. In december paid shows for bands will begin.

To relieve the pressure on our booking committee to schedule very strong shows every weekend, we are actively looking for subtenants to make use of the warehouse space through the week.

If you know a potential subtenant wishing to use our place who is reasonably quiet. Like a dance class, arts/crafts teaching, telemarketing, or any non capital equipment heavy business, leave a message with the answering machine at (408) 741-5056.

Additionaly adds will be run in several papers, realestate news letters and flyers.

- A.B.

THERE ARE THREE KEY AREAS which shall determine if this club lasts more than one month.....

SECURITY, MONEY, PARTICIPATION
(the areas are interdependent)

If Security is lax on crowd control, our patrons and volunteers will not feel safe, will not return and we will no be able to pay bill or keep hold of volunteers.

If Money is short and we cannot make rent, we won't be able to afford proper security.

If Participation is low there is not a strong enough reason to try to keep such a large (300 person capacity) club.

PARTICIPATION

As of early November over 175 people had become Foundation members. It would insure survival unquestionably if we had 175 intelligent self directed volunteers at every show in the next month. If these people brought along just one paying geust besides themselves. The club will stay open.. This is obvious and its simple "Be there!"..be there..and bring your self motivation, bring your awareness, your desire to have a good time. Your can do attitude. Your money too.

If something needs doing, especially in regards to security do it. Don't even wait for some old veteran volunteer to tell you. Vertical command structure is why the world is fucked up. If you like your club just come here in person and give it life. You are the blood and bones of the club. Without you nothing's doing. So become your own magnate on the cutting edge of art. Its just a matter of being there so the good can happen with you.......

The next month is make or break. There will be strong bands that will provide enough cash to keep the place solvent. Otherwise we pack it up in December.

Another excerpt from the AMF newsletter, late 1988

DAVE EC

I found out about Gilman in early 1987, when I was 15, from a high school radio station in El Cerrito where I grew up. The DJ was the singer of a local band that played at Gilman a lot, and he was talking about this "new punk rock club." So I went to the club to check it out and I was pretty blown away, five bands for $5. I had been to a few shows at other places before, and it blew me away that there was no "backstage" at Gilman, the band members were out front hanging out with everyone. I remember shopping carts, Big Wheels, and people playing basketball. I remember the store in the club was giving away demo tapes that had been sent to *Maximum RocknRoll* for review (I still have some of those tapes).

I had heard that you could volunteer there, and right after that first show I wanted to volunteer there. It took me a couple of months to actually do it, but I asked about it that first night. I was really shy and didn't want to screw anything up. I found myself going to Gilman every weekend, almost every show. So, one night I just went in and went for it. I had some friends who were volunteering too, and they encouraged me. Originally I had just wanted to get into the shows for free, and feel like I was a part of something cool. But I soon fell in love with the place, and felt like I was doing something a lot better than school. In late 1987/early 1988, I dropped out of school and became a full-time "Gilman guy." I really wasn't that big of a part of the club though, until it closed down the first time, and the *Maximum RocknRoll* group left.

I was part of the group that re-opened the club, and my involvement increased from there, with the new opportunities that were arising. I wanted to do whatever I could to help, because I felt that I had lost my hangout. It didn't matter that I was only 17, I knew I could help in some way. I was really upset when it closed down. I was getting so much from that place, learning a lot, making friends of all different types, beliefs, and ages, friends that I never thought I'd have, and I had joined a band. It was a whole different world for me from my fairly sheltered upbringing. I had a sense of desperation in wanting to keep the place going, and I got over my shyness real quick. I was pretty much ready to do anything but run the club myself. I'd flyer for shows, book bands, work the store, learn sound, do construction, whatever it took. There was a small handful of other people who felt that way: Jonathan, Pat, Marshall, Eggplant, some others probably that I don't remember. When it re-opened, I was the "store guy," being responsible for the buying for, and general operation of, the store.

We tried to keep the same atmosphere as the original Gilman, and many things were the same, but Tim Yohannan wasn't involved, so it was going to be different in that sense. A lot of the original "cast of characters" didn't come back to help, and when they did come to a show, they'd say that the place had changed. That pissed me off, because I took that in a negative way, and I didn't think it was really that much different.

I started helping out with booking bands to play at the club, I thought that would be the coolest job to have, and gradually moved into doing that more and more. I'd be down at the club three or four times a week to work. There didn't seem to be a shortage of people to work at shows—there seemed to be a shortage of people to really run the place. I worked there until 1993 and didn't leave on good terms. I didn't leave because I got burned out, I left because I felt like I got burned.

I had been booking there for about four years, with a haphazard group of people helping out during that time. I had a dispute with the one other steady book-er, which I tried to resolve at a membership meeting. We had been butting heads because he was into a different genre than I was, a lot harder stuff. What I liked about Gilman the most, and something that I was trying to preserve, was the rela-tively different types of stuff offered there. When I first went there, I had very little knowledge of punk rock, and no political views whatsoever. Gilman gave me a lot of education. I sat through a lot of stuff that I didn't like, and sat through a lot of stuff that I was surprised that I really liked. I took a lot of literature home from the bene-fit shows and learned a lot from those. I was trying to keep a variety there. We were a club for the "underground," and there's more to the "underground" than punk rock. I never thought of Gilman as being "just" a punk rock club. I didn't want it to be just that, I wanted it to be a lot more than that. Towards the end of my time there, it seemed like I was one of the few people there supporting "off the wall" shows and taking chances on things. I remember one person coming up to me after a benefit show I put together there for Big Mountain, and saying to me, "This was a show that really should have been at Ashkenaz (nearby multi-ethnic musical/cultural center)."

The problems started off with him joking about some of the bands I had been booking as too "poppy" or whatever. Then it went to him crossing out or eras-ing bands on the booking board, or changing their name to something derogatory, or writing "emo" next to them, generally giving me a hard time about it. It got to the point where demos or information/messages from bands that were being sent to the club were being hidden or thrown away if he didn't like the bands. I got confirmation from other people that he was doing that. At the meeting, I flat-out asked him if he was doing that, and he said he was, admitting it in front of everyone. So to me, the choice was obvious, he shouldn't be allowed to book there anymore. Instead of making a decision, Gilman offered to bring in a mediator from the City. I said that if we couldn't take care of our own problems, this club is dust, and I walked out. I loved the place but thought it sometimes lacked a spine. I thought they were too passive sometimes, because sometimes you have to be aggressive with getting things done. I felt like I had supported the place for so many years, and the one time I asked them to support me, they didn't. I was very bitter towards Gilman for about a year and a half or two years and stayed away. Really, the only time I go there now is to play shows with the band I'm in. It's still really weird going in there. It's like my old playroom that's been rearranged.

If that incident didn't happen, I don't think I'd still be there now anyway. Everyone gets burned out. Maybe it was just my time to go anyway. I'm older now and I have a kid. If Gilman's still around when he's old enough to go, I'll definitely take him there. Looking back, I got so much out of the place I couldn't stay bitter for-ever. If I didn't have Gilman when I was 15, I can't imagine what I would've gotten into instead. I think it's really important giving kids something to do that's not cheezy, pin-the-tail-on-the-donkey activities at the YMCA. It was something to do and some-where to go that was actually meaningful. I think Gilman kept me a kid in some respects, and kept me from growing up too fast, allowed me to have some fun. Gilman, and the bands I've joined because of it, have been the biggest influences, and had the biggest impact, on my life.

Some other random thoughts and memories:

I wanted to take better care of the bands that played there. They were our livelihood. I wanted to do what I could to make Gilman better for them. I wanted to feed touring bands. I wanted to do sound checks. I wasn't going to cater to a contract rider or huge guarantees, but I thought a simple sound check and cheap food wasn't asking too much. I got zero support from the club on that. I was accused of trying to make it into a rockstar place. I think we lost a lot of bands from coming back because we weren't taking care of them. The "tough shit" attitude might be fine when you're 16 or 17, but when you get in your 20s, and you're on tour, you don't need some young kid giving you some attitude like you're on "his" block. I felt like Gilman had a chip on its shoulder and treated bands, especially "bigger" bands poorly. Bands were being penalized for being popular. The point, I thought, was to try and get people to the club, to pay the bills, so we could then afford to take chances on smaller bands and "experimental" stuff, keep doing what we wanted to do.

Also, the place was getting really shitty-looking and dirty. It was dark, cold, smelly, and lonely. I think we could have kept the place cleaner, not changing everything and taking away the club's character, just keeping it from being a shithole. I'd go down to do booking early and spend time trying to clean the place. I think the problem was that no one there had seen the place in the beginning and knew what it used to be like.

Another thing is that I thought security could have been tighter. Some of the scariest moments in my life were at Gilman. Like the time we had a show with a couple of big New York hardcore bands. It was one of the first shows I ever coordinated. The girlfriend of one of the people doing security that night was spitting on one of the band members while they were on stage playing, and the band member kicked her in the head. The security guy whose girlfriend it was was screaming at me to stop the show. Other people were telling me that we couldn't stop the show and that we had to get the girl out of there. I felt really pressured to do something. Someone told me to tell the band that we might not pay them because of what happened. So I went to tell the band, and then I had their singer screaming at me. It was all really intense and I thought there was going to be a massive brawl. There wasn't, and eventually we did pay them.

And of course I remember the Isocracy shows. They epitomized what Gilman was. I felt they were the "house band."

That first show we had when we re-opened, that was an amazing feeling too.

Another thing I remember is that I think almost everyone who's worked there for a pretty long time has been accused of stealing from the club. I got accused of stealing from the store when I worked there during the *Maximum RocknRoll* years. Nothing ever came of it. I think most of us took advantage of Gilman in some way or another. I didn't steal money, but once I got keys to the place, my band practiced there. We took a few liberties, but I don't think that's too out of line.

1990   photo by Murray B.

ATHENA K.

"That place looks like something from the bowels of Hong Kong!" my dad exclaimed.

"You didn't tell anyone whose dad you were, right?" I asked anxiously, like anyone would know who I was, let alone care.

"No! I just told them that my daughter went there on weekends a lot and I wanted to see it. They were really nice. They even gave me a tour of the place, even though there wasn't much to see."

I was mortified! My dad had gone to Gilman! It turned out that he had been in Berkeley on business and he thought he would stop by to see the place I was always telling him I was going on weekends. Little did he know that we would get really drunk and go there to meet cute punk boys! Ha!

I also heard about my dad's trip to Gilman from my friend Dave EC, who was booking at the club then and who also, it turned out, was the one who gave my dad a tour. I remember whining about how embarrassed I was, but he made me feel better about it. Dave was always like that.

I've always been a fan of punk and hardcore, no matter what the style or substance. As a kid going to shows, I was just happy to be a part of a crowd of people who were having as much fun as I was watching bands. It didn't matter if it was a silly, often terrible, live band like Isocracy, or if it was a serious and heavy band like Christ On Parade. It just didn't matter to me. I was just happy to be in a place where I felt like I fit in, where I could watch bands and make new friends without feeling scared that I was going to get beat up by mean punk girls, or worse, skinhead girls! Gilman was much safer than the clubs in San Francisco that I would occasionally sneak out to. Gilman was that special place I could always go and find a friendly face, see at least one good band, and meet new people. It was also the place that gave me the confidence to become more involved in the punk community.

The Gilman Street Project has been a big part of my life for many, many years. In a sense, I grew up there. I learned a lot through my interactions at the club. I grew up at the end of the BART (Bay Area Rapid Transit) line in the dire suburbs of Concord, California, where the "isms" (sexism, homophobia, racism, etc.) run as rampant as the strip malls and cheap apartment complexes. It was through my interactions with the older friends I met at the club, and through the lyric sheets of the many 7"s I bought from local and touring bands, that I learned that these "isms" are unacceptable. I know it may sound weird that I would learn that from a lyric sheet, but hey, this stuff wasn't being taught in the school I went to! Granted, some of the open-mindedness I eventually grew into came as a result of growing up, traveling, and maturing, but it was because of those lyric sheets that I first thought about these things in an earnest manner. It was again through my interactions with people and bands that I first felt a sense of self-respect about being biracial and strong about being a young woman, two things I was not comfortable with growing up in Concord. It was through watching touring bands whose members' ages were the same or a little older than my own that I realized I could start a band and tour too.

Whenever I think back to some of those crazy nights when I was a kid, I have to laugh. There are so many comical memories, like when my best friend, Monica, stopped Youth of Today's set to ask if anyone had seen the shoe that she lost in the pit. Or the time I was really excited over meeting a certain former member of the Descendents (who I've been a lifelong fan of). I laugh now (I didn't then!) when I remember how much he let me down when he put his hairy hand down the back of my pants, right on my butt cheek. It's funny to remember how nervous I was the first time my first band played there. It always brings a smile to my heart when I remember the faces of the crew of friends I used to go with to see some now defunct, but still loved and remembered bands, like Born Against and Capitol Punishment. There's also a feeling of nostalgia at times, too. I remember feeling nostalgic during Operation Ivy's final show, before their set was even over. I remember feeling sad that Christ On Parade couldn't play their final show due to some assholes fighting during the previous band's set (Neurosis). I feel nostalgia and sadness when I remember good times with friends who are now lost to this world.

The faces have changed a lot over the years that I've frequented the club, but many of the old-timers (jeez, listen to me, I'm only 31!) are still around. Whenever I see Jesse L. there, I remember the time I got Blatz to play my party in my parents' backyard in Concord (what was I thinking?!) Whenever I see Richard the Roadie, I recall me and Monica filling orders at Blacklist Mailorder and him showing me how to use the tape gun, a feat I'm still not good at (long hair and sticky tape don't go well together). When I see Karoline C. there, I sometimes reminisce about booking those early Dread tours, when I would be *so* happy that someone from another state actually wanted to trouble themselves with booking my crappy band!

The last thing I wanted this piece to be was a drippy, nostalgic look back at the good old days, "back in the day," because while Gilman's history is important, its future is just as imperatively vital. While I have fond memories of being a kid among my group of other kid friends, the good times don't stop there. New and awesome raging bands are being formed *all* the time and sometimes I'm lucky enough to catch one of them when they play at Gilman. I'm still convinced that the world's best hardcore punk band is playing in a garage in the middle of nowhere. I'm hoping they tour and come play Gilman.

When Brian approached me about writing something for this book, he suggested I write from the perspective of someone who went from being part of the crowd, to the stage, to touring, and then back to the crowd again, selling records from my own label to kids who are just like I was and repeating the cycle with my new band. I never noticed the progression until it was pointed out to me in that manner. Ultimately, Gilman gave me the courage and inspiration to start my own band, go on tour, and then start a record label. I'm sure I would have never done those things had it not been for the support, stimulation, and encouragement I received from the friends I met through the club.

I still love going to shows at Gilman and watching new and old bands play. I've come to realize through touring and meeting people from out of state how we've been really spoiled here in the Bay Area with such a long-running club around to support our local bands and the myriad touring bands that come through the area. Gilman is still a haven for kids who don't have anywhere else to go. It gives them a sense of identity and security that many lack at home, school, and work. That's not to say that the place hasn't suffered over the years from high school-type politics, or even that it's the quintessential punk heaven, but it is definitely a vitally important space in the Bay Area, in punk history, in my life, and the lives of many others.

RUSSELL

I first went to Gilman in 1987 or 1988. I had just moved to California from Louisiana, and some friends of mine took me along to see a show at Gilman. I thought it was interesting that the people running it were rather young. I was used to going to clubs that were run by some mafia-type to launder money or something. Also, I remember thinking that the people who worked there seemed pretty stuck up, but I was only 15 or so at the time, and pretty impressionable. I thought a punk rock club should be more about personal interaction. But I wanted to help put on shows, since that's what I did ever since I first got into punk, so I started working at Gilman in 1989. Also, I was really broke at the time, and if you worked there, you didn't have to pay to get in. I worked in the store, did sound, front door, sold membership cards, stage managed, etc. I ended up working there about three-and-a-half to four years, mostly running the store, working it on show nights and buying supplies and such during the week. I was going to school in San Francisco, learning about sound equipment and recording and stuff, so it helped me with learning how to do sound at Gilman.

One of the things I liked about Gilman was the fact that it brought different people together to work together and get things done. The punk rock scene has always seemed so fractured and contentious to me. For example, Gilman had straight-edgers and drunks working together and getting things done. I also thought it was good too when folks were living there (I was one of them), because we kept the place clean. When you're there all the time, the smell of the garbage and bathrooms, and the stickiness of the floors gets to you, and you have to clean it. Gilman can really stink sometimes, literally. Another thing I really liked about Gilman was the meetings, and being a part of the decision-making process, arguing and debating about how we were going to run the club. It was idealistic, and sometimes ponderous, but it was good to get a group of like-minded people together to hash out their differences, work out a decision or solution, and put it into action. Unfortunately, and I've seen this happen at other non-profit, or not-for-profit, organizations too, is that someone ends up trying to play "King of the Mountain." It becomes a battle of egos and petty politics. After a while I got sick of that and moved on. I had a major disagreement with the person who was head coordinator at the time, so I left. It showed me that the decisions that were made at the meetings weren't always carried out in the actual running of the club.

Once I left, I didn't go there again, even just to attend a show. Gilman was fun, but it was like a second high school for me. Also, I was twenty-one by then and could go to other places. On top of that, I found out that when I was away on tour with my band, that that particular head coordinator had had me kicked out of Gilman at a meeting! I wasn't even there to say or do anything about it. I was accused of stealing money from the store. I was pissed off and hurt that no one stood up for me at that meeting. I had put a lot of time and energy into that place. I never tried to fight it at another meeting after I got back, because if they were going to kick me out that easily and treat me like that, why would I want to rejoin the place?

I also didn't like the club strictly enforcing the "no drinking" policy. The cops had too much else to deal with in that neighborhood and wouldn't have bothered us. They never came inside the club. I think they should have been a lot more lax about the drinking. If I had a kid, I'd feel a lot better about them drinking at Gilman than if they were out drinking in some bushes, or in a park or something. I don't think people should have been kicked out for drinking in the club—it was hypocritical, since the workers were drinking too. I think they just should have been told to keep it more discreet. There's certainly some things that should be done to get along with the city, but when you're enforcing the city's rules inside the club, then it proves you are being the same as them. Punk rock should be something outside of accepted society and we should be having our own rules, or at least trying to reach agreements, rather than enforcing society's laws on each other. How does Gilman differ from any mainstream club in that respect? Inside of Gilman's walls I think we should have done whatever we wanted. If someone wanted to drink or take drugs there, they should have been able to.

And how come it's only open on the weekends? How come it's not used during the week, like having a cafe or a bookstore there or something? When these things were brought up at meetings before, too many people were defeatist and dismissed them out of hand, saying the city, the city, the city, etc. I thought, since we were having money problems, we should be doing more to try and bring more money in, and also try to give back more to the community, like childcare, more women's self-defense courses, etc. I think they should have more than one type of music there too, it's too narrow in scope. In some ways, I think Gilman has run its course. It's taken too much for granted now.

Right: the punk alphabet, 1990 photo by Murray B.

Below right: this mural still exists today, the last surviving original mural, 1990 photo by Susan S.

Above: store, 1990 photo by Murray B.

Left: 1989 photo by Murray B.

Proposal for a new club/center at 924 Gilman Street

This is an outline of some of the concerns needed to be addressed in attempting to establish a music oriented club at the warehouse space soon to be vacated by 'the Gilman Street Project'. It should be understood that this is NOT a proposal to 'save Gilman', to keep 'it' alive, or even to revive 'it'. Tim Yohannan and others involved in the previous project have made it clear that 'The Gilman Street Project' is to remain dead and should not be linked with whatever new comes into the place.

The former operation, however, does provide a model or starting point for discussing something new. My background is nothing this is six months of involvement with the operation of the GSP. It is inevitable that if this new club does patronize some of the previous customers (at the old location), then certain aspects of the new operation may end up closely resembling the former GSP to some eyes. Enough said of the past.

The purpose of this outline is to present some ideas and figures on paper to provide a basis for some immediate productive discussion by those who have a strong interest in putting in some effort and who have strong ideas about the direction to steer this opportunity. My particular bias is merely towards establishing a place for live music of a broad spectrum to be presented to an ALL AGES audience. That in itself is alternative enough to anything currently available in the East Bay or SF to warrant putting effort into such a project. The key motivating factor to moving fast is that available locations and buildings are hard to come by. 924 Gilman provides a central East Bay locale, plus a building already structurally modified for music shows, plus a potentially very supportive landlord.

A final note: none of the following recommendations (no matter how they are stated) are in any way final; each should be questioned and checked for flaws.

OPERATION / OWNERSHIP

- Ultimate responsibility for this new 'club' (being the legal business partners, signing the lease, signing checks and paying bills on time) should rest on 2-3 people who initially would have to register the partnership, set up a bank account, establish a mailing address for bills (a P.O. box is available), obtain insurance bids for liability and property (potential companies have been explored), and of course meet with the landlord, Jim Widess, who runs the adjoining Caning shop.

- It is advisable to then proceed with the paperwork to try to become a nonprofit (if desired) corporation for purposes of individual financial liability, possibilities of getting grant money for support (depending on the scope of activities), and possible reduced insurance rates. Paperwork to incorporate takes approx. 4-6 months to process.

- Operation decisions can be made democratically by a membership body or a smaller collective of individuals, but input should be made open to all interested persons. In the case of a partnership, those individuals with their necks on the line will inevitably have a stronger say on particular matters and always have the option to ignore certain decisions. In the process of incorporating, a well defined structure of decision-making, board of directors, etc. has to be spelled out.

BOOKING / TYPES OF MUSIC

- It is not desirable to book a narrow spectrum of music for the many reasons of: getting into a rut (shows begin repeating themselves); getting stereotyped and alienating desirable audiences; being hard pressed at times to book strong shows consistently enough to pay the monthly bills; relying on a too small a core of interested persons running too many shows.

- This does not mean we should try to be 'everything to everybody'. Certain genres/bands probably should be restricted, taking into consideration the crowd that they attract and the shows being All Ages (meaning, in this society, no alcohol). Metal anyone?

- It is probably desirable to mix up the types of music (intelligently) on a single bill rather than separating genres to their own night of the week. This helps to broaden people's musical views and is an important aspect to being 'alternative'.

- Booking should not be done by a single person for simple reasons of inevitable burnout and personal musical biases. Rather booking should be done by a committee of persons with different musical contacts. Booking should be also be open to having outside individuals come up with a bill or event to present to the committee for approval and scheduling.

- A single person, however, should have the position of the overall scheduler (possibly a paid position if the calendar becomes very busy with events and the work load too great to be a hobby).

ENTRY COST / NUMBER OF BANDS per show

- Being affordable is also 'alternative'. Charging a dollar a band or less should be striven for. The actual entry price should take into consideration of: not-for-profit operation (?), weekly number of shows and expected attendance, percentage of the door paid to performers, number of lower draw events and activities to be supported by bigger shows, and monthly costs.

- Greater than 4 bands in one particular nighttime show leads to long nights, hectic stage managing and shorter sets for bands. Occasional daytime shows on weekends are a way of presenting more bands on a bill and breaking up the repetition of only Friday and Saturday night shows.

- Having a membership card which costs additional money for first time entry is probably not desirable. The purpose of such a card (such as explaining certain rules or attempting to instill a sense of belonging) would need to be clearly defined (as well as 'membership'). Negative effects on audiences should be considered and if existing, its purpose should not be as a source of income.

- Other types of membership which cost money and may give discounts at the door or put them on a mailing list may be desirable.

OPERATION / STAFFING OF SHOWS

- All volunteer (except for hired security) for the sake of helping out the club and getting in free (but perhaps not seeing all the show) is one option. Additional benefits such as a free future pass for working an entire night (or doing other types of work not at showtime) is another option. A reward system can also improve the quality of work done.

- Shows typically need one overall coordinator, an optional assistant coordinator/trainee and other real jobs of stage managing, door money, hand stamp checker, side door traffic controller, security for band equipment, inside and outside, security and cleanup (oversight?) crews. Also a store/refreshment window with separate money handling needs to be staffed each show.

- Organization and clear job descriptions are important. Coordinators should be signed up weeks in advance whereas the other volunteers may or may not need to be until just before showtime.

- Approved coordinators, sound people, maintenance, garbage and other persons needing access to the club outside of a show need to be issued a set of keys.

STORE / REFRESHMENTS

- All ages means no alcohol means for the older (and younger) 'beer-minded' crowd there should be some decent and enticing alternatives, such as hot food, sandwiches, smoothies, etc. (not just candy and soda).

- Such a menu that customers can expect at every show is important.

- Greater preparation time for such a menu means greater work which hence requires a coordinator of the store for each show, a detailed shopping list, good organization, and perhaps greater benefits for a more demanding chore.

- Expanded scope of refreshments may require registering with the city for the proper licensing.

DECOR IDEAS

- Solicit wall to wall artwork: professional, semi-pro and amateur. Provide or reimburse for materials. Perhaps restrict band-name graffiti a bit. Save one or two pieces of artwork already existing. More 3-D objects.

- Creative use of the ceiling (cool atmospheric lighting). No disco halls.

- Get newer less grungy furniture and side room carpet. Make better use of the 'library' side room - more conducive to reading maybe. Restrict use of it as a bicycle parking lot.

- How clean depends on what won't drive people away.

DANCING POLICY (for the untamed crowds)

- A clearly defined policy should be stated and posted. (Example: No stage-diving (absolutely); Energetic dancing only to the point where it begins to interfere with other audience members' right to enjoy the show.)

- Should the 'swirling' pit be tolerated? Acceptable and non-acceptable dancing is often a judgment call. Responsible and capable people need to recognize the dividing line and enforce the policy.

SECURITY (Very Important)

- Again, a clear, consistent and enforceable policy needs to be set up to deal with troublemakers. They need to be informed right from the very start that their actions and behavior will not be tolerated; that action will be taken at the slightest incident; that after being kicked out that the outside grounds are also off limits. The club cannot become their hangout, otherwise our audience will be scared away and volunteers will get discouraged or burntout always having to deal with crises.

- One outside security (uniformed) and one inside security (nondescript) probably need to be hired.

- Everyone should be allowed in initially (no pre-banned persons). Efforts should be made to identify subsequently banned persons by name (and photo too), so that anyone working door security can know who is banned.

- It is illegal to ban anyone because of their hair (or lack of) or clothing and it is silly to consider it. However known troublemakers of the past and persons fitting the skinhead or fuckup stereotype should be told that they fit the stereotype and be given advance warning (a slip of paper) when they first enter, that any violence, vandalism or simple acts of destroying anyone else's fun will mean their immediate ban from the club.

- Another internal security item concerns the number of keys to be entrusted to volunteers who need access to the club.

OUTREACH (also very important)

- A key to getting participation in running the club is to inform everyone of exactly what is going on: calendar of events, finances, opportunities for involvement, areas that need help and organizing, who the head honchos are, etc. For this, a monthly newsletter (with a mailing distribution) and a newsletter committee to produce it is perhaps optional, but definitely desired.

- A suggestion box and a way for nonactive persons to provide feedback would be helpful.

- PUBLICITY: organization into a committee that will get things done on a weekly basis is a must. Separate art and distribution subcommittees are probably needed for flyering of individual events and calendars. KALX announcements and ticket giveaways are definite possibilities.

Continued next page

- In general, the club needs to work closely <u>with</u> the bands and audience since that is what the (music) club's existence depends on. Bands are probably a great resource for publicity (flyering of their own show at least).

NON- MUSIC SHOW NIGHTS

- Use of the warehouse space during the week is a potential revenue producing resource to be exploited. First it requires approval of the landlord who runs the adjoining wicker repair shop Tues-Fri throughout the day and Sat from 10-2pm. Since one thin wall is shared between his shop and the main warehouse room, amplified music events can't be held during those times nor on Tuesday nights when the landlord occasionally holds classes. Second, expanded use of the space during the week requires oversight probably by the overall scheduler, increasing that persons workload making a likely candidate for a paid position.

- Possibilities include demo tape recordings, movie nights, rental to other organizations who weekly or sporadically need a larger get-together space (possibly need sublease approval from the landlord).

FINANCES / COSTS

Monthly
$2,300	Rent + utilities
$500-800	Security ($50-$100/night, 2 nights/wkend)
$300?	Flyers and misc.publicity
$100?	Phone bill/booking
$35	Alarm
?	Garbage
?	?salaries

$3,500

One-Time
$2,300	last month rent security
$1,500-$5,000	liability and property insurance; may be paid in installments with ins. company finance plan
$3,000	cut rate purchase of GSProject sound equipment from MRR with possible payment plan
$1,000?	additional required sound equipment (monitor speakers)
$500?	repainting, furniture

$8,000-$11,000

Initial Outlay
$2,300	first month rent; possible repayment plan of 1st month rent to MRR if lease signed by Nov. 15
$2,300	last month rent security
$1,000	insurance installment
$500?	necessary equipment and repairs to do first show

$4,000 minimum - $6,000

INCOME

- dependent on: number of music shows per week
average attendance per show
door price
club percentage take of the door
misc. income from the store, demo tapes, and
weekday use of the space

STABLE WORKFORCE / SUMMARY

- necessary committees:
1. Booking - one overall scheduler, pool g...
2. Sound/Stage - crew trained to do stage set...
3. Store - shopping list purchasing,...
4. Publicity - flyering, calendars, news...
5. Show Coordination - training, signup
6. Security - keep track of banned per...
7. Decor (optional) -make contacts, sol...

-necessary individual positions...
1. Overall schedule...
2. Accounting &...
3. Garbage
4. Maintenan...

The above proposal was put together by Jonathan D., the bottom one by Lou E.

INTRODUCTION

[handwritten: bolorlation is the]

The primary goal of this ~~document is provide guidelines for the~~ establishment and operation of an ALL AGES music venue. There have been previous attempts to establish such organizations which have met with varying degrees of success. This attempt to achieve that goal is a step away from the previously attempted lofty ideals of complete volunteerism, but also it is much more ambitious and much more formally organized. If fact you will find the structure to be a mini-government, complete with some bureaucratic overhead.

There are a number of reasons that make this detailed structure necessary:

1. The club needs greater organization to handle the necessary expansion in activities to become financially stable (more so than previous attempts). Also the state requires such a structure to be established when the club files for incorporation, eventually as a nonprofit corporation. Being a nonprofit corporation means the club becomes a financially liable entity of its own (rather than individuals being responsible for the liabilities of the club) that can apply for grants and tax-deductible donations as well as apply for a tax-exempt status.

2. Having a documented organization and operations is also very useful in explaining to insurance companies, future members and potential contributors what we are all about.

3. The longevity of the club is greatly enhanced by including in the structure, ways to safeguard against volunteer burnout, ensure that important jobs get done on time (and not by a small core of overworked individuals), and outreach to new people to join the club's operation.

4. Structure is important to empower the working members as well as keep any individual from becoming too powerful or influential.

The presence of such a detailed structure should fade into the background over time, but the structure at times may be needed for resolving conflicts and crises.

GOALS

The primary mission of this new corporation is to operate a venue that is open to All Ages and that presents alternative music formats that may not have adequate outlets elsewhere. These formats must have adequate support of the members and the volunteer work force, and also be financially viable. Initially the club may be limited to proven successful shows until its financial health improves.

Additional goals of the organization include:

1. A program to provide an outlet and exposure for emerging bands. *[handwritten: MUSI]*

2. To operate on a not-for-profit basis, but with reasonable financial safeguards including reserves.

3. To include membership participation in all aspects of the club's operation. *[handwritten: in co-operative venture]*

4. To provide a learning experience for those members without experience in such an operation.

And if successful: *[handwritten: develop a prototype which can]*

5. Help other regions around the U.S. establish similar All Ages clubs.

Although this document does not yet say how all these goals are to be implemented, it is intended to develop the document and the club with them in mind.

MEMBERSHIP

[handwritten: all volunteer labor/member gov.]

Most all club events are to be open to the public at a regular admission price without the requirement of membership. In the case of certain special events (such as known sellouts) attendance may be restricted to members only or members will be given the first opportunity to purchase tickets to certain activities.

For those who wish to support and keep informed of the club's operation a ten dollar annual <u>regular</u> membership will be offered. A five dollar discount is provided for those who help establish the club by joining between now and January 1, 1989. These members will receive periodic mailings (including the club newsletter), and be entitled to a one dollar discount at all club sponsored events. Also regular members will be allowed to vote for the board of directors annually and attend quarterly membership meetings (which are also board of directors meetings).

[handwritten: working members]

Members who want to get directly involved with a particular aspect of the club's operation can join a committee and become a volunteer. Obtaining *[handwritten: working member]* volunteer status is a position that must be earned and maintained on an ongoing basis by working a minimum of 12 hours a month (and not more than 20 hours a month) on club activities. The benefit of contributing such time and labor is that volunteers can attend all club sponsored events free, they will elect their committee chair persons and they participate in a monthly ~~volunteer~~ meeting/function. *[handwritten: workers]*

Systems are to be implemented to maintain lists of those individuals who wish to become volunteers and to track the hours worked by individuals in support of club activities. The club intends to vigorously monitor for volunteers spending in excess of 20 hours a month. Any such situation identified will be reviewed by the board to determine:

Continued next page

If additional volunteers need to be assigned to the position

or

If the position should be converted to a paid position with appropriate stipend.

An additional type of affiliate membership may be established for individuals (or businesses) that merely want to be on the mailing list or who wish to sponsor the club financially.

ORGANIZATIONAL STRUCTURE

This section details how the club is to be organized. The reader may find it of value to refer to the chart on the following page while reading this section.

Board of Directors

The top level of personnel is the Board of Directors - a body composed of 12 to 15 individuals which maintains oversight of club operations, makes the major financial decisions, sets overall club policy and monitors committee performance. The board will meet a least quarterly and probably monthly initially. Club members are always welcome to attend board meetings on a non-voting basis.

The elected officers are:

President
Vice-President
Secretary
Treasurer

These are the minimum officers required by the state for corporations. They may or may not be involved in the daily operations of the club. A prerequisite to being a candidate for one of these positions is to have served as a committee volunteer for a period of at least one year prior to running for office.

Also the board will have as members at least two outside directors consisting of corporation's attorney and an appropriate civic leader. These two members may be voting or non-voting positions depending on the desires of the membership. The remainder of the board voting members consists of the eight committee chair persons who manage the operational activities that their particular committee is responsible for and are elected annually by the committee members.

General Manager

Finally the club general manager, the person who coordinates day to day operation of the club and its committees, will be a non-voting member. In addition to interfacing with each committee chairman weekly or more often, the general manager will have the authority to resolve timely problems that arise during club operations and will have limited direct spending authority. If the club's operation gets too big the position may need a professional hired manager.

Club Committees

The next organization level down from the board of directors is the actual committees manned by the club's volunteer work force. Members will apply to become a volunteer on a particular committee and are approved for a particular committee through a screening process (to be established). The purpose of the screening process is to match particular skills and aptitudes with the committees needs. Each committee besides performing specific duties assigned to it must perform the following common functions:

o Maintain an operating budget

o Establish and maintain a procedures manual

o Institute a formal training program for new members

These common functions insure that the spending of club funds is properly tracked, potential volunteers can determine a particular committees expectations of them before joining, and that a knowledge vacuum is avoided when committee members depart.

Types of Committees

There are three types of committees within the club's proposed structure:

o Operational Committees: which control a major functional area of the clubs operations. The chair persons of these committees serve as members of the board of directors.

o Sub-Committees: which are created by the operating committees to manage large chunks of work. Chair persons of these committees are also elected by there committee members, but do not participate in the board of directors.

o Special Committees: are appointed by the board of directors to perform special projects of limited duration.

COMMITTEE DESCRIPTIONS

This section details the primary duties of each of the clubs eight operational committees.

Booking Committee

This committee is very important to the club's success. It's members will be the phone contact with bands and will schedule shows and events. The logistics of booking and keeping it open to membership feedback are important in creating booking's structure. The club will live or die based on bookings ability to consistently provide bands that will draw the attendance of both the general public and club members.

Show Operations

This committee runs most of the activities while the club is open including:

o Stage Setup

o Soundboard Operation

o Stage Management

o Admission

o Cleanup

o Volunteer Scheduling for each Show

Store

This committee will manage and staff the refreshment window and work out a consistent high quality menu and supporting shopping list, as well as do the purchasing required.

Publicity

This committee is in charge of flyer creation and distribution, free and paid advertising and general (or targeted) public relations. After the booking committee this committee is most crucial to the club's survival.

Membership

This committee has major tasks of maintaining the membership database, accounting for and collecting dues, running and administering the volunteer program and performing community outreach activities. A major outreach activity will be the club newsletter which will be published by a subcommittee.

Security

This committee is responsible for performing club security functions by hiring professional security personnel and supplementing the professional force with highly trained volunteer personnel. The committee also formulates and recommends security policies to the board. The committee maintains the banned persons list. The committee is important for the safety and enjoyment of the audience as well as the reputation of the club.

Facilities

This committee performs a variety of non-show related functions including:

o Repair and major cleanup operations through a subcommittee for this purpose.

o Planning and organizing the club decor.

o Managing the non-show hours use of the club by both members and outside users. A subcommittee is planned for this function.

Finance

This committee performs the club bookkeeping by tracking both receipts and spending. The finance committee will also form a fund raising subcommittee to solicit outside funds to support the club. The committee is vital to the initial financial well being of the club, since no show revenue will be available initial to finance club activities. The committee will later switch to pursuing non-profit grants and donations.

An Introduction to Gilman St.

The warehouse at 924 Gilman Street in Berkeley operates by a few guidelines and restrictions. The music warehouse aspires to be an affordable all ages no alcohol volunteer-run club. Each of these aspects require more detailed explanations for those unclear of the concepts.

Afforable. San Francisco and the East Bay have a few music shows for low cost entry (i.e. free shows, $1 Tuesdays), but these are normally at 21 and over clubs where money is made from the bar. Hence for us the affordability aspect is linked to all ages and no alcohol. The low price at shows is a sincere effort to not gouge people's wallets in direct contrast to clubs that charge the maximum they think the audience will stand, and then tack on another $3 drink ticket for minors who aren't legally allowed to blow their excess cash on overpriced beer. Our regular audience is under the impression that more bands for less moey is a better deal, so partly for that reason, we put on four or more bands in one evening and charge $5 or $6 dollars. Affordability is also one reason why we are volunteer operated. We understand the economics involved in running a standard nightclub to earn a living for the owner and pay employees, and at present our budget barely handles paying security.

All Ages.

Energy is a key part of all ages shows. The younger crowd has more energy to burn and don't tolerate the motionless standing around (and drinking) type of crowd at most college radio or bar circuit type shows. Bands that put out a lot of energy in their music usually get a greater return at all ages shows. The scarcity of all ages shows is largely due to the younger crowd not patronizing the bar enough to even pay the bartender. Plus the all ages crowd that some bands bring with them are extra security hassles for the club that they'd rather not deal with.

Mad punks, drunk punks, or just drunks.

No Alcohol.

Being a no alcohol club doesn't mean we don't have to deal with alcohol related problems, though. We still have to deal with drunks at the door, drinking outside, cleaning up bottles and broken glass outside after shows so that our neighbors don't get irate.

Volunteer-run.

Important ramifications of volunteerism - have to do shows that we enjoy putting time and effort into. If only one show in ten is inspiring to volunteers that put a lot of time and effort into running the shows, that's not a good enough reason to exist.

\-

It's hard to discuss the club without referring to the past incarnation, the Gilman Street Project, which within two years of existence achieved legendary status in the punk community, partly through its benefactor and spokesmagazine, MaximumRockNRoll. Even if the GSP was never internally quite to the high level that people believed and read about, perhaps the club's greatest service was to inspire people in scenes around the nation and in other countries to try or to think about creating their own 'Gilman'.

Being stubborn and still not totally cogniznt of all the flaws that spelled the old club's doom, the idea behind continuing music shows at the old space was to see if any more mileage could be gotten out of some of the principles set up at the old club and at the same time test to see if the problem was merely structural and/or if the Bay Area community actually did support or tolerate those principles. The verdict is still not in, but one conclusion that we can draw is that the concept of a large membership run organization sharing the large workload of putting on shows at the club is a 'dead whale'.

Booking. Just to clear up some more misconceptions about the clubby bands calling up wanting to book shows. The club is not just another club on the bar circuit. The club is not the farm league for bands aspiring to play the I-Beam or the Kennel Club. We are an alternative to such clubs. It doesn't make sense anyway to develop an underage audience that could even follow the band to such clubs.

The Bay Area is saturated with bands of all types -- far too many for the number of clubs and audience.

We even get calls from bands that when asked what type of music they play (yes, I know bands don't want to be categorized), they say "music for all occasions, we cater our set to the crowd". That's nice and flexible, but personally I question the existence of bands that don't have a purpose, a focus or some message they want to get accross to the audience. Rock stardom and groupies is an abhorrent reason to me.

Written by Jonathan D., 1988

Membership Notes

You do not have to be a member to come to shows. The two main benefits you receive by becoming a member are (1) a $1 discount for admission to all events, and (2) a periodic newsletter informing you of our music calendar, meetings, operations, finances, and volunteer help needs. Also, members are invited to attend and participate in all meetings and members vote for officers (president, vice president and treasurer of the nonprofit corporation).

Membership is $5 (until Jan.1, then $10) and is ANNUAL.

The club needs lots of help and advice in order to operate efficiently and become financially stable. At present we are organized into the following committees:

BOOKING - establish a database of bands; make scheduling decisions; set up special shows; phone call agents and bands; demo tape review; manage press kits; mail booking confirmations

SHOW OPERATIONS

Coordinating - be the oversight manager of all the minor details that need to happen during showtime, including money matters like paying the bands; includes stage managing

Sound/Stage - run the sound mixing board and/or help with the microphones and band equipment on stage

Store - sell refreshments during a show; purchasing supplies

NEWSLETTER/Membership - keep track of membership database; publish a monthly newsletter/zine to inform members of all that goes on

PUBLICITY - make posters and do weekly flyering runs; send press releases to radio stations and newspapers; coordinate the above

FACILITIES/Decor - maintenance and repair; painting, decoration and construction; soliciting artwork

FINANCES - keep track of books, worry about weekly income, advertise for daytime use of building

SECURITY - supplement hired security personnel in trying to establish a safe and fun audience atmosphere; coordinate scheduling of hired security

Committe Update:

BOOKING: scheduling done by committee; primary talking with bands has been taken on by Heather - a godsend. Last minute cancellations and confirmations take up lots of time and are stressful; trying to book far enough ahead to satisfy publicity; organizing paperwork so that finalized confirmations can be mailed.

SHOW OPS: Coordinating - need to train a much larger pool of responsible volunteers; job description still evolving. Sound - popular position to want to get trained for; probably soon to be a waiting list; Marshal's in charge . Store- also popular to work at shows; need to be approved first by Dave before signing up in advance

NEWSLETTER: a rush job; two authors (Andrew and myself, Jonathan); needs to be put out on a monthly basis with an editor who coordinates article writing and layout.

PUBLICITY: large database for free newspaper and radio music calendars computerized; need to evaluate effectiveness; need an overall coordinator of the flyering effort

FACILITIES: emergency construction jobs completed and more planned; plan to move some office operations out of Lou's place to the club side room alcove; artwork solicitation needs a scheduler; high priority to investigate subtenant use of the building during the weekdays.

FINANCES: nonprofit corporate booking keeping started by Ben; presently, I write all checks; payments for immediate club operation first; saving up for rent and monthly bills next; payments for the sound system to MRR; and hopefully soon able to reduce individual startup loans to a maximum of $500 each; fundraising efforts need to get resurrected.

SECURITY: seeking to expand pool of hired in-house crowd control persons appropriate for the club; no one has an axe to grind with the club so far. — J.D.

Above: taken from the AMF newsletter, late 1988

Is proof of membership in 924 Gilman street.

The club has decided to re-instigate its policy of a membership audience. The decision was reached at a general meeting in January after careful considera-tion of some large problems the club was facing. — Due to higher rent and insurance pay-ments, the club has to take in more money. Yearly dues will raise money and let the club keep the door prices low. —The club has rules, (explained be-low,) and if the club does not feel that someone is willing to follow the rules, he or she will not be sold a membership card, and therefore will not be al-lowed into the shows. If this person feels that he should be sold a card, he can address the club at a membership meeting. — Most importantly, the club would like to see more of a sense of community develop. The club hopes that the people who go to shows are not just attendees, but participants.

Members agree to follow the rules of the club.

The club does not want to restrict what you do, but be-cause of police and neighbor-hood pressure, certain rules are necessary. — No drinking, drug use, vandalism, or fighting inside or around the club. Gil-man is not by default "straight-edge," but drinking in public and drug use are illegal. If the Berkeley Police feel that an unusual amount of illegal activ-ity is occurring at a place of business, they will charge the business of what is known as, "creating a nuisance." Creating a nuisance is ample grounds for the city to revoke a use permit, meaning the club would have to shut down. Vandalism, includ-ing littering, gets the neighbors worked up, prompting them to call the police. — No stage-diving or excessively violent dancing during the show. Due to the sue-happy atmosphere we live in, the club cannot allow stagediving, already the cause of a handful of potential lawsuits. As far as dancing is concerned, what is fine at one show could be out-of-hand at another. Use your head and don't be a jerk.

Gilman St. is based on the idea that bands, staff, and audience are all equally important.

Whatever you can do to help keep the club open is greatly appreciated. The club is volunteer run, and while every-one is encouraged to help work the shows, obviously not every-one has the time or desire to do this. However, members are expected to help keep the shows successful and the club open. Please follow the club's rules, they stand for a reason. If you see a fight, don't let it continue. If you see trash outside, pick it up. If you see someone ripping off the club, don't let it go unno-ticed. In addition to the card standing for the member's awareness towards the club, with the membership cards comes a renewed responsibility of the club towards it's mem-bers. There are membership meetings every two weeks and the dates will now be publicly announced. Anyone is free to come and discuss club policy and procedures.

Membership is yearly and nontransferable.

Your card is valid until the end of the month in the year marked. Do not give, sell, or rent your card to anyone, even if you are not going to the show that night. If your card does not fit into your wallet, feel free to trim it up to a quarter inch in each dimension. DO NOT trim off the "Membership valid until" numbers. A card missing validation numbers is invalid. Do not mark or laminate the card. Your card will be required at all shows. Unfortunately, the club cannot keep track of the names of every card purchaser, if your card is lost, a new card must be purchased.

Thank you for becoming a member.

Membership pamphlet after membership requirements were reinstituted in early 1990

ARTICLES OF INCORPORATION

OF

ALTERNATIVE MUSIC FOUNDATION

ONE: The name of this corporation is Alternative Music Foundation.

TWO: This corporation is a nonprofit public benefit corporation and is not organized for the private gain of any person. It is organized under the Nonprofit Public Benefit Corporation Law for charitable purposes. The specific purposes for which this corporation is organized are to educate young people in alternative music formats and in peaceful co-operative ways of working together. The means of providing such education includes, but is not limited to, the maintenance of a performance space and associated facilities for the public performance of alternative music which may not have adequate outlets elsewhere.

THREE: The name and address in the Sate of California of the corporation's initial agent for service of process is Patrick W. ; Oakland, CA .

FOUR:

(a) This corporation is organized and operated exclusively for charitable and educational purposes within the meaning of Section 501(c)(3) of the Internal Revenue Code.

(b) Notwithstanding any other provision of these Articles, the corporation shall not carry on any other activities not permitted to be carried on (1) by a corporation exempt from federal income tax under Section 501(c)(3) of the Internal Revenue Code or (2) by a corporation contributions to which are deductible under Section 170(c)(2) of the Internal Revenue Code.

(c) No substantial part of the activities of this corporation shall consist of carrying on propaganda, or otherwise attempting to influence legislation, and the corporation shall not participate or intervene in any political campaign (including the publishing or distribution of statements) on behalf of any candidate for public office.

FIVE: The names and address of the persons appointed to act the initial directors of the corporation are:

Name	Address
Jonathan D.	Oakland, CA
Louis E	Berkeley, CA
Patrick W.	Oakland, CA

SIX: The property of this corporation is irrevocably dedicated to charitable purposes and no part of the net income or assets of the organization shall ever inure to the benefit of any Director, officer or member thereof or to the benefit of any private person.

On the dissolution or winding up of the corporation, its assets remaining after payment of, or provision for payment of, all debts and liabilities of this corporation, shall be distributed to a nonprofit fund, foundation, or corporation which is organized and operated exclusively for charitable purposes and which has established its tax-exempt status under Section 501(c)(3) of the Internal Revenue Code.

October 19, 1988.

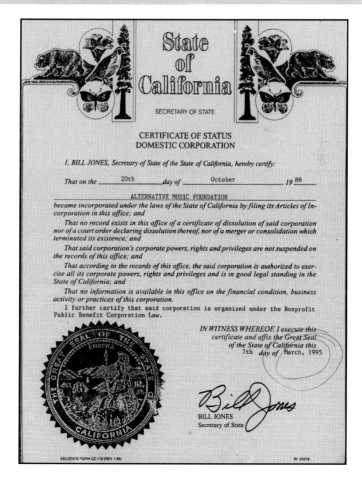

State of California

SECRETARY OF STATE

CERTIFICATE OF STATUS
DOMESTIC CORPORATION

I, BILL JONES, Secretary of State of the State of California, hereby certify:

That on the ___20th___ day of ___October___, 19_88_.

ALTERNATIVE MUSIC FOUNDATION

became incorporated under the laws of the State of California by filing its Articles of Incorporation in this office; and

That no record exists in this office of a certificate of dissolution of said corporation nor of a court order declaring dissolution thereof, nor of a merger or consolidation which terminated its existence; and

That said corporation's corporate powers, rights and privileges are not suspended on the records of this office; and

That according to the records of this office, the said corporation is authorized to exercise all its corporate powers, rights and privileges and is in good legal standing in the State of California; and

That no information is available in this office on the financial condition, business activity or practices of this corporation.

I further certify that said corporation is organized under the Nonprofit Public Benefit Corporation Law.

IN WITNESS WHEREOF, I execute this certificate and affix the Great Seal of the State of California this 7th day of March, 1995

BILL JONES
Secretary of State

SEC/STATE FORM CE-112 (REV. 1-95)

94-25216

924 GILMAN STREET PROJECT BY-LAWS (approved 1991)

These are the by-laws that are filed with the State of California. They do not include the Articles of Incorporation or all of Gilman's day-to-day operational details. These By-Laws are transcribed faithfully from the written original, including most of the formatting. Items in brackets are added for clarification. Please talk to Jesse if you have any questions or leave him a note in his tube (#19).

Definition of a Member:
- Paying Member- buys a membership card.
- Voting Member- comes to at least 2 membership meetings. S/he can speak but not vote at the 1st meeting, then s/he can vote at the 2nd meeting. Plus, a member should do at least one task a month.

Members agree to follow the rules of the club: no drinking, drug use, vandalism, or fighting inside or around the club, and no stage diving or excessively violent dancing during the show. No stealing from the club. No one gets credit from the club.

[Officers of the Corporation (legally required by the State to be 21 or over)]:

On the 3rd Saturday of October the Voting Members will meet for the Annual Election of Officers.

Executive Officer: Oversees the day-to-day operations of the club. Sees different jobs to be done.
Financial Officer: Does NOT get paid. Does accounting, pays bills, files financial statements, and makes these financial records easily accessible to voting members. S/he makes financial reports at membership meetings.
Secretary: S/he will keep a record of voting members. Designates someone to take minutes of each membership meeting and is responsible for keeping records of those meetings.

Each officer has a responsibility to see that other officers are doing their job and they are to delegate their responsibilities to competent others to see that they are done.

[Membership Meetings/Decision Making]:

Quorum = at least 9 Voting Members

Motions are approved by at least 50% of the present voting members.

To change any Articles of Incorporation, Bylaws, or to elect officers, or to hire people, 2/3 of the present Voting Members must approve.

Suspension/Dismissal of any Officer for Dereliction of Duty:
2/3 of present Voting Members must approve suspension. The 2nd meeting following, 2/3 of the present Voting Members must approve dismissal. The following meeting, 2/3 of the present Voting Members must approve a replacement Officer if the previous Officer is dismissed. The other 2 Officers shall see that the responsibilities of the 3rd Officer are done in the meantime.

Membership meetings shall be held every other Saturday at 5 PM at 924 Gilman Street, Berkeley, CA 94710, and are open to the public.

This document was created by the following volunteers:
On 9/24/91, Steve List, Maggie, Zoe, Jim, John, Michael Diehl, Jeff, Jesse.
On 10/1/91, Steve List, Maggie, Jim, John, Michael Diehl, Jeff, Jesse, Don, Valerie, Gar.

Above: 1989   **Right: 1990**

photos by Murray B.

CHAPTER THREE

BATTLE #1

MICHAEL D.

1989-1991

"THAT PLACE IS A FESTERING SORE."
—BERKELEY ZONING BOARD MEMBER, 1991

1991   photo by Murray B.

MICHAEL D.

I first heard about the place in 1986. I heard that meetings were going on with a group of people who were opening up a new club. I was painting at the time, and I heard they were looking for people to do artwork on the walls. I started going there before it opened, became part of the art committee, and did some murals on the walls. I started going to shows there from the very beginning, New Year's Eve, 1986/1987. I was involved in the early punk scene in the late seventies, but had gotten really disenchanted with it before Gilman, due to the violence. I liked the ideas behind Gilman, their willingness to do more experimental-type shows, and slowly got more involved there, booking a few shows eventually. But differences arose between my outlook and Gilman's and I dropped out, and then Gilman closed for a little while in 1988.

1986   artist unknown

When it reopened, one of the people running it, Jonathan D., asked me to come back and check it out again. I started going there more, and started putting on some shows there again myself. I liked going to the meetings. More than the music, the idea of people working together was the hook for me. I was getting more involved and could see that the folks running the space were getting burned out, and when they left eventually, I stepped up and was voted in as head coordinator in late 1989.

I really liked how social Gilman was, too—you could really connect with people there. It seemed like total chaos at first, but eventually I settled into it. At first I felt I was carrying too much of the load, until others stepped up. One of the things I wanted to do was get rid of the racist skinheads who were coming to the shows to cause trouble. I contacted some of the local anti-racist groups and started working with them (two guys in particular, Nando and George, who would become head of security and head coordinator, respectively) to help us deal with the problem. There was one month in particular there that was very intense, basically life or death situations. I thought someone was going to get seriously hurt or killed. The skinheads would mass out front and threaten to attack us. We tried talking with them, and also made it clear we weren't backing down. One night, they did actually come in and start swinging. We were ready, beat them down, and they never really came back after that. There were some we took to court, too, and a couple of them ended up in jail. One of the other skinheads from that night threatened to sue Gilman because his car got messed up by the crowd at Gilman who were throwing things at it and pounding on it as the skinheads tried to get away, but nothing came of it. There were way too many witnesses that saw that the skinheads started it all.

I was head coordinator until late 1991, but George was more or less running things for the last six months I was there before he took over officially. I was burning out from all the work I was doing at Gilman, on top of my fundraising responsibilities for the Berkeley Free Clinic, where I was working at the time. Financially we were struggling too. Other promoters in the area got wind of this and rumors started surfacing about them being interested in "taking over" Gilman. We even had someone from Bill Graham Presents come and talk to me, not with an offer to take over the place, but giving me encouragement to stick with it and not give up, because we were a good "feeder" system for them. Bands would get their start at Gilman, and then once they became more successful, they would "move on" to the "established" clubs (run by Bill Graham Presents). He didn't want his "pipeline" closed down!

Confronting racism was something I didn't have to think twice about, but sexism was something I went through a real mindshift on because of Gilman. I was doing a lot of erotic art at the time and it definitely would not have been considered politically correct. Some of this was also being put into flyers for Gilman shows and I was confronted about being sexist. Also, some of the bands I was booking had sexist lyrics. That wasn't as easy an issue for me. I was strongly against censorship, but I did feel people had a right to speak out against what offended them. I felt that should be a part of the individual shows, as well as Gilman as a whole. But it didn't seem like many people were willing to get up on stage and speak out at shows. People could come to a membership meeting if they wanted to and ask that a certain band not play at Gilman. We'd talk about it and vote about having the band play or not. One night, a band with really offensive sexist, misogynist flyers was physically attacked and beaten up on stage, right when they started playing. We did end up "banning" some bands, but they weren't easy decisions to make. As an early punk rocker, we used to dismiss the politically correct people as "hippies." Now I was having to look closer at the whole issue. Also, I wanted the decisions to be made collectively, to keep the process open to everyone, because I didn't feel the process was entirely open to me during the first couple years of Gilman.

Our financial struggles also impacted our decisions, not only on who we booked, but how we dealt with them, too. There was a show we did with the band

Shattering Gilman's PC illusion, flyer by Jesse T.

Fugazi, where they asked us not to advertise because too many people would come and it would have been a problem. But we needed the money and advertised the show anyway (on top of which, the flyer was very controversial), which made Fugazi really mad at us. Money was a constant worry, whether we'd be able to pay the rent or not, etc. The Berkeley Zoning Board had received complaints from the police and neighbors about drinking/litter/vandalism around the club and, citing a restriction in our original use permit from 1986, wanted us to stop flyering and advertising. We came back to them with a proposal to be allowed to flyer for our shows. We also had volunteers from the club who went and talked to the neighbors in the area, door to door. That really helped. We packed a Zoning Board meeting with one hundred and fifty people, and were granted the authorization to flyer for shows. The Zoning Board said they had never had that many people show up for any one issue before. I think it certainly affected their decision, seeing how organized we were, and how vocal.

Another thing that helped the money situation was bringing back the membership concept. It had been dropped relatively soon after the second group had reopened Gilman in late 1988. It was brought back around the middle of 1990, and we started selling membership cards again. The money that came in because of that was one of the things that helped the club survive. It also helped give people a small sense that it was their club, too.

Another issue which came up toward the end of my time there, was that money seemed to be disappearing. I didn't know who was taking it or where it was going. This just added to my burnout, and I ended up pulling out. By 1992 I was just going to shows there occasionally and it's been a few years since I've been there. I just don't feel as comfortable there now.

There were a number of things I really liked about the club. I liked how fun the place was, the sense of humor, the camaraderie. It reminded me of how punk used to be in the seventies. As an artist, I really enjoyed making the flyers for shows. That was another thing that came out of the early punk scene—the great flyers.

I became more political because of Gilman, and I wanted to not only entertain people there, but also challenge them, politically and artistically. It was frustrating to not be able to do that to the extent I wanted. Gilman helped me deal with my drinking problem too. I knew I couldn't drink there and that helped my resolve to quit. There was lots of drinking and drug use going on there then, and I confronted as much of it as I could.

I look back with a lot of pride on my time at Gilman. One of the things I was most proud of was that I felt we had moved back to more of a collective ideal, like the way the space had started out, but that had been lost along the way. I think that was what saved the club. One of my best memories from Gilman was a show the Offspring were playing. It was during the Gulf War, right when it first started, and the crowd was almost entirely of draft age. When they started playing the song "Tehran," they changed the words to "Baghdad," and all the kids responded, everyone was holding up lighters, it was almost mystical, the intense feeling of community against that war.

When I was younger, I used to dream of being a club manager, so in a way, I lived out my dream.

Classic Michael D.   photo by Murray B.

JESSE TOWNLEY AKA JESSE LUSCIOUS

A couple of years ago, Brian Edge asked me to contribute some words and pictures covering the "Wild West" years at Gilman, roughly late 1989 through 1992. Finally, it's deadline time, and what follows is incomplete and completely capricious in whom it covers and whom it ignores.

This is a brief snapshot of a scene that spread from Benicia and Petaluma, down through Pinole and El Sobrante, through Albany and Berkeley, Oakland and San Leandro, Hayward and Fremont, over to Walnut Creek and Concord, across to San Francisco, and south to San Jose and Santa Cruz. That scene, in those years, covered club shows, skate missions, Tuesday night adventures, backyard keg parties, punk picnics, warehouse parties, weird Benicia toast rituals, coffee worship, and a hundred and one other quirks that every scene boasts of but no one outside of that scene cares about. Below are only a few of the Gilman volunteers from that time—I don't have the time or the memory to memorialize each person in the fashion they deserve. We were a tribe, a scene, full of gossip and secrets and full of unity and rivalry.

The East Bay (Crockett to Berkeley to Hayward) made fun of the West Bay (San Francisco) (and the West Bay took it seriously!) and vice versa, while the equally prolific and rockin' South Bay (San Jose and Santa Cruz) took the attention its immediate northern neighbors were getting as a personal dis and sulked. The North Bay (Santa Rosa, Petaluma, Benicia, and Vallejo) just kind of hung out wherever it felt like and had a good time. Just in the East Bay and Frisco, there was Gilman, Kommotion, the Women's Building, the Sixth Street Rendevous, People's Park, Punk Picnics in Dolores and Golden Gate Parks, Paradigm Studios, Collective Chaos, Eggplant's House, all of the Fraggle/Nana houses, and Your Place Too, not to mention a ton of bars that usually didn't let one in with a fake ID. But this book is about the Gilman Street Project and the people who played, volunteered, and partied there, so I'll try to keep it focused. These years at Gilman were my favorite, my fullest, and my fondest, although I am happily still a volunteer here.

Here's a brief word of introduction: I was born in New Jersey in 1970, and grew up in Philly. I went to my first punk show in September 1986. After briefly living in Ohio, Chicago, and New Haven, me and two companions drove across the country in my 1978 Mazda GLC ("Great Little Car"!) to Frisco to go to the 1989 San Francisco Anarchist Gathering. I had intended on joining an art magazine or some such endeavor. After I talked my way into my first Gilman Street show for free—it was the Anarchist Gathering show with MDC, Dead Silence, Yeastie Girlz, Kondom Nation, etc., on July 20, 1989—and crashing three weeks at infamous UC Berkeley coop Barrington Hall, I was hooked on the East Bay. The band I joined a few months after arriving in California—Blatz—was as much of a house band as any during the first two years I volunteered at Gilman.

I've been a recurring Gilman volunteer in one form or another since that first July night. I've run the snack bar, been stage manager, coordinator, cash box, membership, side door, volunteer and paid security, and was head booker for a year and a half in 1990-91. I've been the Secretary of the Corporation since 1991, which means that I've been responsible for making sure that membership minutes are taken and that I share legal responsibility for Gilman with the other two corporate officers. The only positions I haven't held are working sound or filling either of the other two corporate offices—and I'm not sure if that's an achievement or an indicator of personal stubbornness.

Enough with the bonafides, on with the dirt, er, the "anecdotes"...

"Fuk Ska", "Fuk Lou": After *Maximum RocknRoll* bowed out, Gilman Street re-opened in fall of 1988 with the backing of Marshall Stax (future member of Blatz and Subincision), Pat W., and Lou E. By the time I came to town less than a year later, Gilman's regular mix of underground music, booked solely on a percentage of the door (if that), was being supplemented by a series of "Lou" shows. These were big name ska shows at Gilman for which Lou paid the bands a certain amount out of his own pocket as a guarantee, and that featured big names like Bad Manners and the New York Citizens. He had a reputation among many punks for sleazy personal behavior.

My strongest recollection of his character occurred at a membership meeting in the side room when Jonathan was head of the club. In a depressing discussion about Gilman's money woes, Lou first pushed for installing a bar in the store (which made financial sense but was ethically ridiculous) before suggesting booking more hip hop/rap shows because "that's where the money is." Honestly, his comments were logical in a normal nightclub situation, but unfortunately he was in a completely DIY underground space that was dedicated to being more than just a place for drunk adults to hit on each other to the sound of loud background music. And while DIY hip hop has played Gilman before and after the Lou era, the motivations for booking the genre was never based on how much money could be made by Gilman.

A number of Gilman regulars, especially members of Filth, spraypainted "Fuk Lou" and "Fuk Ska" everywhere in Gilman, mostly in response to his creepy personal reputation, although a certain amount of his nightclub outlook was also targeted. Lou left Gilman by early 1990. He benefited greatly by the business contacts he had made at Gilman, and he eventually became, for a brief time, the preeminent Northern California ska booker at a time when future faves like the Dance Hall Crashers, Skankin' Pickle, Let's Go Bowling, and No Doubt were forming and building their core crowds. As a footnote, he eventually split town with the advance proceeds from a weekend-long outdoor ska festival called "Woodska" and was never heard from again.

Jonathan D. was the head of Gilman when I came onto the scene, and he was a meticulous record-keeper. Before the personal computer came to Gilman five years later, he was writing out all of the show receipts and the monthly income/expense sheets with precise penmanship on graph paper. He went on to become a research scientist, and over the next decade he stopped through the Bay Area in between stints at various labs around the country. While he was around he was moderately quiet (or maybe the rest of us were so fucking loud!) and my main memory of him on a personal level is when we went to see a rare Negativland show in San Francisco after he stepped aside from running Gilman. He kept his low-key sense of humor throughout, which was a tough thing to do, considering all of the mayhem that surrounded Gilman at the time.

Michael D. was the head of Gilman after Jonathan. He was (and still is, as far as I know) the volunteer coordinator of the Berkeley Free Clinic and a long-time member of the OTO (a pagan spiritual group). He had been a part of the local punk scene since possibly the beginning (!?), and stepped up to the Gilman plate in late 1990. His distinctly unkempt appearance, with his long dark hair and his continually askew glasses, combined with his unique dancing style, made him a local landmark. At one point he explained to me that he was harnessing the energy and power of the music for spiritual purposes, but that might have just been a joke on his part. Regardless, his five-foot-five form could be seen leaping about gesturing grandly even during the most thuggish of pits. The brilliant thing was that even the knuckleheads were in awe of him and couldn't figure out what Michael's deal was, so he'd be able to pirouette in an Accused or DI pit without being harmed.

I really got closely involved with the inner workings of Gilman while Michael was in charge. He was also a dedicated visual artist, and his cut-and-paste flyers, with his distinctive handwriting, were legion. He helped organize one of the first visual art shows I'd seen there, as well as booking some sort of solstice-style pagan-themed show with local art bands like Idiot Flesh and Caroliner. I can't remember if those two bands specifically played that show—if not, then the bands were others from the flourishing West Oakland art band scene that also popped up at venues like Merchants and the Heinz Club. Regardless, they were definitely what Dave EC, Stuart, and I (we were the other bookers at the time) called "Michael D." bands that he was putting on the Gilman stage. Other bands included Thinking Fellers Local and Sharkbait. Michael also was into a lot of the punk/funk scene that was exploding locally at the time, so he also got bands like Fungo Mungo, Smokin' Rhythm Prawns, and Psychefunkapus to come in and play. He may have been behind the New Year's Eve, 1989 show with Primus and Mr. Bungle, but I'm not sure.

Anyway, his different musical tastes dovetailed nicely with us other bookers since none of us had too much appreciation for most of the bands he brought in, although the diversity was vital to keeping Gilman vibrant and out of any rut. A lot of the local ska bands, like Skankin' Pickle, went great with the funk/punk bands also, so we could draw two different crowds to the same show.

Our chaos, or "band," Blatz, was practicing once a week at Gilman, splitting nights with Filth and the Vagrants. I was doing booking with Dave EC (drummer for both of those bands) on other nights. Dave, who looked like he was thirty at the age of 19, taught me how to book, and (more importantly) how to say "no." As in, "No, we won't book your band this month or next. Call back in July." He's also the first person I met who loudly proclaimed Gilman as the best club on the planet, no matter what its shortcomings. At the time, L.A. and parts of Northern California were being overrun by pay-to-play hellholes and burly bouncers with chips on their shoulders and Maglites in their hands. Bill Graham was still alive (hsss!) and the Berkeley Square, the Omni, and the Stone were still around booking all of the big money punk tours (which was a lot less than today's big money punk tours, but that's another subject) as well as the crossover and metal tours, and the majority of the local ska shows. Dave went on to play in The Winona Ryders, The Tantrums, and Three Years Down, and is now a proud father.

Stuart, the other main booker at the time, was a real estate agent who apparently dated from the beginning or near the beginning of the Frisco punk scene, and he was always trying to get SVT back together or have The Nuns play. He was booking when I got there, and he usually took care of a lot of the package tours (a lot of which came through Paul Rat of CD Presents and a booker at The Omni). He had a ton of stories that he usually only hinted at, but would slip up when he would say something like, "the first time I saw the Clash..." He kept out of most of the Gilman drama of the time, since he had ten years on most of us and his pals were of the older Frisco art-punk/recovering heroin addict variety—the kind that used to hang out at the Deaf Club and did drugs with Ginger Coyote and Crime. But he was always at shows at Gilman and elsewhere, and, like Michael D. and I, did a lot of flyers for the shows he booked in a very distinctive style.

Booking had a blast mixing up bands and genres on bills, sometimes to excess (the Sharkbait, Boom and the Legion of Doom, Skankin' Pickle, Good Riddance, Aspirin Feast show comes to mind), but on the whole it was a lot of hard work that had a great payoff every time the show went off well. Whether or not the kids showed up, everything was cool as long as the bands rocked. Off the top of my head, the shows I was proudest of in this time period were the Fuckups-Frightwig-Fugazi weekend and the Mentors vs. the Yeastie Girlz show. The F-F-F weekend flyers were plastered all over Telegraph, each one obscene in its own way, and the three shows were all diverse and rockin', although the Fugazi show dwarfed the other two shows attendance-wise. the Mentors vs. the Yeastie Girlz show was different because the two headlining bands couldn't have been more different, the for-

Flyers by Jesse T. for the F-F-F weekend. The Fugazi flyer is with Michael D.'s piece.

mer band being drunken scumbag loser guys singing about sluts and VD over punk-ish metal, and the latter being an a capella politically correct feminist rap band. Both bands were infamous enough that the show drew three hundred-plus to see the carnage—as it happened, the Mentors were so drunk that they couldn't make it through one song without screwing up so badly they had to lurch to a halt, so the Yeastie Girlz walked away the winner by a mile!

PJ and George S. showed up as girlfriend/boyfriend from New York City, their relationship lasted something like three weeks after their arrival. As far as I could tell, they had a positive parting, which was good, because PJ was one tough skitch ("skin bitch") yet a real good person to have on your side. One time I had booked Judge on a Sunday show, and I was heckling them (I think "Straight Edge Revenge" or some other Project X reference) and the guitarist put down his guitar and wanted to fight me. PJ, being a pal from the NYC scene, told him that if it wasn't for me, they wouldn't be playing there, since I booked 'em and loved NYHC as much as any breathing punk fan did at that time (although the recurring machismo has always been a turn-off).

George S. was the brightest shooting star of those days, if only for his quick appearance and leadership ability, and his subsequent drop off the face of the earth. No one, not even his ever-evolving harem, could piece together his actual past, but his earnestness and ideologically driven gentleness made all of us want to trust him.

He succeeded Michael D. as head of Gilman in 1991, after helping to revitalize our security with Nando and Motorhead. He presided over the truly "Wild West" days of Gilman, when the local nazi skins were having their last hurrah before moving to Portland en masse. Gilman was two months behind on rent every month, and Bay Area bands like Green Day, Generator, Downfall, Rancid, Filth, Paxston Quiggly, Neurosis, Anger Means, Blatz, Gr'ups, Econochrist, Jack Acid, Fifteen, Cringer, Grinch, Asbestos Death, Gargoyles, 23 More Minutes, Corrupted Morals, East Bay Mud, Monsula, Fuel, Lungbutter, Jawbreaker, Samiam, The Aborted, Blister, Schlong, Total Fucked, and Sinister Sisters of Satan, were coming up in the

Flyer by Jesse T. and Stuart   Flyer by Jesse T. and Zoe

footsteps of the original Gilman bands like Operation Ivy and Crimpshrine (as well as some who were still around who had pre-dated Gilman, like Mr. T Experience and Special Forces). Other local DIY institutions that were active included *Maximum RocknRoll* fanzine, Epicenter Records and Blacklist Mailorder (MRR being the only survivor today).

As George's right-hand man, this was my favorite Gilman era, a time when I was completely immersed in the people and the bands and the shows. George's one-year of head honcho ended with a fizzle, involving some girl in Rhode Island, a massive Gilman long-distance phone bill, and swirling allegations that he skimmed money from the door receipts. In all honesty, I never saw him take money at any point during this time, and I was involved with counting all of the money nightly. However, I never dealt with actually depositing the proceeds in our bank account or with paying the bills. A friend of mine swears that she and George spent a bunch of show proceeds one time. However, in George's defense I've gotta say that she was/is battling a heroin addiction and I had problems sometimes figuring out when she was being straightforward and when she was "embellishing" reality for her own ends while in the throes of addiction.

People ask me about George stealing from the club as if it was an established fact, and all I can offer them is the allegation above. The circumstantial evidence supporting these allegations, which is that once Mike Stand took over the following year he wrestled Gilman back into the black, isn't convincing, since Gilman had been steadily losing money for years before George took over. Still, people believe what they want to about his reign, and I fear that his otherwise energetic, fun, crazy, and inspirational tenure as head of Gilman is permanently tainted by the questions about money.

Mike Stand, who took over after George, was a funny fucking guy who cracked me up when I first came to Gilman. He had been involved with Gilman off and on since the beginning. Mike was great with making Gilman solvent but he was horrible at dealing with people. He drove out certain long-time volunteers like Russ Wordburger in a fucked-up manner. After a particularly contentious booking meeting, he made me so angry because of his anti-collective intentions that I almost quit Gilman completely. As his "thorn in his side" second in command, I'm sure such a move on my part would have been welcomed by him, but I couldn't stand the thought of him having the satisfaction of adding me as a notch to his metaphorical gun belt, so I stuck it out. Since then we've warily worked together, especially when city-based crises have arisen (Pyramid, DiCon), and although we often are like oil and water when Gilman strategy/processes come up, we've gotten along better as the years pass. Heck, now we even hang out in some of the same social circles and it's almost as if we hadn't had such major ethical differences all those years ago.

Fraggle and Nana, two SoCal expatriates, turned up around the same time I did and hosted a bunch of crazy parties at a number of their houses that are legendary. Starting out with Dementia House, across from the West Oakland BART station, moving to the old Fang house at 8th and Peralta (where the Sinister Sisters of Satan and Bill C. [Fang, Special Forces, MDC] and Aisha [photographer extraordinaire] lived upstairs), and ending with the Pill Hill Zoo House behind 29th & Telegraph, their parties featured almost every local punk band from 1989-1995. Fraggle and Nana ended up working the door at Gilman (like James M. of the Tim Yo Gilman era) for a few years during this time as well. They were dedicated like the rest of us, slogging through the seventeen-person shows (Sloppy Seconds in late 1989) as well as the six hundred-plus-person shows (Fugazi every May 20th). One show, I threw Nana out for the night since she drunkenly kicked her way into instigating a fight in the pit. She didn't appreciate it at the time (that's being polite!) but it wasn't fair to let a regular volunteer do stupid shit that we'd throw out a patron for doing. Fraggle's infamous for being a beer snob, and he actually taught me a ton about fancy-schmancy beer that, thankfully for my wallet, never stuck. Both of them are still in the area and still involved in different parts of the local music scene.

Carrie, who eventually married George S. and had a child with him, was intimately involved with Gilman as a general worker and as security. Tough but nice, she stuck with Gilman throughout the Wild West days and was a voice of intelligence and moderation when it counted. She was an ex-skitch who took very little shit.

At this point Gilman was in the throes of the Wild West days, with great bands and people and just as great debt—we were two to three months behind in our rent for a year or two in this period. There was still a sizeable nazi skinhead problem and a number of regular troublemakers who had been 86'd for years but still hung out most weekend nights outside drinking. Often, these two groups mingled and hung out together. Most of their activity involved hanging out talking shit and being tough guys and gals, not usually physical violence. When it did occur, it was usually five on one or similar skinhead tactics.

At one memorable Rock Against Racism show, which featured local punk band MDC and local hip hop band APG Crew, thirty nazis showed up to start shit and eventually got chased down the street by a bunch of the three hundred audience members in attendance that night.

Other nights Gilman's survival was much more in doubt. One night in particular, the show only drew about thirty people and ten burly nazis showed up across the street and started yelling threats to the three main security people, who were all black—George S., Nando, and Motorhead. The nazis crossed the street and security locked themselves outside to deal with the skins and sent me to guard the side door with a baseball bat. We kept the patrons inside while the nazis were outside in order to keep the situation simple and to make sure unwitting patrons didn't get hurt in a melee. Motorhead had a chain he was swinging around his head, and since he was seven feet tall it must have been a sight to see—whuup, whuup, whuup! Punches were thrown, the nazis ran around the building towards the side door, which I slammed shut quickly, bat in hand. The nazis were eventually driven off a little bloodier than when they showed up, but we were also hurt—I think Nando got a broken nose. Thankfully the racist skins didn't realize that if they had been able to enter Gilman they probably could've overwhelmed the small crowd of patrons and volunteers and caused major damage to Gilman.

Of course, where would they then go to start shit and see and be seen? Would they start busting up all-black bars in East Oakland or brawl with gay bikers at the Stud? These questions will never be answered, because right around this time they started to move up to Portland, Oregon en masse. I think the heat down here was a little too much, perhaps, from activities like the "Reclaim Mayday" antiracist march down San Francisco's Haight Street, during which local nazis were attacked, and from a violent but dedicated group called Bay Area Anti-Racist Action (BAARA). BAARA was originally welcome at Gilman, but then they beat up a band, Total Fucked, who they thought were nazis, on stage at Gilman during a show. We 86'd them for fighting and since then have really avoided working with vigilante-style groups, no matter what their ultimate aims or underlying politics.

You know, there are a ton of people I want to write about, who made our community a living, breathing entity, and there's no way I will be allowed the space to give them all their due. Some of them have written things for this book, others are lost to new beaus, new children, or new convictions (both criminal and philosophical). Some are still my best friends, others are faded to acquaintances or even enemies. So instead of excluding everyone there's no time or space to write about, I'm just gonna list as many people as I can:

Flyer by Jesse T. and Fraggle

Dean Dean the Sex Machine, Ken Wisconsin, Sally and Special Brian, Brian Anger Means, Marcus the Red, Joel W., Eric Y., Kevin D., Elspeth, Ernst, Joey P., Marcus the Anarchist, Marshall Stax, Anna Joy, Annie L., Eggplant, Lance, Gardner, Harry, Janel, Janelle, Scribble, Murray B., Kamala, Mark Public Humiliation, Owen, Jim K., Jim T., Skot P., Russ Wordburger, Motorhead, Rigger, Brett R., Pete and Chelsea, Mike-o the Psycho, Jim Filth, Julia D., Adrienne, Todd, Paula, Karin, Jesse M., Aaron Cometbus, Jerme Spew, Jux, Jim P., Damon, Dan K., Rick S., Alexandria, Ewan, Dana, Larry Livermore, Pat H., Chrisser, David H., Mike Scott, Jeff O., Mark M., Matt F., Lint, Holly, Saul, Billie Joe, Gar, Elliott, Claude, Mike D., Kelsey, Carrie Neighbor, Monica Neighbor, Jorin, Rachel, Jean R., Becca B., Tall Tim, Shane, James W., Robin T., Melissa, Carrie Jean, Tom C., Evan Benicia, Al Sob, Tre Cool, Heather H., Heather P., Lenny, Blythe, Jake H., Jake S., Pete Inc., Steve List, Zoe, John D., Cheryl, Matthew Sinister Sisters, Ariadne, Ben S., John S., Markley, Dave Ed, Ron Grinch, Spider, Noah, Wendy, A-head, Anna B., Kaz, Justin the Monk, Sean Benicia, Sean Lungbutter, Mondia, Salerinda, Orlando, Siberia, Nando, Heather C., a ton of people and a ton of bands. This isn't even close to representative, but it's 10 years and a ton of new faces and fresh bands later. Apologies to the people I know I missed, and for whom I'll smack my forehead as soon as I'm done with this and say, "I can't believe I forgot…!"

For me, Gilman Street was, and is, a mad experiment, a blueprint for the future, and controlled chaos, all in one place.

Editor's note: Jesse is running for Berkeley City Council in 2004

DEAN D. aka DEAN NAKED

I found out about Gilman by coincidence. I moved up to the Bay Area from San Diego when I was 21. I was living in my car. One Friday evening I was going through the *SF Weekly* looking for something to do, this was Sept. 1989. I saw a listing for some bands that were playing in Berkeley. That was my first time going to Gilman. I was very surprised and confused when I first got there. I was used to shows in San Diego that were held at union halls or YMCAs, places like that. So I walked into the place, and there was graffiti everywhere, weird artwork on the walls, punks everywhere. It was obvious it wasn't a place that was just rented out for the night. I thought everyone was really friendly. I talked to a few people, found a place to crash, became friends with some of the folks there, and started going there more, at first just to see the shows. Then my car and all my possessions got stolen, I lost my job, and was living on the streets for a while. One of the people at Gilman that I knew said that they had had problems with people trying to break in and steal the sound equipment, so he asked if I wanted to sleep at Gilman and keep an eye on the place at night. I believe some band gear had actually been stolen out of there once, drums or something like that someone had left there. When people came back the next morning, they found the side door open and the gear was gone.

I ended up living at Gilman for about seven months. That was Feb. to Aug. of 1990. During that time, the club was my life. I slept on the couch in the office. I had no job and just a few possessions. I found out that Gilman was haunted. Chairs would fall over. One of the bathroom doors would close by itself. The bathroom stall doors would slam by themselves. It really threw my sleep patterns off, because I'd be there at night, by myself, and hear all these weird goddamn noises. So I'd spend half the night walking around with an axhandle. I never found out any explanation for this weird stuff. There were a couple times when I did hear people prying on the side door. So I'd walk over to the door and yell "who the fuck's out there?" and hear them run away. I took it upon myself to try and keep the place clean. I would fix the toilets. I would answer the booking phone and leave messages for the bookers.

During this time, there used to be loads of hookers up on San Pablo Avenue. I had met one in passing a few times, on a trip to the liquor store or wherever. One night she was sitting at the bus shelter in front of the Chevron Station and we got talking and she told me that she had been robbed the other night while turning a trick in a car, and nearly beat up. So I told her that if she had nowhere else to go that was safe, and it was a weeknight, to bring her trick to the club, I'd let her in, and she could use the office real quick. She said that would be great, and that she'd give me five dollars for every trick I'd let her turn in there. So, about two or three times a week she'd show up with somebody, I'd let her in, she'd go with him into the office, come back out, give me five dollars, and they'd be on their way. The door to the office would be left unlocked. If there was any problem, I'd come in and deal with it. This lasted a few months. She came to a show once to see what the place was about. I kept it a secret at the time, didn't tell anyone what I was doing, because I knew that they'd put a stop to it and tell me I couldn't do that anymore.

About a month or two after I started living there, one of the security guards, Motorhead, moved in as well. I had the office, he had the sound loft. Bands were practicing there Monday, Tuesday, and sometimes Sunday (when there wasn't a show) nights. People would stop by and hang out. A couple of times there were OTO/Aleister Crowley meetings/readings there, complete with candles, robes, cat o' nine tails, etc. Band demos were recorded on Thursday nights. Saturday afternoons, basket-weaving classes were held by the Caning Shop next door. It was pretty funny seeing 55-year-old women weaving baskets in this hellhole. Apparently, after I left, it turned into Motorhead and about two dozen people staying there, mostly Telegraph Avenue gutter punks. Having that many people living there though did piss the landlord off, and he put a stop to it. I think it started from people crashing there after cleaning up after the shows on weekends, and then progressed to them staying there all week. These were considered the Wild Wild West days. The place was run so chaotically.

I helped out in the store during shows. I started the tip jar. It was one of my meager sources of income. I also recycled all of the empty cans and bottles. I would use Gilman as a job reference. I got more into the ideology of the club. I really liked working at a space that was all-volunteer run. At first I was there just because I had nowhere else to go and nothing else to do, then I got more into the reasons why the club was there in the first place. I didn't like the meetings though. Too much insanity, voting on whether to vote or not, things like that. I had a good gig going on with the liquor store up the street. I was in there so often that I got to be friends with the clerks there. I would tell them who was playing that weekend and what to stock up on, and they would sell me beer for cheap.

I ended up being called Dean Naked after a show where I was naked on stage with Blatz. It came about because one of their singers, who always got naked when they played, was out of town, but the band played anyway. Since he wasn't there, I got up on stage and took off my clothes while they were playing. Of course I was totally drunk. After throwing my clothes into the audience, I ran out the side door, completely naked, and closed the door behind me. Of course it was raining. So I had to go around to the front door, get back in, and try to find my clothes. The name also came from people walking in on me and my girlfriend having sex in the office.

Another show I remember, in 1990, MDC was playing, and a friend and I were down the street drinking, when we heard this loud commotion in the street outside Gilman. We went to check it out and we saw a street full of people carrying sticks and things. When we got closer we saw a Ford Bronco full of skinheads tearing out and across the intersection with all the people in the street beating on it. It turned out that the skins had come to rush the door and fuck up Gilman that night. They definitely chose the wrong night. Later, there was actually a lawsuit brought against Gilman by the skinhead who owned the Bronco, who wanted to sue Gilman for the damage done to his vehicle. Nothing came of it—I think it was thrown out. They did have a private investigator come and check the place out though, one afternoon. I suggested he come to a meeting.

I moved away for a while, then came back in early 1991 and stayed at Gilman again really briefly, but by that time no one could live there anymore. I started working there again sometimes, until I started going to art school, which was late 1991. By then I had realized I had developed a drinking problem, and was spending less and less time at Gilman. Much later, around 1995, out of loneliness, I started going to Gilman again. I missed the place. I missed the sense of community I got out of it. I missed the idea of having something to do with my time, the sense of doing something worthwhile. Gilman was my first experience with people doing something just because they thought it was the right thing to do, and I wanted to be a part of that again. Seeing the people again who worked at keeping the place open inspired me to want to help. I started working in the store again every weekend.

I tried going to the AA meetings at Gilman, and I think that helped some. I think it would have made those first few weeks of attempted sobriety a lot harder if it weren't for Gilman. Friday and Saturday nights were the only nights of the week where I was relatively sober. I knew something had to change because things were getting pretty bad for me. I was suicidal, and tried to have myself committed at Alameda County Mental Health. They wouldn't take me because of my history with alcohol. I went to a treatment center, went on Prozac, and it seemed to work. July 22, 1996 was my last drink. Gilman had a very prominent role in saving my life—the support system of working there and the friends I made there was hugely important to me. I've seen how the club on many occasions gave street kids some focus in their lives. It provided an option to spare-changing and drinking 40s on Telegraph. Suburban kids, too, who feel incredibly misfit, can find that they're not the only ones who feel out of place, like rejects at school, or in life in general. It also provided a place where they could feel comfortable with their sexuality.

I continued working at the store on a continuous basis until about Oct. 1997. Since that time, I just hang out there once in a while on a casual basis, working if they need someone to work. I'll always feel attached to the place. I'm just not there every weekend, anymore, because I'm 31 years old now—I realized one night there that that's pretty old in punk rock years when a 17-year-old called me "sir." I've always wanted to have "geezer" night at Gilman, where everyone sits in rocking chairs, and dresses in overalls, smoking corn cob pipes, lined up in front of the club, on the "porch" so to speak, a bunch of over-30 punks sitting around, talking about the "good old days."

Over the years I've been there, I think the club has definitely changed for the better. The organization the club needed is there, now—it's no longer three months behind in rent, it's no longer hated by the cops and all the neighbors. If the club had continued to be run in the same manner as it had been back in 1990-early 1991, it wouldn't be open at all anymore. But the essence of the place, what goes on there, is the same as it ever was—it's what punk rock really is, hyperkinetic mis-fit teenagers. Just from my own perspective, and I wasn't around during the days when MRR ran the club, but I think that if I had come across the club during the MRR time, that I would have been a little turned off by the place. It struck me, from what I read, as a project for this kind of annoying, intellectual niche of punk rock. It seemed like people were trying to rub their own personal views and ideologies into teenage music for teenagers. Beyond the fact that Gilman is run as a collective, I don't feel there should be too much socialist or anarchist ideology around the place.

Photo by Larry W.

FRAGGLE

I first went to Gilman around 1987/1988. I lived in Southern California at the time and used to come up for shows occasionally. I was amazed when I went to the place for the first time. It was so different from what I was used to in Southern California. It was much more of a family, a sense of belonging—there was graffiti everywhere, and everyone was having a good time, jumping around, toys all over, Big Wheels, stuff like that. In Southern California there'd be fighting, guns, knives, gang stuff. Gilman was a total breath of fresh air.

I moved to the Bay Area in 1989, and Gilman was one of the main reasons I moved there, mostly just to be able to go there more often. I didn't know much about how you could volunteer at Gilman—it took me a few weeks to figure that out. I don't remember what spurred me to volunteer there, it just sorta happened. I first volunteered there around the middle of 1989—I was 22. I had volunteered at a club in Connecticut, Anthrax, for a little bit, but Gilman was my first big experience. Once I took that first step, I was hooked—it was kind of an "overnight" thing. I was there for every show, every weekend. I mostly worked the door, handled the cash. I was happy doing that. I also did some security and booked a few shows. The place just really clicked with me—the people, the atmosphere, all of it. I went there more as a friendship thing than to see a particular band. It was a place to go. It definitely felt like more of a community center to me than just a punk club. The various social circles worked pretty well together at Gilman, but didn't necessarily hang out together outside of Gilman. We'd go to the same parties, things like that. We'd stay at Gilman after the shows a lot. We'd clean up and hang out, sleep there when it was cold and raining, huddling under the heater. Most of us didn't have cars and some of us had nowhere else to go.

I worked there steadily until about 1991, and then sporadically after that until around 1993, when I started volunteering again regularly for a little bit, around two months or so. After that I rarely went again. Once I stopped volunteering, my attendance rate dropped off enormously.

 I don't think I had any particular visions or plans for the place. Especially in the beginning, I was just so awed by it all, it was kind of overwhelming. It felt good just to be part of it. There were things I didn't like about the club. I think it got really cliquish. And I always hated the membership thing. It ended up being just a way to make more money. As far as good things go, one of the really good things about Gilman was that your own peers were doing security, "policing" you I guess is a good way to put it. And if you got drunk or out-of-hand you wouldn't get punched, you'd get taken aside and reasoned with first. You definitely felt like security wasn't going to hurt you or hurt somebody else, as opposed to some big thug with a Maglite, like at other clubs. When I was there I had a real feeling of solidarity with everyone, like if there was a fight I was trying to break up, everyone would help. I don't see/feel that same sense of solidarity there now.

There was one point, during the time I was there regularly, when no one came to the membership meetings—it was usually just the same six people. So when there was a problem, and people got really upset about it, then they'd all show up at a meeting and force through some really asinine rules. Then, two weeks later, it would only be those six people again, and they would revoke it all. I think punks in general just don't stay in decision-making processes like that very long. They have very short attention spans and it just doesn't hold together. My own enthusiasm waxed and waned. There were times when I was working there that I didn't want to come anymore. But for the most part, I liked working there and I liked going there. The people who really cared about the club were usually always there, the key people, like George, Marcus, Scary Mike, Jesse, Nando, myself, and various new people who would always turn up. I think Gilman's reputation made people come and want to volunteer. People were coming from all over the country. I remember some people who came from New York and didn't even want to see the show, they just wanted to work and be a part of Gilman.

Gilman was really important to me in that it helped me open up a lot and made me more comfortable doing things and trying more things. I have lots of good memories from Gilman, and I made lots of good friends. I think Gilman renewed a lot of hope for me. That's something I still have, the idea that not everybody in the world is an asshole.

I think Gilman is still really important to the community and the kids; I think they still need a place like that. I've outgrown it, whether that's a good thing or a bad thing or a jaded thing—whatever. When I go there now, I feel uncomfortable. The sense of belonging is gone, I don't hardly know anyone there anymore. The few people I do know seem kind of burnt out, too. It just doesn't seem as exciting and happening anymore. It doesn't feel like home anymore. But knowing what it was for me—it won't be like that for me again. Those times are gone, there's no going back. Maybe it'll be like that for someone else in the future. Maybe it's like that for someone there now. If I walked in there now and had never seen the place, I'd still think it was an incredible place. Gilman did a number of benefits for me to help pay my medical bills after I got in a couple of accidents in 1991. They were incredibly supportive of me. I can't think of hardly any place other than Gilman that would take care of people that way.

Looking very urbane 1991   photo by Murray B.

STEVE LIST

I first went to Gilman about three months after it first opened. I wasn't too into the bands playing at that time, so for the first two or three years I only went maybe a total of six times. I first heard about it on KALX, they were playing public service announcements about the club, letting people know it was being put together and to come down and help out. I wasn't interested at that time in getting involved in it, but I kept track of what was going on with it. I was curious about it. My first impression of the place was that it was pretty neat. There were a lot of people there, and it seemed like it was open to anybody who wanted to come in. It was like a little community, a community of people who don't fit in anywhere else necessarily. It seemed like almost anyone could fit in at Gilman, as long as they were not violent, and they treated others with respect.

Around 1989 or so, I started going more often, around twice a month. Once I started the List, in June 1990, I started going there pretty much every week, one or two shows a week. I was having fun there. It's one of the few places I can go to and feel as comfortable as I do at home. I started learning more about the bands. When I first started going there I didn't know any of the bands, and what type of music they played. After I started finding some bands I liked, it gave me something else to do, to get away from TV. It gradually became more of a social thing—I'd go there just to visit people and catch up on things. Sometimes I'll find myself outside talking to people the whole show. I think a lot of people go there just to hang out and socialize.

Despite the constant flow of new people coming in, the atmosphere has been pretty consistent over the years. Gilman offers the same thing now as it did when it first opened in 1987. It's been the same type of music all along—that hasn't changed. At first I was a little surprised at how young the people were who ran the place, but now I think that it's probably the best way to run it. The younger people seem to have more motivation and energy, and if it weren't for these younger people, Gilman probably wouldn't have lasted this long. It makes me think that young people should run more things. Gilman's a great learning factory too. A lot of people have gone on to other jobs and taken the skills that they learned at Gilman with them: management skills, interactivity with other people, etc. Gilman's almost like a school in that respect. Older people often get too set in their ways, and the younger people are more willing to listen to others, and adapt as necessary. They're more open to new suggestions.

I've never felt out of place there. I'm probably one of the oldest people (48) that goes there a lot. The music, I think, mainly appeals to younger people, but the atmosphere or environment can be appreciated by all. It is an "all ages" club. I never had any place like this when I was growing up. My mom was involved in a teen center when I was growing up. It was run by adults, not by the kids, and it shut down primarily because it didn't get used by the kids. It wasn't even geared toward input from the kids. I've never worked a show at Gilman. I've hauled the garbage out to the dump occasionally, stuff like that.

Gilman was a major factor in starting the List. If it weren't for Gilman, I probably wouldn't have started the List. At first, the List was pretty much only available at Gilman. Gilman provided a lot of motivation and inspiration, and still does. I still really enjoy doing the List—it's fun for me, and the feedback and thanks I get for doing it is nice too. If I wasn't doing the List, I might not even be going to Gilman now—it'd be easy to drift away from the music scene in general. I think Gilman has made me a lot more open to other people. I've been meeting a lot more people than I would have if I didn't go to Gilman. It's gotten me interested in other people's views, and increased my political awareness—increased my interest in what's going on in the world around me. I'm more open to other beliefs and ideals than I would be if I didn't go to Gilman—it's broadened my horizons quite a lot. The people in general seemed pretty informed at Gilman and help others to learn what's going on.

I think Gilman's more important and effective now than it ever has been, and I see it getting more effective in the future. It's inspired a lot of people to try and do the same thing in their own communities. Or, on another level, it's inspired people to do zines, or start bands, or even start their own business. I'd like to see Gilman do more outreach and help others in other communities set up places like it. I think every city should have a place like Gilman. Gilman's a major part of my life—I enjoy going there a lot, the people are fantastic. There's been some bad nights, but the good has far outweighed the bad. I'll always remember the packed, inspirational, sold-out shows, everybody happy and into it, kids hanging from the rafters. Being hot and sweaty, but having so much fun that I didn't want to be any place else on earth.

Above: 1991   photo by Murray B.

Above: 1991   photo by Susan S.

SUSAN S.

One of the main reasons for the existence of Gilman is to be a vehicle for personal expression. One look at the walls inside, with their countless layers of band names, spraypaint, artwork, tags, stickers, flyers, and absurd commentary will tell you this. It is meant to be a place where anyone can come down, participate, and let their creativity run riot. Although it is often described as being run by a monolithic "collective," Gilman is made up of a diverse collection of individuals. Over and over, I've seen new people get involved, contribute to the club, and grow from the experience. An all ages, volunteer-run club is vital as an example that young people can control their own cultural interests independent of the dominant mainstream culture.

1993   photo by Susan S.

The endurance of Gilman (thirteen years and counting at the time of this writing) is explained by the continual growth of punk rock. Punk hasn't gone away, because it's relevant to the times. Mainstream society is as corrupt and oppressive and disgusting as it ever has been, producing enough pissed off, alienated people to keep punk thriving. In this context, Gilman is a safe zone for punk and others who don't fit into society's straightjacket. For most of those who get involved at Gilman, punk is not only a form of music entertainment, but it's also a counterculture. Values of DIY and resistance to any corporate influence are at the core of Gilman's existance. This, more often than not, causes Gilman to rise above the typical bullshit and rigors associated with some of your average mainstream venues. Of course, there are always exceptions to the rule. I have seen more mind-crushingly boring shows at Gilman than I

1991   photo by Susan S.

care to remember. Because it is established, Gilman lacks the insane punk rock ingenuity of having shows at say, a chewed-up old Filipino nightclub, a club for the deaf, or a spontaneous show at a BART station plaza. But there is still much to be said for stability.

It has been said that politics in its most basic form consists of interactions between people: how we treat each other. Although this is pure idealism, I'm always hoping that Gilman will bring out the best in people. For a long time now, I've been telling others that I have met many of the best people I've ever known through Gilman. The club's sense of community is something that attracted me to it at first, and keeps me coming back. Of course, Gilman has always had its share of personality conflicts, shit-talking, egos, attitudes, animosity, and dysfunction. This just goes to show that for all of our superior punk rock posturing, nobody is free from the mental damage inflicted on us by mainstream society. I've heard people shower Gilman with incredible praise and others say it should burn down. So Gilman isn't perfect, surprise, surprise. But as an example of punk theory put into practice, Gilman stands out with the best of them. At the end of the day, even when the worst happens, Gilman is still worth it.

Record Swap, 1992   photo by Susan S.

1992   photo by Susan S.

CHRIS A.

When I was 13 or 14, I moved from the Bay Area to Humboldt County, a rural area in Northern California. The nearest town was called Garberville, and had about 2000 people. I came across an issue of *Maximum RocknRoll* magazine and then started reading it more often, and followed the beginnings of Gilman. I also was reading *Lookout* magazine, which came out in a nearby town, and that magazine was talking about Gilman as well.

I met Lawrence, who put out *Lookout* magazine and co-founded Lookout Records with David H., at a show in Arcata, where some of the bands on the *Turn It Around* Gilman comp played—this was around March 1988. I was 15 at the time, and had a radio show on a small local radio station. Lawrence and I corresponded for a little bit, and then he asked me if he could come up and be on my radio show. We ended up eventually doing the show together. Through that, I started going to Gilman with him. Prior to that, I had only been to Gilman once, mid-1987, when I was 14, while visiting relatives in the Bay Area. It was exciting to go to the place and see the things put in practice that I had read about. MRR's publicity was a huge part of making Gilman a big deal, nationwide and even globally. I don't think Gilman would have touched as many people without it.

For me, the place lived up to the hype. It wasn't overblown—it was that good. My cousin, who was older than me, had gone with me that first time; it was his first time too, and he ended up working the door that night and making a bunch of friends. It astounded me how human and personable the place was. The music and art was all real exciting. Before going to Gilman, I couldn't really differentiate what made punk rock better then say, Depeche Mode, or other mainstream bands that were on the radio. Then I started seeing this humanity and personality and connection that you just couldn't have if you were a fan of Tina Turner or Bruce Springsteen, for instance. Also, the band members were people my age. I felt really empowered, probably more than I realized at the time, to do things myself, to take myself a little bit more seriously, and to believe that I could have important thoughts, and put them across to others in a fanzine or a song.

So I became a more regular visitor to Gilman, even though it was about a 200-mile trip for much of my teenage years. The radio show was Saturdays, and then we'd either come down to Gilman for the rest of the weekend, or go to Lawrence's house and stuff records or do mail order for Lookout Records—this was late 1988. Some weekends it was a crazy combination of both. I was getting the impression that I was involved in something much bigger than myself.

My further involvement with Lookout Records was a point of connection and a bridge to Gilman, since it was such a fertile ground for great new bands, as well as a great place to meet good people. It was also a difficult place to come into things from, since I had to maintain somewhat of a business relationship with the people in the bands on the label, people who I was friends with. It was different than I think most people's experiences were with Gilman. I moved back to the Bay Area in early 1991, to go to school at UC Berkeley and work at the label full time. I only lasted one semester at college.

Once I started touring with my own bands, I could see the revolution, of sorts, that Gilman had started across America, and the many DIY clubs that had formed, inspired by Gilman. My first band started in summer 1991. I had attempted to form bands prior to that, but they didn't work out. The pinnacle, to me, was being able to play Gilman. We couldn't imagine playing anywhere else. We formed to play at Gilman. For us, the musicianship was really secondary to the camaraderie of having a band, the social status of it. Gilman was able to reach people, or touch them, or connect with them, in a way that other clubs didn't. People even from far away could feel like there was some bit of themselves reflected in the place, and would try to reach it, to see for themselves. There have also been a huge amount of great bands that have provided a soundtrack and attitude for the place—that's been a big component of the "mystique." Punk to me, before Gilman, was a bit sinister, and more closely related to metal. Gilman helped open up new ideas and new ways of approaching punk.

Another thing I think is really great about Gilman, is that as much of an institution as Gilman is, it's maintained a certain irreverence throughout—that's been part of its charm. I never had a problem with the bands I was in being labelled as "Gilman bands," and I don't understand why some of the bands did have a problem with it. Lookout experienced this for a while too, being known somewhat as the "Gilman label." Perhaps it was because of the impression people had that Gilman wasn't serious enough, wasn't real enough. But maybe one of the reasons Gilman still exists is that you need to be like that—you don't have to have those more traditional ways to survive, or even thrive.

Lookout Records would not exist today if it weren't for Gilman. It might have lasted for a short period of time, but the inspiration and source of all the bands wouldn't have been there without Gilman. I certainly wouldn't be where I am now, running this record label, without Gilman. Gilman directly contributed to my experience in understanding the world in which Lookout exists and I now have to guide the label through. That was the place where I "cut my teeth," so to speak, conducting business there, or the donut shop or pizza place up the street. I have no idea what I'd be doing if I didn't have Lookout. I've always taken Lookout seriously and thought that it was something important and valuable, both to me and to the community. I'd like to think that we've given something back to Gilman, or helped it out, as well. Maybe someone is familiar with a band on our label, but not Gilman, and they'll go there to see that band, and really like the place and start working there, or tell their friends to go there, etc. If Gilman needed our help financially, or in some other capacity we could provide, Lookout would contribute what it could, definitely. It would be important to do so, for me personally as well as for Lookout as a whole. We owe it to Gilman to be there for them if necessary—as a relative, as a member of the family.

As far as bands on Lookout being "too big" to play Gilman, or having "outgrown" it, that usually only happens when they've "outgrown" Lookout as well. I'll always want bands on Lookout to play there. I still see Gilman as very important. I'm no longer the 14 or 15-year-old that I was, so sure, Gilman doesn't speak to me in the same way it once did. I wonder, sometimes, if I were 14 or 15 now, would Gilman be exciting? I believe it still would be. There hasn't been a change in how deep of a meaning it has for me, from the excitement of it when I was first discovering it, to seeing how big a role it's played over the years in the job I have now, and how it's changed my life, and what it's done for me. Gilman showed me how a business could be run in an honest, ethical, and straightforward way, and how to treat people fairly and equitably, and also how to have a strong element of humanity and sociability in business dealings.

I became a full-time employee of Lookout Records in 1989, when David H.

left, and became president/owner in late 1996 when Lawrence left. I was 23 at that time. One thing that made it easier to make the decision about running Lookout, and to become responsible for its 14 employees as well, was seeing the strength and power that young people had at Gilman, and drawing inspiration from that, seeing what they could do. It helped me understand my own capabilities, believe in myself, and visualize what I could accomplish. I hope this piece can convey in some small way the gravity of the impact Gilman has had on me.

1994   photo by Murray B.

THESE ARE FROM SPRING 1991.   Page 1 or

Rules: *"The rules is the rules"*

1. No booze or drugs in possession or use in or around the club at any time for any reason. No vandalism in around the club. (Around the club is within two blocks.) This is the biggie, folks.

2. No stagediving or excessively violent dancing during the show.

3. No stealing from the club.

4. There are a limited number of ways to get into a show:
   a. Work during the show or during the week. (see rule #11a)
   b. Pay the full admission and have a valid membership card.
   c. Be in a band performing that night.
   d. Be someone's guest...

5. Only certain people get guests:
   a. One guest per performing band member. *weekly worker list. Coordinator, stage manager* A band gets one roadie in free. Addn'l roadies go on guest list. Roadies don't get guests.
   b. Certain regular workers. This rule is not yet defined.

6. Paid security...
   a. Receive $30 per night.
   b. There are two paid security except on the biggest nights.
   c. On slow nights security pay can be deferred to the next evening.

7. Membership...
   a. Costs $2 and is required for admission to all events.
   b. Membership is yearly and nontransferable.
   c. Do not share membership cards.
   d. Do not share membership cards. (repeat for emphasis)

8. No wearing or open display of swastikas, Nazi regalia, confederate flag or other fascist regalia. Leave or take it off. Security has *discretion* digression over this area.

9. No Liquor or drugs in club at any time for any reason. (repeat for emphasis)

10. No staying overnight at the club, except after weekend shows for cleanup crews or touring bands. Permission must be given by coordinator or director.

11a. Weekly worker list. The following people get into all shows for free because they work during the week *(this isn't totally up to date.)*
   Mike D. — Director, booking
   Gar — name on lease
   George — name on lease
   Marcus — custodial
   Mike Stand — administrative, ambulance
   Jessie — booking
   Dave E.C. — booking
   Stewart — booking
   Jonathan — bookkeeping, advertising
   Marshall — Sound maintenance
   Tall Tim — Sound maintenance
   Radley — Sound maintenance

11b. 86'd list. The following people don't get into shows no matter how much they pay.
   Bruce
   George
   Dirt
   Kyle
   George Bush
   Billie
   Bart
   Patty
   Batman
   Screamer

12. Head of security or coordinator only to call 911 or ask someone else to do so.

13. Bands that get to practice at the club:
   Blatz
   Filth
   The Hated
   Dave E.C.'s bands

14. No one gets credit from the club at all.

15. The side room is not open to he public. Only keyholders (or people directly supervised by keyholders) allowed inside.

16. No one should be in loft unless they are working or have the permission of sound guy or coordinator.

BEN S.

"So this is all?" I said to myself the first time I set foot into 924 Gilman. It was Feb. 1989 and Fang was playing to about 50 semi-bored kids. I remember feeling fucking let down by the joint. There was no energy. I'd built the place up in my mind to be the punk rock mecca, and my first impression was anti-climactic. Shit, I'd been to better shows in Green Bay, Wisconsin.

Gilman was a big reason I moved to the East Bay, at the tender age of 18, along with my band Econochrist. We moved out from Little Rock, Arkansas wanting to live in a big city with a big punk scene and lots of action. We were sick of our redneck hometown and trying to build the scene there.

Gilman and the Bay Area punk scene had been real hyped up in my favorite fanzine, *Maximum RocknRoll*—hell, they founded the project. Many of my all-time favorite bands, like MDC, Christ On Parade, Neurosis, Crucifix, and the Dicks, were from the Bay Area, and I was real excited about the new bands coming out of the East Bay, like Operation Ivy and Crimpshrine. Besides, I felt I had to leave the South and go somewhere fresh. California, a state I'd never been to, seemed like a logical destination, and my bandmates, who were also my best friends, concurred. We just figured we'd move out there, keep playing and maybe get better. Miraculously, it actually worked out.

For me, like many other punks in the East Bay, Gilman provided something I think we were all looking for. A place to find friends, companionship, a sense of belonging, and shelter from a shitty, money-driven world that we didn't want to fit into. Plus, it could be a lot of fucking fun, maybe not every time we went there, but enough to keep us wanting to be a part of it.

The club was, and remains, run by the kids and for the kids. No-bullshit, all-ages shows every weekend since 1987, and making a profit isn't what it's all about. That's an accomplishment unparalleled in the US. Gilman has inspired numerous other cool projects, like ABC No Rio in NYC, and provided a place to play for thousands of bands, including my own. It's a place to hang out for thousands of punks who don't really have anyplace else to call their own.

Me and my buddy Sledge used to go down to Gilman practically every weekend back in the day. We were marginally employed at best, so we'd hang out on Telegraph Avenue all day, then bum a ride or walk to the club before the gig and volunteer to work so we'd get in free. We'd do cleanup or volunteer security or side-door, whatever, it didn't really matter. We were among friends. The bands, workers, and audience were one and the same. I also liked the fact that the place was alcohol-free because I'm straight-edge, and it was good to be at a punk gathering place where booze and drugs weren't the main attraction inside.

My fondest memories of Gilman were from those times of 1989 to about 1994. To me, that's when punk/hardcore music was still really vital and the big MTV, sell-out, commercialization of punk hadn't reared its ugly head yet. I was just way more into the bands of that era and things felt more compelling then.

I remember Operation Ivy's last show, with 600 people packed into the space to see their final raucous and amazing set. I remember playing Christ On Parade's last show—every asshole skinhead in the Bay Area turned up, along with a shitload of leftist punks. I talked shit to the boneheads between songs of our set. One rushed the stage hoping to slug me, only to meet our bassist Mike's boot face-first. Neurosis played next and the assholes kept starting fights, and Neurosis kept stopping to split them up. Scott finally said, "If there's one more fight we're done," and of course, 20 seconds into "Life On Your Knees," one erupted and the show ended. Christ On Parade wound up playing to a roomful of us at their house in downtown Oakland behind the Greyhound Station.

Back then, Gilman could be a really fuckin' scary place to be. On any given night, nazis could show up to intimidate and fuck with people. A ska boy had been stabbed to death, and his friend seriously wounded, by nazi skins up in Sacramento. Not long after that, my band (Econochrist), Filth, Green Day, and some other East Bay bands got into a nasty brawl with about 15 big-ass, corn-fed, nazi skins at a show up there. I remember a packed house at Gilman in 1989 to see Verbal Abuse and Swiz. About a dozen nazis were in the pit fucking with people. They were wearing Skrewdriver shirts and had swastikas on their flight jackets. Martin S., one of the founders of the original Gilman St. Project, told me he didn't feel safe, and left the gig. These nazi fucks, from all over Northern California, were a menace that plagued the club and left blood in their wake. Luckily, most of us didn't want our scene to get destroyed by them. I'd personally seen it happen back down South in towns like Memphis and Dallas, and didn't want it to happen out here.

Things started getting better in late 1989. Jonathan, a bespectacled Cal Berkeley grad-student type, had been the coordinator, and he and most of his crew were too wimpy to enforce the club's no-nazis rule. George Hated, an anarchist black skinhead from New York, showed up and became coordinator. The scene also finally got more militant, and united to stand up against the fascists. Basically we kicked their asses whenever they showed up at Gilman or when we saw them on the streets. The American Front tried to hold a rally at Union Square in San Francisco in May of 1990, and 500 anti-racist protestors showed up and showered them with bottles, ending their little white power fest real fucking quick. They would have been dead if the cops hadn't protected them. Of course, some folks in the scene, like Jeff O. of Fifteen and Jake from Filth, preached a pacifist approach to dealing with the boneheads, but clearly that method hadn't worked in the past, so it was ignored by most of us.

One of my happiest moments at Gilman occurred outside in the street during a Toxic Reasons show, when we routed about 25 nazis who came down to the club. We chased them all the way down Gilman to San Pablo Avenue. I remember black, Asian, and white Berkeley cops trying to hold us back as we punched, kicked, and pelted the white power boneheads with bottles as they ran with their tails between their legs—all the way back to Concord, no doubt. After that gig I can't remember too many more problems with nazis at the club. I mean, assholes still show up, but nothing like that. I certainly don't mean to glorify violence or anything, but those things happened. Nowadays it's rare to see a fight at Gilman. It's hard to believe it's the same place where so much shit went down.

During the Gulf War there were massive anti-war demos in the Bay Area, and every band was using the stage at Gilman to speak out against the war. During the People's Park riots, and during the riots after the pigs who beat Rodney King in L.A. got off, Gilman was again one of the centers of resistance. Back then, punk seemed more political and radical. Bands weren't afraid to speak out and play songs that had real meaning.

I remember seeing Ian M. get the entire sold-out crowd to shut up and listen during "Suggestion," the second time Fugazi played Gilman. I remember seeing a lot of fuckin' awesome touring bands like Born Against, Soulside, Chumbawamba, Nomeansno, Bikini Kill, Nausea, Poison Idea, the Laughing Hyenas, Los Crudos, and many more. Bands like those got my heart pumping and my spine tingling. I could feel the chords hit me in the gut. I felt like they were singing directly to me. The music moved me, but it was more than music, it was something else, a more powerful feeling, and it ran deep. Of course, I also saw a shitload of horrible, down-right boring bands that I wished would get the fuck off the stage and call it quits. But hey, it would be impossible to have eight great shows a month, and one of the beauties of Gilman is that any fucking punk band can play and have a chance.

Now when I step into the club, I rarely see a band that really moves me. I'm an old fart by American punk standards. I'm 30 for Christ's sake and I've been going to punk shows since I was 13 years old. My band is long gone and things are different now. I still consider myself a punk because I don't fit in anywhere else, but today's punk music isn't nearly as compelling to me as the stuff I grew up with. When I go to Gilman now, I don't know everybody there like I used to. The new kids are fine, but I just hope they appreciate the place and respect its history. I still go to Gilman, and I even work sometimes, but now it's only once or twice a month instead of nearly every show.

The club is still a great place to make friends and be around like-minded people. I'm still thankful it exists. In today's watered-down, corporate music world, independent bands need an honest place to play, and the punks still need a place to go. Hell, people I've met at Gilman have become some of my closest friends. I've met people at Gilman who hooked me up with work, housing, and have just helped me out with my problems. More importantly, they've helped me realize I'm not alone, and that there are alternatives to this fuckin' competitive, dog-eat-dog, oppressive, materialistic, earth-raping, dominant culture that we find ourselves in. Gilman is a big part of one of those alternatives.

Back in the day, Gilman was a place that I felt was worth fighting for, despite all of its flaws. It was the center of my circle of friends. We hung out at the shows, but we also went dumpster diving together beforehand, and went to the parties afterwards. We lived, and still live, in overcrowded houses to keep the rent down. We worked together and we supported each other. Back then the fight at Gilman was against nazis, and today the fight is against yuppies and big businesses that could shut the place down, as well as drive us out of our neighborhoods and our homes.

Gilman was, and still is, a place worth fighting for. Sure, other clubs in the Bay Area may have been more fun, cooler, more exciting, punker, or more under-ground, but Gilman has staying power. Hopefully it will remain a vital space to the punk scene. It's a place, and a community, that has yet to live up to its full potential.

City of Berkeley

MODIFICATION APPLICATION

FOR ZONING DIVISION USE ONLY
DATE: 7-19-91
FEE PAID: 86 BY: _____
Zoning District: _____

I (WE) REQUEST MODIFICATION OF USE PERMIT # A 1024

AT: 924 Gilman St., Berkeley, CA 94110 FOR OPERATION OF A youth multi-arts rock music club NAME OF BUSINESS: Alternative Music Foundation

APPLICANT: Michael D PHONE: (w)

HOME ADDRESS: _____ ZIP CODE: _____

CITY: Albany, CA STATE: CA

DESCRIBE BRIEFLY YOUR PROPOSED OPERATION INCLUDING ANY AND ALL CHANGES FROM THE PREVIOUS OPERATION.

It is a volunteer-run music club licensed to operate on weekends with a youth orientation and membership required with alcohol and/or other drug use forbidden as well as violence, vandalism. The change: to drop required condition #7 to allow advertising by newspaper, radio and posting.

Battle #1 started with this innocent request to modify the original use permit to allow more advertising.

TO: ZONING ADJUSTMENT BOARD
FROM: 924 GILMAN STREET PROJECT

SUBJECT: MODIFICATION OF USE PERMIT # A 1024

> This application concerns condition #7: a
> prohibition of advertizing. We are requesting
> either the deletion of the condition or a rewording
> of it so that there can be a listing of events in several
> weekly newspapers and a posting of fliers in certain
> designated areas.

The 924 Gilman Street project is an all-ages, volunteer-run collective.
It is a place where young people can learn to work together socially
to put on music shows and otherwise creatively express themselves. We
have group meetings every other week to make decisions and work on
problems that inevitably arise in any social situation. These
meetings are open to all. Involvement in helping the club continue
is encouraged. 924 Gilman Street provides a sense of community for
many youth who might not otherwise find it.

There are two reasons for requesting this change of condition #7:
the failure of an ideal and increasing expenses. At the original
hearing for this permit we specifically requested the no advertizing
condition -- despite the then Board's saying they thought some
would be desirable. This request came from the ideal that the members
would be loyal to the club and not to specific artists, support
music and not just the best bands. Over the long run, however,
this did not work out. Even with volunteers and popular bands playing
nearly as a benefit, the costs of rent, insurance and maintenance
were not covered.

IMPACT There should be a slight increase in the number of people
attending these week-end shows. The current level, it is awkward to
admit, is already established as a result of publicity. Gilman
shows are listed in the events calendar of some publications, there
have been reviews of many shows, there has been posting of fliers.
We also point out that we are not impacting parking as this stretch
of Gilman Street is mostly non-retail commercial and warehouses and
is closed down in the evenings.

If rewording of the condition is to be considered, our needs (and budget)
would be the standard little box (three column inches) listing the
upcoming bands. These would appear in the East Bay Express,
S.F. Weekly, the Daily Californian, Maximum Rock & Roll. Fliers
would be posted in the general University of California vicinity,
most particularly in the Telegraph Ave. area. We would like to
use radio, particularly the University station KALX.

TO: LT. L____, PATROL DIVISION

FROM: SGT. D____, TEAM 7

SUBJECT: 924 GILMAN Club

As per the attached letter, Michael D____, manager of the Club, has asked for the alteration of the use permit to allow advertising. The officers and supervisors of Team 7 oppose the request. Increased advertising will increase customers and therefore, increase the problems which we currently experience with the 924 Gilman Club.

The problems we experience with the Club when it has a name band playing are as follows:

1. Most of the problems are alcohol related, i.e. drinking in public, drunk, or minors in possession of alcohol. Officers cite violators as often as possible but more often than not, due to the press of business, just have the violators pour out the beverage. Problems with persons littering, urinating, and defecating due to a lack of facilities is common.

2. The hours of operation of the Club are during our busiest hours. On the average, the officers spend 2½ hours each attending to the problems with the Club's patrons. On a Friday night, we have four officers assigned to the NW area of the City which amounts to about 8 hours of service. It is routine to provide almost singular attention to problems surrounding the Club by using the Club as a base of operations. We leave to take a case and return when we clear it.

3. The Club is easily filled and the crowd spills out onto the sidewalk and into the street. When there is a break between band sets, the crowd inside mingles with the crowd outside. Traffic on Gilman Street is impacted since persons stand in, randomly wander into and across the street. They go to their cars or nearby business parking lots and entrances to "hang out" till the music starts again. It is during this time that the alcohol is purchased or consumed, the traffic problems arise, and the fights break out.

4. Most of the patrons of the Club are from out of Berkeley. They come in from Contra Costa and Marin Counties and as far as the Sacramento Valley towns. These persons come into town to party and have little respect or concern for the neighborhood or our community. Youths from Concord have often come in to start fights with the customers at the Club. (Ski Mask/heavy metal types vs. the hippies)

5. Local liquor stores require extra attention since local transient types often buy alcohol for the minors.

often one member of a group is 21 years old and he will buy for everyone. Controlling these sales is a continuing problem during a busy shift.

6. Security needs to be addressed. Presently the security is primarily inside and conducted by employees who wear t-shirts saying "security". On a busy night, there are not enough security employees to control the crowd inside, let alone the outside. Private uniformed security guards need to be employed to control the crowds outside the Club and on the nearby streets.

7. The use permit needs to be expanded to include the furnishing of garbage cans in area, and the cleanup of the area surrounding the Club after closing. This function is now being done by the manager and the Club security staff.

8. The Club needs to create a policy whereby customers are encouraged to stay inside and not congregate outside. We suggest that customers be informed upon entry that if they go outside they will not be allowed to enter again. In this manner, persons in the area just "hanging out" could be asked to leave. The result would be less fights, drinking, and littering.

The bottom line is that the present condition is intolerable and adversely impacts our ability to provide called for services. If the Club cannot be shut down, that I suggest we tighten up the use permit by addressing some of the above concerns.

JE D
10-5-91

Left and above: Part of the normal process for a permit modification request is getting input from the police. This is where it really hit the fan and where it was first made known that the police wanted the club shut down.

Below: The police review led to the permit modification request being denied by the Zoning Board, and the possibility of the use permit being revoked, which would shut the club down.

FOR BOARD ACTION
November 25, 1991

TO: Member of the Zoning Adjustments Board

FROM: Current Planning Staff

SUBJECT: 924 GILMAN STREET - MODIFICATION TO USE PERMIT #A1024

Background/Application

In 1986, Tim Yohannon received Use Permit #A1024 to operate a recreation center including an art gallery, meeting room and dancing/performance area dba Maximum Roc 'N' Roll. Approved hours of operation are 8 PM to 2 AM Friday and Saturday and 2 PM to 10 PM on Sundays. Nine (9) conditions were imposed (see attached) including Condition #7 which prohibits advertising of the events by means of newspapers, radio or posters. Leaflets on the Berkeley High campus or public service announcements on KPFA are allowed.

In 1990, Michael Diehl requested a Transfer of U.P. #A1024, but it was never issued because he did not provide Staff with adequate information on how the club would operate under his ownership. Mr. Diehl is now requesting the deletion of Condition #7 in order to increase both club memberships and revenues. Apparently the club has already been advertising, proposing to transfer ownership of the club in the near future, however, no application has yet been received.

Communications

Seven public hearing notices were mailed, including one to the Fifth-Camelia Neighborhood Association. As of this writing, no comments had been received.

Staff Review

During the past year, both the Code Compliance Officer and the Police Department have received complaints regarding the operation of the club. They appear to stem from a disregard of the imposed conditions. Mr. Diehl describes the club as an "all-ages, volunteer-run collective where young people can learn to work together socially to put on music shows and otherwise creatively express themselves" (see attached Applicant's Statement). Police and members of the nearby neighborhood residential uses see the club as a magnet for rowdy young people who tend to go to the club intoxicated. The club has been accused of overcrowding, with customers' cars parked all over adjoining neighborhoods and "drinking and smoking young adults" damaging city trees and breaking glass. Single-family residents one block to the south on Camelia Street have expressed fear for their safety and some neighbors state that they have been intimidated by the club's patrons. A nearby church has complained about young people hanging out on their property and drinking late at night.

The Current Planning Division has received a memo from the Berkeley Police Department detailing the problems generated by the club (see attached). The memo's final recommendation is that, given the present "intolerable condition", the request to advertise be denied and that, "if the Club cannot be shut down that we tighten the use permit be addressing the concerns."

Staff review of implementation of the 9 conditions reveals the following:

1. No bond was posted for installation of street lights in the vicinity of 924 Gilman Street. Ed Ochoa of the Public Works Department also states that the $1,000 maximum would provide for the installation to two street lights.

2. The Codes and Inspection Department did issue a Building Permit for work done in November 1986.

3. The facility already operates as a commercial dance facility with advertising. The proposed change would formalize this change in character.

4. No specific information has been secured regarding hours of operation except one complaint which questioned whether they were operating after hours.

5. Security has been lax, according to the Berkeley Police Department because security personnel is made up of club members who seem to exert little or no authority in enforcing club rules.

6. Alcohol has been a big problem. Apparently club members either come in intoxicated or they are able to go out and purchase alcoholic beverages since there is a liquor store at the corner of San Pablo Avenue and Gilman Street, two blocks to the east.

7. As pointed out above, the club is presently advertising in the local events calendar sections of newspapers and is posting flyers. The Police Department has indicated that young people as far away as Vallejo are attracted to the facility when name bands appear on the weekends.

8. The use permit is to be transferred again the near future. However, no one has submitted an application to the Current Planning Division.

9. Staff is not aware that any six month review of the project occurred after the use permit was approved. However, complaints seem to have started coming in around mid-1988.

Given the consistent non-compliance with the attached conditions, Staff believes that not only should the present request be disapproved, but that the Zoning Adjustment Board consider holding a public hearing to determine if the club possess sufficient detriment to the neighborhood to warrant revocation proceedings.

Recommendation

Staff recommends that the request to eliminate Condition 7 BE DENIED based on the following findings.

Findings

1. The applicant has failed to live up to the purposes for which the club was founded and, in general, has not met the nine conditions imposed when the club was initially formed. This has resulted in creating a nuisance for the nearby residential neighborhoods and has become a law enforcement problem that can only worsen by allowing advertising as proposed.

Mike L
Senior Planner

To: Mike L.
Berkeley Planning Commission,

I feel given the dire economic situation the club is in it is difficult to see much of a future for 924 Gilman St. Club. Given that the police seem to want to close us down as a public nuisance I am wondering if writing this introduction and update on what I wrote last year in attempt to respond to your request for information is an exercise in futility. I'm looking more at how I can exit out of primary responsibility in as graceful fashion possible over the next 3 months rather than being abruptly closed down.

I have been aware of, consented to last year and have been in basic complaince with the 9 conditions established in 1986 for the club established by Tim Yohannon and Maximum Rock'n'Roll. I honestly thought that last year that the use permit had been reestablished in my name. Our club has sought to keep neighboring businesses, cleaning up after shows and repainting over graffitti and have in the past few months sent a representative from the club to listen to complaints and seek to improve relations. Where possible given our finiancial state we are seeking to redress problems created by those who are our clientele and sychophantic hanger ons.

We not only do not sanction alcohol or drug use in or near the club but several of us spend a considerable amount of time actively discouraging such. Last year I had to clamp down hard on alcohol and drug use problems among our volunteer staff. We have talked several young alcoholics into A. A. programs and have talked of starting an Alcoholics Anonymous program at the club. I am quite aware that a number of patrons including distressingly the underaged come to shows intoxicated. Paid security and myself quite particularly have been spending much of our evening weekends telling people to stop drinking near the club. We are not unappreciative of police support with this. I am quite aware that we need to do better on this. There is a certain group of older punks who do not come to shows but hang out and drink and will not listen to us. We have asked the police to cite them but up until just recently none of this group has been. We have in the past submitted a plan to deal with this working with the police. I am quite willing to do this again. I am opposed to eliminating ins and outs for the club but unless we as a club take much more effective action against this problem of drinking outside the club I can see we may not be given any other choice by the police/city. I do appreciate the efforts made last year by the police to clamp down on alcohol sales to minors. For more discussion on this matter see last year's letter which I never really completed having been overtaken by events including an increased work load at my paid job. I must emphasize that I, like most club members, am a volunteer.

Last year's letter was shared and discussed at 924 Gilman St. club meetings. It was seen as too negative in tone by most others, hardly a good argument for the club continuing. It was also seen as too personal and too personal. We do have attempts to write different job responsibilities out by my predecessors. This we can submit if you would like. We have earlier attempts by writing to explain the concept of Gilman. These we could submit too if you want.

We have been holding membership meetings once every other week since last year. This has lead to a more democratic decision-making process where particularly those who volunteer in running most shows can speak their minds. Grievances against and within the club are often dealt with there. Gradually I have gotten people mostly younguse to idea of taking notes and keeping a record of decisions reached. This meeting process is meant to be educative and more than simply advisory. We are seeking by this process to finally establish bylaws for the nonprofit incorporation and thus finally become free of the real finiancial burden of the state franchise tax.

As of Nov. 1st I plan no longer to be executive director of 924 Gilman ST. and no longer owner. The next two Saturdays may very well establish who will succeed me in this redefined position either in the Alternative Music Foundation or in another corporation preferably nonprofit this time with bylaws clearly established. I would continue in an advisory role probably as secretary if it is clear we will be able to continue then. This frankly does not look likely given the present situation that really needs to be turned around. This may simply be the egotism that if even I couldn't do this right no one or no ones can. It is a reality

that it really has to be more of a team working cohesively together for the concept of Gilman St. to work. It is still too much on my shoulders and that of too few others. I have been doing too poor job because I too stressed/burnt out from continued overload resulting in caffeine-induced insomnia.

We are having an emergency meeting to discuss the future of the club and the present problem of insufficient volunteer security backup. Our present volunteer security are not giving us the support we need. Drinking and the often resulting problem of violence must be dealt with on a collective level if the club is to survive.

Sincerely,

Michael D.

Left and above: letter sent by Michael D., fall, 1991

WE, THE UNDERSIGNED, FEEL THAT 924 GILMAN IS AN IMPORTANT PART OF THIS COMMUNITY'S RESPONSIBILITY TO YOUTH. IT IS ONE OF THE FEW SAFE, DRUG-FREE, REGULARLY OPERATING PLACES FOR PEOPLE OF ALL AGES TO GO. WE CONSIDER THIS CLUB TO BE NECESSARY FOR YOUTH AND OTHER MEMBER OF THE COMMUNITY; PLEASE DO NOT ELIMINATE IT.

| NAME | ADDRESS | AGE |

Above: The first usage of petitions by Gilman, which woud be a key tool, both in this case and in later battles.

BERKELEY DISPUTE RESOLUTION SERVICE

Permit Mediation

15 January 1992

To: Zoning Adjustments Board

Re: 924 GILMAN CLUB

On 14 Jan 92 a facilitated meeting was held at Mt Zion Church which included:

CLUB MEMBERS — George S (Exec Sec'y), Jesse Townley (club sec'y), John H , Carrie C , and Pat W

POLICE — SgtCliff R , Community Services Bureau BPD; Officer Victor B BPD

CHURCH — Pastor M.C. T

Mr S opened the meeting by stating that since he assumed his job as Executive Secretary in November 1991 he has succeeded in significantly reducing the amount of disturbances around the club neighborhood. The police acknowledged that in the past weeks "things have been a lot better...but we still have a good way to go." The police then added that they feared that more advertising would bring in more people, and "the more people, the more problems."

The club responded that they were not requesting to do "more" advertising; they just wanted to continue doing the same amount of limited announcements that they have already been doing for some time. Mr S said that their usual attendance was about 70-90 people and that this size crowd was rarely the cause of any police activity or neighbor concern. A popular group would bring in a capacity crowd of 220, plus many waiting outside for a later entry as some people left. These were the evenings causing most of the police intervention.

Both parties agreed to work together to improve the situation:

1 - The club agreed to send schedules of future events to Sgt R with indications which events might fill the house. ("There aren't as many popular available groups now as there have been in the past.")

2 - Pastor T will inform the club of the scheduled church big evening programs so that the club can avoid booking a big draw at that time.

3 - For popular full-house shows the club will enforce a NO RETURN policy. On these evenings, the club will open (and monitor) side doors to increase ventilation and reduce the need to go outside for fresh air.

4 - The club has started a policy of a more permanent and better-trained security force, which now gets together once a week for training. Sgt R has agreed to attend an upcoming meeting and will work out new ways of communication between the security staff and the police.

5 - NO DRINKING/ NO LOITERING signs will be posted in nearby appropriate areas.

6 - A follow-up meeting of all parties (including the mediator-facilitators) is scheduled on 17 March 1992 at the Mt Zion Church.

The meeting ended in cautious optimism, with all parties awaiting proof-in-the-pudding improved conditions. John H was co-facilitator.

Victor H
co-facilitator

The first usage of the Berkely Dispute Resolution Service, which would be another key tool, both in this case and in later battles

Since 1987 the Gilman St. club has attempted to provide a place to hang out where the pressure to drink can be resisted, a non-alcoholic space, a non-drug space, a place where the subtle and not-so-subtle racist strains in youth culture can be confronted; a safe and non-racist place for everyone.

Lately the club is facing various as yet undefined problems/threats from the city. The club has subsisted for the past 5 years in the most tenuous and marginal manner, expecting every few months to have to close because of continuously inadequate finances.

While the space at 924 Gilman is great in many respects, it is by no means cheap. Rent is $2,735 a month. Additional necessary expenses amount to $495 (approx.). Show totals on an average month in 1991 were 3,175.

1

All personell except security people (3 per show) are unpaid. For the first several years, even security personell were not paid.

The club has existed by a thread for 5 years, hanging on successfully only due to the crying need for a service to youth providing a place to hang out where the pressure to drink can be resisted, where musical groups can come out of the audience and become well known, where kids can get away from both the T.V.s, malls, and Telegraph Avenues of this culture, to enjoy some of their own home made culture, in an atmosphere more alive than T.V. and more positive and safer than hanging out on the street; an atmosphere where some issues can be confronted.

Over the years, the people who run the club

2

with their energy and time have come out of the audience. This group has continually been replenished, despite the burn-out nature of the jobs; the high committment of energy and idealism of this self-replenishing staff and their desire to provide positive activity and space for youth is the only reason this club continues to exist.

What the Police see in this club is the part of society that is attacking the club – the street drinkers and brawlers to whom the very existence of the club is a threat.

A peaceful, non-alcohol club, which they cannot dominate, is a thorn in the side of these people and they cant leave it alone.

Some of the outside problems also come from youth being won over to the Nazi racist agendas of Nazi skinheads – the club is additionally

3

a thorn in their side since it doesnt tolerate expressions of racism of any kind. They find it difficult to leave the place alone.

For the police to wish the club out of existence because of the activities of these groups is the equivalent of getting rid of a chapter of Bnai Brith because it draws negative graffiti, and Anti-Semites hang out near it to hassle members.

What the club needs is to be left alone to continue to attempt to survive. It always needs idealistic and hard nosed volunteer workers (preferably who at least dont hate the music!) and they do seem to come, out of the audience.

What the club needs from the City and Police is some recognition of the job its attempting

4

to do; recognition of what its attempting is enough. From the Police – the help of citing people drinking in the neighborhood would be a great help – its something the club cannot do.

The club would like for the City to hear from Parents whose kids have benefited from its presence, and who support the service that the Gilman club has provided over the years. Letters of support would be deeply appreciated and should be sent to 924 Gilman, Berkeley 94710. these letters will be taken to any upcoming meetings, and will be presented by the club to Zoning Board, Police, or City Council as meetings with these groups occur.

thanks for your help and participation!

5

Outreach letter written by Pat W. (I believe) in early 1991.

artist unknown

January 2nd, 1992

To whom it may concern,

This letter is in regard to the upcoming board meeting concerning 924 Gilman st.,scheduled to be held on the 13th of January. I hope that you take the following aspects of a place like Gilman St. into consideration before making any decisions regarding the aforementioned location.

I moved to the Bay area in 1988 at the age of 17 from Sarasota, Florida, a city with approximately 200,000 residents.In Sarasota, there is relatively no designated public center/place that is legal for a larger than usual group of young people to gather on weekends.A few of the things that I found the youth there interested in meeting to do were to show films, display their art/writing, play/practice in their bands, help local bands/artists get a start by having a legal place to play their music to an audience, or by having means to record demo tapes to distribute, or just as a place to spend some of their free time in a creative enviornment. In my opinion, it is healthy for a community to allow the young people to create for themselves a location to take part in the aforementioned or other such intersets. In Sarasota, the lack of such a place had some definate negative impacts on the community, such as leaving a lot of younger people more apt to get involved with peer groups who were less interested in being productive or in some of the worse cases, getting in trouble with the police. The most logical solution is varying depending on the problems, and needs of different communities.

Upon arrival to Berekely, I heard about 924 Gilman St., and started to go there on a regular basis. I was impressed with the people who were going to the clubs interest and dedication concerning their peers desire to share their views with each other through their music, and art. I found that a lot of people were benifiting from the club in different ways. People were taking interest, and learning about running a small business, about how to work with sound equipment, the correct way to do the book work concerning a small business, how to deal with the problems that stem from keeping an event/show organized when it takes place, and possibly most importantly, how to work together with a group of people successfully. Over the past three years I have continued to frequent Gilman St., and have been left with a really positive feeling from the people that I have met there, and the different ideas that they have given me through their music, and by talking to them personally. In talking to young people from other areas, I have also found that a place such as Gilman St. often works as an inspiration for people in other communities to take part in creating a place where young people can meet in their own enviornment. Similar centers have been set up by adolescents in cities such as

Seattle, WA. , St. Paul, MN. , Gainesville, FL. , N.Y.C. , Eugene, OR. , and many other cities both big, and small.

Over the years, there have been some problems around 924 Gilman St. that I am sure have been drawn to your attention. The biggest issue seems to be that of underage drinking around the club. Those who volunteer to work at an event being held at the club try to prevent, and in no way condone such actions. To enter the club, you must be a member. The fee is $2.00 per year, and upon acceptance of a membership card, one is under agreement not to drink or use drugs in or around the club, and not to fight or vandalise around the club. Every effort is made by the staff to solve any problems which may arise during a show. An example is the new decision to stop the show if there are people fighting or causing a disturbance, and then asking the audience to help create a solution before the show starts again. If that doesn't work then the show is stopped, and no refunds are given. I agree that there are bad aspects to having a community center for the local youth but overall I feel that the good aspects outweigh the bad when looked at closely, and fairly.

Yours truly,

Brad L

To Whom This May Concern:

Approximately 5 years ago my son, Michael began his association with "The Gilman Street Project" (as it was known in its infancy) and as I continue to call it.

As he talked about membership meetings, issues to be voted on, I realized he and his compatriots were applying the basic democratic process as a part of their lives. I find, years later, that his experiences there have been a personal learning and growth experience in organisational skills, marketing, finance, security as well as development of the skills necessary to work with the public and volunteerism, which we've all been called upon to do.

He also has made a serious life altering decision regarding his personal life, to become and remain a non-substance user. This decision was based directly on his involvment with the people of the club and they support him in his efforts.

The young people who attend "The Gilman" may not dress and wear their hair in an acceptable, tasteful fashion to us "baby boomers", but, I do vividly remember a time when another generation thought our attire, hair and music was totally unacceptable.

Please consider that anytime you assemble a large group of people there will not always be harmony. The Gilman Street people do try to "police" themselves and welcome assistance from the Berkeley Police Department.

There is just not enough places for underage people to go to dance, listen to music and just plain commiserate. The establishment consistantly denies young people a place to go, citing "insurance" problems and "fire codes" as reason to close them up. This has been going on for years and years. Can't we try and work with these kids to keep the place open, make it a safe place for these kids to go.

Thank you for you attention.

Jeannine M. W

El Cerrito, Ca.

Dear members of the Berkeley Board Of Adjustment:

I am the person to whom your body issued the original permit for the Gilman Street Project many years ago, and I'd like to say a few words because of the hearing you are now conducting.

Gilman Street Project was begun as a vehicle for younger people to learn to take responsibility for themselves, to provide a community center where they could produce their own music, form their own bands, conduct their own art projects, and learn the ins-and-outs of dealing with the public.

We encountered many problems along the way. City bureaucracy was one—it took us 9 months of paying rent with no revenue coming in before we could even open our doors, and costs of about $40,000. At various times, we had to deal with some expected troublesome areas, such as a small minority of problem kids trying to ruin things for the great majority of well-behaved and well-motivaed young people. It should be noted here that this project always endeavored to be a membership club, based on a no alcohol, no drugs, no violence policy. But trying to keep away those who don't agree with that stance is not easy, and at times we required the assistance of the Berkeley Police, with whom we've met several times over the years. When the skinhead phenomena grew a few years back, it was necessary to increase our security procedres even more, now trying to not only patrol a few blocks in all directions for drinkers causing trouble, but for groups of violent hoodlums who were hellbent on trying to get the progressive Gilman Street Project shut down because of its anti-racist stance.

All of these efforts to create, and then sustain, a community-run youth center are incredibly draining, especially on a group of people that are trying to be independent, don't ask for or receive any kind of government grants, and who run on a shoestring budget, trying to keep expenses and door prices very low so that most all young people can afford to participate there. There are very few other examples of this kind of self-run centers in this country, which has made Gilman Street famous the world round, and not just in youth music culture circles. Articles or mention of it have appeared in periodicals ranging from Rolling Stone to the Wall Street Journal.

This kind of project should not ever be considered for closing by the City of Berkeley. Quite the opposite, the City should be trying to find ways to continue and increase support for it. Not only is Gilman Street not costing the City a penny, but it sets an example that is being immitated now in many other cities around the country. Sure there are some negative side effects, such as occasionally having to ask for a police visit or having to deal with a few drinkers out to cause trouble, but this does not weigh at all compared to the immense service this kind of project provides. Literaaly hundreds of bands have formed and gotten their start just because the place exists. All sorts of creative endeavors have been able to flourish as a result, providing a chunk of today's intelligent youth with an outlet and mode of self-expression, something which I believed Berkeley always stood for and encouraged. If Gilman Street Project were to be closed down or shackled in such a way as to render it compromised in the eyes of youth, then it is highly likely that all the positive energy that's gone into building this community effort will either lie dormant, or more likely, will curdle and find a much more negative avenue for release. This would be tragic for the young people who have found a place to call their own, and for the city itself, another sign that even in progressive Berkeley, kids are not even second-class citizens.

I have been active in this community for 16 years, doing a weekly radio show on both KPFA and KALX, publish a monthly magazine dedicated to music and politics, and have helped start a community-run not-for-profit record store in San Francisco. Yet my years of trying to get Gilman Street Project off the ground are the most memorable. The place is not perfect, and reflects all the symptoms of woe that plague society in general. But I have never seen an idea as noble as this one continue to struggle and grow as this one has. It deserves your forthright support and congratulations.

Tim Yohannan

SOME OF THE SUPPORT LETTERS RECEIVED IN JANUARY, 1992

January 24, 1992

TO: Members of the Zoning Adjustments Board
FROM: The 924 Gilman Street Project

CONCERNING: 924 Gilman Street

Our original intent in coming before the Board was to resolve a
non-compliance situation. For two years, 924 Gilman had been
running small display ads in several local weekly newspapers and
posting flyers in the Telegraph Ave. area. This violated a
condition in our use permit. We asked that the condition be
removed or changed to specify a limited amount of advertising --
to "legitimize" this publicity.

However, staff review and police comment have brought out more
pressing issues of crowds hanging out in front of the Club, drinking
in areas adjacent to the building, some neighborhood complaints,
and non-compliances. It is clear that our original request be put
on hold until the control of nuisances and the non-compliances are
worked out. We would appreciate guidance whether to reapply at a
later date, leave the matter open pending review, or something else.

As for steps taken to address police, staff, Board members'
concerns: The meeting, as requested by the Board, with the
Berkeley Dispute Resolution Service was held. Mr. H   's
report has been distributed.

A few additional items:

1. Not only will shows certain to be at or near capacity have a
   "no-ins-and-outs" rule, but in cases where there are too many
   people around the building we will also apply the rule. This
   was done at the Jan. 17 show, and it will continue.

2. Further discouragement of drinking and nuisance behavior will be
   made by Gilman security by cancelling hand stamps and denying
   re-entry. This was done last week, and it will continue.

3. We want to have beat officers attend our security meetings
   frequently. Communication between the police and Gilman
   security will profit from on-going discussion.

4. Outside trash cans will be placed during shows by the building
   and across the street.

5. A crosswalk for Gilman Street is being evaluated.

6. As for non-compliance issues: Staff requested a transfer of
   the use permit to the new director. The form has been submitted.

7. Regarding installing street lights "if improvements are necessary."
   There are lights along Gilman Street (every pole) and all the
   side streets except Tenth towards Harrison (two blocks away).
   After talking with Ed O   in Public Works and with Chuck
   D   in Traffic Engineering it seems that necessity in
   this case is not decided by them. Further contacts will be made.

We feel that a sound start has been made towards controlling
nuisances and resolving issues of non-compliance. We will
be at the Board's Jan. 27 meeting to continue work on this matter.

Thank you.

                              The 924 Gilman Street Project

**The second address to the Board regarding the permit modification
(after working on the issues the police raised).**

City Of Berkeley
Board Of Adjustments
NOTICE OF DECISION

USE PERMIT NO. __AA1024__ /VARIANCE NO. __1177__

OTHER _____

MEETING DATE: __1/27/92__

PROJECT LOCATION: __924 Gilman Street__

APPLICANT: __Michael D__ (_____ , Albany, CA)

BOARD ACTION: __APPROVED modification of Use Permit #A1024 and Variance #1177__

to revise condition 7 regarding advertising and add new conditions 9 through 14.

REQUIRED CONDITION(S) AND FINDING(S): See revised conditions on attached sheet.

REQUIRED FINDINGS AND CONDITIONS:

1. Subject to review and approval by the Public Works Department, the applicant shall bond for the installation of street lights on Ninth and Tenth Streets from Camelia to Harrison Streets and on Gilman and Camelia Streets from Ninth to Tenth Streets, to a maximum of $1000.

2. The building shall be upgraded and improved as required by Codes and Inspection.

3. The facility shall operate as described in the application as a membership facility, not as a commercial dance facility.

4. The hours of operation are limited to 8 AM to 2 AM Friday and Saturday, Sunday from 2 PM to 10 PM. Weeknight, evening use for rehearsals and organizational meeting may occur between 6 PM and 10 PM. Performances or shows are prohibited except during the specified weekend evenings. Changes in hours must be approved by the Board.

5. Security shall be provided for all performances, and shall include at least two people at the entrance, two inside the hall, and two on the exterior. These personnel shall be easily identifiable by means of clothing or badges, and can be members of the organization. Hired security personnel is not necessary.

6. No alcohol shall be provided on the premises nor shall it be brought into the facility by members.

7. Announcements of events will be allowed in newspaper entertainment listings, public service announcements on KALX and through the posting of fliers. No newspaper display advertising is permitted.

8. The permit is subject to review by the Board upon receipt by the Current Planning Section of verifiable complaint of detriment or non-compliance with conditions.

9. The Gilman Street project shall notify the Community Services Department of the dates and times of all future events, and indicate which events might generate a full house.

10. The Gilman Street Project will conduct regular security training for staff. The Project shall notify the Community Services Department of the time and location of the training sessions.

11. For popular, full-house shows, the club will enforce a "no-ins-and-outs: rule. The club will open and monitor side doors to increase the ventilation and reduce the need to go outside for fresh air. Hand stamps will be used to identify patrons who enter the club.

12. Outside trash cans will be placed by the building and across the street during shows.

13. No drinking and loitering notices shall be posted inside the club and on all promotional and advertising materials, club literature and admission tickets.

14. Staff shall review compliance with permit conditions as modified within six months from the date of issuance.

And so it came to pass that the permit modification was approved, and Gilman lived happily ever after...

CHAPTER FOUR

NEW SHERIFF IN TOWN

GEORGE S.

1991-1992

"...A CHAOTIC DANCE OF INFORMATION AND PASSION AND BRUISES."

-EGGPLANT

photo by Larry W.

GEORGE S. AKA GEORGE HATED (TAKEN FROM *P.U.N.K.* ZINE)

"PLEASE DON'T CALL ME KING GEORGE"
GEORGE HATED SPEAKS

ARE THE FINANCIAL PROBLEMS THAT GILMAN IS FACING TODAY UNPRECEDENTED OR ARE THEY THE NORM COMPARED TO WHAT GILMAN HAS FACED IN THE PAST?

They go along kind of with what's been happening since the place opened in 1986. There are less bands now. There are less headliners now. There are less people still into it now. So things have changed somewhat but it's still just endemic of society as a whole, the same thing that's going on everywhere else: Nobody's got any money.

SO GILMAN HAS PRETTY MUCH BEEN IN A CONSTANT STATE OF DEBT.

We run, on average, a month behind on rent. There are surprises every month that go. Anywhere from 2 to 4 to 5 to 6 hundred bucks. It all kind of depends.

IS THE LANDLORD PRETTY COOL ABOUT IT?

He has to be because even if he wanted to rerent this place, for example, the place across the street has been sitting there for about a year and a half, just 'cause it's industrial space and nobody's got the money to rent it. He can't get rid of us any more than we can get rid of him.

HE MUST BE PRETTY TOLERANT TO LET THIS PLACE EXIST.

He kind of has to. He couldn't rent it out. From what I understand when he rented it to them at first in 1986 the space had been idle for 4 years, he hadn't been able to rent it. And now he's making some sort of guaranteed income from it every month. He can't afford to lose us and we can't afford to move.

HOW LONG HAVE YOU PERSONALLY BEEN INVOLVED WITH GILMAN?

A little over 2 years. I got up here Christmas of 1989. 2 years, not long at all. Less than half the people still work here.

SO YOU'RE PRETTY MUCH NEW SCHOOL THEN.

Yeah by all means, I don't deny it.

ARE GILMAN'S PROBLEMS A COMBINATION OF BOTH LOCAL GOVERNMENT AND JUST GENERAL MONEY PROBLEMS?

Yeah it's local government, it's money problems, it's the people that come here somewhat. There's this swing it seems in the punk scene now. It's like back to '77. It's a really retro, no future, I don't care, I'm just gonna get drunk and break things sort of attitude. Cause when I first got into the punk scene it was like '78 and people were really odd. I mean it was much different than just leather jackets and mohawks. There were alot more ideas around but with the overall feeling that nothing really mattered and it seems that things are swinging back that way now.... which is a problem.

DO YOU SEE THAT AS A PROBLEM FOR THE LOCAL SCENE?

For the scene in general and for anybody who sees themselves as alternative because half of it is is getting sold again from metal bands playing punk rock standards to bands like Nirvana being entirely accepted by the masses to the latest drunk punk thing. Yeah, it's a problem. It involves people caring less and more attention thrown on us seeing people caring less.

ONE THING THAT REALLY IMPRESSES ME ABOUT GILMAN THOUGH IS THAT THERE'S STILL HELL OF DIVERSITY AND THERE ARE ALOT OF COOL PEOPLE HERE ▪ AND YOU'RE REALLY KEEPING TO THE PUNK VALUES. I MEAN, YOU'RE STRUGGLING BUT YOU'RE STILL MAKING AN EFFORT IN THAT DIRECTION.

It's an important place. I've said alot of times that I really wouldn't care if another band ever played here just as long as people have a place to go where they can feel safe. That's why I'm here. Some of the music I like, some of it I don't. I can't remember the last time I saw a band that I really really liked but it matters more that this place be here every friday and saturday night for people. And during the week. It's an imperative, 'cause there's too few places to go where you can do nothing if you want, y'know.

IT'S A SAFE PLACE. IT'S A FRIENDLY PLACE. IT'S NOT COLD AND HOSTILE.

It's not the high stress of Telegraph of the buy, buy, buy and the police constantly. It's simple and you can get away from home if home's bothering you and just relax, I hope.

WHAT ARE THE GREATEST REWARDS THAT YOU GET FROM PARTICIPATING?

That's a good question. It goes half and half. It's like this megalomanic martyr thing, 'cause half of me enjoys being needed. It validates existance, you don't exist until somebody knows you do and then you matter. The other half is living up to my ideals of doing everything I can to make a difference, somewhere. No matter how infinitessimal it is. I just feel that I have to do something because the world is so swung against most of the people that come here, that somebody's got to do something. Anything, just even something small that's just keeping this place open. It's not alot to ask but it's something that's really, really important.

WHAT, DO YOU FIND, ARE THE BIGGEST DRAWBACKS?

My health.

MENTAL AND PHYSICAL?

Yeah. Physically more than mentally, I mean mentally it's kinda stressful but it always passes. Physically, the place is kinda running me down. I mean, I'm 26, which is plus or minus, it doesn't really matter, you're only as old as you think you are. But I had a hernia operation last year and I probably need to go back in for another one and I have leukemia but I'm still in remission, which is good. My diet's okay but the stress, just in general is running me down. I can feel myself a little more tired every weekend but I'll do it till I can't.

HOW DID THE DEAL WITH THE ZONING BOARD GO?

Okay; In fact it went alot easier than I had anticipated, which is good. There was really nothing for them to decide at this last meeting because we had met with the police and as long as the police at least, seem to be happy, they were willing to work with us to a point. So we get all our advertising, except we cant do box ads, but we cant afford to do box ads, so again, it's okay. We'll be in entertainment listings. We can be on KALX and any other radio station that we can get away with and we can flyer anywhere we want. So all, totalled it went pretty well. We had to agree to things like no ins and outs on big shows but thats up to our interpretation what we decide a big show is. We're supposed to send the police a schedule of shows that we think are gonna be a problem but again, we have to interpret that for them. So as long as they're there, and we know we can get in touch with them but we still have entire control over when we decide the shows sold out and when we decide there are no ins and outs and when we decide "Well, maybe we should tell the cops that tonight might be bad". Thats the crux of the matter. Thats what I wanted. We still have full control over the place. We haven't given anything away which is good, so far. We have to go back in front of the board in 6 months and we're meeting with the police again on St. Patrick's Day. But the police really don't seem to care terribly much right now, they really don't.

YOU MEAN THEY'RE INDIFFERENT. THEY DON'T CARE IF YOU EXIST OR NOT?

Well, Sergeant R___, who is the police officer in Beckeley that we had the "biggest" problem with, he's a public relations officer or something. When we asked very simply "What could we do to make you happy" said very simply "Nothing short of closing the club would make me happy." But since he's not gonna get that he doesn't seem to care very much. If he really, really wanted to close the club, it would be closed. It would be really, really easy for the police to do, if they really wanted to get rid of us. So right now I look at it as...things are okay, not great, but okay.

I THINK THAT GILMAN'S RECENTLY ADOPTED POLICY THAT ATTENDEES INTERVENE TO STOP VIOLENCE AT SHOWS IS COOL. DO YOU THINK THAT GILMAN'S REGULAR ATTENDEES ARE AGAINST THE VIOLENCE AND THE MACHO ATTITUDES?

Some are. It's a two sided question 'cause it makes me nervous sometimes 'cause we've had situations where mobs of people have decided to do something and that gets easily, easily out of control. Being the security coordinator here it puts me in an odd position 'cause part of me says "9 out of 10 times my staff can handle it if they're there", but the other half of me says "It's really really good that people wanna get involved" but it really depends on the night. Some nights, like last night (the Aborted, Jack Acid, Rancid, Paxston Quiggly on 8th of February). On the other hand, the night before, Neurosis, most of the people there were only interested in dragging their knuckles and flexing their muscles, so it's really dependant on the night. I'd say 35 to 40 percent of the people that come here, not regularly, just come here period really do care about The things that happen here and really do care about the violence and the macho attitudes and the testosterone overload but I'd say close to 60 percent really couldn't care less or even enjoy it. Y'know, again, it's a validation for existance. "I'm a man and this is why I matter because I can run backwards in the pit and knock everybody over" and it makes people notice them and, I guess thats what they're searching for. I guess thats what were all searching for in one sense or another.

ANYTHING ELSE TO SAY?

Just that, I hope that one way or another, since I hope to be leaving the country in September, by then somebody has decided that this place is important enough that they could sacrifice a year of their life and take over the directorship because I don't want to feel that I'm just bailing out and leaving it like "Oh well, that's the end of that, I did my part". I want this place to be here. I think this place is still viable and it could be viable 10 years from now. It has to change to suit the people that come here but I hope that it's still here. Id hate to think that if I left that everything would just drop off. That would really, really bother me and that's influencing my decision somewhat I need to get out of society, I need to get off of concrete, I need to get away from cities and away from people and away from the daily grind. But at the same time part of me says "this is so important that maybe I should be thinking of more than just myself". I dunno, it's a quandry. It goes again, back to the martyr concept. Can I put myself in front of the needs of 150-200 people? I dunno which weighs more.

1992   photo by Murray B.

JOHN H.

I first went to Gilman around 1991 to see a movie. The showing was *The Cabinet of Dr. Caligari*, but the real attraction was the Club Foot Orchestra. They had composed a complete musical background for the silent film, and they were going to give a live performance of this work. There on the wall behind the stage a screen was hung, and to the right the eight members of the orchestra—saxophone, violin, guitars, drums, synthesizer, keyboard. So, twenty feet away: the crafted, eerie expressionist film of 1919, and real live people playing frame-by-frame counterpoint of thoughtful, lyrical music. Wonderful. And, afterwards, being able to walk right up and talk with the musicians. Talk about being inside the art!

I was impressed. It was all very well done. And a pleasant surprise: the usual lines separating performer and audience barely existed in this Gilman place.

I knew little about punk music, but I listened a bit to KALX and came across a band—Nomeansno—which I liked. I saw that the band was going to play at Gilman. I went. Again, that same good feeling of involvement.

I would have remained the occasional audience person, but I kept hearing from various sources that Gilman needed help; not just more volunteers, but people who would get involved in an ongoing basis. Over the years, I had put much time and energy into community work: neighborhood organizing, People's Park ("If you want a swimming pool, start digging. If you don't want it, start shoveling the dirt back in. Who ever shovels the fastest wins.") Being impressed by what I'd seen at Gilman, I went to a (*gasp!*) Gilman meeting. Again: a group working together. And that was the start of my involvement there.

One thing going on at that time was some sort of pressure from the city on Gilman's putting up flyers, about the use permit not allowing it. When Gilman first opened, a "no advertising" condition in the Gilman use permit had been requested by Tim Yohannan, et al. The idea was that the DIY/community/music event was more important than which bands were playing. Within six months it became clear that not enough people were willing to exchange their five dollars for such an event. Ta-dah! the Gilman Flyer, and the condition (in spirit) was history. So, four years later, a big Gilman task was preparation for going before the Board of Adjustments to have this condition eliminated, or at least eased.

I offered to help. A letter was prepared explaining what we wanted. A hearing date was set with the Zoning Department and fees paid. Several of us (including George H. and Gar) went to the Zoning Board meeting. Around 11:00, the "924 Gilman Street" item came up on the agenda, and the shit hit the fan.

Right off, on hearing the address announced, a Board member spoke out: "I know that place! It's a festering sore!" (The source of the phrase, "Berkeley's Own 'Festering Sore,'" as seen on Gilman countout forms.) The next thing was the staff presentation of a four-page report from the Berkeley Police Department detailing many incidents (fights, alcohol drinking, litter, vandalism) at Gilman, which the police were involved in or received complaints about.

A lot of problems the city had with the club came out. The rest of the Board time was spent with Board members talking with each other and with us about these problems. The majority of the Board basically supported the club, but wanted something done about the destructive behavior going on outside in the neighborhood leading to all these complaints. The final result was that we would work with the police under the guidance of the Berkeley Dispute Resolution office. There would be more security, more picking up of litter after the shows. We were given six months and then had to come back to the Board to see how things were going.

So we worked on the litter and vandalism. We met several times with the beat cops, especially Officer R. who advised and encouraged us. The Dispute Resolution group also gave us feedback as to how well the "resolution" was coming along.

After six months we went back to the board. The police said we had done what we needed to do. Conditions in the use permit were worked on about such things as ins-and-outs, trash cans, and frequency of security patrols. The slate was clean. Oh, and the advertising matter resulted in flyers being okay in certain areas—listed in newspaper calendars was okay, no display ads in newspapers.

The next thing: a local, commercial property owner in the area started urging other nearby businesses to write letters to the city to get our use permit revoked, citing litter, graffiti,vandalism, etc. Some businesses did actually write letters. On speaking with these people, we learned that no one knew much about Gilman—there had been little contact. One person said she didn't even know of the existence of the club, but saw the beer bottles and litter on doorsteps, believed the commercial landlord's blaming a teenage hangout two blocks away, and wrote the letter. So, we made special effort at cleaning up—going back to the stores and offices to make sure they were okay about how things were going. The city was aware of this, and no official action was taken.

Around this same time, the Gilman Street Merchants and Business Association (Gilman Street MBA—catchy, huh?) was organized, primarily by REI three blocks away on San Pablo. The whole area was a kind of Wild West: every few weeks there were reports of a purse-snatching, a car window smashed to get the cell phone, expensive mechanic's tools stolen, armfuls of clothes removed from display racks into the getaway car at the curb. Walgreens was twice held up by gangs with guns. (One ended in a shootout at the Bay Bridge toll plaza: four Billy-the-Kids in the shoreline mud versus the police forces of three cities. Unbelievable!)

There was also a fair amount of prostitution going on. Social issues and misogyny aside, the occasional dickheads yelling from their passing cars, "How much, baby?" made just walking around the area a little threatening. Besides, the condoms scattered around were "left there by those kids." Ditto the drug dealing: the syringes were "left there by those kids." And there was the "Dead Guy," a cadaverous man who dragged himself around reportedly selling cocaine. There was at least one case where no one thought he was a Gilman patron.

I talked Gilman into joining the Association (after all, GAMBA was definitely DIY), and even became part of the group leading it. I think it helped make the club part of the neighborhood. Before this, some people's impression of us was, as one person expressed it, that all we did was make money and didn't give a shit. People started talking among themselves more, to exchange information, and to feel less isolated. People saw that Gilman was actively part of improving the area.

Members of the Association chipped in and hired a uniformed security guard to patrol Gilman Street from San Pablo Avenue to Sixth Street. The guard—a very competent guy who soon left the guard gig and went on to better things—even came to a couple of Gilman meetings. Organized people got more attention from City Hall. The police worked better in the area because the merchants and residents talked with them more, giving them accurate and timely information; and there were fewer vacant buildings. The whole tone of the area changed. Building owners kept the litter picked up. The occurrence of prostitution, opportunity crimes, cruising cars, and holdups lessened to the normal every-once-in-a-while. In about three years, the Association withered away.

Next came the banana incident when, during a show, two women in the Insaints band took off clothing and added a bit of a sex show to the band's set. This event might have just transmogrified into Gilman legend, but unfortunately, in the audience was a somewhat well-known contributor to the national punk music scene who, having brought flowers for one of the performing band members, felt his "heterosexual rights were being violated." He called the cops.

This resulted in one of the women being charged with some kind of lewdness (later dismissed) and the city's zoning officer urging the Zoning Board to set a public permit-revocation hearing, i.e., to close the club. We got an attorney who guided us on dealing with zoning law and how to prepare for an appeal just in case.

Soon, a Zoning Board meeting had the agenda item of setting a date for the hearing. Our attorney was told that our item would be at 9:45; he went to have dinner with some friends. At 6:30, the Board's chair said, "Well, it looks like there are a lot of people here interested in 924 Gilman—let's deal with it now." My heart stopped. The bastards tricked our defense away. The zoning chief gave her report on how serious the police and she thought the event was. And then, the Board members started discussing it, and amazingly, they seemed almost amused by the whole thing. The chair asked if there was a motion; heads shook. Silence. Next agenda item. And that was it: no revocation hearing, no scolding, the zoning chief in a bubble, the moral fabric of the East Bay deemed intact. I think that shows how the Zoning Board felt about 924 Gilman—or, at least, about what complaints were important. Why the Chair thought it okay to bring the item up before its promised time I never found out, but there were rumors that the chair knew Tim Yo in high school. Sam the lawyer seemed quite content.

The next big city involvement was Pyramid Brewery. For years, on the other side of Gilman Street from the club, there had always been these empty manufacturing buildings, a whole square block, thousands of square feet on which infrequent attention was paid to those who drank, relieved themselves, or used it as a squat—an accommodating blank, the ideal Gilman neighbor (and ideal for some of Berkeley's homeless and for those who avoided dump fees by leaving tires, mattresses, and piles of rubbish). But then, one fall day in September, 1995, into Gilman's pastoral life came a zoning notice. Pyramid Brewing of Seattle wanted to build a large (80,000 square foot) brewery with attached 250-customer restaurant/brew pub—right across the street. The wide-open frontier was about to be filled up.

It was clear that arguments opposing Pyramid would have very little weight. The area's zoning encouraged manufacturing uses, the brewery jobs were union, the zoning allowed the restaurant as "ancillary" use, more than 100 off-street parking spaces were in the ground plan, Pyramid was bringing jobs and tax revenue to the City, no city official or planner would go for the idea of letting a trashed-out block just sit there until something really cool came along.

Nevertheless, there were issues. Our concern was, how would Pyramid interact with us? Would there be a culture clash? Would they be afraid and only deal with us through the police? Would Gilman be blamed for everything? Would they simply see Gilman as frightening customers away?

For the next several months, a group of Gilman regulars worked on this problem. We went to a preliminary hearing, three of us went to Seattle on Pyramid's invitation to get a guided tour of the restaurant/pub there, and we talked with city officials and several times with the company's president. In preparing for the public zoning hearing, Charles L. and Lindsay K. ran meetings where we prepared a letter for the Zoning Board and rehearsed our presentation. Concerns included city hiring policies, traffic, parking, drunk pub customers, lighting, retail in the manufacturing zone, conflict resolution, and security people.

At the hearing, around a hundred Gilman supporters showed up, all quietly in their seats at the 6:30 starting time. The Board looked over the agenda, and announced that the Pyramid item would be taken up at 10:00; the hundred quietly filed out and three hours later filed back.

We gave our presentation as a group, each with a specific topic, each under the three-minute time limit, stepping right up to the speaker's lectern in turn. (Afterwards, the zoning officer told me that that was one of the most professional presentations he had seen). The Board, sympathetic with Gilman's concerns about dealing with conflicts, spent maybe half an hour asking questions of our speakers and Pyramid's people. (They did ignore our suggestion to close Eighth Street at Gilman). Unbelievable as it may seem, the Gilman folks sort of charmed the Board.

Pyramid's use permit, as prepared by the Zoning Department, has the following language:

- Because the youth club is an important youth resource
  for the City of Berkeley, the operators of the proposed
  brew pub will adopt the following actions to ensure that
  the brew pub is operated in a manner which is compatible
  with the continuing operation of 924 Gilman
- There will be regular meetings the first six months
  between ...
- The brew pub must provide at least one security guard
  specifically to monitor interaction between pub and youth
  club patrons
- Shared responsibility ...

The entire experience with Pyramid, the Zoning Department, and within Gilman could be characterized as one of mutual respect. No demonizing—including by Gilman. Much thoughtfulness and listening. After the place opened, we met with the restaurant manager for several months. And then, because there really weren't any conflicts to work out, we all decided to let the meetings become much less frequent. An anecdote: I came to Gilman one Saturday around 6:00 and there was the Pyramid Brewpub manager hunkered in a chair in Gilman's side room. I said something about no meeting, and he replied that he was on his break and he had come over to Gilman to hide. No Pyramid employee would find him and ask those "Where's the ..." or "What should we do about ..." questions.

Things were pretty quiet after that until late 1998, when the DiCon Fiberoptics Company fell on us. DiCon had been in a building across Eighth Street making fiber optic cable switching equipment ever since the club opened. During the dot-com/internet/Silicon Valley boom, their business skyrocketed, and they went from about 50 employees to over 400 in less than a year. They started expanding to other buildings in the immediate area, enlarging their "campus." They also started having evening shifts, which meant that on Fridays their employees (mostly non-English-speaking Asian women) were mingling with Gilman patrons (talk about culture clash). DiCon had six or seven exotic palm trees planted (without protective posts or anything) in the curbless dirt strip along Eighth Street, right where everybody had parked for years and continued to do so.

Maybe I'm being defensive, but I remember the graffiti occurring once a month or so, and it was mostly the typical two or three cinder block tag. The aftershow cleanup did a pretty good job. Occasionally, I'd get a call and I'd go paint over or pick up things. Moreover, Eighth Street was (and still is) a sort of no-man's-land on which many users dumped trash. Gilman received blame for much of it. I often talked with their maintenance guy; we got along quite well. Up until this expansion, DiCon seemed okay with how Gilman was dealing with graffiti, bottles, and trash on their property. After all, Eighth Street was no San Mateo high tech park.

Then something changed. DiCon's owners went to the city and complained. They said that their buildings were being vandalized every week and it was hurting their business. Kids with machetes were chopping down the palm trees and DiCon was afraid for the safety of their employees (Palm trees break off at nodes in their trunks, giving the appearance of being severed with a blade). DiCon threatened that if the city did not stop this they would have to move out of Berkeley, taking 400 jobs with them. This focused the minds of the city's Planning and Economic Development personnel.

For the next several months, Gilman and the city's Planning Department fenced with each other. Mike Stand became Gilman's pointman in this whole affair. Meetings were held in city conference rooms where proposals and counterproposals were declared. At one point, they wanted Gilman to have a couple of uniformed security guards in a car driving around the area reporting incidents of alcohol/drug use, vandalism, etc. to the police. With DiCon not participating in the discussions (they wouldn't even speak to us), in no plan would we ever be able to have a mutual agreement on what each of our obligations were, and we'd be left open to limitless expectations and complaints. We offered counterproposals. DiCon had security guards on duty in the evenings (we talked a lot with them and, overall, things worked well). Staff at the permit counter said there were no applications for work permits for any of the addresses that DiCon was moving into.

The Planning Department people found we were in noncompliance with a condition in our use permit of ten years previous: Gilman was to pay $1000 towards street lighting on the block. This was a common kind of clause in permits to get businesses to pay for improvements which helped their businesses. Gilman hadn't paid it. But the city must not have demanded it back in 1987—I never saw a dunning notice in five years, and besides, now there were street lights everywhere. No matter: a condition is a condition; we paid the $1000. They also found some kind of entertainment tax from way back for $120 that we hadn't paid (nor been notified of). No matter, a tax is a tax, etc.

It appeared that our supportive beat officers had been sidelined by the desk officers. They had a police lieutenant (lieutenant, not patrolman) park across the street on a Saturday night at 10:00 PM and videotape the Gilman folk hanging around outside the club, apparently to catch vandalizing, graffiti, littering, drunkenness, and Satan worshipping on tape (no tape was later waved about as evidence of Gilman violations). We were told that Telegraph Avenue cops would now be patrolling the area, i.e., not the regular Beat #17 wusses. A city code enforcement guy caught a Gilmanoid tagging a DiCon wall. In addition, he reported later (frequently and at length) that he had seen a young man and woman in a car take their shirts off and disappear below window level.

We had many letters of support from area businesses. Of course, there were letters from Bay Area Gilman goers, but there were letters from many parents as well. We had a web site petition which got, as I remember it, 7000 signatures. Granted, someone from Perth, Australia is not exactly a voting constituent, but all this showed that Gilman had considerable stability. It was not just a warehouse squat.

Then, one day the word went out that DiCon was going to have a liaison person come to the meetings. So, the city set up a big meeting in one of the upstairs dining rooms at Pyramid. Planning people, police department officials, a Berkeley Dispute Resolution guy, Gilman representatives, and the DiCon liaison person. We went back and forth. Gilman agreed to meet with DiCon, and work on a MOU (Memorandum of Understanding). With that, the city was out of the negotiating loop, out of the scene, gone. Gilman, the liaison person, and the BDR guy met together several times. We talked about obligations, but the time between meetings increased. Then, there just wasn't another one. As I remember it, it was as if DiCon just lost interest. Somehow, the generational attack on entrepreneurial freedom had ceased. The city of Berkeley's responsibility was fulfilled. Gilman paid more attention to the condition of DiCon property, but things went on pretty much as before. Except that about a year later, DiCon moved out of all the buildings and took their campus with its 400 jobs to Richmond.

I hope these stories provide some sort of historical record of Gilman's interacting in the larger Berkeley community. Not only can this be a how-to guide, but it is also to show that Gilman has standing and respect in the community and has, as well, a responsibility in the community. I see this history tending to get lost in the constant turnover of people working for the club. Without these realizations, we have the idea and feeling that Gilman is always on the edge of being shut down. It's all very punk, but it's also a confession of weakness, of being victims rather than participants.

So, Gilman in the Berkeley/East Bay municipal world: a city and larger community which supports what Gilman is all about; a core of people who work very hard; our audience (a sort of entity) and community; a few who harm people and property; the ease and satisfaction of demonizing Gilman.

We have always been basically supported by elected officials and their appointees to commissions and boards. Many city staffers—police, city manager's office, public works— go out of their way to help us. There are people all over—in stores, offices, professions—-who went to Gilman shows in the past and still feel a loyalty to the place. (They have been referred to as being—as in the post-college-graduation phrase—"five or ten years out.") Gilman, held in kind of awe by young people scattered worldwide, contributes to Berkeley's reputation of tolerance and innovation.

During a year of weekend after weekend after weekend, 30,000 wildly assorted young people bring themselves to Gilman to be part of the scene and to have a good time. The shows are safe, bands go on, the rent is paid, three full trash carts are put out at the curb almost every week for pickup, most of the trash around the club is picked up, when graffiti appears it is soon buffed, security people spend a lot of time confronting: "Get out of ...", "You can't ...", "You'll have to leave ...",

"You're 86'd", "We'll call the police ..." (There's the almost serious idea of security T-shirts reading, "I took a punch for Gilman.") And a wonderful memory: Will, Dave, and Sam carrying paint, rollers, solvents, rags up Eighth Street into a cold, January 1:00 AM darkness to remove some particularly offensive graffiti a Gilman patron had applied earlier that evening. I want to add that Gilman meetings (please, no rude guffaws) do deal with a vast number of problems, and, by and large, solve them.

All the time we have to work on getting more people to volunteer and then not getting resentful or burned out, to have everyone— audience, bands, volunteers —have the feeling we made another Gilman show (great or not so great) work, maybe even feel that we deserve to applaud ourselves.

There are all kinds of reasons people do harm; sometimes Gilman doesn't exert enough group pressure (when Gilman is just a treehouse for teenagers), sometimes individuals hate Gilman, some are just ignorant, sometimes we are dealing with family dynamics and social conditions, and sometimes vandalism is just in the human genes (vide: Vandals, 455 AD). Gilman does a pretty good job dealing with each of these. We can't (and, of course, wouldn't) just sit back and blame others.

We could diminish being "Other" by making more contact with people in the neighborhood. We could be more involved with the Berkeley Youth Commission and Berkeley High School projects: art, music, films, drama. There are civic projects, like creek restoration—you know, Codornices Creek, up at the end of Eighth Street, with all the bottles and trash in it. Anything involving the betterment of the Gilman area. Some newspapers accept articles.

And finally, the best way to stick it to the Man is to have Gilman live well and long.

2000   photo by Lauren L.

MARCUS P.

I first started going to Gilman in 1988. I would come down from Sacramento for the shows fairly regularly. I then moved to the Bay Area in 1991 and worked at Gilman for about two years. I had heard about Gilman through *Maximum RocknRoll* magazine. The first time I went I thought it was pretty much exactly the way it had been written about. There were lots of things bouncing around, basketballs, etc. I think one of the first shows I went to was an Isocracy show. The one thing I was surprised at was that there weren't many people at the show. The Sacramento shows I had been going to were very different. Those were shows held at rented-out "regular" clubs and they were extremely dangerous to go to. The skinhead scene seemed to be at its height right around then. Gilman was nice because it didn't have anywhere near the same danger level. It seemed like the center of the punk scene and I wanted to help out there. It was one of the main reasons for me moving to the Bay Area.

When I was working there, the turnout for shows was pretty bad. I could never understand why it wasn't more supported. It never really felt like it was widely supported, and I still don't think it is today. One of the big reasons, of course, is that once you turn 21 and can go to bars, you stop going to Gilman. Also, at that time, there were a lot of really bad bands. But I really liked the people I was working with, and it was a good place to meet new people. It was primarily a social outlet for me. For almost two years I was there every weekend. During that period, it was hugely important to me. It was important to me because I felt like it put me in the center of the punk scene. I felt like I was part of something somewhat vibrant and alive. In the bigger sense, I never felt like I was part of some huge, important project or anything like that. It was just a fun thing to do.

I felt that Gilman being volunteer-run was important, as well as having a place for bands to play that wasn't "pay-to-play." But gradually I got pretty burned out. During that period Gilman always seemed like it was on the verge of shutting down, being behind in rent, etc. I initially felt like I was going to keep working there until it shut down. But Gilman kept going, and I couldn't.

I still go occasionally. I'm really happy that it's still going on, I think it's as important as ever. It fills the niche for people who can't go to bars and don't have a lot of money to go see bands. It seems now that attendance there is better than ever, and that there are a lot better shows going on there. My most memorable night was the first time Chumbawamba played there. There was such a great sense of community, from the people working, from the bands, and from the people attending. And I'll always remember the smell of the place.

SHOWS: EVERYBODY'S ALWAY'S TOO CONCERNED ABOUT THE DUMB STUFF AT SHOWS, LIKE THE PARTICULAR BANDS AND THE CLUBS THEY PLAY AT, NOT THE IMPORTANT STUFF...LIKE THE WAY YOUR CLOTHES SMELL AFTER THE SHOW. I REMEMBER AFTER THE FIRST SHOWS I WENT TO, MY CLOTHES WOULD SMELL LIKE BEER AND SWEAT AND WEED AND CIGARETTES FOR A WHOLE WEEK AFTER THE SHOW, EVEN IF I HADN'T SEEN ANYONE DRINKING BEER OR SMOKING POT AT THE SHOW. IT WAS LIKE BRINGING PART OF THE SHOW HOME WITH ME. I REMEMBER SOMEONE AT GILMAN COMPLAINING THAT AFTER SHOWS THEIR CLOTHES STUNK AND WHEN THEY BLEW THEIR NOSE THEIR SNOT WAS BLACK. THEY WERE COMPLAINING!! I ALWAYS THOUGHT THAT WAS THE RADDEST PART OF GOING TO SHOWS. THAT, AND GETTING TO AND BACK FROM THE SHOW, WHICH USUALLY WOUND UP IN SOME SORT OF MISADVENTURE INVOLVING MISSED BUSSES AND GETTING LOST AND AVOIDING COPS AND THUGS. I NEVER HAD A CAR, AND THE SHOWS WERE ALWAYS IN SOME BAD NEIGHBORHOOD AND OFTEN IN A CITY I WAS UNFAMILIAR WITH. GETTING THERE WAS HALF THE FUN.....

Taken from a piece written by "Skrub" for *Absolutely Zippo* fanzine

ERNST

I first went to Gilman in 1989 to see Neurosis open for Green Day. My younger brother had told me about the place. We lived in Chico, California (a few hours away) and I couldn't always get rides there. I was a senior in high school in Chico, a little rural town. I thought Gilman was a really cool place, a Martin Scorcese-type of club, lots of spooky looking people, and graffiti everywhere. I had heard a lot about it. We actually had a good club in Chico at the time, too, so it wasn't that strange to me to see a functional club for punk shows. I don't think I went to another show at Gilman that year.

After a year of college, I came out to the Bay Area for the summer and started playing in a band in the Bay Area. The first place I went to was Gilman to see if I could find a place to live. I had heard that you could sleep at Gilman if you needed to, which turned out to be sort of true. Gilman was my central social point for a month or so while trying to meet up with people to try and find a place to live. I was living in a car at the time. That was when Jesse was booking and George was the head coordinator, and I started hanging out with them a lot, and spent a lot of time at Gilman. It was a real community then, a "pirate den," a sense of close-knit craziness; all the people I hung out with were involved there in some way. Working there just kinda grew out of always being there. I worked the door, did clean up, learned how to run the sound board, my band practiced there, my girlfriend did a lot of the stage managing, etc. I had wanted to learn how to run a soundboard for a while, how to mix and record bands, do live sound. It seemed like the funnest thing to do, since I'm not terribly good at dealing with people. I didn't go to the meetings much, unless I happened to be there when they were held, and even then I didn't contribute much, except to shoot fireworks at people. I was there a little of 1990 and most of 1991. I just worked occasionally after that for a few years, then just went to shows there.

I think it's become more of a collective over the years. When I was there the decisions were mostly all made by one or two people. But, having more people involved in the decision-making process can make it harder to make a decision, as well. But I think it's worth the extra work because I don't think one or two people should be making all the rules. It's a fascinating laboratory for all that stuff because most everyone is really young, without a lot of previous activist/collective experience. I didn't really think that much about me being part of an activist group, it was just something fun I did with my friends. And over the years, I've started to feel more negative about the perception of an activist part of Gilman, because I feel it doesn't succeed terribly well in a lot of ways in being activist that other similarly run clubs across the country do. These other clubs seem more interested in community outreach as well. Putting on shows is just one of their functions, as opposed to being their only function, like Gilman. I don't mean this as a criticism so much of Gilman, more of the apathy prevalent in the Bay Area in general. In the small towns where these other clubs I'm referring to are, the motivation level and excitement level is much higher, predominantly because so little goes on there. In the Bay Area, it's almost like there's too much going on and people are overwhelmed by having too much to choose from and end up doing nothing. I saw Gilman as just another club. And I don't really know what would make it anything but just a club.

From a band member's perspective, I have a huge quarrel with Gilman because of the low pay for bands. It's possibly the only place I've ever played where fifty percent of the door goes to the club. That's way higher than anywhere else. It's frustrating, as a band, to play on a bill where 300 people come to the show and you get paid fifteen dollars. I've never sat down and taken a look at where all the money at Gilman goes, but when you're in a band, and you feel like you've put a lot of work into your music and your shows, and all the bands on the bill get what seems like a tiny little cut of what looks like a big audience, it's very frustrating. I grew up with the idea of Gilman being the model for how a club should be run, but now, having been touring and seeing how other clubs are run, I don't think that anymore.

Those criticisms aside, I think Gilman had a big impact on me, more than I realized at the time. Gilman taught me how to be in a band, how to tour, how to cooperate with other bands. I learned the mechanics of things. Bottom-rung musicians, like myself, are tradesmen in a certain sense, and you do need to learn how to do some things professionally, even if your ultimate goal is to just go out and have fun and do crazy stuff. You have to know how some things work or you're stuck forever. Another thing I learned at Gilman was the etiquette/protocol of running the stage/bands smoothly and efficiently, like having set times for the bands to play, helping them off/on stage with their equipment, things like that, stage managing, basically. That doesn't seem to happen very often at the other places I've played. Also, Gilman's sound system was really good. After I went back to college, I was helping put on shows there and I persuaded the school to buy a sound system and helped put that together. That was a copy of the system at Gilman and from what I learned at Gilman. And I liked the heckling of bands that went on at Gilman, that was always fun. And I remember the crazy Blatz shows, them throwing out squid at the audience, or spraying the audience with rotten milk out of an inflatable goat's ass, or chopping things up with an electric chainsaw. They generally always made a big mess when they played.

Where's the stage? Part two,   1992   photo by Murray B.

In all fairness, in some ways Gilman can never live up to its reputation. Gilman has been around long enough now to almost have become a myth. So much has been touted about it and ideallized that it seems like it could never be as good as the way you imagine it in your head. People come from all over the country, all over the world even, to see what it's like, expecting it to be the best place ever. Nothing could ever live up to that. Sometimes I feel like we should just burn it down and start again.

MARCUS DA ANARCHIST

SHITTING ON SCUMLEBUTH WIFE

MARCUS DA ANARCHIST

WHAT DID I DO AT GILMAN? CHIT MAN, WHAT DID I NOT DO THAR. I'VE DONE EVERY JOB AT GILMAN EXEPT SOUND & MOST OF DA TIMES I WOULD DO MORE THAN JUST ONE JOB A SHOW. I USUALLY JUGGLED ABOUT 4-6 JOBS A NITE THAR, JUST TA KEEP THANGZ RUNNING SMOOTH AZ POSSIBLE, & TA KEEP GEORGE HATED FROM GETTING A BIGGER ULCER.

MY FIRST IMPRESSION OF GILMAN WAZ A VERY LONG TIME AGO. I WENT TO GILMAN ABOUT DA TIME THEY FIRST OPENED. I THOUGHT IT WAZ A GRAND THANG, ALMOST AZ COOL AZ DA FARM (I WAZ MORE INTA DA FARM FOR BEING A POOR HOMIE FROM DA CITY, YA KNOW EASIER TA FUCKIN GET TA!!!), BUT AZ I WAZ GETTING OLDER & PUNK SHOWS WERE GETTING MORE SCARCE FOR UNDER AGE CHILDREN IN SAN FRAN-FUCKINCISCO, I SAW MYSELF GOING TA GILMAN ST. PROJECT. DA FACT IT WAZ A VOLUNTER-RUN CLUB REALLY IMPRESSED ME. VERY SOON I WAZ APPLYING MYSELF TA HELPING IT RUN & MOST IMPORTANT, MAKING NEW FRIENDZ, THAT TODAY ARE STILL GOOD FRIENDZ.

NO NAZI AZZWHOLES

THAR ARE MANY STRENGTHS & WEAKNESSES TA GILMAN. I FIRST STARTED GOING TA GILMAN IT WAZ MUCH, MUCH, MUCH LOOSER THAN IT IZ TODAY. CHIT, DE'RE WOULD BE SHOWS THAR FULL OF EM FUCKIN NAZI'S SKINNERS!! BEING A MULTI-BREED MEXICAN, I WAZ VERY AGAINST NAZI'S. INFACT I WAZ A TARGET FOR 'UM FEW NAZI GROUPS FROM DAT CITY BY DA BAY BECAUSE I WAZ REALLY INTO COUNTER DEFENSES AGAINST DEM & THEIR FUCKED UP ACTIONS. THEN GILMAN ALL OF A SUDDEN GOT SOME BACKBONE AND DECIDED NOT TO LET THESE CREEPS COME AROUND. THAR WERE LOTS OF FIGHTS, LOTS OF BASEBALL BATS, CHAINS, & BLOOD.

BUT ALL IN ALL IT WORKED & STILL TODAY GILMAN DOESN'T ALLOW NAZI FACIST ASSHOLES AROUT DA PLACE. I HAD, I WIFF MANY OTHERS, VISIONS GALORE FOR GILMAN, & DA BAY AREA, IF NOT DA WORLD. BUT, ALAS I MUST SAY, GILMAN CAN ALSO BE A CRUSHER OF SPIRITS.

Ye see, PUNK FUCKIN ROCK waz not az populer az it iz today, these darz ye can be a fuckin yuppie fuck wiff punk hair, so every struggle ta keep thangs going waz wiff tooth & naik!! At Gilman we wanted ta do much more, like maybe having da store opened during da week & having a cafe style of things. Also, we really would of liked ta do more for da community that lived around da place. All these great idea's were crushed, mostly thanx ta facist "Willow" when he took over. See, gilman waz in da red, & while he did do good in getting gilman out of da red, he also waz not a good person ta other's who worked thar for a long time. Unfortunately, he lied & cheated people ——

ta make himself look good. Dat's when I really got disillusioned, especially when we had fought long & hard ta keep facisum out of gilman. All of a sudden, here iz gilman being run by facist-by-heart asshole. My last straw waz broke when he set up russ (Lordburger/Lungbutter) who ran da store for plenty of year wiff a uncommon pride. "Willow" told lies & got him 86ed. They had butted heads long before "Willow" took over.

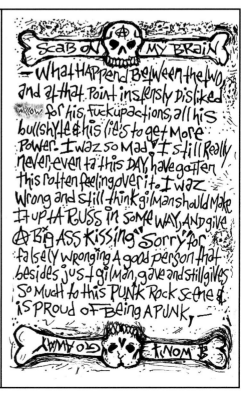

OUT OF DA WAY, PECK.

—Being head honcho and ta make thang's short, "Willow" falsely accused russ of stealing money's, wich waz complelely false!!! Then "Willow" went to a meetin— without russ even being thar! A stand up for himself, and got him 86ed (wich he still iz to this DAY!) I waz so pissed off by this ass-h*le & all of the people that jumped the gun behind this little twerp, that I instantly went on strike, wich lasted a cuple of years— (dam scabs) I did that mainly because I waz a witness of "Willow's" @ chump.

SCAB ON MY BRAIN

—What happend between the two, and at that point instensly disliked "Willow" for his fuckupactions, all his bullshyte & his lie's to get more power. I waz so mad. I still really never, even ta this day, have gotten this rotten feeling over it. I waz wrong and still think gilman should make it up ta russ in some way, and give a big ass kissing "sorry" for falsely wronging a good person that besides just gilman, gave and still gives so much to this PUNK rock scene & is proud of being a punk.

OUT OF DA WAY, MOMB

SH*TE It's NoT LiKe He's Ditching Dead Baby's in Rafters! I Learned plenty of skills from gilman, as far as how ta Run shows. A couple years after starting MY s!rike I started Draw-ing flier's Agian (thanx ta Ben A-Head). Putting on MY own shows & Doing sound with Russ (A punk genuis for Doin Sound. I After a lot of Nagging ta give MY shows a name, I finelly caved in and started calling MY endeavors "PYRATE PUNX" (MY two favrite thangs PYRACY & PUNK). The Basis of It spilled inta some indoor CLUB, money-making shows (HAR, HAR, HAR, yea like thars is a lot of CASH flowin PUNK, HAR!) Eventually, ON A SAKE TOUR, →

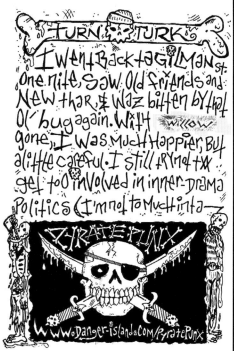

TURN TURK

I Went Back ta GiLMan st. one nite, Saw Old friends and New thar, & waz bitten by that Ol' bug again. With willow gone, I was Much Happier, But a little careful. I still try not ta get too involved in inner-Drama Politics (I'm not to Much inta —

WWW.Danger-island.com/PyratePunx

WALK together open commitees. I'm more of a take charge kind of ASS H*LE!) Well, then I started doin f (yer's again for gilman and booking show's UNDER "DA BLACK FLAG"!!!

All in all, through DA THICK and thin gilman st. Project should, I Hope Always shall survive as A D.I.Y. or die venue, If It Does not then It's not Really gilman st. Anymore. Mainstream has It's place, we have OURS, and when I mean OURS I mean OURS! Thanx ta Me Parents, PYRATE PUPSZ DA BATTLE AXE. VIVA LIBERTAD! contacts: PyratePunx.com or PyratePunx@aol.com

'96 — photo by Ayumi N.

MIKE GOODBAR AKA SCARY MIKE

I was into metal and some of the metal kids were getting into punk. A friend of mine in the ninth grade was going to a show at Gilman—this was early 1987. I went with him and it was a big, chaotic experience. As small as Gilman is, when there's a lot of people there, it looks much bigger, and when you're 15, all the older folks look like giants, and when they have mohawks and spiked leather jackets, they look even bigger. It was an easy transition from metal to punk once I saw how approachable the punk bands were. They weren't dicks to their fans like the metal bands were—even the small, local ones. Punk just seemed so much more accepting of everyone overall. There's a place for everyone in the punk scene, even if you didn't fit into one of the "cooler" cliques.

Shortly afterward, I learned more about what the place was about, and I kinda fell in love with it, because it had some social ethics that I liked. Things like: it was affordable, the whole scene was that way. I was used to spending $10 on a record, and here they were $5 and $6. I also liked the way Gilman was run. It was sorta run on a Berkeley "commie" ethic. I knew it was volunteer-run and started working there occasionally early on, doing clean-up and stuff at first, then cash-box and so on. I knew from the beginning that I wanted to work there. I did that until the first shutdown in 1988.

I joined the group who wanted to re-open Gilman, the AMF. We kinda felt jilted that there was this great thing that was being closed on us, and we wanted to do something about it. So, it opened up again, and in spring 1989 I moved away for about a year and a half and didn't start coming to Gilman again until late 1990/early 1991. There had been a lot of change—a whole new slew of people were running it and hanging out there. I had to start all over, basically, with getting started working there again. It was definitely a clique then and it took time to be accepted, to show that you weren't just working to get in for free, that you wanted to help, and that Gilman meant something to you. I started posting flyers for shows, and was making some too from time to time. I was collecting old magazines for graphics—I got really into it, cutting and pasting, tracing logos, etc. I really liked the creative aspects of it.

Then I started taking an interest in the Gilman store and working there more often. I wanted more of an intellectual challenge than flyering was offering. I worked in the store from 1992/1993 to 1996, about four years. The tips helped too, since I wasn't working a full-time job. It seemed like the fun, hip position. It wasn't just the social aspects I liked—it was the challenge of it, running it tighter, doing the ordering, inventorying, accounting, etc. It gave me a sense of real responsibility. Because of my lack of good grades, I couldn't get a work permit to get an established job, so it wasn't until I was 18 that I could get real jobs. And those didn't really give me much responsibility or sense of accomplishment—you just ended up feeling like a sucker, doing shitwork for someone else. There wasn't anything else around where I could have gotten as much responsibility at such an early age, like I did at Gilman. People need to feel needed, and Gilman provides that opportunity. It also provides a vocational education. At meetings, 14-year-olds have an opportunity to deal with issues sometimes as complex as those faced by 46-year-olds involved with big business corporations. In the regular world a person would have to have really good grades and upper class status to get access to the right job or situation that would provide the same experiences that Gilman does to anyone who's interested.

Since 1996, I've just worked on occasion, helping out here and there. I needed to slow down or I would've burned out completely. I was also treasurer on the board of directors at Gilman from 1994 to 1999. The place has grown on me over the years, and I've enjoyed watching it grow and change too, like seeing the filing system for paperwork change from it simply stuffing it in a paper bag, to a tight, rigid, formal setup. Every head coordinator has seemed to take it further—the collective consciousness seems to keep maturing and evolving. Gilman's helluv organized now and has survived many things that would've ended many other clubs. Gilman's become a part of me, a part of my life. It was important to me in the sense that it was a place to grow up in as a teen, and as a young adult it provided something to be involved in, and I was glad to put in so much of my energy. It was a place where I "belonged." I had been involved with different political causes before, but they seemed to have a lot of baggage and infighting. Gilman didn't place unreasonable demands on me, either. I'll always care about the place and want to help if needed. I was able to quit smoking and doing certain drugs at different times, but quitting Gilman, and completely severing myself from it, would be hard for me. It's not something that can just be cast off for me.

Exercising the right of freedom of religion, 1988   photo by Murray B.

JERME S.

Something happens to you when you put your life on the line for something you believe in. Although I no longer work at 924 Gilman, it will always be a place that I consider one of the best experiences of my life. I grew up watching bands come and go, volunteers pledge undying allegiance to the club only to quit months later, various folks trying to use the club as platforms for their own agendas, and of course, all the knuckleheads who came to make someone's life unpleasant for one reason or another. Yet there were a few dedicated people who stuck with it and put in an incredible amount of hours so that "the kids" would have a place to watch bands and hang out.

At some point, in the nine years that I worked at the Gilman Street Project off and on, I started working security. It was something I took very seriously, and if you asked most of the people I threw out over that time, or even a few of the people I worked with—a little too seriously. It was very hard to not just start cracking skulls when a few morons would come in and attempt to run the place. I had watched it happen as a young punk rocker: at almost every show I went to there was some jackass in the pit or out front making a really cool show very unfun for a few people.

I decided early on as a bouncer that I would make the people who were used to intimidating others feel very uncomfortable and unwelcome. I figured it would be the least I could do for a space where I had spent years meeting very cool people and watching bands that to this day I am blown away by. My job meant dealing with the part of the crowd that wasn't cool or nice. The segment of the audience that had come to act out, or through the course of the evening had decided that they were going to have fun at someone else's expense. I found that it made me believe in the club even more, but I also found that it made me more jaded about the people who patronized it through the years I worked at 924 Gilman.

At the second show I worked, the level of commitment that those working Gilman was shown to me. A large group of white power skinheads decided to show up and make a pseudo attempt at rushing the door. It was a total shock to me—not the violence, but the complete lack of a goal behind their attack. They never once tried to actually go inside the club, choosing to slug it out with anyone brave enough to face them out front. I can remember rushing outside to face an enemy I had no dealings with, over a place that I had really no allegiance to. How quickly that changed as I witnessed people taking great steps to ward off a large group of assholes bent on ruining a larger group's weekend. During the evening I learned why they had picked that particular night to come down and brawl with us. MDC was headlining, and the skinheads had a feud with them that went back years. Apparently they took MDC's show at Gilman as an opportunity to come down and fuck shit up. One of the things that stood out very clearly was MDC's roadie/friend Pierre. That guy seemed so insane, tall, muscular, missing teeth, jailhouse tattoos, and wired way too tight. I didn't get a chance to talk to him much that night, but years later I ran into him. Even though I didn't know him, I brought up that night from years back and instantly we had something in common. It was weird to think back on my first years at Gilman, since by that point it had changed so much.

I was to find out over the next year or so that the skinheads, and other fuckups, would use just about anything as an excuse. Any reason to come down and try and make life hell for those that volunteered. It's a goal they achieved on many nights, making our nights at the shows long and tiring.

Years later, two junkies tried to ruin my weekend by running me down with their car. They were down the street from the club—after almost all the people, patrons and workers alike, had gone home—starting trouble and making the nightly cleanup crew's lives hard. Apparently one of them grabbed a trash bag away from one of the kids and threw it over a barbed wire fence. So then it was my job to walk down the street and make them go away. After a brief verbal altercation, which was elevated into an almost all-out fight when one of them pulled a knife, I convinced them they should leave. As I walked back down the street I could hear them gunning the engine of their car as they came driving down the street. I figured they would just buzz by us, trying to get even for me facing down the one junkie who had pulled the knife. I could quickly hear the engine getting closer. As much as I didn't want to, I looked over my shoulder to see how close they were going to get. The car was about twenty feet behind us and it was immediately obvious that they were going to hit me with it. I had enough reaction time to jump up onto my tiptoes. The car's fender slammed into my left calf and my right hip was slammed by the top front corner. I slid back on the hood and bounced off the windshield into the air, up and over the rest of the car. I found out later that I had been tossed into the air with so much force that I did a full-gainer with a twist. I also was told that I had gone into the air high enough so that when I was coming down I hit the guy I was walking with in the back of the head. I landed on the cement in a sprawled-out sprinter position. The first thing that came to mind was to get up and chase the car so that they couldn't get away. Of course they got away, but I think I gave one hell of a chase to the corner.

It's appropriate that one of my last shows working as security involved a large brawl in front of the club. A small group of losers, who had been previously thrown out for one reason or another, had shown up. I met them at the door as they tried to enter and told them that they were not welcome inside that night, or any other night in the future. After some arguing on their part, and me simply explaining that they weren't welcome and to go away, a punch was thrown. One of them slugged me in the side of the head as I turned to tell another one of their friends to get out from behind me. What happened next was me, Raif, Dean, and Andrew ended up in the street with twelve of them brawling. They were very bent on seeing me go down, and I was swarmed pretty much the whole time. After what seemed like twenty minutes, but was probably only five or ten, cop cars started showing up. As they ran off, I marveled at the fact that I was still standing. Made me chuckle a little to think about, that if this had been the time with the skinheads, I'd be searching the gutter for my teeth once I came to.

In reading the last couple of paragraphs, I realize I'm making shows at Gilman out to be very violent and out of control. I wanted to talk about a side of Gilman that I didn't think many others would write about. Even though most of what I had to deal with was tedious and sometimes violent, I could still recognize the part of Gilman that made it stand alone. A lot of really amazing events occurred at Gilman over the years. I watched a lot of people grow up inside the graffiti-covered walls. I got to see young kids come in, unsure of their place and/or abilities in the world, and discover that they could make a difference in how things are run. Working security didn't bring me in contact with the smartest or fun-seeking parts of a show's crowd. Even still, over the years I met a lot of people who made lasting impressions on me, good and bad.

1991   photo by Murray B.

**Above, left, and below: photos by
Larry W.**

CHAPTER FIVE

OUT OF THE RED

MIKE S.

1992-1993

"IT CAN BE DARK, COLD, SMELLY, AND LONELY."

-DAVE EC

photo by Larry W.

MIKE STAND

I first saw the flyers that MRR put up in record stores in 1986 before they even had a location. I was only fourteen then and didn't have a car, so I didn't go there until about four to six months or so after it opened. I was fifteen by that time (summer 1987). I hadn't been to many other places to see shows, other than church basements and people's backyards. I don't think I had been to any actual clubs before Gilman. That was pretty much my first exposure to organized, cohesive punk rock in one location. I lived in the East Bay, but about 30-40 miles away, way out in the suburbs. It was pretty hard to get to Gilman for a while. Finally I had to convince my friends to take me occasionally. I didn't have any money at the time, and I heard that if you worked at the show, you could get in for free. I was kinda always the type of person who wanted to get involved with stuff anyway, so it wasn't like I was just doing it to get in for free, it was almost like something to do, and, at least for me, it made the show more exciting. So I started working shows just a few months after I started going, about late summer/early fall of 1987. I even knew, without having been to many other commercial venues, that it was community-oriented, and I liked the sort of utilitarian aspect of it—you all came together, and got to see a huge number of bands every Friday and Saturday night. I liked the "bulk" aspect of it. I think that was what impressed me the most. It was a lot of bands, a lot of people, every weekend night. That really appealed to me at the time. And that there were really great interesting people involved with the club at that time that I got to meet. Growing up in the suburbs, you didn't have a lot of contact with people between the ages of eighteen and thirty-five, basically. You had the kids you went to school with, and then your teachers, and that was it, other than your parents. It was nice to meet people of all ages and from all different places, and get a much broader view of life than what you had in the suburbs.

Even before I started going to shows, I was interested in the music, because the people were better. I could tell right away that the people into punk rock were better than the people who were into say, bad hair metal, for instance. It just seemed natural to me to go to a place like Gilman and surround myself with a cooler crowd of people than I had been. Right from the start, even before I went to Gilman, punk rock was more than just the music—it was the people, the sense of community and activity.

For the first year or year-and-a-half that I went to the club, it was hard for me to get to the meetings, so I rarely went. The meetings were on Sundays back then. I worked occasionally during my first year there, then once I turned sixteen and could drive, I started working more. I just worked the door basically. The other jobs, like stage manager or show coordinator, were usually worked by people older than me, who seemed more worldly and knew more about how things worked there, so I didn't pursue those jobs. I was taken by surprise by the shutdown in fall 1988. I wasn't paying too much attention up to that point. I wasn't part of the meetings about starting it up again after the closure either, although I did know some of the people involved.

Pretty quickly I got involved with working again after it reopened in late 1988. After working the door again for a few shows, I was pulled aside by one of the main people helping to run the space and was asked to get more involved in the space. I think it was because I knew how to do math! At first I was helping with the count-outs after the show, but I couldn't always stay late, so I started stage managing instead. I really liked that, getting to meet people, hang out, be as helpful as I could. I started going to meetings a lot. I would go there during the week, do some desk-top publishing-type things, help with the calendar, stuff like that. That's when I started getting exposed to the behind-the-scenes type stuff, and learned about organization, etc. I felt really comfortable working with the second group that took over running Gilman; I felt like we had a good bunch of people. There just weren't a lot of people involved, in particular not a lot of "kids" involved—it was mostly older people. But everyone coming to the meetings seemed to have a common vision and a common goal for what the club should be and what kind of shows we should put on. That was probably the most fun I had working shows, up to about 1989. It was tough for us though, financially—a 60-person show was a good-sized show. I don't think we ever had a sold-out show.

During 1989-1990 I was a senior in high school and working more, so I went to a lot less shows. I had gained a lot of self-confidence from working at Gilman. It was invaluable to me in getting involved with my high school newspaper. Also, I started my own business silk-screening T-shirts in my garage. My experiences at Gilman definitely enabled me to take on bigger things in life. In 1991, I started working a graveyard shift at my job. After graduating, I was at Gilman even less. Then I heard that the head coordinator at the time, George, was leaving, and I started coming to meetings again. A group had approached Gilman about wanting a benefit show to help their cause, and I got involved in helping put that together, and it ended up blossoming into this three-day festival. During this time, I was at Gilman all the time, and a couple people approached me about taking over the head coordinator position, but at first I didn't really want to. Ultimately, there were three people who said they'd do it, but not do it alone. That was me, Brian S., and Ken S. We were going to co-coordinate. We announced it at a meeting.

The club was in dismal financial shape at the time. We were three months behind in rent. We had some huge phone bills ($300-$500) left to pay. The club was a pig sty, people had been living there, the office smelled like a trash heap, theft was rampant, people were stealing cash, they were stealing stuff from the store, people were letting their friends in for free in epidemic proportions. There was no accounting for anything. People were spending Gilman's money recklessly. That was the first thing I did—I said, we're not spending any money on anything, period. We're going to get the phone bills paid, and the rent paid, and we're not spending any more money until we do. There were maybe a couple hundred dollars in the bank account. Then we started some pretty extreme booking, and started calling in a lot of favors to have "bigger" bands come play a lot and help bail us out. I started asking reliable old friends to come down and help work, especially the door, because I couldn't trust a lot of the old people to break their habits. We started to climb out of debt really fast. After about four to five months, we were finally caught up with the rent. We paid the phone bills pretty quick. I would deposit the cash in the bank that night after the show—we wouldn't leave it in the club overnight. More than once, someone had pried open the strongbox in the club and taken the money. I wouldn't let anyone else do the countout at the end of the night. I watched the money like a hawk.

It was a good time to try and get the club out of debt, with the rising popularity of Green Day and Rancid, along with others like Econochrist and Jawbreaker, and Lookout Records. Gilman is a really—I won't say *easy* organization to run from a business standpoint—but it's fairly straightforward. You don't have any inventory to take care of; you don't have any assets other than the sound system and the money from the door at the end of a show. The bookkeeping is very straightforward, money is split with the bands (Gilman was taking fifty percent at the time). The security guards were being paid as independent contractors, so we didn't have to worry about payroll taxes. At the time, we were blowing off sales tax, so we didn't have to worry about figuring out sales tax on the stuff we sold in the store. We went round and round with the membership thing. Ultimately we decided on $2 yearly membership with $5/$6 doors. The membership fee provided significant additional income for us. Compared to a regular club, it somewhat took the place of alcohol sales. The membership money wasn't split with the bands. I felt it was one of the keys to our continuing financial solvency. Sometimes things that are good ideas for one reason end up being good ideas for other reasons. The membership concept started out as a way to help foster the community aspect of Gilman, but really turned out mostly as a big financial help. I don't think Gilman would lose its sense of community if we dumped the yearly membership, but it would be a lot harder to make ends meet money-wise.

We started having a lot more $6 shows. I felt it was necessary, but others at the club fought it pretty hard. It did help us get out of debt faster, but put us on a similar level price-wise to other venues in the area. We were no longer always the cheapest alternative. I wanted to run the club at a profit, or at least pay our own way. I wanted to end the "clubhouse" atmosphere, to put an end to people running the club for themselves. Gilman should be run for the kids who have nowhere else to go, who don't have enough money to go see Marilyn Manson for $17.50, or who really don't want to.

I wanted to open Gilman up at the level of the people coming to the shows. Unfortunately, what I ended up sacrificing was that Gilman was less and less for the people working the shows. Because of that, fewer people were working the shows, my life got harder, and I burned out faster. I wanted to book some of the larger bands at Gilman, so kids wouldn't have to go to Berkeley Square or some other bar to see them. I wanted to make Gilman safer, too, have the security be effective, but as unobtrusive as possible. I wanted Gilman to be as drug and alcohol-free as possible. It was twelve months that I was in the head coordinator role. After about three months, Brian S. wasn't able to spend as much time there, so he pulled out, and Ken S. was doing mostly booking. John H. offered to help with the bookkeeping, which helped out immensely. Dave EC and Dan K. helped with booking. I worked almost every show and wouldn't let anyone else deal with the money. That was one of my failings—I wouldn't trust anybody. After I announced my resignation, and knew that I would have to find other people and show them how to do things, I loosened up a bit. I think I pushed a lot of people away, and that wasn't a good thing.

Branwyn took over from me, and I still tell people that she saved my life. I took the head coordinator position as a last resort, because no one else wanted to do it. We had things pretty squared away by then. At the time I announced I was leaving, we had over $4,000 in the bank, and when I left, three months later, we had close to $10,000 in the bank. It seemed like all or nothing, crowd-wise. We'd have six shows a month with about sixty people per show, and four shows a month with 250-400 people. It was hard for us to find a constant middle ground. I think that led to a lot of burnout. I moved farther away from Gilman and didn't even go to a show there for three months after I resigned. But over the years I have kept a hand in, like helping with the Pyramid Brewery fight and the DiCon fight. I still feel a connection

190

to the place, a necessity to help when needed, just like those who helped me when I asked. For me, the club's always been about the individual people involved, and my feelings about the club are strongly intertwined with those individuals who helped me out.

I still have the memories of amazing, inspiring shows, like Op Ivy's last show and the first time Chumbawamba played there. I would not be doing anything close to what I'm doing with my life now if it hadn't been for Gilman. I got a lot of confidence in how to deal with people older than me. I learned a lot about business as well. To see that it's possible to take something that a lot of people saw as a lost cause and a total failure and to show them that it could be saved showed me that almost any business can be saved. I went to work for a company that was slowly dying, and we turned it around, at least for a period of time. It showed me that just by changing a few small habits, you can vastly change the direction that a large organization is going in, whether it's a non-profit collective or a commercial business. If a business is losing money slowly, it's probably able to make money. That's my take on things. Now I run my own business, and a lot of what I do on a daily basis is based on working at Gilman. Learning how to manage people who aren't getting paid is where you really learn how to manage people. Also, striving to not fuck people over—mutual respect. Just because everyone around you is sleazy doesn't mean you have to be sleazy. If you lie to people and fuck them over, you're going to get lied to and fucked over in return. In closing, I think Gilman does a really good job of delivering music to people, but that's about it, and people get their own sense of community out of it, despite the fact that there's not much going on besides music. The club has a way of chewing people up and spitting them out, and it's important to recognize how much work goes into a place like that. There are very few businesses that have stayed open as long as Gilman and have been doing pretty much the exact same thing as the day they opened.

Gilman Show Staff,

You have probably noticed a few changes in the way we are running shows lately. These are changes designed to get a tighter grip on the financial situation here. Please help us out by asking us if you have questions about the new procedures. If you think some of the new stuff sucks, tell us, tell us why, and we will change it.

We also need your help in other areas. Please help us get the shows started as quickly as possible. When security clears house, go to the store as soon as possible. Be patient and polite while we stamp hands and discuss the night's show. Do the job you signed up for and help newer workers do their jobs.

Realize that you are a role model for other workers and the membership at large. Take an active role in stopping fights and discouraging theft. Don't expect special privileges because you work at the club or are "hella old school." If you need to make a personal call, use the pay phone. Don't loan out you membership card. Your friends still have to pay to see the show. (If they can't afford it get them involved in working.)

Gilman is changing rapidly in other areas. Try to keep the warehouse, especially the side business office, clean and neat. The only reason people should get sick coming to Gilman is if the band stinks. Help us keep expenses down to a minimum. Don't waste membership cards, flyers, or supplies. If you need to buy something for the club, ask someone first and make sure it is absolutely essential. Things are really lean right now, and if you can afford to pay for it yourself, please do.

Thank you for your help. You guys are the real backbone of the club and the only reason we have made it this far.

Brian
Mike
Robert
Jesse

If you signed up on the work list just to get in free, you're at the wrong club.

By signing up to work at Gilman, you have become a vital part of the show, a vital part of the club, and a vital part of the scene. You are the most important part of the club, don't forget that.

You have signed up for a particular job, for a particular shift. This is your focus. But working any position means working every position. Working part of the show means working all of the show. When you sign up to work be prepared to work all night, fulfilling a variety of functions.

No one is doing you a favor by signing you up to work. It is hard work with little tangible reward. The reward comes after the show, tonight, tomorrow, five years from now when you realize that you have been responsible for keeping our club and our scene alive.

If you see a job that is not being done, DO IT. If you don't, who will? If you end up stuck somewhere you're not signed up for, tell a coordinator. They will hunt down the person who signed up for the spot.

Once again, let me stress that the job you signed up to do is your primary responsibility, but your duty is making sure the show runs well.

Remember, without you there would be no club. The membership at large, and the community as a whole, owe you our respect and thanks.

Sincerely

Mike Stand

P.S. Please come to the membership meetings, the 1st and 3rd Saturdays of every month at 5PM.

KEN S.

Drawn by the Shining beacon of the San Francisco Bay's Punk Rock Mecca, I moved to The Kitchen Floor of David Hayes of Very Small Records and Dave Mello from Schlong's Emeryville apartment for a few ...uh months in the summer of 1992. Off of San Pablo, Down an occasionally hooker filled alley land marked by the Giant "MR. EGG ROLL" sign/fast food greasepit, I owe those guys eternal gratitude for allowing me to Sleep on their floor, Get trapped in by Opossums (In California! Hell?), Drink heaps of OLY and occasionally help magic Marker color the covers of the latest Very Small release. I had met them by setting up house shows in my hometown of Auburn, Alabama over the past few years, through word of mouth it had become a regular stopover through the south for many a bay area band -- ranging from Jack Acid and Green Day to Neurosis and Plaid Retina.

O to 60 in seconds flat, I mean there would be a show once every two months in Alabama, and here We'd go to a show every night!!!! Always at some different venue all over the Bay Area, but seemingly never at Gilman. Being from out of town you have this vision that it's a punk Rock Megalopolis every night at Gilman, and everyone always goes there no matter what, not seeing or understanding the Shrugged shoulders and lackadaisical "I'll wait for a good Show" of most jaded scensters that I too, sadly possess all too well by now.

But Man!!! It's what I came here for -- Hundreds of punks going completely out of control to Rad punk sounds!!! Just like in the Smeary photos in *Maximum RocknRoll*!!! Sign me up!!! So somewhere around my third week here(remember Gilman Only does shows on the weekends) I was finally successful in getting someone to drag me over there (Toby the drummer from the late, Great, and recently then departed Filth) to an afternoon Matinee show with the then new band Johnny Peebucks and the Swinging Udders and the South Bay's Slip (with a pre-Rancid Lars) and I oddly wondered where everyone was!!! There were like 40 people there! NO ONE was going anywhere near nuts!!! There was barely anyone there to go Nuts!!!, very sparse, Gilman's a big space, it takes a lot of folks to fill it up and make it seem like there's a crowd. And suprisingly this seemed pretty common then, there weren't a lot of shows going on.

I Missed a lot of the Chaos and politics that had gone on a year or two previously, but Gilman seemed in a slump. I was kind of dumbfounded though that Gilman Wasn't holding its own with Just Weekend nights, amazing shows one after the other, and found that the booking was really, really sparsely done. Dave EC would drop an Occasional amazing Blockbuster show of Gilman's old guard inbetween weeks of Cancelled and no shows, and the other people who had begun doing booking backing out or having stopped coming in months ago. Gilman Had five-Six years on developed its crusty old-timers already, marked with a swarmy " I was here Opening Night and helped nail in the Basketball Hoop" attitude that miraculously, (and still miraculously today) discounts "Where the hell have you been since then" Unmercilessly (and necessarily) retorted back at least once a month. Theres little laurel resting in Punk Rock, always stuff to build, learn and grow from fueled by new faces that discounts that kind of High School Style "But I'm a senior" nonsense. Who Cares!

Mike Stand was starting as head coordinator, a remarkably together and organized guy and after a few, painful Gilman General meetings I got set up to do Booking. I had keys and would trek over from San

Francisco on BART every Monday night to sit there and answer a constantly ringing phone from Hopefuls around the bay and across the country. I would make the long trek from North Berkely Bart, Grab a slice of Pizza (so often I have a hard time eating it now having been fed off it for two years, now it's a Burrito Joint run by McDonalds), and sit there and answer incessant calls from bands like Mindslam and Shotmaker who would call every fifteen minutes to see if there was a show for them yet. Yeesh.

Gilman is a cave when you're the only person there, with stale coffee left over from the Weekend before festering in the Store. A Completely dark and creepy main hall, Sometimes freezing cold, and the phone calls only interrupted by the occasional Band stopping by with a demo or the Non-stop banging on the door, asking who it is and having a screaming little guy (er..James) shout over and over again "IT's the CAN MAN!!! It's the CAN MAN!!!" You let him in, He scurried around picked up all the aluminum cans from that weekend's shows and hurried off. Okay, No problem. Whew.

I think if there was a contribution I made to Gilman Street it was just by showing up regularly weekly, and making sure there were shows almost every weekend. I think Since then the booking has continued pretty on course like that. At the time I worked at both Mordam Records and *Maximum RocknRoll* and had a good overview of the Bay area and National punk scene, so was able to draw from a lot of different sources and scenes to make some good shows. On a personal level, it made a newcomer to the area instantly in touch with a lot of people and I made some really lasting and wonderful friendships with amazing people from then. And was able later to start my label, prank, with a lot of the folks I met during that time.

Booking at Gilman is a difficult task as truly there are more bands, especially touring bands, that want to play there and base their west Coast tour around getting a solid date at Gilman. Often sadly after they dredge through miserable shows across the country and pine hopes on the East Bay's Punk Rock Central only to find twenty people looking bored into 25 cent cups of coffee all night. It makes it hard to accommodate all the touring bands and have it be a breeding ground for locals, as there are usually only a few that would draw enough people to headline their own shows. We restarted cheap new Band nights again to clear the roster of local bands that wanted to play, But for better or worse would group like sounding bands to build an audience, I.E. a pop punk night, a hardcore night, a Geeky punk night, usually worked to get a crowd out and pay the bills, but unfortunately defeated the cross Pollination of sounds that Early Gilman seemed to accomplish. Some of my most memorable shows were of complete sore thumb bands winning an audience over -- the electrifying appearance of SF's Ripoffs in the middle of a Queers/Rancid show, the Later, thrashier Grimple devastating the crowd expecting a pop punk band when opening for Chaos UK, Schlong's acoustic country Band Three Finger Spread plunked in the middle of a total Powerviolence thrash show of Man Is The Bastard and Rorschach, Japan's Mighty, all-female Gaia Levelling the Riot Grrl crowd in the middle of a Bikini Kill show. The blockbuster shows generally pay Gilman's Rent, but sometimes happen a few months apart or clump together all at once. It's a drain on the people who have to show up and work the show to have no one there and typically it's those shows that drag on for hours. Bands arriving late, more touring bands trying to jump on a show with four touring bands and thirty people there, People needing to borrow equipment or take an hour to set up, a drummer or bassist goes AWOL, whatever.

The early Nineties actually was rife with Headliners, bands set to jump onto the mainstream and sadly later, right before I quit doing booking, there arrived bands there to work it with a goal of popularity superceding community, art, politics, or at least it seemed that way. The Explosion of majors onto Punk Rock had the adverse effect of really changing band's expectations even small bands. I Bear no ill will towards any of those bands that chose that path, some did well, some got destroyed, it was their choice, but it was pretty sad when small crusty punk bands start looking at the real estate section of the paper and wondering where their house in the Berkeley hills is going to be. It's the wrong way to raise the bar in Punk Rock, there are more positive examples of goals to reach for (and luckily I think even more now) than a major label crapshoot.

There was tension with that, the policy of No Major bands hammered out at Saturdays first and third 5 O'clock meetings as friends and bands that had been at Gilman from the beginning took their leave. The meetings were painful, sometimes more of a learning experience in cooperative bargaining and agreement than actually accomplishing anything. Going around the circle of members until the same point had been articulated over and over in a myriad of different ways. Sometimes drama-filled, my particular drama was being later stupidly railroaded out of Gilman in a Secret three person "Hey can you come down to the club" meeting because someone in the higher-ups at the time was dating one of the other bookers. Later came back to a general meeting, discussed my problems with booking, wanted to organize it better, set up some guidelines and responsibilities for people who do booking and this was so soundly rejected by the other party, who at the end just had a groundless "well, I don't get along with you" that came off as dumb as it sounds in a room full of people.

Mostly however the meetings were arguing over whether to give free sodas for roadies, whether to admit someone back into the club or bounce someone out, and generally riveting subjects like whether to buy new lights or a different brand of Juice at the store, etc. I remember setting up a record Swap there and arguing on a time to start it, and a bunch of people said "well I don't want to get up and go there early, so let's start it at Noon". That won a show of hands, and the swap comes around with a bunch of restless and angry record sellers and buyers wondering why the swap was starting later than any other record swaps and none of the said folks being seen all day. Ho-hum, How it works, ass backwards sometimes, but necessary nonetheless.

Biafra got beat up. Miriam Got arrested. I was at both shows and left early before the chaos. The Biafra thing was a really low point of Gilman. Biafra or some random kid nobody knows, That kind of stuff shouldn't be tolerated by anyone at Gilman or any other punk show. I found myself about a year ago breaking up one of those punk rough and tumble slam dancing that starts to escalate into two guys roughing each other up and was like goddamn it! I'm like the oldest person here, You eighteen year old kids have flexible bones! Pitch in here will ya??? Go Nuts, Sure, Hurt people no. If You're such a tough Punk fighting boy (or girl), take it to the front lines at Corporate chain Stores, banks and fast food restaurants. I dare you. See you're not so tough!!!

In Biafra's case Basically, the very Dead Kennedys sounding Fixtures were headlining a show and some sort of scuffle erupted. Biafra got pinned between a table, some people started kicking him and damaged one of his knees while the gilman house security was dealing with another fight outside. I wasn't there, the guys left town and hid out, Biafra would call my house, and talk to my-oh-so-removed from Punk rock girlfriend of the time who would then ask "who's this guy who keeps calling up??" He knew me via Mordam, and was hoping to catch the people involved before they left town. Since they were yelling "sellout" at the time of beating him up, there was a vague feeling of egging on from the vibe of a very anti-Punk Business/anti-success *Maximum RocknRoll* of the time. I think that credits the intelligence and political motivation of the thugs involved more than I would personally give, I think vague punk notions topped off with a lot of booze and testosterone was probably more a factor. By yelling "Sellout" however, this gave it some rooting in the very entrenched old San Francisco Punk Rock Politics and personality clashes, deep fissures dating back to the late 1970's and early 1980's that became impossible to heal after this incident. To his Credit, Biafra still continues to support local and international bands, comes to Gilman and if you've listened to a lot of the Alternative Tentacles catalog as a whole, experimentation definitely takes precedence over making sure thing hit selling records (Ground floor for Vagtazo Halottkemek and Stickdog!). It's my hope that no one ever has to come to Gilman or any other punk show and fear that kind of violence, it ruined enough scenes, bands, concert halls and people's involvement with punk in the 1980's.

The Insaints' Miriam was another story all together. David Hayes and I split after Grimple to go drink Beer at his house before they played. We had seen The Insaints at Your Place too a few months before, a lot of nudity and so-so punk rock. Like the Aborted, sort of shock-core. Whatever. I can't really think of a single instance (sorry Jesse) where Nudity and a Punk rock concert has been combined to be a pleasurable experience for me, usually it's "eeeeew, get the fuck off the stage!!!" Hey guy from the fleshies -- Take notes! Anyway, I guess She was ahem...Pleasuring herself with a Fruit on stage for the "all ages, no racist, sexist, no homophobic bands" audience until some other fruit (also somehow related to Dead Kennedys) ran down the street and called the cops. The hilarious thing about that is You have NEVER heard of more cop cars getting there as quickly as "Public female nudity at Eighth and gilman" over a police scanner, there were like eight cop cars within ten minutes! There was a city council meeting, there was a legal defense benefit with Rancid and a bunch of other bands. It got tossed out but there was a lot of heat and tension, hand wringing special emergency Gilman meetings before it saw itself out.

I decided to Quit. Burnt from the Railroading incident, tired of the long two hour each way commute on public transit, and also an unfortunate and ridiculously groundless run in with the Berkeley Police outside of North Berkeley BART (yes, all Cops are not all good people), I'd had enough. I think also coming from working at college radio for years with a similar cooperative structure has its advantages saddled with an equal amount of compromises. I decided to move on to my own project, a record label Prank that started with a 12" EP by Gilman favorites Dead And Gone. There was a panic who would take over booking, just like there was a panic when Mike Stand quit being coordinator, a panic when Branwyn quit being coordinator, and even though there's that intial fear of who will fill those shoes, no one ever does, but somehow a new person steps up bringing their own personality, views and ideas to the project and it continues. That's the strength of Gilman, New blood, Fresh faces, new injection of enthusiasm and energy to make something out of the place. A great experiment, some failure, lots of success.

And yes, I did get to see Hundreds of Punks go nuts, absolutely beserk with some of my best friends and to some of the best music.

Favorite moments that stick out in the memory cells being Sam McPheeters of Born Against doing a weird squiggly hand clapping dance across the stage to absolutely devastating back up of thrash and Irony. Getting to sing with my friends in Spitboy. Watching southern California's Crossed Out's singer lumber across the stage as Bassist Eric W.'s Eye rolled back in his head and their drummer tried to kill his drumset. Watching Martin From Los Crudos from the old perched sound booth cut a line straight through a gigantic Slam pit and crowd of hundreds of folks still singing the whole time. Booking "sacto Punk night" on a night where virtually every Punk band from Oakland (Rancid, Econochrist, Grimple, Spitboy) was playing Petaluma's Phoenix theatre; while the Horny Mormons and Pounded Clown put on a great show, it goes down as the worst door take ever -- six people paid! Assfort from Tokyo firmly staking a claim for International hardcore by blasting a completely blazing set Before Swing Kids and Assuck. Sacto's Lil' Bunnies getting thrown off the stage after five minutes. Watching the throng of hundreds of crazy girls and guys bounce up and down to Bikini Kill. Sitting outside the front of Gilman Catching up with Jeremy and Richard the Roadie more times than I can count. Catching up on the latest Business with a true Hero of Gilman Street John H. Dividing up the band's money at the end of the night and being awed as people kicked down to a touring band down on their luck. Diving off stage with my short lived side project Nuclear Armed Hogs!!! The manic psychotic energy of early El Dopa Shows. The Clunky last Green Day show at Gilman. The simultaneous terrible, hopeful and wonderful sounds of bands of High School Kids on New band night. Charged fists in the air as people sing back lyrics to Avail, Citizen Fish or Dead And Gone. And having to sit out many a show as there were just plain too many punks, Going nuts.

1996   photo by Ayumi N.

JULIE R.

924 Gilman Street

smell of sweat, smoke, and drying spray paint

official mosh recipe

I can't believe 924 Gilman has been around for so long. I came here a few times when I was in high school (1990-1991), being oh so cool and sneaking out to the suburbs into the big, cool college town of Berkeley. It was after high school that I really started being a regular at Gilman Street. Every weekend my friends and I would pile in the car and go to a show.

shortage of volunteers

So my friend, the coordinator, said, let Julie work the door,

shy and out of place

When I first started hanging out at Gilman, I felt like I wasn't punk enough and didn't belong there since I lacked tattoos and piercings and a bunch of punk patches on my clothes. One night I was working the door, I flagged down a guy who was so excited to get inside that he forgot his change. When I handed him his money, He said, "Wow, an honest punk!"

I was at Gilman for the riot grrl thing, the sellout band thing, other things. . . I worked a lot of shows, made a few friends.

I just showed up because it was comforting – a second home.

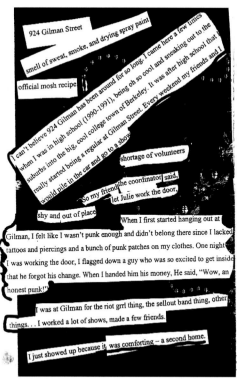

there was a meeting the coordinator and some regulars were caught drinking inside the club during a show. I knew none of these people personally, I didn't want them to be permanently 86'd from the club, but I

didn't want them to get away with a slap on the wrist either! I suggested that in addition to being 86'd from the club for 2 months (?), they should have to write a 1000 word essay and read it on stage during a show. The idea was adopted, and I got dirty looks from 4 or 5 people I didn't know for a while. When the time came for them to get on stage and read their essays, they read them at once over the roar of a band. It was an unintelligible shouting match, but at least they held up their end of the bargain.

I was hoping that they would be made an example of for the sole reason that

After spending time working at shows and learning how much commitment effort and time it took to keep the place running

I didn't want to see Gilman shut down because of people drinking

I have spent a lot of energy defending Gilman when people say it's a lame place with too many rules to losers who would rather support a bar than a non-profit organization because they think bars are cooler.

That doesn't mean that Gilman Street is perfect. I realized long time ago, I love Gilman St (and the punk scene) kind of like the way I love my family.

There are things that happen that piss me off and there are fuck-ups and flaws, but there is still a lot of good stuff to not take for granted.

Criticisms? Gilman St punk scene?

When people complain about the rules

when people show up and bitch and complain and then never go to a meeting to present a creative solution. mall punks

disturbing. To see a young woman behave like a common groupie at a mainstream stadium cock rock concert went against everything I knew. The fact that the band didn't stop playing, that her friends didn't try to stop her from embarrassing herself, that security did not remove her for being so drunk upset me even more.

Boys are on stage more than grrls. Boys mosh while their grrlfriends hold their jackets. The same little high school dramas of 2 grrls fighting over a dopey guy, they're not, thinking when punk boys act like jocks and punk grrls act like cheerleaders especially when it comes to gender roles. I'd like to see some change. I have seen a lot of shit at Gilman.

Share the control of the stage with more than just the bands playing

I had to wonder if any of the people there that night really appreciate how much hard work it has taken to keep the club open.

Gilman St. is a haven and a sanctuary. It needs to be protected more than ever

If Gilman St no longer existed, what would all of you be doing on Friday and Saturday night?

Gilman provides a space for people to loose their shit, be creative form a band, perform solo, write a fanzine,get recognition for contributing something positive!

Some things I would like to see: more non-show activities like work shops

a broader range of musical styles welcomed into the club. I don't like it when certain bands play and attract jock types who start fights and act like assholes toward women. I don't like seeing the scene get stuck in a rut.

I met a lot of great people

The only way punk can be a threat to society is to be intelligent, political, and organized.

The group effort on behalf of Gilman realizing how many people were there to support the club,

There are nights there when things have seemed magical and I think it's the people who make it that way.

I think, at least in Berkeley, that punk idealism has a lot of direct connection and parallels to the idealism of people in college about changing the world and doing things differently. Well what about when we're older?

I still consider myself punk- in a broad definition of the word- I still try to be open to new ideas, and do my best to live my life in a way that upholds my ideals (I still fuck up sometimes though). I think I would have given up a lot sooner and became "normal" if it wasn't for all the things I learned at Gilman Street.

MIKE H.

I first found out about Gilman by seeing a photo of the Eighth and Gilman Street signs on the back of some East Bay punk band's album, maybe one of Rancid's early records, I don't remember exactly. I grew up in New Jersey, and I moved to the Bay Area in 1992 with a friend because we figured it was the farthest we could get from Jersey without leaving the country. Being around Gilman and the Bay Area punk scene was also a motivation for moving. We had heard that there was some sense of community there, which Jersey didn't have. We thought it was going to be one giant, happy community, where all the punks got along. I would mess with my friends back in Jersey when we first got to the East Bay by telling them that Gilman was in the center of town, and there were all these houses around Gilman, and every other house was a punk house.

My first impression of Gilman when I got there was that it was a shithole, but still pretty amazing. I thought it was going to be a lot smaller. I felt the sense of community there right from the start. It's a little scary moving somewhere new, but at Gilman I felt I had a home away from home. I went to shows there for a couple months before I started working there. A friend asked me to help out there, so I did. It was the first time I had seen a whole bunch of people working together to try and make something happen and not care about the profits, just trying to keep the place alive so people had a place to go. I started with helping out at the record table and then moved on to helping run the shows as assistant coordinator. That was for about a year. Then I went on tour with a band, and when I came back, the head of security at the time had just quit. The next thing I knew, I was head of security.

I lasted a year or so as head of security until I got burned out and couldn't do it anymore. I feel every band has a right to play there, but there were times when I'd see a certain band's name up on the board for an upcoming show that I knew had a violent audience, and I'd just think, oh my god, they booked them again. We'd get the same people giving us shit every show for about six months, then they'd disappear and another group would take their place. You'd get so sick and tired of telling people, "you can't drink here," over and over that you'd just want to go and drink yourself. We tried to keep people from drinking within a two block radius of the club, due to the mess the people who were drinking would make. Depending on the show, we'd have from one to five people working security for the night. I didn't have too much formal dealing with the police. There was one beat cop I remember who was really into the place and would help us out if we needed it. He even gave us his cell phone number to call if there was a problem that we needed help with so we wouldn't have to call 911 and have it on our record. On the other hand, there was the police surveillance that occurred every show for a while when one of our neighbors, DiCon, was trying to close us down. Nothing came of it, we just ignored them and did our usual job.

I stopped working there completely after stepping down as head of security. My general statement now to people who ask why I don't work there anymore is, "It was fun, but now it's not." It was very tiring and frustrating to put so much work into trying to have a community space, and have the people who were attending not care at all. A lot of times I got the sense that a lot of those people would rather see it close than stay open. I think they knew what Gilman was about, they just chose not to care, the punk credo, "Go fuck yourself." That's what burned me out the fastest, made me the most jaded. Some bands were like that too. I couldn't understand why people who were into punk and punk music would hate, and try to destroy, the one place that consistently gave them just that. Even the times of rallying and coming together against the Brew Pub and DiCon, it was mostly the Gilman workers and their parents and friends who came out in support of the place, not the Gilman patrons/audience, not the bands. One of the things that helped seal my decision to leave Gilman was noticing that on my way there, I was actually hoping that something would happen at the show that night, hoping to get into it with somebody, take out my frustrations on them. I knew then that it was time to get out. Your diplomatic skills erode pretty quickly when you're dealing with the same assholes night after night and you know what they're going to do and say. Words just end up being useless. My philosophy for working security was just to never throw the first punch.

On the positive side, the reason I stayed as long as I did was the other workers at Gilman. For us, it definitely was a community center. We went there to hang out, help out—who was playing on stage wasn't important. For the audience, it was just a music club. They were going there just because of who was playing. I think to get a feeling of actual community, you had to work there. There was a great support team at Gilman when I was working there, also. John H. and Pat W., they really cared about the place and contributed a lot, outside of the actual running of the shows. That was one of the great things about Gilman, the people who did work there were really passionate about the place. This passion did lead to difficult decision-making at times, though, since we were all opinionated and had no real leader as such. It sometimes would take a couple months to make a simple decision, since everyone's opinion counted. Whenever there was a problem, we'd all get together and figure out a solution. That was very spectacular, given how young most of us were.

One thing that needs to be pointed out, and credit given where it's due, is that Gilman's really been helped by the bands that have come from there and gotten a lot bigger. Everyone gives them shit for being "sellouts," but they really helped put Gilman on the map by mentioning it positively in their interviews and liner notes and such. That brought in a lot of people and really solidified Gilman financially. Green Day opened a lot of parents' eyes to the place. I would be at Gilman hanging out with friends on a Saturday or Sunday morning, and parents and their kids would show up, 10-year-olds and 15-year-olds, just wanting to see Gilman. So we'd let them in and give them a little tour. If I have a kid, I hope they can experience a place like that.

I hope Gilman will be around forever, so many others can experience it and learn from it. I took away a real sense of responsibility from working there, a sense of duty almost. And some of the friends I made there will be friends for life. Even if we don't talk much, we'll always have this bond, this relationship from working there together. I think Gilman's a great stepping stone for people. You learn a lot, you grow a lot, but just eventually, it's time to move on. You get older, but the general age of people around you stays the same.

HAWK

I grew up in the Washington, DC area. I was heavily influenced by "the DC sound and style," you know, Dischord and all that. Well, the bands I was really into, like Swiz, Soulside, Marginal Man, Ignition, etc., were all gone by 1993 and there really weren't too many new bands picking up the slack. Meanwhile, I had been reading for some time about 924 Gilman Street in the pages of *Maximum RocknRoll*, *Flipside*, and many other zines. Suddenly all the new and vital bands, i.e. Samiam, Econochrist, Jawbreaker, and John Henry West, were from the San Francisco Bay Area, and the "scene" in Northern California seemed to be thriving with punk volunteer-run projects like Epicenter, Blacklist, MRR, and Gilman. Not to mention, I grew up, like many from the East Coast, romanticizing California in general. A few of my friends moved to the Bay Area and told me it was the place to be. Well, after two blizzards in the winter of 1992-1993, I decided California was the place for me.

So I arrived in the Bay Area ready to couch surf, borrow money, and take in the "scene." I went to Gilman right away and volunteered for cleanup duty in order to get in for free. I did various jobs, from side door to hand stamp, before moving on to volunteer security. Pretty soon I was paid security, which made me a few enemies among the usual troublemakers and Gilman staff alike because of my fiery temper. By this time, I lived in a warehouse with two other Gilman staff members, reviewed zines at MRR, worked at a "punk" job with many Gilman regulars and staffers (Vantastic, which was a wheelchair-accessible van service) and I was also in a band with a Gilman booker. I started to come to his booking nights, and since I had five years or so experience booking bands in DC, I became a booking assistant in charge of reviewing the tapes, CDs, and records that came in so the bookers had an idea of what a band sounded like and what kind of show they would fit on. Once I actually started booking shows, I usually showed up to stage manage them too. Pretty soon all the bookers quit and I became "head booker," and trained all the new bookers that came and went for the next few years. I was a booker from 1993 to 1997, which was double the length of any previous booker.

My first impression of the space was that it was much smaller than it appeared in zines. It also was dirtier, and had way more "crusties" than I'd ever seen in my life. I was also surprised at all the mohawks, spiky hair, patches, and dog collars, not to mention the circle pit. All these things had died out in the mid-'80s on the East Coast. I couldn't believe some of the bands they let play there either. One of the first shows I saw there included a band who mocked rape on their stickers and in their lyrics. The paid audience for that show consisted of about 15 people who were yelling things, throwing things, and holding up picket signs to protest this band. I was however, impressed by the smooth operation of the club and the egalitarian way they paid the bands.

After three years of booking and going to nearly every show, I started to get burned out and went to fewer and fewer shows. I still booked most of the shows, but I can't say I really liked too many of the bands, and I didn't want to spend my weekends listening to bands I didn't like. I still booked bands that people wanted to hear, but few of them appealed to me at this point. All the bands I was into when I moved out here had now broken up, and once again, I didn't see too many bands picking up the slack. I was also tired of all the flack I took from the security guards and other collective members for the way the shows went or the bands behaved.

Everyone complained to me if I booked bands they thought sucked, or acted like assholes, or the bill didn't draw enough people, or drew too many.

I was treated as the token "emo" guy by many, but I am proud of the fact that a lot of bands play Gilman now that would never have considered it before. I think I broadened Gilman's horizons a little. I am also proud of the fact that Gilman did much better financially during my tenure as booker than before. I think I helped get rid of a lot of the "rock star" mentality that was tolerated before. I was glad to be a part of the successful fight to ban major label bands from playing at Gilman. I also helped start "new band night," which Gilman does when we have trouble with a bill on a particular night. We only charge $3, and all the money goes to Gilman, but bands get to play here faster than they normally would. Some of the bands that played the first "new band nights" included AFI, Screw 32, and Link 80.

I don't know if I ever would have stopped booking at Gilman had I not moved to NYC for a year. During that year I realized how nice it was not to be booking bands for the first time in nine or ten years. I still got phone calls from Montana in the middle of the night, but not nearly as often as before. And only a couple bands slept on my floor that year. It was a breath of fresh air.

I don't think Gilman was ever my main focus for an extended period of time, which, in hindsight, is probably why I lasted so long. I was in bands, had girlfriends, and jobs that Gilman took a back seat to. My experience volunteering there was everything from exhilarating to frustrating. I saw so many amazing shows, met so many great people, helped raise money for several worthy causes, and in general had great times. There was the occasional violent episode at a show, or rift amongst collective members on certain issues, but ultimately I have truly fond memories.

I learned many things from the Gilman Street Collective. I learned how to get along in a collective. I learned the history of West Coast punk rock and all kinds of information on thousands of bands and people. I think I gained a real sense of accomplishment from my time as a collective member. I think I helped Gilman and Gilman helped me.

924 Gilman wouldn't have lasted this long if it didn't have many strengths. Gilman has always relied on the constant renewable energy of the seemingly endless stream of dedicated punk rockers that come and go. To me, the most obvious weakness is the fact that the people who go to the shows, including the volunteers at the shows and the bands who play there, rarely go to the meetings and really get involved. They often complain and tarnish Gilman's image, but don't really do anything to try and change what they feel is wrong with Gilman.

Here are some of my favorite stories and anecdotes from my time at Gilman:

I'll always remember the time Jello Biafra's leg was broken. I was working paid security at the time. I remember being inside while the band was playing and noticing that, although there were only thirty or forty people up front, a handful of assholes were moshing extra hard and slamming into the crowd. Suddenly I was called outside because a band that had been banned from Gilman for racist and sexist lyrics and comments was trying to get in. A large scuffle ensued, and it turned into a brief fight in the street between Gilman security and staff and the banned band and their friends. I was called back inside in time to see Jello lying on the floor screaming out in pain. Apparently, from what I gathered from witnesses, Jello had tried to be a pit monitor, and when the troublemakers slammed into him, he pushed back, only to be knocked down awkwardly, breaking his leg. Outside, we confronted the people who pushed Jello down. They swung a chain at us and made their getaway. I remember a bloodied paper towel that supposedly had Jello's blood on it hung in the office for years.

photo by Emilie V.

One time someone erased two months of booked shows from the dry erase board in the office and we had to try to remember what bands were booked on what bills and when. I think we ended up rebooking most of those shows. Which was almost as hard as when Gilman was closed for earthquake retrofitting for a month and we booked out of Andrew's (fellow booker) house. To say it was disorganized is an understatement.

Another great memory is Gilman's tenth anniversary weekend shows. Let's just say certain people started rumors that Green Day, Jawbreaker, Crimpshrine, and Operation Ivy might play. Gilman staffers fell prey to the gossip as well. Even some of the members of the bands mentioned showed up to see what was going on. I think several hundred people, up to the last minute of those shows, thought their favorite band was going to reunite at any minute. But alas, none of those bands played.

Of course my greatest memory, and another way Gilman will be a part of my life forever, is the story of how I met my wife there. Her name is Emilie and she came to a collective meeting to pitch the idea of doing a photo documentary project on the collective. I just so happened to volunteer to be the liaison between Emilie and Gilman for this project. We quickly fell in love and eloped within a year. It's perfect knowing that we met doing what we love, photography for Emilie and music for me.

I got involved and stayed involved and will always feel connected to Gilman because it's the only long-lasting entity that's doing it for the kids, not to the kids. Punk rock pretty much saved my life, and working at Gilman is my way of paying back punk rock. This is a place where people can fit in for not fitting in anywhere else. You can be a part, not apart. It is as vital today as the day it started, and every day in between.

Sneakin' in, 1995   photo by Sita R.

Vandalism raises community concern

By Alex Coolman
Contributing Writer

Members of the music club 924 Gilman St. collected trash Sunday in an effort to clean up both the club's neighborhood and its reputation in the community.

About fifteen volunteers filled a city-donated dumpster with paper, glass and other debris from the area between and Seventh and Tenth avenues on Gilman St.

Cleanup participants aimed to demonstrate their commitment to the community in the face of concerns expressed by some local businesses and residents that the club is bringing graffiti and litter to the streets, according to 924 Gilman St. director Mike Stand.

"We are part of the neighborhood and we have a duty to help keep the neighborhood clean, regardless of who does the damages," Stand said.

924 Gilman St. operates primarily by the volunteer labor of its members, who each pay a $3 dollar annual membership fee.

The club has been the subject of several letters written to the Berkeley Zoning Office by businesses and residents who feel the city has not paid enough attention to vandalism occurring in the area, according to Eighth Avenue resident Billy Williams.

"Everyone has a right to have a business," said Williams. "But your business participants don't have the right to destroy another person's property."

Arthur McIntosh, who owns property on Gilman between Eighth and Ninth avenues, described graffiti, litter, broken glass, loud noise and public defecation as some of the problems he attributes to club members.

"Since they've been there we've had graffiti a number of times and always after the weekend," McIntosh said.

Members of 924 Gilman St. contend that the vandalism in the area has many sources and that the club has been unfairly singled out.

Stand argues that the area has long been plagued by prostitution and drug dealing, problems that are greater obstacles to neighborhood safety than the club's presence.

"We're caught up in the gentrification of the neighborhood," Stand said. "People are rightly worried, but we had nothing to do with (prostitution or drugs)."

Next door to the club, workers at Allied Radiator Co. pointed out that much of the graffiti afflicting the area appears to be related to gangs rather than music.

"You can see the writing, that it isn't something these guys (at 924 Gilman) would write," Allied manager Pat Watson said. "They never did it on our building so I really doubt it's these guys."

Several participants in the cleanup said they believe that much of the garbage they were picking up originated elsewhere.

"I wish some of the neighbors who complain would come clean up, because what I've found is that at least half the garbage is generated by the businesses who complain," said Larry Livermore, one of the original founders of the club.

McIntosh agreed that there were "several levels of problems," but said he felt 924 Gilman St. was "not beneficial for the community in general."

"I don't think they add anything to the community. They don't bring anything to the community economically, that's for sure," he added.

Williams said he considered Sunday's cleanup beneficial but emphasized the need for more communication on all sides.

"Unless you communicate with people and the business properties in neighborhoods ... you're not going to be able to accomplish much," he said.

"Young kids, they need a place to go to blow off steam," said Williams. "It needs to be other than infringing on other people's benefits."

A meeting is scheduled for Wednesday at 11 a.m. to discuss the matter with city officials. Those interested in attending should meet at the corner of Eighth Avenue and Gilman Street.

Article taken from the *Daily Cal*, March 1993

Three women and a banana

Berkeley punk's onstage sex pushes the envelope — and the district attorney's buttons

By Meredith May
SPECIAL TO THE EXAMINER

BERKELEY — There's a low-profile club where the punks come out at night.

There are no signs or flyers advertising the club and you can't find a listing in the phone book for 924 Gilman St., which has played host to an occasional subversive performance. But so far nothing compares to what Insaints lead singer Marian Anderson did with two other women and a banana on stage.

The 24-year-old blue-haired punk singer faces a July 12 jury trial in Berkeley Municipal Court on three counts of obscenity and lewd conduct in what may be the first case of its kind in Berkeley.

The charges stem from an April 3 show at 924 Gilman (as the club is called), in which Anderson performed a live sex act on stage with two other women and the fruit in question, according to police reports. During the 30-minute performance the three women also urinated on one another.

The scene was too much for audience member Carlo Cardona — ironically a former Dead Kennedys punk rocker — who left the club to call the cops.

"I was totally shocked at what was going on," said Cardona. "I like punk music, but since I regained my faith in Jesus, I don't agree with some punk ethics. I went to see music, not a kinky lesbian sex show."

After the performance, Anderson, who refused police requests to clothe herself, was booked in the buff on suspicion of lewd and lascivious conduct, indecent exposure and engaging in obscene conduct before a live audience in a public place. She pleaded not guilty to all three misdemeanors May 25.

"Sure I'm guilty of obscenity, but I don't think to be obscene is wrong and something that should be penalized," said Anderson. "I'm not hurting anyone, and anyone who is offended has the free will to leave. I'm only asking they give me my free right to express myself."

Anderson said she had been performing "sex 'n' rock 'n' roll" in Bay Area clubs for about a year, with no problems. She said she hadn't informed the management at 924 Gilman about the content of her show, but said it was on a par with other punk stage antics.

Malachi West, part of the all-volunteer management of 924 Gilman, worked security during Anderson's show and said Cardona seemed to be the only one offended by the three women.

"A band should be able to do whatever they want on stage," West said. "Really, we don't think this issue is that important."

"I do everything from golden showers to fisting to sex on stage," said Anderson. "I do it because it's fun and shocking and it's a chance for me to be an exhibitionist. It's unfortunate that the district attorney is wasting city money on this when there are more important issues of crime and violence that need his attention."

Deputy District Attorney Darryl Stallworth, who pressed the charges against Anderson, said obscenity couldn't be considered an individual right because it affected others, most specifically the minors who frequent the all-ages, no-alcohol club.

"There are First Amendment rights, but some things are not protected by the Constitution, like obscenity," Stallworth said. "She may theorize that what she did was performance art, but something is offensive if it goes against the community's standard of decency, and the police report was generated by an audience member who thought it was indecent. It will be up to the jury to decide if her act offends the community."

If convicted, Anderson would at the most spend a year in county jail, but it's more likely, said Stallworth, that she would receive some combination of probation, fine and community service.

Anderson scored a point when the Berkeley City Zoning Board decided April 26 in a 7-1 vote that the incident didn't warrant a hearing to revoke 924 Gilman's use permit.

"The main response from the board was that this one act may have overstepped the bounds, but Berkeley needs more alcohol-free places like this where kids can release their energy," said Berkeley Zoning Board administrator Vivian Kahn. "Then maybe we wouldn't have the problems we do on Telegraph Avenue."

The infamous Insaints episode. Article taken from the *SF Examiner* 1993 (exact date unknown)

CHAPTER SIX

SEX & VIOLENCE

BRANWYN B.

1993-1994

"I DON'T KNOW IF I COULD RUN GILMAN ANY BETTER NOW THAT I'M OLDER AND MORE EXPERIENCED, BECAUSE I NO LONGER HAVE THAT YOUTHFUL IDEALISM, AND I THINK YOU NEED THAT HERE."

–BRANWYN B.

1992   photo by Susan S.

BRANWYN B.

I first went to Gilman during my sophomore year in high school in 1989. I went with my best friend and her boyfriend, who was familiar with the place. It was a ska show and my curfew was 11:00 PM. I had a really awful time. I can't believe I went back. I didn't know anybody else. Also, there was a woman there who'd brought in a small baby with no earplugs or ear protection at all, and I thought it was really horrible that the club let her do that. I didn't really have anyone to hang out with because my friend was off with her boyfriend. The whole punk rock thing was new to me. I was living in Daly City and pretty isolated from the whole thing. It was kind of intimidating. But with nothing better to do, we went back. I was really shy back then, and if someone hadn't taken me back, I wouldn't have gone on my own. I started to get to know more people there, and a lot were really cool, and sort of took us under their wings.

The whole set-up there, the volunteer collective thing, was completely foreign to me. I never volunteered to work a show then, but I thought the concepts were cool. I went there for about two years before I started doing anything there. I got tired of not knowing when shows were, and never seeing any flyers, or when I did see them, you couldn't read them. So I volunteered to take over being flyer coordinator, and started making flyers and going to meetings. The head coordinator at the time, Mike Stand, started entrusting me with more responsibilities. The first time I actually worked at a show was around 1992/1993, and I was the assistant coordinator. I had never worked the door before or anything. It was a pretty small show, and some nazis showed up, looking for trouble, so I had a little excitement my first night. It wasn't very long after that that Mike said he was going to be stepping down. He called me and told me his last day was going to be August 3rd. August 3rd is my birthday, and I had this sinking feeling that I was going to

Flyer by Branwyn B.

get a club for my birthday. I really didn't want it to happen, because I had seen all the stress that Mike had. But when Tim Yohannan came to me and told me I should take it over, I started thinking about it. I thought, if he thinks I can do it, maybe I can. It also was appealing because there had never been a woman running the club before.

As always, I had no idea what I was getting into. I was only twenty years old, and had only had two minimum wage jobs before that, with not much responsibility. I had hardly worked at the club at all, just the flyers and assistant coordinating a couple of shows, and going to meetings. I had done a couple zines and was a full-time college student. It was my first experience in collectives, my first management experience. It still kind of shocks me to this day that people wanted me to be their general manager. Eventually, I decided to go for it. I figured it was worth a shot. If I did a horrible job, I could step down. My parents were really supportive, they were telling me that it would be such great work experience, and that it would look really good on a resumé. At the time I thought they were full of it, but it was true. My mom had gone to a few shows there, sometimes by herself, and my grand-mother (who was over eighty) ended up going to a show there too. It was a lot of responsibility. Gilman is an institution, people all over the world know about it. People think they named the freeway exit after the club! I didn't want to screw up, and I didn't know if I'd be able to handle the stress. People at the club were very supportive, too, maybe just because no one else wanted to do it! Maybe I was just the biggest sucker they could find!

photo by Brian E.

Once I was running it, I was kind of a hardass. I wanted the shows to begin and end on time, etc. I was head coordi-nator for a year. I had a lot of lofty goals at first. I wanted better organization. I was getting sick of the three or four hour-long meetings. I was compiling the meeting minutes and collecting as many flyers from the club as I could from over the years, trying to make some kind of historical record. I redid all the forms for doing paperwork, show tallies, etc. Divvying up the money at the end of the night was one of the hardest things at first, because I had so little experience doing that—figuring out how much each band should get. We gave out no guarantees and accepted no con-tracts/riders. I was taking 17-18 units at school, didn't have a regular paying job, but was putting in about 20-30 hours a week at Gilman, working the shows, meet-ings, admin., etc.

Flyer by Branwyn B.

After about seven to eight months, I was getting burned out, and Charles L., who had been taking on more and more responsibility there, ended up splitting the position with me—we were co-head coor-dinators. He was doing the show coordi-nation, and I was doing more of the behind-the-scenes type stuff. When the incident with Jello Biafra happened (where his leg was injured in a fight), I dealt with the police and wrote up a press release and sent it off to local newspapers, MTV, etc. We had gotten a request for informa-tion from MTV, and stories were appearing in the local papers as well about the inci-dent, so we wanted our side put out there, to alleviate the misinformation. From what I could tell, though, none of the writers for the local papers actually read the press release. It was kind of pointless. As I recall, MTV actually gave the most balanced presentation, as astonishing as that sounds. MTV contacted Gilman another time also. It was when they were shooting *The Real World* in San Francisco. I got a call one night from one of their producers, who told me that some of the cast from *The Real World* were coming to one of our shows, and asked if we could let their cameras in. Of course, I said no. The guy acted so shocked that I had actually said no to him. I told him when our membership meetings were and that he could come and ask at a meeting if he was really interested. Of course, he never came to a meeting. Another incident that happened was the night the singer of a band on

stage was engaging in a sex act with one of the audience members. Another audience member felt this was too much and called the police. The band member was arrested and heat came down on the

Puppet show that reenacted the infamous Insaints' "sex show."
photos by Susan S.

club. Yet another incident I remember was one night a kid ended up getting cut somehow, and to me it looked like it needed stitches. So I called 911, and before the response units got there, the kid took off and went to the hospital with friends. The response ended up being multiple cop cars and a fire truck. I approached one of the officers to tell him what had happened, and he accused me of trying to block his entrance into the club. He said that if I did it again he would arrest me, which was baffling to me since I was standing behind him and was not in between him and the door. He said there were reports of a stabbing at the club, that a 911 call had reported a stabbing. I told him I was the one who called 911, and that I had never said anything about a stabbing. I ended up getting into an argument with him. I probably could have handled it better, but he could've too. Community relations have always been really important to Gilman—our survival depends on it. I believe the club had a hand in helping start the Gilman Street Merchants Association, which was already in place when I

Sept. 25 Fri. Green Day

★RANCID★

OILER

Night Shift

Krupted Peasant Farmers

$6 + membership card ($2/year) **8 pm**

924 Gilman St.
Berkeley 525-9926. Take the 9 bus from Berk. BART.
All ages, no drugs/alcohol.

no ins & outs at sold out shows

Sat. Sept. 26, 8 pm-Plaid Retina, Schlong, Blister, False Sacrament Raoul()
Sun. Sept. 27, 5 pm-Chumbawumba, Vee Tee Glow Sunls, Letch Patrol, Qore)

Flyer by Branwyn B.

started managing the club. All the members of the association contributed money to pay for a security guard for the area. He was mostly around Walgreen's, up at the corner of Gilman and San Pablo. Occasionally he'd come to the club and say hi.

Running the place kind of ruins the whole experience, because you're worrying about so much. When you're just a patron, you can sit back and enjoy the chaos—you're not thinking about if an incident will attract the police, or having to come down on a Sunday afternoon and clean up trash or graffiti. Even after I stopped working there, if I saw someone doing something they shouldn't, I would still catch myself thinking, "That person shouldn't be doing that." Or if the toilet paper rolls were low or empty, I'd be thinking, "I should go replace them." In a way, that's good—everyone who goes there should be worrying, or thinking, about things like that, because it's a community, it's a collective, it's run by the membership, it's run by the people who attend the shows, and whoever attends the shows should be doing whatever they can to help out and protect the place. You get a whole new perspective. I certainly used to complain about how things were run there before I started working there. That's why I did start getting involved—put up or shut up. I realized I was being a big hypocrite. You have no right to complain about anything if you're not willing to help out. If people approached me with complaints, I'd suggest they attend a Gilman meeting, and maybe start helping out in that area. For the most part, they never would.

Flyer by Branwyn B.

Eventually, I found myself turning more and more responsibility over to Charles, and was thinking about stepping down. Near the end of my time there, there were some people who were caught drinking alcohol during a show. During the meeting where their punishment was being discussed, I raised my hand and said that I had done the same thing sometimes during shows before I started working there, and now I was running the club. I wanted people to take that into account before deciding on a punishment, because the punishments they were considering were pretty harsh. This resulted in my being punished as well. A lot of the people there felt that since I was the head coordinator, it would be a good idea to make an example out of me. I did drink inside during shows a few times after I had become head coordinator, but not ones I was actually working at. I stopped doing it after a while because I realized it was stupid and pointless and hypocritical. So they decided on a punishment for me, and a lot of it was just ridiculous. I was banned from going to shows for a month, but they still wanted me to come in and work during the week. They wanted me to clean the bathrooms for a month, stuff like that. Some of the punishments ended up being retracted. I was bitter for a little while, but I also took responsibility for what I'd done. So I was definitely leaning towards quitting at that point. Yes, I had fucked up, but this all seemed like too much. So that, combined with everything else, led me to step down.

Gilman was a really great experience, and I don't regret doing it at all, but the club does tend to sap the life out of people, if they let it. I'm proud of my accomplishments there. There were things I could have done better, but also, I was just a 20-year-old kid. Some people came up to me after I left and told me they thought I was a bitch while I was running the place, but I think you kind of have to be sometimes to get things done. There are other ways to motivate people, but sometimes that's all you have left, if nothing else works. Tim Y. told me once, a few months after I became head coordinator, that while he was running the place it brought out the fascist in him, and I totally knew what he was talking about! Other people told me it was the best they had ever seen the place run.

Flyer by Branwyn B.

So, I continued on for a few weeks, and then left the area on a vacation. I really enjoyed relaxing and not having to worry about the place, so I called Charles from my vacation and told him I was going to quit. I knew the place would be in good hands with him. I learned a lot about how to deal with people, how to approach various situations, how to multi-task, how to delegate, how to be creative in motivating people, and how to be more assertive. Punk rock in general has been a huge influence on the person I am today. I have a corporate job now, and a lot of the skills I brought to this job, I got at Gilman. I don't feel very punk rock anymore, but it's still a big influence on me, everything from the way I watch the news, to the way I interact with people, to the way I think about things. I don't know if I could run Gilman any better now that I'm older and more experienced, because I no longer have that youthful idealism, and I think you need that, because the whole concept behind Gilman is idealistic. There aren't that many people out there willing or motivated enough to volunteer their time and energy to do what is often a thankless job. The core groups there over the years have always been small, but they've shown some of the best qualities and aspects that humanity can have. When I would get frustrated and upset that more people weren't helping, seemingly always one of the people we did have would go out of their way to do something great, and it would make me really happy. I really want to thank everyone who helped while I was there, I couldn't have done it without them. I want to encourage others to get involved there and not take Gilman for granted. I still go occasionally. It's no longer a place I go to primarily to see friends, since I don't know as many people who go there anymore. Now I'll just go to see a band I like. A piece of me will always be there—it was like a second home to me for a long time.

GILMAN GAZETTE

Volume I Issue I   Late February 1993

My involvement in "the scene" began as, and continues to be, a Bay Area experience; specifically, the East Bay. Born and bred here, I am not familiar with the scenes of other areas. But one thing many non-locals have communicated (in person or thru the mail) to me is how lucky we are to have 924 Gilman St. Being a non-profit, all-ages venue that caters to punx, Gilman is indeed unique. I will even venture to call Gilman a rare gem in this world where the norm is your average 21-up bar with a $10 cover charge and two drink minimum. In most places, if bands want to play, somebody has to be the lucky host and put it on in their house (where acoustics ain't too grand). If the house-mates don't object, you can bet the neighbors will, and will promptly call the fuzz. The house residents can be arrested, and any money collected, confiscated.

The occasional house-party is fine, but in order to build a strong scene (the band base), something more stable is ideal. Gilman provides a reasonably reliable, low-cost, space for fledgling bands to test the waters, and the old-hands to continue pleasing their adoring fans. True, I get burnt out on the place every-so-often, as other regulars similarly do, but I catch myself from becoming too jaded. You see, these people telling me how lucky we are here point out how much we can sometimes take for granted. Especially my fellow "new-schoolers" and I who weren't around before Gilman.

Yes, there is more to life then punk rock shows, but imagine what the Bay Area would be like without Gilman. These are some questions to ponder; how many other all age venues are there? ones in the $5 range? or give free admission when you volunteer? ones that have more then the occasional punk band? ones that would give your novice band a chance? I could go on, but you get the picture.

Gilman is a good thing, beyond the convenience of shows every weekend. Hey man, it's for the kids! Seriously, where would under-aged tikes like myself go? And because of the all-volunteer (wo)man power, the cover charge is kept comparatively low. A lot of people have worked really hard to make Gilman as successful as it has been despite all the obstacles. These people do not receive pay-checks. They have jobs on the outside, go to school, whatever, and put aside time to do the shit and behind the scenes work. I hope you are as appreciative as you should be. And I hope you're doing your part, because "it is your Club."

What is your part, you may ask? Well, the bottom line is to refrain from doing things that will get the Club up poop creek. I put this news letter together because Gilman is in a heap of troubles at the moment (that will be explained in greater detail later on...). Things that would put us in very bad standing include: grafitti, littering (that includes smashing bottles, you punk rock Messiah you), loud obnoxious drinking, harassing those out for an evening stroll, and general idiocy. I am, of course, not suggesting that any of ya'll could be guilty of such things...Never!

The point is, use your head. Fuck-ups threaten the Club's standing, which would affect us all. If you've got to fuck-shit-up, do it somewhere else, or at least do it quietly and covertly in a manner that won't mess things up for the rest of us. Also, if you see somebody, say, drinking near the Club, don't be afraid to ask them not to, or not be as obvious.

If you think what we ask of you just ain't punk...deal with it, or get out and fuck off.   -Räzl

The area around 924 Gilman is gradually changing. Less steel-door warehouses and light industry. Increasing high-tech offices. Increasing retail stores with concerns about appearances and what discourages customers.

But the area is hardly South of Market chic. It gets a lot of hard use: a freeway access, trash loaded trucks heading for the dump, a main route for pedestrians to the race track, a seemingly good place for heroin dealing and prostitution. With this there is litter, grafitti, car break-ins, vandalism, broken bottles, burglaries, etc.

Now, what's happening is that many people believe the Club is the cause, directly or indirectly, of the vandalism and crime. After all, some of the litter/grafitti/broken glass is being done by some people coming to the shows. Also, crowds of youth hanging out or scattered around in cars is very conspicuous. Furthermore, people working in the neighborhood come to work Monday and see more trash than when they left on Friday. So, who clearly uses the area during the weekend? 924 Gilman, of course. Car break-ins? Burglaries? 924 Gilman, of course.

If the fear, resentment, and accusations ("They just make money and don't give a shit about anyone.") continue, the Club will get closed down. Even now, the Zoning Office is threatening to recommend that our permit be revoked. Each of us has to see that our own littering, grafitti, and trashing is cut way down. Be cool. Help Gilman security. What we can't prevent we clean up.

We must get the community to realize that other things than 924 Gilman goes on here. Many other people drink beer, have spray paint, and throw down food wrappings. Recently a guy was caught breaking into a car. It is believed that he broke into more than 50 cars. Unfortunately, many don't realize that he had nothing to do with the Club. A Gilman community association is being formed to deal with area security. We will be part of it. Businesses should be

brought into this group. More will be informed. We might want to set up information meetings with the residential neighbors.

We need to be a part of the community: talk with our neighbors, be responsive, sponsor neighborhood clean-ups.

We cannot remain just some foreighn "THEM" that others are directing their blame and fears on. All of us in this community can help each other. We sure need it. The others can, at least, feel relief when a lot of fear and resentment fade away.   -John H

Come to the neighborhood clean-up we are sponsoring on Sunday, February 28 at noon. Other members of the community will be involved and a pot-luck is planned (so bring food). The city will be providing a dumpster and maybe rakes and the like. Keep your ears open for future announcements of meetings with the Zoning Commission or community. We can show our dedication with numbers. Also, look out for the letter writing campaign and petition that we will probably be starting in the near future. These tactics have been successful in the past when we were up similar creeks. Attend regular Gilman membership meetings (every first and third Saturday of the month at 5pm) and any emergency meetings called. The next meeting is on March 6. If you have any further questions about the clean-up, or Gilman's situation and how you can help, either call Gilman at 510.524.8180 (a real person may answer) or Mike Stand at [........] (your message will be returned). You could also write me c/o *Sour Mash* PO Box [...], Berkeley CA [....]. Include your address and/or local phone number.

GILMAN GAZETTE

Volume I Issue II   Early July 1993

To begin with, if you (this goes out to all who attend shows, not just those who volunteer at them) have never attended a **membership meeting**, you should definitely do so. If you have been to one before, please continue to attend as often as possible. At these meetings club policy is discussed and voted upon, and the basic mental work of putting shows together is done. In a nutshell, anything and everything that might affect the club is discussed. For example, a past meeting's decision was to help pay, along with other Gilman area businesses, the salary of a security guard who patrols the area until about 10pm. Not only does this help with our public relations (very important to the club's standing), but the guard helps to control grafitti and destruction of property, which is something we often get blamed for, whether it's caused by Gilman members or not. Membership meetings are normally held every first and third Saturday of the month at 5pm, but are currently being held every Saturday because of a crisis I will be discussing next.....

For the last year or so, Mike Stand has been in charge of Gilman - I suppose we would call that position *General Coordinator*. He has done a wonderful job of making the club financially stable, in addition to fulfilling the basics of the job; essentially making sure things get done. However, come August 3, Mike will be stepping down from that position. Finding a replacement is no longer a problem, but we do desperately need old and new volunteers to help us make the transition, organize, etc. There will be a shifting of responsibilities, and positions will most likely need to be filled. Furthermore, volunteers are *always* needed for a variety of jobs including; making and posting flyers for shows, working the doors at shows, clean-up before and after shows, etc. Not only does volunteering provide the personal satisfaction of helping a non-profit organization as unique as Gilman, but doing so will also result in free admittance to a show(s) of choice. If you are interested, either attend a meeting (you should do that anyway) or show up around 7pm before the show.

Another problem the club is currently dealing with is that of the arrest of Marian Anderson, singer for the Insaints. As many of you probably know, her arrest was a result of alleged events that occurred at a show they played at Gilman a while back. I will not get into the specifics right now, but she will be going to trial around July 12, and if you would like to know how you can help her (and thus, indirectly help the club), please attend a meeting very soon. Artistic rights are in jeopardy.

GILMAN GAZETTE

Vol. I   No. III   Mid-July, 1993

Welcome to the third issue of the *Gilman Gazette*. The name I have been writing under for these newsletters, Räzl (pronounced "Razzle"), is the one I use for my zine (*Sour Mash*). But you can call me Branwyn if you prefer. Last issue, I was merely the lowly "flyer coordinator," but HA! I am now running the club (starting in August, anyway) as "general coordinator." The Head-honcho. The all-powerful wizard. The Big Cheese. The punk rock goddess. Actually, I'm not really into that dictator shit, so please come volunteer and help out.

Today I received a letter from a Brian from San Jose, whom I assume was responding to the two issues of the *Gilman Gazette* I have published so far. Not only do I appreciate the effort he made to express his concerns, but I also agree with, and was inspired by, a few of the things he had to say. Unfortunately, I feel that much else of what he wrote was unjustified and representative of ignorance.

Unlike Brian, I haven't been going to shows at Gilman since the beginning. In fact, I haven't even been involved in the behind-the-scenes politics of it all for more then 9 or 10 months, so everything I "know" about the old days is simply what I've been told by people who were there. But I do care very much about Gilman continuing to be open for all ages at a reasonable price, despite the jaded apathy inherent in much of "the scene," either because of burn-out, elitist attitudes, or laziness. Now that Gilman is financially stable (for now, at least) - thanks to a lot of work by Mike Stand and the other volunteers - we are going to focus on improving other areas of the club. The only way this can be achieved is if a large variety of people remain/become involved in every aspect of running the club. Membership meetings exist for this very purpose, and they must be well-attended. The importance of attending meetings is something I've adamantly stressed in the past *Gazette*s. I also suggest it in person to many people.

Gilman has acquired a blemished name from a lot of people and bands for a variety of reasons, some justified and some not. One of my main goals as the new General Coordinator will be to remedy that less-then-pristine record, starting with increasing the cooperation between the traditionally rivalling East and West Bays. But again, this can only happen with the support of a variety of people who attend membership meetings (at least occasionally). People who bitch about Gilman, but then never show up with ideas and energy at meetings, will do nothing but annoy me and others who have, and do, work so hard for the club.

Brian writes, "I think people with elitist attitudes should be dismissed and no longer allowed to be directly involved with policy at Gilman St.," and that "anyone who walks through the door at Gilman St. should be allowed direct involvement with Gilman policy..." Well, in case I didn't make myself quite clear enough, as I have said repeatedly, membership meetings exist so that a variety of people may affect Gilman policy. But we can't *force* people to attend them, and if they aren't going to show up on their own, what are we supposed to do? Read their minds?! Out-of-towners can write (as Brian did - I really do appreciate his effort!). But apathetic wind-bags deserve anything they set themselves up for.

Organizations like Gilman and *Maximumrocknroll*, etc, are always getting accused of catering to an elite group of insiders. In some cases this may be true (although, I know for a fact that Gilman, at least, charges admission even for the "in-crowd"), but in many more, those doing the accusing are simply incorrect. Non-profit, volunteer-run organizations rely on the time and energy of those willing to donate it. Unfortunately, more often then not, a regular core of volunteers develops, who out of *necessity*, appear to dominate the situation. This is not necessarily a conscious, power-hungry decision, but rather, reality in the face of limited (wo)man-power and resources. Without a few "aggressive" personalities, believe me, all of you who benefit from the various "D.I.Y." organizations would be up shit-creek.

Those who regularly attend Gilman meetings and work shows are not seeking benevolent status. They simply care about the club. The Bay Area is extremely lucky to have a place like Gilman St., and everyone should - rather, *must* - understand that.

Concerning Brian's dissatisfaction with the required membership cards ("...only Berkeley and S.F. residents should have to buy a membership."), they really do exist for a reason. I myself had a problem with them until Mike Stand explained to me the fact that while inflation has been rising, Gilman's door price has remained the same. About a year ago, it was decided at a meeting that all shows, from then on, would be no more then $5,

when previously, some had been $6. Part of that decision was that the price of membership cards would be raised from $2 to $3. In the long-run, that would *save* attendees money because membership only has to be bought once a year, the extra dinero from which helping to combat our rising costs due to inflation, not being covered by an increased door price. See what I'm saying? I know it really sucks for people from out-of-town just visiting for the weekend, but would you rather have us arbitrarily raise our door price from show to show, as other venues do (not to mention the drink tickets they make minors buy, if they let people under 21 in at all?)?

In closing, Brian commented, "If Gilman wants to be what it once was, then it needs to take the first step. (Personally, I'm sick of it all.)" As I already mentioned, I wasn't around for Gilman's early days, but anyone must be able to figure out that regression to those times, for better or for worse, would be impossible because of the very nature of the club as a volunteer-run venue. New people with new ideas are always going to be getting involved. Brian had plenty of complaints, but absolutely no suggestions for improving the situation. Exactly what sort of steps would he like us to take? What the fuck are we supposed to do if nobody is interested in getting off their butts to help those with the "elitist attitudes" run Gilman St.?

My point in writing this was not to berate Brian at all. It's just that lately I have been noticing that there are a number of things concerning Gilman that are very misunderstood by a great many - sometimes even by those that work at the club. If you, as a 924 Gilman St. member, are going to shell out those bucks to attend a show there, you have a right to know what's going on, and why. You have a right to understand the basis for the few rules that do exist. And you have a right to be part of the decision-making process.

*

924 Gilman St. is an all-ages (no alcohol allowed in or around the club), non-profit, volunteer-run club located in Berkeley at the corner of 8th and Gilman. *

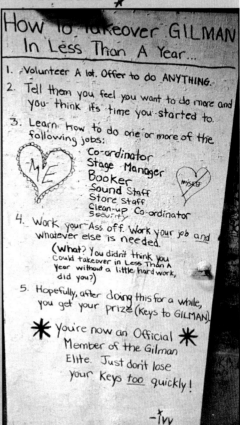

photo by Larry W.

JAKE KELLY

This thing is hard to write. I didn't like the interview that Brian did with me, so I asked him if I could simply rewrite it. But how are you supposed to sum up the past ten or so years in a page or two? Furthermore, what do you want to know? Do you want the dirt, to hear about personal conflicts that had no place in the club? Do you want to hear about being held down due to weird politics that I still fail to understand to this day? Do you want to hear about collective decisions that were made based on personal preference and the ever-present contest for popularity, as opposed to doing what's best for the club itself? How about the collective's willingness to continually rely on unreliable people, not realizing it until it was too late? Or would you rather I look at my experiences at Gilman through rose-colored lenses and talk about how everyone was cool to one another and every show rocked and had hundreds of people in attendance? I'll do both, and I'll do neither at the same time.

The fact of the matter is that not every show featured the most wonderful bands known to man, and there were certainly not hundreds of kids piling on top of each other to get a glimpse of their favorite musician. Quite a few of the volunteers that some of you might remember as being these incredible, awesome people turned out to be elitist power-hungry assholes that didn't want the club to belong to anyone except themselves and their handpicked group of friends. Many people did their best to protect their position in the club and didn't want to share the knowledge and experience with the next person to come along. Those on top truly believe that they are the best ones for the job and no one else will ever be able to replace them, or even come close to being an equivalent. The problem with that mentality is that new people with fresh ideas and perspectives are needed to help make things move onward and upward. Instead, those with radical and thought-provoking ideas will almost always be misunderstood and pushed aside due to the selfishness of the ones that are already present and would rather just keep everything safe and sedate with no one getting out of line. Yet at the same time, there's always that underlying slogan "If you don't like how things are, come help change them and don't just talk shit."

No, they'd rather just have you talk shit. That way you're not a real threat to anyone, and easily written off. It's not really "your" club inasmuch as it's "their" club and maybe it can belong to you too if they're willing to share. And "they" are people whose active days of volunteering ended long before you even knew the club existed. "They" are people who don't care about fostering a community in which even your band will eventually get a chance to shine on the same stage as certain people whose faces are now all over MTV and mainstream music magazines. "They" are people who almost always tow the "it's all about the workers" line while rarely meaning it and are only saying it so they look good in front of their much younger, more enthusiastic peers.

I've been asked to not name names in the interest of fairness, perspective, and taking the high road. This also means that I probably should not dredge up specific incidents because it won't be very hard to figure out who I'm talking about in the process. Good. At this point, it's no longer worth my time to remember such things and such people whose lives must be empty and unfulfilling then and now. There were many times throughout the years where I felt like I was being pushed too far and just wanted to walk away. At one point I did, but came back for some crazy reason. Perhaps I am a glutton for punishment. Or maybe I cared about the club enough to put aside the petty personal differences and simply forge on. Either/or is a plausible explanation for me. It took a very long time for me to feel accepted at the club as a volunteer, and as a patron. Many obstacles were thrown in my way, for a variety of reasons depending on who you talk to. But I'm still here, for better or worse.

When I found out about Gilman, it was at a time when I did not know of any local punk bands besides ones that had broken up many years before and are now taking up space in your record collection and history books. So it took me a while to actually get around to going to the place, but once I went, I was sold. Gilman looked like what a punk club ought to look like—a dingy warehouse with band graffiti all over the walls. When I found out you could work and get in for free, that was even better. That made me feel like anyone could get involved and do things, so when me and a couple friends found ourselves at the club on my sixteenth birthday, I signed up for cleanup duty. Over the next several years, I would show up early and volunteer. Not on a particularly consistent basis, but when I wanted to. We won't get into the trials and tribulations of my being in a band and having a hard time getting shows…face it, it's hard to get booked at the club where everyone wants to play, and that's the end of that. In 1997, I found myself in downtown Berkeley panhandling for beer money, and had nothing to do. So instead of being bored on Telegraph Avenue, I trekked on down to the club and signed up for just about anything they had to offer. I wound up taking over the cleanup coordinator position, and I'll be honest and say that I didn't do the greatest job in the world, but I guess it was better than not having anyone filling the position at all.

To spare you the details and in-depth history, I'll just say that I've been the cleanup coordinator, worked in the stoar (spelled that way for reasons I don't question), made flyers, booked shows, cleaned up graffiti, and even worn a security shirt a few times. We're not counting the standard day-to-day volunteer positions that you can sign up for, but I've done all of that except work the cash box…I'm just not comfortable handling hundreds, if not thousands, of dollars. At the time of this writing, I am the co-head of booking and wondering if it is my time to move on and let someone else handle things. While I do love the club and get a lot out of being involved with it, I also do not want to be like these people that have nothing else going for them and the club is basically the only thing they have in their lives. I don't want to fall into the trap of feeling like no one can replace me, because everyone knows that this is a bullshit mentality to have. When your time is up, step out gracefully and allow someone else the chance to pick up where you left off and see what comes out of it.

I don't know where to go with this. I've started and stopped this rant so many times, but it's got to be done. Gilman has done a lot for me…it's given me a place to play, as well as a place to live when times were tough. I'm a better person coming out of it than I was going in at the beginning. I dealt with a lot of stupid shit over the years, but it comes with the territory, and like your parents used to say, it builds character. You suck it up and deal with it to the best of your abilities and try not to lose your mind in the process. Therefore, I salute all of the Gilman volunteers, past, present, and future. Even the ones I can't stand, for it is those people that inspired me to stick around and say "Yeah, I'm still here and doing a good job and you're not, so you can kiss my ass." Hopefully they've found whatever it is they were looking for to make them happy.

I imagine the ultimate point of this book is to inspire people to start their own venues for live music and whatever else your community has to offer. I hope this happens. But do understand that it is not going to be a good time all the time. You'll have to put up with more bullshit and headaches than you imagined possible. The burnout factor is certainly there, as it will most likely be you and a skeleton crew of people dealing with everything while the majority of people take it for granted. Just try to not abuse your relationship with the bands you book and the patrons that pay to get in and support your club. I wouldn't trade what I've done at Gilman for anything and in the end, I can look back at the past ten years and say that it was a wild and crazy ride, but it was worth it in the end.

Now my tale has been told.

Editor's note: Jake has been the "voice of Gilman" (on the show info line) for many years.

1992   photo by Susan S.

CHRIS H.

Steve List gave me a copy of the List outside a show in San Francisco that I had gone to and told me about 924 Gilman and that I should check it out. I moved to Berkeley in mid 1994, after I had gotten my graduate degree in consciousness studies at JFK University, my studies mostly centering around Native American spirituality, and first went to Gilman shortly thereafter. That first show happened to be a big sold-out show. I couldn't get in, but I remember seeing lots of happy, sweaty people inside, and lots of heat pouring out of the side door. I came back the next night, enjoyed the show, and helped out with cleanup afterward. I really liked the music there, that's what really does it for me as far as the club goes, I've always been about the music. I had mixed feelings though, because I was older and this is a pretty young-audienced club. I wasn't sure if it was appropriate for me to be here, or if I'd fit in. I knew it was "all ages," but that generally indicates a younger crowd. So, I was just going to play it by ear, and see how it went, see if I was welcomed or not, see if people thought I should be there or not. I lived close by, so I'd go there every week.

Gradually people got to know me, and did welcome me to be a part of the place. For the first couple years I was going, I mainly just attended shows as a fan, occasionally doing cleanup afterward. There was a group in Berkeley that I was studying Native American drumming with, and through them, in 1995, I attended a four day visionquest in sweat lodges. I had a vision on the third day, of an anarchy symbol, with the circle made out of clouds in the sky, and the "A" was a guitarist with his feet spread wide and his guitar forming the crossbar of the "A". The top of the "A" was a mohawk made out of ice crystal clouds. I came away with the feeling that nature liked what I was doing at this punk rock club and wanted me to continue. It was a pretty clear sign to me that the spirits liked what I was doing and wanted me to get more involved. I saw it as a calling, and decided to make a commitment to Gilman and help in any way I could with whatever they needed. At that time they needed help working the store, so I worked there until late 1996 or so, eventually becoming store manager. I also started doing occasional booking there around that time. I got really into hardcore, it really touched a nerve with me, and I wanted to have more of those types of bands at Gilman. Gradually I started doing more booking, and mid 1997 I became a regular booker, as well as continuing as store manager. I did that until late 1998, when I was asked to leave booking because of the type of shows and bands I was booking. It wasn't done at a meeting, I was told to step down during one of the weeknights I was there doing booking. The crowds that came to see these bands weren't always the best behaved, and sometimes caused problems for Gilman. The channels of communication weren't the best about this issue, and I think it could have been negotiated and talked about. But rather than fight it, I stepped down from booking. I was feeling a little burned out anyway and it was getting to be too much for me. In a way, I was grateful. If I felt like it was wrong, I would have fought it. I wasn't here to push my own way or make a name for myself for my own benefit, I just wanted to fit in where I was needed, and if I wasn't needed anymore, then okay. I did notice afterwards though that I had "withdrawal" symptons. One of the best parts about booking for me was talking to the bands, and I didn't have that anymore, and I missed it a lot. I did ask that they continue to book hardcore bands, though, because I felt that I had done a lot of work to get those kinds of bands into Gilman. I felt they were a facet of the community that was underrepresented at Gilman.

I stayed on as store manager until late 2000. I came back to booking in late 2000 when I ran for head of booking, and was voted in. I didn't want to be the "head of" two things, so I stepped down from being store manager. I also didn't want to be known just as a hardcore booker, so I tried to be as diverse as I could, and book different types of shows as well as those I really loved. I rely on inner guidance a lot, and I'll seek answers from deep within as to whether a show should happen or not. Sometimes I'd go up to the loft (where the sound board used to be) before a show and say a prayer and ask for protection for the club, and to not have a certain undesired element show up to start fights, etc. I believe strongly in that kind of stuff and I don't expect others to believe it. I didn't have as much experience and history with this type of music, and the mentality it attracted, as others at the club who had seen and experienced it firsthand. I was a bit naive in thinking that it was always going to be okay and what was the fuss all about. I had always focused on hardcore from a positive perspective rather than a "tough guy" perspective. I think now people have changed their opnion of me and they're able to see that I'm not all about just one genre of music.

Gilman's really important to me and I love it deeply, because I see it's such a good thing for kids and for the community. It's bigger than any one of us. It's almost an organic entity that seems to draw to it the people it needs to help it run, or "live." Lots of people have come and gone, but it's still stayed strong and stood up to threats to its existence. I've felt the energy and strength of the place pretty strongly at times, seeing it like a big tree with deep roots connected to the earth, and branches that spread out far into the community. It's much bigger than the size of its building, and reaches a lot of people, all over the world. Music is that universal language that helps unify people. Even if you can't hear or understand the lyrics, the emotions come through, and that's what touches my heart and my soul. Because of Gilman, I've gone from hating myself to loving myself, and appreciating who I am, and therefore appreciating other people more. It gave me a sense of purpose, a sense of belonging, a place in the world where I feel at home, where I feel good and my life makes sense. Being here just feels so right. It may sound corny, or schmaltzy, or whatever, to say that, but it's so true. I think I had my first adolescence at Gilman. I don't remember having much of a "teenage-hood" until I came here. Gilman is family. It isn't easy working here, though—this isn't a place where your ego gets massaged. There's not a lot of "thank yous" for working here.

I'm not looking so much at what I can get out of the club—it's what I can put in. One thing I don't like is the tendency I see for Gilman becoming more "institutionalized," with governing boards and more and more rules and regulations, codifying more of what Gilman is. I don't ever want to see that happen to this club. I want to see it stay fresh, and keep what happens next a mystery rather than something predictable. There's a balance we have to achieve between being punk rock/anarchic and continuing to exist/stay open in "regular" society and the city of Berkeley. This stems out of the movement currently underway to make the Gilman "manual," a guide as to how to do the various jobs at Gilman, so if someone key leaves unexpectedly, there would be instructions for the next person as to how to do that particular job. But I think being thrown into a job and making it up as you go along is healthy, keeps things from staying too much the same, and keeps things evolving.

CELIA S.

Gilman was very important and meaningful to me at one point, but that gradually became lost, that certain feeling for me, that strong sense of "we," and that's why I stopped working there. I can't say if that was due to me changing, or the people I knew there leaving, or perhaps a combination of both. As the Friday/Saturday night shows got less and less interesting for me and others there, we tried to find something else to do to utilize the space. We had book groups meet there, movie nights, art shows, "fashion" shows, things like that. We had some self

Art show, 1997   photo by Sita R.

defense classes and training for security there too. That helped give women more confidence to help do security. The number of women doing security increased during the time I was there. We even attempted to have art classes there, but it fell through, didn't work out. There also were some puppet and mask-making classes there during the week, but that didn't last very long either, I think mostly because there wasn't much storage space there. Gilman has a lot of shitwork that needs to be done to keep it running, it isn't all "fun." But to me,

doing the hard part is what bonds the workers, gives a sense of accomplishment for the greater good—it brings you closer to those who are willing to do that with you. The threats we faced, legal and physical, brought us closer together, gave us a common "enemy," helped us define ourselves, and helped us figure out exactly what we were doing. It takes a certain kind of person to commit to any project, let alone a volunteer one, because it's not always easy and fun, it's hard work. You have to be willing to rely on each other, that's a really important part of having a community.

I wasn't really into punk music when I started going there. My brother took me there in 1988 when I was fifteen. It didn't really do much for me, and I didn't go there again until 1991 or 1992 for a Spitboy/Paxston Quiggly show. That show really inspired me. There were these really strong women up on stage, kicking ass, and I was floored! That's what really got me into punk and into Gilman, this sense of these really strong women who could fucking do anything! I wanted to be around that. I was working at Uprisings at the time, a collective bakery near Gilman, and a friend of mine at the bakery also worked at Gilman, and was encouraging me to work there too, so I knew about the volunteer aspect of Gilman. Also, I had worked in a bunch of collectives before, and that was what also drew me to Gilman. It certainly made it easier for me to have an "introduction," so to speak, rather than just walking in cold and not knowing anyone there. I worked the front door for a long time, and I went to the meetings. I think the meetings were the most important part of Gilman, the ability to choose what you wanted to have happen there, and how to go about making it happen. It was inspiring and empowering, it was your club, your space. Like in the other collectives I was involved with, the people were fairly smart there and could figure out how to do all the things that needed to be done. The motivation to learn was high because it was something you really wanted to know how to do, to help this place that you believed in to run better. Gilman was made up of a much younger group of people than the other collectives I worked at (free clinic, bakery, martial arts studio), but they all seemed to function about the same.

I quickly stepped up my involvement there and wanted to help run the place. I don't remember a lot of other women being involved, but I always felt comfortable there and that my opinion was respected at the meetings. What I didn't like was the macho boy crap at the shows, the fighting, violent dancing, etc.—that would piss me off. It would be kinda depressing, too. I had hoped that "we" could be different, and not have the same crap that "normal" society has.

I had trained in martial arts for a number of years, so moving into doing security at Gilman was a pretty easy transition for me. Being more physically confident, I became more willing to not look away from confrontations, to step in and help. Gilman wanted to have more women doing security as well. Doing security also felt like I was doing something a little more "skilled." I never got into any face to face fights, I just would use certain holds and such to lead people out, get them out of the club. The training also helped in learning how to take a punch. Mostly though, it was just using your verbal skills, your diplomatic skills, resolving the situation without violence. Also, as a woman, I didn't feel the need to respond to challenges from guys who I had to deal with. You could work security without fighting, just get a group together if there's something you can't deal with yourself. I didn't feel like I was protecting the people there so much as I was protecting the space. To do security, it seems like you have to be an asshole, or be perceived as an asshole or authority figure, all the time, and that's a real drag, because this place was supposed to be about not having authority figures. And I think that's why security are the only people being paid, because that sucks. I felt like I was somebody's mother, a lot. Or a babysitter. It really wore on my nerves. We're supposed to all be in this together and here these jerks are fucking it up by acting stupid. I didn't understand why people had to be that way, why they needed babysitters.

I would hear "Gilman sucks" from a lot of people, even some of my friends too, and I would tell them to come to meetings, come and help make it different if you want, rather than just complaining. I had my "Gilman" friends and my "other" friends, and my "other" friends would always talk total shit about Gilman. For most it was because you couldn't drink there. For some of the others, I think it was because they didn't want to belong to a "place" in that way, they just wanted to see some bands and then leave. And of course, some people just like to complain. There's a reason for every rule in a collective—sometimes you might have to hunt for it, but it'll be there. There's not rules just for rules' sake. One of the biggest complaints I heard among the hardcore Gilman workers was that it was hard to have a life outside of Gilman, and I don't know how long you can live that way, to have this "thing" that takes over your life. But that's been true to a certain extent with all the collectives I've been involved with—it becomes your social life too. As long as you're enjoying that, that's fine, but if you want something outside of that, then it can get difficult. It's so very much like family, those people are so important to you. I lived with all Gilman workers, it was always around me.

Gilman opened up a whole other way of being for me, and I never really realized it until I turned twenty-five and started going to college. I had lived in this insulated punk world and grown up without realizing it. Gilman had a certain ethical standard. I felt people worked there and did stuff there because they felt it was the right thing to do. That moral/ethical code is what helps keep us all connected, knowing what the right thing to do is and then doing it. I learned that people had made a choice to live this way, there was a reason for it. I learned at college that the rest of the world isn't like that, there's a much different set of ethics out there, much more selfish. Through punk, and Gilman was a vehicle within that, I was able to meet this huge network of people, go on tour with bands, see the world, have so many opportunities I wouldn't have had otherwise. It established a connection with people all over, showed you that there were other like-minded folks out there, and made the world a smaller place, not quite so distant. It gave me the feeling that we could do anything, and Gilman was very symbolic of that. That was a huge impact on me.

Another important connection for me, that I made through Gilman, was the Local 510 Trade Union. A number of people from Gilman ended up working there, about ten or so. It pays well—good benefits, job security, call up when you want to work—it was another place that I got that feeling of community from. It changed my life in a big way, allowed me to afford to go to college, buy in on a house, etc. And the skills learned from the Union went back in to Gilman—setting up the art shows, minor construction, things like that. Those are the kinds of things that make Gilman more of a symbol that it's a community and not just a music club, and that it permeates throughout all these different things in your life, and has a lasting positive impact. I don't know if I do anything that feels that meaningful now, like Gilman did. I've wanted to ask other people who used to work at Gilman, "what did you replace it with?"

I think my strong point at Gilman was helping people deal with something they were uncomfortable with, empowering them with the confidence that it was their space too, and let's step up and deal with the problem. I've dropped out and come back a couple times at Gilman. As long as some of the people I knew were still there, like when my brother was head coordinator for a time, I had an interest in working there. When the people I knew were all gone, so was my interest. I ended up working there for about six years in all. I started working there in 1993 when Branwyn was head coordinator, left in late 1998/early 1999, then came back again

for a short period in 2002. This last time was a lot harder for me—I hardly knew anyone there, and everyone was so young. Gilman had been having some problems, and asked me to help out with security again. It seemed a strange motivation for me to work there again just because they needed it. It felt like a sense of obligation, rather than working there because I really wanted to.

Movie night, 1997   photo by Sita R.

I really didn't like it this time. It seemed even more like babysitting, rather than a community. It didn't feel like there was a "we" anymore at all. It didn't feel like there was any meaning for anyone, even the workers. I even started rallying to close the place, saying that if nobody's enjoying it anymore, let's just stop. Some people agreed wholeheartedly, others just laughed. I was suggesting it partially in jest, but it was also said with the assumption that someone else would come in and open it up again. And if no one did, then you know for certain that it's outlived its usefulness. It would seem too hard for me to choose, after fighting for the place for so long, to admit that it's outlived its usefulness.

It's kind of hard for me to "just" go to a show now—you come to enjoy having a role at the show. I don't think it's ego, I think it helps add meaning to it, it makes it more into something that you're doing as a group. It's hard for the people who've committed themselves to Gilman to leave when they're burned out. I think you have to have faith that when you leave, someone else will take on what you were doing and you won't be leaving a hole. And sometimes a vacuum is needed to really motivate someone to step forward and take on more responsibility. And as for the possibility of working there only part-time, while it might lessen the burnout rate, it can be sorta depressing too, because it would mean that it's not great enough or inspiring enough to put your whole heart and focus into. And I think that having that certain vision or idea is what's lacking there now. What would be great now? What would get people all excited and turned on now? Have we done it all and seen it all? I hope not. Is wild enthusiasm just inherent in the young? I really miss being excited about something, but I don't know what would get me excited now.

Clockwise from left: photos by Susan S., Murray B., Larry W., Larry W.

GILMAN DOESN'T ALWAYS ROCK

RICHARD

I had read the initial articles in *Maximum RocknRoll* magazine in 1986 about the Gilman Street Project coming together and then opening up, so I knew it existed. But it didn't do much for me at the time, because my previous experience of seeing bands and knowledge of music was limited to big name bands. I didn't care much for small, local bands. I lived in Sacramento at the time and first went to Gilman almost by accident, maybe it was fate. I was on my way to another club and the car I was driving literally almost died at the Gilman Street exit on the freeway. So I ended up going to the show at Gilman instead. This was June, 1987. I was totally blown away, it was so great. Every band seemed like the best band in the world to me, everything clicked, everything suddenly made sense. I saw people my own age, or a little older, running the space, and no fights. And it had this sense of permanence too. Most of the other clubs I had been to felt temporary, if not overall, then definitely for punk rock. I remember the person at the front door being horribly mean, but once I got past her, it was like this magic wonderland.

I was sixteen—my social skills were pretty limited at the time, and it was hard for me to talk to people, so for the first couple of years I went there I was basically just an observer. I moved to the Bay Area in 1989 and got involved in a couple volunteer projects in San Francisco. These helped build my confidence and social skills. After a couple years or so, I burned out on these projects and was looking for something else. I started going to Gilman more and started working there about 1993. I felt like I had to do something, I wanted to contribute, so I chose Gilman. I definitely feel like if you're part of a community, you have to put something back in. I was really into live music, I had been touring as a roadie for a couple years, and I wanted to help put on shows, so working at Gilman was an obvious choice. I had learned from the other projects I was in about burnout, so I was determined not to take on too much at Gilman, to pace myself. My goal was to be there until it stopped or closed. I started out working the door, then learned how to do sound. I did sound for a while before becoming the sound coordinator. Did that for a while before settling in to what I do now, which is occasional building maintenance as needed. I keep a hand in and want to contribute what I can. I don't want to be resentful of the place. I want it to be as magical as when I first went there in 1987.

I'm getting more of an adult perspective on it now. It's more of a social experiment for me now then a place for awesome shows. There are still good shows there, it's just that I don't have that crazy sixteen-year-old enthusiasm anymore, just a need to continue to contribute in some way. There are nights occasionally when that magic returns though. Of course, there are also nights when you just want it to end. It's all tempered by the realization that for me, if I burned out on Gilman, there'd be nowhere else for me to go. I haven't found anyplace else that interests me. The whole bar scene doesn't appeal to me. It seems to be made up of lost dreams and lost hopes. Hanging out with your friends at the bar might seem fun, but I'd rather try to connect with 16-year-olds or 20-year-olds at Gilman who are trying to do something constructive, taking the potential of Gilman and making it what they want it to be. I see kids working there at twelve or thirteen and, at least twice a week, when they're working at Gilman, people will listen to them and treat them as an adult. I've never felt old at Gilman either, maybe because I keep in touch with the people there and it's not all new faces when I go. I go there for inspiration, to have fun, and see friends. I'm thirty now, and I'm still learning when I go there, I'm still being challenged.

Some of the things I like about Gilman are that people are held to the same level of conduct regardless if it's their first night working or if they're running the place as head coordinator, and that it's also held the same tenets/foundations since the beginning for what goes on there: no bands on major labels can play there, no sexist/racist/homophobic activities are allowed there, etc. I totally agree with those things. Another thing I like about Gilman is that you can't have a huge ego there. You'll either get burned out or pushed out. So the people that do last—maybe they're not the sanest, but everyone works together pretty well. Through my going on tour with bands, and seeing lots of other all ages places across the country, I've been able to compare them with Gilman, and I think Gilman is the best place. It's been around a long time and had time to learn from its mistakes and smooth out the rough spots. On the other hand, I think Gilman is pretty underutilized. It's only used two or three times a week, while rent and utilities are for the whole month. People are trying, or have tried, to use it more, but it doesn't seem to last. I don't know what the answer is for that. Maybe if we had a full-time person who just worked at Gilman and could interact and coordinate with the community, it could happen. But it's all volunteer and the people there have to work, go to school, etc., too, and there's little time or energy left over to do much more than just keep Gilman afloat. I wish we could go that next step, buying the place, get that real sense of permanence. It's month to month now, always has been, and it's usually a struggle to make rent. I think it affects the volunteers too, that there's no long-term vision. I think there'd be more enthusiasm in the place if we purchased the building.

Gilman can be like this sometimes   Photo by Larry W.

☆ Membership Meetings

★ You can - and should - come to membership meetings and contribute to the running of the club.

★ All decisions affecting the club are decided by the members at meetings. We vote by standard parliamentary process with a minimum quorum of 9 members and a 50% majority needed to approve a measure. Two-thirds majority is needed to change any articles of incorporation or bylaws, to hire anyone, or to elect officers.

★ Meetings are every first and third Saturday of each month at 5 pm.

☆ Membership Rules

This list of rules is only meant as a general guide: Come to a membership meeting if you are interested in seeing a complete list of all 924 Gilman Street's policies and rules.

★ There is no drinking of alcohol or taking of illegal drugs in or around the club (meaning within two blocks of the club). This is not a moralist measure but a necessary condition of our all-ages status.

★ Vandalism in or around the club is prohibited. Please respect our neighbors for tolerating our club the last seven years, and also respect the very limited resources we have inside the club. (Artwork and the like is encourage within the club walls, unless paint fumes get too strong.)

★ No one is allowed in the loft unless they are working or they have the permission of the sound person or coordinator.

★ In the case of some large shows, ins-and-outs may not be allowed.

★ Violence or overly aggressive dancing will not be tolerated, and this includes stage-diving and crowd-launching. We must enforce this because of our insurance.

page two

☆ Doin' It For the Kids Since '86

Entering upon its eighth year, 924 Gilman Street continues as a truly unique community-oriented, non-profit, independent venue open to people of all ages.

This is not just *a club.*
THIS IS YOUR CLUB!

Gilman is based on the fact that bands, audience and staff are all equally important to the success of a show.

This was compiled and produced by Branwyn, heavily based on a similar such pamphlet from two years previous, and on 924 Gilman Street collectively passed by-laws, rules and policies.

☆ Club 924 Gilman Street

☆ Membership

March 1994

★ Gilman Street is entirely volunteer-run (except for one or two regular, paid security) and requires the cooperation of all its members for maximum enjoyment and safety for all.
☆ Any member, whether officially working that night or not, is encouraged - and expected - to help enforce our rules, and should be respected for doing so.

★ If somebody is hurting the club it is in your interest to stop them: If you do not feel safe confronting the person, find a show worker (who can at least point out security or the coordinator) and explain to him/her the situation.

★ Gilman is a labor of love... Neither regular nor occasional volunteers are becoming rich off this - we do it in support of the ideals the club represent. We understand the importance of such an inclusive, unique, community-oriented, non-profit, cooperative venue (especially as the word "alternative" becomes increasingly appropriated by the status quo to the point of demoralizing embitterment).

☆ Membership Requirements

★ 924 Gilman Street operates as a membership collective and proof of membership is required of everyone for admittance to all shows.
☆ Proof comes in the form of a membership card, which you probably judt purchased.
☆ And hey, read the back of your card if you haven't already.

★ The annual membership card is presently sold for $1, is non-transferable (we reserve the right to confiscate shared cards), and must be signed at the time of purchase.

★ Purchase of a membership card signifies the holder's agreement to follow all club policies. You are a member as long as you don't violate any of the rules of the club; if you do violate the rules you will either be removed from the club temporarily or banned completely.

page one

☆ Violent individuals will be removed from the club. Overly aggressive dancers will be warned to calm down, and if the behavior persists, s/he will be removed.

★ Gilman Street reserves the right to refuse service to anyone. We also reserve the right to eject anyone from the club and confiscate their membership.

★ Gilman Street reserves the right to "86" a person who is known to have violated the rules of the club. (This has been reserved for very serious - rare - circumstances.)

★ Gilman Street does not knowingly advocate racist/race hate organizations or people, and people wearing obvious indicators of these beliefs will not be allowed to enter the club (or will be removed in the event they slip past us).
☆ Bands known to be racist, homophobic or mysogynist will not be booked.

★ There are a limited number of ways to get into a show:
☆ Pay the full admission and have a membership card.
☆ Volunteer:
• Work during the show (get there early).
• Work during the week; jobs must be pre-approved at a meeting, or if that is not convenient, upon the coordinator's consideration.
☆ Be in a band performing that night.

page three

☆ Win tickets on the radio or be someone's guest. Only certain people get guests:
• One guest per performing band member.
• A band may get one roadie.
• Certain regular workers.
★ Only the head of security or the coordinator should call 911 or ask someone else to do so; police involvement should be kept to a bare minimum.
☆ Violent incidences at Gilman are few and far-between (especially when compared to other venues) because we are self-policing, and because it is the responsibility of all members of the Gilman Street community to see that the club stays safe and inclusive.

★ Absolutely no illegal acts are allowed in or around the club.

Anyone caught breaking any of these rules will be disciplined in the manner deemed fit by security and/or the show coordinator (or any night's worker if the former aren't available).

★
Show info: 510.525.9926

★
Booking: 510.524.8180
☆
Send demos with a lyric sheet to:
Attn: Booking
Alternative Music Foundation
P.O. Box 1058
Berkeley, CA 94701

page four

4 JUNE 94

Are you a part of the Upper Class at GILMAN? do you have SERVANTS, whose Lives are less meaningful and significant than yours?

Do you come to shows but never work the Shows? is it someone elses job? Do they owe it to you to keep this club going? Does someone else owe it to you to keep this club going?

if so, CONGRATULATIONS! you are a part of the GILMAN UPPERCLASS.

Posted by Pat W., 1994

P.O. Box 1058 Berkeley, California 94701

Alternative Music Foundation

924 Gilman Street Project

May 22, 1994

On the evening of Saturday May 7, 1994 during the show at the 924 Gilman Street Project in Berkeley, ex-DEAD KENNEDY's singer and Alternative Tentacles head honcho Jello Biafra was involved in an altercation with at least four other patrons of the club. Before audience members and Gilman Security personnel could separate the group, Biafra had sustained moderate head injuries and extensive knee damage which will require an operation and physical therapy.

At a special membership meeting the following timeline of the incident was pieced together from eyewitness accounts and police information:

A young man nicknamed "Cretin" was slam-dancing and knocked into Biafra's knee twice, possibly breaking it. After a short pushing and shouting match between Cretin and Biafra which resulted in a struggle on the venue's floor, a friend of Cretin's, "Sphincter," and possibly "Spider," joined the melee. As other audience members tried to separate the combatants, a fourth assailant, "Little John," kicked and punched Biafra at least 3 times in the head while one of the other assailants held him down.

After the fight was broken up, the police were called at Biafra's request. Meanwhile Gilman Security attempted to discuss the incident with two of those involved and a female companion outside the club, and Cretin brandished a chain with a padlock on it at security. A tense discussion ended without violence and the participants left in a blue Chevrolet truck with Arizona plates before the police arrived. When Sphincter, Little John and one other returned to the club minutes later they were interviewed, but because of a lack of evidence, were released by the police. Emergency personnel examined Biafra's injuries and members of one of the performing bands drove him to Alta Bates Hospital to receive medical treatment.

The membership of 924 Gilman Street voted to hold a benefit for Biafra's medical expenses, from which Gilman is donating its usual 50% cut as well as the bands' payment to set up an Emergency Medical Fund for Biafra (donations accepted at the address above - checks should be written to Alternative Music Foundation). In addition we voted to cooperate fully with the police investigation.

The Gilman Street Project is an all-ages, volunteer-run collective dedicated to presenting alternative music, theater, and art. Neither stage-diving nor excessively violent dancing are allowed. Started on December 31, 1986, by the local fanzine MAXIMUMROCKNROLL, the Project has open membership meetings the 1st and 3rd Saturdays of every month at 5pm.

Please direct any further questions or information to Gilman's Head Coordinator, Branwyn
B   , at (510)

Club press release after the incident received media attention

CHAPTER SEVEN

BATTLE #2

CHARLES L.

1994-1997

"IT'S COMMON IN WHATEVER HISTORY THAT PUNKS WILL GET BLAMED."

—CHRIS S.

Photo by Emilie V

CHARLES L

I was one of the people who came to the Bay Area with the point of going to Gilman. I never really thought of Gilman as a place just to "attend." Gilman set an example for people everywhere, and I wanted to be part of that. I had done so many other things, but they all seemed so small, and I wanted to do something that was big. From what I had read about it, I expected Gilman to be big and glorious, and when I first saw it, it was anything but that. I walked down there from the UC Berkeley campus with my roommate (it was during the day) and when I first got there, I couldn't believe it. First, for some reason I thought Gilman would be open 24/7, people hanging out, etc., like this super community space. Second, there was no sign, nothing going on. I was absolutely amazed. It's funny how that perspective changes over time. I volunteered from day one. I don't think I ever went to a show there without working. I initially came out to the Bay Area between my sophomore and junior year of college (1993). I spent the summer working at Gilman every weekend, during the time when Gilman was three to four months behind on rent and no one ever showed up for shows. I was just glad to be there, and it was just so much fun to be with the other people who were working. And there were so few people attending, that it seemed to be mostly just us running around and having fun at the club.

When I came back to the Bay Area for a second time, about a year later, when I actually ended up moving out here, I lived here for several months before going down to Gilman. One of the coordinators at the time, Trevor, kept encouraging me to go down and help out again. So I started working at Gilman again, and the next thing I knew, I was one of the coordinators. Branwyn was running the club at the time. I ended up taking on more and more responsibilities and it all snowballed into me becoming head coordinator in 1994, all within about six months of me starting working there again. Branwyn and I were initially going to be co-head coordinators. But that didn't seem to last too long, before I took it on myself. The Jello Biafra incident happened during this period, turned into a big deal, and got a lot of publicity. There was a big fight outside and the club's security was all outside dealing with it. At the same time, there was an altercation inside that resulted in Jello having his leg injured. Subsequently, Jello's insurance company was threatening to sue us, and there was a lot of fear that Gilman would be closed because of it. We had lots of meetings trying to find out exactly what happened. But the people who were accused of attacking Jello weren't talked to about it, weren't given a chance to give their side of it. In fact, it was decided at a meeting that they would be invited to the club and then kept in the side room while the police were called. This shocked and horrified me. There were a lot of people at the club who were adamant about this. There was also talk of vigilante squads and such. So I went and found the accused people and had them write down what they had to say about it and what they saw or did during the incident. I then brought these statements back to the club. I didn't want to be involved with turning people over to the cops. And those statements uncovered some aspects and information that disputed the allegations that it was an unprovoked attack. What ended up happening was that the "suspects" all left town, Jello's insurance company didn't sue, and Jello held a spoken word performance at Gilman to help pay his medical bills. We issued a "press release" to newspapers and magazines stating what had happened and our take on it, since there was so much misinformation going around *(see last page of previous chap-*

ter—editor). MTV got a hold of it and had a small blurb on their network "news." Even though I strongly disagreed with how this incident was being handled, I had become part of a family at Gilman, and I couldn't walk away from them. Dissension is just part of the community. Back then it did really feel so much like a family.

My first couple years there seemed to be the "golden age" of Gilman, because we were just making money hand over fist. Punk seemed to be going through a major resurgence. There were a lot of cool bands and a lot of people were coming to see them. There were lots of really big shows with lines going around the block. There were also a lot of people who were very interested in working at Gilman. We stopped our paid advertisements because we didn't need them. Word of mouth and the List seemed to work fine. Because the shows were so big we had a big security staff and almost every

Alternative Music Foundation
for Club 924 Gilman Street

Press Release

Media attention on the Bay Area punk scene has recently increased as a result of the career moves of certain bands. However, a given band's individual, personal decisions are what is best for that band only, and must not be taken out of context.

924 Gilman Street exists as a safe, inclusive, community-oriented venue for those who do not feel represented by the status quo. People of all ages are welcome since alcohol and violence are prohibited, as are racism, sexism, and homophobia. Gilman will cease to exist if through *cooptive* exploitation we are prevented from continuing as a true alternative.

We are part of an underground movement and intend to remain so. *We have a right to self-determination that should be respected by the mass media.*

924 Gilman Street Membership

show had not only a coordinator but also multiple co-coordinators. You really had to stay on top of things. And there was a lot of money to be dealt with. This was also the time we started to try and document things, coordinator rules and procedures, etc. Myself and some of the other people involved there had experience with other collectives, and we started incorporating more of a "procedural" feel to Gilman, particularly the meetings. The meetings became more and more essential to the running of the club. Gilman seemed to become less of a hangout and more of a serious place. I don't think Gilman had been called, or even thought of as, a collective, up until that point. We became almost a political-social body, with a responsibility to itself and to the community. I think this was also partially fostered by the fact that I felt uncomfortable having so much responsibility over so many people, and that the decisions that I was supposed to be making were having an effect over this large of a group. I wanted more of these decisions to be made at meetings and involve everyone else. I didn't want to think of myself as the boss, just as an administrator. If you were involved with the running of the club, the meetings were becoming something that you couldn't miss. If you did miss one, the next time you came to Gilman you could find it completely different! We were coming up with new projects all the time, like a photo board, announcement board, record/zine table, etc. We were deciding things like who could come in to take pictures, whether they got in for free or not, whether or not so and so should have a key, whether or nor this play or that event can happen, who's a booker, who's not a booker, who can practice here, who can't practice here, who's on a major label, who's not on a major label, etc.

The DIY fest came out of my initial feeling that there wasn't any substantial difference between the political scene and the punk scene (this feeling changed later), and that we should have a gathering of people from different communities who share the same vision of existing outside the corporate structure. I spent months preparing it. I felt it was really important to be able to share all the great talent and energy I saw out there with those who maybe weren't "in the loop." I thought it turned out great, I was just sorry that we didn't follow through and finish publishing the information we gathered from it, and that we didn't have more of them. I'd say that was the highlight of my time at Gilman.

But what comes really close is the time we packed the Berkeley City Council meeting about the Pyramid Brewery with all these people supporting Gilman, kids and adults alike. We had heard that a brew pub was moving in across the street from Gilman. This was during a time when Gilman was being blamed for everything bad that was happening in the neighborhood: graffiti, litter, vandalism, etc. As Gilman was becoming more and more popular, the surrounding area was becoming more and more gentrified. We felt that if the "upscaling" of the neighborhood continued, we could be pushed out. Also, with a bar being across the street, people could be getting drunk and coming over to our club and starting fights, etc. We had lots of meetings, and lots of people I had never seen before were getting involved with helping us. "Gilman's gonna close" became a rallying cry across the community. There had been cries of "wolf" before, but we felt like this time there was a serious and legitimate threat to Gilman's existence. There was even quiet talk among our staff of moving Gilman. We became very involved with the Berkeley Zoning Board, attending all the pertinent meetings, and they took us very seriously. It was amazing to me how seriously they took us, and very empowering. We had always felt up until that point that Gilman was always just hanging on by a thread, but what became quite clear was that Gilman was anything but. It was the first time I was able to see that Gilman meant a lot not just to us, but to the city as well, and that we were something that they considered important, not just a bunch of obnoxious kids they wished they could get rid of. The brewery took us pretty seriously too, and even flew a number of us up to Seattle to see their operation and what they were all about. Eventually they were allowed to move in across the street, but a number of conditions were placed on them by the zoning board, including having to meet with us, street/traffic lights, etc. It turned out all okay though, because the brewery people have been really cool with us, and really accommodating. I don't think there have ever been any problems since they opened.

Out of an incident involving a long-time Gilman worker accused of multiple incidents of sexual harassment at Gilman (who, faced with the choice of either having the issue brought up at a general membership meeting or "retiring," chose to "retire") came a need to create policies, rules, etc., about how to deal with grievances and social uncomfortability and such. Things sounded good on paper when we were sitting around talking about them, but when it came down to actually making them work, it was impossible. After months of arguing and debate, we created a grievance council. I could tell you how it was supposed to work, but I don't think it would be a very good idea to publicize it, because I wouldn't want anyone to use it as a model. It was a bad idea. Or maybe it was a good idea that turned out bad in practice. One of the main points of this council was anonymity. They could investigate incidents without it being brought to a general membership meeting and perhaps wrongly embarrassing someone. It gets really tough, though, when the alleged incidents occur away from Gilman. Say someone who attends Gilman doesn't want someone else to be allowed into Gilman because of what they did elsewhere, things like that. The council wasn't around very long when things exploded, and we should have seen it coming. At a general membership meeting, one person accused another regular patron of Gilman of unwanted sexual advances, which occurred at a location other than Gilman. An investigating council was called, I was one of the council members, and things became so messy and so ugly. I hated being on it. Before any conclusion was reached, and before all the evidence/information was gathered, one of the council members decided to publish the information they had. This to me was a heinous crime, because they had collected that information in Gilman's name. Not only did they publish it online, but also flyers, seriously harassing, were placed around the accused person's home and around Gilman. The police ended up getting involved and the accused person ended up getting arrested. The person was tried and found guilty and spent some time in jail. I can't say whether the person was guilty or not. One of the things that became clear is that no one in that council was in a position to be able to make that decision. Shortly afterward, the council idea was dropped.

I lasted about a year or so after that as head coordinator. I was looking at pursuing more and more serious jobs, and I wouldn't have the time to do both. Also, I found I had become incredibly antisocial. I couldn't go anywhere without the stigma of Gilman attached to me. On top of that, all my friends were five to ten years younger than me—I felt like I was being socially dwarfed. I needed to get out, I needed to grow. I approached Chris S. a few times about taking over as head coordinator, and eventually he did. To be honest, I think I stayed too long, and in some ways Gilman had a negative effect on me. I don't want to be a boss of anybody again, ever. I wish that I had more fun towards the end. I consider that a closed period in my life now. I don't think about it very much anymore. Objectively, I don't have any negative feelings about Gilman. I think it's a great place and I think it's a good thing—I'm really glad it exists, it's just that I'm really, really bummed that I put so much time into something that I ended up feeling so bad about. I feel that I put a large portion of my life into Gilman and instead of getting a lot of positive feedback, I got a lot of negative feedback. That weighed really heavily on me. I'm sorry for that in my life. I feel in that respect that Gilman had a negative impact on my life. I don't think it soured me on collectives or community projects—I think it soured me on punk, and punk spirit. I got pissed off at the community for blaming me for decisions made at Gilman. People seemed to just get angry at me for what Gilman decided. People blamed me for what happened to the person who was sent to jail regarding the unwanted sexual advances. People blamed me for getting kicked out when they were drunk. People blamed me because they got older and Gilman got younger. "It's Charles' fault that Gilman isn't the way it used to be, etc." No, Gilman isn't the way it used to be, because *you* aren't the way *you* used to be.

The issue over whether to pay the head coordinator a monthly stipend was another example. Someone at Gilman proposed giving me a monthly stipend of $200. I hadn't even thought about getting money from Gilman. I was working three jobs and working at Gilman about twenty hours a week. I eventually was talked into it. I wasn't very comfortable with the idea—no one else other than security had ever been paid there. It lasted for about a year. I ended up stopping it once I got some better jobs. It wasn't as if I wasn't in enough trouble as it was, being the administrator of the club, and then it became even worse with the stipend. It became awful—people actually made up songs about it and sang them stage. It was only $200 a month—it wasn't like I was rollin' in dough. I think it came to about $2.50 an hour, a whole lot less than security was making. I felt like the same people who talked me into taking it were the same people who threw mud at me for having it. I really feel like the saying that Gilman has, "Gilman eats its own," is true, it does. It builds people up, and then as soon as they're up there, it tears them down. I watched it happen over and over again. Very few of the past head coordinators go to Gilman anymore. I've only gone to one or two shows since I left.

One of the things I realized was that punk has a lot to do with your age. I found I wasn't identifying anymore with the people who were going to Gilman. I wasn't thinking about destroying something anymore, I was thinking about creating something. I did take away a sense of accomplishment, a sense that I had done something with my life, crossed a hurdle, carried a weight. There are definitely some good things that happened in that period, I have some good memories. My bitterness or anger isn't directed at Gilman, it's directed at some of the crap that came out of the punk community as a whole. I still can't fit in with "normal" people, they won't let me! I'm still a punk rock jerk that says exactly what's on my mind,

Metal fest   photo courtesy of Charles L.

and I don't say it very nice, either. I remember the punk proms, Slap A Ham fests, geekfests, I really enjoyed those. I remember the metal fest—that was great, it was gorgeous, awesome! We had about eight bands, made T-shirts, and everybody dressed up. Events like that generated so much energy and excitement. If those types of things were held at regular nightclubs, people would just think it was a money-making scheme. At Gilman, it was for the community, and you could just have fun with it. Those were the kinds of things that made me feel good about working there. People could smile and not take themselves so seriously. I wouldn't say Gilman was taken for granted. I would say that the people who didn't appreciate Gilman were the people who were too old to appreciate it anymore. When I think back about Gilman, I'd rather think about the good than the bad.

Punk Prom '97

photo courtesy of Charles L.

WORK OUTSIDE OF THE SYSTEM? WANT TO LEARN?

FOR THOSE WHO WANT TO HELP EXTEND
THE ANTI-CORPORATE COMMUNITY:
924 GILMAN IS HOSTING A DO IT YOURSELF
FESTIVAL THE WEEKEND OF
JULY 26, 27, AND 28
COME HELP TEACH AND LEARN

INFORMAL WORKSHOPS WILL BE HELD AS FOLLOWS

FRI 26
12-1 PM CHECK IN/INTRO
1-3 PM ZINES/PUBLISHING
4-6 PM RADIO STATIONS

SAT 27
1-3 PM MUSIC VENUES
4-6 PM DIY BUSINESSES

SUN 29
12-2 PM BOOKING TOURS
3-5 PM RECORD LABELS
5:30-7:30 PM RECORD STORES/DISTRIBUTION
CHECK OUT/PARTY/POT LUCK

924 GILMAN IS A NOT-FOR-PROFIT MEMBERSHIP RUN
PERFORMANCE/COMMUNITY SPACE THAT DOES NOT
TOLERATE RACISM, SEXISM, HOMOPHOBIA, OR BIG
BUSINESS

DO IT YOURSELF FESTIVAL

July 26, 27, 28, 1996

924 Gilman is hosting a festival of DIY organizations and those who want to learn about them and you are invited!

This three day weekend will offer roundtable discussions each afternoon. They will be recorded and distributed for those who cannot attend. Opportunity for text will also be discussed.
Lectures will not be given. The workshops will be organized so that people can relate their personal experiences and questions can be answered in a non-hierarchical fashion.
Loose agendas and facilitators will be established before the workshop to aid in procedure.
Each evening will have bands. Organizations are encouraged to come and table at each show. Free entry for tables not selling material.

FRI 26
12-1 PM CHECK IN
1-3 PM ZINES/PUBLISHING
4-6 PM RADIO
8 PM SHOW

SAT 27
1-3 PM VENUES
4-6 PM DIY BUSINESSES
8 PM SHOW

SUN 29
12-2 PM BOOKING
3-5 PM LABELS
5:30-7:30 PM DISTRO
CHECK OUT/ PARTY

ALREADY ATTENDING:
Lookout Records, Profane Existence, Fat Records, Kill Rock Stars, Underdog Records, Sla, A-Ham, Allied Records, Zafio Records, Ebullition, Alternative Tentacles, Vacuum Distr., Mordam, La Mala Yerba 'zine, Pressure Drop Press, Cinderblock T-Shirts, Punks With Presse Leave Home Booking, Wingnut Records, Epicenter and 924 Gilman
We need people to commit to attending workshops and help organize.
PLEASE CALL CHARLES L AT (510)

LEARN HOW, HELP TEACH OTHERS

924 GILMAN'S DIY WEEKEND

924 Gilman hosted its first Do-It-Yourself Festival the weekend of July 27-29, and the experiment in self-education and community building was a success. We held workshops on **zines and publishing, radio(pirate and college), venues (both clubs and house parties), businesses (collective and ownership), venues (tours and clubs), labels, and distribution.** Each workshop was packed, 30 to 60 people sitting in rented chairs on a hot afternoon, relating their experiences on how to better run their 'zines, businesses, labels, and shows without selling out to "The Man." There were no panels, or lectures given by those officially chosen to be "in the know." Workshops were organized to function collectively, people asking for, and contributing, information as they wanted. Big and little sat in a circle together- from AK Press to Alternative Tentacles with small town beginners- to improve our scene, our businesses, and our community, and start new ones. Compared to your average "punk" gathering, not one asshole showed up to ruin it, everyone contributed or at least listened. And it was far from being only punk- collective businesses, "pirate" radio, political publishers- everyone against the capitalist norm worked together. Everyone helped each other out, teaching and learning from one another's' experiences.

Gilman took a big step towards becoming the community space it hopes to be. We want to continue to act as a community-building space, hosting and organizing gatherings and workshops. Last year we hosted the Born of Fire gathering (and hope for another). Occasionally we offer the space to art shows, as well. Every Wednesday we hold a mask and puppet making workshop for kids and "non-kids". AK Press tables at most shows and we run our own record distribution here in the club. Even Chaos Days has chosen to organize educational workshops to be held at Gilman. We hope by offering our space and our experience that we can spread the Do-It-Yourself community and ethic as well as support the existing groups in our area.

For those who missed the DIY Festival, despair not for the entire weekend was taped and notes were taken. Services exchange lists, for those looking for or offering help, were passed around at each workshop. People were asked to contribute (and you still can, if you have experience you want to offer people) to a publication on each workshop. All these will be wrapped up in a release on the workshops as soon as we can get 'em together. If you are interested or wanna help, call (510) on Fridays or leave a message. A *BIG* thank you to all the people who worked so hard to make this weekend work and to all the people who came to contribute.

DIY meeting 1996   photo by Sita R.

CLAYTON M.

I first heard about Gilman around 1993 or 1994 through *Maximum RocknRoll* magazine when I was in high school and living in Southern California. I ended up going to college at UC Berkeley, and a big motivation to go there was Gilman and the East Bay punk scene. The first time I went to Gilman was an Avail show in 1995, and it was amazing, it was everything I wanted in shows. The friend I went to that show with knew one of the people working there, and so I got to meet some of the people running the show. It was weird to me to see that punks were running the place, I was used to the sleazy "promoters" running the shows in SoCal. It shocked me that everyone at Gilman was a volunteer too, it sounded great to me that anybody could get involved. Also with the volunteer aspect, if you think you can run things better, you can jump in and try your hand at it. I knew from that very first night that I wanted to get involved there.

After I moved to the East Bay I started volunteering there right away. I knew Ed, who I had met that first night, and some others from Gilman who were in the same dorm as me at UCB, and those were the people who I fell in with. I felt I fit in pretty quickly because of the people I knew from the start. If I hadn't known anyone I might not have gotten started, or lasted very long. My very first day in town was spent with folks I knew or met through Gilman, and it just continued from there. I worked there every weekend. One thing I realized pretty quickly was that some of the people who worked at Gilman were jerks, and sometimes I'd have to explain to someone who had a bad experience there that these are real people, and some aren't the nicest, but don't judge the place just on one or two jerks. I worked the side door mostly at first and tried to be as nice as I could, knowing that people would be getting an impression of the entire place from the interactions they had with the workers. I worked there from '95 until 2000, doing the side door, booking, sound, then I worked occasionally for a year or so after that, and now I don't work there at all, but I still go to shows there now and then.

Gilman was my social life at the time, so, to be honest, a big part of me being there was that I didn't have anything else to do. Instead of, say, being a regular at a bar, it was being a regular at Gilman—that's where my friends were. It was a clubhouse in a way; the bands were secondary, after that first intial rush and excitement. There was also the sense of doing something good. I've always had a tendency to see the negative or bad side of life, and Gilman gave me a chance to see the good side. It certainly wasn't perfect there, but we were all trying really hard to make the place the best that we could. We were mostly just kids, and kids should be allowed to make mistakes.

The taking on of responsibility wasn't something I think most people there really thought too much about initially. It just sort of happens. You wake up one day and realize you're helping run a music club/community center. At first I felt it was like such a privilege to work at Gilman and help run a space like that. I don't know if other people felt that or not, but for me, and where I grew up, we had nothing like it, and to have a place like Gilman seemed amazing. I felt Gilman succeeded because we chose to take on the responsibility involved in running the place, it wasn't something we were required to do. I ended up dropping out of college during my first semester and Gilman was a real anchor for me. I was homeless because I had to leave the dorms. Although Gilman may have played a part in my dropping out, I wasn't very happy at school and probably would have left anyway. UCB seemed like thirty thousand kids all stepping on each other to get ahead. Gilman was a handful of kids working together to make something good happen. If it wasn't for Gilman, I probably would have just moved back down to Southern California and been really depressed. Gilman showed me that I don't have to have a college degree and I don't need some special high-end job to be happy, or even to survive. I got to know people who were making due with a lot less, working jobs where they didn't have to sell their souls, and having lives that didn't revolve around going to work and trying to make more money than their neighbors. Gilman really helped me get out of the suburban, tract-house, conservative, middle class, Southern California mindset that I grew up in. Gilman gave me an opportunity to be productive and do something that I cared about, during a time when I wasn't sure if I cared about anything.

During the various "crises" at Gilman, this feeling of belonging was further solidified. The sense of community and "us vs. them" during our battles with the brew pub, and later with DiCon, became really strong. Going to the meetings, rallying everyone, "fighting the good fight," really helped bring us together. The sense of urgency, that we might lose everything we had worked for, really inspired us and made us work harder. It forced us to look closer at what we were doing at Gilman and what our level of commitment really was. It helped fight our cynicism too. We would talk shit about the place all the time, joke about burning the place down, but when a real threat came along, the facades were dropped and our real feelings came out. It was a martyr-complex in a way too—you want to do your part and keep the place open, but you also want to be seen as making all these personal sacrifices as well, you wanted a little bit of attention for how much you were giving up to work at Gilman. Our cynicism was certainly noticed by audience members too and perhaps alienated some of them from working at Gilman or maybe even coming back to a show there again, but it helped keep us all sane, allowed us to blow off steam so we could keep working there. Like when we were doing booking, we'd talk shit about bands and how much they sucked, then have to get on the phone and be nice to them. We had a rule: "everything said in this room doesn't leave this room." After a while, we had developed a tendency to focus on the bad nights, dwell on them too much, rather than the good nights, almost like we expected every show to be good, took it for granted. Same with the bands that played there. No one in the bands would say anything if the show went well, but if one band member mistakenly wasn't allowed back in because their hand stamp rubbed off or something like that, it's "fuck Gilman."

The amount of workers at Gilman rose and fell during my time there, sometimes too few, sometimes too many, sometimes just right. The "skilled" positions were harder to keep staffed, partly due to our own mistakes. We would take on too much responsibility individually sometimes and not leave enough for others, so if someone would get burned out, there wouldn't be anyone trained to take their place. We ended up being fairly gun-shy as well sometimes about investing time and effort into training new people, because of the number of times someone would show interest for a couple weeks, then vanish. It became hard to trust people to do what they said they were going to do.

One of the more difficult things we did at Gilman was in dealing with a long-time worker who was accused multiple times of sexually harassing women at the club. I felt we dealt with it really well. We talked with the person and gave them the option of staying if they changed their behavior, or leaving if they didn't. That person chose to leave. It also had the effect of opening up the sound equipment, and the chance to run it, to the collective. It had been monopolized before; now more people were able to get involved.

My best times at Gilman were when my best friend, Chris S. was head coordinator. I was head of booking and head of sound at the time, and he and I had really good communication. We were "benevolent dictators" in a sense, but we always felt that we acted in the best interest of the club. With a large collective, consensus is pretty tough, and democracy isn't easy either—both ways someone is bound to end up disappointed. I think with consensus you'd really need a strong leader or core group who could sway everyone one way or another. There is no "process" of becoming a member, like over a certain period of time, etc. Once you buy a membership card, you have the same status as everyone else, and that just seemed how it should be. It's worked, somehow, all these years. Everyone should have a say—this is their place, even if they've just been here once.

I started booking in 1996 and was head of booking from 1997 to 1998. Booking was really hard, because you had to take so much into consideration and try to be fair to everyone: the local bands, the touring bands, the audience, the people working the show, etc. You just can't win; someone always is unhappy and feels like they're being slighted. I got so frustrated by people complaining, that I spray-painted on the wall, "If you don't like this place, come help change it." As far as my doing sound goes, I had no previous experience with sound equipment, and learned how to run the sound board from scratch. At the time I started learning it, I was at

Above: photo by Emilie V.

Below: 2000   photo by Lauren L.

Gilman four to five days a week between booking and working the shows. I'd even go there when it was empty sometimes and hang out. It gave me a different perspective than during the busy-ness of a show. I could reflect on all the amazing things that had happened at Gilman over the past fifteen years or so. It also gave me a chance to really look at the physical structure of the place, read the graffiti, check out the art. The whole place has its own kind of beauty and magic. There wasn't so much "tagging" back then, more little quips and quotes and things that were interesting.

During my last year or so there, when I was falling away from the place, I

Clayton's story, 2000   photo by Lauren L.

wrote out a section of a book that I really liked up on the wall. It was a story (from *Numbers In The Dark* by Italo Calvino) that meant a lot to me, and I wanted to put it up somewhere that people could read it. During the five years when I worked there regularly, I felt more at home there than any of the places I was actually living in at the time. Gilman was where I grew up, gained a sense of responsibility, and developed my general philosophies of life, both good and bad. It's a place to blame and credit at the same time. It's gotten me to where I am, which is both good and bad. I learned how to speak up and say what I think, that was the biggest plus I took away from Gilman. I also learned how to not take on more than I could handle. I think I definitely got more out of Gilman than I put in, even for as much as I did put in. I didn't want to become one of those people who would talk about how great it used to be and how it sucks now. I didn't want to forget how much it meant to me, and how much it can mean to other people. That's why I got the 924 tattoo, so I wouldn't forget. I'm so grateful to all the people who worked there before I did, who kept the place going so when I came along it was there for me too. It's pretty amazing that it's passed through as many hands as it has and still survived. Gilman was only ever as good or bad as the people who went there and the people who worked there, the people who made it up and made it what it is/was. Unfortunately it seems to be human nature, that the bad will stick out in your memory stronger than the good. It seems easier to find someone to blame and harder to find someone to thank.

For me, Gilman is best encapsulated by this: at the first show I went to there, I was just another oblivious kid dancing around to a band. Three years later, I went on tour with that same band, doing sound for them, selling radical literature, and seeing the world around me. Gilman's opened up a lot of doors for me, and had a hand in all my successes as well as all my mistakes. I still go to shows there occasionally now, and I'll still find myself up in the old sound loft sometimes, looking out at everything and everyone and find myself thinking "this is great." The "midnight basketball" (after the shows) is still a draw for me as well. It brings together Gilman workers from all different eras. Chris S. and I still talk sometimes about going back and working there again if the place were really in trouble. I still feel a lot of guilt about not working there anymore. And I feel that we missed some opportunities to make the space into more of a community center, used seven days a week. I regret not having been able to accomplish that. We did get some things done, like putting in the video projector and screen. I was involved in putting on movie nights for a little while. I don't have very much in my life that I'm proud of, but Gilman is one thing I did that I'll always be proud of.

ZARAH

I was in high school, 14 years old, and I was dating a boy who had gone to Gilman a bunch of times, and his friends all hung out there, and he wanted me to go. Right around this time I was detained by the police for smoking pot in a park, so I ended up being grounded by my parents for six or nine months or something. I was able to go to my first show at Gilman in early 1995. My parents were still really paranoid about me using drugs, so they dropped us off and picked us up there.

It was a pretty good, big, pop-punk show. If I had shown up at a crusty show I probably would have been really freaked out. I remember everyone being really nice. It seemed like almost everyone was older than I was. I remember getting in line, realizing I didn't have a membership card, and having to get in another line, and being confused about the lines.

Gilman was dirty, it was small, but it was impressive because of how many people were there. I was meeting lots of people right away (people my age). I was in love with the place from the first time I saw it, even though it was, you know, gross.

It was about four months till I went again, because I was still grounded, and my best friend at the time, Eve, who I had gone to that first show with, was away for a while. When she got back, we started going again. I was still sort of intimidated by the whole thing; I didn't really feel like I was "punk" enough to go there. The people I had met that first night were all really young kids around my age, and the older people all seemed to be like, "We paid our dues, who the fuck are you? You're just a little kid who'll think this is stupid in two years."

When I did go back, it was right in the middle of the brew pub hoopla. The second time I ever went to Gilman, it was to a membership meeting. There were about 35 people there and it was pretty intense. It seemed an important issue to me, but I didn't want to get too involved since I was still in school. I couldn't get to a lot of the zoning board meetings and things like that.

I did want to work at Gilman. I saw these other people working there who were about my age, and thought I could do it too. I worked there every weekend, my parents driving me there and back. They were really cool about it.

I worked side door, front door, etc., for a while and then let it be known that I wanted to get more involved, take on more responsibility. Eventually, when I was 15, I started training as a coordinator and stage manager with a number of other people, learning how every aspect of the club worked. I learned a lot. It gave me an interesting perspective on the behind-the-scenes efforts. I wanted to be 15 and running the club, and I really wanted the recognition for being able to do so. Looking back on it now, maybe that was a little weird, egotistical, whatever. I believe a lot more now in doing something for the sake of doing it and getting it done, rather than doing it to be recognized.

Once the training process started, it was hard to stop. It was kinda this whole "snowball" thing. I think that the people training us were excited that we were so excited.

One thing that happened during this time was that a longtime worker at Gilman was accused of ongoing harassment of women at Gilman, either those working, playing in bands, or simply attending. Some of the people at the club started getting really freaked out about it all and wanted that person gone.

The small core group of us women who worked there regularly got together and had a meeting. We decided that things had to change with this person or we were all going to leave. So we met with this person and more or less delivered an ultimatum: "We feel uncomfortable with your actions, what are you going to do about it?" The response from the worker was, "Whatever, I'll just leave."

Some of the people at Gilman weren't happy with how we dealt with it, feeling that it should have been decided at a regular membership meeting. But we felt like it would have been a lot worse for that person to make "public" an issue like being accused of sexual harassment. We felt like it could have been better dealt with privately. It was an issue that a lot of people there didn't want to talk about with others who didn't spend a lot of time at the club. While it is the right of the membership to know, it seems like there should be a "second" membership or something, because while it's great that everyone who attends becomes a member and can have their say, they can reduce the "weight" of the vote of people who have put blood, sweat, and definitely tears, into the place, by just showing up for a meeting now and then.

Shortly after this incident was the beginning of the dreaded "committee" as well, the "conflict management committee" or something like that—I can't remember the official title. If you were having problems within Gilman, you could get an "impartial committee" together, and they would research what was going on.

I hated them—it was like the fucking police, it was crazy. I learned so much about conflict management at Gilman, but none of it from any of these "committees." The first "case" involved the singer of a local band who was accused of slapping their partner at Gilman, pushing a Gilman worker up against a wall, and harassing other people there. A move was made to kick that person out and one of those "committees" was formed to "get the facts." They didn't find enough to warrant kicking the person out, but a number of us wouldn't work the shows that this person's band played at.

One big problem that came out of this "committee" concept was that people stopped differentiating between things that happened at Gilman and things that happened away from Gilman. The next "case" was a person who claimed at a membership meeting that they were raped (somewhere away from Gilman) by someone who attends Gilman. This person wanted the accused rapist kicked out of Gilman and wanted Gilman to deal with the situation. It became a huge, unbelievable, contentious nightmare that resulted in the accused rapist going to jail. Lines were drawn and people were at each other's throats. It was one of the most controversial things that ever happened at Gilman. The "committee" concept died soon after, but the damage was done. I'll never feel that it was our place to "research" and "investigate" people that attended the club.

The next thing I remember was the summer when I was 17, getting ready to start my senior year in high school. Some of the regular key people at Gilman were burning out and showing up less, or were on tour with a band, etc., so for that summer it was the head coordinator at the time, Charles, and me, running the club. I was going to high school and running a punk club! I'd leave school on Friday, head to Gilman, work over the weekend, and go back to school on Monday.

I remember a huge fight at a Sunday show. It was the first time I had seen real violence. It was like a barroom brawl. Punches were flying everywhere. That was in 1996.

At the beginning of my time of being heavily involved in Gilman, I got really mean, and I don't know why. I got called on it and tried to do better. I ended growing up really, really fast. I lost all my friends at school because I wasn't able to hang out with them on weekends; I was always at Gilman.

I took a break from Gilman after I graduated from high school. I got a place to live, got a job, got more into the "normal" world. I was planning on going back to Gilman, and did for a little while, about nine months or so, but it wasn't the same for me, and I stopped going. I just couldn't anymore, because if I started working there again I would have to be completely involved, and I can't do that now. For me it's all or nothing. I think it's that way for a lot of people there, past and present. You get too personally involved with the place; it consumes your life. I think you just become a martyr. I've seen people try and scale down their involvement there, to "do less" than they used to, but it just doesn't seem to work.

I think I got what I wanted from Gilman. The only other thing I wanted to do (that I never did) was to be head coordinator. It's hard for me even to just attend shows there now, because I don't really know what to do with myself. I find myself asking the people working if they need any help. I've never really been to Gilman and not worked (since my first few times there); I don't know how to do that anymore.

I learned a lot of great job skills at Gilman—I can sit and talk to a roomful of people now and feel comfortable. I learned how to work with co-workers, conflict management, etc. I gained confidence and responsibility. I think most of what I learned and took away from Gilman was good. I feel like I was there forever. I feel like I was there for a whole lifetime. People think it amazing when they find out I worked at a club for five years and I'm only 20!

What I wanted to see was more women involved, and more things like Punk Proms and art shows. As for the question of whether I thought of it as a community center or a "punk club," I think from the time the doors were unlocked until just before the show started, it was a community center. After the show got underway, it was a punk club. I got the impression that most people shared that view. I think it turned into way more of a punk club than people wanted it to. I think that by the time I got there, it was already too ingrained in people that it was a punk club. I think it would have been great if we could have had art supplies, or sewing supplies, or whatever, for people to use while they were there. But we never got it together to do that.

To say that Gilman's a failure is bullshit. It reinvents itself every five years or so, I think. It becomes something different, to different people. I felt like I made a difference. The little bit of thanks that we did get meant so much to me.

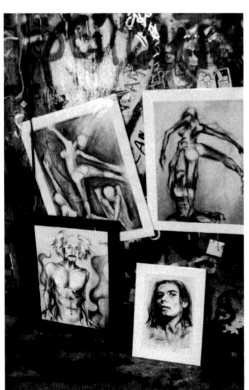

From one of the art shows   photo by Emilie V.

JESSICA S.

I first heard about Gilman in 1994 or 1995, when I was fourteen or fifteen. I believe it was from a music magazine like *Spin*, or something, that had an article on Green Day or Rancid that mentioned Gilman. I lived in Los Angeles at the time and moved to the East Bay shortly after that and started going to Gilman. I remember the first time I went, Oct. 1995. I ended up meeting a few people and felt welcome there. In fact, I ended up working the show that very first night. It was much different than what I was used to in LA, much friendlier, more down-to-earth, and smaller. I did mostly the small jobs, front door, cleanup, etc.

Before I moved to the East Bay, I used to call the "Gilman Hotline" to hear what was going on. That's how I found out you could volunteer to work there. I was so excited about Gilman, going there, and getting to work there, that it didn't really make me nervous or anything beforehand, just a little intimidated once I got there. I just showed up and asked to work. I worked at Gilman until early 1997, when I ended up moving back to LA. Then I moved back to the East Bay in 1998 and worked at Gilman again until 2000, this time including being a show coordinator.

I never really had a plan for what I wanted to do there. I was just so enamored with the idea of Gilman, at first from what I had read about it when I lived in LA, and then from going there once I moved to the East Bay. I wanted to be a part of it, I wanted to do things there, help however I could, live with people who also worked there, etc. I was so in love with the music from the beginning that that is what I think drove me, realizing I could be a part of that at Gilman. It wasn't really the feeling of community or collectivism that did it for me. I did feel more of that later, but it was really the music for me.

It also was a combination of little things—the midnight basketball, the $.25 sodas, the people who I met who I ended up trading tapes with, etc. I also learned a lot, too, from the AK Press book tables, fanzines, and other literature tables, that frequently were at Gilman. It gave me a part of my life that was really satisfying and inspiring, that stuck with me even when I wasn't there. I learned a work ethic that didn't revolve around getting a good "grade" or earning money, it was doing work and contributing for the love and care of something or someone. I felt indebted in a way to this great place for providing somewhere where the bands I loved could play, and I wanted to give something back. I learned about the value of volunteering, and how it can make you feel much more rewarded than just being compensated monetarily. I didn't go to the meetings much, and didn't participate in the decision-making or policy-making very often. Looking back now, I kinda wish I had.

I had some personality conflicts with people there, as is to be expected when working with a group, but overall my Gilman experience was really positive. I did end up hanging out with a group of other workers at Gilman for a while that drank a lot, and I did too. We'd work half the show, then go drink. Looking back now, I don't really like that particular time in my life and having done those things. I was around people sometimes who were doing really hard drugs too, and I could have ended up like that. It seemed a lot easier at the time to make friends with the "partyers," and since punk was about rebellion, we felt like we were "rebelling" against the Gilman "establishment."

After I moved away and came back in 1998, a number of the people I used to hang out with and party with had left, and I started taking Gilman a lot more seriously. That's when the community aspect started becoming more important than the music aspect. I was around during the brew pub and DiCon battles. I couldn't understand how those businesses couldn't see how special Gilman was, how important it was for it to survive, and how it could be seen as a threat to anyone. The slight degree of "public nuisance" that happens there should not undermine all the good that Gilman has done. Gilman had so much more creativity within its walls than a brew pub or a technological place—it could draw so many different people in.

The best thing I took from my time at Gilman was that it made me feel like I could go out and do anything I wanted if I set my mind to it. Also that I could be a vital part of the music community, even if I wasn't in a band. I was given the opportunity there to interact with all different types of people, young, old, rich, poor, white, black, men, women. I experienced quite a bit of personal growth at Gilman. It wasn't just "something to do" for me, it was a passion, and to be able to be involved with something you're passionate about feels amazing.

I believe Gilman inspired me to change my career path also. I originally was going to be an economics major, but changed it to American Studies Within Music And Verse. I wanted to pursue something I was really into, as opposed to what I "should" pursue. My parents were really into me going to Gilman too. My mom told me she always wanted to be around music but never really had a place to go to. Telling people you've worked at, and helped run, a music club, might sound amazing and impressive to them, but it's mainly because they haven't been exposed to places like Gilman, and seen just how easy it is to get involved. Gilman gave me a real focus, gave me ideas, challenged me to do something with my life other than sit in front of the TV or get fucked up. Maybe all I really did there was check hand stamps at the door, or sweep up trash, or help the show run a little more smoothly, but what I took away from it was so much more. I'd be a lot more boring of a person if it wasn't for Gilman, a lot more lame, a lot more stuck up.

I used to collect things from Gilman that would remind me of a certain show, a certain night. Little scribblings, drawings, receipts, they'd all go in a box, things that most people would probably throw out, because it was so important to me to document this amazing, inspiring, hopeful period of time. How many people can say that they have such a strong, positive, emotional tie to a prolonged period in their life? When I go through all that stuff I saved, the emotions are there still. Again, for me, at first it was just for the music, then it became a community for me, a group of friends. I used to just go there to see certain bands, then I found myself going because I knew my friends would be there, regardless of what bands were playing.

I guess now it's kinda come full circle, because I don't work there anymore and just go there once in a while to see certain bands. I really don't have the time or energy to work there anymore. Plus, I don't feel the excitement and sense of possibility that it used to have for me. Still, sometimes I think about all the people out there calling the show info line at Gilman, like I did, and being inspired by the idea of Gilman. Maybe they live too far away and can never go there and experience the reality, but the idea of the place, the existence of the place, the potential of the place, could lead them in the same direction, even if it's just in their heads.

LARRY W.

I guess I've been going to Gilman for about four years (as of 1999), which isn't very long in terms of the history of the club, or in terms of how long many other people have been involved. People sometimes ask me if I have pictures of certain bands from the '80s, or even from the early '90s, like Green Day, and I don't. In historical terms, I'm a newcomer.

My identity is that of "picture man." I'm interested in photography and people, and after that, in specific people and places they gather. I started out trying to do street photography on Telegraph Avenue (in Berkeley) around 1991. Since I was trying to teach myself, and had no monetary motive, I photographed what interested me, both visually and culturally. That turned out to be the alternative types, usually young, homeless street kids, gutter punks, house punks, high school kids hanging out, the various kinds of nomads that constantly come and go through Berkeley, etc. One kid in particular, called Trey, suggested that if I wanted to do this, why didn't I just go to Gilman? That started it.

My first impression of Gilman was that I was out of place; that I was in a different world—mainly because of the age difference. Also, it is in the nature of what I do that I usually can't take the time to introduce myself or explain what I'm doing. Sometimes I try to say a few words to put people at ease, but even that can often destroy the mood of what I'm after—which, ultimately, is truth—so a lot of times I just keep my mouth shut and shoot. My first time at Gilman some people were cooperative, some were suspicious, a few were nasty (calling me "granddad," which I'm not—I have one child, ten years old); but no one threw me out (I later learned that this is one of the distinctions of the place—you have to do something truly egregious to be ejected). I learned that it was my attitude and demeanor that made the difference. As long as I didn't think I was doing anything to harm anyone, my activity was accepted. Also, I genuinely like the people who go there, virtually every one of them; this is not something I could fake, so I hope it comes across. I grew up in a small, isolated town in the Midwest, and I *wish* I'd had something like Gilman, since I was a misfit where I was. In some part, Gilman is a chance for a second, different, and more to-my-liking, teenage experience.

I take so many pictures there because I'm trying to become good at it, and stay good. I like the people and I like the emotions generated by the bands. I like people who can let go completely. On the street, people who let go completely can be self-destructive, but Gilman is a safe environment where some things are "as if," where it is safe to experiment with feelings and actions, and then come back. I also have the feeling that Gilman is an important place, and as time goes on people will want to know what happened there, what it was like.

I recently started going to the Saturday meetings, and I've offered my two-cents worth a few times, particularly on matters that I'm familiar with from my years as a carpenter/contractor. But usually I just listen. I think it is good for me to know what goes on, since my pictures are now such an intimate part of the club, even if I don't take any other part in the normal operations. I may have more to offer; others can decide if they want to call on me.

The issue of the relative strengths/weaknesses of the space is a very big question. Many people have said to me, and I can't disagree with them, that the biggest weakness is that the club is run by a clique or cliques that stand aloof from the regular people who attend shows. Gilman is like a punk high school, and the social life of any high school is run by cliques. This is human nature, and it holds true everywhere, not just in high schools. I think anyone who is bothered by this needs to look at themselves, and why they are going to Gilman. Part of the point of "punk" is that we are all worthwhile, even if we are geeks who don't fit in. I don't hang out in the staff room, though I suppose I could, partly because I don't belong there, and partly because I don't think that that is the real "scene" that is happening. Furthermore, the people who do spend time in the staff room are held together by the fact that their unpaid labor is what makes the club happen, it is real work and not at all easy, it involves sacrifices and absorbs a lot of their precious hours of life, and all this sometimes makes it hard for them to mingle with the casual attendees.

The greatest strength of the club is the obvious: that most of the music played there is real, heartfelt, and played with intensity. In a social sense, the strength of the club is that every kid is given the opportunity to be him or herself in an age-appropriate way in a non-judgemental setting. I would hope in a lot of cases that specific kids are "going through a phase"—that they won't try to be this way when they are forty. But we all make the best of what the draw of life deals us. If the situation calls for rebellion and outrage, then do it, for as long as it takes. If it is suppressed, then it will just happen later in ways that may be more disruptive to a person's development. I've seen a lot more mental health at Gilman than I've seen in some other social settings. If I were one to worry about the future of the society we live in, Gilman would actually give me hope.

In Shakespearean tragedy, the hero's fatal flaw is simply the flip side of his greatest strength. One of the club's strengths is that it is politically correct on many key issues—bands and people who are racist, sexist, homophobic, aligned with big corporations, etc., are not allowed. This is good. But it also leads to several consequences. One is that several bands and movements which are important parts of the local and international punk scene are not represented, as if they did not exist. Of course one club can't reflect everything, anyway, and I'm not suggesting that nazis be given equal time, since they don't deserve it. But the consequence for the club is that it takes on, if I may put it this way, a certain sort of socialist sterility which is typical of long-standing collectives. Some have said that the same thing happened to *Maximum RocknRoll*. I think it is inevitable to some degree. One positive result of the club's position is that the politicians in town are fully aware of the club's PC credentials, and are reluctant to mess with it. In many other places an outfit like DiCon would have destroyed the club long ago, but not here, thank God.

Gilman has impacted my life the most by simply accepting me for what I am: an older guy who is interested in recording and examining the world and people around him through images. It is a fact that some of my pictures are unpleasant, or show people in unflattering ways. I am not misanthropic; such images reflect my interest in eternal verities. People, for example, will always seek out intoxicants, and some people will always overdo it. They can be idiots for the moment (we all have been), and we can still identify with them and love them. It is also a fact that some of my pictures present people in odd or surrealistic ways. Put briefly, this reflects my attempt to see through the veil of ordinary reality, to attain glimpses of truth that are usually hidden beneath mundane appearances. Gilman has given me freedom to pursue these ideas.

And paradoxically, Gilman has helped me to deal with the fact of my own aging, because my age difference from most of the regulars puts the issue in a healthy perspective for me. Superficially I'm not at all like that teenage house punk with the spiked hair; but like it or not, someday he'll be a lot like me, and he had better accept the fact—unless he really does plan on dying young. And I, in turn, have to accept that I'm not young like him, that I had my chance and made my choices, and that I am here, right where I ought to be. I'll be 60 when the year 2000 rolls around. That spiked punk has his whole life, if he knows it; I have a lot less. But we're alike in that we have to use the time we do have as best we can.

Changes in the club over the years? For better or worse? The simple survival of the club is highly notable. I personally haven't seen any great changes except in ways that are intrinsic to the punk movement itself. The movement is over twenty years old, long in the tooth, full of bands that just repeat earlier ideas, and yet it all keeps reinventing itself somehow. The same is true of this club. It is old, the staff has heard it all before and sometimes feels jaded, and yet the collective soul (and the soul of the collective) keeps rising from the ashes to give one more stirring account of itself. Perhaps a little of the magic has gone out in recent years, or perhaps it is just me. Perhaps it is millennial ennui, or perhaps punk itself is dead. I don't know because I am too close. But also, I don't care, because the seeds of something new are right there in the dung, sprouting beyond language even as we speak and try to analyze.

**PHOTOS
BY
LARRY W.**

PHOTOS BY LARRY W.

SITA R.

At age thirteen I was making the transition from the eighth grade into high school, but I was also leaving San Francisco and moving back to my East Bay roots. Expressing myself and making friends who shared my interests were the most important part of my young life. An enormous part of every teen's life is music. Music defines our interests as people and is a way in which we express ourselves. While the majority of the country is exposed to popular mainstream music, they often only get to see their favorite bands in arena-sized shows. I found Gilman to be such an amazing experience because I could see any show I wanted in a much more intimate venue and was often being exposed to much more unique and inspiring music being performed by my peers.

Gilman had so much to offer me. It provided a place where I could be myself, learn the responsibilities of running a non-profit collective and make life-long friends. It gave young kids a place to explore their talents by playing music or participating in art shows and other events. From my personal experience, Gilman gave me the opportunity to explore my true passion, photography. I was asked by the members of the club to be the Gilman photographer, which later was approved at a membership meeting. They wanted photos for display in the club. I was fourteen at the time and I was given the opportunity to document both people and bands at as many shows as I wished. I worked as the Gilman photographer steadily for about six years. I have now graduated with a degree in photography and am currently working as a freelance photographer. Gilman was the place that inspired me, and when the opportunity presented itself, I volunteered to document what was going on there every weekend. My work was publicly displayed in the entryway for all to see as they entered the club. This was a wonderful experience and due to this constant exposure, it truly led me to pursue my passion. After about two years I started doing other jobs as well: front door, security, stage manager, and eventually coordinating shows. I worked there until late 1999.

I will never regret the amount of time and energy that I invested in coordinating and photographing the events that took place during my span at the club. Keeping it afloat seemed to be a constant struggle and while I have moved on, I would not hesitate for a second if Gilman needed help and were in danger of shutting down. It seems to be a constant struggle to keep that club alive. I only hope that people can recognize what an important place Gilman truly is and what a beneficial experience it provides for all teens and young adults, as well as providing a place for aspiring musicians.

Art show, 1997   photo by Sita R.

EMILIE V.

The first time I was at a show at Gilman I saw the minutes from the past collective meeting posted on the wall. Known around the world for its punk shows, the fact that Gilman was a DIY venue, a collective that was thriving, inspired me. Gilman is such a visual space—the graffitied walls are conjured up almost anytime you think of the place—but there was this invisible collective behind it all. I decided to go to a meeting and talk about the idea of doing a photo essay on Gilman that looked beyond the music. I brought samples of my work to share and defended my intentions. There was debate and dissension, but ultimately the project was okayed. As an outsider at the time, it was important to me to go through this process before shooting. Gilman (the club) and Gilman (the collective) were like home and family to many (as it turns out, this extended to me in a special way—while shooting the project I met a guy who is now my husband and father to my two kids). When I "finished" the project almost a year later, I posted an essay on the wall at Gilman—images along with text. The project explored what (who?) the collective was and how it functioned, bringing a bit of the collective to those who only went to Gilman for shows. Some of those images are included here.

924 Gilman is an all ages, alcohol-free, volunteer run, non-profit, collective music venue. Gilman has always been a part of the underground scene and now mainstream media mentions it as the place where bands like Green Day and Rancid got their start. But one of the most remarkable things about Gilman, the fact that it is a collective, is often overlooked. It is a collective that has survived for over ten years, is an outlet for socially responsible expression, and as a punk club exists for the fans and the bands, not to make money.

This photo essay is dedicated to the collective behind the club.

Gilman membership meetings are held
the first and third Saturdays of
every month. Everyone is welcome.

"...membership makes the decisions...
it's the give and take of having a
community, egalitarian, membership run
club... it can be very difficult."
    - Charles, co-head coordinator

Each show has a crew of volunteers who, in exchange for
working part of the show, get in free. About an hour before
the show begins volunteers sign up for specific tasks
ranging from checking hand stamps to clean-up.

If you want to stereotype, the best shows at Gilman are usually girl bands and queer shows... everybody's nice, there are no fights... and the people have a lot less attitude... well, some of them..." - *Lindsay, a Gilman stage manager*

No racist,
homophobic,
misogynistic,
or major label
bands are booked
to play at Gilman.

Secuirty is a
crucial part
of the smooth
functioning of
the club. The
regular security
staff are the
only paid members
of the collective,
all other positions
are volunteer only.

"...paying security
was the only way
to have someone
willing to show up
on a mightly basis
and risk his or
her life," explains
a long-time Gilman
member.

No money is guaranteed to any band up front. Half the money made
at the door goes back to the collective and the other half is
divided up between the bands. After a show Gilman staff (usually
one or two coordinators and a stage manager or booker) discuss
how much they think each band should be paid, based on draw, distance
traveled and any other issues relevant to that show. The Gilman workers
then meet with at least one member of each band and discuss the suggested
amounts. Usually everyone agrees, but sometimes a band offers some of
its cut to another band who might be touring or had to drive a long
distance to the show.

Gilman is a
community
center,
not just
a punk club.
Regular
community
events range
from youth
art shows
to 12-step
meetings.

emilie

LAUREN L.

I can't really remember how long I've been working at Gilman. I started when I was in high school, I think 1996 or 1997. I worked the front door, etc., for a year of so before I started working the store. I first went to a show there in 1994, when I was thirteen—a friend in high school took me. I'll always remember the second show I went to there, which was Bikini Kill. My first impression of the place was the amazing difference between the outside and the inside, so normal and unmarked outside versus graffitied chaos inside. I was pretty intrigued by the place, started going there more, and eventually started working there when I was about fifteen. Pretty soon I was working there every weekend. My move to working in the store came after a night at Gilman when I was really drunk, sitting outside, feeling sick, and Dean, who worked the store at the time, came out and hung out with me and kept me company. We became friends, I started working the store pretty regularly, and when he had to leave for a while, he asked me and my friend Stephanie if we could take over running the store while he was gone. We said okay. I was a little apprehensive (being only fifteen or sixteen years old), but also excited about it. I remember talking to my parents about it and they were really supportive. They were really supportive of the place in general. My mom even dropped off a couch there once! When my younger brother was having problems, my parents wanted me to take him to Gilman. They saw Gilman as a place that could teach him responsibility and help him out.

I really liked working in the "stoar" (as it became known), and rarely missed a weekend. I think I took a month off one December, but otherwise I was always there, for about six years. I really believe in what's going on at Gilman. Music is important to me, but it's not my driving force in life. I worked at Gilman because of the sense of community and because of the people I met there. It's a pretty incredible experience to be involved in a place where you get to see people grow up, to watch them become coordinators or bookers, it's pretty awesome. I've never really put much importance on age because I've seen so many amazing things from young people at Gilman.

Another thing Gilman did for me was to introduce me to zines. They had a huge impact on my life, along with Gilman. They helped foster a strong sense of trust of others in our community. I ended up bringing zines back into the stoar to sell. It had been a while since anyone had sold zines there and I think they're a really important part of punk and a natural thing to have at Gilman.

And, of course, Gilman put me in "light-bulb" mode, gave me the inspiration that I could do this stuff too (zines/bands). It's shown me that I don't need a big established gallery to show my work, I can set my own show up. I don't need a publisher to put my writing out, I can print it myself. My next project, the Copy Cafe, wouldn't have even been an idea without my having worked at Gilman. What I learned there and experienced there has enabled and inspired me to try and put together my own space where people can come and do art, zines, etc., as well as enjoy good food, and, of course, coffee (one of the things I wanted to be known for at Gilman was making the best coffee). I see the two spaces as sister projects, complementing one another, working together.

I've never felt unsafe or threatened at Gilman—it's been my second home. I'm comfortable enough there to speak up when guys say stupid shit to me or other women; I don't have to accept that kind of stuff, I know that the other people there will back me up. But there were things happening there that I was unaware of. The issue of sexism came up pretty prominently at Gilman when a woman who was working there for the first time wanted to quit doing her shift about halfway through because she said she couldn't handle it. The person coordinating the show that night said that if she didn't finish the shift she'd have to pay or leave. She argued about it and eventually one of the guys doing security ended up having to escort her out. She came to the next Gilman meeting and said that Gilman was unsafe for women and that security was too heavy-handed. This prompted a lot of discussion about sexism at Gilman, including stopping one show and having a meeting right then and there. This led to the forming of a women's group, and regular meetings started being held, open to all, not just women working at Gilman. One thing I noticed that came of these meetings was that during shows women were coming to me in the stoar and telling me about incidents that were happening that they didn't feel comfortable telling the guys doing security or coordinating the show. They didn't feel like they would be taken seriously. Gilman is no utopia, unfortunately many of the same things happen there as happen out in the rest of the world. The difference is that we can do something about it, we don't have to sit back and take it. We

> *"There is a theme that runs through punk rock about fighting a revolution. Anger and aggression are just as much a part of the scene as the music is, but sometimes I wonder what we are fighting against when we just keep fighting each other. This includes the internal schism between the roles of men and women in the scene. There is this girl who used to hang around here and at almost every show someone would grab her tits. I watched her stand up for herself after getting physically torn down and rarely did anyone stand up with her. This consistent degradation denied her the right to fully contribute what she could to the community she wanted to be a part of. Hate to sound like an idealist, but I did not get involved in Gilman to get beat down or beat up. I came here because I love the music and saw the potential of what can happen with it."*   *— Rachel S.*

don't have to just reconcile ourselves to "that's just the way it is." I found it a lot more comfortable to speak up at the women's group meetings, much more so than at the regular Gilman meetings. This was partly my personality—I'm not really that outspoken in certain situations—and partly that there are usually so few women at the regular meetings. I thought it was very interesting that I felt so much more at ease talking to a group of women as opposed to a group of men. This group is just in the beginning stages, it's been about a month now that we've been meeting, about 10-25 women attending each meeting. It's basically a support group, helping each other with things that are happening in our community, not necessarily just at Gilman. I've gotten a lot of confidence from working, and just being, at Gilman over the years, but in just a handful of women's group meetings I became even more confident and more ready to deal with situations. Getting harassed every single day, just because of your gender, really wears on you, really beats you down, and having a place to vent, or share ideas/solutions, and be supported really helps. It's brought out a whole new dimension to Gilman for me. A number of women in the group are women I've seen at Gilman for years and never talked to, and it's been really cool to get to know them. It's opened up yet another avenue for personal connection, which is the whole reason why I worked there.

     My decision to leave Gilman was a really hard one to make and it took about a year for me to finally make it. Basically, I was getting burned out. I was taking on too much else in my life and something had to give. Going to art school took its toll on me as well. It was like living two lives, the art world and the Gilman/punk world, clean and dirty, (somewhat) superficial and gritty reality. It was all getting pretty confusing to me. So I really had to start questioning why I was at Gilman. Some nights I'd love it, but more and more I wouldn't... Taking the photos I did for my art school project brought me back in touch with the Gilman I really loved, all the subtleties and nuances which captivated me. That ended up carrying me for a while, but gradually I would lose interest again. This kind of up and down ride kept happening. Another thing that moved me was when people would leave messages/drawings for me on the walls, things I'd find later, encouraging things, greetings, affection, things I'd come across seemingly just when I needed them most, bringing back great memories and feelings. Also, there was the anonymous messages, where people just wrote whatever was in their head at the time, for no one in particular, little gems of dialogue. And those will be there for the life of the club, the life of the building even, since they may be painted over, but they'll still be there, hidden underneath. The same with all the stuff I've written or drawn in the stoar over the last six or seven years. A piece of me will always be in that building. And that's why I've always regarded Gilman as much more than a building—it's got a life of its own, it's not inanimate. Who knows how many times the walls have been painted over, how deep the layers are, how much history they contain.

But, bottom line is, it's a thankless job, and that does eventually get to you. It's hard to maintain the same level of excitement about something over a sustained period of time when it seems like no one is appreciating what you do. All I ever seemed to hear was complaints about the place. So I gradually started taking longer and longer "vacations." It was strange at first, because I had no idea what to do on a Friday or Saturday night. But, on the night before I was leaving for about a month and a half, I kinda knew that that was probably going to be the end of my deep commitment to the place, to working there all the time. It was a pretty emotional night... After that I was there less and less. It was really hard to leave, but I just couldn't bring myself to go anymore. I'd be sitting at home thinking about going, but I couldn't do it. And there was definitely withdrawals and regrets after quitting. Those were hard to overcome. Part of it was missing the good things about Gilman and part was fear of what's going to happen next, what will I do now. Everyone uses Gilman for something. There's a reason that you work there and then there's the "other" reason, like feeding an insecurity, fulfilling some inner need, or giving some sense of importance or purpose, having a place where everyone knows you. It was all of those things for me. It was where I grew up and learned about life. It felt a lot like a romantic relationship, one where you grow, learn, share, have good times and bad, then just find that you've grown apart, it's just not the same anymore, the spark is gone, the memories remain. I felt like I had to rebuild myself a little bit, like I had lost part of my identity. I was no longer "Lauren from the stoar."

Gilman's been the biggest influence in my life. It's given me a lot more confidence, a strong sense of responsibility, and it's given me the ideas I have for how I want to live my life. It's taught me how to live and work within a community structure, within a collective. How I see the world now is very different after being at Gilman, I've seen a different way that life can be lived.

There were three main things that I wanted to see and do at Gilman: zines, art, and more women involved, and to a certain degree that was all accomplished. The bonds I formed while working on these things and just the place in general, with the other people I worked with there, are really strong and intense. I know that if I ever needed help with anything that those people would be there for me, just like if they needed any help from me, I would be there for them. It's interesting how that has worked too, because I don't really see these people outside of Gilman, I don't really know that much about their personal lives, yet we have this connection. I can't think of any other situation I would be in that would provide those kinds of bonds.

PHOTOS BY LAUREN L. (THIS PAGE AND NEXT TWO)

I wanted to show that there was more to the club than the band playing on stage—there's a lot of craziness that goes on there during the shows that people generally don't notice. Also, since Gilman is so visually overwhelming (inside) and, with the bands playing onstage it's bright and loud, it's easy to overlook the little things, the off-moments, the quiet interludes that Gilman is full of–those are the things that I wanted to capture. Gilman is completely different during the day. The skylight illuminates all the dark corners and you can see all the drawings and graffiti on the walls and furniture, everything takes on a different look, different shadows, different highlights. The space is only used two or three times a week, so this is what it's like most of the time, quiet, yet intense. I like being there by myself when it's empty, you can feel every single person who's ever walked through there, you can feel the heaviness in the walls, in the air. I wanted the essence, not just the obvious. The graffiti, for example, is the mark that some people have left there, a little bit of themselves left behind.

DISPUTE RESOLUTION, GILMAN STREET STYLE...

September 6, 1996, membership passed Pat W_____'s mediation proposal, with the amendments that paid workers and the head coordinator cannot be mediators and mediators must keep all details of mediations confidential (unless presenting them to the membership as per Pat's proposal.

November 2, 1996, as the _____ situation unraveled, we decided to not have any personal-type (non-show related) dispute resolutions occur until a new, thorough dispute process is in place.

December 7, 1996, the following dispute resolution proposal passes:

Here's the general overview:
Disputes must directly involve Gilman patrons, workers, and/or bands. Any finding of fact by the 5 mediators is reached by consensus. If a mediator violates the strict code of confidentiality, s/he is 86'd for 6 months and can never be on a dispute resolution committee again.

1. Someone asks for a dispute resolution group to resolve a situation. This request can occur within a membership meeting or directly to a meeting facilitator or other officer of the club. The request can be in person or in writing, and can also come from a third party who's asking for a dispute resolution on behalf of an involved party.
2. At the soonest membership meeting, the membership will appoint the dispute resolution group. Before the membership is asked for volunteers, the following statement will be made: "By raising your hand and volunteering to be on this group you are agreeing to place yourself under gag order regarding what your group is dealing with indefinitely, except when it is time to formally report back to the general membership. This is unchanged if you decide to quit the group." The top five vote recipients will be the full group.
3. The top three vote recipients will meet outside of the membership meeting with the complainant and determine which of the following situations will occur:
    a. No dispute resolution officially involving Gilman will occur.
    b. Mediation is wanted by both parties. Group members are eligible to act as mediators if the complainant wishes. The group is responsible to set up the mediation, to be informed of the outcome, and to report the outcome of the mediation to the general membership.
    c. A fact-finding group will convene. This happens if the group wants more facts or if both parties don't want mediation. Fact-finding is to be done by the top five vote recipients. Fact finding must be done within two membership meetings. The people who carry out the fact finding process can request, from general membership, an extension, and receive it by a majority of positive votes.
    d. The issue is too heavy or potentially legally damaging to the club. The complainant will be referred to some person or outside group who can assist the complainant. The complainant can return at any time and request more help.
4. The group will return to the membership meeting with one of the following reports:
    a. No action was taken
    b. Mediation is complete
    c. A Recommendation based on facts found
    d. No action was taken by the club, but a referral to some other agency or body was made

- If there is a Gilman-related issue that you wish to be resolved through this process, please contact one of the officers (Chris S_____, Tyler, or Jesse) or a meeting facilitator (Jesse or Jemuel) and they will forward your request to the membership as laid out above.
- Please attempt to resolve the conflict on your own before involving the Gilman dispute resolution process. Thanks!

Some info on the Mediation-Grievance Committee/Dispute Resolution issue. There was a more indepth version I had, but it was six pages long and gave me a headache trying to read it, so I didn't reproduce it here.

if someone has a problem with another person at Gilman, there needs to be a clear & accepted way to approach solving the problem.

A Mediation Process for Gilman.

Member desiring solution of problem with another gilman person asks the meeting, thru chair for a volunteer mediator. Chair asks for volunteers willing to mediate. these persons raise their hands & identify themselves. After the meeting, person desiring mediation talks to their choice from among the volunteers. This mediator talks to all parties involved, and consults with pertinent staff (workers). If this (chosen) mediator fails to find a solution thats agreeable to both parties, she/he states at the next general meeting "we will need to have a full mediation on "x's" issue; i have been unable to resolve it." Then chair of meeting asks for volunteers to be a part of a 5 person mediation panel. these are then voted on by secret ballot, each member writing downn their 5 choices on a pc. of paper, with the top 5 vote getters becoming the 5 mediators. If candidates for this volunteer mediation wish to make a short statement as to why they are qualified, they should be able to do so. Both parties and all witnesses available are inter- viewed separately and if possible together, with the idea of finding a resolution acceptable to both parties. If no such solution is found, and at the request of one of the parties, the entire case is brought to the membership at the regular meeting, starting with a briefing from the 5 mediators on the progress of the issue, including all details of the case to date. Membership Meeting then investigates the case further (if appropriate) and takes whatever action it decides is fair desires.

An open letter to the Membership of 924 Gilman.

As a former director of the project, and someone who spent the better part of a large chunk of my life hanging around the warehouse, I am totally appalled by the level of violence that I have seen at the club recently. It was not always this way, and it doesn't have to continue to be this way.

The first thing you have to decide is if this level of violence is acceptable or not. Gilman, the East Bay, and the "scene" are all different places now than they were when I worked shows every Friday and Saturday night. Maybe fights at the club are just a fact of life, something that can only be controlled, not prevented. Maybe Gilman, as a microcosm of society, is only reflecting to an ever more hostile America. Maybe you believe that "life is conflict" and the evil in the world needs to be repelled "by any means necessary" wherever you are, at any time.

I don't believe any of that, and I would hope that few of you feel that way. However, I hear security staff brag about the shots they got in, and talk about their guns. I see people who I know are "the good guys," people who have worked at the club, who I know are intelligent, responsible people, provoke or take part in fist-fights. It makes me sick. One of Gilman's founding values was a commitment to non-violence. It seems to me that has non-violence has been replaced by an attitude of "If we're right, it's OK." Caesar, Hitler, Nixon, and George Bush would all be proud. There is a top-to-bottom problem here.

Let me explain how I feel: Whether or not stupidity and ignorance should be met with violence on the street, whether or not, it the world outside our door, aggression should be met with counter-aggression, there is no place for violence inside the club. Kids are getting beat up at home, beat up at school, and beat up in their neighborhood. Gilman should be a haven, not more of the same. Our club should be better than the world outside, not a grimy mirror.

Grabbing someone, tackling someone, or dragging someone outside can help diffuse a situation, throwing a punch has never broken up a fight, and never will. Our security guards should never have to throw punches. Everybody 'looses it' once in a while, that is understandable. But the idea that it's okay to kick or punch someone once or twice if they're a troublemaker is a page right out of the LAPD handbook. Is it OK for a security guard to go down the street and have a fight with someone as long as they take their shirt off first? Maybe if you base your code of ethics on John Wayne movies and Gomer Pyle reruns. Get a grip.

The violence can be stopped, and here's how. Some of these measures seem a little extreme, but I think we have an extreme situation.

First, all club flyering and newspaper advertising should be stopped starting now. Advertising should be limited to a calendar passed out at shows, the phone line, and radio stations. I even think that the club should consider a blackout of information from The List. (I will personally help Steve offset any additional cost if he wants to make two versions of The List. One, with our shows listed, to mail and pass out at Gilman, and another to pass out at other shows and leave at the record stores on Telegraph.) Blacking out information will help keep some of the trash away, and more importantly, help raise awareness that the club will not stand for this kind of stupidity any more.

Next, we need to eliminate the troublemakers. If some idiot comes to a show with a Swastika on his jacket or a T-Shirt with some misogynist crap printed on it, we aren't going to change his mind by engaging him in a shouting match that turns into a spitting match, that turns into a brawl. Anyone breaking the rules of the club regarding aggressively offensive behavior should be given his money back and kicked out, before the fighting starts. If he came with friends, let them have their money back too, if they agree to leave. Constant troublemakers need to be 86'ed. If they get in a show, even if they aren't causing trouble yet, should be kicked out with a refund. You can change someone's mind a lot faster by kicking him out of the scene than by kicking his ass.

We need to take serious fights more seriously. If any security guard or member who is trying to break up a fight gets hit, inside or out, the music should stop and the lights should go on. The second time it happens in a night, the music should stop for 20 minutes. The third time it happens, the show should be stopped. We need to let the crowd know that fights will not be tolerated. A show is listening, dancing, meeting, and learning, not taunting and fighting.

We all know that the bands that are on a bill affect the temperament of the audience. Booking needs to take responsibility for the bands they book, and bands have to take responsibility for what kinds of crowds follow them. This was common sense a few years ago, "Walk Together, Rock Together," etc. (If I booked or played a show that sent someone to the hospital, I would feel like shit. Some people seem to wear it as a badge of honor.)

Shows that will tend towards violence should be limited to four or even three bands. (Prices should be adjusted accordingly.) The less time people spend drinking and puffing their chests, the less fights will occur.

In the early 80's, violence in the scene closed all the cool clubs in the Bay Area. It was a big reason Gilman came together, and a big reason that non-violence was a founding tenement. Fights at shows are a bigger threat to the club than micro-beer and Warner Brothers combined. We argue about free sodas for bands, and kids are leaving shows with broken noses and concussions!

Thank you,

Mike "Stand"
3/2/96

THE GILMAN NEWSLETTER

June 96

GILMAN STREET IS AN ALL AGES, NOT FOR PROFIT, MEMBERSHIP CLUB THAT DOES NOT TOLERATE RACISM, SEXISM, HOMOPHOBIA, OR MISOGYNY.

We actually got our shit together enough to put out a second (amazingly boring) issue of the NEW gilman newsletter. We need help! This is our voice and we want everyone to be involved. If you feel like you can contribute intelligent or amusing ideas come to a newsletter meeting on the 2nd and 4th Saturdays of the month at 5PM.
newsletter motto of the month: "why talk shit when you can write shit"

THE GILMAN NEWSLETTER

august 96

GILMAN STREET IS AN ALL AGES, NOT FOR PROFIT, MEMBERSHIP CLUB THAT DOES NOT TOLERATE RACISM, SEXISM, HOMOPHOBIA, OR MISOGYNY.

WOW! The forth issue and it's hasn't gotten any better or easier. If you have opinions that you actually want anyone else to hear please come to a newsletter meeting on the 2nd and 4th Saturdays of each month or send us mail.
p.o. box 1058 berkeley CA 94701. All are welcome.

THE GILMAN NEWSLETTER

October 96

GILMAN STREET IS AN ALL AGES, NOT FOR PROFIT, MEMBERSHIP CLUB THAT DOES NOT TOLERATE RACISM, HOMOPHOBIA, OR MISOGYNY.

Issue #5, & the 1st to deal (a little) with death (insert cliche about death & taxes here). We're still here, and now is when friends are most important. Enough seriousness, 2nd & 4th Saturdays of each month when we "organize" this beast- all help/contributions welcomed.
mail to: p.o. box 1058, Berkeley CA 94701

The 924 Gilman Street Project is an all-ages, volunteer-run, alcohol & drug-free alternative cultural center. We mostly put on d.i.y. punk music shows, although we've had plays, art shows, and occasionally various other music shows (like ska, rap, folk, flamenco, industrial/noise). All shows are $5 and under, and we require everyone to have a membership card ($2 annual fee) & therefore be a member of the collective. All the major rules (no stage diving, excessively violent dancing, alcohol/drugs in or around the club) are printed on the back of the cards. No racist, misogynist, or homophobic acts will be booked. People can show up 1 hour before the doors open to volunteer to work and get in free. We have membership meetings that are open to everyone the first and third Saturdays of each month at 5PM at the club. We make decisions by a 2/3 or 50% majority vote (depending on the subject up for a vote) whenever we can't reach a consensus. We are a legal not-for-profit corporation under the laws of the state of California with 3 corporate officers.

ITEMS FROM
1996 NEWSLETTERS

CHARLES' JADED RANT

Do you remember high-school? Are you still in high school? What did they call you? Geek, nerd, freak, wimp, pussy, fag, lesbo, twerp, retard, homo, spaz, lard ass, fatso; do these sound familiar? These are the reasons why I and most of the people I know ended up punk. We were rejects that couldn't get accepted anywhere else: The politic came later, when we needed to build our own community, outside of the one that made us want to puke. When did cool become part of it? Now that M TV sells punk to anyone buying, where do the rejects go? How do we deal with the cool, popular Berkeley scenester punks? What of the Oakland punks who spend more $ on their outfits and hair than I do on rent? How did cool = punk? You know what, cool SUCKS.

SOMETHING BY PAT

Gilman owes (me) (us) (the world) something.

Gilman doesn't meet our expectations.

The scene would be better without Gilman, it'd be more raw. Well, go and live in Bakersfield if you want to experience real life. This is East Bay 1996, not LA 1982, not SF 1977, not New York 1996, or Berkeley in the 60's. What the fuck is this Gilman that doesn't meet your expectations? Do you know?

1. It's a big building that costs $3000 a month to rent.

2. It's the 25+/- people who regularly give up their weekends without pay and work to make the shows happen.

3. It's the money that they collect at the door, which goes to the landlord who then pays the bank that holds the mortgage.

4. It's the head volunteer (head coordinator Charles) who the volunteers and members voted recently to pay- the idea being he's being paid such a small amount of money (amounts to about $1.25 an hour) that no one would keep the job for the money...

5. It's the 2 or 3 regular security people who are paid a percentage of the door. The idea is to interest them in staying here, even if it is for the money, to protect the rest of the workers from the BURNOUT of dealing with security. The original MRR club closed in part because of the burnout of the volunteers in dealing with the expectable and regular security problems (there were no paid security in the first club).

6. The sound people do not get paid- so how can they owe you anything?

7. The store people do not get paid- how can they owe you anything?

8. The flyer people do not get paid- how can they owe you anything?

9. The booking people do not get paid- how can they owe you anything?

10. The trash people do not get paid- how can they owe you anything?

11. Yes- Gilman is a big black hole eating up the labor of all these people; just like a regular job you have to find time elsewhere to maintain your life, do the wash, do homework, etc. It eats up your life to a degree.

What you get back is knowing that we have a place to meet that belongs to us: not to the STATE, the YMCA, the Methodist Church, Bill Graham Presents, the UC Regents, your uncle, your mom, or anyone else.

If you work, you get back something for we, not for you. Now isn't that stupid?

I wrote this in June 1994:

"Gilman continues to exist because of the idealism of the few."

This is really a shame, because the original vision for Gilman was as a community effort. It turns out that as it is, it's a free gift to the (passive) community from the committed few.

In April 1996: This is still true, but it may be evolving into a real community generated effort/structure.

Pat W   . April 12, 1996

GET INVOLVED!!!
GILMAN NEEDS VOLUNTEERS

the gilman record table needs responsible help ordering records, pricing records, and assisting with paying bands/labels. talk to chris or come to a membership meeting. record table volunteers get into shows free.

volunteers are needed for both posting flyers and creating artwork for flyers. talk to sammy or come to a membership meeting. flyering gets you into shows free.

every show people are needed to work many positions such as front door, side door, security, clean up, membership, store, or even coat check sometimes. if you'd be interested come to a show by 7pm and ask for the coordinator. you only have to work half the show and get to enjoy the rest free.

the gilman newsletter desperately needs nearly articulate people to write lame opinionated rantings about anything from gilman to dental hygiene. you wanna? then come to a newsletter meeting the 2nd and 4th Saturday of the month.

Gilman needs responsible volunteers to remove graffiti. this requires communicating with neighbors about whatever complaints they might have and removing spray paint, stickers- etc. wanna help? ask Steve or come to a meeting. you'd get in to shows free whether you'd had to work that week or not.

the gilman "stoar" needs help. you have to be responsible, ok with numbers, and able to deal with mike. if you fit the description talk to mike.

teach a class, organize an art show, start a zine library, mad and crazy kung-fu fighting, teach me how to use this damned computer. anything. this is ALL of OUR place. use it.

CELIA'S UNJADED RANT

chARLES WAS SAYING THAT he was going to write an article about being a geek and getting into punk rock. But he's too jaded and cynical and would just end up complaining about something or another. I got in to punk rock because of the girls. Punk girls are the raddest thing in the world. I remember being 17 at a Paxton Quiggly show and watching Bronwyn scream her fucking head off and thinking ooohhh, this is why people like punk rock (which incidentally is also the same feeling I had the first time I came while having sex). And I remember feeling ultimately very geeky telling her that I thought she was rad. It seems like there is a history of misfit=punker that is getting very awkward now that punk is being shoved down the throats of every teenager around the world. Does that still make us misfits? Does societal acceptance change what we are doing?

Yeah, I'd say it does. It makes it so we almost can't pride ourselves on our outcast (although it seems like half the teenage punk boys I meet still do). What we are doing is fucking amazing though. We are creating a world, a self sufficient, or as close to as we can, world of creativity, life-sustaining community. We RUN A PUNK CLUB, WE have a huge movement of alternative press composed of fanzine writers, printing presses (we print our own books! posters, record covers, etc.), we have a school locally where the principal is a punk, a lot of the punks I know do social work, counselling and the like, we have a martial arts school that is sliding scale and super rad, a bunch of bookstores, like bound together in S.F. that sells raD lefty anarchy books, and AK press, that prints them, a group that does community gardening, another that serves free vegetarian food, every fucking day, a punk owned business that makes t-shirts for bands, people who breathe fire, create comics, put on art shows, work at a collectively run recycling, composting and worm selling business, and it goes on and on. We are doing it. It's not perfect, and a lot of us have to work really hard at shitty jobs that we hate to make it possible for us to do the things we love, but we are doing it.

ITEMS FROM 1996 NEWSLETTERS

Something by Ed.

America's got a two week attention span. That's always been my theory. No matter how big the tragedy or the piece of news is, it gets old in a couple of weeks. So if I started talking about something that happened in January, most of you probably wouldn't give a shit.

I knew a kid named Ben. It's hard to call him a kid, really. He's 16, but acts more mature than a lot of "adults" I know. He ran away from home when he was 15. It came down to a choice between staying at home and following his parents' rules or trying to make it on his own. It was the choice his parents gave him, the "my way or the highway" mentality. But even more than the fact that he ran away or anything that Ben did when he was living at home, what really pissed his parents of is that Ben was able to make it on his own. He didn't run back to mommy and daddy whenever he got in trouble, like they hoped he would. He was acting like an adult, not necessarily his parents' concept of an adult, but he made decisions and took responsibility for the consequences.

They couldn't handle that. I guess it was fine to give Ben an ultimatum, but when he actually called his parents on their bluff, then there was a problem. Their solution was to have a couple of cops snatch Ben when he was meeting his father for coffee. They tossed him into rehab and no one has talked to him since. His parents wouldn't let me write him a letter or tell me where he was. I hear he's now somewhere in Virginia.

I can't really say whether or not his parents made the right choice by putting Ben in rehab, but their methods were totally off. Ben was not any sort of addict, except maybe to cigarettes. He was living with me at the time he was taken away and never asked for money or help from anyone. He was taking care of himself and his parents couldn't handle that. (Ed forgot to mention that Ben had been a coordinator at gilman for quite some time-Chris)

The never ending troubles of Ben the disappearing coordinator:

So last we had heard of Ben he had been captured by his parents and sent to a school for boys or something like that in Richmond Virginia. Recently he'd been home for a family visit and decided to escape instead of return to Richmond. Last Friday he came down to Gilman before the Piss Jar show and his Dad showed u/ with a couple geens who snatched him back to teenage misfit special school. We probably won't see him till he's 18. Bye-bye Ben- we'll miss you. Oh yeah, I don't care how long Ben is gone the shoes in the office are for him when he returns. thanks-chris.

"Gilman's getting rich off us!" by Ed

So what happens in the office during the last band that is so important, anyway? It's Count-Out! Whoo hoo! This is when we figure out how much to pay the bands and security guards after counting money and filling out a bunch of paperwork. Fun stuff, really.

We start by counting up all the money that we made that night and pay our Big Bad Bruisers (security guards) their cut. They usually get 10% (together, not each) of the door if we have two security guards working that night and 5-7% if we only have one. On nights when we bring in over $1000, their percentage progressively drops.

Next we split the money between the club and the bands. Our usual split is 50/50, but we can make exceptions for smaller shows and give more money to the bands. Sometimes we give all the money to the bands, but we never keep more than 50%.

Now the hard part is figuring out how much the bands should get paid. We don't actually decide this, we just make suggestions based on draw (how many people came to see the band) and distance (how far away they're from). But we always let the bands have the final say. While we want to pay our local headliners fairly, we also don't want to leave anyone without enough gas money to get home (or at least to the next stop on their tour). What can I say? We're nice guys.

Our half of the money goes to pay the rent, insurance, bills, and all that other shit we need to keep the club running. We don't pay ourselves (except for Charles, but he's still po').

WORKER-CYNIC TERMINAL

It is easy to be disillusioned by working at 924 Gilman. The work is hard. There is no "rock star status" or even thanks most of the time for all the work you do. You have to give up most of yourself to the club. Then the club itself even has this habit of eating its own. You get so much shit from both inside and out that you begin to forget why you came here in the first place; the responsibility becomes your primary motivation, not the joy.

But every once and a while I put on a record at home and I remember. I remember how good the music can make me feel, how important the lyrics, the feeling, can be to me. I remember going to see bands that pumped my heart, electrified my brain, made me scream, even if i didn't remember all the words. I remember dancing until I was slick with sweat and still be leaping back for more, for the bonding of dancing with people I didn't know but who always looked out for me, slapped hands and backs between songs. I remember jumping around my room, or closing my eyes and dreaming to the music of my favorite records. I remember how important it was to me to openly flaunt normalcy, the normal that never accepted me anyway (I grew up in steel- town PA). I love the scene of like minded rejects and rebels. It feels so good that so many people are working so hard to play, produce, and support the music, scene, and politics that supported me. I was so eager for the opportunity to give back, to join the crew of workers who labor to keep our scene alive and powerful. I need these reminders and I hope other people remember them, too. I hope that the work we do helps other people feel these ways, too. The infighting is shit- why do we do it? I still love our scene, our music, our politics, regardless of how cynical I may get. I hope all the terminal cynics can take a moment to remember, as I do.   -charles

---

ITEMS FROM 1996 NEWSLETTERS

Having fun at Gilman (for a change)

Before I ever even came to Gilman, I had heard and read so much about it and the community it was home to. Being from southern California (where the only consistant venues for shows are either large halls with asshole security guards or sleazy bars trying to cash in, neither creating much of a sense of community), I was amazed that there could be such a place where people came together to do more than just see a few bands play. Gilman was always described to me as a place where people who didn't fit in with mainstream society could come together and create an alternative to that mainstream; a place where they could create their own close-knit community based on the exchange of ideas and have fun together as a community (as you can see I'm going to abuse this word alot in this article).

When I arrived here and started coming to shows, I was a little disappointed. Gilman was still unbelievably better than anything I had ever experienced at the venues for shows back home, but it didn't live up to the legendary stories passed along to me. I still saw Gilman as something extremely worthwhile and have since dedicated much of my time to helping it live or, but I can't help wishing that it was more of the community space all the long-time Gilman scenesters never fail to describe while justifying their lack of interest in getting involved here. I'm sick of hearing about how great it used to be; I want us, the Gilman membership, to start having fun at Gilman again (not just coming to a show, watching a few bands, talking to the same people we always talk to and then going home, that's how its done everywhere else, and its fucking boring). I'm not the only one who feels this way.

After a recent membership meeting, I was talking to some friends who dedicate much of their time to this place, and they began telling me how they feel the same. As we talked about the lack of a sense of community, more and more of the people who put so much of themselves into running Gilman came up and said that they agree and that something needs to be done. So we're going to do it.

We just had Punk Prom and we want to do more things like it. We want to make Friday and Saturday nights at Gilman more than just shows. We want people to come here for the fun they are going to get out of interacting with the diverse people that make up the Gilman membership, not just for the bands.

We want to start having events here that don't revolve around bands. Events like movie nights, pot lucks, art shows, etc. We just had a wedding party for Chris Dodge here and it was great. People just came, hung out with old friends, talked to people they wouldn't ordinarily have had the opportunity to meet, ate food, and watched a couple bands make fools of themselves on stage. People had fun and it didn't revolve around the bands that played; it revolved around being here for the sake of having fun together. We need to do more things like that involving the general membership.

I guess the whole point of writing this article is to start people thinking. We need ideas and people willing to make those ideas happen. If you think of something that might make coming to Gilman more fun and exciting, talk about it with other people you know who come here or bring it to a membership meeting. This place doesn't just belong to the people who work here, it belongs to all of us. It's our responsibility to make it fun, and I for one want to start trying to live up to that responsibility.

by clayton

GILMAN BITES

First off, the Gilman Log has been eliminated in the interest of having a monthly colunm about what is happening at our space in a little more detail than the Gilman Meeting Notes. This is my column, so I can't swear to be *completely* objective, but I will try.

For the last few months, the Gilman membership has been debating the concept of a mediation/ disciplary council for workers and patrons who have problems with other worker or patrons beyond the normal capacity for the club to handle. Most interpersonal problems that occur here can be handled by talking things out, asking for help from "senior" club volunteers (ie head of booking, coordinator, stage manager, corporate officers, etc), or going to a membership meeting. But sometimes people don't feel comfortable flaunting dirty laundry in a public meeting or going to other "senior" members who may come across as "the man" or be a problem as well. These problems may be uncomfortable subjects, like sexual harassment or personality conflicts, that can be too sensitive for a membership meeting. And the membership has a habit of draging things out painfully and embarrassingly long or going on witch hunts that can fry relatively innocent people. Several ideas were given and a touchy debate raged (literally) for weeks on the best way to create a new "department" in Gilman. The result was this: a person who has a problem with a regular worker or patron and feels that they have tried every means available to them to work it out can come to a membership meeting and ask the facilitator to ask for volunteers for mediation. The person can then choose, anonomously, who they feel can be the best mediator for them. If that does not work, they can return and ask agian for mediation. This time a council of up to five can volunteer, an election occuring if there are more. Paid workers (security) and the head coordinator (presuming he/she has already done their best to work this out) are exempted from this group. All of these mediators are to keep all information private. If this does not work, it goes to the membership. It sounds like beauracracy and hopefully it rarely has to be used, but there are times when private discussions on personnel issues are the only way to fairly resolve things. It has already been put to the test, and I hear it worked great.

The extensive sound improvements are nearing their finish. The new speaker, new monitor, and new aplifier to run them are all installed and running. We don't yet have our new monitor board (which our head sound person, Radley, is donating), but he promises it soon. The new sound booth is finished and even in its reduced size, it takes up alot of room on the floor. There are alot of new discussions to be held on how to increase capacity be building shelves for band equipment and platforms for patrons. We have yet to decide what to do with the old sound loft. I'm really interested in what people think about our improvements, expecially since we spent over half of our savings on them.

The managers from the brew pub that is moving in across the street have shown up at the last few meeting and we are having a series of outside of memebership meetings to work out the details of smooth running betweenthe two establishments.

Lastly, some good news and some really bad news. The good first- we have had some really excellent shows this month: Avail, Gauze and Assfort from Japan, and at the last moment, Zeni Geva. The bad news in that our mostly friendly street punk from Boston, Frank Depression, died from internal bleeding resulting from a bar fight in Boston on August 23, 1996. Frank has been in the punk scene for well over a decade and and, regardless of the differences between him and the club, he has always been, when it came down to the line, a club supporter. We will all miss Frank. I will alot.

-Charles L

Ouch! Don't step on me, asshole! by charles

"I'm not your stepping stone." A lyric from a song that everone has heard, if not coved in a band they play in. If not, I'm sure you've heard the line "Its just a phase." I've heard it so much it makes me sick. But Gilman is a mix of both and if you are here long enough you begin to see it, over and over again. People show up, they love the place, they come every night, they want to play every show, they want to volunteer for everything. Then the excitement wanes. They think working here is boring. They want to hang out with their friends- people who they usually have met here. They want to play other clubs because their draw, after playing Gilman for years, has gotten too big- the money is better, they get treated better, the politics are easier, they can play to more and "different" kinds of people (not Gilman punks). So they leave and new, fresh, and idealistic faces replace them.

I guess it is a "phase," a fact of life as people get "older," more "mature." The politic they supported when they were kids just desn't fit in with their lives any more. It keeps the scene alive, brings in fresh blood, the next generation. The people who are left behind, like me and many other "old school" (total crap) Gilman workers, are just stuck in their rebellious adocensece. It stinks, but it happens all the time and who can resent your old friends when they "change."

The list of ex-Gilmanites is thousands long. Some names are so obvious that to list them is being redundant- just read "Rolling Stone" or "Spin". They are on the cover half the time. The others are clear to most of us but maybe not to the casual observer (hence this article). They are old Gilman punx who don't seem to feel comfortable here anymore- no booze, we're "uncool" now, they don't get the respect, the special treatment, they deserve. All you have to do is work the door for a couple shows and fight with all the people who yell at you because they deserve to get in free, give you attitude, flip you off for just helping out where they used to. Bands begin to demand longer guest lists, special favors, spread attitude that some call "rock star." The ideology which they once fought for, helped establish, doesn't work any more. Yet not one of them cares enough to show up at a meeting to try to change it.

But this is just whining. This has been going on for years. No one will ever mention their names out loud in fear of talking shit about their old friends, the now all too powerful "scenesters." I know I won't start the ball rolling. But they are out there and they are walking out of our scene, if slowly. And you know who is getting walked on.

ITEMS FROM 1996 NEWSLETTERS

Battle #2 started with the plans for a microbrewery and restaurant/bar to be built across the street from 924 Gilman. Below is a letter the club submitted to the zoning board.

Concerns of 924 Gilman Regarding Proposed Brew Pub at 901 Gilman

What is 924 Gilman?

924 Gilman Street is the only consistently all-ages alcohol-free youth center in the bay area, best known as the premier underground music venue in the nation. 924 Gilman is run by youth for youth. Anyone who wants to get involved can. It is a volunteer-run collective which has existed in the same location since 1986. Gilman has hosted amateur theater, spoken word, art shows, self-defense courses, and numerous political and community benefits over the years.

924 Gilman actively opposes racism, sexism and homophobia. Its low door prices, informal atmosphere and commitment to a fun, safe, alcohol and drug free space for local youth has created a strong sense of community among otherwise alienated kids. The sense of accomplishment that youth gain is unparalleled in the bay area.

We have survived as a viable alternative to commercial pop music. Nationally famous bands such as Green Day, Rancid, The Offspring, and Jawbreaker grew out of this supportive community. It is an important stop on the international d.i.y. (do-it-yourself) music circuit.

We only oppose the proposed large bar and restaurant: we welcome the skilled jobs that the proposed brewery will bring to this low-income industrial section of Berkeley.

Potential Problems/Possible Solutions

Why are we opposed? Our greatest concern is that every problem that arises between patron of the brew pub and members of 924 Gilman will be "blamed" on the club and that the club, which has been in existence in 1986, will end up losing its permit. In the past few years there have been a minimal number of problems involving the club and the city, including police calls. We consider ourselves a good member of the business community which provides a valuable service to the citizens of Berkeley and the East Bay, namely as a place for young people to gather in a safe all-ages, alcohol and drug free environment.

1.   The presence of a retail establishment will reduce the viability of the West Berkeley as an industrial area, which the city needs to remain dynamic and able to grow.

Possible Solution: If the application for a zoning permit is allowed, that this will be the last retail establishment allowed on Gilman Street in West Berkeley.

2.   The presence of a restaurant/bar across the street from 924 Gilman, an all ages, youth center with an explicit no alcohol policy, as well as in a neighborhood with a homeless shelter in it, may present a negative influence.

3.   The proposed brew pub is an "upscale" establishment, which will be located in a working class neighborhood. Many residents will not be able to afford to patronize it, which may cause resentment among residents who will see problems arising from the brew pub including increased rent, increased traffic, and increased crime, but no benefits.

Possible Solution: Require that a certain percentage of employees be West Berkeley residents.

4.   We are extremely concerned that conflicts will arise between members of 924 Gilman and patrons of the brew pub, particularly during large shows. We wish to be a good neighbor to all businesses in the neighborhood, and before the brew pub's zoning permit is approved we think that special steps should be taken to ensure we work out any potential problems.

Possible Solution: Before zoning is approved, we would like to meet with the management of the brew pub at the Berkeley Dispute Resolution Center to address and attempt to resolve potential problems. We would like the brew pub to agree to implement the suggestions of of the Dispute Resolution Center before their permit is approved. We would like to set up monthly meetings between the management of 924 Gilman and the management of the brew pub to address problems which may arise in an informal manner, which will decrease the likelihood that either of us will have problems. We would specifically like the brew pub to acknowledge that a certain amount of socializing happens outside the club at 924 Gilman.

We would like an acknowledgment by the zoning board, and in the zoning permit for the brew pub that any problems that occur between the patrons of the brew pub and the members of 924 Gilman are mutual and not just the fault of 924 Gilman. In addition we would like acknowledgment by the brew pub and the city that all problems occurring between 7th and 8th, and Harrison and Camelia are the shared responsibility of both 924 Gilman and the brew pub. We are extremely interested in setting up a system whereby friction between the two businesses and their patrons can be dealt with in an informal manner.

5.   We are extremely concerned that drunk and disorderly patrons of the brew pub will cause problems with the members of 924 Gilman, many of whom are minors. Many of the people who go to 924 Gilman feel they are marginalized members of society who seem to be targets for less accepting members of society. One of the reasons for 924 Gilman's location in an industrial area is to stay out of the way of the kind of people who harass the members.

Possible Solution: Have the brew pub provide paid security on their premises at all times. Security at the brew pub and 924 Gilman shall work together. They should attempt to become sensitized to the problems of each other's patrons.

6.   The current plan for parking at the brew pub is woefully inadequate. It assumes that most patrons of the brew pub will use street parking (25% of the brew pub parking is allocated to 8th Street.) Many of these spaces are currently used by members of 924 Gilman Street and neighborhood residents, who we feel will be negatively impacted if the current plan is implemented.

Possible Solution: Require that the brew pub provide enough on site parking for all patrons, not just employees. We additionally feel that this lot should be enclosed and patrolled by security guards.

In addition to the solutions proposed, we believe that a reduction of the size of the restaurant and an earlier closing time will alleviate the pressure on 924 Gilman and the community.

7.   We are worried that patrons of the brew pub may cause property damage in the neighborhood, particularly towards the premises of 924 Gilman. We are further concerned that currently, 924 Gilman is held accountable for may incidents of minor vandalism in the neighborhood. We have an excellent record and reputation with our neighbors for dealing with these incidents in an informal manner but we are worried that we will be held accountable for damages caused by patrons of the brew pub and that this may detrimentally affect our status before the zoning board.

Possible Solution: We have found security and cleanup crews solve this problem.

8.   The brew pub will greatly increase traffic in the neighborhood, both vehicular and pedestrian. There have been several incidents of pedestrians being hit by cars around 8th and Gilman in the past year, and we see these incidents only increasing if the brew pub goes in.

Possible Solution: Put a traffic light at the corner of 8th and Gilman. This would in itself cause several problems -- creating a blockage to a major freeway artery in the city as well as costing a great deal of money. We would like the brew pub to commission another traffic study, conducted at peak times (including large band performances at 924 Gilman and at closing time at the bingo parlor at San Pablo and Gilman) to determine the best way to minimize the traffic impact of the brew pub on Gilman Street. We feel the best solution would be an alternative traffic plan that diverts the majority of the brewery traffic off Gilman Street altogether. This could be accomplished by locating the front of the brew pub on Harrison Street and blocking 8th and/or 7th on the north side of Gilman Street. This would minimize the potential of negative interactions of older patrons from brew pub with the patrons of the youth oriented 924 Gilman Street Club.

9.   The brew pub, an "upscale" establishment, will likely attract expensive cars, which will tend to increase the likelihood of "opportunity theft" against brew pub patrons' property in the neighborhood, particularly if the current parking proposal is allowed.

Possible Solutions: Floodlights on the side of the building on 8th street between Gilman and Harrison would decrease the petty crime around the brew pub. The best solution, however, would be lighted, patrolled, on site parking for patrons.

10.   Drunk Driving. We are concerned that the presence of a brew pub will increase drunk driving on Gilman Street, exacerbating an already dangerous traffic situation for pedestrians on the street.

Possible Solution: Require the brew pub to sponsor mandatory training for all brew pub employees who will serve alcohol, to ensure that they know when to cut patrons off before they reach legal limits for impaired or drunk driving (around one drink an hour for most people.)

Thank you for your consideration.

The Membership of 924 Gilman

Planning Meeting Brew Pub
Tuesday 10/17/95 7PM

After extensive discussion, we decided our goal:
** As a collective, we oppose the bar & restaurant because of many problems- to let this project pass we present certain solutions. **
Basically, this allows us to oppose the retail part of the project (no one was against having a brewery employing 50-60 people move in) while simultaneously making our concerns known, presenting solutions, and hopefully securing <u>our</u> future (as a unique alcohol and drug-free youth center) with the city in the process. A formal list of problems and solutions should appear somewhere on this bulletin board.

**We broke up into 3 groups: Media/Punk Rock/Radical Outreach, Political/Neighborhood Strategies, and Negotiation. Here's what each group came up with & their next meeting date:
MEDIA/PUNK ROCK/RADICAL OUTREACH:
We'll be sending out press releases with contact names/numbers of spokespeople to the following:
-All punk rock and radical outreach (zines, radio shows, etc.) possible
-Local papers (EXPRESS, BAY GUARDIAN), local radio stations (KALX, KZSU, KUSF), and local print media (Chronicle, Examiner, Tribune).
-Glossy magazines (Rolling Stone, Spin).
-Various places on the Internet
We will <u>not</u> be doing MTV or local TV news stations.
We're writing a press release (for approval by Saturday's membership meeting) and re-writing the petition on THURSDAY OCT. 19 @ 4PM. Future meetings of this group will be posted here & on phone line.
POLITICAL & NEIGHBORHOOD OUTREACH
We'll be ringing doorbells and flyering nearby residents, meeting individually with the Pastor, the beat cops & possibly Sgt. R   , PicNPac, Ashkenaz, Allied Radiator, Long Haul/Infoshop, and Linda M   (our City Council Representative). In addition, we're starting a postcard campaign to the Zoning Board (postcards courtesy of Punks With Presses), at the Public Hearing we'll be telling the Zoning Board our story & concerns, and documenting that story & sending it to the City Council members and other city politicos.
The next meeting is SATURDAY OCT. 21 @ 4PM.
NEGOTIATION
We're going to present a formal (& legal) version of our concerns/solutions to the Zoning Board. We're also documenting current accidents/crime for comparison to the future. NEXT MEETING WILL BE POSTED HERE & ON SHOW INFO LINE - STAY TUNED!

****Many thanks to the 41+ people who showed up!***

For Immediate Release:
October 22,1995

Berkeley, CA- 924 Gilman Street is in jeopardy. The only consistently all-ages alcohol-free youth center in the bay area, best known as the premier underground punk venue in the nation, is threatened by an out-of-state brewery's plan to open an upscale bar and restaurant directly across the street. The project, which is currently under review by the Berkeley Zoning Board, includes plans for a 250-seat restaurant/bar, a 100,000 sq. ft. brewery, and only 70 indoor parking spaces.
924 Gilman is run by youth for youth. Anyone who want to get involved can. In addition to being the breeding ground for such current acts as GREEN DAY, OFFSPRING, RANCID, and JAWBREAKER, it is a volunteer-run collective, which has existed at the same location since 1986. Besides being an important stop on the international d.i.y. (do-it-yourself) music circuit, Gilman has hosted amateur theater, spoken word, art shows, self-defense courses, and numerous political and community benefits over the years. It actively opposes racism, sexism, and homophobia. Its low prices, informal atmosphere, and commitment to a fun, safe, alcohol and drug-free space for local youth has created a strong sense of community among otherwise alienated kids. The sense of accomplishment that youth gain is unparalleled in the bay area.

We only oppose the proposed large bar and restaurant; we welcome the jobs that the proposed brewery will bring to this low-income industrial section of Berkeley. The irony of local residents being unable to afford the restaurant/bar's prices (a.k.a. gentrification) is one of many concerns, which include massive problems with traffic, parking, drunk driving, and potential culture clashes. We also question the wisdom of putting a bar directly across the street from a community center that actively discourages alcohol and drug use.
Increased police presence and both wealthy businesses and young, upwardly-mobile clientele clamoring for a more upscale dining and drinking environment will quickly spell the end for 924 Gilman's unique community center. Our current location was chosen for its relative isolation from retail and residential neighborhoods, thereby allowing our alternative community to thrive.
The Zoning Board meets to decide this issue Monday, October 30th, at the North Berkeley Senior Center, located at Hearst and Martin Luther King Jr. Blvd. in Berkeley at 7:15 p.m.

Above: press release issued by Gilman

Below and right: Gilman's petition

To The Berkeley Zoning Commision and The Berkeley City Council:
We are opposed to the proposed project at 901 Gilman Street as it stands now, specifically the 250-seat family restaurant/bar. We foresee massive problems with traffic, parking, drunk drivers, gentrification, and potential conflicts between 924 Gilman's patrons and the bar's patrons. We also question the wisdom of locating a bar directly across the street from the East Bay's only all ages, youth-run, alcohol-free alternative cultural center. We've been working for and with bay area youth for 9 years in this location.   -Supporters of the 924 Gilman Street Project

NAME	ADDRESS	PHONE

WHAT YOU CAN DO!
1:Sign Petition
2:Write letter
   Address it "To Whom It May Concern" & tell the Zoning Board/City Council "What Gilman means to you" & the potential problems that can shut down this valuable resource to youth, etc., or whatever you think will help. Please give it to us at the front door or mail it to the address below.
3:Fill out postcard
4:Get parents to call their
   city council members
5:Get involved with a group
6:Distribute Petitions to
   other scenes/cities
7:Your own idea here
Thank you for your help!
Gilman Street P.O.Box 1058 Berkeley, CA 94701
Show Info/Update (510)525-9926 Office/Booking 524-8180

**ZONING BOARD MEETING
Monday October 30, 1995
7:15 PM**

FELLOW GILMAN ST COMMUNITY MEMBERS:

An addition to our neighborhood is being made in the next few months that will change the aspect of our community drastically. In the warehouse at 901 Gilman St. a large, "upscale" microbrewery is being built by an out of town business called Hart Brewing. Besides the strong smell and increased traffic that such a business will incur, Hart Brewing feels it necessary to help sell their product that they must also have a 350 seating pub/resturant. This is a primarily industrial and residential neighborhood, a fact that has been intentionally protected as such by the "West Berkeley Plan" until recently with the building of Office Max and Jimmy Beans as well as other retail outlets. The purpose of the plan was to maintain this area as a viable neighborhood and encourage industrial jobs (in comparison to low paying retail jobs) in Berkeley.

The restaurant planned for our neighborhood is *not* a simple vehicle for the selling of their beer; it is one of the largest in Berkeley. Hart Brewing is very anxious for the "prestige" of having "Brewed in Berkeley" on their bottles.. The increased traffic, parking, crime, and intoxication of a 350 seating pub seems not to be a concern, for Hart Brewing is sure that this will be a perfect location for their business. We are frightened by the prospect of an enormous bar being placed in the middle of our neighborhood. I think that we're all aware of the already signifigantly overcrowed 6th and Gilman intersection. Besides the obvious problems of intoxication and crowding, we foresee a rise in property values and along with it, rents and property taxes. We have to pay for their moving in to our community.

The permit to allow Hart Brewing to begin construction has already passed the zoning board, despite large protest. We are appealing to the City Council. To stop our new neighbor from moving in, as seen from experience at the zoning board, seems unlikely. Too much money is pushing this upon us for Berkeley to refuse. But with our appeal we hope to at least shrink the coming problems. We need more support and you can help by writing letters expressing your concern for our neighborhood. These are the points that we are fighting for:

1. We want Hart Brewing to reduce its proposed capacity from 350 to something more reasonable for an industrial/residential neighborhood.

2. We want a reduction in operating hours and

3. an increase in on site parking.

4. We want a reduction in the availability of take out purchases.

5. We want an assurance of our security by the hiring, by Hart Brewing, of guards to keep their patrons in control.

6. And, most of all, we want a recognition by the City Council that we are a viable community that must be protected *as it is* and not as an increasing retail strip for high priced businesses.

The letters need to be presented to the City Council before the appeal, which will occur in the near future, so they need to be finished this week, if possible. When finished, please call   for it to be picked up. Please help, for we can only keep ourselves safe by working togther.

Freud R

Above: another part of Gilman's community outreach program in dealing with the brew pub
Below: the conditions imposed upon the brew pub by the zoning board
11/13/95

12) The project is across the street from 924 Gilman Street, a unique all-ages non-alcoholic youth club with a valid Use Permit. Because the youth club is an important youth resource for the City of Berkeley, the operators of the proposed brew pub will adopt the following actions to ensure that the brew-pub is operated in a manner which is compatible with the continuing operation of 924 Gilman. Such actions shall include: 1) the provision of at least one security guard on Friday and Saturday evenings to, among other activities, monitor interactions between brew pub patrons and youth club patrons; 2) hold regular meetings of a designated brew-pub liaison with a liaison for the youth club to be held not less than once per month in the first six months after the opening of the brew-pub, and as often as requested by the representatives of 924 Gilman thereafter; 3) first use of the Berkeley Dispute Resolution service whenever possible to seek to resolve disputes that cannot be amicably resolved between the two liaisons; and 4) a recognition that there is a shared responsibility to maintain safety and security in the area and to resolve disputes between the club and the brew-pub privately whenever possible.

ZONING BOARD RESULTS!!!

Monday's Zoning Board Meeting saw 100+ Gilman supporters pack the room, and most of us stayed until 2 AM for the decision.

Although the board recognized us as "a cultural institution" and as a "valuable community resource," they approved the 350-seat bar/restaurant <u>with</u> some important concessions to us. The brewery managers & security must meet with us at least once a month, and the board suggested that we try to work out potential conflicts without involving the city or the cops. A traffic light & lots of bright lighting will be installed at 8th & Gilman. The board is recommending that the Berkeley law mandating $500 for each sucessive 911 call within 90 days be waived for the Gilman Street Project. The brew pub has a 6 month review in front of the Board.

Anyone can appeal the Zoning Board's decision to the City Coucil within 10 days of their decision becoming official.

WHAT NOW?

Come to our membership meeting

<u>THIS SATURDAY AT 5PM</u>

and we'll decide our course of action & the pros & cons of various approaches.

Below: letter the club sent to the zoning board after the decision to allow the brew pub to open.

Introduction

For almost ten years, The corner of Gilan and Eight Streets in Berkeley has been host to a unique and very special institution. To an outside observer, the club might seem to be just another nightclub, albeit with a slightly younger audience. However, the club is much more than that. "The Gilman Street Project" is an all-ages, youth oriented, volenteer-run, non-profit performance space and community center. All patrons are required to be members, and for many of the members, the club is the most important institution in their life.

People that don't "fit in" anywhere else can be comfortable at the club. A kid whose home life is racked by violence and hostility can come down to a space where respect for women, gays and people all races is actively enforced. Someone whose social life is dominated by the hopelessness, and petty posturing of 'hanging' on Telegraph can come to the club and be and take an active role in making something good happen.

The club has always been a fragile institution, and the members are obviously very protective of the environment. 924 Gilman has it's own way of doing things that is not always obvious or apparent. People who are not familiar with the club or the 'scene' can be alienated, and at the same time alienating. While 924 Gilman welcomes everyone, they must insist that anyone inside the club respect the principal rules: No alcohol or drug use, no violence, and no displays of racism, homophobia, or misogyny.

Situation

When the members of 924 Gilman learned of the proposed Brewery and Restaurant that was to open across the street, many of them feared the worst. The club members brought up their concerns with the City's Zoning Board, and the Management of Hart Brewing. As a result, a number of agreements have been made between the parties. We feel that smooth operation between the two establishments can only occur if the letter and spirit of the agreements are followed by all parties.

Agreements

The Zoning Board Meeting of 11/13/95 became a forum to determine how the Restaurant and the club would be able to coexist. The City of Berkeley's Conditional Use Permit for 911 Gilman (no. A2359) contains a few specific terms that must be followed. As stated in the report "Because the youth club is an important youth resource for the City of Berkeley, the operators of the proposed brew pub will adopt the following actions to ensure that the brew-pub is operated in a manner which is compatible with the continuing operation of 924 Gilman."

- The Brew-pub must provide at least one security guard on Friday and Saturday nights between 7pm and closing specifically to monitor interaction between brewpub and youth club patrons. It was recommended that this be a uniformed, unarmed "rent-a-cop" rather than a t-shirted "bouncer." If desired, 924 Gilman will provide this person with a radio by which he can quickly contact our head security monitor so that they can easily work in tandem.

- There will be regular meetings between designated Brew Pub liaison and youth club liaison, not less than once per month for the first six months of operations and as often as requested by 924 Gilman thereafter.

- The parties will make "First Use" of the Berkeley Dispute Resolution Service to resolve differences that cannot be resolved between the liaisons.

- There will be an acknowledgement of "Shared responsibility." Situations during shows should be resolved without involving the Police. A 911 call by either establishment involving the other will appear on both establishments records.

- On site sales of bottled beer will be handled responsibly. When members of the club visited the Seattle brew-pub they were impressed by the tasteful manner in which beer for off-site sale was displayed, and expect that the display will be similar here. The zoning board was quite concerned with this aspect of the establishment, and if they determine it to be a nuisance they will restrict weekend off-site sales.

After the Zoning Board's decision was released, four club members visited the Seattle operation. They met with John S   , and agreed on a few additional points.

- There will be a section in the employee manual explaining the unique nature of the club. This is exteremely important. We need to know that all employees of the brew pub understand our club, and can respond to questions from the patrons in an appropriate manner.

- Monthly meetings between security personnel from both establishments will be held. This is separate meeting in addition to the aforementioned monthly meeting. These meetings could be very short, possibly just before a show. We just want to make sure that all people responsible for security in the area "touch base" once in a while.

- There will be a commitment to resolving disputes privately.

Conclusion

With the proper precautions and planning, the the Brew-pub and 924 Gilman will be able to operate across the street from each other without significant problems.

Below: an article written in 1996 for *Slingshot*, a local newspaper published by a Bay Area infoshop.

Gilman St Gentrification
written by Charles Long, ed. by Lindsay Krisel and Pat Wright

924 Gilman, an all ages, punk community/performance space located in West Berkeley since 1986 is finding its once quiet, industrial/warehouse location increasingly crowded out by upscale "brew pubs", restaurants, and retail stores meant to appeal to a more moneyed crowd.

The Gilman Street Project chose this location for its relative isolation, where it can avoid confrontations with police, merchants, jocks, "yuppies", and other people who might object to "funny colored hair" or "punk attitudes". This region and others like it, industrial areas right off the highway, have been attracting a larger and larger crowd as Berkeley and its industrial areas gets more trendy to those with money. This area of Berkeley is supposedly protected as an industrial/warehouse area by the West Berkeley Plan, approved by the City Council in 1993.

The zoning board of Berkeley has cited us as a valuable and delicate resource in the Bay Area (when over 100 punks show up at their meetings to apply pressure) yet allows new businesses that potentially threaten us to unbalance the "delicate" balance they point out. The zoning board's approval of Hart Brewing building a brew pub at 901 Gilman, across from an all ages, no drugs or alcohol space, is ridiculous! This bar opens in September and is to be larger than the Gilman Street Project, maybe even larger than Spenger's, the largest bar in Berkeley. Other new businesses have been approved in the last month.

The zoning board has just approved a new restaurant and three retail stores that violate the West Berkeley Plan in word and spirit regardless of our vehement objection. The zoning board staff and the owners had been "working for over a year" to devise a plan to make these new businesses work, despite of their continued threat to existing businesses (including us) and zoning violations.

With the infiltration of upscale businesses, we are afraid of a sudden lack of parking and street danger due to all the new traffic (several people have already been hit in front of our club by cars coming off the highway or from other businesses), that the rent for the area will rise with the increasing gentrification of the neighborhood, or that our new neighbors will object to the "obnoxious" punks that attend our space. We are, of course, in active resistance to the influx of businesses which threaten to push us out of our neighborhood.

The West Berkeley Plan was created to protect industrial and warehouse jobs and businesses (Gilman rents a warehouse space). Yet the pressure from big money pushes the line further each year as warehouse space becomes more available and industry drops. This plan protects us from retail, foodservice, or bars. Yet the zoning board of Berkeley has allowed several upscale restaurants and businesses to move into the Gilman corridor: Jimmy Beans, Office Depot, Hart Brewing, and other retail stores that attract clientele beyond the region's financial means. Our patrons have already been refused service or find the prices well outside the limit of their wallets.

We are, of course, in active resistance to the influx of businesses which threaten to push us out of our neighborhood. We also fully support the West Berkeley plan in all its intentions for this area.

What can we do to resist the continued invasion of upscale businesses into our neighborhood; businesses that, by their very existence, threaten ours, if the city will not respect the concerns of existing spaces or even their own rulings? It seems that money may win out over the kids again unless there is a serious turn around.

The following four pages contain an article that was reprinted from *Maximum RocknRoll* (Jan. 1997).

GILMANGILMANGILMANGILMANGILMANGILMAN

Gilman Street. 10 years old Dec. 31, 1996. 10 Years since Soup, AMQA, Silkworms, Christ On Parade, and Impulse Manslaughter first took the now well-worn stage.10 years of insanity, desperation, togetherness, and great times. Who could possibly have thought it would ever last this long? But passion and dedication have overcome exhaustion and frustration time and again. From a handful of people sitting in an empty warehouse in July '86 planning the beginning, to a handful of people sitting in a now vital part of the community, planning the future, Gilman battles along.

On the surface, not much has seemed to change, the place just looks more trashed. But new people continue to come along and get involved and gradually, subtly, evolution takes place. Attending a recent meeting, the bulk of the discussion centered around mediation councils and investigative committees, things unheard of in the meetings of 10 years ago. Financially as well, things are better now than ever before, including some months of turning a decent profit, allowing for club improvements and setting something aside for months that aren't so good.

Gilman continues to be a place that provides opportunities to people that can be found practically nowhere else. Where else could a 16 year old be given a chance to run a club/community center on any given night? Where else could someone with no background in sound be given a chance to run the soundboard? This place is run by people whose commitment and resolve have overcome lack of experience and skill. It seems as the average age of the people running the space has gotten younger, the more successful the space has become. Easily over a thousand shows/events have taken place here in its ten years of existence, totally amazing given the amount of work involved in putting on just one, and considering it's mostly all volunteer.

What does the future hold? The area around the club is gradually changing, a micro-brewery pub/restaurant is moving in across the street, Office Depot and Walgreens have appeared, and a nearby junkyard has supposedly been sold with possible development to follow. What was once an industrial wasteland is now becoming upscale. Will Gilman fit in? Are crises necessary to garner support, tighten bonds, and keep things exciting? I talked to some of the current staff, what follows are their thoughts. If you'd like to be a part of this ongoing legend (or start a legend of your own) — GET INVOLVED! You can make a difference, just as these individuals have. Article/interview by Brian Edge

First Impressions/ Why Get Involved

Charles: I first came here four years ago after hearing about the place while living in St. Louis. I was so anxious to contribute. The punk scene had given me so much, and here was a way to contribute back. I loved the place. I was intimidated at first about asking to work, but I overcame that and just went for it, and it turned out to be so easy to get involved and fit in with the group that was working at the time. I think the people who work here, including present day, are really open towards others getting involved. It seemed more like Gilman offering me something rather than me offering Gilman something.

Jesse: It was about seven years ago and I was really impressed with the whole thing and started working at the next show. It was just such a comfortable place, it felt like a totally natural extention to then volunteer here. I'd been involved in other political groups previously and thought of Gilman as an "action" in itself. It was putting ideas/ideals into action, for the most part in positive ways. When I first got involved things were very "loose" here, a lot more out of control. For me though, those were the funnest times, I felt so connected with everyone. We'd meet at Gilman sometime during the week and then go out skating, whatever, together as a group. It was kind of like the "wild west", especially compared to now. Then, as different people came along to "run" things, it got more under control, more organized, more financially stable. Sometimes we were up to three months behind in rent. It's a lot more serious now, and in some ways, conservative. But it establishes balance and enables us to survive.

Clayton: I thought, "Wow, this is how it should be!" It was so much better than other places I was used to in LA. I felt like I could trust people here and felt comfortable. That was about a year ago. Then one night my friend Ed asked me to work and I've been working ever since. Now this is where my best friends are, this is where I spend my time. The meetings themselves weren't too intimidating, but some of the personalities were. But working with those people and getting to know them removed the intimidation, no matter how they came across in meetings, I could have my say just as much as they could. I think things are more balanced now than when I first started.

Ed: I first came here about 2 1/2 years ago from San Diego and thought it looked like a dump. But that was kinda cool because it didn't look like a club, it just looked like a space where bands play and people write shit all over the walls. It seemed honest and energetic, without the prepackaged feel of things like where I came from. I felt like I had to get involved, to keep things going, I was really impressed. Some things have gotten better since I've been here, some things have gotten worse. There's a lot more people involved now which is good, but on the other hand there's a lot more shit talking than how it used to be. And since there's so many people involved, it's now harder for new people to get involved. Now it seems like more of a solid hierarchy, I hate to apply that word to Gilman, but it does apply. It doesn't seem to me like anyone could start coming here and say that they want to get involved and start coordinating shows and actually have it happen. It's sad that there's a lot of politics at Gilman.

Sita: I first came here when I was seven! Then off and on till I was 13, then I started working here. I thought it was a lot of fun here, I loved the atmosphere, I loved the people, and the "look" of punk rock, they looked so different from everybody else. So I've been working here about 3 years now, just this past year I've started coordinating shows. When I first started working things seemed pretty bad, a lot of really violent shows, but over the years it's gotten a lot better, more under control. More people have gotten involved but not many of those have taken on much responsibility, like coordinating shows, etc.

Zarah: I first came here about 1 1/2 years ago, it was really overwhelming. The place looked really small, the staff members looked really intimidating, the crowd looked really big, and I felt scared to be there. But once I started talking to people and getting to know them it was okay. My friend started volunteering here, and then I started volunteering here, and I liked it a lot. You get to meet a lot of people. I've been working here about a year now. Over that year I think things have gotten better here as far as security/violence goes. It's more under control now.

Strengths/Weaknesses of the Space

Charles: Sometimes people lose their perspective. They become ego-oriented, competitive, jealous. It really brings things down. The strength is the unity, the working together, the fighting together to accomplish something worthwhile. Like when I first got here, there was next to nobody running the club, maybe 1 or 2 coordinators, 1 security person, and an irregular staff of volunteers. Now there's 3 or 4 coordinators on any given night, 2 stage managers, 2 or more security people, a regular volunteer staff, cleanup coordinator, booking staff, etc. Now it's much more of a team effort. We're all really anxious to have more people work here. Unfortunately, the more responsibility you take on, the more you become a target for criticism and nitpicking. Another change is that Gilman has never analyzed itself so closely before. We're able to better deal with problems now that we've never been able to deal with before—like sexism, homophobia, or harassment issues. There's greater awareness and greater commitment. It's a tough balance though, because with a larger staff there's a greater potential for infighting.

Ryan: There's still 2 shows here every weekend, bands get paid pretty reasonably, still $5 door, and neighborhood issues (like the brew-pub moving in next door) have shown that the zoning board of Berkeley and other community members think of Gilman as a valuable place to Berkeley.

Charles: We had over a hundred people show up to the zoning board meeting concerning the brew-pub to support us, lots of people got involved to ensure our survival. It was very inspiring. So we're still here, giving people opportunities to get involved, make what they want out of the place. What really gets me powered up isn't that bands play here, but that people get to have the opportunity to allow bands to play here, as well as having a space to do so many other things with as well. Every time the club changes hands it becomes a new club to a certain extent, with new opportunities for new people to get involved and learn that they have power, that they can do things, that they can produce something. Who cares if it's bands, an art show, or just using the place as a laundry room. For me it's not the performance itself, it's the organization. The means are much more important than the end result. It's not so much the physical changes in the club that's important as the mental changes in the people who work here. People are learning that they can control their own lives, they don't have to be victims all the time. So it doesn't matter if there's "just" punk shows here, it provides opportunities and examples.

Jesse: Being more organized allows more fairness. Dealing with others becomes a huge production. I think things are really good now. We co-founded the Gilman Street Merchants Association to help deal with neighborhood issues, we're financially sound, although sometimes I think it would be better if we weren't. We'd take more risks, gamble a little more. So many people have been brought up in the Gilman of now. The connection to the lean and mean days just isn't there. But it still really appeals to me in an ideological sense, plus I live really close, hah! One of the strengths, as well as one of the weaknesses, are the membership meetings. Weakness in the sense of when they turn into PC witchhunts, strength in the sense of anyone being able to attend and have

their say.

Clayton: Strengths are that the power is more distributed now. The head coordinator isn't the one making every decision, more people are involved. The membership meetings are a definite strength, that's where most of the decisions are made. Even decisions made outside of the meetings—booking for instance—consideration for the entire membership has to be kept in mind. I can't book or not book bands just because I like or dislike them, I have to think of everybody else as well. Weaknesses are how to deal with a person who's acting out of line. How to deal with it in a collective sense. Another strength is the kinship; sometimes I lose sight of it until I pull myself away from it, like when I realize I haven't spent time with anybody

who doesn't work here for a while. This is my family now, these are the people I trust more than anybody else, my best friends. The houses I've lived in have been "Gilman" houses, where everybody who lives there works at Gilman. I don't really come here because a certain band is playing, it's because my friends are here, even though I don't usually get to spend that much time with them because we're all working, just being around them is enough. Sometimes I fall into the feeling that if I don't do it, who else is going to. I think sometimes everybody feels that pressure, that if they're not here it's just not going to go right, but now I feel there's enough people that more people can take breaks or skip shows. It seems like more of a community effort, that if one person decides it's time to move on, another will step forward to fill their shoes. That's how it's been over the years.

Ed: The strengths and weaknesses are the people involved. Anyone can come to a meeting and work towards changing the

space towards what they want. I think it's harder now for people to find out about how Gilman works, how it's volunteer staffed and collectively run. I think that before, when there was a lot less people, you couldn't help but notice these things. You would walk in and say "You know, something's really different about this place, why is that?". And that's what made people really want to get involved, it was more open. It seems that since now we're more comfortable with our staff and the number of people who come here and volunteer, people aren't encouraged so much to try and get more involved. I think it's really important to make it clear to everyone that they can get involved, they should get involved, and that we want them to get involved.

Sita: Sometimes it's hard to be depended on, to feel like I have to be here. I didn't ask for that, but on the other hand, it can be fun too, it can be fun to have that responsibility, to feel needed, to be respected. It's a collective, it's all up to the membership, it's all up to you. You do it because you want to. I didn't know for the longest time that all I had to do was ask to take on more responsibility and do different things. I was always afraid to. I think more should be done to make it clear and easy for people who want to do more. Gilman provides this great place for people to go, to hang out, or learn things. It's a real nice social setting. It supports what you want to do as an individual. As far as the weaknesses go, it seems that the problems are more individual problems or little group problems, as opposed to involving the whole collective. Our landlord is a big part of why we've survived here, he's been so supportive. Also because of the city of Berkeley, it's open to things like this, I don't know if other areas of the country would be. This club has had more of an impact on the surrounding community than most people realize. I've worked at schools before and little kids know about it, and their parents are totally for it, things like that.

Zarah: Nitpicking and petty fights are a weakness. When I first started here things seemed very tight knit, it was a joy to see everyone every weekend. Now it's kind of become more like work and less like fun, but that seems to be getting better too. Strengths are us learning how to work together.

Things Learned/Gained Personally

Charles: I learned a great deal about organization, commitment, people, collectivism. Helping others is the best! It's one of the greatest rewards. Also, some of the other political groups I've been involved in just produced a lot of talk, Gilman produces results. We produce something every weekend. That's really rewarding too.

Clayton: I've become much less of an introvert, I've learned how to deal with people better, I've learned how to use authority without abusing it. Also I've learned how to do sound, mix bands, I had no

GILMANGILMANGILMANGILMANGILMANGILMAN

background in sound and probably would never have the opportunity anywhere else but here. I've learned how to adapt well and quickly. Like for booking, you become the sole representative of Gilman for these bands from all over the country, you have to treat these people fairly whether you like their band or lyrics or not, and try to be as helpful as you can. You become protective of the space, whether I'm signed up to work or not, I'm still thinking that way and keeping an eye out for things.

Ed: What I've learned mostly is that you can run a collective, you can get it to work, you don't have to stay within the traditional boundaries of what a club is supposed to be like.

Sita: I've learned how to run a place like this, I've learned how to go start a place like this on my own if I wanted to. I don't know if I could do it, but I would know how.

Zarah: I've learned how to calm myself down, how to talk to peop sponsibility, how it feels to be appreciated, confidence, realizing that it can't be all fun, sometimes it's work. It makes me happy that I can be a part of such a big thing, something way bigger than myself. I think I learn more here than at school. It's hard to balance what I see at Gilman with what I see at school. Like dealing with huge fights here, then going to school and having to listen to people talk about petty little things like boyfriend problems. It makes you grow up faster. If I didn't have Gilman I don't know what I'd be doing, probably freaking out or something.

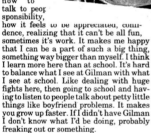

The Future

Charles: I'd like to see more things like the DIY festival, I'd like to see more things happen here other than just shows. I'd also like to see the perspectives of the people who work here extended beyond just the performance of shows. Another thing I'd like is a tighter bond amongst the people here, more communication, more understanding about what goes on between the various departments/committees, etc.

Jesse: I think the future holds being more of a political entity in the city. It's become an institution. Also, I'd like to see more weird stuff happen here, more crazy booking and mixing of bands. It amazes me that it's been here ten years.

Clayton: We book so far in advance it

seems like it will always keep going. As far as improvements go, we still need to improve on dealing with each other in a fair way. I'd like to see the development of the community space aspect go much further. I don't know how many times I've sat down and made up a list of things that I'd like to see happen here. I don't know if there's enough energy left over after just putting on the two shows a week for the people here to do much else, but I'd like to think so.

Ed: I'd like it to be run more as a collective. I'd like to see more of a decentralization of the power. The feeling like everyone is equal, there is no boss. I'd like to see more things happen than just shows. Shows are a huge part of what punk is all about, but I think a more important part is what people are actually doing to build the community, to actually do something besides just have a good time on the weekends. I think the most important thing for people to take into account is that anyone who comes here is a part of the club and they can do whatever they like with that. If, for them, being a part of the club means watching a band once a month, that's up to them, but, if for them, being a part of the club means they want to do something more with it, then they can. Don't be intimidated with the structure of the place.

Sita: I'd like to see more "regular" workers or new people get more involved, take on more responsibility, do more things, let us take more time off. I'd like to see more things like the DIY festival, I think we should support doing that kind of thing, not just at the Gilman space, but other places as well, expand more. We can't do it all ourselves, but we can teach others how to do it, and hopefully they'll survive, like we've survived.

Zarah: I'd like to see more things like the DIY festival, more things where we can act like a community. My favorite part about Gilman is the little things we do, like Haloween, decorating, costumes, things like that, or prom night, Christmas shows, that stuff makes me really happy. The future looks really positive to me.

DIY FESTIVAL

July 26, 27, 28 1996 924 Gilman held what I think has been its single most important event so far. It was called the "Do It Yourself" festival and offered roundtable discussions on zines/publishing, radio, venues, DIY businesses, booking, labels, and distribution. 30 to 60 people attended each workshop and it was inspiring to see organizations and individuals working together to improve and expand the community around them. What follows are thoughts from some of the people who made it happen. Brian Edge.

Brian: Where did the idea come from?

Charles: It's been a long standing idea of mine soon after I got involved with Gilman. I've been involved in the political activism community and there's lots of different conferences there, anarchist conferences, Food Not Bombs conferences, etc., and it seems there's a real active community that involves the DIY scene. It just seemed like the festival should happen, that people should come together, not just to educate others, but to create more of a sense of community. There's just too many people out there that are doing things that don't contact each other. I would say that the festival was a success, it needs more follow up, and it might be hard to maintain that, but we're encouraging people to do so. I tried to get others involved, but it was very difficult. For one thing, the staff here is pretty stretched as it is, and on top of that there were people who just didn't feel that it would work.

Brian: What made you feel it would work?

Charles: I've been involved in other collective/DIY projects and I feel there are shared values and similarities/interests that would enable us to all work together.

Ryan: I think this year the festival was mostly punk businesses/groups but there were a handful of organizations from outside the punk scene and hopefully we can expand on that in the future.

Charles: Underlying all the groups, a certain ideology exists, and that is the attempt to create an alternative community. There wasn't a conscious attempt on my part to bring in groups outside the punk scene, because in my mind, these groups are all similar and I don't see a lot of difference between Gilman and New Earth Press (a worker run collective) for instance, and the invitation was open to all. I think if we could understand the similarities better, we could operate ourselves better. I think we limit ourselves by claiming that the only people who share our ideology are those into punk. These other groups outside the punk scene have taken a lot of the ideas we also have and applied them to real life, working, operating, producing.

Brian: Where does the motivation come to try to work towards this change if you meet so much resistance just trying to have a meeting about it? Where does the energy come from to overcome such barriers even at the very beginning?

Charles: Because there are groups out there outside the punk scene that are cre-

GILMANGILMANGILMANGILMANGILMANGILMAN

ating and existing and there are fragments within the punk scene that are creating and existing and it's just a matter of persistence until people become aware of it and start working together. I think there should be an increased awareness of what supports us, and what supports us can be extended, and that there are other people out there that have the same ethics doing different things.

Brian: Do you think you've come to the realization that punk isn't going to accomplish very much by itself, that it needs as much support as possible from as many com-munities as possible?

Charles: I think that punk needs to stop thinking only about music and about cliques, and start includ-ing others with its ide-

olo-
gies
and be-
liefs, I
think it
needs to be
adult, so to
speak, and be
ready to grow out of
its adolescent phase.

Brian: Do you think that it will ever happen? It seems to have been that way since the beginning, then people get frustrated and then they leave completely, they don't work at trying to make things differ-ent, they just vanish.

Charles: I think people grow up and leave because there's no space for people who are moving into wanting to support themselves, not wanting to be living at minimum wage jobs for the rest of their lives and living in a house with everyone just turning 18 and being on their own for the first time. People want to be able to move on and grow and I think there needs to be space made for these people.

Brian: Do you reach a point where you get too frustrated because you're not accom-plishing what you thought you'd accom-plish when you first got excited and into things?

Ryan: As you get older you get a bit less myopic and you try to apply that enthusi-asm and energy to a larger view, a bigger plan, perhaps like starting a worker collec-tive or something to make a living off of.

Brian: One thing that wasn't brought up at the festival was the huge issue about making a living off of punk. Should people feel comfortable with that?

Charles: I think so. I think it's ridiculous to think that we should create an alterna-tive community, then have to step outside that community to work some shit job to

support that community. The community should be self supporting. If we all really believe in the things we espouse, than why shouldn't it be all inclusive of our lives, not only just our performance spaces and our music produc-tion, but our food and the maintenance of our lives, etc. Make a real, full alter-native to the rest of the world. Why not take the be-liefs you

have
and
apply
them to
all your life
rather than
just a section of
it. I'm against the exploitation that so often occurs making a living off punk. I think there's a definite differ-ence between exploitation and support-ing yourself.

Brian: With all the eagerness in the punk scene to point fingers at people who are supposedly doing "too well", what is "com-fortable", what's "too much", how would you come up with some kind of parameters as to what's exploitation and what's not?

Charles: I couldn't define it for anyone other than myself and the conditions I set for my own life. I think the fingerpointing

should be more at performance than at the money that someone is making. If someone is selling their product cheaply and help-ing small independent groups while mak-ing a good deal of money, more power to them. I think why some organizations should be volunteer oriented is the lack of efficiency. If Gilman was efficient and suc-cessful enough to have $5 doors, $2 mem-berships, and also pay a staff, I think it should do it. On the other hand, volunteer organizations are more capable of being community oriented, of involving more people, hiring oriented organizations have to be more selective, you can't hire every-one, staff will be limited. Some businesses you wouldn't be able to run on a volunteer basis, the motivation just wouldn't be there, neither would the commitment. People treat volunteer organizations like they can come and go and it doesn't mat-ter, but if you take on certain responsi-bilities, it does become like a job and you can't flake or someone else gets stuck with doing your job. In a work oriented world there's competition and if you can't fill the bill your business gets replaced by another that can.

Brian: Getting back to the festival itself, did you have cer-tain expecta-tions going in, were they met?

Charles: I think

it
went
awe-
some, I was
really im-
pressed, the
turnout was a lot
larger than I ex-
pected, people's feed-
back and energy levels
were a lot higher than I expected.

Ryan: The respect level was higher than I expected.

Charles: There were some people who I did expect more from. There were some "pillars of the community" who ei-ther didn't show up or contributed very little.

Brian: What would you like to see happen for the next one?

Charles: Different workshops, different topics. I'd like to see other organizations get involved and have them present their ideas. We might also experiment with dif-ferent formats, presentations in some in-stances rather than collective oriented, a tax workshop for instance. Roundtable dis-cussions are good for ideas, but actual factual content needs to be presented.

For more information or to contribute call (510) 524-8180 Friday afternoons or leave a message anytime.

Lindsay Krisel, Charles Long, Chris Sparks (top), and Mike Limon

"Save Our Neighborhood," Gilman Street Punkers Plead

Allowing new brew pub to move in across the street would be "like placing an adult bookstore across from the Catholic church."

By Karen D. Brown

It was a surreal night indeed. About seventy punk rockers sat quietly through a seven-hour Berkeley Zoning Adjustment Board hearing to protest, of all things, the presence of alcohol on their block.

Members of the Gilman Street punk-rock collective—their mohawks, flourescent hair, and multiple piercing looking splendid against the formal white plaster of the meeting room—put on their best bedside manner for the board. In two-minute turns, they talked about the unique inclusiveness of their club, 924 Gilman Street. They described the fragility of its substance-free pledge, and the already tense relationship between punks and

the rest of the world. But primarily, they urged the board to modify the use permit for a new micro-brewery in West Berkeley.

Seattle-based Hart Brewing Company, maker of Pyramid-brand beers, had applied to put an 82,000-square-foot manufacturing plant and 10,000-square-foot brew-pub at 901 Gilman Street, where a building has been standing abandoned for years. But across the street is 924 Gilman Street, a popular social spot for those under drinking age. The club doesn't allow drinking, at least in theory, in or around its premises.

Gilman members have no problem with the brewery itself, which could bring about 35 new jobs in light manufacturing to the area.

It's only the attached restaurant they fear will change the neighborhood's character. "It's a little ridiculous to put a Cadillac dealership across the street from a housing project," said Gilman Street member and local resident Freud Reia.

One fear is that a brew-pub on the block could make it impossible to keep alcohol away from 924 Gilman, threatening the club's very existence. "It's like placing an adult book store across the street from a Catholic Church," according to one young speaker.

What's more, 924 Gilman members revel in their counter-culture freedom, and they don't expect patrons of an upscale bar to be tolerant of their often eccentric looks and behavior. So they asked

By Ken Holt

the zoning board to recognize the club's precarious role in the community when considering the conditions of the brewery permit.

The city of Berkeley has its own incentive to protect the area from gentrification. The West Berkeley Plan restricts new retail development in West Berkeley as a way to keep rents affordable for light industry. But at 346 seats and 10,000 square feet, the brew-pub would be one of the largest eating establishments in Berkeley, similar in size to Spengers Fish Grotto; Hart Brewing argued that it needed that much restaurant space to offset other costs. The company has estimated hiring about fifty employees for the brew-pub.

The city's planning commission had recommended approval of the full space, concluding that the benefits of the brewery would excuse the impact of the restaurant—characterized as an "ancillary use" of the brewery.

At the hearing, "The zoning board listened to us and respected our issues," said Gilman Street's head coordinator, Charles Long. The protest was an important organizing tool for the club, Long said, and sent a message to its critics. "Most of the people who spoke are under 21. They were able to speak and present opposition to a very large corporation. The kids can do what they want to do. They can defend their own space. They can defend their own community."

"It was a good way to go before the zoning board in a positive way and say, 'Here are all the people supporting the club," agreed Mike Limon, 23, a club member who's also its former director. He remembers the last time Gilman Street members appeared before the zoning board. Three years ago, they successfully defended their own use permit after the board received complaints about noise, litter, and graffiti in the neighborhood. That's why club members this time wanted to make a pre-emptive strike.

Zoning board chairman David Blake said the young people's behavior was better than that of most protesters at public hearings, and, in fact, it was older people in

continued on page 22

the audience who had to be hushed for speaking out of turn. The club members made the point, Blake said, that abrasive looks don't always translate to bad attitude. "If there was a feeling of that, I think it was dissipated [at the meeting]," Blake said.

Besides, he added, Gilman Street has become a sort of sacred cow for city officials. "They're a *non-alcoholic* club for kids. Nobody wants to mess with that."

On a recent Saturday night, the crowd at 924 Gilman Street bobs near the stage to a raucous band appropriately called Loudmouth. "NO STAGE DIVING," warns a sign. One young couple takes a nap on a couch. "Masturbation 14 times a week is OK," reads a piece of graffiti. The Gilman Street Project was founded in 1987 by a group of punk-music lovers, who set it up as

a nonprofit, volunteer-run club. It's known nationwide for independent music, and has helped launch now-famous bands such as Green Day and Rancid.

Every Friday and Saturday night, five or six bands play for a cover charge of about $5. Anyone wishing to partake pays a one-time $2 fee to become a member. Members can attend biweekly meetings to discuss the future of the club, which doubles as a community center and site for various workshops on issues such as AIDS and alcoholism.

The no-alcohol rule is how the club keeps its doors open to all ages, but collective members admit that alcohol is still a problem at the club. "It's controlled chaos, the way it is," admits Long, a 25-year-old who doesn't drink. "We have no way of grading people by their intoxication," Long told the zoning board. "We're not going to sit there with a Breathalyzer." Introducing a pub across the street, he says, "is going to make my job a hundred times harder."

Paula Ruiz, sixteen, is circulating a petition against the pub outside the club's doors. She gestures towards a liquor store two blocks away. "People are going to drink here, no matter what we do," she admits. "But it would bring in more people and cause more trouble."

In fact, Paul Santos, 21, who drove in from San Leandro for a Gilman show, says the brew-pub would make drinking more convenient. "We wouldn't have to walk all the way up the street."

Gilman members also fear that alcohol could exacerbate what is likely to be a culture clash. Show-goers span the economic and fashion spectrum, but the club is meant to be a haven for punk fans and the otherwise alienated—in fact, it's supposed to be a sanctuary from the very people they say go to brew-pubs. "I don't like sports and I don't like jockos," says member Chris Donohue, eighteen.

John Stoddard, Hart Brewing's spokesman at the zoning hearing, said such assumptions have been overblown. "The restaurant has been misconstrued as some kind of yuppie hang-out," he told the board. "It's a family establishment."

Gilman members question that distinction. "I think it's quite obvious it's not going to be Gilman fare," said Long. "This is a micro-brewery and a bar. All you have to do is go to Bison [Brewery] or Jupiter and use them as an example."

Gilman members are also worried about behavior of their own people. "It's a rebellion community," Long said. "We don't control each other."

"Look at the people in this room," Donohue added at the meeting. "You think they're respectable? Wait until you see the rest of them. They're crass and abrasive."

con't from previous page

Club members worry that if relations get out of control, the police are likely to pay 924 Gilman Street unwanted attention; they asked the zoning board for guarantees that people with pierced lips and orange buzz cuts won't automatically be blamed for neighborhood tension. The board agreed to draw up a statement declaring equal responsibility among the parties if fights break out or vandalism occurs. "It's something we can at least establish in the record," Planning Director Marks said. "I don't know what authority we have."

The club already employs two security guards to help discourage clashes in the neighborhood. The zoning board required Hart Brewing to do the same.

Deputy Police Chief Roy Meisner said he welcomes a more upscale influence in the neighborhood. "When it looks tawdry, that's when crime is more prevalent." Club members' tolerance of the brew-pub crowd, he added, will be critical. "I would hope that people at 924 won't hold it against them if they come to check out the music."

For his part, Stoddard promises that Hart Brewing's doors will be open to club members, whatever their attire. "Everyone in that club that's over 21 is a potential customer of ours."

But integration, even peacefully done, may not be an unmitigated gain; Gilman members don't particularly want to expand their appeal. "We're worried we'll become another Berkeley Square," Long said.

By the zoning hearing's end, Hart got most of what it asked for. The zoning board approved the permit, but required Hart Brewing to meet every month with Gilman representatives and go through dispute resolution before the restaurant opens. To deal with the new crowds, Hart will also have to spend about $200,000 on a new traffic signal and street lighting, and hire two security guards to keep bar customers under control. The company will provide about sixty parking spaces for patrons, but its staff will park on the street. The zoning board did not, as Gilman members asked, require the company to reduce the size of the restaurant, close it earlier than 11:00 p.m., or limit off-premises beer sales.

Long said the club considered appealing the board's decision with the City Council, but Blake convinced them that this was probably the best deal they could expect.

The next step is living together. Mike Limon has volunteered to be the club's liaison with Stoddard in the wake of the tense zoning fight. "It's going to be hard for [some club members] to shift gears and work with him," Limon said. "I'm a professional now. I have a nice pair of pants and a shirt, so I can talk to the guy."

Above article taken from *East Bay Express* 11/24/95

HArd-CoRe HeAveN

No part-time punks allowed at Berkeley's Gilman Street nightclub

By JOE GAROFOLI
Staff writer

When two East Bay punk bands returned home for gigs this month, they remembered their roots. But those memories have as much to do with the ethic they learned inside a tiny, red-brick building in Berkeley called 924 Gilman

BRIAN ROBINSON, 23, and Angelique Gibbons, 21, share a hug during a break between bands at Gilman Street. Both are from Modesto.

Street as their working class upbringings in Rodeo and Albany.

Inside that club, the heart of punk rock tries to remain pure despite the tempting offers waved by commercialism. An all-ages, no-alcohol club where young punkers won't pay more than five bucks to thrash away to bands like Spitboy, Swinging Utters and Nuclear Armed Hogs.

But there's a slight problem. Ever since Rodeo's own Green Day became a multi-platinum-selling band last year, you can't pick up a copy of Rolling Stone, Spin or other mainstream magazines without some mention of the 600-person, general admission venue a few miles west of the UC-Berkeley campus. This collective, run solely by volunteers, has become one of the meccas of the punk-rock revival. Bands from Japan, Hawaii, England and the Czech Republic are playing there now, along with local punkers cutting their teeth. Foreigners stop by in mid-afternoon to just see the place.

Yeah, the occasional record company rep has popped in, the regulars concede sheepishly. The good news is that increased attention has helped the collective buy a computer several months ago for business. But there's a rub under 924 Gilman's studded collar: They want to preserve their

■ THIS WEEKEND

Friday: Juke, Media Blitz, Wet-Nap.
Saturday: A.F.I., Heckle, Struggle Buggies, the Force.
$5 plus $2 annual membership. 525-9926.

Please see **CLUB**, Page 2F

Club

FROM PAGE 1F

enclave, but not be seen as hostile to young kids looking for a place to listen to music each weekend.

As Gilman's answering machine message says, "we do not book racist, sexist or homophobic bands or major label bands or bands that don't know anything about Gilman." Next to a sign at the entrance listing the unwanteds is a hand-written note adding "and hippies."

"They've taken great pains not to be (commercial)," says Richard Gargano, aka Lucky Dog. He's a punker who grew up in Pinole and San Pablo, and has played Gilman probably 40 times. "It changes things if MTV is coming in every weekend to show what's cool about punk rock. It makes people plastic and fake. People would just start posing for the cameras instead of just hanging out."

Inside it's a punker's playhouse. Spray-painted band names, designs and random "verse" cover every square inch of the walls, ceilings and cross-beams. Before a show, punkers drape themselves over beaten up couches randomly strewn about a space roughly the size of eight single-car garages.

On card tables in the back, you can buy independent discs, tapes and T-shirts from bands like Krupted Peasant Farmerz. You can buy soda, chips or candy in a small room near the back. And yeah, you see a lot of colored hair in the crowd, which ranges from mid-teens to early 20s, depending on the show. Nearly everybody is pierced somewhere and most of the fashions here can't be found on the racks at Macy's.

Part of the punk ethos is that you don't "sell out" — compromise your core values for attention, power or the almighty buck. Even being perceived that way can be dangerous. Ask Jello Biafra. In May 1994, the Dead Kennedys' frontman — a punk pioneer who probably wouldn't be considered a sell-out by most mainstream definitions — broke his leg inside the club after he got caught up in some errant slam-dancing.

What happened next depends on whom you ask. Some say once the slammers found out who he was, Biafra was kicked in the head, beaten and called a sell-out. Gilman insiders say club regulars came to his aid, and attribute the incident to newcomers, unfamiliar with the club — kids who think they're punk because they have a mohawk and a lip ring. Crowds are younger there now (more 13 and 14-year-olds) and some longtimers scoff at the newcomers' ignorance of the punk ethic.

"Punk rock is cool now," says Ross, a 23-year-old San Franciscan who has come here once or twice a month for the last four years. "Two years ago, these are the same guys who listened to Heavy D. Some jock who thinks that it's cool to take people out in the mosh pit. I can see that there may be people who are trying to find out what works for them. That's fine. But don't wreck my scene if you're doing it."

Some of the longtimers who've hung at Gilman since its inception seven years ago wrestle with that conflict in the face of increasing media attention. Everybody interviewed for this story insisted that they were speaking as individuals and not for the club. J. Freud Reia, a volunteer at the club, predicts that once the punk resurgence fades, the posers will disappear.

"That cycle will go away," Reia says. "That's fine, either way. When you're dealing with Gilman Street, you're going to be left with the people who are still standing when that change happens. It's a lifestyle choice. Some of the kids who are doing it now will end up making it a lifestyle choice to live outside the mainstream, and some won't."

But once you've donned the trappings of the mainstream, it's difficult to return. This month, two alumni who helped expose the "Gilman scene" to a wider audience through their international success returned to the Bay Area. And they did a couple of things that reflected the punk ethic in 1995 terms.

Rancid, featuring two former Albany High School students, cut prices to $10 for each of the two shows they played at the Fillmore in San Francisco. That's half the price of most Fillmore shows and probably far less than a band that performed on "Saturday Night Live" the previous month could fetch.

Green Day, which played the Oakland Coliseum Arena two weeks ago, cut ticket prices to $15. That's pretty much unheard of for an arena show, especially by a band featured on the cover of a recent edition of Rolling Stone. Both of these bands remember the old days. Before they played for thousands, both played for dozens of punkers at Gilman.

A longtime Gilman regular, who personally knows members of Rancid and Green Day, echoes what many feel: "I'm really happy for those guys and their success," says 24-year-old Nondo Lopez, the head of security at Gilman.

But to the regulars, the spirit of Gilman will always be more important than the performers who have moved beyond. Older regulars talk about preserving Gilman "for the kids."

That desire still motivates 19-year-old Ed Easton. One of the first places Easton sought out when he moved to Berkeley from San Diego was 924 Gilman. Now he coordinates events there. He's into the music, but he's also into the soul of the place.

"I've been to a lot of places that are sort of like this and they're all usually run by owners who just want to make money," Easton says. "This is as close to the ideal as it gets."

Above article taken from the *West County Times* 12/27/95

Artist unknown

CHAPTER EIGHT

BATTLE #3

CHRIS S.

1997-2000

"GILMAN GAVE ME THE FEELING THAT WE COULD DO ANYTHING."

—CELIA S.

2001   photo by Lauren L.

CHRIS S.

I first started at Gilman in late 1994, at a Zafio Records showcase. I got to talking with one of the people working the Gilman record table, and he invited me to help work the record table. I ended up working at Gilman almost every weekend for the next five or so years, in various capacities, ultimately as head coordinator of the place. It came at a point in my life where there wasn't a whole lot else going on, and my sister and my roommate were working at Gilman all the time and I would go there with them. At first I didn't really see it as an important place, I just liked having something to do and having somewhere to go where I felt comfortable. Starting out working at the record table turned out to be a good way to go for me. It was low-key and low-stress, and I could meet all the "regulars" and get to know people gradually. I'm not really comfortable socially in large groups of people, so working there gave me a way to meet people on my own terms. I was impressed that I could feel as comfortable there as I did. I could be depressed, unemployed, pathetic even, and work there, contribute there, and not be judged or put down. I was at a real low point in my life, really struggling for answers, and being at Gilman really helped me keep myself together, gave me focus. It ended up turning out the opposite of what I initially thought of the place. I didn't have to worry if my hair wasn't spiked, or I didn't have a mohawk, or whatever. People there accepted me as I was, I didn't have to be afraid of being an "outsider." I wasn't really that involved in the punk scene before I started working at Gilman. It was a good introduction, not necessarily to the music, but to the activist/constructive side.

Eventually the other people involved with the record table dropped out or moved elsewhere in the club, and I ran it. After about four to six months I started stage managing. I liked that because I enjoyed meeting all the bands, getting to know the people in them, hearing their tour stories, etc. It was fun, I was like the club's "host," the "maitre d'." Another of the things I liked about the club was that we seemed to do everything the "wrong" way or the "hard" way. Everything that would have been a really good idea for us to do, we refused to do, including more liberal policies, guarantees, more than just water for the bands, etc., and this was done purely out of stubbornness. I thought it was great, it kept us small, it kept us real. I don't think bands should have to "hurt" to play at Gilman, but there's other venues for those who want more than we were willing to give them. And I think most of the bands who play at Gilman understand that. They understand that they'll be playing to 15 to 22-year-olds who can't afford big ticket prices to see arena shows. And a lot of these fans are people who want to see bands that can't play at bigger, more established clubs in this area.

I don't really remember how the transition to head coordinator came about. I started getting more involved in the politics of the club, and Charles L., the head coordinator at the time, and I started talking a lot about the place during the shows. The last six months or so that Charles was there I could tell he wasn't very happy. It was really hard for him to be enthusiastic anymore and it was uncomfortable for me. (Ironically, the same thing happened between me and the head coordinators after me, Sammy and Jemuel, a few years later when I was stepping down. I turned into a real asshole and was hard to be around. It was definitely time for me to go). Also, Charles had a forty hour a week job by then, so I started working with him more and more at the club, helping him out and learning the head coordinator position. It was something I was interested in doing and seemed like a natural transition, although, to be honest, if there had been someone else that really wanted to do it, I never would have done it. I had never been exposed to the dealings of a small business within the community and its interaction with local politics. Seeing us represent ourselves before the city zoning board, like during the brew pub and DiCon issues, was amazing to me. I had never really thought about that route being available to "ordinary" people, let alone a bunch of ragtag kids. Ending up as head coordinator at Gilman kinda followed along with my understanding of collectives—responsibility tends to fall on those who are ready to take it on. I was ready to take on that responsibility when Charles moved on to other things. It wasn't something I actively pursued, it just happened that way. And that was an adorable aspect of the club, there were no specific qualifications necessary, just having the desire to learn and commit was enough. Also, I was fortunate enough to be there during a time when we had a lot of regular, experienced volunteers. That made things a lot easier for me, I had a lot of support. That's one aspect of the history of the club to point out, that the head coordinator gets a lot of credit, but there's a number of other people involved that have so much to do with the successful running of the place. There were a number of nights where I'd just show up and not have to do a thing; the other folks ran the shows just fine.

Gilman was my main focus most of the years I was there. I wasn't really interested in doing much else. It was my social life, my responsibility, my job. For a couple years or so, it was the only thing I did. I ended up being known as "Chris from Gilman," that's what people associated me with, that's where they knew me from, it gave me an identity. I had a great time working with a number of the people there—that's what I really enjoyed, getting to know some really great people. I also really enjoyed seeing these people come into their own over the years there, seeing their confidence build, seeing the transition from kids to adults, enjoying the camaraderie, the atmosphere. My favorite times at Gilman were sitting in the side room/office after a big or hectic show, when everyone had gone except for the workers, and just basking in that sense of relief, as well as accomplishment, of having gotten through it. These were people I probably never would have met otherwise, and now, through these experiences together, were people that I'm never going to forget. I remember the little social events we had for the workers too, movie nights, etc., those were great—no bands, no general public, just us. My impression of the club is that it was started up for the public and the bands, but in my opinion, it's really all about the people who work there, those are the people to whom the place matters most.

There were a few things that changed or were fine-tuned while I was there. We expanded the number of bookers from two or three to about eight or so, revamped the store, started a dedicated neighborhood cleanup, put up flyers from our shows in the office to give the place a little sense of history, stuff like that. DiCon was a big battle, and I don't know what would have happened to us without John H., he was vitally important. That struggle also really changed how we dealt with the neighborhood in general—there was a lot of PR we had to do to survive, it wasn't just security and cleanup. I tried to be as accomodating and open to DiCon, Pyramid, our difficult neighbor at the end of the block, etc., as I could. I knew impressions were important and I tried to present Gilman as being a responsive and concerned part of the community, rather than a rebellious, antagonistic thorn in everyone's side. I think it was good in a lot of ways for DiCon to call us on our shit—it made us take responsibility for problems we were, in fact, responsible for. It forced us to come togther and actually work at being the "good neighbor" we thought we were. I felt a lot of pressure during that time, a lot of fear that we would be shut down. I panicked and didn't really know how to deal with it at all. I remember making some pretty ridiculous, over-reactionary flyers and things like that. Luckily there were some really level-headed people at the club who helped us through it all.

Gilman was basically really simple for me. I needed to find certain people that I could relate to and find something that I could work at, and toward, and Gilman provided that for me. Also, I could just step in and help with an established, existing place, I didn't have to create it from scratch. I feel that all the head coordinators before me really had to fight to create and shape the place—I just was able to continue what they had set up, and I really benefitted from that. I really don't know who I'd be right now if it wasn't for Gilman. I definitely got more out of Gilman than I put in. How can I put a value on being given a new life, or a life in the first place? No amount of work given back would equal that. And I did put a lot of hours in. I felt I wouldn't really have any authority over anyone, or the right to tell anyone what to do, unless I put in more hours than anyone else. I felt like I should be the first person to get there and the last one to leave, so if I asked someone to walk down the street and pick up bottles, they wouldn't be inclined to say, "Well, I don't see you doing it, so why should I?" I thought that's how management should act—if you want people to have respect for you, then you should put in twice the effort as anyone else. Of course, towards the end of my time there, that was a lot harder for me, and I ended up getting burned out and being there less and less. I think the people who take on this much responsibility want to overexert themselves and burn out, to a certain degree, because it's the only way out, the only way to break the ties, beat the guilt, once you're in so deep. And, of course, it gets tiring dealing with the same complaints over and over, too: bands aren't getting enough money, people can't drink, etc., everyone takes the place for granted. I was head coordinator for about three or four years, but the last year or so, I wasn't doing very much. I used to worry a lot that once I left, the place would fall apart, that no one would step up and take over. But of course, someone did. There always seems to be someone that comes along with the same enthusiasm and same feelings that you once had, and is willing to put the time and effort in to keep the place going.

Another negative aspect of working there was that it kinda ruined music for me. I remember when I first started going to shows that I was so excited about a lot of bands. But after working at Gilman for years, and seeing all those shows, I'm at the point where I don't really care anymore. I can't really sit through a show anymore. After about fifteen or twenty minutes I need to go do something else. And I've been conditioned to always feel like I'm working security. If a fight breaks out, even if it's someplace other than Gilman, my first reaction is to go and calm people down and break it up.

I feel a little empty now, not having something to work on. Of course, it would be a lot harder for me now to find the time to do something like that, since I'm working a regular forty-hour week. It's a lot like a relationship. It's something that becomes a part of you, and when it's over, it's scary to have to go out and try to find something else to fulfull those same needs. So, despite the fact that I felt really burned out and not really happy with the place when I left, and that I have a hard time going back there now, a part of me is still waiting for the call to go back. If no one wanted to be head coordinator anymore, I feel like I would have no choice but to go back there and do it. That feeling and that devotion, to a certain extent, is still there.

RACHEL SIEBERT

PUNK ROCK PRAXIS: WOMEN AT 924 GILMAN STREET

I arrived at Gilman early to set up sound equipment. I put my motorcycle helmet and jacket away and went up on stage to put mics in stands. None of the other sound volunteers wanted to work the show; one said he couldn't stand the amount of testosterone the headlining band generated, another didn't particularly like hardcore, so my Friday night was set.

The doors opened at eight and slowly people began to arrive. Piles of drum kits, amps, and electric guitars came in. The opening bands began to play and kids shuttled in and out; in to watch a band, out to their hot-boxed cars to drink from bagged bottles and smoke pot. This was usual at Gilman on weekend nights. As the evening went on, more inebriated men came in. Women with high hair and dark lip-liner were under their arms. They stood at the sidelines of the dance floor while the guys pulled off their shirts exposing homemade tattoos of gothic letters O.B.H.C. (Oakland Brand HardCore) and threw their fists around on the dance floor, running in circles and yelling. The music was fast and aggressive. Between two songs the lead singer spoke to the crowd about the importance of scene unity— "We all have to work together in order for hardcore to exist!" The band ripped into a song about kids who look hardcore but do stupid shit and give the scene a bad name. The anger in the club was as thick as the sweat that came off their bodies.

> I just want to objectify my girlfriend, I like her because she is hot between the sheets, I just want to show her off at parties, and dress her up as if she walks the streets.
> —Tribe 8, "Manipulation"

The set ended and the band cleared the stage so the last one could get on. I was in the sound booth setting levels on the board when I looked out to the stage to see if the next band was ready. Staring back at me was a full-sized female blow-up doll. I was stunned. Before running on stage to pull off heads, I mentally reviewed my options: a) find the guy who booked the show and tell him to get the doll off the stage, or b) do it myself. I got out of the sound booth, seething, and approached the stage.

"Excuse me, what the fuck is going on?" I asked the bassist, behind clenched teeth.

"What do you mean?" he looked at me briefly before pulling his bass out of its case.

"The doll," I said pointing out the obvious.

"Oh that. It's just a joke."

"I don't find it funny, and I would like you to get it off the stage." I was not containing the anger in my voice very well.

"It's just a joke," he said again, turning his back to me to tune his bass.

"I don't find it fuckin' funny!"

I climbed on stage and moved toward the doll. The lead singer caught my motion and came toward me. What would this take? I thought.

"Aren't the implications of this real obvious? What do you think you are telling your audience?" I asked, after he tried to explain himself out of the situation. I got nowhere. The bassist looked at me like I was a bitchy militant feminist. He was totally drunk and had no logical facilities at his disposal. As I was about to walk away, Celia came up behind me wearing a Gilman Security shirt. She stood taller than any five-foot woman I had ever seen. She was backed by Dolce, and Sita was one step behind them. Sita caught the doll after the bassist finally flung it off stage.

> Good girls don't, but I do, and just because I do it don't mean I want to with you. Good girls don't, but I do, motherfucker don't fuck with me or you'll be through, I'll kill you.
> — Raooul, "Good Girls Don't, But I Do"

Back in the sound booth, I begrudgingly ran sound for their set. They opened with an explanation about the doll and an apology. After the show was done, I cleaned up the sound equipment and told another volunteer about the incident.

"It doesn't surprise me," he said, with a raised eyebrow, "the last time they played here you were on stage setting up mics for the drummer and he had his eyes down your tank top the entire time."

At the front entrance of Gilman there is a statement painted on the wall which reads that no racism, sexism, or homophobia is tolerated in the club. The bands that are booked there cannot be signed to a major label record company, for the sole purpose of supporting independent labels and entrepreneurs in a small scene, rather than supporting corporate America. For more than a decade, Gilman has been pivotal in the development and continuation of a scene that takes the time to question American values, create great music, and have fun.

In this moment, I want to document what some of the values are around Gilman, said or unsaid, whether they just get lip-service or are actually lived. Specifically, I want to address the values around gender and sexism at Gilman as they are experienced. At the beginning of 1999, I acquired the position of sound coordinator at Gilman. Because I am now more engaged in the club than I ever have been, I have the chance to see the vital role women play in the club and how the values around Gilman enable us to be seen in a scene that is historically sexist. This essay is written from my personal experience; in no way am I speaking for, or on the behalf of, the Gilman community. The values I talk about are ones that are the most reoccurring themes I have noticed at Gilman, but may not express the personal views of some of the members. I have been a Gilman member since I was thirteen and it is through this community, intertwined with music and politics, that I have found my voice as a woman.

Punk was first publicly acknowledged on a large scale when the Sex Pistols became popular in the 1970s for their vulgar appearance and language. They proved to be a media blitz and disappeared from the public eye like a flaming bag of dogshit. However, their influence still exists. They questioned societal and political systems through anger, aggression, cynicism, and suicide, which characterize punk to this day. (I use the term punk loosely to encompass a myriad of sub-groups in a musical underground that incorporates many nuanced factions). Recently there

> Remember, punk is more than teenage rebellion.
> — Filth, "The List"

has been a recurrence of punk culture in pop-culture that is stereotyped with morbid fashions such as black fingernails and brightly colored hair. Sadly, not much of the political flavor of punk has reached mainstream media except for Marilyn Manson t-shirts sporting slogans such as "Kill your parents," though this hardly touches the punk values I have learned at Gilman. But then again, people tell me Gilman is a very special place. Fashions and fads come and go, attendance and volunteer support for shows waxes and wanes, but Gilman is still a strong influence both in the local punk rock community and in larger contexts.

Contemporary music in general, rock 'n' roll in particular, and punk rock specifically, are male-defined and generated. Simon Reynolds and Joy Press, in their book *Sex Revolts: Gender, Rebellion and Rock 'n' Roll* (1), describe with great detail and theory the historical sexism in rock and punk. They noticed that while Iggy Pop was exploring the homoerotic side of musical idolatry, bands like the Clash were defining masculinity as a brother-in-arms, fight-to-the-death, "response to the pains of post-industrial adolescence." (2) Both sides are androcentric and neither side of this framework addresses women as anything more than minor characters in a play written, produced, cast, and staged by men. Most of the time, women are relegated to the role of groupies who desire male performers for their music, are had at will by the rocker, but possess little agency themselves. This is the gendered foundation of both rock and punk, which form an immediate barrier for the female participants in the scene.

When I was thirteen, I found that I was turned off by the lyrically empty music I heard on the radio. A friend of mine introduced me to a band that lived in my own neighborhood and had lyrics about how alcohol affected their families, and how they felt put out in school. I gravitated toward them because they had words for the problems I was dealing with. For my first show, I told my mom I was going to an eighth grade dance but cut out to go to Gilman, just two blocks away from my middle school. My friends and I paid the two dollars for our membership cards, another five bux for the show, and walked in. My eyes adjusted to the dim light and I

> Father passed out again, passed out on the couch again, I left home at an early age, I had to get far away.
> — Downfall, "New Regulations"

looked around at the crowd. I immediately felt young and awkward. When I was in high school and hanging around Gilman, I would call the pre-pubescent kids in the crowd Cabbage Patch punx. I felt that tension then, but more clearly I remember what was on stage. From the back of the room I could see a large banner of bones in the shape of a fish behind an all-guy band. A clear and strong bass line thumped through me. My friends and I could only stay a little while before our mothers would be waiting to pick us up in front of the school, and we left before the headlining band. But that did not matter, I did not care who I was watching, I just wanted to be at Gilman. Six years later, I figured out that I saw Fishbone my first night at Gilman, and they weren't even headlining. Because the originators of Gilman established it as a non-profit organization and a collective, small bands who had no chance of being heard on corporate radio flourished around Gilman. Gilman was the space where their voices were heard, and I heard them.

> From across the room I spotted him there, I said, come here baby, then I grabbed his butt and decided OOOOh yeah, so I took him to my car and exploited him there... took him to a party, showed him off on my arm, I said give me some head bitch, so he did... made him take me home, he tried to kiss me good night, I said, lay off baby, I'll call you later, but I never did.
> — Raooul, "I Had Richie Bucher"

Right out of middle school, five friends of mine started a band called Raooul. They played shows at Gilman and eventually came out with a seven inch record on a well known independent local label. When I was living in Washington, I met a few young women who were familiar with the group even though it was already five years since the band broke up and it was based two states away. Raooul disintegrated within two years of playing together, a flash in the pan as far as longevity goes for bands, but they still resonate in the underground punk community. This is in part due to the fact that they had good distribution for their record, but another aspect of their attraction is that they were all fifteen years old and able to communicate vital parts of their lives through music. American society does not teach young women to have a voice, much less use that voice to address topics like objectification. "I Had Richie Bucher" is a disturbingly self-conscious song written as an inversion of a scenario women face when being sexually objectified by men. The song is about a girl using a boy, who happens to be older and established in the Gilman scene, for sexual favors and discarding him in the end.

Although Gilman struck me as a haven when I was a teenager, I realize now that it is caught between the sexist history of punk and the freedom that its space conceivably creates for women. This is layered under the sexism inherent in American patriarchical politics, capitalism, and the greater American society whose values touch Gilman simply because the people who make Gilman are raised in America. Conceptually, the absence of making music for the sole purpose of profit creates a space where the raw truth of sexism in society can be addressed. The truth hurts and does not make a lot of money in record sales, so it is filtered out in corporate capitalism. Functioning within a collective and not in a hierarchy, women have a greater chance to be a part of the process and the creation of the Gilman scene rather than being relegated to a minor role. Business meetings at Gilman are bi-monthly, democratic, and open to anyone who wants to be involved. Limited access to money and political exclusion have historically contained women in America. Even though Gilman obliterates those two factors of sexism, women are still objectified within the club. It is then apparent how socialized people are to doubt the abilities of women.

At the same time that Gilman is a place where women can employ many different roles, people are still disrespectful of them. If I run the sound system with a man, bands address him for assistance before they approach me. In this situation I feel like I am either being disregarded or am invisible. Because punk is a boy's club, I am often looked past. Conversely, I had to explain to a fellow (male) volunteer why I should not have to wear less revealing clothes if someone in a band is looking down my shirt when I am doing my job. While my technical abilities are overlooked, I am treated as a spectacle. This is no different than what women face outside of Gilman, but at least in Gilman I have the social mobility to do something about it.

> Baby... you got wings to fly, but you won't say goodbye, 'cause in my latest rage, I bought you a cage.
> — Victim's Family, "Caged Bird"

Bands communicate through songs, writers communicate through words, and workers communicate through actions. I believe that the presence of so many women doing intricate jobs enables Gilman to function, and is in itself a profound protest to sexism. Gilman is a small fraction of punk rock, and an even smaller fraction of the United States, but it is very influential for what it represents. Kids who come to punk shows also live and function in society. They are not just reclusive alcoholics, pale junkies, or aggressive anarchists. They have jobs and go to school. Some even pay their parking tickets. So if someone recognizes me as a woman with technical ability and responsibility, they will take that into the other parts of their lives. During one hardcore show, a singer in a band from the east coast was speaking in between songs about how he was not racist, homophobic or sexist, "except for girls with mustaches," he said, "I hate girls with mustaches." I heard this, I fumed, and disappeared into the ladies room with a thick, black pen and drew a big, curly mustache on my face. As soon as his set was done I was on stage, with the mustache, to set up for the next band. He looked at me and his chin dropped to the ground. Other band members began to apologize profusely for their singer's comment. When my friend got back from Washington, DC six months later, she told me that the incident had made news in the east coast grapevine.

> I can not learn to walk until I learn to crawl, but I'll have to kick and pound to break this fucking wall
> — Good Grief, "Why Wait?"

Seven years of being influenced by local punk music, intense voices, and hard working volunteers has supported me and many other women in punk rock. We do not exist in a vacuum and are influential to each other and larger society. We are seen and will continue to be seen, and will grow stronger through the tension that exists within punk and its own self-critical awareness of sexism.

(1) Simon Reynolds and Joy Press, *Sex Revolts: Gender, Rebellion and Rock 'n' Roll*, Harvard University Press, Cambridge, 1995.
(2) William Finnegan, "Rocket Science," *The New Yorker*, November 16, 1998.

Above: 1991   photos by Susan S.

Entrance to penisland? Photo by Larry W.   **1987   photo by Cammie T.**

LEIGH VEGA

July, 1996

Claire had naturally red hair, was creative and outspoken, and was 16 years old. She behaved in a way that reflected her undeniable beauty and possessed one important characteristic that drew me to her: like the tides of an attractive and stunning sea, her confidence was guaranteed to always claw its way repeatedly up the stretch of any coast.

I was an equally attractive 16-year-old, dark-haired, opinionated, and incomprehensively outspoken (I had a French accent that overshadowed any point I tried to make with a European past I was having trouble leaving behind). I was confident, but needed someone to understand my points, then translate and dictate them to the outside world on my behalf; that's how Claire fit so perfectly into my life, carrying my ideas and energy on the crest of every wave.

November, 1996

Claire and I visited the Gilman Street Project for the first time. She was operating under the pretense that it was a mecca for punk rock and all those that operated in alliance with its underground movement. I had only heard of it through the tales of traveling punks in France whom referred to it as "le temple des toilettes degoutant," or, in English, the "temple of the disgusting bathrooms."

We arrived, did not volunteer, and danced in the middle of a nearly motionless semi-circle. There were butt-flaps and mohawks. There was a ska band. There was moshing tame enough that she and I could participate and remain unscathed. We found ourselves terribly happy and beaming with sweat. I, who expected nothing, and Claire, who expected everything, left equally satisfied. That is because Gilman is, and always will be, a malleable and entrancing figment of every respective imagination.

July, 1999

I was moving out to the Bay Area for college. I had learned more about the history of Gilman and began to feel its relevance and importance increase with every connection I made. It happens to everyone, I suppose: the tendency to view Gilman as a place you can go to become part of something bigger than yourself, to depend on it to make you part of the bigger picture. To maybe even shape and mold it and leave a mark that people who come after you will admire and revere.

Folklore.

To be part of the tall tale.

Claire had become a Hare Krishna, my French accent had long since deteriorated, and I suddenly felt an incredible weight on my shoulders to make a mark on Gilman. I decided that I didn't want to watch the show anymore—I wanted, desperately, to be part of what ran it.

November, 1999

Every evening, after I had been assigned my volunteer position for the night, I would walk down the street and sit on a log by myself, waiting for the show to start. It had been harder than I suspected to talk to people. And nobody talked to me. It was easier to sit down the street on the log than to attempt social interaction with a seemingly impenetrable group of punk rockers. How had it happened that when I was 16, I was free and outspoken and confident, but now at 21 I was intimidated and nervous and shy?

I attributed the change to the introduction of a new and fundamental element of the Gilman experience: The Side Room.

The side room carries with it tremendous myth and mystique. It is where the workers hang out during the show. It is significantly quieter than the rest of the club. Its walls are plastered with flyers of old shows, each adding to the weight of Gilman's importance, surrounding you, holding the room up.

I didn't get my first kiss there. I didn't find myself there. I was petrified. I felt unguarded and tiny because I couldn't think of anything worthwhile to say to what was supposed to be my community but somehow remained unapproachable and intimidating. I thought that if I had Claire there, I might be more comfortable. I felt like I needed something confident there to save me from drowning, to push me, gasping for air, up that deafeningly quiet shore.

July, 2001

Smitty and I met in college. If Claire's confidence had been the tides, then Smitty was a buoy; floating, anchored, attractively bright. Much like the 16-year-old me, he didn't really care what Gilman thought of him. He started coming down to volunteer, and while he wouldn't get me to the shore, his friendliness at least kept my head above water. Cool, calm, and casual, he entered the side room. I spent waves of energy trying to just make decent eye contact, and he effortlessly slid in and earned everybody's respect with between 20 and 25 well thought-out moves.

Chess:

There was a time when, at any given moment during a show, you could walk into the side room and see two Gilman volunteers hunched over a narrow coffee table, arms crossed, eyes focused, playing chess. I theorize that each player envisioned the king of the game to be a symbol for him or herself, and that the rest of the workers were their personal game-pieces, their faithful and subservient pawns. This made the game very personal, and your status at the club was directly proportional to how many times you'd had an opponent in checkmate.

Smitty was much better than I at chess. Whenever he missed a show, I, not being able to hold my own, returned to the log.

November, 2001

One night I worked the front door. I was excited because I had been appointed to work cashbox, and that is a position that requires the club to trust in you somewhat. All my thoughts began to follow that same neurotic vein: "they asked me to count the money, I must be making some progress," "they let me help sign up workers, they must think I am responsible," "I get to work side door, that means I am *allowed* to wear a security t-shirt, I'm really doing well!!!" Of course, some of my thoughts were ridiculously inaccurate.

One night, not a single person said "hi." I worked second half even though I knew I could miss BART. Somebody stole my jacket. I had to hold back tears as I stood outside the shut BART gates in the freezing cold. As I curled up in the backyard of some North Berkeley home to sleep, I thought about how sad I was that after a year, I didn't know anybody well enough at the club to go back and ask for a place to stay for the night.

July, 2002

"Naively optimistic": the #1 phrase to describe the future workers of the club.

"Realistic to the point of pessimism": the #1 phrase to describe those currently enlisted.

"Burnt out": the #1 phrase to describe Gilman ex-patriots.

November, 2002

People, realizing that I wasn't going to go away, began talking to me. As soon as I got everything I had been chasing after, as soon as I got to the shore and stood sturdily as the waves crashed at my feet, I promptly began taking everything for granted.

No, I am being too hard on myself. Before, though, if somebody had asked me how I was doing, my entire night would have been engulfed in a euphoric glee because somebody took note of my presence. Now, if someone asks me how I am doing they'd generally be surprised if I could sincerely answer, "well."

Now, instead of lusting after the club, I complain like we have been married for 20 years and it has gained quite a bit of unnecessary weight.

But I love it. I am committed to it, like a hundred others. It draws me back to it over and over again. I have learned to speak up. My consistent presence has drawn out from other workers an emotion that is not unlike respect, but isn't quite like it, either.

There are less mohawks and buttflaps and more calf-length skirts and white belts. Everybody is shaping it, everybody's ideas are crashing and dueling and occasionally cooperating. I became confident when I realized that almost everybody's story of Gilman is similar in one way: they thought it would be one thing and then it was another. Everybody is part of the folklore. Everybody is drowning. And Gilman is the ocean.

Photo by Pat W.

SEAN M.

I first heard about Gilman from an article in *BAM* magazine in 1996, about the band Green Day, that mentioned Gilman Street. I went there with a friend during the day, and we weren't sure we had the right address, so we knocked on the front door, and there just happened to be someone there. We checked it out and first went to a show there in 1997, when I was fifteen or sixteen. I had won tickets on KALX (the UC Berkeley college station) to a Gilman show, but my parents wouldn't let me go. So I went anyway, telling my parents I was spending the night at a friend's house. It was an exciting show and a good experience. It really felt lke a community to me, I felt a bond with the other people there.

I started working there a couple months after that first show, mostly because I had met one of the people who worked there and I had developed a big crush. I didn't have a very good relationship with my parents, and tried to get out of the house as much as possible. They really didn't want me going there and staying out late. So I'd go to the meetings and volunteer for the first half of the show and then go home. I was making good friends and wanted to be a part of something that I thought was pretty important. I liked that it was all ages, inexpensive, low key, and that the members of the bands that played there were ordinary people like me, not big stars on pedestals.

I've worked there about five years now, primarily in the store. It seems to have pretty much stayed the same, generally. The age of the audience seems to have stayed really young, but the age of most of the workers has gotten older, since a core group of us has been there a while now. We're trying to do more there, and make it more of a community space rather than just a place where you can see bands. It also seems like the younger people aren't as involved now as we were when we were younger. It doesn't seem like a whole lot of new people are volunteering. It also seems like there's a greater amount of disrespect being shown towards the club and the people who work there. We've been making more of an effort to let everyone who comes there know that it's all volunteer run, and you can help out if you want. It doesn't seem like it's enough though. I get the feeling that no one's paying attention, no one's listening.

I really see it as a community center. I also think of it as my home. I haven't been able to work there a lot lately, I've been feeling burnt out. But it comes and goes. I'll probably go back there soon and do more things. I've learned how to deal with people better, how to be more responsible, and how a small business is run. It's shown me a way that I'd like to run my own business someday, in a not so typical "business" way, more idealistically. I've seen at Gilman that it can work.

I feel a little parental at times with the younger kids there. I don't mind it too much. I think maybe I can help these kids in some way, help them feel more accepted, more comfortable, welcome them to be a part of Gilman. I try to give them a chance, rather than be negative and cynical towards them from the outset, hoping that maybe they'll feel the same way about the place as I do. I remember people being nice to me and encouraging me when I first started going there, and that's how I try to be to others now.

I think there's a romantic aspect to Gilman in a sense, the possibilities are endless, so much potential to do pretty much anything you want. Gilman provides a place of hope, a place where you can make your ideals a reality. It's changed my perspective on life, it's shown me how things could be, spoiled me in the sense that now I want things to be that way outside of Gilman too. It's hard for me to hold regular jobs, because I don't have the motivation for the sacrifice a job demands, the rewards aren't enough. Sometimes Gilman gets that way too, where I'm feeling like I have to be there, rather than wanting to be there. If I was getting paid for working at Gilman, sometimes it would be good, because if I was feeling burnt out, at least I would be making some money, but mostly I'm glad that I don't get paid, because it wouldn't feel as special, and it would make it feel more like a job.

I think the most important thing for me about Gilman is the people there, particularly the people I work with. I think the music is just a vehicle for bringing people together and sharing ideas, building more of a community. I've played there in a band as well as worked there and I think by working there I'm giving and making a difference, as opposed to when I'm on stage, which feels more selfish.

One thing that's hard about putting this all down on paper, is that I really don't want to try and reproduce the feelings I have at Gilman outside of Gilman— it's its own special little world. In trying to tell others about the place, I don't think they'll be able to understand the impact it's had on me. Even some of my friends get bummed when I can't hang out with them on Friday and Saturday nights because I'm at Gilman. One of the best times I remember I had there was when I was hanging out in the office once after a show and looking at all the old flyers on the walls, understanding the "inside" jokes on some of them, and really getting a feeling of being a part of history, and being a part of this community.

The next generation of Gilman workers?   Photo by Larry W.

DAN W.

I first went to Gilman in late 1993 or early 1994, when I was seventeen or eighteen, to see a band, Rancid, who I had just heard about and really liked. I had been to big rock shows before, but that was my first time to a relatively small punk club. I had never been that close to the bands before. The people seemed friendly, and I really liked the place. I started going there about once a month or so, and once I moved to the East Bay, about five years later, I started going almost every weekend. It took me a while to figure out how the place worked, and I didn't really know you could volunteer there until much later after I first started going. I was working two or three jobs at that point anyway, so I didn't have a lot of free time.

After I had moved to the East Bay, in 1999, I started working at a local record shop, and Gilman's head coordinator at the time, Chris S., used to come in all the time, and would bug me about volunteering at Gilman. He wanted me to get involved with booking. Eventually I went down and started doing it and ended up liking it. It was awkward at first, because the people who were already doing booking when I started didn't really seem to get along very well. Lines seemed to be drawn around music genres, and the type of bands being booked. There was no "head of booking," either, to try and facilitate things. I worked with one of the other bookers there for about a year before I was approved as a full-time booker.

Booking is separate from the membership in a way, because many times immediate decisions have to be made—you can't wait until a meeting usually. The long term decisions/policies were dealt with at membership meetings. I'm very pro "mixed" bills. I like to see different types of bands together, rather than all similar bands on the same night. It can be hard to motivate yourself to book bands you don't like, but you try and establish a balance as best you can between those you do like and those you don't. Also, I don't think the main purpose of the club is to build up the local scene, so much as being there to support the touring bands, especially those that can't get shows anywhere else. It goes back and forth with the local versus touring band issue. It can be really hard, if not impossible, to please everyone. You have to establish a strong local base to support those touring bands who can't headline. I don't think it's ever been "officially" established exactly what Gilman's purpose actually is (locals vs. touring). We try to balance it as best we can.

We get so many bands calling us who want all ages shows. It would be really helpful if there were more venues that they could choose from. It would really take the pressure off us. It's hard to say no to bands, but what else can we do? We can't have shows every night. We'll pick out a headliner or two and try to build a show around them. If we just threw bands on bills as they called, there would be a lot of really bad shows. Each week we get about ten to thirty demos, just of local bands wanting a show. On top of that, we get the phone calls from both the local bands and the touring bands who want shows. Some months we get as many as three hundred bands contacting us. We try to put two to three touring bands on each bill, at most, with two to three local bands. So, with two shows a week, five bands a show, we only have slots for forty to fifty bands a month, twenty to thirty local, twenty to thirty touring. And not all those slots can be filled with "new" bands. A number of those slots we need to fill with established local bands that can draw, and sometimes, if there's no suitable alternatives, the same band will get multiple shows. You can see the difficulty in trying to get everyone a show—it's impossible. "Touring" season used to be generally over the summer, but it seems to be getting longer each year. We're booking four to five months ahead at this point. The amount of bands looking for shows (local and touring) seems to have stayed roughly the same over the couple years I've been booking there. The biggest impact has been the significant increase in venues closing down in the Bay Area. It puts a greater load on us. We're trying to do more Sunday shows, but that puts a bigger load on the workers.

We're fairly solid financially, but our costs go up each year (rent, insurance, etc.). When I first started working there, we figured we needed about 150 people per show to break even. Now that figure has increased to needing about 250 people per show. Since there aren't that many "headliners" around right now, we'll put together shows based on two or three "medium" drawing bands. With those shows, mixed bills are more successful because the different types of bands probably aren't going to have the same fans, so you're drawing from a larger group.

The current group of bookers is pretty good about showing up to the shows they book, so if there's problems with fighting or assholes, they'll be there to see it and help deal with it, maybe influencing their decisions in the future. We try to be selective about who we book, in the sense that we are all-volunteer, and we're not looking to make more work for ourselves in dealing with problems or putting the club in jeopardy with the city. There was a show recently that ended up costing Gilman $1500 to $2000 to repair damage to the club as well as to surrounding businesses. We don't see booking just from a "business" standpoint. In fact, I don't think any of the current bookers see that as their first priority, but you definitely have to take it into consideration for the club in the long term. Also, it's not just to make money for the club, we'd like to have enough people come so we can pay the bands pretty well, especially the touring bands. We split the door 50/50 with the bands (after about ten percent has been taken out to pay the people working security that night). Over the last year or so, since we were doing better financially, we had been giving more to the bands, particularly the touring bands, but since our costs have risen lately again, we've been sticking to the 50/50 split. If no one shows up for a show, though, we'll usually just give all the money to the bands. We try to look out for the bands as best we can.

We don't get that much feedback, positive or negative, from the bands first-hand. We'll hear most of the complaints second or third-hand, or on the internet, etc. Complaints will be about how the shows were run, how much they got paid, etc. I haven't played in a band, so I can't compare if we pay that much worse than other places. I do know that other places will do guarantees, which we don't do. There are bands that support us, and will play Gilman and make much less than they would at other places. We provide water for the bands—that's about it. I think we probably have the worst rider of any club ever. There hasn't been too much discussion at the meetings about providing anything else.

My biggest thing is trying to provide as diverse a mixture of shows as we can. To try and have at least one show a month that just about any one person in the area would want to go to. I've been booking there long enough now to have the confidence to put my own stamp, or flavor, into the shows I'm putting together, to know what will work and what won't. I don't really have any interest in booking at another place as a paying job. I just enjoy being a part of things, and helping out the bands, having fun. The community center aspect of Gilman comes and goes—sometimes it's utilized as such, sometimes it's not, but the music club aspect pays the bills and allows the community center part to exist.

I don't see an endpoint yet in my working there, I still really enjoy it, and I don't see myself getting tired of going there anytime soon. Gilman's really helped me in working with others, understanding them better, and getting along with them. It's been such a huge part of my life for the past eight years or so. I've met a lot of great people and seen a lot of great bands. It's not easy to put into words, I think people have to come and see for themselves.

Flyer by Dan W.

Photo by Larry W.

MEGAN MARCH

de ar clayton,   h   Spring 2003

I'm writing this letter to you from a kitchen table in Florida, where the only distractions I can hear is the slow hum of the train, or the meaow of a cat that sounds like a person.

For four years, Brian has been asking me for my contribution to that book about Gilman he's been putting together, and I still can't find the voice to tell that many people I don't know about a place that means so much to me. Like a best friend who've I've fallen in and out of love with, Gilman is a constant in my life that has been there for me the past 14 years, in some way or another. The past few months, I haven't done sound more than a few times, and I feel slightly jelous watching everybody get 924 tatoos. I wish I'd went ahead and gotten mine when I was 16, so at least I'd have something to regret.

Anyway, I figured since you we a major partner in crime around the time I learned sound, at least you'd read my letter. A little background first.....

I don't remember the specific shows very well, but according to my sister Tanya, she took me to my first show at Gilman when I was six. Lots of people have told me how lucky it is to come from a family who already owns all the records you'd spend your allowence on, but trust me, it wasn't till a few years ago that I discovered the hidden truth. Although I thought my sister was the toughest shit in town, being 12 years older than me, she really was just the smart outspoken kid who hung out with all the tough scensters, who read a lot. I've come to have more respect for her from this, because she hasn't ended up dead, boring, or brain dead like a lot of her friends. At the age of 32, this woman who saw Gilman at the begining is raising a son and raising hell with her DIY punk ethics and I couldn't be more proud.

I didn't start going to Gilman on my own or start volunteering till I was 12. There was a small group of us who came every weekend-regardless of who was playing. Similar to my friends, Gilman gave us a steady place to go on the weekends when there was no school, and we were avoiding going home. My parents kept a lazy eye on me, which allowed my stomping ground to stretch out of Oakland, through the vains of bus and train, from the outskirts of Berkeley to San Francisco, where my sister lived. I mostly stayed with her in the city-reducing my dad to a voice on the other end of the phone.

When my sister moved to Spain, I returned home to discover that my mom had left, and my dad was in the same emotional state as an empty mason jar. By the time I was 16, I'd learned how to play bass, was learning guitar, and had aquired my sister's old VW Rabbit which I still drive occasionally today. Frustrated with gender issues in band dynamics—I wanted to be a part of the scene which required a skill → something not everybody knew.

Sweaty palmed, and not quite sure what I was asking for, I introduced myself to Rachel S. She was the sound co-orinator at the time, and showed me all the ropes. She introduced me to Richard, and I think you, Clayton. Rachel became really busy with school, leaving me in the hands of you and Richard. The time I sprained my ankel replacing fuses in the mains with Richard on a school night was probably the first time in a long time I knew I could trust somebody over 25.

The best times ever ~~were~~ were when you and I made fun of the bands in the sound booth, when 2øø backs were turned.

I don't think you were there the night when ~~[crossed out]~~ played their 10 yr. Aniverversery show. I took a 5 min. break to dance with my friend Margaret, and the lead singer threw an aresol can out into the crowd, which hit me in the head. I came to in the back room, bleeding like you wouldn't believe. Lucky Rachel was there to work the rest of the show - Chris Sparks took ~~to~~ me to get ice cream, and I told him my life story so I wouldn't pass out into a coma. Later I drove myself home and made my dad go with me to the emergancy room where they sewed me up. I always thought it was fucked up how ~~[crossed out]~~, who made hundreds of dollars off their shows at Gilman, refused to take responsibility for their irrisponsible actions. At their next show they appologised for their violent sets, but words are cheap when a collectivly run punk club has to pay for a violent bands mistakes. It took me a while to feel safe at those types of shows again - and realize it's the meatheads who are the jerks, not Gilman.

I think alot of women struggle with gender issues at Gilman, but it's more of a general issue in the punk scene, than at Gilman in perticular. I remember feeling really insulted when a meeting was called to discuss wether or not gilman was a sexist place, and some one said that Gilman was male oriented. How's that? I feel Gilman has been a major support in my life - I was encuraged to work shows by myself at the age of 18, and when you're working the sound board, that's 5+ hrs. of either sinking or keeping your head above water. ~~They~~ As a younger woman I have never been in the majority, ~~but that's really all in the back [crossed out]~~ but that ~~[crossed out]~~ hasn't held me back at Gilman - I don't think anybody there would allow it. *True, it's harder as a woman, but not impossible

It's been 4 years since I learned sound, and since then, there's more people involved, giving everybody more time to do other things. I play drums and Gilman basketball - both give me plenty of cuts and brusis. All my house mates are Gilman workers too, I guess that makes things convinent.

I know the club is slowly getting smaller, with all it's layers of paint, spit, sweat and blood ground into the walls, it's what gives Gilman it's unique & familiar smell. I feel privilaged to have a place like Gilman, ~~to~~ as an all ages venue where my band to play, where I've made my best friends, learned to make amazing basketball shots from the sound booth, write love letters on the stoar walls, learn sound, get stiches, and become slightly deaf in my right ear.

Watch your back next time we play basketball clayton, you and Arron maybe taller, but when I fall down, I get up faster.

heart,

Megan March

2000   photo by Megan M.

TYLER HUTTON

Damn, we know how to dress: patched, ripped, cutoff articles of clothing; creepers and fishnets on pale legs; simple black jackets with leopard print; tight pants; arm and leg tattoos worn like an old shirt. And mohawks, spiked hair, ratty hair, shaved heads, fringe cuts—we can cut our fucking hair! And sometimes we have attitudes, abrasive and rugged like our clothing. Did I mention that, more often than not, our music sounds tough, too? It is style.

When I first came to the club at the corner of Gilman and Eighth Street, in 1996, I was a shoddy dresser. I benefited from being around that bastion of modern punk fashion; I look rather nice now in Converse and thrift store shirts. Then, I was approaching the end of high school in the affluent suburb of Danville and I didn't enjoy looking at the name brand clothing of everyone around me in school. The folks with character, my new friends, were the punk rockers—the drunk, stoned, rebellious, and confused folk at my high school. God, the patches were exciting.

1991   photo by Susan S.

In 1996, approaching the end of high school after failed years of playing sports I didn't like and attempts at fitting in with the majority of the people at my school, I found 924 Gilman Street. I would like to say that I found the club and had some sort of epiphany, a flash of insight that told me that I was okay and I had found people that I could relate to, but that was not the case. The people at the club seemed just as foreign and oppositional as the football players at my high school. I clung to the person I came to the club with. I didn't know what to think.

I had realized, though, that I had stumbled onto something different than I was accustomed to. It seemed that while the dynamic of interpersonal relations and the push for popularity were the same, the requirements for those things were skewed. Someone who, like myself, was terribly unequipped for the high school social scene could find a social niche in the odd environment of 924 Gilman Street. I was a fat kid, a smart kid—and I was heckled for both of these among people my age, away from the club.

I just spoke with Jennifer, who is our customer service representative at a company called PAYCHEX. Every month, we report the earnings of paid security guards so the proper taxes can be taken out of our bank account. I was surprised when I found out that we pay taxes on our security guard payments, as opposed to a shadier system involving "under the table" payments and an adequate amount of deniability to the IRS, but paying taxes is just one of the decisions that was made to ensure the stability and longevity of the club.

I am the treasurer—have been the treasurer for almost a year. It is one of those elected offices at the club—like secretary, executive director, head coordinator. I am doing something that needs to be done—bland paperwork that nobody knows I do. And this work has made me realize, however recently, the extent of the work required to keep the club running.

We have bookers that come in during the week, spending hours of time planning shows and dealing with difficult people. We have people who run the store, selling soft drinks and zines and chips and candy, and it is almost run as an enterprise separate from the club. We have people who come to our twice-monthly membership meetings to think for the club and vote. We have coordinators and stage managers scrambling about inside and outside the building during shows—also dealing with difficult people. We have security guards who throw people out and tell them not to drink. We have volunteers who work at the shows, a cast of hundreds over the years, taking money and stamping wrists. We have people clean up. It is a mammoth fucking operation. It is a mammoth operation and it is ours.

I made new friends in high school—people who mirrored my sense of style, attitude towards the world, and matched me in the consumption of alcohol. They were fantastic people, but as people do, we grew apart.

I found myself, in the summer of 1998, among a new group of friends. These people were very passionate about punk rock and booze and the suburban necessity of killing time and waiting for something cool to happen. We frequently went west through the Caldecott Tunnel on Highway 24, around to Interstate 80 strafing the bay, and up to Gilman Street.

One evening, mid-summer, we brought a case of Blackthorn cider and drank it behind dumpsters a block away from the club. I remember I drank more than one bottle of cider in the clear night, the stars strangely bright and crisp through the city light. I remember one of the girls we were with, because she was beautiful and radiant. But I don't remember any of the bands that played in 1998.

The year was a blur of alcohol and people, but it brought me closer to the club. That year, Gilman Street became a refuge that I would run to—escaping the mundane life of the suburbs and community college.

2000   photo by Lauren L.

The office at the club, off to the right after entering through the front door, is a safe place. There are couches to sit on and a desk to prop your feet on. Two closets hold files, phones, binders, a stereo, personal belongings. Two narrow, dirty windows with bent blinds look out onto the street and on a busy night the line of patrons waiting to get in runs past them. A lockable desk houses a donated computer with printer. An enclosure with mail slots for the workers is nailed to the wall in the corner.

I have seen bleeding people taken to the office for first aid. I have seen people passed out, sleeping on the couch. I have seen large men in red security shirts playing chess on the table over coffee.

Flyers cover the walls. One wall is covered with old flyers advertising old bands. Studying the flyers while working at a show and realizing that I was at most of the events recounted leaves me with a feeling that this place is home. It is very important in a world where I feel out of place in my hometown.

At the end of 1998, my drinking picked up and peaked at a wholly unmanageable level. Amid the rainy nights of November, I was reunited with an old friend and started on a simple path to darkness, shooting heroin and cocaine in San Francisco's Mission District. The life of alleys and crime consumed me, and I did not return to 924 Gilman Street for almost a year.

Sid got thrown out of the club permanently, "86'ed," after being too drunk too often and causing minor altercations. He was a short, solidly built gutter-punk with facial tattoos, in his late teens. He still hung out in front of the club, seeing friends and killing time.

Sid was very likeable, when sober, and I had the opportunity to talk with him on a few occasions. All that was required for him to get back into the club was for him to attend a membership meeting and request re-entry. The people at the membership meeting would be forgiving—they always are considering the courage and accountability necessary for someone to show up and explain themselves. Terms would be set. It is a very civil process.

I explained this to Sid a few times. I did not want to see him standing out in the street or sitting on a corner while a band he liked was playing. He reacted positively and said that he would show up to a meeting, asking when the next one was.

He never showed.

In the middle of 1999, I returned to the club, clean and sober, and found the community that I had left a year earlier still intact. Life without booze and other inebriants requires passionate diversions and positive action. I became a volunteer, as I had done before to get into shows with no money, but I began to push to be more a part of the club.

The summer of 1999 stood in direct contrast to that season in 1998. The previous year I had stumbled through the neighborhood and into the doorway at 924 Gilman Street, under the Caning Shop sign, and I had returned, as the same person, with a different agenda. Suddenly, Gilman was something to get involved with —not something to use as a diversion.

I was, and still am, a large person. So it was natural that I would become a security guard. I volunteered, taking no money. The duties were simple: disallow people to drink in and around the club; pull stagedivers off the crowd; stop fights. I felt obligated, bound to the club—as though terrible things would happen if I didn't show up. But those incidents were usually fated to happen and were dealt with by those loyal to the club, without me.

The building at the corner of Gilman and Eighth Street is in the middle of a neighborhood that is being crept upon by yuppie culture. The Pyramid Brewery has moved in across the street; bland boutiques line Fourth Street; more money is being funneled into the area. I had heard stories about the neighborhood in the time that the club opened. I had heard that it was way away from everything —in the middle of an industrial neighborhood that shut down for the weekend at 5:00 PM on Fridays.

The current money interests would like to keep the neighborhood appealing, and have come into conflict with us—having patrons that do not always meet their standards of appearance and behavior.

The police presence in the neighborhood is ever-increasing, and there have been positive and negative sides to our interaction. There are police that are aggressive, constantly patrolling the neighborhood and looking at our patrons as a threat to it. But, we have had positive experiences with

2000   photo by Lauren L.

local law enforcement that try to understand the sort of operation we have and have either kept their distance or lent a hand when it was needed. As a security guard, I always detested calling the police. They are an outside force, and it is always best if we can deal with trouble and conflict within our community. But, there have been times—with an excessive amount of violence in or around the club, for example— that it has been necessary to call them. We can only hope for the least amount of conflict when they are involved.

Most of the disputes that we have had with our neighbors have been resolved—including the most pressing disputes involving the Berkeley Zoning Board or other parts of the local political machine.

Toward the end of 1999, the club seemed to be going through a transitional phase with workers coming and going. One night, breaking their quiet conversation on the couch in the office, Chris S., the Head Coordinator, and Mike H., the head of security, turned to me. Mike asked me if I would like to be paid. "Do you want a job?" he said. I agreed.

Being a paid security guard left me with a legitimate obligation to the club. At the end of every show I would receive money for attempting to keep the place safe. There were many altercations and quarrels between security guards at Gilman St. and people who wanted to drink, wanted to fight—with us, sometimes. These incidents were too many to enumerate. Blows were exchanged sporadically throughout the months of 2000. Sometime early that year I became the head of security, which to me only meant that Mike would not be around. The prospect of being in charge of security and making decisions in stressful situations was not

1997   photo by Pat W.

appealing. Since I had worked at the club, I had the privilege of standing behind strong-willed people like Mike H., and had backed them in their decisions.

Working security at 924 Gilman Street spawned an intense personal growth. When I began, I was not used to saying things and standing by them. I was "laid-back" and apathetic when tension arose. By the end of my time as a security guard at the club, I could make a decision and stand by it—most of the time. I became used to the selflessness involved in enforcing rules that you sometimes do not agree with, and the selfishness of others. I had been serving something that I deemed worth service—the club and community of 924 Gilman Street.

I had asked myself what the point of all this is. Why do I continue to go to the club to see shows? Why do I still volunteer my time? Why do I travel, almost every weekend, to a place relatively far away from my house? I found the answer a few days ago.

I had been out all weekend—at a show in San Rafael on Friday and at the Contra Costa County Fair on Saturday, during the day. The days had involved quite a bit of traveling by van, on a BART train, and by bus through four counties and seven cities. It was late on Saturday night and I was getting off a bus on San Pablo to walk to the club. A feeling of peace flushed through my body. I had been jolted around the whole of the Bay Area and, though I was tired and upset, I felt that I had found my way home again.

"I love this," I said to my companion.

"What?" she asked.

"This place. The way it makes me feel." I said.

"Whatever," she responded.

And we walked three blocks to the club, and friends were there in the street, and the night was warm and clear.

ROBYN M. (REPRINTED FROM HER COLUMN IN *HEARTATTACK*, AUGUST 1999)

We hadn't been in Berkeley for a full week yet. In fact, all of our worldly possessions were still packed up in a fifteen-foot Budget truck and parked in back of my aunt's barn. We were still in search of a place to live. We hadn't found jobs. We were beyond exhaustion after the six-day drive across the country. But we're pretty fucking punk (defined loosely), so before we even found the small, over-priced apartment we now call home, we found Gilman Street.

Back on the East Coast, those of us who cared to discuss politics, amidst herds of the apolitical, heard about Gilman Street as the infamous Bay Area club where punk rock meets leftist politics. Collectively organized and operated, the club maintains a commitment to non-racist, non-classist, non-sexist, non-heterosexist music promotion. It stands as a force both in Bay Area punk rock and the Berkeley community, challenging conceptions of punk as fleeting, irresponsible, apathetic, and elitist. Part of the excitement about our relocation to the Berkeley area was our eager anticipation to once again witness the political potency of punk, metal, and hardcore.

Mike and I almost drove right by the club. It is a fairly innocuous building, mostly distinguishable by the collection of kids with dreadlocks and faded clothing standing out front. It appears to be a pretty large and fairly diverse crowd for a Phobia show, but a relatively local band (to remain unnamed) is also playing and we had already heard the buzz about these punk rockstars. We learned that this band play Gilman quite often, and therefore have developed quite a following (though I am still wondering exactly why). So perhaps many people were there to see the hometown heroes. Or perhaps kids just come to most shows at Gilman, help with some of the set-up or clean-up, hang out with friends, and watch the bands.

We sit outside for a little bit, scoping out the scene, forgetting that we are no longer in Massachusetts and therefore would not see anyone we knew. After heading inside, I immediately start reading all of the newspaper clippings hanging on the walls detailing the history of Gilman Street—its legal run-ins with neighboring businesses, its support from other local businesses, and its significance in Bay Area punk rock. I glance over a statement written boldly on the wall forbidding sexism, racism, classism, homophobia, alcohol, and stagediving inside the club. And then I head to the distro tables—the essential fixture of any punk/hardcore show, ensuring that kids can arm themselves with the latest in punk rock merchandise. One woman has a pretty interesting setup, with books and zines covering topics ranging from vegan cooking to bell hooks on race and representation. After hearing we are new to the Bay Area, she suggests we check out a vegan restaurant in San Francisco. And I am thinking, "I can dig this. People are so nice around here. And they seem to really appreciate this scene and this club."

The first band goes on, and the long-haired, B.C. Rich-playing, metal kid starts talking about the brutality and inhumanity of our economic war on Iraq, and I'm thinking, "This fucking kid rocks! Who says all metal kids are braindead?" And then I hear a few people in the crowd yell out some crap about "shut up and play." The kid on stage looks a bit flustered, but keeps going. This happens a few more times during the band's set.

Next, My Lai, the band we were originally there to see, is tearing shit up during their first song. They do some pretty technical stuff, and the sound in the club is decent enough to capture it well. After their first song, the vocalist encourages those dancing to be cautious of those who may or may not want to be slammed. One can tell by murmurs in the crowd that—among some—this doesn't go over well. My Lai play their second song. Afterwards, the singer begins to explain the premise of their third song when someone from the crowd tells him to "shut up and play." And then a bit of a verbal confrontation emerges between the witty man with the microphone and the drunk kid who thinks that being punk means one has to be an asshole. My Lai plays their third song. More noise from the crowd about "we just want to have fun and dance." Fourth song. Comments from guys who just wanna have fun. Verbal confrontation. Fifth song. Comments from guys who just wanna have fun. Verbal confrontation. I think it was during this hostile exchange of words and insults that the band's vocalist says something that had been running through my mind. He talks about how psyched he was to play Gilman because he had heard so much about this club and it being a place where people come together to exchange ideas, hang out with friends, and listen to the music they love. He regarded it as a club where people would be encouraged to communicate with one another, whether it be outside, at the distro table, or on stage. And then he admits his recent disillusionment.

There are those in the crowd who shout their support of My Lai, but they are overpowered, if not actually outnumbered.

After My Lai's set, I go outside to get some fresh air, because unfortunately those at Gilman Street failed to disallow smoking along with racism, sexism, homophobia, alcohol, and stagediving. I overhear a group of rowdy and obnoxious boys complaining about the "faggots" and "pussies" whom had just exited the stage. I don't have to eavesdrop. They are talking loudly enough so anyone standing in relative proximity could hear. Nice. That's all I have to say about that. Really fucking nice.

I head back inside to pee, only to find a few women crowded around the bathroom sink drinking beers, and a drunk guy taking a piss on the floor of the women's bathroom.

Back outside, I hear the beginnings of a fight that would inevitably draw negative attention to the club.

The relatively-local band mentioned at the beginning open their set with, "We are not much for talking in between songs so here goes..." and they play straight through until, "This last song is dedicated to those who come here to escape the bullshit of everyday life and just wanna have some fun." An attempted jab at the previous bands? An effort to give their fans what they came to see? Either way, the kids ate it up—circle pits, slam dancing, head bopping, and even some hardcore-inspired sing-alongs and mosh parts.

Phobia plays. Decent stuff. Afterwards, I go to the bathroom to wash my hands and see tampon applicators on the floor and more women guzzling down their brewskis.

On our way to the car, we see a few police cars and a bunch of people crowded around a commotion. Rather than rubber-necking, we keep going, so I don't really know what the deal was that night. I am guessing that there was some kind of fight and things blew out of control. But based on all of the things I had read regarding Gilman's dealings with neighboring businesses and the Berkeley police, I assume that for every time the cops have to disperse the crowd at the end of a show, it becomes more difficult for the club to maintain its standing in the community. Excess police visits = increasing hostility between the city of Berkeley and

Gilman Street coordinators = problems for Gilman Street next time one of their neighbors complains about vandalism.

When punk is DIY, when it is collective, when it does attempt to exist outside the conventions of popular culture, it is the punk kids themselves who threaten its survival. It's like the word "destroy," left over from too much adolescent indulgence of the Sex Pistols, just reverberates itself in the punk rock ear over and over

> *"I couldn't understand why people who were into punk and punk music would hate, and try to destroy, the one place that consistently gave them just that."*
>
> *—Mike H.*

again with no concern for direction or productive destruction. Pissing and spilling beer on the floor of the bathroom may be pretty punk if it is Stephen Forbes' private bathroom suite, but it's just inconsiderate and disrespectful if other kids have to come clean it up at the end of a show. Heckling bandmembers who are simply trying to explain the premises or significance of their music is not punk, just arrogant and obnoxious. It creates an atmosphere where bands new to the area do not feel welcome simply because they do not know the protocol for appropriate time elapsed between songs. Severe intoxication is so often the setting stage for acting like an asshole—instigating fights, getting a little rough on the dance floor, throwing up, breaking shit—so I wonder why all of the alcohol consumption in and around the club.

And if kids aren't threatening the physical existence of Gilman Street—the space to put on punk rock shows—they are at least threatening the intellectual existence of Gilman Street in the "shut up and play" approach to punk rock. "Shut up and play" disallows band members to connect with the crowd on some basis other than the impersonal exchanges between rock band and rock fan. "Shut up and play" terminates all onstage discussion of politics, therefore relegating political, cultural, and subcultural conversations to a secondary position in the scene. "Shut up and play" forces bands to be about "playing music and having fun" even if those aren't the only two priorities. "Shut up and play" not only hinders the possibilities of political discourse, but it can also interfere with the experimental elements of music-making and public performance. "Shut up and play" limits the creativity and possibility of a scene that claims to rest itself on breaking boundaries, challenging conventions, and fostering community.

I didn't expect to hear "shut up and play" at Gilman Street. Perhaps my expectations were too high going in. I didn't expect to see kids defacing the building and disrespecting the bands. I didn't expect fights and police cars. I expected more distro tables like the one where I met my first Bay Area acquaintance. Basically, I naively expected punk to be smarter on the West Coast. Or I had hoped it would be. So far it isn't. I hope I'm mistaken.

I think I'll start going to Gilman Street collective meetings to find out what those who keep the place up and running think of some of the crap that goes on there. It was difficult to decipher most people's reactions to what I thought was blatant selfishness and disrespect on the part of a few. Kudos to the woman who yelled "KEEP TALKING" during My Lai's set...my thoughts precisely.

COMETBUS
ten years
at gilman
(a scrapbook)

30¢ / FREE!

This was a special issue of *Cometbus* done for the ten year anniversary of Gilman, and handed out at that weekend's (Jan. 3, 4, 5, 1997) shows only. The following seven pages contain excerpts.

I WANTED TO DO SOMETHING SPECIAL FOR GILMAN'S TEN YEAR ANNIVERSARY, AND ONLY DECIDED ON THIS LAST WEEK. FOR A YEAR NOW PEOPLE HAVE BEEN GATHERING STUFF AND TALKING ABOUT PUTTING OUT A BOOK ABOUT GILMAN TO CELEBRATE THE TEN YEAR ANNIVERSARY, BUT NOW THE ANNIVERSARY IS HERE AND THE BOOK IS NOWHERE NEAR DONE. WHAT DO THEY THINK, THE TEN YEAR ANNIVERSARY WILL COME AROUND TWICE? I WANTED TO HAVE SOMETHING TO CELEBRATE NOW. THIS IS JUST A FEW SCATTERED SCRAPS I DUG UP IN A HURRY, NOT ANY SORT OF DEFINITIVE HISTORY AND CERTAINLY NOT UNBIASED. IT'S ABOUT THE PEOPLE INVOLVED WITH THE CLUB, AND THEIR IDEAS AND STRUGGLES, AND ABOUT HOW THE PEOPLE AND IDEAS AND THE CLUB ITSELF HAS CHANGED AND EVOLVED OVER THE YEARS. THIS IS A LIMITED EDITION HALF-ISSUE ONLY AVAILABLE AT GILMAN THE WEEKEND OF JAN 3-5, 1997.

x Aaron

AN EARLY MEETING.

THE MEETINGS STARTED IN JUNE 1986. THE FIRST ONE WAS MAYBE TEN OF US, INCLUDING ALL FOUR MEMBERS OF S.F. BAND SHORT DOGS GROW. THEY SAID THE CLUB HAD TO HAVE A BAR, OR IT WOULD NEVER LAST. CONSTRUCTION BEGAN IN THE MONTHS FOLLOWING. SOUNDPROOFING AND NEW SEWER PIPES WERE PUT IN, THE BATHROOMS AND THE LADDER TO THE LOFT AND THE FRONT DOOR WERE ALL RE-DONE. ACTUALLY ALMOST EVERYTHING WAS RE-DONE. UP TO CODE, BY THE BOOK, ALL BY VOLUNTEERS.

COVER: THE GILMAN BATHROOM + STAIRS TO LOFT BEFORE CONSTRUCTION. BELOW: SHORT DOGS GROW-A GREAT BAND, BUT WRONG. ALL THESE PIX BY MURRAY B. EVERYTHING IN HERE IS EDITED BASED ON LACK OF SPACE AND/OR RELEVANCY, AND I APOLOGIZE IN ADVANCE IF SOMETHING IS OUT OF CONTEXT.

CITYSIDE

The Gilman Street Project

In the beginning, though, Yohannon and other staff members of the magazine ended up in charge of much of the organizing and supervision. "We begged and pleaded for people with the slightest amount of expertise to help, because the rest of us didn't know jackshit!" he said, laughing. He shook his head in disbelief as he recounted how so much of the construction hinged more on serendipity than on careful planning.

"One day this weird little group showed up—four people, all the same height, similar build, all dressed in black, similar personalities..."

"We're here to do the soundproofing," one told Yohannon while the others busied themselves with measuring tapes and utility knives. By the end of the day the job was almost completely finished, and the unknown quartet left as quietly as they had come.

"They were 'The Men in Black,'" Yohannon chuckled, "even though one of them was a woman. Then there were 'The Big Guys,' both over 6'2", 230 pounds, who showed up and announced that they'd build our bathrooms in two days flat. It was surreal, sort of like the mysterious gangs that pop up in the movie *The Wanderers*."

IF JUST SHOUTING ABOUT IT ISN'T ENOUGH FOR YOU ANYMORE.....

WE FORMED COMMITEES, HAD MEETINGS, MORE MEETINGS, WENT TO CITY COUNCIL MEETINGS, PRINTED UP PROPAGANDA, AND SPREAD THE WORD LIKE MISSIONARIES.

LATE 1986 PAMPHLET BY MIKE MIRO EXPLAINING THE PROJECT AND CALLING FOR SUPPORT.

ISN'T IT TIME WE CREATED A REAL ALTERNATIVE?

Hey! There's a new club in Berkeley, graveyard to the scene.

Located at the corner of 8th and Gilman, the 300 capacity "Warehouse" (it has no official name) is the result of collaboration among some of the people who put on the "New Method" and "Own's Pizza" shows, MAXIMUM ROCKNROLL, and many volunteers who helped transform fairly raw warehouse space into a viable venue.

It's easy to be cynical about high ideals and ambitious goals, especially in the music biz. That's one of the problems with the scene now. Cynicism seems even less justifiable (this early in the game) when so many people have worked so hard for nothing but the satisfaction of seeing the Warehouse succeed in creating a new sense of community in the underground. Let's give it a chance, help to make it work. The Gilman Street Warehouse Project is, as far as I know, unique in the Bay Area. In Berkeley, especially, we don't have much alternative.

SOUP'S SETLIST. THEY WERE THE FIRST BAND TO PLAY GILMAN.

ARMY SONG
TAKE A DAY
G.Q.U.
CON-TROLL
HANGNOUT w/MESELF
CHATTER
C.S.P. → G.A.
TRAIN SONG
FUCK WITH WHITEY
RESUME
SMALL
YOUR KIND
RAIN
TWINKLE

A far-from-subdued Gilman Street crowd vents its energy at a live music melee.

FROM THE KALX PROGRAM GUIDE→

NEW METHOD WAS A WAREHOUSE SPACE IN EMERYVILLE THAT HAD DONE SHOWS ON AND OFF FOR YEARS. OWN'S PIZZA WAS AT ALCATRAZ AND ADELINE, WHERE THE NEW METHOD SHOWS RELOCATED BRIEFLY. GILMAN STOOD A CHANCE AT BEING A CROSS BETWEEN THE LOOSE, DRUNK, ANARCHISTIC APPROACH OF THE NEW METHOD PEOPLE, AND MRR'S STABILITY AND SENSE OF ORDER. DIDN'T WORK OUT THOUGH. ALL THE NEW METHOD PEOPLE GOT FRUSTRATED AND DROPPED OUT BEFORE LONG.

January 29, 1987 ■

GOLDEN GATER ■

Gilman Street encourages individual initiative, so artists are at work covering concrete walls with colorful murals. One group has even started a small store that carries refreshments, magazines and records from local bands. The profits are put back into the project.

A typical show — if there is such a thing — might include blues, punk and world-beat bands, poets, films, and considerable creative mayhem from the audience.

Past evenings have been livened by a game of "Twister," a running battle between two people in mock-FBI mufti armed with automatic Uzi waterguns, and a scavenger hunt that turned up everything from "Garbage Pail Kids" to a picture of someone's mother in a bouffant hairdo.

What's duller than a punk show? Not much, says Tim Yohannan, 41, editor of the Berkeley punk fanzine, *Maximum RockNRoll*. "Punk has become predictable, a cliché. Nowadays you can pretty well tell what a show will be like *before* you ever go to it. We intend to change that."

"We" is a coalition of punks, artists, political activists, and the *Maximum RockNRoll* family, who have rented a 3,000-square-foot warehouse in an industrial section of Berkeley. Since December the warehouse has put on shows every Friday and Saturday night without advertising its bills. People don't know what they're getting until they're inside. "This gives the warehouse an element of unpredictability and keeps it from becoming just another club," says Yohannan. "We don't want people to show up for what they know they like. Rather, we want to expose them to bands which they won't normally see, but would like."

If you don't like what you see, don't fret. An open-mike period follows every band's set. Members of the audience can comment on or criticize the band, and one band member gets equal time to respond. The space also offers video, film, comedy, one-act plays, and poetry readings. You must be a member of the warehouse to participate, which means shelling out two dollars and promising to adhere to three rules: no violence, no vandalism, and no alcohol.

Offstage it's up to the Mind Fuck Committee to "start or create a weird atmosphere." On tap is South Africa night: everyone will receive a racial classification at the door and be segregated for the remainder of the evening; "blacks" will be pulled out of the audience and interrogated. "We want to knock people out of their complacency without hurting them physically," says one committee member.

REALLY, THE WHOLE THING WAS PRETTY WEIRD. A SCIENTIFIC APPROACH. TRYING TO CREATE ARTIFICIALLY EVERYTHING WE HAD ALWAYS VALVED THAT HAD COME, AND COULD ONLY COME, NATURALLY. A "MINDFUCK COMMITTEE" TO CREATE SPONTANEITY. NO ADVERTISING AT ALL, TO CREATE THE DESIRE TO COME TO THE CLUB REGARDLESS OF WHO WAS PLAYING. MEMBERSHIP CARDS TO CREATE THE FEELING OF COMMUNITY, THOUGH OF COURSE THEY DID JUST THE OPPOSITE, ALIENATING ALMOST EVERYONE. OH, THE PROJECT WAS YOUNG AND WE WERE EXPERIMENTING. WE DROPPED THE NO ADVERTISING POLICY AFTER JUST A FEW MONTHS. STILL, TEN YEARS LATER, WE HAVE THE STUPID MEMBERSHIP FEE. IT'S A HUGE MISTAKE, BUT TRYING TO CONVINCE SOMEONE TO LOSE $6,000 ANNUAL INCOME IS A HARD ARGUMENT TO WIN.

Rock star throws dead animals at the audience

The leader of the shock-rock group Feederz stunned fans when he appeared on stage with live insects glued to his head — and tossed dead animals into the audience.

"It was a total glorification of death and destruction and killing," said Nick Van Eyck, who had attended the shocking concert in Berkeley, Calif.

"This guy had a dead cat wrapped around his arm and something that looked like live crickets cemented to his head."

Witnesses said fans were about equally divided in their reaction to Feederz leader Frank Discussion's antics. Some stomped and squashed the animals carcasses that were thrown into the audience while others screamed in objection. The humane society was alerted. But the group apparently broke no laws and was not charged, reports said.

THE INFAMOUS FEEDERZ SHOW THAT MADE IT INTO THE WEEKLY WORLD NEWS! THE FUNNY THING IS THAT THE ARTICLE IS TRUE. IT SEEMED THAT SURVIVAL RESEARCH LABS HAD A CONNECTION AT THE SPCA WHO WOULD GIVE THEM PILES OF DEAD PETS FOR THEIR MACHINES. FRANK DISCUSSION MERELY BUMMED ONE OFF THEM.

THE GILMAN LOUNGE: OUR LITTLE HAVEN AND SICKLY TEEN ORGY ROOM UNTIL TIM THREW OUT ALL THE COUCHES AND MATTRESSES AND BROUGHT IN A BUNCH OF UNCOMFORTABLE BRAND NEW AIRPORT CHAIRS. ONE THING TO SAY FOR THE AIRPORT CHAIRS THOUGH, THEY SURE WERE DURABLE. THERE ARE STILL SOME AROUND GILMAN, AND A LOT ON VARIOUS EASTBAY PORCHES. THE REMAINS OF THE PHOTOWALL ARE IN THE MEN'S BATHROOM, AND THE LOUNGE IS NOW THE LOCKED OFFICE.

And although the great majority of those involved in the Gilman Street Project is somehow involved with the punk scene, members tend to eschew that label too. Perhaps it's because "punk" has come to mean some snarling caricature instead of being a description of a do-it-yourself musical (and personal) philosophy. As a result, the booking committee has actively sought out practitioners of other "non-commercial" forms, like reggae and folk, hoping that exposure to different ideas will bring a new vitality to "the scene" and broaden horizons.

The club opened its doors on New Year's Eve last year, but early on the popularity and energy of the punk scene began to overshadow the presence of other music and art forms at the Gilman. That's when the club split Friday and Saturday into different themes. Saturday nights are predominantly punk, while on Friday nights, as club regular Mark Davies puts it, "pretty much anything goes."

IT'S FUNNY HOW MUCH PUNKS ARE EMBARRASSED BY THEIR OWN CULTURE. OH, WE ARE SO "OPEN MINDED", ALWAYS STRIVING TOWARD "DIVERSITY" AND TRYING TO "EXPAND OUR HORIZONS". WE WANT DESPERATELY TO BRING IN OTHER CULTURES AND PEOPLE OF OTHER CULTURES TO OUR SHOWS. IT'S WEIRD AT BEST. WHAT ARE WE TRYING TO PROVE? IT'S PATRONIZING, AND IT'S JUST DISHONEST. WE CARE MORE ABOUT PATTING OURSELF ON THE BACK FOR BEING WORLDLY AND DIVERSE THAN WE DO ABOUT ACTUALLY CHECKING OUT OTHER CULTURES. IF WE CARED THAT MUCH WE COULD WALK TO ASHKENAZ INSTEAD OF THE LIQUOR STORE. ANYWAY, FRIDAY NIGHTS WAS GIVEN OVER TO THE "WEIRD" BANDS AND MOST OF US STAYED HOME. WHEN IT CAME TIME TO DO A COMPILATION OF GILMAN ST. BANDS, THINKIN' FELLERS UNION LOCAL 282, PERHAPS THE MOST GILMAN BAND OF ALL, WITH ALL 5 MEMBERS WORKING NEARLY EVERY SHOW, WERE NEVER ASKED. "TOO WEIRD".

PERHAPS I AM BEING TOO CRITICAL? YOU'RE MOST CRITICAL OF YOURSELF. GILMAN WASN'T MYSELF, BUT I WAS FIRMLY ENTRENCHED IN IT, AND I TOOK THE SUCCESSES AND DISAPPOINTMENTS PERSONALLY. IT'S IMPORTANT TO BE CRITICAL AND LEARN FROM MISTAKES, ESPECIALLY IN THE CASE OF GILMAN WHERE "THE OLD DAYS" ARE LOOKED BACK ON SO SENTIMENTALLY. IT'S EASY TO FALL INTO THAT SENTIMENTALITY, BUT IT DISTORTS THE REAL PICTURE. FOR ME, AND A LOT OF OTHERS, THE "OLD DAYS" AT GILMAN WERE REALLY EXCITING BUT ALSO REALLY FRUSTRATING. SINCE THOSE DAYS, GILMAN HAS RARELY BEEN SO EXCITING, BUT I THINK IT'S ONLY GOTTEN MORE HONEST AND SUPPORTIVE, BECOME MORE OF A REAL, OPEN COMMUNITY, AND MORE OF A DEMOCRACY.

Gilman Street's Unique Project

By Roya Camp   *The Voice*

You kind of hope your kids don't dress like this, swear like this, *smoke* like this. You can only hope they act like this, talk like this, care like this.

The members of the Gilman Street Project are an odd assortment of human beings. By the admission of "Clawed," a project member, the warehouse at 924 Gilman St. is "a place where misfits can get together."

It is instructive to listen to Clawed.

"People come to shows like this to escape the monotony of society," the baby-faced adolescent said before the Saturday night punk rock line up revved into life with the Petaluma group, "Trap A Poodle."

The 150 members had been assembled by the unwilling elite that runs Gilman St.; adults tending toward their mid-thirties. Martin, speaking for the organizers, stated the problem: what had started as a collective, emphasizing individuality, had become just another consumer-oriented rock club, without any input or enthusiasm from the people who were supposed to be running it.

Much was said, little resolved. After two hours the people resolved they wanted to hear the bands slated for that night, and they resolved to continue the meeting the next day.

Will Gilman St. close down, as the reluctantly-ruling elite threatened? Unlikely. They called for new energy, new input, and I'm passing that call along to you. If you enjoy alternative music and alternative lifestyles, if you're glad kids today have opportunities to get wild that we were denied (jeez, when did I become my dad?), if you want to get involved, but can't make yourself boat down to Nicaragua to pick coffee beans, take your energy and talent down to Gilman St. and see what you can do.

THE DAILY CALIFORNIAN — WEDNESDAY, MARCH 9, 1988 — At Gilman St.

PUNKS (AND YOUTH OF TODAY) AT WINCHELL'S AFTER A GILMAN SHOW. THE SHOWS HAD BECOME JUST A WARM-UP FOR THE LATENIGHT AFTER-SHOW HEDGEDIVING AND HANGING OUT. I COUNTED 80 PEOPLE AT WINCHELL'S ONE NIGHT. WHEN GILMAN CLOSED FOR THOSE FEW MONTHS, I COUNTED, LIKE, ONE OR TWO PEOPLE AT WINCHELL'S. I WONDERED WHO ALL THOSE PEOPLE WERE WHOM I HAD SPENT EVERY WEEKEND BONDING WITH. IT HAD SURE FELT LIKE FRIENDSHIP, BUT IT WASN'T.

THIS LETTER WAS THE BEGINNING OF THE END FOR THE MRR ERA AT GILMAN. TIM TOOK ON A PATERNAL ROLE AT GILMAN, AND GOT ALL THE PROBLEMS THAT COME WITH BEING A PARENT. YES, HE HAD SUPPORTED US AND GUIDED US, AND IT WAS A THANKLESS JOB. BUT LIKE ALL PARENTS, HE LECTURED US TO BE MORE RESPONS-IBLE, BUT DIDN'T SEEM WILLING TO GIVE UP ANY OF HIS OWN AUTHORITY. HE WANTED MORE PEOPLE TO DO THE WORK, BUT ONLY IF IT WAS DONE HIS WAY. HE WANTED US TO FEEL IT WAS OUR CLUB, AND AFTER ALL, IT WAS OUR CLUB, AND MAYBE WE DIDN'T THINK IT NEEDED TO BE SWEPT EVERY NIGHT. MAYBE WE DIDN'T FEEL LIKE WATCHING EVERY STUPID BAND. WE WERE THANK-FUL OF TIM FOR THE WORK THAT HE'D DONE, BUT HE WAS GETTING TO BE A PAIN IN THE ASS. HE HAD DONE AN AMAZING, GUTSY THING BY PUTTING IN THE MRR MONEY AND HELPING LAY THE GROUNDWORK FOR GILMAN. TEN MONTHS LATER WHEN HE DID PULL OUT OF GILMAN FOR REAL, THE FOUNDATION WAS STRONG ENOUGH TO CARRY ON WITH COMPLETELY NEW PEOPLE. SADLY, TIM HAD TO LEAVE AND CLOSE GILMAN IN ORDER TO SEE THAT IT REALLY COULD WORK WITHOUT HIM.

There Is More To Life Than The Grateful Dead

LA PUMA, DECEMBER 8, 1988

Unfortunately, nothing lasts forever, and the Gilman Street Project was no exception. Instead of all the members helping out, as time went on the burden seemed to fall on the shoulders of a smaller and smaller group of people. Many of them associated with Maximum Rock and Roll, a monthly punk/hardcore music and politics magazine published in Berkeley. As Tim Yohannan, editor of MRR, states in the October issue, "If any one single cause could be cited for the membership decision to close, it could be said that burnout was it." Due to this and other problems, it was decided on September 11 that the Gilman Street Project should close after that night's show.

A Fresh Start

This was not the end, but rather a new beginning. Once again, a group of concerned music fans started holding meetings. They adopted the name the Alternative Music Foundation. The AMF took over the Gilman Street Project's lease and bought the sound system. The AMF has not thought up a new name yet, but most people who go there still refer to it as "Gilman." Most people agree that the AMF is doing a good job. The atmosphere hasn't changed too much, the faces are basically the same as before and the interior has remained in its original state.

The difference between the AMF club and the Gilman Street Project is the way in which it is run. Under the new system, not everyone has to be a member to attend the shows. The people in the AMF realize that not everyone can or wants to work at shows. By realizing this fact, the people at the AMF hope to avoid the burnout that plagued the Gilman Street Project.

ANOTHER OPEN LETTER TO MEMBERS...

The motivation for me in becoming an initial director of this club was to preserve and expand on what was special about the old Gilman Street Project by trying to start afresh, ironing out some faults with the old operation and by opening the doors to the diverse hordes like-minded people who have a personal emphasis of music over money.

My personal vision for the club includes: attracting knowledgeable people in the alternative music world to use their knowledge and contacts to educate audiences of new, exciting and creative groups through intelligent booking; support creativity and artwork in flyering and publicity and inside the club; being open to all types of people willing to put in time and effort to support what it is that makes the club special and not 'just another nightclub on the circuit'.

The club cannot progress further without a clear statement of its purpose for its directors (current or soon to be elected) to act upon. Too much time and energy is being wasted in conflict of direction in the present leadership. I feel silly for even having to make this statement and I will feel guilty and ashamed if the work put into this club so far becomes exploited and perverted into a stepping stone for a very commercial music venue.

Jonathan Denlinger

PART OF AN OPEN LETTER FROM JONATHAN, PART OF AN ATTEMPT TO WRESTLE POWER AWAY FROM LOU, THE CREEPY BUSINESSMAN WHO STEPPED IN AS FATHER FIGURE WHEN TIM LEFT. EVENTUALLY LOU WAS RUN OUT, HIS HOUSE COVERED IN GRAFFITI, HIS NEW ATTEMPT AT A SEPERATE CLUB THWARTED. BUT HE WAS WHAT GILMAN NEEDED BRIEFLY TO GET BACK ON IT'S FEET. HE WAS ORGANIZED, MOTIVATED, AND RICH. JUST ONE OF A LONG LINE OF CHARACTERS AT GILMAN OVER THE YEARS WHO WERE EITHER CROOKED OR SLEAZY OR BOTH. THEY TEND TO OVERSHADOW THE QUIET BEHIND-THE-SCENES TYPES LIKE JONATHAN AND MICHAEL D AND A HUNDRED OTHERS WHO DID SO MUCH WORK AND RISKED SO MUCH AND NEVER DEMANDED A THING IN RETURN.

MAYBE I AM TOO
PICKY ABOUT LITTLE
THINGS, BUT THESE
DIFFERENT MEMBER-
SHIP CARDS DO GIVE
A CLUE AS TO THE
CHANGES IN GILMAN
OVER THE YEARS.

That wasn't always the case. By the mid-'80s, punk rock's youthful energy had begun to disappear as consumerism settled in, corporate sponsorships muscled forward, venues closed down, and unity dissolved. Most of all, not a single regular all-ages club survived in the the Bay Area.

Livermore is currently writing his thesis on the Gilman scene and he naturally has a lot to say. In his words, Gilman Street is the "Mecca of the punk rock universe…the most significant place in the punk rock scene today" and "the modern equivalent of the Fillmore or the Avalon."

TWO POPULAR LIES — BAM MAGAZINE 1990

READER'S CHOICE

BEST HARDCORE MUSIC

Gilman Street Project. Ten years after the first and only Sex Pistols' US tour, stage dives, slam dancing, mohawks, and exciting hardcore music still live. And, less pretentiously and far more vitally than anywhere else I've been lately, it lives at the Gilman Street Project.

E.B.EXPRESS

AL'S FLIER. A LOT OF LOCAL BANDS MADE
A POINT OF REFUSING PAYMENT FROM GILMAN.

EPILOGUE: THE FOCUS OF THIS MAGAZINE IS ON THE FIRST THREE YEARS OF GILMAN, BECAUSE THOSE ARE THE ONLY ONES I KNOW WELL. AFTER THAT I DROPPED OUT OF THE COMMITEES, STOPPED WORKING THE DOOR, AND ONLY CAME TO MEETINGS WHEN THEY THREATENED TO 86 ME FOR DRINKING IN THE GIRL'S BATHROOM. OH, EVERYTHING GOT SO MUCH BETTER. I CAME TO GILMAN AND GOT TO STOP WORRYING ABOUT THE CLUB AND START REALLY ENJOYING IT. THE WHOLE SCENE CHANGED AND GOT LOOSER, SEXIER, MORE DARING THAN IT HAD EVER BEEN BEFORE. NOT AS SELF-CONCIOUS, NOT TRYING TO BE SOMETHING IT WASN'T. A COMMUNITY SPIRIT GREW ORGANICALLY, NOT FORCED OR ARTIFICIALLY CREATED. IF THE SECURITY CAUGHT YOU DRINKING THEY WOULD SMILE AND SHAKE THEIR HEAD. IF YOU SMASHED A BOTTLE THEY WOULD HAND YOU A BROOM. NOW THAT EVERYONE WASN'T TRYING SO HARD TO BE FUN AND SPONTANEOUS, GILMAN BECAME FUN AND SPONTANEOUS. NOT JUST ON WEEK-ENDS, BUT SEVEN DAYS A WEEK, BANDS REHEARSING, PLAYING, PEOPLE HANGING OUT, TALKING SHIT, SHOOTING HOOP. AND THAT'S THE WAY IT'S BEEN EVER SINCE, FOR SEVEN YEARS. SO, HAPPY BIRTHDAY GILMAN, AND THANKS TO THE PEOPLE WHO HAD THE GUTS TO LAY THE GROUNDWORK, AND THE PEOPLE WHO HAD THE GUTS TO CHANGE IT, AND STICK WITH IT, THROUGH TEN LONG YEARS. DAMN.

Happy Birthday, Gilman st.!!

(THAT'S ME + MY DAD JOINING THE CELEBRATION)

IF THERE WAS A CAUSE, NO MATTER HOW HOPELESS OR RIDICULOUS, THERE WAS A BENEFIT FOR IT AT GILMAN. THIS IS THE DOOR POSTER FROM THE COMETBUS BENEFIT SHOW WHICH SUCEEDED IN GETTING ME OUT OF DEBT WITH THE PRINTER.

onehour
sevenminutes
in the
gilman stoar

Photo montage by Lauren L.

Battle #3 started with complaints of vandalism and graffiti filed with the city by a neighboring business in Oct. 1998. Below is a report/policy review sent to the zoning board by Gilman in response to the complaints.

924 Gilman St. Project Policy Review, December 1998 - Final

The Membership of the 924 Gilman Street Project is greatly concerned about our immediate neighborhood. In an effort to provide an environment suitable for residence, entertainment, dining, retail, light manufacturing, storage/distribution, professional services, and high-tech R&D, we are revising and reaffirming a number of security policies that relate to the quality of life in and around our building both during events and during the week.

The Project has a number of policies not listed here. The most important ones in regards to our neighborhood are specified in our use permit and reproduced below:

- Security shall be provided for all performances, and shall include at least two people at the entrance, two inside the hall, and two on the exterior. These personnel shall be easily identifiable by means of clothing or badges, and can be members of the organization. Hired security personnel is not necessary.
- For popular, full-house shows, the club will enforce a "no-in-and-outs" rule.
- "No drinking [or] loitering" notices shall be posted inside the club and on all promotional and advertising materials, club literature and admission tickets.

86 list.

- We are responsible not only for our building, but also the surrounding neighborhood.
- Security and staff have the right to "86" (bar) anyone from the show.
- Anyone who is 86'ed is required not only to leave our building but also to leave the surrounding neighborhood.
- Anyone who has paid their admission and is later 86'ed can receive a refund at staff's discretion. If they have traveled to the show with friends, their friends can opt to have their handstamps cancelled and receive a refund. If this is so, they are also required to leave the neighborhood for the duration of the evening.
- Patrons will be 86'ed for the following reasons (among others.)
    - Drinking or drug use inside the Project.
    - Drinking or drug use in public in the immediate neighborhood.
    - Violent behavior inside or around the Project.
    - Being intoxicated while inside the Project.
    - Defacing property in the surrounding neighborhood.
- The Project will keep a list of all 86'ed members. The list will be divided into two sections, the "Membership Reviewed" section and the "Security's Discretion" section.
- The master 86 list will be kept in the computer in the office, and a fresh copy will be posted at the front door.
- After a member is 86'ed security is responsible for hand writing their name on the "Security's Discretion" section of the 86 list at the front door. After the show, (or the next day) the Head of Security will double-check to make sure that the name was added to the computer file, and if the name is not clear on the front-door printout, a new printout will be made.
- No one on the 86 list will be allowed inside the Project at any time, except to address a membership meeting.
- At each membership meeting, the membership will review any additions to the "Security's" section of the 86 list. The membership will review the situation. The 86'd member will have the opportunity to address the meeting if they feel that they were unfairly barred from the Project. The membership will vote on each 86'ed member and either remove them from the list, add them to the "Reviewed" section of the list, or leave them on the "Security's" section pending further review.
- Under no circumstances should an 86'ed member be allowed into a show as a paid audience member, a band member, a guest, or a volunteer. Only a majority vote at a membership meeting can remove a name from the 86 list.

During the Show

- No one who is visibly intoxicated will be allowed inside the Project or allowed to remain in the surrounding neighborhood.

- Under no circumstances should an 86'ed member be allowed into a show as a paid audience member, a band member, a guest, or a volunteer. 86'd members are not allowed in the surrounding neighborhood.
- Each show has at least six clearly identified security personnel who are responsible for the inside, entrances, and area surrounding the Project.
- 924 Gilman will hire an additional paid, unarmed, uniformed security person dedicated to patrolling the peripheral neighborhood around the Project (7th to 9th, Camelia to Harrison) each Friday and Saturday night from 9PM to 1AM (Possibly 7PM to 1AM during the winter months.)
- This perimeter security person has been on regular duty since December 12th.
- This perimeter security person may use a bicycle, provided by the Project, to aid in the patrol of the neighborhood.
- This perimeter security person will have a two-way radio to communicate with the other security staff.

- This perimeter security person is hired to prevent vandalism and public drinking in the neighborhood, but is not responsible for the interior of the Project, the immediate sidewalk around the Project.
- This perimeter security person will pay special attention to the East side of 8th Street. (DiCon, P.Kelly, etc.)
- On especially busy nights, additional guards may be hired for peripheral patrol.

After the show

- The Project will ensure that a landscape person circles the neighborhood before 10AM on Sunday Morning, removing litter from doorways, bushes, sidewalks, etc, in the immediate neighborhood area. The landscaper will be either a club volunteer or a client of Berkeley-Oakland Support Services (BOSS.) The landscaper will also notify Project personnel of any Graffiti or property damage.

Other Issues

- The Project will participate in the cost of installation of high powered lights to illuminate the steps and front of the DiCon building and Paul Kelly's office.
- The Project will participate in the cost of cost of replacing the palm trees planted by DiCon with heartier, **indigenous** plants, and protecting those plants from parking accidents.
- The Project will continue to sponsor periodic neighborhood cleanups in concert with other neighborhood organizations and businesses.

Background:

The 924 Gilman Street Project is an all-ages, volunteer-run, alcohol and drug-free alternative cultural center. We mostly put on "Do It Yourself" punk music shows, although we've had plays, art shows, and occasionally various other genres (like ska, hip-hop, folk, flamenco, and industrial/noise.) We have held benefit concerts for such varied organizations as Rock Against Racism, Food Not Bombs, various battered women shelters, and various local underground record labels. We also have weekly Alcoholics Anonymous, Narcotics Anonymous, and Youth Narcotics Anonymous meetings. We have also held first aid, self-defense, and mask-making classes for our volunteers and patrons. All shows are $5 and under, and we require everyone to have a membership card ($2 annual fee) and therefore be a member of the collective. All of the major rules (no stage diving, excessively violent dancing, or alcohol/drugs in or around the Project) are printed on the back of the card. No racist, misogynist, or homophobic acts are ever booked. We have membership meetings that are open to everyone the first and third Saturdays of each month at 5PM at the Project. We make decisions by a 2/3 or 50% majority vote (depending on the subject up for a vote) whenever we can't reach a consensus. We are a legal not-for-profit corporation under the laws of the state of California with 3 corporate officers.

924 Gilman St. Project
Alternative Music Foundation

PO BOX 1058
Berkeley, CA 94701

December 19, 1998

Wendy C   , AICP
Deputy Planning Director
Planning & Development Department
2118 Milvia St. Ste. 300
Berkeley, CA 94704

Ms. C   .,

The 924 Gilman St. Project appreciates the time you took to speak with John H   and the memo that you sent to us following that conversation.

After reviewing your suggestions at our weekly meeting, we had the following observations.

1. Hiring a security guard from a professional security service would not be as effective as hiring a Project member to perform the perimeter security. Our past experiments with "Rent-a-Cop" services have proven them inadequate at best, dangerous at worst. Every paid security person has started as a Project member and volunteer.

2. In order to provide affordable entertainment for youth, the Project runs with a minimum of overhead. All the workers at the Project are volunteers, except for a number of paid security staff compensated on a sliding scale.

3. Outside security, unfamiliar with our Project's membership, goals, and history, charged with notifying the police at any possible infraction, would cause an undue amount of strain on the City's law enforcement services, without addressing root causes.

Enclosed you will find the final revision of our policy review. Although we are hesitant to employ all of your recommendations, we still feel that we can, in your words, "show the City a good faith effort to minimize neighborhood problems."

Sincerely,

Mike L.   , Member   John H   ., Neighborhood Outreach

Above: the letter that accompanied the policy review on the preceding two pages.
Below: DiCon's press release.

DiCon
FIBEROPTICS, INC
1331 EIGHTH STREET
BERKELEY, CA 94710
TEL. (510)
FAX (510)

FOR IMMEDIATE RELEASE

In response to inquiries from the press and other interested parties, DiCon Fiberoptics submits the following statement regarding issues of vandalism against DiCon and their relatedness to events at the "924 Club", an underage alternative music club located at 924 Gilman Street.

Over an eight-year period, DiCon has endured repeated acts of vandalism including bottle breaking, graffiti and destruction of property. These acts of vandalism coincide with events at the 924 Gilman club, which is located one block from DiCon. On numerous occasions, DiCon has confronted and secured agreement from the club representative to address and resolve the problem. Unfortunately, the vandalism continued and in fact worsened.

In a continuing effort to find a solution, stop the vandalism and increase the security in the area, DiCon alerted the City of Berkeley Planning and Development Department to the problem. Subsequently, the City has undertaken an investigation and is working towards an ultimate resolution to the ongoing problem.

DiCon Fiberoptics is a privately held manufacturer of fiberoptic components for the telecommunications industry. DiCon currently employs 220 people and has been operating at 1331 Eighth Street in Berkeley since 1991.

924 Gilman St. Project
Alternative Music Foundation

PO BOX 1058
Berkeley, CA 94701

January 24, 1999

Concerning: 924 Gilman St.

Members of the Berkeley City Council and Zoning Adjustments Board,

The 924 Gilman St. Project is a non-profit, volunteer run, all ages performance space and community center in West Berkeley. For the last 13 years, we have produced alcohol and drug free performances, hosted community events and provided space for Alcoholics Anonymous and Narcotics Anonymous meetings.

Recently, complaints from one of our neighbors, DiCon Fiberoptics, have prompted an investigation of our operation by the Planning and Development Department and the Berkeley Police.

DiCon refuses to meet with us, even refusing a request for a meeting made on our behalf by Wendy C___, the Deputy Planning Director. We feel that the only way to achieve a lasting solution is to meet face to face with DiCon's management. We need to hear their concerns and possible solutions, and we would like to present them with our ideas. This is how neighbors co-exist. Our successful interaction with Pyramid Breweries over the past two years proves the success of direct cooperation.

Enclosed you will find letters that have been sent to us for forwarding to the City. These letters, clearly demonstrate three things:

- The majority of our neighbors feel that we operate in a responsible and responsive manner.
- We are a vital part of the social **and** economic fabric of Berkeley.
- We have touched the lives of people all over the world.

We have also provided the City Clerk and the Secretary of the Zoning Board with a copy of a statement signed by our supporters. Over 4,500 concerned people took the time to sign the document at the club or attach their name via the Internet.

Sincerely,

Mike L___, Member

January 27, 1999

Ken B___
Dicon Fiber Optics Inc.
1331 8th Street
Berkeley, CA 94710

Dear Mr. B___ :

We received a call from Mike L___ of the Gilman Youth Club concerning problems that have developed principally around trash and graffiti. We are familiar with dealing with community problems related to the club as we have done mediations with community groups and businesses and the club in the past.

Berkeley Dispute Resolution Service (BDRS) is a voluntary mediation service which helps the citizens of Berkeley and Albany resolve problems simply. We are strictly neutral: we do not represent anyone's point of view.

If your company is interested, we would be willing to facilitate a meeting with representatives of your company and of the club. At that meeting, problems your employees are having with club members could be discussed with the aim of reaching some agreements. We could then focus energy on creating an atmosphere where problems could be solved through better understanding and cooperation.

To this end, we would set-up a facilitated meeting between representatives of both the club and your company. If this is of interest to you, we should decide who should be at the table in order to get a handle on taking action. Hopefully this will make your employees feel they can come and go without fear and that trash, graffiti, and drinking on the street can be controlled and minimized.

I called you and left a message today and hope we will be able to talk about the proposed meeting.

Yours truly,

Dan R___
Senior Case Manager

DR:amf

cc: Mike L___

Please support The 924 Gilman St. Project!

What's Going On?

The 924 Gilman St. Project, a non-profit, volunteer-run, alcohol/drug-free performance space and community center, is being singled out as the cause of all problems in the eight to ten blocks surrounding our building.

The ultimate goal appears to be the complete removal of our organization and services from the community.

We have a successful track record negotiating and collectively resolving issues with our neighbors. In the current situation, however, we feel that we are not being recognized for our efforts to resolve the various issues. As a result, we are being steamrolled into a hearing before the Berkeley Zoning Adjustments Board.

Our normal method of dealing with complaints of graffiti and litter in the neighborhood has been to work directly with the affected parties, cleaning up any damage, paying for repair, and working to minimize repeat occurrences.

Our requests for conflict resolution have been ignored. Instead, we are the target of video surveillance and misleading and questionable investigative tactics by individual city employees.

Why is this bad?

The 924 Gilman St. Project benefits the City of Berkeley and the entire Bay Area in a number of ways. The Project provides an alternative to the despair and isolation of street life or minimum-wage jobs. Musicians who often have no other available venue get a place to perform. Project volunteers learn valuable organizational, business, technical, artistic, and career skills. The Project provides a place for young people to network and find role models with similar experiences and interests. Many volunteers have gone on to become successful artists, join trade unions, operate small businesses, or pursue advanced educational degrees.

We estimate that a government-funded youth center and job training facility offering a subset of the services we organically provide would cost taxpayers over $200,000 per year. However, the 924 Gilman St. Project is completely self-sustaining, operating for over twelve years without one cent of funding from government or corporate grants.

What Can You Do?

Please write a letter of support to the Berkeley Zoning Office. Let the City know that you respect our efforts to provide a safe, affordable environment for youth and to work directly with our neighbors.

We'd like to show that support for the Project comes from people everywhere in all walks of life. So, whether you live in Berkeley, Richmond, Livermore, or London; whether you're a current or former Project atendee, or a parent, teacher, counselor, or friend of a club member, please send a letter on personal stationary, company/organization letterhead, or even plain binder paper!

If you need help getting started, we've included a few sample letters. If you need more information, see the phone, web, and email contact information at the bottom of the page.

We have included an envelope, addressed to The 924 Gilman St. Project. We will file a copy of all correspondence, and pass the original on to the Zoning Office. If you would rather send your letter directly to the City, the address is:

City of Berkeley
Zoning Office
2120 Milvia St.
Berkeley, CA 94704

Who are we?

The 924 Gilman Street Project is an all-ages, volunteer-run, alcohol and drug-free alternative cultural center. We hold benefit concerts for such varied organizations as Rock Against Racism, Food Not Bombs, and battered women shelters. In addition to weekly Alcoholics Anonymous, Narcotics Anonymous, and Youth Narcotics Anonymous meetings, we hold first aid, self-defense, and mask-making classes for our volunteers and patrons.

Our Friday and Saturday evening performances feature musicians ranging in age from their early teens on up, in bands that operate outside of the corporate media ("major label") structure. No racist, misogynist, or homophobic acts are ever booked.

Membership meetings are open to everyone the first and third Saturdays of each month at 5PM at 924 Gilman St. We are a non-profit corporation under the laws of the state of California.

We have existed as a community providing a needed youth service for twelve years. Please help us continue in a spirit of cooperation.

I support the 924 Gilman St. Project!

I support the 924 Gilman St. Project's efforts to provide a safe, pleasant, and affordable performance space in Berkeley. I feel that the 924 Gilman St. project is an important resource in the community, and I trust the Project's membership to resolve any potential conflicts with their neighbors.

1.		
Signature	print name	city of residence

924 Gilman St. Project
Alternative Music Foundation

PO BOX 1058
Berkeley, CA 94701

February 13, 1999

Dr. Ho L.
President, DiCon Fiberoptics
1331 8th St.
Berkeley, CA 94710

Dr. L ,

Thank you for taking the time to meet with me on February 5. Let me restate how concerned I am that you and some of your employees are dissatisfied with the current state of our neighborhood. At that meeting, you asked me to send a memo to you detailing the increased measures that we have recently taken to further minimize graffiti and litter in our immediate area.

Please see the attached document, "Policy Review - December 1998." It details the additional measures we implemented after having been made aware of your concerns by the City.

Not mentioned in the document is the positive relationship between our security staff and yours. Our security staff has taken the time to speak with your weekend guard, and your guard has been quite generous in sharing his concerns, knowledge, and expertise.

We still feel that a mediated discussion between our two organizations would be helpful at this time. If you agree, please contact Dan R   at Berkeley Dispute Resolution Services. His number is (510)

Sincerely,

Mike L   , Member

---

924 Gilman St. Project
Alternative Music Foundation

PO BOX 1058
Berkeley, CA 94701

February 13, 1999

Concerning: 924 Gilman St.

Members of the Berkeley City Council and Zoning Adjustments Board,

Enclosed you will find additional letters that have been sent to us in the past few weeks for forwarding to the City. As before, these letters, clearly demonstrate that we are a vital part of the social **and** economic fabric of Berkeley and we have touched the lives of people all over the world.

We have been trying, with limited success to communicate with DiCon Fiberoptics, whose complaints have prompted an investigation of our operation by the Planning and Development Department and the Berkeley Police. (Mentioned in our letter of 1/24/99.)

We still feel that the only way to achieve a lasting solution is to meet face to face with DiCon's management. We need to hear their concerns and possible solutions, and we would like to present them with our ideas. This is how neighbors co-exist. Our successful interaction with Pyramid Breweries over the past two years proves the success of direct cooperation.

The Berkeley Dispute Resolution Service, at our request, has contacted DiCon and offered to set up mediation. DiCon originally refused, then agreed, then refused. One of our representatives met with DiCon officials without the BDRS and we now realize the importance of having them involved. We would also like to invite Wendy C   and other members of the City's Planning and Development Department, as well as other interested City or neighborhood parties.

We have also provided the City Clerk and the Secretary of the Zoning Board with a copy of a statement signed by our supporters. Over 8,500 concerned people took the time to sign the document at the club or attach their name via the Internet.

The 924 Gilman St. Project is a non-profit, volunteer run, all ages performance space and community center in West Berkeley. For the last 13 years, we have produced alcohol and drug free performances, hosted community events and provided space for Alcoholics Anonymous and Narcotics Anonymous meetings.

Sincerely,

Mike L   , Member

Gilman fights neighbor to stay in business

by Katie Flynn

The only all age, punk rock music mecca in Berkeley, 924 Gilman, is under attack. Complaints of vandalism by a nearby business launched a police crackdown, and prompted Gilman into a fight against a possible closure.

The Gilman, located near the corner of Gilman and San Pablo for over twelve years, has hosted such bands as Greenday, Rancid, Operation Ivy and Black fork. It has also welcomed many BHS benefit concerts with school groups like the Mooches, Mr. Harlequin, and Eye Claudia.

Four months ago, Gilman's neighbors of ten years DiCon Fiberoptics, began complaining to city economic developers about vandalism and the damaging of four decorative palm trees in their parking lot shared with Gilman.

After receiving the complaints, the city economic developers sent Zoning Complaint Officials to check out the scene around Gilman. The officials caught two teens tagging on one of DiCon's walls.

All Graffiti was removed immediately and the offenders were removed from the club.

"If there is vandalism, the way Gilman deals with it is to talk with the owner and paint it right away," stated John Hart, Gilman volunteer. "We have a new person come out every Sunday morning and pick up any trash around Gilman and people to paint over graffiti. But DiCon says they don't want those things to

happen in the first place."

Soon after this incident, and the damage to four of DiCon's palm trees, Berkeley Police, equipped with video cameras, joined the crowds of punks outside the club.

"Two or three times the police

PHOTO BY REBECCA WEISSMAN
A palm tree DiCon Fiberoptics says Gilman-goers vandalized.

were here video. taping and following kids to see what they were doing," explains Chris Sparks, head coordinator of Gilman. "As far as we know they haven't been doing any video taping lately."

DiCon has refused to negotiate directly with Gilman volunteers, and instead goes through various city departments.

"I talked to DiCon last Friday for the first time. They said that there was nothing to negotiate, and they

were not willing to discuss the subject to any great length," says Sparks.

Wendy Cosin, Berkeley Deputy Planning Director, is one of the city officials contacted by DiCon. She

explained in The Bay Guardian that "we've had reports of vandalism that appear to be associated with the club. We're trying to work with the club and the police department to see how extensive the problem is."

Concerns over a possible permit revocation hearing in the near future have been quelled, yet Sparks maintains he is "always afraid the club is going to get shut down."

DiCon has distributed a press release, stating their position. In it, the company explains that "it has endured repeated acts of vandalism, including bottle breaking, graffiti, and destruction of property."

So far, the Berkeley Planning Department has recommended that Gilman add more security guards. Although the city suggested uniformed guards from established services, Gilman contended with adding one more of their own security 'workers per night, and holding security meetings.

The two feuding neighbors are making the first steps in resolving the issue. They will both attend meetings with the Berkeley Dispute Resolution, an organization which helps Berkeley residents negotiate problems.

Gilman has received much support from other neighbors, and letters from the Pyramid Brewery, Lookout Records, are being sent to city departments. Petitions in support of the Gilman have received almost 8,000 signatures all together and will also be sent to city officials.

Above: article taken from the Berkeley High school newspaper.
Below: article taken from the *SF Bay Guardian* weekly newspaper (01/06/99).

Seen but not heard

Berkeley police are cracking down on venerable punk club 924 Gilman. Is the city no longer safe for counterculture? **By A. Clay Thompson**

THE BEIGE WAREHOUSE at the corner of Eighth and Gilman Streets in northwest Berkeley is a hub of the Bay Area's youth culture. Every weekend for the last 11 years, 924 Gilman has hosted underground bands from around the bay and around the world. Local heroes like Green Day and Rancid got their start in the all-ages joint, where they shared the stage with international cult favorites like Japan's Ruins and Canada's NoMeansNo and subterranean sound makers like Dystopia and Neurosis.

Lately, the all-volunteer, nonprofit, membership-run space has hosted visitors from outside the world of Mohawks, dreadlocks, piercings, and tattoos. On at least two Friday nights in December, Berkeley police parked across the street from 924 Gilman, recording clubgoers' movements with video and still cameras. And officials

in the city planning department are making noises about revoking the space's permit.

The cause of all this governmental sound and fury: some graffiti in the neighborhood and the occasional underage drinker.

"It's ridiculous. It's incredibly unjust," said club coordinator Chris

Sparks, who first walked through the club's battered brown doors 10 years ago. "It's like you see a bunch of punks and it's OK to assume they're committing a crime."

Wendy Cosin, deputy planning director with Berkeley's Planning and Development Department, explained the city's rationale for putting 924 Gilman under the microscope. "We've had reports of vandalism that appear to be associated with the club. We're trying to work with the club and work with the police department to see how extensive the problem is," Cosin told us. "There have been complaints about the drinking of alcoholic beverages" in the vicinity of the club.

Cosin said the department is considering a permit revocation hearing—which could spell the end of another Bay Area counterculture institution.

The club spends $500 a year on paint to combat the tagging that shows up occasionally on its walls and on those of neighboring businesses, and it has just hired two people to clean graffiti every Sunday. Club members are also stepping up security to prevent drinking in and around the warehouse.

But the city's idea of security seems to differ from that of the club's organizers. The planning department suggested that the club hire uniformed, gun-toting guards — a notion that doesn't sit well with the punks, crusties, hip-hoppers, and hardcore aficionados who frequent the joint.

Gilman has a red-shirted cadre of volunteer bouncers and security workers on hand to break up occasional punch-ups and paint assaults at shows. Their tactics differ from those of the standard rent-a-cop — a much

continued next page

despised figure in punk circles.

"Security guards don't know how to deal with people in the punk community," said Colin Ascher, a Gilman security conscript. "How is that kid going to react to that guy with a gun or nightstick? We *explain* to people why they shouldn't do something. Hiring security would destroy the whole feeling of the club." And at $75 and up per cop per night, the club can't afford it.

Gilman staffers and city officials say a neighboring high-tech firm's annoyance with the club prompted the city's newfound interest in the space. They say they are willing to address any complaints the company, Dicon Fiber Optics, may have.

"All they have to do is call," Sparks said. "We're right across the street." Club members have spent recent weeks canvassing the neighborhood for support and helpful suggestions.

Calls from the *Bay Guardian* to Dicon went unreturned.

Capt. Bobby Miller, press liaison for the Berkeley Police Department, was unaware of the Gilman Street surveillance. The *Bay Guardian* was unable to contact Lt. Bob Maloney, who is responsible for the operation.

A recent Friday night outside the club found teenagers and twenty-somethings guzzling sodas, smoking cigarettes, sitting on the curb discussing life, and generally doing what young people do. Spray cans and beer bottles were nowhere to be found — if there were underage drinkers, they had likely found spots blocks from the club, where the ubiquitous red-shirts couldn't harass them.

Inside, a Canadian sludge-rock act known as Seized blasted through mega-bassy metallic dirges as the crowd moshed front and center. At the edges of the packed room clubgoers picked through stacks of self-

produced underground CDs and vinyl and pored over a table of books by the likes of Noam Chomsky and Emma Goldman, on sale from local agit-lit distributors AK Press.

As usual, there was no booze to be found in the club, no pot smoke wafting toward the rafters, and no brawls. The only drama occurred when a teenage hardcore fan discovered his wallet had been nabbed while he was walking through the neighborhood.

City council member Kriss Worthington is worried about the club's fate. Worthington told the *Bay Guardian* he'll go to bat for Gilman if the issue of the club's permit comes before the council. "Usually there is a way to work out compromises with the neighbors and businesses," Worthington said. "It is important to maintain as much of our alternative culture and as many of the creative things that the young people are making as possible." ∎

Below: article taken from the *East Bay Express*, April 9, 1999

924 GILMAN VS DICON FIBEROPTICS

The Search for Peace on Gilman Street

Can a growing high-tech company and a venerable all-ages punk club coexist in peace and harmony? Not so far.

BY TIM KINGSTON

DICon Fiberoptics Inc. is apparently not familiar with what it takes to be a good neighbor in Berkeley. For the past few months the high-tech manufacturing firm has been busy trying to make life miserable for the folks at 924 Gilman (also known as the Gilman Street Project)— Berkeley's venerable all-ages, alcohol-free punk club. DICon has been—in the words of Wendy Cosin, Berkeley's deputy planning director—"vociferously" complaining about graffiti, broken beer bottles, and acts of vandalism allegedly perpetrated by the club's patrons.

Even if you haven't heard of the Gilman Street Project, established in 1987 and located in what used to be a predominantly industrial area, you've probably heard of some of the bands that the club has helped launch: Green Day, Rancid, Operation Ivy, and Neurosis, among others. But there can be little doubt that DICon knew of 924 Gilman when it moved into its current location in the early 1990s—or else it was blind to the all-ages punk club directly across the street.

Given the club's history of occasional difficulties with neighbors and the authorities, DICon's complaints are, not surprisingly, making 924 Gilman nervous. In the past, the complaints have ranged from litter outside the local church to

From left, Chris Sparks, Jesse Luscious, and Krissy M. of 924 Gilman

graffiti, and the occasional public drunk—yet all these seem managable compared to the current standoff. "I know personally from talking with Ho Lee, president of DICon, that he will not be satisfied until we are gone," says Mike Limon, former coordinator of the collective and today a club point person in dealings with city officials and DICon. "I had a short meeting with him [several months ago]. I offered him partial solutions —we could go the extra mile to make sure everything is in top shape. He just said, 'There is nothing to negotiate. You need to control your people.'"

The latest flurry of DICon complaints came about as the result of vandalism to some palm trees the company planted on 8th Street last November. Standing outside 924 Gilman, with the sound of a ska band rocking out in the background, Chris Sparks, the Gilman Street Project's current coordinator, says the problems go beyond the so-called "palm tree incident." "This is the result of years of miscommunication," Sparks says. "We have heard complaints of graffiti [from DICon], then it was nothing more and we assumed it was okay, no complaints." Asked if he thinks DICon won't be satisfied until the

club closes, Sparks responds, "They are indifferent to our survival. They want to run their business. They are self-centered enough that they think they don't have to communicate with the neighborhood. They [see themselves as a] big important company that Berkeley can't do without."

Repeated calls to DICon president Ho Lee and the company's head of human relations, Ken Brown, went unreturned. Attempts to contact company officials in person were rebuffed by a distinctly uncomfortable receptionist, who relayed a curt message from

con't
next
page

Brown: "I was told we have no comment at this time." DiCon manager Ettie Nixon even refused to supply a basic description of what the company does or even a quarterly report or the names of corporate management.

Berkeley officials insist that DiCon has never intimated, let alone demanded, that the city close Gilman Street Project, but that's not to imply pressure is not being applied. "It is my understanding that DiCon's position is the club is a city problem and the city should deal with it," says Calvin Fong, an aide to the area's representative on the Berkeley City Council, Linda Maio. That view places the city between a rock and a hard place. DiCon is one of Berkeley's fastest-growing companies. It provides two hundred jobs—a figure that is expected to double inside two years. And in accordance with the hard-won West Berkeley development plan, the company provides clean manufacturing and jobs, not to mention a steady tax revenue stream.

Yet the Gilman Street Project provides one of the East Bay's only music venues open to underage patrons. The club allows no drinking or drugs and provides an enviably friendly environment for many a teen who would otherwise be hanging out on Telegraph, in malls, or on street corners in a fashion that has aggravated older generations for eons.

"There have been a number of complaints off and on for many years," says the city's Wendy Cosin. "We began meeting with club members in January. We would rather work things out and see if we could come to an agreement about how the club can be managed, without going through the process of revoking a permit or changing the conditions of the permit."

The most recent

meeting between the city and club took place in late March. The city offered a series of proposals in hopes of resolving the DiCon-Gilman dispute. Ideas on the table include additional street lighting on 8th Street, beefed-up club security, restrictions on "ins and outs," improved cleanup, and new "No Drinking and Loitering Signs." The Gilman collective will consider the city's proposals and

offer its response by the middle of next week.

From the perspective of the Gilman Street Project volunteers, the main sticking point has been beefed-up security. The city is asking the club to hire a third-party security group to supplement Gilman's sweatshirted crew, but inside Gilman they're balking at outside security, noting that their punky patrons do not respond well to authority figures. Yet Limon wonders if a concession would even make a difference. "The main problem we are having is that we don't feel any of these things laid out here will do anything to mollify DiCon," he says.

City officials are slightly more hopeful that they can hammer out an accord between what Wendy Cosin describes as "different cultures." "We in the city are trying to help build bridges between the business, the city, and the 924 club," Cosin says. "I don't think [DiCon] wants [924 Gilman] out. They just don't want there to be problems." Yet negotiation, let alone neighborly collaboration, does not seem to be on DiCon's radar screen. In contrast, when Pyramid Brewery, Allied Radiators, or anyone else in the neighborhood has a problem after a show they call Gilman Street Project. Chris Sparks says volunteers promptly show up the next morning to paint out graffiti, sweep broken glass, and make any necessary repairs. The club even stores tins of paint that match most buildings in the area for instant graffiti eradication.

Indeed, so deeply has 924 Gilman managed to embed itself in the community that when word of its latest troubles surfaced, members of the club were able to blitz the Berkeley City Council with three-inch stacks of letters of support from local businesses near the club, including Pyramid Brewery (directly across the street), Allied Radiators (next door), Happy DoNuts, Reliance Antiques, the Working Glass shop, and Ed Kirwan Graphic Arts. That Alex Krallis, general manager of the Pyramid Ale House, wrote a letter supporting Gilman Street Project is particularly noteworthy. Things have come full circle since the brewery first opened. At first,

Krallis notes, members of the Gilman Street Project did not want the brewery to open across the street, fearing a clash between drunken yuppies and club members, or the overimbibing of their own patrons at Pyramid. But Krallis and other Pyramid employees eventually won them over. Now the security forces at both establishments are coordinated. Both sides agree that Gilman's volunteers will deal with their problematic patrons and Pyramid's paid guards will do the same for the Docker crowd, regardless of where the incident occurs. "There have been a few isolated incidents," Krallis says. "To this day there is not a stick of graffiti on the building. If there have been problems, they come right over. [But there has been] nothing. No clashes, no staring across the street at each other.

"I don't understand what is going on that side. I am just trying to be a good neighbor."

Even Linda Maio, who is widely viewed as the City Council swing vote, supports the club. Maio got involved early on, shortly after the club opened. There were early problems involving graffiti, fights, and public drunkenness, but Maio says the collective members moved rapidly to troubleshoot. "They went ringing doorbells and went door to door to meet neighbors and find out what they had to do," Maio says. "They are amazingly responsible. Every once in a while there is a little blip. There is no drinking there, but they don't have complete control over everyone." But DiCon has flatly refused to talk to representatives of the club's volunteer collective. The company even backed out of its offer to work with the Berkeley Dispute Resolution Service, Limon says. "Talk to any of the neighbors," says Jim Widess, the club's landlord and owner of the Caning Shop. "They are supportive [of 924 Gilman]. But DiCon just refuses to talk. It is the Berkeley way to work things out. It may be a cultural thing. I don't know." To the city's Calvin Fong, that is "the crux of the problem."

Meanwhile, many of the club's patrons seem blissfully ignorant of the battle over 924 Gilman's fate. The only sign of conflict is a cryptic "Save Gilman"

sign that hangs on the wall behind the main stage. One recent Friday night, the Alkaline Trio, a Chicago-based band on tour, gamely blasted out classic three-chord pop-punk. Outside, all that could be heard was a dull roar. Inside, the club felt almost homey. The cavernous room, spattered with brightly colored graffiti, was filled with a well-behaved mob of youth who looked far more interested in the music than causing trouble. At the risk of being snarled at, adorable is the word that came to mind about the punks there, not threatening.

"This collective is alive. It survives on a spirit of cooperation," muses Sparks outside the club as another group, the Chinkees, played their own variation of fast ska. "We are disregarded as a chaotic group of miscreants, but that is not the case. This is where seventeen-year-olds are responsible for thousands of dollars of equipment. We are responsible for our space. It is the energy that makes this place go. That is more exciting than the bands that come here."

So is DiCon interested in finding a middle ground that will keep both sides happy? "I did not think so at first," muses Maio. "They have not been here that long to become an embedded part of the town. But with more conversations and more dialogue and more awareness, and with more participation by the club itself, I am really quite hopeful they will start to think of how they can get what they need and still allow them to function. The club needs to be a part of that solution." ∎

Below: article taken from the May/June 1999 issue of *Punk Planet*, written by Ben Sizemore.

924 NO MORE?
GILMAN STREET UNDER FIRE

Staffers at the 924 Gilman Street Project, Berkeley's punk mecca, sent out the SOS signal late last year. City officials were threatening to revoke the club's use permits due to a neighboring high-tech firm's complaints about petty vandalism. 924 Gilman's fate—finding itself caught in the crosshairs of city paper-pushers and businesses—is emblematic of a wider war for territory tearing apart the San Francisco Bay Area.

During 924 Gilman's 12 year existence, the space has hosted nearly every important underground punk band—from Fugazi to Born Against to Bikini Kill to Neurosis to Operation Ivy, just to name a few. Over that same time, over 3,000 lesser known bands have also taken the stage. The all-ages, volunteer-run, membership-driven performance space has been a mainstay of the region's cultural life since day one.

In addition to hosting bands and hundreds of their fans, in December 1998, the club began playing unwitting host to undercover Berkeley cops. On at least two occasions that month, an undercover police officer rolled up in an unmarked car and shot video of 924 Gilman patrons as they congregated on the

sidewalk outside the beige-brick warehouse space. Complaints about graffiti, broken bottles, and two chopped-down palm trees from a nearby tech biz called DiCon Fiber Optics prompted the COINTELPRO-style surveillance. DiCon had moved in across 8th St. from the club in 1991.

Also in December, local planning department official Wendy Cosin told local media the city was considering yanking Gilman's permits because of graffiti and underage drinking.

"The city is trying to put a squeeze on Gilman because they want to show they support business," explained Chris Sparks, Gilman head coordinator for the past two years. He feels the city's approach is dead wrong. According to Sparks, the club gets scapegoated for any problems occurring in the rapidly gentrifying light-industrial neighborhood Gilman calls home. DiCon has never talked directly with coordinators of the club about its problems, instead running straight to the city.

con't next page

The club promptly paints over any graffiti that sprouts up in it's vicinity, whether it's related to the club or not. Gilman volunteers also spend time before and after every show picking up any trash and bottles that may have been left behind. "Gilman just wants to be good neighbors," explains Sparks. The club has long made an effort to cooperate with its neighbors and the city to deal with any problems associated with the space. "We're showing the city how committed we are to being responsible to the community," sums up Sparks.

If, as the city has threatened, the club comes up for a permit revocation hearing, it may find itself closed—or worse. The city may slap Gilman with new demands—like hiring paid security, barring "ins and outs," or creating an 18-and-over age limit. Sparks would rather see the space close for good than put up with such concessions. "We're not going to hire a fucking rent-a-cop, it goes against the whole spirit of Gilman," said Sparks. "The idea is to police yourself and to control your own space."

Jesse Luscious—frontman for the band the Criminals—has been working at Gilman ever since he moved to Berkeley from Philadelphia in 1989. He says the climate at the club nowadays in terms of drinking, fighting, and "fucking shit up" is the calmest he can remember since he arrived. Luscious is helping to spearhead Gilman's fight back with a letter writing and petition campaign designed to show the city how much support the club has. Luscious and others have collected over 7,000 e-mailed signatures on a "Save Gilman" petition with signatures from as far away as Serbia and Japan. The petitions has been turned into the city council, zoning board and mayor—as have numerous letters of support from city businesses.

Ironically the Pyramid Brew Pub, whose move into a warehouse across the street from Gilman a few years back prompted worry that the club would be shut down, wrote a glowing letter supporting the club to the city citing their ability to peacefully coexist. City council members like Kriss Worthington have also publicly voiced sympathy for the space.

The counterattack by Gilman seems to be working and Luscious is hopeful the club can win this latest bout with the powers that be. A positive resolution looks within the clubs reach. Gilman has contacted the Berkeley Resolution Service (an oh-so-Berkeley mediation team) and hopes they can get DiCon to meet with the club and hash out some sort of compromise.

Wendy Cosin, Deputy Planning Director with Berkeley's Planning and Development Department told *Punk Planet*, "The city has no plans to go to the zoning board to revoke the club's license. We think we'll be able to work things out with the club." Cosin was unaware if there had been a rise in the severity or number of complaints about the club.

DiCon was contacted for this article but would not discuss the situation with *Punk Planet*.

TROUBLE IN BOHEMIA

While it looks like 924 Gilman may have won this round, it is getting harder and harder for Bay Area counterculture institutions and to survive. The face of the region is culturally strip-mined. Rent control laws, once some of the strongest in the country, have been gutted. Artists, the poor, the young, activists and and people of color are being displaced as the white-collar cyber yuppies sweep in like a plague of locusts.

In an October 1998 special issue entitled "The Economic Cleansing of San Francisco," the *San Francisco Bay Guardian* reported some very telling statistics. For instance: the median rent for a vacant one bedroom apartment in San Francisco has increased more than 56% from $800 to $1,245 in the past four years. To afford the median rent for a vacant one-bedroom apartment, a person making $6 a hour and paying the accepted one-third of their income for rent would have to work 143 hours a week! The paper cited a survey of SF Tenants Union cases showing that for tenants who changed their addresses in the past year, nearly half left the city entirely. Between 1994 and 1996, the gap between rich and poor in San Francisco has increased by nearly 40%, the biggest two-year increase in the history of the Tenants Union survey.

"The Bay Area has changed in the last 10 years," said UC Berkeley professor Richard Walker, an expert on gentrification. "It has gotten richer, bigger, higher land prices, more traffic, with rapid changes in employment. In west Berkeley, there has been a lot of development in biotech, software and trendy retail gentrification like the 4th St. upscale shopping area [a boutique-zone that is rapidly slithering toward Gilman]."

In Berkeley, the average cost of a one-bedroom apartment has increased from $600 per month in 1996, to approximately $1,000

per month today. Neighboring Oakland has seen its rents increase an average of 10 percent annually in recent years.

Walker points out that local landlords went to the state legislature to bypass liberal Berkeley pols and get municipal rent control laws done away with. The lobbying by landlords resulted in a new state rent control law that went into effect on January 1st of this year. Under the new law, it is impossible for cities like Berkeley to regulate the prices for vacant apartments. Previously, Berkeley and several other California cities, maintained limits on how much landlords could jack up rent for vacant apartments. Before the law's passage a Berkley landlord couldn't evict someone simply to raise the rent—a profitable plan when rent control keeps property owners from substantially increasing rents on occupied units. Thanks to the Costa-Hawkings state rent control law, that safeguard is out the window.

YOUTH-PHOBIA ON PARADE

The assault on Gilman goes hand in hand with the overall assault on youth in the Bay Area. "Everybody wants the youth dollar but they don't want the youth behavior," Walker explains. "We just want to police everybody but not admit that there are any human problems, we want sanitize our cities and our lives." Gilman, serving tens of thousands of young people each year, is one of the only places left that area youth can go to for entertainment and certainly one of the only spaces youth have some control over. Its closure would create a huge void.

This void is hightened among Bay Area homeless youth, among whom Gilman functions as not just a place to see shows but a second home and a safe haven. After finding themselves criminalized for existing in the one of the tightest rental markets in America, the Bay Area's homeless youth are now watching their hangout hang in the balance.

The famed tolerance of the Bay Area hasn't extended to homeless youth lately. In the fall of 1998, Berkeley spent $80,000 on a paramilitary police operation aimed primarily at sweeping homeless kids and small-time weed dealers off Telegraph Avenue, one of the city's major shopping strips. The operation consisted of stepped-up foot patrols, surveillance, and the presence of a gargantuan midnight-black "mobile substation." When public outcry seemed to have halted the operation after a month, local muckrakers discovered that the police department had simply continued the program surreptitiously, albeit at a reduced level.

Rachel McLean, of the Haight Ashbury Youth Outreach Team, a group that helps homeless young people get off the streets, remembers what it was like when she was homeless in the early '90s: "Haight St. used to be used clothing stores and old beat up shops. It was a place where all the freaks hung out, that's what it was for and that's why people liked it but now all the stores cater to a more upscale yuppie tourist crowd."

McLean feels that the Haight's gentrification has led to a significant increase in the criminalization of homelessness these days. "When I was on the streets we never used to get tickets for sitting on the sidewalks or sleeping in the park," she explains. "Nowadays kids get tickets for blocking the sidewalk and trespassing when they sit in front of businesses." When the kids can't pay off the tickets, the tickets become arrest warrants.

Jennifer Ruel, a youth worker with Berkeley's Chaplaincy to the Homeless, was herself arrested for sitting on the sidewalk on a busy retail drag. She reports an increase "in pressure on youth, with cops harassing kids where they are sleeping and giving out more tickets for things like trespassing and jaywalking." Since its task force began, the city has handed out hundreds of citations and made dozens of arrests—mostly for petty offenses. According to Ruel, one homeless kid got taken to the county jail because her dog had no license.

Across the Bay in San Francisco's Haight Ashbury District, the situation is similar. In 1997, fueled by media hype, the city mounted a major drive to purge nearby Golden Gate park of homeless encampments. The offensive entailed helicopters equipped with searchlights, foot patrols, the closure of large chunks of the park, and the decimation of dozens of trees, since—according to the city—the foliage could be used for cover by the homeless.

"People come here to see the culture and the culture of Berkeley and the Haight is youth culture. Ironically it's that culture that's under attack by the generation that created it in the '60s," concludes Rachel.

San Francisco's Coalition on Homelessness reports that in 1998 the SFPD issued 17,512 citations for crimes such as sleeping, camping and blocking the sidewalk. The current number of people living on the streets of San Francisco is a whopping 10,000 to 12,000 in a city of only 780,000. There are only 3,000 total shelter beds, many of which are in dirty, crowded and dangerous spaces. Over 1,200 of San Francisco's homeless are currently lan-guishing on waiting lists for substance abuse treatment programs. The rent for the cheapest 10% of vacant apartments in the city far exceeds the incomes of low wage workers, poor families, and dis-abled people. All this in an era of supposed economic prosperity for America.

TOUGH ALL OVER

Epicenter Records and the Bound Together Anarchist Bookstore have also had their problems staying afloat in the ever-gentrifying Bay Area. Bound Together, a small Haight Street enterprise, has seen their rent skyrocket twelvefold since 1983. Tom Alder of Bound Together says the story is lucky because, with no rent control laws for small businesses, the rent could have gone even higher. Even with that small bit of luck, the economy of the Bay Area is causing many prob-lems for Bound Together. Alder reports that "collective members are moving out of town because they can't afford it here anymore and owner move in evictions have taken their toll."

Kate Short from Epicenter, a DIY record store and meeting space, echoes Alder's sentiment. "People don't have enough time to volunteer at the store because it is getting so expensive to live here so everyone has to work more." Epicenter, which also provides free meeting space for groups like Food Not Bombs and Prisoners' Literature Project, currently pays $3,000 a month in rent, up from $1,700 in 1990. With so much money going towards rent, the store doesn't make enough money to restock promptly and currently has half the inventory it once had. "We've had to prostitute ourselves to make ends meet by renting out artist studio space in places where Blacklist [a volunteer mail-order] and the zine library used to be," explains Kate. The store can't have shows anymore due to a broken water pipe fiasco which resulted in a lawsuit and the computer compa-ny upstairs always whining to the landlord about Epicenter. The possibility of a new collectively run book or record store being able to open up in the Haight or the Mission today is slim to none.

Countless other subterranean cultural spaces have been shut due to the rent wars. In San Francisco, a gang of venues including Klub Komotion, the Nidus space, House Of Debauchery, the Chameleon, the Trocadero and Star Cleaners have closed their doors. Most of the aforementioned spaces were of the underground, non-commercial variety.

LOOKING BACK, LOOKING FORWARD

Martin Sprouse, one of the founding members of the original Gilman collective, remembers why the location was picked: "It was a com-pletely out of the way light industrial area just factories and warehouses."

Kamala Parks, another Gilman founder recalls finding the ware-house: "The landlord was cool, it was $2,000 a month, a perfect site with no neighbors. There was nothing going on there at night. As punks you want to attract as little attention to yourself as possible."

Since its first show on December 31, 1986, the club has been all ages, drug and alcohol free, volunteer and collectively run. No bands with major label ties, and no bands with racist, sexist, or homophobic lyrics are allowed to play. Violence in the club has never been tolerat-ed. "To keep down violence, the idea was you wouldn't let people fuck things up if everybody felt like part of the place, part of a community," said Sprouse. Racist skins aren't allowed in the club and if you start shit the crowd, the staff and the volunteer security will stand together to kick you out. From the beginning the club took painstaking care to do everything legally so the place couldn't be closed on a technicality.

According to Sprouse, Gilman's own audience—quite often Nazi skins begging for a beat down or tough punks with something to prove—was its biggest threat back in the day; now it seems to be money. "Once again, yuppies could ruin something. They have no regard for any past culture or past community," Sprouse told *Punk Planet.* "They just come in and take over. Closing Gilman would show total disregard to an amazing idea." ◉

Below (and next page): the report from the Berkeley Zoning Board on 924 Gilman's use permit after a review was held on March 24, 1999, spurred by DiCon's complaints about the club.

924 GILMAN STREET CLUB
REPORT REGARDING CONDITIONS OF USE PERMIT

CONDITION #1:   Subject to review and approval by the Public Works Department, the applicant shall bond for the installation of street lights on Ninth and Tenth Streets from Camellia to Harrison Streets and on Gilman and Camellia Streets from Ninth to Tenth Streets, to a maximum of $1,000.

Status/Comment: This condition was never implemented. The Club's December '98 Policy Statement indicates they are willing to participate in the cost of installing high-powered lights to illuminate the steps and front of the DiCon building and Paul K____'s architectural offices. The statement also indicates willingness to participate in the cost of replacing plants destroyed on Dicon property.

Implementation:
- The City will provide additional lighting on Eighth Street. The Alternative Music Foundation shall pay $1,000 to the Department of Public Works by April 15, 1999.

CONDITION # 5:   Security shall be provided for all entrances, and shall include at least two people at the entrance, two inside the hall and two on the exterior. These personnel shall be easily identifiable by means of clothing or badges and can be members of the organization. Hired security personnel is not necessary.

Status/Comment: The Club's December, 1998 Policy Statement recognizes the need for additional security measures in the neighborhood. The Club's Policy Statement states that, as of December 12, an additional paid, unarmed uniformed security person was hired and has been dedicated to patrolling the peripheral neighborhood, specifically the area between 7th and 9th Streets, and Camellia to Harrison Streets, each Friday and Saturday night from 9PM to 1AM (possibly 7PM to 1AM during the winter months). The Statement indicates that the perimeter security person shall have a two-way radio and may use a bicycle; and that additional perimeter security may be hired for busy nights.

Implementation:
The increased security proposed in the Policy Statement is a step in the right direction, however, to be effective, the following revisions are needed:
- Two paid, unarmed uniformed security rovers shall be dedicated to patrolling the peripheral neighborhood, specifically 7th to 9th Streets; Camellia to Harrison Streets, each Friday and Saturday night from 9PM to 1AM (possibly 7PM to 1AM during the winter months).   They shall each carry a cell phone and shall immediately contact the Police Department at ____ (non-emergency number) where there are instances of trespassing on private property, graffiti, vandalism, or drunken or abusive behavior.
- Every Monday morning, the Club shall provide the names of the security staff, their times on duty and a list of any incidents to the Zoning Enforcement Officer. Information can

be reported to the City either by telephone (   ) or by e-mail
(.@   ).
- A specific Club member shall be designated as liaison regarding security with the City of Berkeley. The name of the security liaison shall be provided to the Zoning Enforcement Officer. This information shall be kept up to date.

CONDITION #9:   The Gilman St. Project shall notify the Planning & Community Development Dept. of the dates and times of all future events, and indicate which events might/ generate a full house.

Status/Comment: Noncompliance

Recommendation:
- Every Monday, the Club shall provide the schedule for the next four (4) weeks to the Zoning Enforcement Officer. Information can be reported to the City either by telephone (   ) or by e-mail (   ).
- Full house shall be defined as 90% capacity.

CONDITION #10: The Gilman Street Project will conduct regular security training for staff. The Project shall notify the Planning & Community Development Department of the time and location of the training sessions.

Status/Comment: Noncompliance. The Club Policy Statement includes rules for member behavior and information on under what circumstances members will be 86'd and barred from entrance.

Recommendation:
- On the first Monday each quarter of the year (January, April, July, October), the Club shall provide information on the last security training, including a list of the people trained, and on the time and location of the next scheduled training.

CONDITION #11: For popular, full-house shows, the Club will enforce a "no-ins-and-outs" rule. The Club will open and monitor side doors to increase the ventilation and reduce the need to go outside for fresh air. Hand stamps will be used to identify patrons who enter the club.

Status/Comment: The Club's policy includes the statement that "for popular, full-house shows", the Club will enforce a "no-in-and-outs" rule.

Recommendation:
- Capacity of the Club is 220 persons. "Full house" shall be defined as 90% capacity. When the Club reaches 90% capacity (198), the "no-ins-and-outs" rule shall be enforced.

CONDITION #12: Outside trash cans will be placed by the building and across the street during the shows.

Status/Comment: Noncompliance. The Club's Policy Statement indicates that a "landscape person circles the neighborhood before 10AM on Sunday morning, removing litter from doorways, bushes, sidewalks, etc. in the immediate neighborhood area. Said person is also to notify the Project personnel of any graffiti or property damage". It appears that Club members are cleaning up directly in front of the Club only.

Recommendation:
Regular clean up as called for in the Policy Statement is the right direction, however, more specificity is needed.
- The Club shall take responsibility for clean-up after events. Trash and litter left on both sides of the street in the gutter, on the sidewalk, or immediately adjacent to the sidewalk shall be cleaned up every Saturday and Sunday morning after an event by noon in the following area: Gilman, between San Pablo Avenue and Seventh Street, and Eighth Street, between Harrison and Camilia.

CONDITION #13: "No drinking and loitering" notices shall be posted inside the club and on all promotional and advertising materials, club literature and admission tickets.

Status/Comment: Noncompliance. This statement was not included on the few posters submitted by the group. Rather than "no loitering", staff suggests that notices read "no drinking or drugs".

Recommendation:
- The "no drinking and drugs" notices shall be included on the promotional and advertising materials. A copy of each notice shall be included with the information submitted to the Zoning Enforcement Officer weekly.
- Two "no drinking and drugs" signs shall be posted outside the Club on both the Gilman and 8th Streets sides. The signs shall be 2 ft x 2 ft in size and shall be designed to minimize graffiti. The signs shall be approved by the Zoning Enforcement Officer prior to installation.

924 Gilman St. Project
Alternative Music Foundation

PO BOX 1058
Berkeley, CA 94701

April 11, 1999

Wendy C   , AICP
Deputy Planning Director
Planning & Development Department
2118 Milvia St. Ste. 300
Berkeley, CA 94704

Ms. C   ,

Thank you for the time you and the other City staff spent with us on Mar. 24. We appreciate all of your observations and suggestions regarding compliance to our use permit. After discussing your suggestions with our membership at large we have decided to do everything we need to do to become compliant with our use permit #AA1024-1177 (last revised Jan. 27, 1992.)

Condition #1: We were to have bonded "for the installation of streetlights on Ninth and Tenths Streets..." Enclosed you will find a check for $1000 payable to the City of Berkeley. Please send a confirmation of receipt to our Controller, John H   , at the address on this letterhead.

Condition #9: You had indicated that condition #9 of our use permit states, "The Gilman St. Project shall notify the Planning & Community Development Dept. of the dates and times of all future events, and indicate which events might generate a full house." The actual wording of the condition is, "The Gilman St. Project shall notify the *Community Services Department* of the dates and times of all future events, and indicate which events might generate a full house." To that end, we have been relaying our event calendar to Lt. Bob M   of the Berkeley Police. The City of Berkeley web site[1] lists Lt. M   as Command Staff for the Community Services Bureau. **We feel that we are in compliance with this condition.**

Condition #10: As with #9, we are in compliance, as we have notified the Lt. M   of our regular security training meetings.

Condition #12: We have resumed our practice of putting trash cans across Eighth Street during shows. If The Pyramid Brewery Restaurant (across Gilman) wishes us to place trash cans on the sidewalk in front of their building, we will be happy to do so.

Condition #13: Notices informing our members that no drinking, drug use or vandalism will be tolerated around the club have always been posted inside the club. All promotional materials indicate that drinking and drug use are not permitted at the club. We will ensure that all promotional materials and notices in the club clearly indicate that drinking and drug use are not allowed inside the club, and drinking, drug use, and loitering are not tolerated in the surrounding neighborhood.

We have also decided to delay making any commitments to the City not outlined by our use permit or December Policy Statement, until we have had the ability to meet in a moderated environment with the owners and senior management of DiCon Fiberoptics.

Sincerely,

Mike L   , Member

Letter sent from the club to the zoning board in response to the club's use permit review.

Below: a draft of the "communication and action" protocol proposed by the club, May 1999.

Introduction

This document outlines a communication and action protocol for DiCon Fiberoptics and The 924 Gilman St. Project. The following guidelines are intended to help DiCon and 924 Gilman agree on the obligations and responsibilities from each party to the other.

Note: This version is a draft from Mike L   , 924 Gilman. DiCon, and 924 Gilman will make changes, and the 924 Gilman membership and DiCon senior management will approve the final version.

Preparation

Over the next two weeks 924 Gilman will make sure that they have matching paint for all DiCon buildings.

Kevin _____ (DiCon) will provide store mixing codes where they exist, or chips where more appropriate.

Assuming that John H   (924 Gilman) has all codes and chips by May 24, 924 Gilman will have matching paint ready by June 7.

For any buildings where matching may be inaccurate, Kevin and John may arrange tests as paint is mixed.

For each event at 924 Gilman, DiCon Security will be aware of the identity of the 924 Gilman Head Security Person and Show Coordinator .

924 Gilman will hire a groundskeeper to circle the neighborhood each Sunday morning to remove litter and notify 924 Gilman of any graffiti or damage.

Notification:

Approximately 30 minutes to one hour before an event, the DiCon and 924 Gilman Security will meet, discuss the evenings event, and make sure that all contact information (cell phone #'s, etc.) is up-to-date.

If an incident of litter, graffiti, damage, or trespassing is noticed by DiCon employees or security during a 924 Gilman event, DiCon Security will notify the 924 Gilman Head Security Person or Show Coordinator as soon as convenient.

If an incident of litter, graffiti, damage, or trespassing is noticed by or reported to DiCon employees after a 924 Gilman event, Edda N   (DiCon) will contact Chris S   (Gilman) via voice mail at 510-   .

If an incident of graffiti or damage is noticed or reported to 924 Gilman personnel, 924 Gilman will notify Edda via voice-mail

Response:

Graffiti

924 Gilman will make every effort to paint over or remove graffiti before 8 am Monday or within 48 hours of notification. While effort will be made to completely remove any traces of disfigurement, the goal of this initial response is to obscure the graffiti to prevent other incidents, rather than flawless repair.

After the initial repair, if DiCon feels that the repair is inadequate, they should contact John H   at 510-   . 924 Gilman will then take additional steps until the repair is to DiCon's satisfaction. This may take some time, as new paint matches may have to be made, or professional painters hired.

If, at any time, DiCon is dissatisfied with the timeliness or completeness of 924 Gilman's response, they should contact Mike L   at 510-

Damage

924 Gilman will make every attempt to reduce further damage, remove debris, etc by 8 am Monday or within 48 hours of notification.

924 Gilman will contact Edda N   to discuss further repair or reparations.

Follow-up:

924 Gilman and DiCon will contact each other immediately if any phone numbers or contact names change.

924 Gilman and DiCon will have monthly meetings for the next three months to discuss the effectiveness and adherence to the above guidelines. After the initial three months if either party would like to meet, they can organize a meeting through Mike L   and Edda N .

924 Gilman is willing to participate, with DiCon Security and the BPD, in any efforts that will help DiCon night shift employees feel safer in their neighborhood.

And 924 Gilman and DiCon lived happily ever after...

A SAMPLING OF SUPPORT LETTERS RECEIVED IN 1999

On this page, and the next ten, is a sampling of the many letters Gilman received during its dealings with DiCon in 1999. They exemplify the impact Gilman has had, not just locally, not just nationally, but globally as well.

```
    The Zoning Advisory Board,
  .fice of Economic Development,
:ity Councilmembers, and
Mayor Shirley Dean
City of Berkeley

                                                        Aug 4, 1999


     Enclosed is the third and final batch of letters of support and petitions
in favor of 924 Gilman Street's continuing existence in Berkeley. After the past
8 months of tension, we have, with the help of our neighbors, our patrons, our
volunteers, and the City, reached a point of positive dialog with our neighbor
DiCon Fiberoptics. We feel we have communicated the positive social and cultural
contributions of the Gilman Street Project to both DiCon and to parts of the
city government who were previously unaware of those contributions.
     We remain very accessible if there are any questions or concerns in the
future.

                   Thank you for your attention,

                              Jesse Townley
                              Secretary, 924 Gilman Street
```

```
                              Allied Radiator
                              920 Gilman Street
                              Berkeley, CA  94710


          City of Berkeley
          Zoning Office
          2120 Milvia St
          Berkeley, CA  94704



          RE: 924 Gilman Street Project


          Our business is right next door to 924 Gilman St. Over these
          last 11 years of the club's tenancy, we have found the kids
          to be respectful and good a neighbor.

          Any earlier problems with graffiti or trash has long ago
          been resolved.  We found that when we had any complaints
          with the club, we could talk with the kids and they were
          very responsive to our concerns.

          We respect them as our neighbor.  They are doing no harm.
          Incidentally, one of my employees used to attend the club.
          Today, he is an excellent and responsible mechanic.

          Berkeley should be proud that it supports such a unique
          outlet that 924 Gilman St Project provides for the young
          people of the area.


                    Sincerely,



                    Pat W        , owner
```

Subject: Please don't shut GILMAN down

City of Berkeley Zoning Office
2120 Milvia St.
Berkeley, Ca 94704

To Whom It may Concern,

My name is Ayumi N   . I am a foreign student from Japan majoring
Photojournalism at San Francisco State University.

The reason why I chose to come to San Francisco 3 years ago was the music
scene in the Bay Area. Especially, when I was still in Japan, I had heard
so much about the 924 Gilman St. Project and I was so impressed with the
kind of music and energy that people have produced from a place like Gilman.

Coming to Bay Area, going to Gilman and meet the people or feel
the music had given me one of the biggest motivations to decide what
I would like to do in my life.

My future goal is becoming a music photojournalist who can make a bridge
between this country and Japan or else with the pictures I take.
I have produced so many pictures at Gilman. I am also planning to
publish my photodocumentary on the punk rock scene including the people I
met at Gilman.

Gilman is not only world-wide known, but also it has been giving a
tremendous amount of encouragement to the youth who support music scenes
in the world. Especially, it's a non-prifit, volunteer-run,
alcohol/drug-free performance space and community center for all ages.
It's such a unieque and unprecedented place where it can give a great
influence to the increadble number of people in the world.

I know that a lot of bands from Japan are so inspired by the people who have played at
Gilman and try to come to the U.S.A. and play there. It
is one of the dream places to play for so many people now.

It is too unfortunate if the place has to be completely removed. Gilman
has been there for a long time. And it occupies an important part of the
history in the Bay Area music scene. It would affect not only the music
scene, but also it would hurt too many numbers of people's hearts, if it
had to shut it down.

Please do not shut it down and take the freedom and dream away from us.
And please understand what Gilman means to a lot of us.

Thank you very much.
    Sincerely,
        Ayumi N

1997   photo by Ayumi N.

To Whom It May Concern:

My name is Jake K   , and I am a 21 year old resident of the Bay Area since June of 1988. I am also one of the many homeless youths that the city of Berkeley is attempting to sweep under the rug, and it seems like you're trying to do the same to the club that I have faithfully attended since I was fifteen years old. This is appalling.

Before I started going to 924 Gilman, I was an active alcoholic/drug addict hell-bent on suicide. When I actually started going to the club, I was pleased that there was a place for young punk rock kids like me to go, see a few bands, and escape the problems I had at home and at school, if only for a few hours. I went on to volunteer for many a show when I was short on the five-dollar admission. By doing this, I got to see exactly what 924 Gilman and its volunteers accomplish week after week, year after year, and it is amazing. I have cleaned up after shows, sold membership cards, made sure nobody was sneaking in the back door, etc. I have even worked in Gilman's snack bar, and have helped out with security on very few occasions. I've learned way more about responsibility and friendship than I ever would have in school. I would much rather be the responsible, active, caring person that I am today than the apathetic self-destructive wreck that I once was. I also learned that hating people for skin color and sexual preference isn't right either, as I was once a gaybashing Nazi skinhead so long ago. I was also motivated to get involved with my "scene," and contribute the talents that I have.

When the Pyramid Brewery made plans to move into Gilman's neighborhood, I was scared. I thought Gilman was going to be shut down in favor of yet another yuppie watering hole and that I wasn't going to have anywhere to go on the weekends. I'd rather go watch a couple bands and do something productive with my life than contribute to a boring life of sitting at home watching the football game and getting drunk. That's what my dad does with his life, and he's one of the most miserable, depressed people I've ever encountered in my life. You people worry about kids drinking at shows. Kids are going to drink if they so desire, and you're not going to stop them. If anything, you're encouraging it with the amount of "hip" microbreweries and liquor stores all over this city. By the way, for every one underage drinker at a Gilman show, there's two or three at the same show that aren't indulging. I quit drinking almost two years ago, by the way, and despised the atmosphere of bars when I did.

I, along with many people, feel safe at Gilman. In my hometown of Alameda, various jocks and racists because of who I was and how I dressed physically assaulted me. Visiting my father in Pennsylvania, carloads of rednecks occasionally drove by calling me a "faggot," because of my dyed hair and choice of clothing. Here in Berkeley and at Gilman, I don't have to worry about that. Isn't Berkeley a city of tolerance for those that are different from the status quo? I love Berkeley for that very reason. When I walk down Telegraph and see all the homeless kids, wingnuts, and everyone just being alive, there's no other place I'd rather be. It sure beats where I came from.

Sure, there's a few "bad eggs" that come to Gilman. There's at least one in every batch. But a majority of these kids are nice kids who just happen to look a little bit different. There's nothing wrong with that at all. This is America, and we do have the right to look however we want, whether it would get us that fancy lawyer's job or not. Gilman's volunteers are a responsible lot; otherwise they wouldn't take the time to clean up the neighborhood of graffiti and trash. The security staff wouldn't work so hard to make sure nobody drinks or does drugs in the club, and there would most certainly be stagediving allowed as well. Don't forget the fact that Narcotics Anonymous hosts weekly meetings at the club, which helps out a lot of people.

Here's another thought: if you were really so concerned with the neighborhood around Gilman, you'd arrest the drug dealers and crackheads around Gilman and San Pablo. Then again, you're not doing it in People's Park, so why would you do it here? Use your petty video surveillance for the real criminals, not a bunch of kids having a good time. Actually, don't use your video cameras at all. Also: for a brief time, I worked at a tele-fundraising place called Stephen Dunn and Associates. I put Gilman on the job application and during the interview, we talked more about my work at the club than we did about my old $9 an hour job doing surveys for the electric company!!

Did you know that Dicon is unwilling to take this to dispute resolution? Why don't you tell Dicon to put lights in their parking lots? Why don't you tell them to lock their precious parking lots at night, which would keep people from using them as a drinking spot? Did you know that well over eight thousand people from around the country and even the world have signed Gilman's petitions at shows and on the Internet and have sent letters much like mine? What does that tell you? Or do you even care about anything except for yourselves and who lines your pockets with more money?

Please don't shut 924 Gilman down. If this situation goes to the zoning board, I promise to be there. I'm well known around here for being a loudmouth and I will be more than happy to voice my opinion on these matters. What's more important, the money that Dicon makes for the city or the fact that the kids need a place to go? It would also cost more for the city to open a youth center, so there's another great idea to keep Gilman alive. And where would you rather have kids go, anyway? To a frat party where there is, believe it or not, underage drinking, and a high possibility of date rape? Would you rather have these kids out on the streets every Friday and Saturday bored and seeing how much trouble they could cause? If Gilman did in fact lose their license, you would probably see a lot more in the name of crime and drug problems. You'd probably see so much more graffiti in the West Berkeley area, you'd think that the area right now is clean by comparison. This entire situation is completely the opposite of what I'd expect from a city like Berkeley. Besides, even my mother supports the idea of Gilman, and she's hardly ever thought anything I did was productive!

Sincerely,

Jake K

Gilman member for six years

P.S. Just remember that what goes around comes around, and one of these "punks" that you're trying to sweep under the rug may one day be the government official that cuts your social security.

---

this is a letter to tell you how important 924 GILMAN is in me and my kids lives. i attend A.A. meetings there, and that saves my life. then on weekends i take my eight year old there to see shows, because i believe that the gilman organization (not to mention the music) is important to the education of my child. we have fun together and we've made quite a few friends there who all support one another in a safe, family-like environment. my daughter has seen a place where people work together to make things happen, talk things over when there's a problem, and just belong when it's apparent that there is no other place to belong. i am asking you to not get rid of what you don't understand.   the gilman serves this community, and it would really suck if you threw it away.   ANNIE S

January 20, 1999

Gail W. & Michael L

Orinda, Ca.

Dear Berkeley Zoning Board:

We are expressing our concerns about the upcoming permit revocation hearing on 924 Gilman, aka The 924 Gilman Street Project. This youth center has been an integral part of our daughter's life since May of 1994. She began attending several of their music shows on weekends when she was 14 and has volunteered as their store manager for the last 1 1/2 years. At the age of 18 now, she considers 924 Gilman an integral part of her life.

At first, we were skeptical of having our daughter attend a club in Berkeley where she knew few people, but soon realized there were few locations in the Bay Area where she could listen to alternative music due to her age. We would drive her from the "safe" and quiet confines of Orinda to a neighborhood unfamiliar to us in west Berkeley. We were often worried about her safety, but soon realized that with 100-200 young people attending this club, and not hearing any negative reports, we looked forward to hearing about her activities with her many friends. Soon she carpooled with several of her friends from Miramonte High School on weekends.

Lauren would describe in detail the security measures 924 Gilman took to insure the safety of their members. We felt that Lauren was in a safe environment not only at the club but when walking to where we would pick her up a few blocks away. She enjoyed the diversity of the members, the music, and the feeling she could get involved and work to provide an enjoyable experience for the young attendees.

Lauren began to volunteer at the front door where she would collect money, sell membership cards, and clean up after shows. Because of her hard work and dedication, she and a friend from Orinda were asked to work in the store and within 3 months become the store managers. They were responsible for opening the store, selling merchandise, using a cash register, dealing with customers, eventually becoming the store managers.

Because of this volunteer experience and the skills learned at 924 Gilman, Lauren was able to secure a counter job at The Bread Garden, a bakery in Berkeley, where she has worked for a year and a half. Both of these experiences have helped her become more responsible, more organized, and self assured.

We realize that 924 Gilman has had an important part not only.in our daughter's life, but in the East Bay from where the club draws its membership. It is the only "all ages" alternative music club where they can get involved in something bigger than themselves. Many friendships have been made there.

We feel that it would be detrimental to this community to close this club which has provided not only a safe and secure atmosphere for young people, but has provided job skills through volunteerism. We hope the Berkeley Zoning Board will not take away these opportunities to this young Berkeley community.

Sincerely,

Gail W. L   & Michael L

I'm no longer a resident of Berkeley, so maybe this letter won't mean much, but I had to write. It would be a real shame if the city forced 924 Gilman to close. It's a revered institution to millions of youth across the world who dream of creating something as vibrant and enduring in their own cities. Many of the clubgoers, they're punks, and I realize that some people look at them and think they're all a bunch of vandals and troublemakers, but that's not what 924 Gilman is about. The Project is the only thing I've come across that channels the youthful energy into something truly constructive, creative, and even utopian.

Down here, in LA, young adults have a harder time getting together to pull off projects like Gilman, and often just burn out. A lot of them get frustrated and devolve into well entertained zombies who contribute nothing back to the community but their taxes. A few end up on drugs.

The punks won't disappear from the city streets if 924 Gilman disappears. They'll still go to Berkeley for the same reason the hippies have migrated there, because they're cut from the same cloth: they want to "be free." Gilman, conversely, encourages people to "be responsible." I think they do a pretty good job, and the fact that they do it on a shoestring volunteer crew is commendable.

924 Gilman has been an asset to Berkeley and the surrounding communities for over a decade. Of course, it's important to maintain the local economy, but please consider the true cost to your community.

John K
Los Angeles, California

January 14, 1999

City of Berkeley Zoning Office
2120 Milvia St.
Berkeley, CA 94704

To Whom It May Concern:

For the past 12 years I have been a member of the Alternative Music
Foundation, commonly known as 924 Gilman Street. I became
involved in Gilman when I was in college, studying for my degree
and playing music with several bands. At the time the bay area was
a truly desolate place with regard to all-ages venues. In fact, before
924 Gilman opened its doors in 1987 there was nowhere safe in the
entire bay area for kids to see local and nationally known punk and
alternative bands perform. I volunteered, along with dozens of other
local members of the east bay music community to build a place
where young people could hear and play music.

Since then 924 Gilman has become more than just an all-ages
nightclub. It has become something of an institution. 924 Gilman
has been the proving ground for internationally known bands and
has put the city of Berkeley (and the East Bay) on the map once again
as a place that breeds individualism, art and youth culture. And the
incredible thing is that 924 Gilman has succeeded in doing so without
running a bar, without engaging in crass commercialism and without
treating the kids who keep it going with disrespect. It has also done
this while promoting social tolerance, non-violence and the fine idea
that personal involvement does indeed count for something in
society. Add to these fine accomplishments the fact that 924 Gilman
also serves the community by hosting AA meetings and other groups
during the week when it is not being used as a music venue and we
have a real asset to the community as a whole and proof to youth-
haters that kids, when given the opportunity, can really create
something constructive and special that we can all be proud of.

Unfortunately over the past 12 years 924 Gilman has also been
repeatedly threatened with closure due to, at best, ignorance of its
mission, purpose and place in the community, and at worst, mean-
spirited ageism and anti-youth sentiment. The latest salvo comes
from a business that moved into the neighborhood due the
attractiveness of low rent and now finds themselves made
uncomfortable by an established institution in the neighborhood. I
find it simply amazing that the City of Berkeley would even bother to
honor this complaint with their time and resources, let alone go to
the trouble of reviewing the use permit for 924 Gilman. I equate the
complainants with the sort of folks who buy a home in the path of an
airport runway and then proceed to bombard both the city and the
airport with complaints about the jet noise. The simple fact is that
the club was there first and has been there for quite a long time. I
find it impossible to believe that 924 Gilman's current detractors
could have moved into the neighborhood without knowing whom
they would be sharing the neighborhood with.

In summary, I believe that 924 Gilman provides an asset to the City
of Berkeley and the entire East Bay community by providing a much
needed focal point for young people to congregate at, listen to music,
perform music, get involved in community organizations and, most
importantly of all, to truly feel that there is a place of their own right
here in the bay area. I support 924 Gilman to this day, even though
I'm hardly part of their larger demographic anymore because I'm
proud of the institution I helped build 12 years ago. I have traveled
all over the world and whether I'm in Prague, Amsterdam, London,
Paris, New York, Los Angeles, Seattle, Chicago, New Orleans or even
Great Falls, when I meet a teenager and they find out I'm a musician
from the East Bay, the first thing they want to hear about is 924
Gilman. I can't imagine that the City of Berkeley's zoning board
wants to wipe all that away with the swipe of a pen.

Sincerely,

Joseph S
toyboat Industries

Kids are in trouble these days, and what sort of outlets do we have? The kids in the punk scene have a different sort of outlet. We listen to music that affects our lives, and changes who we are. We run around, think for ourselves, think about the world and the way it is, and make the effort to educate and enlighten ourselves. We arent just a bunch of kids trying to cause trouble. The truth of it is, that we are a bunch of kids who are trying to make things better. And a lot of us go about it the wrong way.

The Gilman is a place that brings pure joy into the hearts, minds, and lives of kids all over the Bay Area. Kids spend so much time listening to a band, relating to a band, thinking about a band. And then, this band, which the kid loves so much, comes around to a worldwide famous punk landmark, and the kid has a chance to see them.

This chance comes to them in an ideal environment. No alcohol. No drugs of any kind. No violence. Kids all around them, there for the same reason. Which automatically means, kids with similar values and opinions, because they listen to the same band. And we all know there is a close relationship between a kid's opinions, ideas, and morals, and the music they listen to.

I live in Menlo Park, and there arent many kids here I can relate to. I keep an ear open for shows where some of my favorite bands play. Which is the gilman. I go there, see a band, and meet kids. I met one of my best friends at the Gilman. I saw, and heard, who i consider to be, one of the smartest men in punk rock, Jello Biafra, speak. And i dont plan on letting it shut down without a fight. In all honesty, I will cry if the Gilman gets shut down.

I know the city is in a hard position. The Gilman has been there for a bit over a decade...how many of the people who live in that area were there before the Gilman? This is not unlike the San Francisco SOMA conflict, and most of the people knew about the club when they bought their homes.

I'm really not sure if the city recognizes how huge of an impact this will have on kids lives. And not just the kids. In the careers of countless bands. The hearts of old punks. If the Gilman is shut down, lives will change, drastically, for the worse. Instead of kids gathering at the Gilman to punk out together, in a safe environment, kids are going to disperse, throughout the city, and turn to streets and abandoned buildings. Avoiding this change is in the best intrest of the city. And more importantly, in the best intrest of the lives of hundreds of kids, and a movement.

Sincerely,
Juli F   , 15 years old
Menlo Park

June 16, 1999

Berkeley Zoning Commission
2120 Milvia Street
Berkeley, CA 94704

Re: The Gilman Street Project

To Whom it May Concern:

I am a member of the Gilman Street Project and have been since I first visited it in 1995. I am twenty-four years old and gainfully employed at the business indicated on the letterhead. The sense of community and opportunity I felt on my first visit to Gilman is ultimately the reason I came to the Bay Area. Gilman supports the idea of free speech and individualism which is paramount to every resident of this city.

Here is a personal example of the Gilman Street staff's *recent* generosity and community spirit: you may recall a house burning down this winter, a five-alarm blaze in which a firefighter was killed. The landlord is being investigated for negligence. My current roommate lived there at the time, along with other friends. The firefighter had a large funeral and many people showed their support for his family. My friends escaped with the clothes on their backs. Gilman was part of the effort to get these victims back on their feet by scheduling a benefit show. What other non-profit, community-based, entirely self-run organization could manage this as enthusiastically as Gilman Street??

What parent/relative/friend wouldn't rather see a young person playing basketball or watching a hard-working band than roaming the streets aimlessly, drinking or doing drugs? Having a place for people to go and enjoy themselves is what community is all about.

The staff at Gilman are intelligent, hard-working people who have kept a community institution going strong for eleven years. Please consider what Gilman Street means to its members and the city of Berkeley, and the effort the staff has made to appease and co-exist with DiCon in the past and right now. A compromise can be reached, just as long as both sides of the story are heard.

Sincerely,

Julie G

City of Berkeley Zoning Office
2120 Milvia Street
Berkeley, CA 94704

To Whom It May Concern:

I am writing about the proposed permit denial to the 924 Gilman Street Project. I started going to Gilman street when I attended Lowell High School in San Francisco. Gilman street was the only club that a teenager could attend that played good music. And since I don't believe in drugs or alcohol, it was one of the only places where I could enjoy the music I liked in a safe, nonconfrontational environment. Gilman Street was a mecca for all of my friends and I really think it helped me get through high school without turning to alcohol or drugs like so many others.

In fact, now that I am graduating from Yale in May, I look back at my high school experience and see what a positive impact Gilman Street made on my life. I hope that someday I can open a similar club that offers a place for youth to come together and enjoy music that promotes political awareness and camaraderie. I was always thankful that I grew up in an area where a club like Gilman could exist; there are no such clubs in CT and I see how harmful the scene has been to the kids here.

If you deny a permit to Gilman Street, you are denying hundreds of kids the opportunity to have a safe place to enjoy music and to share ideas. Do you know what kids do when they don't have a place to go? They get bored. And what do bored kids do? Well, they drink, do drugs, screw their life up-- boredom breeds despair. And you want to do that to a whole generation of kids just because some big business is leering over your shoulder? That's just such a sad excuse.

I hate to think that the Berkeley Zoning Office is seriously considering selling out the youth and leaders of tomorrow by closing down Gilman Street. 924 Gilman Street helped me stay off the streets and gave me a place to go and feel accepted when I was growing up. Just because we look different doesn't mean we're not going to have political power someday.

Look at me-- I feel like Gilman Street was a formative experience in my life. I am graduating in May with a 3.7 GPA from Yale, one of the top universities in the nation; I have won a Fulbright Grant to study Archival Science in British Columbia. And I intend to move back to the Bay Area when I get my Masters so that I can be part of the thriving intellectual and music community that a club like Gilman Street make possible.

Again, I implore you to let Gilman Street have its permit,

Kathleen B

Kathleen B
Timothy Dwight College, 1999
Yale University
New Haven, CT 06520

MOUNTAIN HARDWEAR

950 - A GILMAN STREET
BERKELEY, CA 94710

510 (EXT.)
510 (FAX)

FAX / MEMO / LETTER

DATE: 3-22-99
OF PAGES TO FOLLOW: 0
FROM: MARTIN Z
TO: MAYOR AND CITY COUNCIL OF BERKELEY
REGARDING: THE 924 GILMAN ST. PROJECT

DEAR MAYOR AND CITY COUNCIL:

I AM WRITING THIS LETTER IN SUPPORT OF THE 924 GILMAN ST. PROJECT. I HAVE WORKED AT MOUNTAIN HARDWEAR, WHICH IS LOCATED ACROSS THE STREET FROM 924 GILMAN, FOR THE LAST 5 YEARS. THE 924 GILMAN ST. PROJECT IS A FANTASTIC NEIGHBOR AND A TREMENDOUS ASSET TO THE COMMUNITY!

924 GILMAN IS ONE OF THE ONLY PLACES WHERE YOUNG PEOPLE CAN ENJOY MUSIC IN AN ALCOHOL AND DRUG FREE ENVIRONMENT. THEY CONTRIBUTE POSITIVELY TO THE COMMUNITY BY RAISING MONEY FOR WORTHWHILE CAUSES AND BY OFFERING VARIOUS EDUCATIONAL PROGRAMS. EVERY CONTACT I HAVE HAD WITH THE MEMBERS OR VOLUNTEERS OF 924 HAS BEEN PLEASANT AND POSITIVE. THEY HAVE A TREMENDOUS SENSE OF COMMUNITY. I WISH ALL OUR NEIGHBORS WERE AS EASY AND PLEASANT TO WORK WITH.

ALL THE MOUNTAIN HARDWEAR EMPLOYEES SUPPORT THE 924 GILMAN ST. PROJECT, THIS INCLUDES THE MANAGEMENT TEAM OF MOUNTAIN HARDWEAR.

I WOULD LIKE TO BE NOTIFIED OF ANY HEARINGS (INCLUDING THE BERKELEY ZONING ADJUSTMENTS BOARD) REGARDING THE 924 GILMAN ST. PROJECT. WE DO NOT WANT TO LOOSE 924 GILMAN AS A NEIGHBOR.

PLEASE CONSIDER THE INTERESTS OF THE COMMUNITY OVER THE VESTED INTERESTS OF THE VOCAL MINORITY WHO HAVE A FINANCIAL INTEREST IN THIS MATTER. PLEASE USE THE "TOOLS" OF THE CITY TO HELP THE COMMUNITY, NOT HARM IT.

SINCERELY,

MARTIN Z

3/11/99

Dear Zoning Committee,
First of all please read this letter, I put a lot of effort into it!

For over a year now I have frequently visited 924 Gilman Street. I am 14
years old and just starting high school and many times get very depressed
because of social and academic pressure. I enjoy going to Gilman because
it is a place where I can go and hang out with a diverse group of
intelligent people who are open to hearing other people,s ideas.

Sometimes I feel alone, but as Rancid says (a band that started out at
Gilman), „When I,ve got the music I,ve got a place to go.%. For me
Gilman is the place to go. Every time I go there I learn something new
and am able to look at the world with a heightened point of view.

It is said that, „All men are created equal.%. This obviously is not
true. People are oppressed because of their points of views, race,
gender, sexual orientation as well as numerous other categories. One
place that I feel that , „All people are created equal%. is at the Gilman.
People are always willing to listen to my ideas and I am never shunned
away because I have different ideas. Even the security there is nice and
doesn,t ever act superior to anyone else in the club.

I understand that people have been complaining that Gilman is a magnet
for underage drinking and the illegal use of drugs. For me, going to the
Gilman has many times prevented me from using drugs or drinking, because
when I am there I feel so good that I don,t need to drink or use drugs.
instead the music and good vibes from everyone around me gives me fuel to
live my life drug free.

I think that the same thing goes for tagging as drinking and using
drugs.
The Gilman street project gives youth other things to do instead of being
in gangs or grafting. After 4 hours of listening to people preach about
how we should take care of the world people would feel like hypocrites
going and tagging up the place. There their will be graffiti no matter
where people go and it is untrue to say that no one at the gilman has ever
graffitied, but the only reason that their is graffiti at the gilman is
not because there are a certain kind of people, but because their are
people their in general.

All over the country there are youth basketball leagues to keep kids of
the street, but for those of us that are not in great physical condition
or are interested in other things we are provided nothing except the
Gilman. For me the Gilman provides the opportunity to engage my mind and
further my knowledge about important issues community in our community
(ie. racism, sexism, political issues etc.). If you take this away from
me and all of the people who like to go to the Gilman I assure you that
there will be more underage drinking, illegal use of drugs, tagging and
ignorance.

Sincerely,

Nathan M

S.F., 94110

To Whom It May Concern:

I have been a patron of 924 Gilman Street for over four years. I first started attending shows at the club during my freshman year in high school. I am now a freshman at UC Santa Cruz and an active volunteer at the club. The club was a community for me during high school, and continues to be one even though I no longer live in the Bay Area.

One of the things Berkeley likes to pride its self on is its diversity. I wouldn't be shocked to see a not for profit youth club such as Gilman being swept under the carpet in favor of industry, (read: money) in any other city. However, for the City of Berkeley to do such a thing would be for it to sell out what makes it such an interesting place: the wide variety of people that co-exist there.

Gilman does more than provide a place for youth to congregate on weekend nights in a safe, fun place: It is a working model of diversity. At Gilman, I am working along side people from ages 13 to 60. Some are working class, some are middle and upper class. There are a wide variety of educational, ethnic, familial and cultural backgrounds. Yet we are all peers, all equals, volunteering our time together. There is no where else in my life that this is true: not at school or at work or in my family or circle of non-Gilman friends. I learn a lot from all these people, people I would never come in contact with as equals in any other setting. Gilman is a true study in diversity, and that in and of itself is worth more than any money Di Con pays their workers or brings to Berkeley.

Sincerely,

Megan W

Megan W

January 20, 1999

City of Berkeley Zoning Office
2120 Milvia Street
Berkeley, CA 94704

Dear Sirs and Madams:

I cannot place enough emphasis upon the importance of the 924 Gilman Street Project to the city of Berkeley.

I recognize Gilman's importance from a variety of perspectives: as a UC Berkeley-educated public librarian who works closely with young people, as a fan of punk rock who has been attending shows at Gilman for the past ten years, as the sister of a professional rock musician, and as an individual who cares deeply about the cultural excellence that the Gilman Street Project has brought to the city of Berkeley.

I know how important it is to take care of our young people: my Master's Degree is in Library and Information Studies with an emphasis on service to young people, including youth at risk. Both my education and my personal experience have taught me that teenagers are *not* the easiest population to serve--that's why they need committed, caring adults who are willing to be a little flexible. Kids can get into trouble, and even at my suburban library we see fist fights, litter, and acts of vandalism. When we as adults perceive trouble, however, we need to be sure we do not overreact, especially when the young people concerned are competently taking care of things themselves. That's why it's so exciting that through the Gilman Street Project, young people *can* take responsibility for themselves and for their music scene.

Whether just for the evening or as a lifestyle, Gilman provides young people with healthy opportunities and the chance to participate in a genuinely cool and creative activity that can be free of drugs, alcohol, racism, and violence. Speaking as someone who works hard to develop programs that will interest young people, it's inspirational that no adult spent time and money creating Gilman as a program for youth, even though it functions as recreational, job training, and intervention programs. No adult could have created Gilman, in fact, because it has worked so well for so long only *because* it came from the young people themselves. This do-it-yourself (or *DIY*, the punk rock philosophy) attitude is the key to Gilman's success. For more than ten years, members of the Gilman Street Project have been volunteering to do it themselves with dedication, organization, and commitment: they book the bands, they play in the bands, and they comprise the audience; what's more, they provide security and clean up the neighborhood after every show.

Members of the Gilman Street Project, although they may seem like outsiders, are not outlaws. Gilman's positive attitude toward the law is evident when Project members don't hesitate to call the police when

it's necessary, whether to protect audience members or the general public. These kids are not criminals or gang members at war with the community--they are *part* of the community, and they care about their neighborhood, their scene, and their city. Their sense of community is in no way negated by a few isolated instances of trouble. It is crucial that we understand this; it is needless to react with suspicion and hostility, and we cannot afford to alienate those who are, fundamentally, doing such good work.

I have traveled the United States while on tour with my brother's punk rock band, and I've found that very few cities are lucky enough to have a nightclub like Gilman. In many cities, there are *no* clubs which are open to people under the age of 21. Even the few all-ages clubs I've seen, and they are uncommon, have serious problems. Many are poorly run, and thus plagued with violence and hatred; after we were threatened by racist skinheads at a club in Eugene, Oregon, we fled before the band even had a chance to play. At other clubs, the few teenagers who came told me their parents feared for their safety--because of the neighborhood *and* because of the other people in the audience. On the other hand, many nightclubs have security guards no better than hired thugs, and audience members get hurt; it can even be deadly when security and audience do not trust one another. (Remember the killing at the Berkeley Square?) The Gilman Street Project holds itself to a very high standard, and despite its outward signs of rebelliousness, Gilman is a safe and welcoming club. It is safe because the audience is loyal, the security is trustworthy, and both understand each other; this is especially true because the people who provide security are derived *from* the audience.

Punk rock has been very good to Berkeley, and vice versa. While even from the narrowest vantage point it is clear that the Gilman Street Project, as a successful nightclub, brings business to its neighborhood, the economic and cultural benefits of Gilman are much further-reaching. Berkeley, unlike many cities, is home to numerous record stores, record labels, bands, bookstores, musical equipment stores, and "alternative" shops and services; these thrive, in part, because the music scene thrives. People come from all over the country (and from other countries) to visit Berkeley because of the city's long connection with punk rock; many people come specifically to visit 924 Gilman Street. But Berkeley has not just played an important part in the history of punk--it continues to host a vital and exciting scene, and Gilman's role in this cannot be overlooked. Other cities may have just a few punk rock shows a month, but because of Gilman, Berkeley has at least two shows every week of the year. In addition to providing a profitable venue for established bands on national tours, the frequency of shows at Gilman gives beginning local bands, often teenagers, a chance to play as well--a combination which engenders success for a club as well as a scene. The success of Gilman is success for the city of Berkeley.

The 924 Gilman Street Project should be celebrated by the City of Berkeley, not regarded with suspicion, and its members should be congratulated for their continuing good work. I encourage the members of the Zoning Board, and all City of Berkeley employees, to defend Gilman against this attack, because Gilman is of vital importance to the City of Berkeley. The Gilman Street Project is a positive force in the lives of many young people, it provides a creative outlet for the disenfranchised, it is good for the greater economy, it has enormous historical significance, and its presence is crucial to Berkeley's continued cultural excellence. I thank you very much for your time, and I would be pleased to discuss this further if you have any questions.

Sincerely,

Nicole R

Nicole R

January 21, 1999

To the Berkeley Zoning Board,

My name is Alex K   and I am the General Manager of Pyramid Brewery Alehouse. I came down from Seattle to start the Pyramid Alehouse Project in August of 1996. From the first month to the present I have had a positive and good relationship with the 924 Club. In a way we have come full circle. In the beginning of our relationship the 924 Club did not want us to be their neighbors, siting there might be issues with our Alehouse customers and the kids showing up for their shows. We met every month in the pre-opening stages to go over situations that might arise and if they did how to correct them.   When the Alehouse opened in February of 1997 we had both security companies meet in the event any of these issues arose.

The fact is from our opening to the present we have had no problems between us. It was always interesting to me that problems might arise, I never thought there would be any problems.   The San Francisco Chronicle also wrote a little article about our coexistence with the same results of nothing really happening between us. The 924 Club was one of the first neighbors that I have met and continue a relationship with, if they are forced to move out I will be very disappointed.

If you have any further questions please feel free to contact me at 510-extension   , Monday through Friday.

Sincerely,

Alex K
General Manager
Pyramid Alehouse
901 Gilman St.
Berkeley, Ca. 94710

S. Scott K
PO Box
Boulder, CO 80302

City of Berkeley Zoning Office
c/o Alternative Music Foundation
PO Box 1058
Berkeley, CA 94701

To Whom It May Concern:

It was brought to my attention recently that the future of the Gilman Street Project was in jeopardy, and I wanted to write a letter to add my voice to others who believe that closing the club would be a terrible mistake. I understand you on the board may question the validity of an outsider point-of-view, but you also must understand the impact that the project has had on the outside world. When I was a teenager and started learning about Gilman, it seemed like an idealistic vision that wouldn't work. However, the longevity of the project has proved me wrong. It is a community club where anyone is welcome, and the activities aren't limited to music, but include poetry readings, art expositions, and other diverse events that otherwise wouldn't be possible at other venues. It is a haven where drugs and alcohol are not welcome, but the members understand today's world enough to offer Alcoholics Anonymous and Narcotics Anonymous meetings to those in need of help. It is a place that stands for noble ideals and supports an anti-racist, anti-sexist, and anti-homophobic stance. The project accomplishes all of these goals while still remaining self-sustained, yet affordable for local youth. Ultimately, all these positive efforts mingled with the aforementioned longevity have made the project an operational role model. People across the United States and Europe look to Gilman as the blueprint for what they wish they had, or are trying to create in their communities.

It appears that the problems of graffiti, litter, and other infractions are not substantial enough to revoke the club's permits. This is especially true because the project is willing to work with the city and community to find a compromise that will be sufficient for everyone involved. It is true that this place may be geared for the counter-culture, but it does not exclude anyone. Gilman is about building community, and building a place where coexistence across the lines of difference is not a foolish dream, but a reality. I do not see the benefits of revoking the Gilman Street Project's permits as outweighing the cost of removing this landmark institution.

S. Scott K

Dearest whom ever this concerns ,

I am from New Jersey . I have never personally experienced 924 Gilman Street ,
but it really hit me close to home today when I heard there was a threat of it closing .

The musicians from the Gilman Street scene have always inspired me . It is such a
meaningful endeavor that a group of young people could get together and create a safe
haven for their fellow peers . They have created more than a club , they have produced a
healthy environment for promoting the well-being of teens . Fundraisers have taken place
there . Many people have learned self - defense there , which may very well save their lives
someday . But most of all , it is a safe haven for youths of all walks of life to express
themselves .

Things like racism , drug and alcohol abuse , and violence are harshly looked down
upon . Gilman Street is a real benefit to the community's youth , whether most people
realize it or not . People think of punk and the music associated with it as bad news . They
treat the right to express yourself the way you choose as a crime . But these macho
tendencies normally associated with punk are strewn aside at the club . Just listen to what
some of the local bands have to say . Guaranteed you will find some truly inspirational
lyrics .

So many people have worked so hard to get this going , and keep it alive , I would
just hate to see it go . Though I can't speak for them , I'm sure the club is trying hard to
comply with the demands . I believe with a little sacrifice on the club's part , this issue can
be resolved with both sides fully satisfied .

To most Americans , famous movie stars , actors , singers , etc . are their icons .
They are the people whom they look up to . For me , and a handful of other like - minded
kids , the Bay Area music scene is who we look up to , and 924 Gilman Street is the seat
of this scene . It's impossible to sum up in words just how much it means to me .
Someday , I hope to visit this place . I'm sure I speak for all of us when I say that when
Gilman Street was born , a star was born , and we don't want to see it die out . We don't
want to lose Gilman Street .

Sincerely ,

Mike S

My name is Ryan B   . I'm fourteen years old, and I live pretty close
to 924 Gilman in Albany. I lived about a block away from it on Stannage until
I was 6. The first time I went there was in 1987, when I was 3 years old. My
sister took me. That club has been a part of my life for as long as I can
remember. It has always been a place where I can go to just hang out, listen
to my favorite kind of music, be myself, and just be totally comfortable. It's
really a second home to me.

I'm straight-edge (don't smoke, drink, or do drugs) like a lot of people
who go to Gilman. I have never broken any laws while in gilman, or anywhere
around it. The people who do, usually go at least a couple blocks away to
drink or do anything like that. If they were doing it out front, or inside,
Gilman security would kick their asses out in a second. They won't even let
people in the club that they've seen drinking outside in the bushes, or
fighting. Even so, in all the times I've been there I've only seen two fights,
and have only seen 6 people not allowed to come into a show. And I've never,
ever seen graffiti being written outside, or inside of the club by the punks
who frequent it. I swear to you that I see more drunks and drunk people coming
out of the Pyramid Brewery I've seen in all the time I've been going to Gilman

Gilman security is doing a really good job. They're there to keep the
club in order, which they do well. Usually, people will run off if they're
breaking the law and they see the black-on-red of a gilman security t-shirt.
It wouldn't be the same if we had rent-a-cops and beat officers controlling
things. Punks typically don't like cops, and from the apparent surveillance of
the club, among other things, cops don't seem to like us much either. Gilman
is the perfect example of a peer group policing itself. If someone is doing
something that's against the rules, a whole bunch of people will tell them to
get out, and if they won't, they get dragged out by security. After the
Grimple (a band) show a while back, the Gilman staff warned people that if
they ever saw as many people drinking at a show as that night, the show would
be shut down. It's worked this way for over a decade, and I see no reason for
it to stop now.

No alchohol, cigarettes, or other restricted items are sold at Gilman.
People have to go somewhere else to get them. No laws have been broken by the
club, it's staff, or almost all of it's members. When my sister went to
France, people there knew about 924 Gilman, and wanted to hear about what it
was like from her. Don't let a few people ruin something so special, so
unique, for the rest of us. I don't know if you can understand what I mean by
this, but Gilman is the only place in the world where I've felt like
everything was okay, everything was right. As Jesse Michaels of Operation Ivy
put it, I was experiencing " the reconciled world." I'll put the full quote at
the end. Gilman is nothing like the other clubs I've been to in San Francisco
or Berkeley. There is a really powerful sensation I get when I go there. I
can't imagine a place that would make me more excited and happy. In short,
Gilman is a club by the kids, for the kids, and of the kids. Don't take that
away from us.

Ryan

"Music is an indirect force for change, because it provides an anchor
against human tragedy. In this sense, it works towards a reconciled world. It
can also be the direct experience of change. At certain points during some
shows, the reconciled world is already here, at least in that second, at that
place.

Operation Ivy was very lucky to have experienced this.

Those seconds reveal that the momentum that drives a subculture is more
important than any particular band.

The momentum is made of all the people who stay interested, and keep
their sense of urgency and hope." - Jesse Michaels

CHAPTER NINE

WHO'DA THUNK IT?

SAMMY G. / JEMUEL G

2000-2002

"*I COULD BE A VITAL PART OF THE MUSIC COMMUNITY, EVEN IF I WASN'T IN A BAND.*"

— JESSICA S.

Photo by Paul C.

SAMMY G.

I moved to the East Bay in 1994, when I was just starting high school. I heard about Gilman through a friend at school. I didn't know any of the bands or much about punk. I ended up going there to check it out. I remember walking in and looking around and thinking, god, how am I going to explain this to somebody? How am I going to explain what this place is? I didn't understand it at all—there was graffiti everywhere, people with metal stuck in their face, mohawks, stuff I hadn't seen much of, if at all, before.

I sat there for a while, just soaking it all in. Then they started clearing everyone out of the club before the show started and someone yelled at me to get out! I got so scared! But I went out, paid, came back in, and watched the first band. It was just this wall of noise. I couldn't even tell it was music!

I went once more about two months later after winning tickets on the UC Berkeley radio station KALX. Two weeks later, I went a third time. I was there early again and the show coordinator for that night asked me if I wanted to work and get in free. I said okay and he put me at the cash box, and first-timers aren't really supposed to work cash box. But the coordinator said I was okay and so I did it, and ended up working almost every show after that for the next two and a half years, and about eighty percent of the shows for about the next six years total. Gilman was the first time anyone in my life, that I can remember, had given me any responsibility. It was the first "job" I had ever had outside of mowing lawns or shoveling snow. It was the first time I had someone I didn't know count on me. I felt this obligation of sorts to keep coming back.

Gilman was where I learned about the punk scene and the music. I would hear a band I liked, buy all their records, read all the interviews with them I could find, learn what their influences were, and then go buy all those records too.

Gilman seemed welcoming to me, if not in an outright sense where people came up to you and said hello, then in the sense where you didn't feel "unwelcome." Even if you were insecure, a loner, not particularly social, you got the feeling that it was okay to go there as much as you wanted, that it was open to all. It definitely wasn't the music for me at first, or even the desire to meet people, it was just that it was something to do, it was interesting, and I felt comfortable there, not pressured or insecure. Also, the people running the place never talked down to me. I felt more of an equal there than I had anywhere else. It seemed pretty culturally diverse to me too, a place where there were all different types of people.

I worked pretty much all the jobs there for the first two or three years, but mostly in the store. There was even consideration of me being the store manager when I was fifteen, but I wasn't that great at math, so I didn't do it, and people were okay with that. I liked the fact that you could be bad at something, even fail at something, and you could have a place there, find something that you could do there. That was one of the things that kept me coming back.

Eventually I started coordinating shows and that seemed to go pretty good, so I was doing that more and more. When Chris S., the head coordinator at the time (1999), announced he was leaving, me and another person there, Jemuel, were the leading candidates to take over, since we were working there so much and coordinating a lot of the shows already. I wasn't sure I could do it myself, so it was decided that both of us would co-head coordinate. You don't really realize how much work it is to run the place until you actually do it. And you can't really "train" for the position either, there's so many little things you just have to pick up as you go along. I knew the basics, but you can't explain everything, mostly you just have to jump in and do it. That's kind of the way all the positions are at Gilman, you have to learn fast. Learning how to adapt quickly also helped me with my regular job at a fund-raising group. I went from an entry-level position, making phone calls and not knowing what I was doing, to managing a room full of thirty people within a year there. I had never been in charge of people before working at Gilman. I had never had any kind of managerial training or experience. That's what I learned the most of as head coordinator.

I was able to get by at the fund-raising group working twenty to twenty-five hours a week, so I stayed there an extra two years so I could work at Gilman and not have to work a forty hour a week job. I didn't really like the job, but I made the sacrifice for Gilman. I think working there hurt me in some ways, fried me, but it was worth it for me to be able to put more time in at Gilman. After becoming co-head coordinator, my time at Gilman fluctuated. Sometimes I'd be there too much, over-stressed, other times I'd be there too little, leaving it all to Jemuel. It was hard to achieve a balance. I don't know if it was because I wasn't really ready for it, or I had been there too long already, or what. On top of that, I had a hard time admitting that I was flailing. I feel like I could have handled it better and just come right out and told people the truth. I think I hurt Gilman by what I did; I flaked on the club, and I definitely regret doing that. I regret that period more than any other time I was there.

I had lots of plans and ideas that I wanted to implement when I first took over. One of the things I wanted to do was to make it easier for every head coordinator after me. I was trying to make it more organized. I wanted the show coordinating staff to meet every two weeks, to work out problems, do scheduling, etc. I also wanted to get out of having to be there for every show. I had been to almost every show for a lot of years and I wanted to stop doing that. I think I've worked more shows than anybody else who's worked at Gilman. The ideas I had for better organization depended on more work from everyone else. But most of the other people weren't interested in doing this extra work. I was trying to give everyone autonomy. I wanted security, booking, store, sound, all to be their own entities, to meet and decide things within their own subgroup, handle it on their own. I wanted to have about thirty people on the staff so everyone could work less, and we could get more done. But I couldn't convince the people who were working a lot to work less, and I couldn't convince the people who were working a little to work a little more. We couldn't get thirty people. That was pretty discouraging.

We also discussed two ideas to help the club financially. One was to increase the door price from five dollars to six. The other was to have shows every Sunday. Neither of these ideas went through. I also wanted a more comprehensive web site, written and produced by the collective, that posted info on how to get involved, job descriptions for the various positions, the "chain of command," meetings, bulletins, etc. I wanted a schedule in the office for who was working the main positions each show (sound, security head, coordinator, store). Most of the ideas I brought up ended up getting shot down at meetings, and this discouragement accelerated my burnout. Also, people would bring up projects or ideas at meetings that they wanted implemented, we'd all agree it was a good idea, and then, when it wasn't put into action, they'd blame me. I couldn't do everything. I needed them to carry some of the load. If they wanted these ideas carried out, they could organize it and carry it out, but they didn't. These kinds of things would build up in me and occasionally I'd lose it and blow up at somebody. I think I had more of a reputation as an asshole than probably any other head coordinator. I think it was easy for people to criticize me. I wasn't as easy to get along with as the head coordinator before me, Chris S., I was younger, more closed off, more surly. I just tried to see past it and do the best job I could. Chris S. helped me a lot when things were really stressing me out. I wanted to gradually ease out of the head coordinator position as more people stepped up and did more, but that didn't happen, or not quickly enough, and I burned out and split. People were flaking on me, and I ended up flaking on Gilman.

It wasn't all pain, of course. I did like things about being head coordinator. The things I liked most about it were the things I got to do that helped change the club, and also seeing the potential in someone and being able to bring that out of them. When I first started working there, I was very irresponsible and immature. But the more responsibilities I was given, the more responsible and mature I became. Because I was given a chance, I wanted to give others that chance too. Seeing people change really had an impact on me, seeing them make themselves into better people without having to be told to. The atmosphere at Gilman inspires that. I think a huge portion of my maturity came from working at Gilman. Being able to realize this and then try to give something back was very rewarding. It's also rewarding to see an idea you have be put into place and work successfully. It makes you feel like you're an important part of the place and that your contributions matter. Every day that that place stays open is a communal event based on everyone's work. I was in a postion where I could make things better at a place that made me better. That's what I would tell the people who were interested in working at Gilman, or explain to the parents who only see that their kids are coming home drunk or smelling of cigarettes and think that Gilman is bad news. I think that if you really get involved at Gilman, it will make you a better person. But these rewards were things that I had to look for. They're not always obvious and sometimes you just have to trust that they're there. Gilman doesn't offer much, if any, direct positive feedback. You have to be fairly self-reliant for your motivation and inspiration. Mostly it was the little things, triumphs, smiles, meeting a cool new person, etc., things that would happen maybe once or twice a month, that kept me going there, working there, made me love it.

I've learned a lot from working at Gilman, and it's definitely changed me as a person. When I first started there, the head coordinator at the time didn't like me, and with good reason. I was an obnoxious, annoying fifteen-year-old kid who was always around, poking his nose into everything. I worked there for two years before becoming a show coordinator. I felt I had proven myself responsible enough long before I was actually allowed to coordinate a show, long before I was given keys to the place. But I stuck it out, I knew I had a place there, that it was a communal thing, and anyone could participate. It didn't matter that he didn't like me, I could work there if I wanted to. And I did want to. I'd do any job they asked me to. I matured a lot faster because I worked at Gilman. I can't imagine any other scenario where I would have grown up that fast. I have much more of a sense of who I am now. It taught me how to deal with people, taught me what I'm capable of and not capable of, what's worth sacrificing for and what's not. Gilman taught me that having a goal for selfish reasons is ridiculous. My outlook now is how my actions and contributions affect or help the group, rather than just myself. Gilman has ingrained that in me.

The skills I got from working there, and the people I met, far outweighed just seeing good bands. That's why it felt more like a community center to me rather than just a music club. I was never really involved there for the music, I was never really involved there to "network." I've put my work at Gilman on a number of resumes, and when I told them it was volunteer, people couldn't believe I did that much work for free. But Gilman couldn't possibly pay the head coordinator, even minimum wage, for all the hours they put in. They couldn't afford it. And I felt that the money they would put towards someone's salary would be better spent on maintenance or improvements or something like that. With that said, I do think a small monthly stipend is appropriate if there's only one head coordinator, or have at least two head coordinators. It's just too much for one person.

The entire time I worked there, up until this past year, I had wanted to work there my entire life. I had dreams of winning the lottery, or having a book of mine become a big seller and buying the club. Then I would buy the house down the street where the guy who always complains about Gilman lives, and turning it into a "band hotel." I wanted the "festering sore" (Gilman's nickname to some city employees) to continue to ooze in the face of the rampant sterile development in the area. I always thought I would be involved on some level. I wanted to change the pattern where people left (particularly head coordinators) and never came back. I think the best thing that former head coordinators can do is to come to the meetings, offer their insight and experience. That's what I want to try and do, that and maybe coordinate a show once a month or something. I keep meaning to go to the next meeting and find out what's going on. I keep meaning to come back...

To be honest, now that I've been away from Gilman for a little while, I can see the load it was on me, and the toll it was taking on me. It feels like the first time in seven years that I haven't had two jobs. I can see why the other folks haven't come back. Now I can go to school if I want, go on tour with a band, do other things like that. I feel like I put off or turned down a lot of things to work at Gilman. I don't feel resentful about it, that's just the way it was. It does make it harder to go back though, because now, I do want to do some of those other things...

2001   Photo by Ace M.

JEMUEL GARDNER

CAKE FIGHT

So I was going to write about what Gilman means to me and how important it is, but changed my mind. That's boring. If people wanted to read about people's experiences and thoughts on the club, they'd buy some book, a collection of essays and interviews about 924 Gilman Street maybe. I'm sure there are several out there, available through Amazon.com or your local Barnes and Noble.

No, I won't be telling you anything about the place. I already gave you the address, which probably was a mistake. I shall instead tell you a story about something that happened in the side room at Gilman. The story is very true and one of the most amazing things I've ever been a part of. I suppose this could be a "being there" description of Gilman, thus being defacto about Gilman. But I prefer to think of it as a story, preferably told to young children late at night.

The Gilman side room is where the magic happens. Not really, but considering "the magic" doesn't happen on stage, the side room might as well take over as "where-it-all-goes-down." It is actually where the volunteers hide from the bands and people seeing the bands. It's where we play chess and talk shit about Gilman. It's usually a mess, like all of Gilman, and has a collection of various oddities. For this specific story, aside from the normal mess, there is a half-eaten birthday cake on the table.

In the side room is me and two other guys. One who I don't know, but will call Brian, and Ilya. Ilya I do know. He's kind of new there and not quite fitting in. But he doesn't quite fit in anywhere. Lots of people like him show up there, myself included. They are playing chess and I'm watching them.

During this time in my involvement with the club all I really did was watch people. Just a fly on the wall.

Enter Liesl. She's a story in herself. The infamous Liesl. Very well known, very disliked in some circles. Once I went on a crusade to find out why so many people didn't like her, but like my crusade to carve my intials in the "Niles" sign in the Niles hills or my crusade to weigh more than 130 pounds, it was fruitless. I had no solid answers or stories as to why people booed and hissed when she entered the club. The only theory I could find is that she was vocal, opinionated, and a girl. I myself adored her. She was my punk rock hero. She was so fun and energetic. Her constant babbling was never inane or chit chatty. She was always thinking, even if it was pooh pooh fifteen-year-old thoughts (Come on, admit it! Everything you thought at fifteen sucked too.) So I was her fan.

Enter Liesl. She comes in and asks Ilya for a cigarette. He says he doesn't have one, but Lauren does. Would she, Liesl, be so kind as to bum one for him as well? Liesl says sure and exits.

"Ew," says Brian. "Are you friends with her?"

Ilya stammers, no, he's not. "I just wanted to get a cigarette."

I'm tsk-tsking here, because I know Ilya and Liesl are friends enough, and Ilya just wants to fit in. And it's not like I can blame him, wanting to be "one of the guys." I did stupid things to fit in too... when I was twelve!

But what's done is done...

This next part is a little hard to believe and I feel I need to again confirm that this actually happened. This is true. Brian suggests to Ilya that they throw cake at Liesl when she comes back in with Ilya's cigarette. It's absurd, but not really. Most everyone here is around high school age, so it's completely reasonable to assume there are high school mentalities around. They're dominant, really. If you are so nice and innocent that you find it hard to believe two sixteen to twenty-year-olds would conspire a food fight against someone because she was unpopular, you are a better person than most and are best staying in Canada or home school or where it was that made you such a freak.

But true enough, there they sat when she came back. Spoons of cake pointed, stupid grins. She comes in, throws him a cigarette; "There you go." And then she sees their intent. "What? You two going to throw cake at me?"

"Uh huh," they nod.

She puts her hand on her hip, smokes her cigarette. Classic cool girl pose. She waits. "Well? What are you waiting for?" They don't do anything. She laughs. "Well, aren't ya or are ya? I thought you were going to throw cake at me?" She's totally goading them on, making fun of them. Ilya gets brave for a second and bends his spoon in preparation to let go. She says, "But let me warn you, if you do, I'll tear you a new asshole." He changes his mind.

Brian speaks up. "We'll do it when you leave." Ilya agrees this is the best plan of action.

"Yeah, when you leave."

Liesl gets a good laugh at this. "You fucking pussies! You get this idea to throw cake at me, you don't have the balls to do it. Then you say you'll do it when my back is turned! No, no. Not going to happen. You're going to throw cake at me, at my face (at which point I'll beat the living shit out of both of you) or you both can go home."

I was loving it. Liesl is maybe four or five years younger than them, skinny as a rod, but she is totally bullying them. Punk rock hero. It goes on with this, her telling them to do it and them stammering. So I did the only thing I could do. I picked up a handful of cake and threw it at Ilya.

They both go "huh." Brian retaliates. I'm hit. Ilya throws a piece at Liesl, but misses. I throw a chunk at him. Liesl jumps on Ilya and hits him. Brian and I give it to each other. All this is in fun, mind you. Liesl jumping on Ilya, threatening to throw cake at innocent girls. It was all done with a smile, a smirk. It was fun, even though it was stupid, lame, and high school.

In the end all of us had cake but Liesl, as things work out that way in life and in bad movies. Brian and I shook hands and cleaned up the mess. I told Ilya I thought it was lame he didn't stand up for Liesl, because he really was friends with her. Then Jake came in and whined, "I was going to eat that cake."

1987   photo by Cammie T.

BEN DITCH

AFTER HOURS AT GILMAN ST.
BY BEN DITCH

AT GILMAN STREET, AT LEAST SINCE I'VE BEEN GOING THERE, THERE'S ALWAYS BEEN A LOOSE KNIT GROUP OF PEOPLE WHO ARE JUST BUMMING AROUND IN THE OFFICE, KICKIN' IT IN THE STOAR OR HANGING OUT IN THE ALLEY WAY A COUPLE OF BLOCKS AWAY (IF YOU KNOW WHAT I MEAN, WINK) WAITING FOR THE SHOWS TO END SO THEY CAN GET ON WITH SOME REAL FUN.

IT WASN'T LONG AFTER I STARTED GOING TO GILMAN THAT I BEGAN TO BECOME ONE OF THESE PEOPLE, SHOWING UP WHEN THE SHOW WAS HALF WAY THROUGH, OR A LOT OF TIMES COMPLETELY OVER WITH NO IDEA OF WHO WAS EVEN PLAYING. IT'S ALWAYS BEEN COMFORTING TO KNOW THAT WHEN THERES NOTHING TO DO ON A FRIDAY OR SATURDAY NIGHT THERE'LL AT LEAST BE A BIG POT OF FREE COFFEE AND A FEW FRIENDLY FACES DOWN AT THE CLUB REGARDLESS OF WHAT SHITTY BAND IS PLAYING.

MOST OF THE PEOPLE WHO COMPRISE THE GROUP I SPEAK OF, AT ONE TIME

①

OR ANOTHER WERE AT THE CLUB EVERY WEEKEND RAIN OR SHINE, WORKING, CONTRIBUTING THEIR TIME AND COMING TO SEE THE CLUB AS A SECOND HOME IN MANY CASES. NOW WE LURK IN THE CORNERS. WAITING.

MIDNIGHT BASKETBALL

AS FAR AS I KNOW, AFTER HOURS ACTIVITIES STARTED WITH MIDNIGHT BASKETBALL. I'VE ALWAYS THOUGHT THAT THE BEST THING ABOUT THE MIDNIGHT B-BALL IS THAT IT OFFERS EVERYTHING THAT YOU WANT FROM A SHOW BUT SELDOM GET. YOU GET TO MEET A BUNCH OF NEW PEOPLE AND IF YOU DON'T GET THEIR NAMES THROUGH YOUR THICK SKULL NO ONE WILL PASS TO YOU (THUS NEW FRIENDSHIPS ARE BORN). YOU GET TO FEEL LIKE YOU'RE ACTUALLY PART OF A COMMUNITY. THERE'S A SENSE OF COMRADERY AND ACCEPTENCE OFTEN TIMES LACKING AT THE SHOWS. YOU GET TO RUN AROUND AND SWEAT OUT ALL THAT PENT UP ENERGY FROM DRINKING TOO MUCH COFFEE AND THEN STANDING AROUND AT THE SHOW FEELING JITTERY AND AWKWARD

②

B-BALL ONE OFFS
- PLAYING A WHOLE GAME ON OFFICE CHAIRS
- PILLOW FIGHT BREAK OUT
- PLAYING AGAINST A DUDE IN AN APE SUIT
- PLAYING CALIFORNIA VS OREGON AND LOSING (NEVER AGAIN)

1998   photo by Sita R.

AND LAST, BUT NOT LEAST YOU GET TO LAUGH AT HOW BAD PUNKS ARE AT SPORTS.

B-BALL INJURIES

CELIA GOT HIT IN THE FACE BY HER OWN TEAM MATE AND HAD TO START COLLEGE WITH A BLACK EYE, AS CAN BE SEEN ON HER STUDENT ID. ASHLEY FELL ON HIS ELBOW, WHICH WAS BRUIZED FOR TWO WEEKS. A LUMP REMAINS. THE FIRST TIME HE EVER PLAYED, JEMUEL JUMPED FOR THE BALL AND LANDED ON HIS KNEES ON THE CONCRETE FLOOR. OUCH! ROBERT TUMBLED AND ROLLED CAUSING MORE INJURIES THAN HE RECEIVED. MEGAN GOT HIT IN THE FACE WITH THE BALL AND WE ALL HAD TO STOP PLAYING AND SPEND THE NEXT 15 MINS SEARCHING FOR HER LIP PEIRCING. I GOT FLIPPED OVER SOMEONES BACK AND WAS FROZEN IN MID AIR FOR A SPLIT SECOND BEFORE COMING CRASHING DOWN TO THE GROUND DIRECTLY ON MY HIP. I HAD TO LIMP AROUND IN CIRCLES FOR 10 MINS.

MOVIE NIGHTS

BEFORE THE PURCHASING OF THE FANCY PROJECTOR AND THE SCREEN THAT OPENS AND CLOSES ON ITS OWN, AND BEFORE THE LEGITAMIZING OF THE WHOLE THING, ROBERT AND I, AS WELL AS AN EVER ROTATING CAST OF FRIENDS WOULD HAVE GILMAN MOVIE NIGHTS OF OUR OWN. IT ALL STARTED ONE NIGHT WHEN WE DECIDED TO BORROW A TV AND VCR SO WE COULD WATCH MOVIES AT HELLARITY (OUR HOUSE). SO WHERE BETTER TO

③

GO TO THAN GILMAN? JUST ONE CALL TO A KEY HOLDER (WHO SHALL REMAIN NAMELESS) AND WE WERE IN.

URBAN BOWLING ASSAULT

THIS WAS SO COOL! AFTER THE SHOWS WERE OVER AND EVERYONE HAD CLEARED OUT, WE (THE PUNKS) WOULD BOWL IN THE MIDDLE OF FUCKING 8TH ST. IT WAS GREAT. WE HAD LIKE 3 OR 4 BOWLING BALLS AND A SET OF PINS AND WE WOULD DRAG A COUCH OUT ONTO THE STREET TO PUT BEHIND THE PINS SO THAT THE BALL WOULDN'T ROLL AWAY. EVERY ONCE IN A WHILE A CAR WOULD WANT TO PASS, SO WE WOULD HAVE TO STOP PLAYING AND DRAG THE COUCH TO THE SIDE OF THE STREET. ONE TIME SOME GUY DROVE HIS CAR INTO THE PINS BEFORE ANYONE COULD MOVE THEM.

FOR THE MOST PART THE COPS WOULDN'T DO ANYTHING EXEPT FOR DRIVE BY AND LAUGH AT US, BUT ONE TIME A COP VAN PULLED UP RIGHT BEHIND US AND STOPPED THERE WITH ITS HEADLIGHTS HITTING US FULL BLAST.

④

BEST MOVIE WATCHED AT GILMAN:
THE DAY THE EARTH STOOD STILL.
WORST MOVIE WATCHED AT GILMAN:
HEAVY METAL (EUGH!)

WE KIND OF FREAKED OUT BUT DECIDED TO KEEP ON BOWLING. THEY STAYED THERE WATCHING US FOR LIKE 15 OR 20 MINS BEFORE TELLING US TO MAKE SURE THAT WE LET TRAFFIC GET THROUGH, AND THEN THEY LEFT.

SOMETIMES PEOPLE WOULD MISS THE COUCH COMPLETELY, SENDING THE BALL ROLLING OFF INTO THE SUNSET UNTIL IT EVENTUALLY FOUND ITS WAY TO THE GUTTER, OR IT HIT A PARKED CAR. ASIDE FROM THE TRADITIONAL BOWLING STYLE, PEOPLE WOULD BOWL ON SKATEBOARDS, ROLLER SKATES AND BICYCLES. SOMETIMES THEY WOULD FORGET ABOUT THE BOWLING BALL COMPLETELY AND JUST LAUNCH THEMSELVES INTO THE PINS.

⑤

2000   photo by Lauren L.

CHLOE

Why Gilman? I feel like people ask me that a lot. Why devote my weekends to a smelly, dirty punk rock club that never really did anything for me? Why stress out over trying to run a show when I could be watching the show, unscathed? I mean, they don't even pay me! What's my problem?

I think those questions answer themselves. It's not just a sense of personal responsibility (although that is part of it), but also the fact that Gilman has given me more of a community and a family than I've ever felt anywhere else in my life...Sometimes it seems like they're more of a family to me than my "real" family is, as cliche as that sounds. The fact is, without Gilman I don't know where the fuck I'd be, but I know that I'd definitely be in a much worse place than I am right now. I was thinking about this the other day, talking to a friend who started out volunteering at Gilman when I did (almost two years ago) and has since "grown out" of the scene. She was telling me how she's all grown up now and how punk rock is just a phase for discontented quasi-rebellious teenagers, and hearing her say all these jaded things made me truly realize how fucking great it is to be involved with Gilman, and how lucky I am to be a part of it. I mean, I could be doing so much worse. I could be fucking flipping burgers or sitting in a parking lot drinking Budweiser and listening to rap metal. But instead I somehow stumbled upon this amazing community where I'm not only able to enjoy real independent music, but also become a part of the community and of the club itself, to learn how things run and eventually run them myself, to feel like I actually belong. Not really feeling at home with my family in my nice neighborhood, or at my school with all the apathetic, liberal-by-denial kids there, I'm able to go to Gilman and actually be myself (again, sorry for all the cliches). As stressful as it can sometimes get having to find kids to work shitty posi-hardcore shows, or scrambling to find a last-minute coordinator, it seems like I always end up having fun, laughing through the stress, or the drama, or whatever the problem is this week.

The fact that I'm sixteen and already in a position of authority as far as coordinating shows and working in the stoar is very important to me—I feel like too often teenagers (and especially teenage girls) are not taken seriously, and sometimes for good reason. I think it's necessary to show that age doesn't really matter in this case, that just because I'm still legally a minor doesn't mean I don't know how to handle a show or work a cash register. It's just another thing that makes me realize why I love the punk scene so much: it's inspiring to me that I've been able to do this, that I wasn't constrained by my age and other people's consequent perceptions of me. It's a testament to how open-minded people can be that I do what I do at Gilman. And it's not just me—some of the most together and responsible workers at Gilman are kids under twenty. Of course, the age range is important too, that's another reason why Gilman is so rad: it proves that punk isn't just for young kids like me. A lot of the workers ae well into their late twenties and thirties, and are still contributing to the scene, still get excited over new bands and new ideas.

What really matters to me is the fact that Gilman has enabled me to transcend the role of spectator that is practically inescapable in almost any other subculture I could be involved in at this point. I mean, you don't see teenyboppers operating the cameras on MTV, but it's the fuck'n punks that run Gilman, right? And that's so important, that I'm able to take part in the creation and propagation of something that means so much to me. I take pride in the fact that, on some small level, I'm contributing to the continuation of something that has inspired me so much, and hopefully I'm enabling it to keep going, so that someday another fourteen-year-old girl will stumble upon Gilman like I did two years ago, and find in it something that strikes her as profoundly as it did me.

So people ask me why I'm getting "924" tattooed on my wrist. "Are you crazy?" Shock, disbelief, and condescension flash over their faces. "You won't want that in five years." And, you know, maybe I won't. But at this point in my life Gilman has done so much for me, and I feel like I've given so much of myself to it, that it's really impossible for it not to have left a lasting impression on me. I know that, even though I've only been around for two years, Gilman has pretty much become a part of me. Yeah, it's a love/hate relationship, and sometimes I get pretty fucking pissed off having to be there, but in the end I know that by the time next Friday rolls around, I'll be stoked 'cause I know that I'll end up at Gilman that night and, shit, is there any other place I'd rather be?

Left: photo by Lauren L.   Above: photo by Emilie V.

Below: photo by Emilie V.

JOE G.

My name is Joe. I'm currently the sound coordinator at Gilman, which involves a number of different sound-related responsibilities:

a) I'm in charge of making sure the sound system as a whole is in good condition, which means fixing things or making sure things are fixed;

b) I'm in charge of buying sound-related equipment, like mic stands or cables;

c) I'm responsible for training new sound people;

d) I make sure that there is at least one sound person responsible for doing sound at every show. If I can't find someone, that means that I do sound.

Of course, because the people at Gilman are so good, everyone helps with all of the

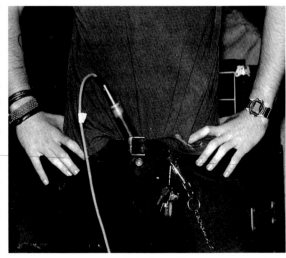

Photo by Larry W.

above. I also get to help out with other tasks, from filling in on nights we have open volunteer positions, to helping suggest numbers for paying bands, to doing cleanup.

I've been the sound coordinator since June, 2000, but I've been doing cleanup and sound since March, 2000.

I went to my first Gilman show in December of 1996. I don't remember what bands played, but I remember being intimidated. It was somewhere new to me, and I didn't know anyone there.

I didn't go to another show for a few months. Slowly, I started going more often, until I was coming to shows every week. I liked the music, but so many things about the place still intimidated me. I knew a little bit of its monumental history; so many people there seemed to know each other (and I didn't know any of them); many bands were famous and had been around forever.

As I started to grow slightly more familiar with the place, I began to spend more time at shows and look around a little more. Eventually, I read some meeting notes that said that they had been looking for more people to help with sound, but had found some. I could have kicked myself: there was an opportunity to get more involved in a way I would have loved, but I had missed it.

I decided that Gilman was the type of place I wanted to support, and I should try to make sure that another opportunity didn't pass me by. At one particularly slow show, I worked up enough courage to talk to the main sound person. She told me that she was training some new people right then, but that if I was still interested in a few months, she could start to show me some stuff.

In the meantime, I began to get involved in other small ways. I helped clean up a few times; I started going to meetings; I began to talk to some other volunteers.

Just as I was beginning to think that she had forgotten, Rachel came up to me and asked if I was still interested in learning sound. She was patient and nice to me, answering any questions I had and helping me get acquainted with the other sound people. Someone without her understanding may have mistaken my reticence, a result only of my being intimidated by her knowledge, experience, and ease at mixing sound, for antipathy, but she treated me with only kindness.

I slowly learned how to make things work. I remember when I first did a show by myself: I was pretty slow, and the sound wasn't so great, but I was so proud that I was practically bursting. Heh.

After a short while, I was doing sound pretty regularly. Rachel told me that she would be graduating and moving soon, and asked if I would be interested in being the sound coordinator. A few weeks later, I was approved by the collective, and have been the coordinator since.

The best thing that Gilman does is to bring people together. It provides a social gathering place, and that's nice. More importantly, though, it is a place for people to meet new people.

Sometimes people meet for very specific reasons: maybe they're both participating in the DIY Skillshare conferences that happen at Gilman. Sometimes the meeting isn't planned, but there's still a specific common interest, like when people sell zines, or set up tables with info about veganism, politics, or DIY networks.

Photo by Larry W.

Gilman can also bring people together, even if they're not both at Gilman at the same time; it's nice to have a space that has flyers and information that will reach the right people.

Gilman brings people together in another way, too, that most people probably don't even think about. When people go to Gilman, they know that they will be at a space that doesn't tolerate sexism, homophobia, and racism. They see other people that reject the notion that you have to live a passive, normal, boring life. They meet people that are working for what they believe in: volunteering to support and keep alive a place that represents so many of the ideals that all of us have, but aren't represented in mainstream society. Even if someone goes to a show at Gilman and doesn't talk to anyone else, they can still feel closer to the whole group of people: a sense of community can grow.

Gilman has quite a bit of notoriety as a DIY space. That very strongly works in its favor. It's extremely difficult for a space to stay open for any length of time; people are often excited about the idea of opening a new space, and will volunteer to help set it up, but then slowly start to work less and less as the novelty wears off and the reality of the space requiring a lot of unglamorous, hard work starts to weigh on them. Because Gilman has so much history, I think it attracts more people and bands, and retains workers, more easily than other spaces. That's not to say that it's easy: there are a lot of times when it seems like, were it not for a few dedicated souls, Gilman could not stay open.

A space like Gilman requires a sort of critical mass of energy. Below that level of energy, people start to work less; shows happen less or with more problems; fewer bands come through; people work even less. Above that critical level, bands support the place; people show up and see something worth supporting; more volunteers join and people do more, and better shows happen. It's pretty clear that Gilman will continue to have enough dedicated workers to stay above that critical mass, and therefore to stay alive, for quite a while to come.

In some ways, Gilman is a victim of its own ideals. Having a collective is great, but it's really tough to keep going. Some of the things I like most about Gilman are a result of what it stands for: all ages, cheap shows, no alcohol allowed. The problem is that those policies cause a place to take in less money. That's okay; people just have to keep in mind that we're not some typical bar or club, and our shows are going to be different.

In other ways, Gilman is a victim of circumstances: land in Berkeley isn't cheap, and its price is going up all the time. That means that Gilman's rent goes up, and Gilman's space becomes more attractive to developers. Also, Gilman now has neighbors that don't quite understand what Gilman is about. Even though Gilman was there before they were, they can still complain about the small inconveniences that come along with a place like Gilman.

Gilman can also be a victim of the attitudes that sometimes plague the punk

Photo by Emilie V.

community. Punk has always been extremely quick to turn and attack its own; the slightest perception of violating the mythical punk rock code can cause people to weaken their support for, or even speak out against, members and groups that have supported them for years. Punk is about tearing down institutions and avoiding hero worship, but people can be too quick to prove their punkness by going overboard by attacking those that don't deserve it. I think some punks also tend to view things as either pure or worthless, with no in-between allowance for pragmatism; maybe this is a result of trying too hard to avoid putting people and groups on pedestals, maybe it's because so many punks have been disillusioned in the past and are now quick to distrust, in an attempt to avoid building new illusions. Finally, people involved in the punk community often end up there because they've rejected many typical social conventions and norms; for some people, this translates into a distrust of social relationships altogether, and that can make it difficult for them to become a member of a community. All of these attitudes and prejudices have to be overcome by people that contribute and support Gilman.

I believe Gilman should concentrate on providing a place for local and touring bands that don't have other places to play. I think most people would agree with that, and it's an idea that gets talked about a lot, but it really takes an effort to make sure that Gilman really works toward that ideal. It's really easy to fall into the trap of booking larger, more exciting bands, but there are other places that are better for those bands to play. Gilman should stick to its roots.

Of course, there are things beyond shows that Gilman is great for. In the past, it's had art shows, film viewings, and plays. Those are all great, and Gilman should try to make itself available for more of those in the future.

There are also more private uses of the space that work out well. Alcoholics Anonymous and Narcotics Anonymous meet there; demos are recorded there; bands practice there. Those things aren't public in the way that a show is, but they all help support the community.

I've learned a lot of practical things from Gilman. Mixing sound is a good skill to have; even if you don't use the knowledge to actually mix sound, a lot of the experience carries over and can help with recording, playing, or just appreciating music. I've also learned a lot about keeping equipment going: fixing and cleaning electrical equipment like the soundboard, DIs, and various adapters, cables, and connectors; cannibalizing mic stands; having copious amounts of duct tape on hand.

I've also learned a lot of useful things about how venues and bands work. I never realized the incredible amount of work that it takes to keep a place like Gilman going. Normally, you go to a show and just pay attention to the bands; all the other people that keep the show running smoothly sort of fade into the background. Beyond them, there are all sorts of people that work for the show but aren't there. I've also learned what sort of things a band should and shouldn't do. After seeing enough bands, you start to realize that the ones that seem organized and have smooth-running sets aren't just lucky: they work at it.

Probably more importantly, though, I've learned things about dealing with people. I have to interact a little bit with the bands when I'm setting them up; I have to work with the stage manager and show coordinator to make sure things keep moving; I have to communicate with the entire collective to let them know what sound issues there are, talk about new equipment, let them know my concerns. Individually, all of my dealings with other people at Gilman seem tiny; together, they've really gotten me more comfortable with working and talking with people in everything I do.

So many people have said it that by now it's cliche, but Gilman changed my life. When sound isn't working right, or takes a long time to get set up, a whole room-ful of people know it; there's no time to sit back and wait for things to fix themselves. Working sound has forced me to be assertive: I have to step in and make sure things are set up right and everything is where it needs to be. That same attitude, in some ways, carries over to the rest of my life.

I've also met a lot of people and made a lot of friends through Gilman. One of the nice side effects about volunteering for something you believe in is that there's a pretty good chance you'll get along with the other volunteers.

Another more indirect way that Gilman has affected me is that it's given me something to care about and believe in. I like what I do during the week, but it's not really something I can be passionate about. Supporting a place that shares my ideals lets me feel that I'm doing something and working for change.

I've never mixed sound anywhere else. I have done a few things that are slightly related, and have been somewhat useful: my formal education has been in electrical engineering; I have some experience with small electronics, both on my own and through volunteering at Free Radio Berkeley; I've recorded some things on my own and done simple audio processing on them on my computer.

Really, though, none of that is necessary. I think most people don't realize that we can train pretty much anyone that's interested in how to work sound.

2000   photo by Lauren L.

When I was growing up, I never really had much interest in popular music. My friends were into the top 40 lists and everything, but I pretty much only followed along because they did.

In second grade, a kid named Brandon moved in across the street. We ended up becoming best friends all the way through junior high. My main exposure to '80s music was from him: every week, he would collect the rankings of the most popular singles, and talk about up-and-coming bands.

As I started to get a little bit older, and more willing to try things on my own, I started to find some stuff that I was a little interested in. Growing up in the suburbs like I did doesn't expose one to much outside the mainstream, so the music I listened to was pretty much limited to what I could hear on radio stations. Something about the oldies and early rock bands caught my attention, but they still weren't something that could really get me excited.

Eventually I went off to college, and discovered college radio. The place where I went, the University of Illinois in Urbana-Champaign, stuck to bland alternative music during the day, but during the night, they gave the DJs a little more freedom. Here I found another little piece of the puzzle: music that was willing to be different, that wasn't going to get wide, mainstream acceptance, and was perfectly fine with that. The attitude was great, but I still didn't find anything that really fit me. I did get exposed to a much wider variety of music than I had seen before, and started to learn that it's worth it to try new things.

One day, my brother suggested I go see a band that was performing locally. I had all sorts of excuses why I shouldn't go (too busy, had to get up early the next day, and so on), but I finally decided that it was worth giving it a try. I didn't really know anything about the band, what type of music they would play, or anything.

The venue was a non-denominational church that some local kids rented for the night. I don't remember anything about the opening bands, but I still remember that pop-punk band and how they changed my life.

Almost nothing about the show was like I expected. First of all, the music was better than just about anything I had heard before in my life. I couldn't understand why they weren't hugely popular and on all the radio stations and MTV. The people there amazed me, as well. Seeing people dance—really letting go and just enjoying the music—was a new experience for me.

Maybe the best thing about the show, though, was the attitude of everyone involved. The people running it were just some kids. The band wasn't snotty and self-absorbed: they moved their own equipment, and talked to people before and after the show. There wasn't a huge stage or barriers between the band and the audience. Some kid sprayed the band with silly string, but there weren't any bouncers to beat him up.

For the next few days after the show, I was almost giddy with excitement. Here, for the first time, was something I could identify with.

I didn't really have any friends that were into the same music, so I was forced to find out what else I liked on my own. I started going to all sorts of different shows, without knowing anything about the bands or what genre of music it was going to be. Over the next few years, I started to refine my tastes.

At some random show later on, I was just about to leave when I spotted someone I thought I recognized. While I was looking at him and trying to remember who it was, he came up to me and it finally struck me: it was Brandon, the kid I used to know! His ride was leaving soon, so we could only catch up for a few minutes. After high school, he had left home and moved out to Berkeley. He was now pretty much just traveling across the country, tagging along with bands on tour.

Our both getting into punk rock independently was amazing enough; its bringing us together, after more than half a decade of separation, was incredible. I thought that would be pretty much the last I saw of him.

And it was, for a while. I graduated, and decided to go to Berkeley for grad school. For a few years, I studied and went to shows. One day, out of the blue, I got some mail: Brandon was coming out to Berkeley, for good. He was going to go to school here as well.

Sometimes when we're sitting in Gilman together, watching the show, I marvel at the way that punk rock has affected our lives and kept us in contact. The more I'm around, though, the more I realize that our story is not altogether unusual: punk rock brings people together. Some people argue about what punk is, but it's clear to me. I can sum up what punk means to me, and what Gilman most symbolizes, in one word: community.

New Band Nights at Gilman are a good idea: it's important for new bands to get a chance to play somewhere. The best part about them, though, is that they are often young kids, and bring lots of relatives to see them play. It's sort of funny to look around on these Gilman Parent Nights and see tons of moms and dads, sort of bobbing their heads trying to fit in, videotaping and snapping pictures like their child was in the school play.

Sometimes people will see the sound person tearing stuff down on stage after a band has played, and think they're in the band. New sound people usually say something like "Oh, I'm not with the band." No! The correct answer is, "You liked our set? Thanks! Too bad you won't have another chance to see us... this is our last show," or anything to that effect. The more outrageous the thing is that you get someone to believe, the more points you get.

A while ago, some of us were talking about what we would title the book that told the story of our time at Gilman. My title: "No, You Can't Have More Vocals In The Monitor." Sammy's title: "Everyone's In My Way." Hm, maybe those are only funny if you work there.

Not all the bands that play at Gilman are entirely human.   **Photo by Larry W.**

BEN DE LA T.

Too many people give up,
and too many people never stop chasing.

I love Gilman for what I see in it, I guess.
I think it's a very different place for me
than it is for a lot of folks.
For me, it's a small tangible version of Anarchy.

Gilman, I can breathe in and live through
Its walls change and vibrate color
like my home, my heart's dwellings
Those walls celebrate my security
and I attach a lot of comfort to them

I don't know where Gilman began really
for me it just sort of appeared

I've heard whispers trading through the air,
lightly touching my ears on soft winds
they tickle me like beauty caressing my soul
the stories, they add dimension, age
it becomes like a legend that I am re-living

However, ideals are the most important thing to me
purpose or intent, if neither are pure
I usually choose not to involve myself, my time, my heart

Yet, Gilman has a way of constantly repairing itself
It has the hum of an old engine
and you can hear it grinding its way to some new peaceful dimension
It is constantly evolving into new generations

And that I believe is the heart of it
no matter who may attempt to control the forum
however depressed and malnourished it may appear,
children bring it life

We get force fed ideology that we hate
We plunge through the destruction of the reigning bodies
We watch our parents' generation massacre the world
We burn with the pressure to look molded.
turn sour and cold inside, move in ways that scream boredom

Pressure is shoved down our throats, by our parents, our schools,
our friends, TV, magazines, security for the future,
capitalism, societal norms
With that, I scream NO!!!

I am not normal, I am not satisfied
I want loud music to numb me
make this psychotic world disappear

You can find me amidst blue mohawks and black dreads
    tatooed fists and slashed jeans
I want blinding movements of raging children
I want to release my anger, vent my frustrations
pound deadly silence into the air
    what have you done to this world?
    and why did I wake up in it?

Gilman was my refuge. At 16 I was released from a drug rehabilitation center for teenagers. I was told that I was faulted, broken like a machine. I could never enjoy life like others could. I had no idea of this at the time, however, I did find myself quite isolated. I remember the first time I went to Gilman, I didn't know how to get there from the North Berkeley BART station, but luckily I saw some obvious punks (black clothes, dirty as hell), they took me along with them. That was the first time, in a long time, I had been accepted so easily, without even having to prove myself. It was nice. I've stayed a loyal fan of Gilman ever since. I worked roughly two years as head of security, seeing as I had grown bigger, I felt it was my duty to protect the club. I met a lot of great people there, and I wouldn't be the same without it. Much love to all whom I have met and cherished there, and love to the building itself.

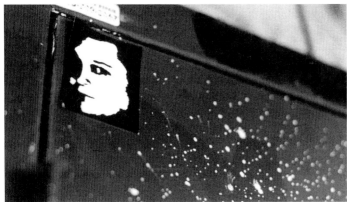

Photo by Adam T.

Photo by Lauren L.

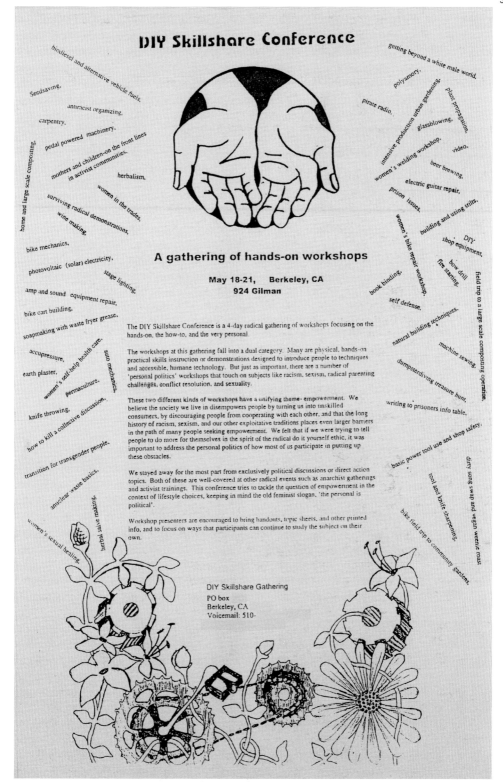

DIY Skillshare Conference

A gathering of hands-on workshops

May 18-21, Berkeley, CA
924 Gilman

The DIY Skillshare Conference is a 4-day radical gathering of workshops focusing on the hands-on, the how-to, and the very personal.

The workshops at this gathering fall into a dual category. Many are physical, hands-on practical skills instruction or demonstrations designed to introduce people to techniques and accessible, humane technology. But just as important, there are a number of 'personal politics' workshops that touch on subjects like racism, sexism, radical parenting challenges, conflict resolution, and sexuality.

These two different kinds of workshops have a unifying theme- empowerment. We believe the society we live in disempowers people by turning us into unskilled consumers, by discouraging people from cooperating with each other, and that the long history of racism, sexism, and our other exploitative traditions places even larger barriers in the path of many people seeking empowerment. We felt that if we were trying to tell people to do more for themselves in the spirit of the radical do it yourself ethic, it was important to address the personal politics of how most of us participate in putting up these obstacles.

We stayed away for the most part from exclusively political discussions or direct action topics. Both of these are well-covered at other radical events such as anarchist gatherings and activist trainings. This conference tries to tackle the question of empowerment in the context of lifestyle choices, keeping in mind the old feminist slogan, 'the personal is political'.

Workshop presenters are encouraged to bring handouts, topic sheets, and other printed info, and to focus on ways that participants can continue to study the subject on their own.

DIY Skillshare Gathering
PO box
Berkeley, CA
Voicemail: 510-

Above: Skillshare 2000

**Below (and on following page): the schedule for the 2001 Skillshare Workshops
(some of which were held at Gilman)**

```
Subject: Tentative DIY Skillshare Workshop Schedule 4/05

DIY Skillshare Conference Workshop Schedule      (subject to change!)
It's here, the long-awaited schedule. THere might be more workshops ad
changes might happen, but the conference will look more or less like t
(If you didn't get this message from the listserve and it was forwarde
please see the end of this schedule for more information about the con

Note following workshops not yet on the schedule: Grief workshop,
Handling Your Legal Case and Staying in Control of Your Lawyer,
Emergency Care for Drug Overdose, Herbalism, and the following
tentative workshops: Sexually Transmitted Diseases- Prevention,
Diagnosis, and Treatment Options , Lime Plastering a Straw Bale Wall
Workparty, Rescue Breathing, Pepperspray/Teargas First Aid

----Thursday 4/19:----

***10 am-noon:
Permaculture Design
Build a Cob Oven (work party to take place all day, still tentative)
Homemade Biodiesel Fuel (this workshop takes place 10 am-1 pm)
Cooking for a Crowd with Food Not Bombs (you'll be making our lunch!)

*** 11 AM- How to Hammer A Nail Microworkshop (15 min)

***noon-1 pm  (our 1-hour timeslot for short microworkshops)
How to Drive A Screw (15 minutes)
Steam Distillation of Essential Oils (1 hour)
Questions and Answers about Vasectomy (30 min?)
Bike Repair Basics
(cob oven continues)
(biodiesel continues)
(Food Not Bombs cooking continues)


***1 pm-2 pm lunch

***2-4 pm:
Welding 2-6 pm
Build a Sneaky Covert Mobile FM Radio Antenna (4 hour workshop)
Everyday Perfect Health (do-it-yourself wellness care)
Make your Own Sex Toys
Cultivating Edible Mushrooms (30 minutes)
Build a Greywater System (4 hour workshop)

***4:30-6:30 pm:
Widening Circles
Beyond the Whiteness: A Challenging White Supremacy Workshop
Bike Repair Basics- Site Visit to the Bat Cave Bike Library in North
Oakland
How to Hammer A Nail and How to Drive A Screw repeat
(Pirate Radio, Greywater, Welding workshops continue)
----Friday, 4/20:-----

***10 am-noon:
Do-It-Yourself Emergency Medicine
Alternative and Community Currencies
Building Instruments From Scrap Materials: Marimbas
Plant Propogation

Cooking with Food Not Bombs


***noon-1 pm microworkshops:

Making Herbal Tinctures By Percolation (1 Hour)
Darn Those Socks (15 minutes)
Bike Repair- Flat Tires(15 minutes), followed by
How to Change A Flat Car Tire (30 Minutes)
(Food Not Bombs continues)

***1 pm-2 pm lunch

***2 pm-4 pm:
Welding 2-6 pm
Girl Army Self Defense Workshop For Everyone
How to Crochet Hats
Solar Electricity
Community Garden Design and Layout
How To Bust Your Nuts (and break loose bolts and other stuck fasteners
(1 hour)

***4:30-6:30:
Silkscreen Printing (tentative)
Automobile Alcohol Fuels
```

Radical Women's Health Care
Sewing!
Kissing- the Oral Majority
Easy to Build Pedal Power Washing Machine
Capoeira
(Welding continues)

-----Saturday, 4/21:----

Glassblowing- offered in several timeslots today
***10-noon:
Electrical Wiring
Auto Mechanics (three hours)
Community Garden Installation Workday (all day)

Keeping Chickens In The City
Coping with Trauma
How to Drill A Hole microworkshop (15 minutes)
Bike Repair Basics
Cooking with Food Not Bombs

***noon-1 pm:
Basic Seed Saving (1 hour, there will be a lunchtime seed swap
following)
Sawing a Board (15 minutes)
How to Change Your Oil
Building Simple Solar Cookers (1 hour)
Carpentry/electrical wiring work party with Christmas in April (all
day)
Straightness and How to Get It microworkshop (15 minutes), followed by
Sawing A Board microworkshop (15 minutes)
(Community Garden Installation continues)
(Food Not Bombs continues)

***1-2 lunch, w/discussion about a June workparty- the Pollinators
***2-4 pm:
Welding 2-6 pm
Community Garden Installation (2-6) workparty
Alternative Fibers and Drop Spindle Spinning
Biotech Forum: How to Avoid and Resist Biotechnology
(followed by : How to Pop Perfect Popcorn Every Time, 15 minute micro)
Reusing Old Bike Inner Tube
Herbal Healing for the Urinary Tract
Bike Repair Basics
What's Wrong With Our Schools? (tentative)
(Carpentry workparty continues)
(Community garden installation workparty continues)

***4:30-6:30 pm:
Border Activism 101: How to Get Involved
Making and Using Stilts
Shiatsu Massage
Renewable Energy Issues and Energy Efficient Construction and Design
More Bike Repair Basics
How to Drill a Hole microworkshop and Sawing a Board microworkshop
(welding continues, workparties continue))

------Sunday, 4/22------

***10 am-noon:
Surviving Radical Demonstrations
Make Your Own Shoes
Making Biodiesel in a Community Scale Processor
Video and Activism
Bike Repair Basics- Community Bicycle Projects

Urban Gardens Bike Tour (4 hours, bring a lunch)

***noon-1 pm:
Q&A about Solar Panels (1 hour)
Straightness and How to Get It (15 minutes)
Bike Repair Basics
Hip Hop- Freestyling (two hours, continues into lunch)
How to Jump Start A Car (30 Minutes)

***1-2 PM lunch, (Hip Hop-Freestyling workshop continues)
***1-2:30 (special timeslot for People's Park program)
Organic Gardening in People's Park garden, followed by:
***3-4:30
Medicinal Weed Walk in People's Park Garden

regular timeslots:
***2-4 pm:
Welding 2-6 pm
Bicultural/Immigrant Identity and Radical Subcultures discussion
Tool Resurrection and Sharpening Clinic

CHAPTER TEN

KEEPING IT GOING

DAVE S.

2002-2004

"THE BEST WAY TO STICK IT TO THE MAN IS TO HAVE GILMAN LIVE WELL AND LONG."

- JOHN H.

Photo by Larry W.

DAVE SCATTERED

I first heard about Gilman from my friend's older brother. He told us about the club and gave us a tape of Green Day. We liked what we heard, and he told us that they were playing a show at Gilman. We went there and saw the show—this was 1989. I grew up in the East Bay and that was the first show I ever went to. I was scared of Gilman at first, it was all new to me, and I didn't know what was going on. I was only 13 then. It was about six months later that I went to another show. It was the only place I knew of for punk shows, or hell, any show in general. I didn't work there at first. I was mostly interested in just hanging out with my friends and destroying everything. In 1994, after going there for a number of years, I came to see it as a place I wanted to see stay open, so I started helping out a little bit. I didn't really want to get that involved, just pitch in on a casual basis. Plus, working there got me into the show for free. That continued until about 1998, when I started getting more heavily involved and working there more, doing front door, side door, security, and cleanup. I started to see the place as something I really wanted to be a part of, rather than just something to do for the night. It took me a long time to realize what the club really was.

Of the people that I met at the club, about half weren't really that into working there, and half were really encouraging to me. Being encouraged certainly helped me to get involved more there, but being encouraged or pushed along doesn't always work for everyone. Now that I'm in that position, I try to take people on a case by case basis, as to whether I encourage them or let them go at their own pace. I try to get the word out as best I can that Gilman is all-volunteer and that everyone is encouraged to help out, but I know that working there isn't for everyone. Plus, the burnout factor is pretty high. It will fluctuate, from having lots of regular workers, to having very few. I started coordinating shows on a casual basis and that continued until I was elected head coordinator in 2002. I wasn't really looking to be head coordinator, but people voted me in. I thought a lot about it, and there really was no one else that was willing to do the job right, so I said okay. At first I was excited, but also nervous, because I didn't really know what the job entailed to the full extent. After about two months though, I really got the hang of it and I started enjoying it. About halfway through the year I got really stressed out and wasn't planning on doing it again the following year (yearly elections are held in Nov.) I ended up finding someone (Alex) to run with me as co-heads of coordinating. We split the responsibilities as equally as we can.

I think the structure of the place is pretty good right now—the biggest problem we have is finding dedicated workers, we need people ready to commit for more than just a month or two. There's good and bad to the spontaneity of just picking up volunteers for the night. It's good in that it exposes new people to working at Gilman, and and gives them life experience. For us, it provides looseness to the atmosphere. It can also be bad in that the experience level is way down, and it can make certain situations really hard to deal with, less people who know what's going on and can step in in a pinch. As far as the bands go, booking is their main point of contact, and that's the one area where we do have a fairly stable and experienced group. That's helped immensely. One thing I've been trying to do is to train more people to be show coordinators, and train more show coordinators to be head coordinators. Maybe by encouraging them more and involving them more, more people will stick around longer.

We still have groups of jerks that come to the shows and cause problems, but it's not nearly as bad, or as often, as it used to be. I do neighborhood cleanup, collecting trash and painting over graffiti. That and security are our only paying jobs, the jobs no one wants to do. It's sad that our neighborhood is still getting trashed. I think most of the kids that come here know not to do that. There's some obvious graffiti that is related to us, but most if it has nothing to do with the club, we just get blamed for it. We clean it up as fast as we can and try to keep a good relationship with our neighbors. Gilman spends about $200 a month to do neighborhood cleanup. The graffiti problem has lessened recently, the ongoing problem is kids drinking in the area and throwing their bottles all over the place and making a mess in people's yards. Overall though, I feel our relations with the neighborhood are pretty good right now, and we work hard at trying to keep it that way. We address complaints as soon as we are notified, and let people know that our membership meetings are the first and third Saturdays of each month, and that everyone is welcome to attend.

For the future I'd like to implement a recycling program. We waste a lot of paper, bottles, cans, etc., and it usually all just gets dumped in the trash. Like almost everyone else, I'd like to see the space used for more than just shows. We have a great opportunity to help out the community around us. In the past we have had yoga classes, a knitting circle, self-defense classes, NA meetings, and even an electronic music workshop.

I see Gilman mainly as a music club, but I'd like to see the community center aspects developed and utilized more. It's a place that's taken for granted by almost everyone, especially since it's been around for so long. Maybe there's something we can do to change that—we'll see. It's going to take some fresh, new utilization of the space to really make an impact on people. It's the potential of the space that really appeals to me, as opposed to the way it's actually being used now.

My favorite parts of being part of the collective have been seeing the enjoyment that people get from going to the club, knowing that I had a hand in making it all possible, and from seeing all the great bands that have played there. I've really liked a lot of those bands, and getting the opportunity to meet them and talk with them. The music still means a lot to me. Gilman has given me a great sense of accomplishment. We have a successful club that is run outside of the mainstream. Score one for the punx!

photo by Annie B.

JANELLE HESSIG

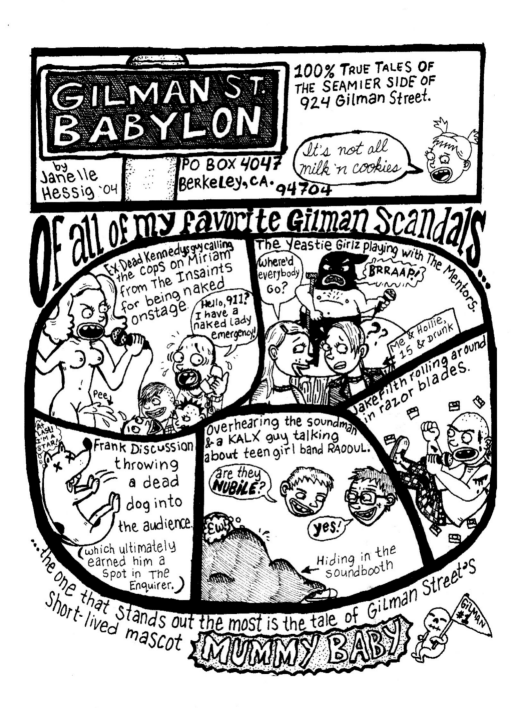

It began with an open crypt at the Piedmont Cemetery.

Holy shit!

A Skull!

whoa!

I'll call him "Lil Jerme"

Mummy Baby!

They took the skulls home & proceeded to clean them in the front room.

WHAT THE FUCK?!?

Hey! I pay rent here too, you know!

A housemate freaked out & called the cops. Jerme Spew was tipped off before they got to his house, so he ran.

Don't worry Mummy Baby

No one will come between us

EVER!

He took Mummy Baby to Gilman & hid him in the sound booth

Wait...

ZIPPO

SOUP

Blatz

You're Not Marshall StAX!

Lint found Jerme's lil bundle of joy in its hiding place. He called the cops & struck a deal: In exchange for Mummy Baby's safe return, Gilman St. would take no heat.

So Gilman dodged yet another bullet.

And although Mummy Baby was indeed returned to the cemetery, his ghost is still occasionally spotted wandering through the pit, searching for his true love.

Oh Jerme!

END

The 924 Gilman Street Project

www.924gilman.org

Navigate:
Index
Calendar
Booking
History
Contact

BOOKING INFO
Send a recorded form of your music (cassette, vinyl, CD) to the Gilman booking address:
ALTERNATIVE MUSIC FOUNDATION
P.O. BOX 1058
BERKELEY, CA.
94701

The 924 Gilman Street Project

We ask that you wait three to four weeks before following up via the Gilman booking line. This gives the bookers an adequate amount of time to review and process your material. The booking and office phone line is (510) 524-8180. Booking nights and hours are on Tuesdays and Wednesdays from 7-9 PM, Pacific Standard Time. As for email, there is no longer a central Gilman booking email address. Most of the bookers have their own email addresses, and it is their choice if they wish to deal with your band in that medium.
Call Tuesdays for Jake, Nick, and Jemuel.
Call Wednesdays for Dan, Naoma, and Chris.

Remember that we only do weekend shows (Friday/Saturday), with the occasional Sunday matinee. Because of this and the fact that many bands want to get booked at Gilman, please don't take it personally if we aren't able to accommodate your band in any reasonable amount of time, or sometimes even at all. If you are persistent, it is in all likelihood that you will eventually get a show. To give everyone a heads up, it has been known to take a very LONG time to get booked, and an individual band's experiences in regard to how long it takes can vary.

When you call in to the booking line and leave a message, we do listen to what you have to say about your interest in getting booked, but we usually don't have the time to respond to each and every request unless we have something to offer immediately. Please remember that we are volunteers—with outside jobs, activities, and loved ones—doing the best that we can. Patience is a virtue and try to keep a positive attitude.

Our booking is often done up to three months in advance, especially during the summer months. Summertime is touring season and out-of-towners get the first crack at open dates and we try to set up shows around who's coming to town, but keep in mind—not every single touring band gets booked. If you are contacting us for a date that is not on our booking board yet, we will politely tell you so and ask you to call back when the time is appropriate. Let's be honest here—there is no reason as to why we should start booking shows for bands that are touring in five months or more. Keep it within the three-month time frame and that will be fine.

BOOKING POLICIES:
We are generally willing to consider most bands, within reason. However, we do not book racist, sexist/mysoginist, homophobic, or major label bands. Our "no major label" rule also applies to bands that are on record labels where 95% of their sales are done through major labels or major-owned distributors within the United States. More mainstream or "college rock" bands will most likely not be booked, but that is also up to the interpretation of the individual booker of what that means. We like to keep our underground scene as far out of the corporate eye as we can. We do not do monetary guarantees, nor have we ever. Certain booking agents like to think otherwise, but the truth lies here. We generally do not do written contracts, although we have in the past. We also reserve the right to alter those contracts where applicable, i.e. crossing out everything that does not apply to the regular Gilman process. We do not do food riders (don't even ask), but you are entitled to one free bottled water per band member.

HOW WE PAY BANDS:
We take 10% off the total of the five-dollar door take and give it to our only paid staff—our security guards. The remaining door money is split 50/50 between the house and the bands. The band money is divided up based on two considerations: the distance traveled to get to the club, as well as the drawing power based on the approximate mass of audience members watching during the band's set. Our staff for the night comes up with suggested divvied-up amounts and then bands are more than welcome to negotiate amongst themselves. It's a fair and honest process and for the most part, it works for the club and the bands.

924 Gilman Street - Constructed and Maintained By Volunteers.

Taken from the Gilman web site, late 2003

Poster from Gilman's fifteen-year anniversary weekend Feb. 01-03, 2002

Maximum RocknRoll's 20th anniversary weekend 29-30, March 2002. The entire inside of Gilman was plastered with enlarged copies of MRR covers. Above photos by Chris B. Below photos by Paul C.

Information on the following five pages is from a few years back but basically still valid.

MEMORANDUM OF UNDERSTANDING

LOAD-IN: 7:00P.M. Ask for the stage manager, although they will probably come to you.

SOUNDCHECK: Sound checks must be scheduled in advance; call 510-⊣   to request a sound check. Sound checks are not guaranteed.

SET TIME: The average set time is 30 minutes. However, nothing is decided in advance. The stage manager of the evening will determine the times based on the circumstances at the show.

PAYMENT
Every show is five dollars unless otherwise noted. However, each patron of the club must pay $2 for a membership card (that's good for one year). The money received from the membership cards goes directly to the club. The $5 entry charge received at the door is separate, about 9%* is taken off the top to pay security guards. The remaining money is split 50/50 between the house and the bands. The coordinators and booker come up with suggestions on what the bands should get paid based on the distance a band has traveled to the show and the amount of people they drew. These are merely suggestions; ultimately it's up to the bands.

GUESTLIST/RIDERS
Bands get one guest per member. Bands from 300 miles away or more get a crew guest. These bands also receive free coffee/water in the stoar, when they ask for it.

DIRECTIONS:

*Security is paid based on how many security guards work the show and how much money there is to deal with. For shows where the door is under $1000, security gets 7-10% of the door based on coordinator discretion (an average of $40). For shows where the door is over $1000, security gets 10% of the first $1000 and 3-10% of the remaining money.

Gilman Street
Suggested Booking folks policy

1) People entrusted with booking privileges should keep standard hours and should be in at those hours. These hours must be posted. Barring vacation, illness or death, every attempt should be made to keep those hours and/or have someone cover. Repeated "no shows", as documented by the head coordinator, other bookers or Gilman Membershi,p will result in the revoking of booking privileges. It is expected that you will be there at least three out of every four times.

2) Only people entrusted with booking privileges should make alterations to the booking board, unless changes are voted/decided upon at a general membership meeting. Aall other booking should be coordinated with a booker, it's really no big deal.

3) Demo tapes will be kept in the security closet. They can be "checked out" by Bookers and/or people approved by the Bookers, through a dated "Sign out" sheet. This way, when a band calls, it will be simple to refer them to who has the tape.They will be retained six months after receipt. Any "graft" promo material (CD's, records, posters, etc.) sent after a show is confirmed is a "perk" and free for the booking folks doing the show to take home. Records, tapes and CD's sent by local bands for general booking fall under the same category as demo tapes.

4) A form will be provided for the booking agent for each show they book. On it, the line-up for the night, phone numbers and contact people, load in, percentage and special needs for pay out at the end of the night, whether anyone is sharing equipment or needs to borrow anything, whether they are on tour/local, etc..These must be filled out in advance and left available for the coordinator and stage manager for that show.

5) Bookers will keep a detailed phone log, whether working from Gilman or home. If working from home, this log should be xeroxed from time to time and brought to the club, or just review them from time to time with other bookers.

COORDINATOR IN-TRAINING
RESPONSIBILITIES:

COORDINATOR:

1. COUNT OUT- START UP MONEY, SECURITY SPLIT, BAND CUT, HOUSE CUT, MEMBERSHIP, PAY SPIEL, PAPERWORK, CLEAN UP, DROPS.

BENEFITS, TOURING BANDS, ABSENTEE BANDS, WHEN NOT TO SPLIT 50/50, EXTRA GUESTS, DAMAGED EQUIPMENT, EXTRA BANDS.

2. WORKERS- PRIORITIZING SIGN UP (TRUST, TIME), CLEAN UP, SIDE DOOR, '86ED WORKERS, JOB DESCRIPTION, 'DISCIPLINE' (SOBRIETY, PERFORMANCE), SCHEDULE, DIPLOMACY.

3. CLUB PERFORMANCE-

SECURITY- SNEAK INS, '86ED, DRINKERS IN AND AROUND, COPS (WHEN TO CALL, HOW TO DEAL WITH)OR AMBULANCE, DIPLOMACY, WHEN TO BAR, VIOLENT DANCING OR STAGEDIVING, NAZIS, HOMOPHOBES, SEXIST MATERIALS OR ACTIONS, GRAFFITTI, BAND SHIT, FIGHTS, CHILDISH SHIT, WHERE AND WHEN PEOPLE CAN GO OR STORE STUFF, WHEN TO CALL PAID SECURITY, WHO CAN STAY HERE

RESPONSIBILITY- THIS CLUB IS YOUR ASS; THINK ABOUT IT. EVERYTHING IS YOUR RESPONSIBILTY. THE SHIT THAT GOES DOWN WILL LAND ON YOUR HEAD FIRST. MAKE SURE THAT OTHER PEOPLE DO THEIR JOBS.

IF SOMEONE FLAKES OR WE DON'T HAVE THE WORKERS, YOU DO IT.

ALSO THINK OF LAWSUITS. THEY CAN SUE US, WE CAN'T SUE THEM.

DON'T FORGET THE BALANCE OF AUTHORITY. WATCH PEOPLE BUT DON'T STOP THEM FROM DOING THEIR JOBS

YOUR RESPONSIBILITIES EXCEDE THAT OF A REGULAR VOLUNTEER. BY TAKING ON MORE RESPONSIBILTY (AND THEREFORE MORE AUTHORITY) YOU ARE EXPECTED TO LIVE UP TO IT. YOU CAN'T DISAPPEAR, YOU CAN'T JUST DECIDE NOT TO SHOW UP (ADVANCE NOTICE), MAKE OUT DOWN THE STREET, GO OUT AND GET DRUNK OR STONED, CAN'T HANG OUT IN THE OFFICE, YOU CAN'T LEAVE EARLY UNLESS YOU HAVE SOMEONE TO COVER.

GENERAL WORK- DROPS, CARDS, OPENING AND CLOSING THE CLUB, WORKERS, SECURITY, PAYOUT, GUESTLISTS (DON'T GET TAKEN OR FORGET THEM. HOW TO DEAL WITH MISSING LISTS), DIPLOMACY W/ SOUND OR STORE

ADDITIONAL WORK-

TRAIN TO STAGEMANAGE AND OPERATE THE STORE (YOU WILL HAVE TO COVER). THESE ARE NOT A STEP DOWN FROM COORDINATING. THIS IS PART OF THE SMOOTH RUNNING OF THE CLUB. ANYTHING ELSE YOU LEARN- THE STORE, SOUND, IS A PLUS.

IT WOULD BE COOL TO HAVE A PERMANENT STAFF OF PEOPLE COMMITTED TO RUNNING THE CLUB WHO CAN DO ANYTHING THAT IS CALLED FOR. THIS IS WHAT WE WILL BE.

GROUNDSKEEPER JOB

The "job" is to have the area around Gilman clean <u>before</u> Monday morning. This is
so that when there is graffiti on people's houses and buildings it is removed
as soon as possible and so that the area looks on Monday (when people
come to work) pretty much as it did on Friday.

In other words, the job is , besides respecting our neighbors, so that people won't say
after the week-end, " Well, it wasn't like this Friday. All this trash and
vandalism is since those kids were here Friday and Saturday nights." So that
people won't say, "All they do is make money and don't give a shit."

The area of responsibility is from Camilia to Harrison and from Ninth to Seventh.
Not all areas require the same level of attention . There could be some
obvious Gilman graffiti or trash beyond these boundaries and the
Groundskeeper should either deal with it if not too complicated or ask for
help.

924 GILMAN

Sweep front sidewalk and side parking area past Caning Shop enclosure --
including gutters and removing crap from struggling plantings along wall.
Bike rack can stay outside, against the wall.

Buff any graffiti and remove any stickers from walls and windows. Don't bother about
fliers on telephone poles.

If <u>empty</u> refuse carts are out at curb (Saturday night co-ordinator and/or clean-up
crew flaked) bring them inside. If they are <u>full</u>, call John H (-).
Maybe the City didn 't empty them Saturday morning or maybe a special pick-
up has been requested for Monday or Tuesday.

EIGHTH STREET (Gilman to Camelia)

Buff any graffiti: on walls, fence slats, posts, side walks.

If there is a piece of litter bigger than a pile of three issues of Spin magazine: pick it
up. Any bottles or piles of broken glass: pick it up.

Pay special attention to E. Paul's building and plantings.

GILMAN STREET -- Seventh to Ninth

Specifically: Allied Radiator, Pyramid, 950 Gilman (Bennett J 's building), The
Working Glass (899 Gilman at 7th)

Pretty much the same level of pick-up. Check with Pyramid before painting over
anything. Graffiti only at 899 Gilman.

CAMELIA -- Eighth to Seventh

Special attention to the north side of the street: Bill R and Jonah in the Flesh Suit
building for graffiti, litter, and damage to things.

OTHER AREAS
Ninth Street; Check for graffiti and obvious Gilman litter (e.g. a bag of empty beer
bottles). Pay special attention to the building just north of Gilman on Ninth—
white walls and down behind hedges.

eventh Street (between Gilman and Camelia): Buff graffiti on east side and pick up
bottles.

PAYMENT

The payment is $40.00 a week for keeping the area free of graffiti and obvious
Gilman trash. It is understood that there could be on one week-end an unusually
large amount of graffiti. Part of the clean-up could carry over to the next week.

No advance payment. No partial payment, such as for doing half of the work.

Determining how much can be carried over, whether the work is complete and done
competently is up to John H or somebody else who takes over this
responsibility. Grievances can always be brought to the membership meetings.

FINANCES

Keep checkbook:
- Neat and unconfusing so that months old entries are easily understandable
- Entries accurate as to description and amounts
- Balanced at least monthly - more frequently allows easier correcting of errors
- Secure

Drop plastic deposit bags in bank 's drop chute weekly -- soon after last show of the week-end. Every few weeks, request a handful of new plastic deposit bags. Get show sheets: make sure count-out sheet is accurate, mail checks to bands who left before split, log payroll and income figures, and (later) assure bank agrees on bag deposit figure.

Payroll taxes: at end of month, phone Paychex (our payroll service) what each security person (not trainees) was paid; they will compute gross pay and taxes. From the statement received a few days later, enter taxes withdrawn from our account into check book. Keep statement for easy access.

Prepare monthly financial statement.

Keep track of our three charge accounts. Make sure the charges are allowed and the billing accurate. Maintain good relations: pay promptly

Post Office Box: Get all non-booking mail weekly from PO box. Deal with the letters, bills, etc. Make sure annual (Jan.31) box fee is paid -- if too late, box will be canceled.

Take care of bank accounts: signature cards, order new checks, track down unexplained entries, such as "pre-authorized debit."

Pay monthly rent and fee for City's refuse cart service to Jim W , building owner.

Reimburse people who front money for supplies, equipment, etc. Reimburse people for vandalism repair. Reimburse people for medical bills. Some of these -- especially those of large amounts - will need group approval. File receipts.

Pay annual insurance premium -- policy expires mid-June. Contact agent two months prior to expiration to make sure there are no surprises and paperwork is filled out on time. This premium ($4378 in 2002) is covered by making adequate monthly set-asides during the prior twelve months.

Gilman goes to the polls!

we're gonna have our annual underlineelections for the 3 "officers of the corporation" at the Saturday Novmber 1 meeting (5PM). Officers must be 21 or older by California State Law. Nominees who accept their nominations have a few minutes to "campaign" at the October 18th meeting if they wish. Voting will be by secret ballot. Officer: just receive at least 2/3 of vote. Nominations are closed at the end of the October 18th meeting. Current officers are:

Executive Officer- Tyler, Secretary- Jesse, Treasurer- Jemuel

Executive Officer
Oversees the day-to-day operations of the club. Sees different jobs to be done.

Secretary
Keeps a record of voting members. Designates someone to take minutes of each membership meeting and is responsible for keeping records of those meetings.

Treasurer
Does accounting, pays bills, files financial statements, and makes these financial statements easily accessible to voting members. Makes financial reports at membership meetings.

COUNTOUT

924 Gilman Street • Berkeley's Own "Festering Sore"

Date: _____ Countout Person(s): _____

• Set aside $50 from door money for cash box.

1. Count rest of door money (don't include Memberships) $ _____
2. Deduct Money for Security $ _____

Name(s)   Pay

_____ $ _____
_____ $ _____

3. Total Money Remaining (for Bands & House) $ _____
4. Total Money for Bands $ _____

Note: This is a legal document, so sign with your real name

Band Name	First Split	Adjustments	Final Payment	Signature
_____	$ _____	$ _____	$ _____	
_____	$ _____	$ _____	$ _____	
_____	$ _____	$ _____	$ _____	
_____	$ _____	$ _____	$ _____	
_____	$ _____	$ _____	$ _____	

>>> HOUSE INCOME <<<

5. Gilman's cut (#3 minus #4) $ _____
6. Membership Money $ _____
7. Money from Bands (xtra guests, etc.) $ _____
8. Total House Income (Add #5,#6, #7) $ _____

*** ADJUSTMENTS ***

Money to Mail to Bands by Check (plus) $ _____

(Please get a 'Pay to the order of' name, address and phone # on the backside)

Other (Explain): _____ (plus or minus) $ _____

TOTAL DEPOSIT (verify that money is same as total) $ _____

• Attach both tally sheets, worklist, guestlist, radio list, and the deposit bag plastic doohicky to this sheet. Punch them and put them in the 3 ring binder.
• Put the deposit slip and all the money in the deposit bag. Put the deposit bag in the safe.
• Put the coordinator keys on top of the bag.

Go home. Get some sleep.

jdd 5/00

WORKLIST

_____ coordinator   _____ assistant coordinator   _____ stage manager

_____ cashbox first half   _____ cashbox second half

_____ handstamp first half   _____ handstamp second half

_____ handcheck first half   _____ handcheck second half

_____ membership (first half only)

_____ store head   _____ store assistant

_____ side door   _____ side door

_____ head security   _____ paid security

_____ volunteer security   _____ volunteer security (big shows only)

_____ volunteer security (big shows only)   _____ volunteer security (big shows only)

_____ cleanup coordinator   _____ cleanup

_____ cleanup   _____ cleanup

_____ cleanup (big shows only)   _____ cleanup (big shows only)

_____ flyers   _____ other (explain)

_____   _____
_____   _____
_____   _____

page total

MEMBERSHIP MEETINGS

Membership meetings are where policy and direction for the club is made/decided. Meetings are held twice a month and open to everyone. A quorum is considered to be nine voting members. Without a quorum the meeting will be cancelled. There are generally about 10-20 members at a meeting.

Some "highlights" taken from past meeting minutes:
(not much in the way of minutes prior to 1993)

07/10/93 — no media cameras allowed inside

11/20/93 — allowing religious rituals to be decided on a case-by-case basis

04/02/94 — booking agents are not to be used unless Gilman can get phone numbers for band members also

05/21/94 — nudity okay at Gilman

05/20/95 — proposal submitted to have tie-dyed security shirts with the words "Be Kind" on them, failed

08/06/95 — the owner of the liquor store up the street was beaten up by a Gilman patron and lots of items were stolen. The patron was banned from Gilman and the store reimbursed

08/19/95 — head coordinator will receive stipend of $200 per month (later rescinded)

09/16/95 — two "official" Gilman photographers chosen, they will take two photos of each band each night

11/04/95 — monthly cleanups started, to be held the last Sun of each month

03/02/96 — all security will be approved by membership

03/16/96 — Chris and Lydia to be married at Gilman in May

04/06/96 — 20 Russian kids (victims of Chernobyl radiation leak), in the US for medical treatment, will be allowed into a show for free with their teacher

04/20/96 — security pay scale approved as follows: for 2 paid security guards, 10% up to $1000 total door; after $1000, show coordinator's discretion; if 1 paid security, about 7% of door; if 3 paid security, between 10-15% under $1000 total door; percentage is, as always, taken out of the total door before the 50/50 split

04/20/96 — no drinking/drugs in Gilman, 7 days/week, 24 hours/day

05/18/96 — band guest list policy reaffirmed, one guest per band, extra guests taken out of band's pay

05/18/96 — proposal submitted for using Gilman as a residence hotel, failed

06/15/96 — proposal to help the Urban Creek Council with defraying the costs of recent vandalism to equipment used to nearby creek, passed

08/03/96 — community service hours can still be worked off at Gilman

09/07/96 — mask-making classes to be held Thursdays at Gilman

12/21/96 — dispute resolution process adopted

02/15/97 — Indian dance classes held Tuesday nights at Gilman

03/15/97 — free HIV testing to be held before an upcoming show, $1 off admission to all who are tested

06/21/97 — affirmed earlier decision that there is no policy against booking bands that are religious

07/05/97 — decision made to compile a concise, precise statement of Gilman's operating procedures and the neighborhood situation, complete with contact names and numbers, sending it to city reps, zoning board staff, and neighbors (business and residential)

01/17/98 — proposal submitted to honor the original "lifetime" mebership cards from 1986, failed

02/21/98 — 924 Gilman Street Homeless Youth Advisory Group formed, will advise the city of Berkeley's Homeless Task Force as per their request

06/06/98 — payroll taxes withheld from paid security

07/18/98 — worker guest list policy: if working that night, one guest per volunteer security, sound, stoar, coordinator; whether working or not that night, one guest per paid security, booker, head coordinator; whether present or not that night, one guest per corporate officer

03/06/99 — Gilman to pay the repair/replacement costs for multiple car windshields broken during a recent show

09/18/99 — $3000 approved to defray costs of medical care for a member of security who didn't have insurance, and was injured during a show

12/18/99 — approved reimbursement for medical costs for a patron injured at a show; approved reimbursement for multiple car tires slashed during a show

06/03/00 — stage manager gets one guest when working

08/19/00 — major label definition is as follows: If a record label has 95% or more of its total US sales through either a major label or a major label distributor, the label's bands cannot play at Gilman. A major label is defined as one of the"big four", and a major label distributor is defined as a distributor having any percentage of ownership by one or more of the "big four"

10/07/00 — no pets allowed inside when bands are playing

11/04/00 — video projector and screen purchase approved

12/16/00 — the first "known" case of a volunteer having to be ejected by security (drunk? belligerent?)

03/03/01 — $40/week groundskeeper position approved

05/19/01 — complaints from another neighboring business (on Tenth Street), meetings with Berkeley Dispute Resolution Service, Berkeley Public Works Dept, and the building owner to discuss/rectify vandalism and renovations

07/07/01 — touring bands get two roadies in for free plus guests, band members get one bottle of water from stoar free on the night they play

10/20/01 — more vandalism costs: four front windows on two cars

11/17/01 — official web site: 924gilman.org

01/19/02 — approved weekday usage: quilting/sewing workshop, salsa dancing lessons, art workshop (zines/artwork), book club

03/02/02 — at a recent show, police in unmarked car were hassling security and videotaping outside of club for approx 45 min. Police area supervisor contacted, was unaware of activity

03/16/02 — descriptions of volunteer jobs posted in lobby

05/18/02 — more approved weekday usage: music workshop, yoga, self-publishing, juggling—circus training; security staff to become a collective, no "head of security"

07/20/02 — sexism/racism workshops to be held before/during regular membership meetings

08/03/02 — neighboring business (not DiCon) threatening to sue the club because of graffiti on their building, Gilman pays $500 to clean building

08/17/02 — Berkelely police very positive about the club, they want club members to meet with the organizers of a new skate park and offer advice

11/02/02 — two very young girls seen hanging out with much older guy and kissing him, club will monitor situation

11/16/02 — older guy mentioned above was arrested by police for outstanding warrants

01/04/03 — cable to be installed for ease of KALX live broadcasts; question: does the club take action on slanderous/accusatory graffiti inside? no proposal submitted; flyer volunteers will get in to one show free for each show flyer they make or help with distribution

02/15/03 — security collective reinstates "head of security" position

03/01/03 — pyrotechnics inside discussed, specific guidelines for what is allowed are established

03/15/03 — fire marshalls came to inspect building based on a written complaint, nothing found

05/03/03 — on-line flyer library being assembled

05/17/03 — angry neighbor came to club, complaining of car break-ins and his kids being kept up by noisy patrons, security will patrol there more often, it was also noted that this neighbor pulled a gun on a club patron; flyers will be posted in the area warning people about an increase in car break-ins

07/05/03 — Gilman Street Music Distro to be restarted, no consignment, all bought up front, hope to open in early 2004

09/06/03 — offered money to Pyramid Brewery to help with repairs to their vandalized bathroom (declined by Pyramid)

09/20/03 — proposal for gym memberships for security memebers fails

10/18/03 — parent of young patron called and left a phone message concerned about the club, she said her child goes to the club a lot and is often drunk, she has seen lots of passed out kids at the club and said that the club should pay more attention to young kids and take care of them, she wants to hear back from the club or she will call the police, two club members spoke with her; discussion ensued on how to better police alcohol consumption

12/06/03 — discussion about giving a band less money if they cause problems during their show, no proposal submitted

12/20/03 — paid bathroom cleanup position established, $25/wk

NOTES TAKEN AT MEMBERSHIP MEETINGS IN JUNE

Minutes From June 1, 1996

* MAC artists propose to paint the walls white for upcoming art show. It passes Y-7, N-5, A-0.

* Proposal to hold benefit for Gilman-like club in Richmond, VA passed. Y-18, N-0, A-1.

* Smiley proposed that he be un-86'ed for the Gravediggers show on June 16 so that he can play with the band at their final show. He must be sober that night and he will continue to be 86ed after that show. Passed Y-17, N-6, A-5.

* It is proposed that the Gravediggers not be allowed to play on June 16. It fails. Y-7, N-14, A-0.

* Proposal that the person who emptied the fire extinguisher inside the club must pay to have it re-filled. Passed unanimously.

* Radley and Charles propose that Gilman buys new sound equipment. It passes.

* clayton is approved as a booker.

* A flyer will be posted asking for input on a proposal for a Gilman volunteer disciplinary committee.

* Accusations are made that Jerme kept a kid's backpack while working the front door and refused to give it back. Charles says Jerme did so with Charles' approval because the backpack was left as collateral. Tabled until next meeting.

Minutes from June 15, 1996

* Carol from the Urban Creek Council announced that her organization is working to restore the nearby creek. Their equipment has been vandalized. She asks for our help in preventing future vandalism. She also wanted to know if any Gilman members would be interested in helping with creek maintenance. Charles suggested we make flyers and said that Gilman patrons were probably responsible for the vandalism. Rory suggested we hold a benefit to help pay for the damage, this will be decided at the next meeting.

* Elbi joe will run a mask making/puppet workshop Wednesdays 11a.m.-7p.m. A storage space for their materials may eventuallily be built. Passed unanimously.

* $400 was just spent on purchaing new microphones, which were long overdue.

* Proposal that the soundbooth be moved to the space the record store is currently occupying. It would tremendously improve the soundperson's perception of the overall live sound. The primary drawback is potential damage to the soundboard because of the vulnerable location. Richard and Radley have offered to do all the work. Radley will provide a new, better soundboard for free. Approved Y-12, N-2, A-1.

* Russ and clayton are currently training to do sound, but more people are still being sought.

* Radley estimates that sound improvements will cost $5,000, but will greatly improve sound quality. These improvements include one new monitor, another speaker, and a vocal speaker power amp. Radley will obtain this equipment at cost. Sita proposes that we wait, because of possible trouble with the brew-pub. Charles proposes that we wait and talk to John Hart about finances. The subject is tabled.

* Charles encouraged people to come help out with the DIY festival. So far he and Jesse have been doing all of the work. 3 p.m.-7 p.m. Fridays.

* A proposal is made that there be an informal party on Sunday July 28th at the end of the DIY fest. No bands will be booked, but bands might be able to jump up and play. Passed unanimously.

* A clean-up day will be held on Sunday June 23rd. 3pm. Free pizza.

* Jerme responded to recent accusations made against him.

Membership meetings are held the first and third Saturdays at 5 p.m. Everyone is welcome. You can vote at your seond meeting. This month's meetings will be on the 6th and 20th.

Gilman will not be hosting any part of Chaos Days this year. Those of you who were around last year might remember, among other incidents, the near-riot that broke out by the side of the club. It was a hundred-person boot party with a small handful of security people trying to keep one guy from getting killed. Guess what, it wasn't fun. As much as we support independent music, we have to consider the safety of our patrons (YOU) and the club's continued existence (i.e. how likely the cops are to shut us down). Choas Days is still happening and we hope it works out for everyone involved. We're just not going to be a part of it.

A sample of complete meeting minutes, taken from a couple of meetings in 1996. This was originally printed in one of the Gilman newsletters.

A SAMPLING OF MEMBERSHIP CARDS FROM OVER THE YEARS

(courtesy of Susan S.)

Over the next four pages is a sampling of Gilman's finances from over the years.

1986 — Expenses
construction — $12,788
equipment   — $6,075
rent/ins.   — $20,365

1987 — Expenses
maintenance   — $803
sound equip   — $3788
operating exp — $38,700

1987 — Income
receipts — $32,303

DATE	DOOR	HOUSE	Comment	BANDS
May				
5/6/88	1840	886		Op Ivy, Neighborhood Watch, No Warning
5/7/88	638	218		Feederz, Dwarves, Vomit Launch
5/13/88	598	199		Dead Silence, Dissent, BHT
5/14/88	333	323	Benefit	Dead Silence, Dissent
5/15/88	795	225		Naked Raygun, Mr. T-X
5/20/88	2174	775		Fugazi, Beatnigs, Crimpshrine
5/21/88	789	263		Christ On Parade, Surrogate Brains
5/27/88	524	174	AltFri	Non, Caroliner, FrankMoore
5/28/88	456	114		Fagan Babies, Division
		3177	4 wkds	
June				
6/3/88	395	130		Screeching Weasel, Bitch Fight
6/4/88	1831	611		Op Ivy, Sc. Weasel, Corrupted Morals
6/10/88	1438	479		Dag Nasty, No Use For A Name, MK Ultra
6/11/88	2158	888		SNFU, Neurosis, 647-F
6/17/88	189	73	Prom Night	SDT, The Idiot, Yeastie Girlz
6/18/88	123	113	Benefit	Max. Albacore Reekage, Social Disease
6/24/88	2180	730	R Against R	Beatnigs, MDC, Op Ivy
6/25/88	909	300		Capitol Punishment, NoFx, Stikky
		3324	4 wkds	
July				
7/1/88	671	268		Neurosis, Melvins, Lethal Gospel
7/2/88	381	127		Conditionz, Breakaway
7/4/88	750	250		Isocracy, Crimpshrine, Lookouts
7/8/88	245	81		Eyeball, Surrogate Brains, Steel Pole Bathtub
7/9/88	511	240	40% door	Special Forces, Malicious Grind
7/15/88	589	236		Eyeball, PHC, Shit Howdy
7/16/88	540	245		Crimpshrine, Offspring, I Am the Hamster
7/17/88	798	345		Corrupted Morals, MDC, For Peace
7/22/88	359	144	AltFri	Dot 3, Looch Bajar,...
7/23/88	218	178	Benefit	Kamala & Karnivores, Swollen Boss Toad
7/29/88	616	247		Neurosis, SDT, A Priori
7/30/88	620	304		Sweet Baby Jesus, A Priori, Koel Family
		2665	5 wkds	
August				
8/5/88	413	165		Surrogate Brains, Brain Dead, For Peace
8/6/88	1502	601		Soulside, Swiz, Mr. T-X, PED
8/7/88	1678	672		Youth of Today, Bold, Underdog
8/12/88	326	126	AltFri	Stick Dog, Skeleton Moses,...
8/13/88	538	215		Last Option, Reason to Believe
8/19/88	1735	595		Op Ivy, Lazy Cowgirls, Dwarves, Creamers
8/20/88	1037	414		Victims Family, Moral Crux. Cringer
8/21/88	145	0		SOC, Fearless Iranians, Ex Pistos
8/26/88	733	366	$6 door price	MDC, Isocracy
8/27/88	430	170	50% door	Capitol Punishment, Wimpy Dicks, Hated
		3324	5 wkds	
September				
9/2/88	1209	605	$129m	Doughboys, Stikky
9/3/88	241	241	$47m	No Use For A Name, Vagrants, Skin Flutes
9/10/88	1490	745		Final Conflict, Neurosis, Apocalypse
9/11/88			last show	Savage Republic, Steel Pole Bathtub
		1591	2 wkds	

SUMMARY 1993		Rent/ Utilities	Insurance/ Taxes	Capital Equip.	Flyers / Advertis.	Phone	Supplies	GAMBA	Misc	Total Monthly Costs
Jan		0	0	40.59 ✓	27.53	80.63	0	0	10.00	$158.75
Feb		2,875	416.79 ⁄	27.05 ✓	66.07	21.47	0	0	35.00	$3,441.38
Mar		2,875	1,720.00 ⁄	147.79 ✓	35.20	100.86	38.28	0	5.00	$4,922.13
Apr		2,875	0	0	50.25	59.30	807.16	0	30.65	$3,822.36
May		2,875	0	0	65.25	143.77	0	500	430.00	$4,014.02
Jun		2,875	0	587.10	56.46	87.80	27.92	250	91.35	$3,975.63
Jul		2,875	0	234.16 ✓	77.27	108.73	0	250	323.70	$3,868.86
Aug		2,875	0	228.29 ✓	103.11	183.47	235.77	269.83	115.05	$4,010.52
Sept		2,875	0	1940.86	20.66	36.87	31.36	250	345.70	$5,500.45
Oct		2,875	0	677.70	86.99	149.05	0	250	203.02	$4,241.76
Nov		2,950	0	1446.52 ⁄	94.09	132.45	17.58	250	124.40	$5,015.04
Dec		2,950	4,309.89	87.91 ⁄	58.02	85.37	14.06	0	669.92	$8,175.17
YEAR TOTALS		31,775.00	6,446.68	5417.97	740.90	1189.77	1172.13	2019.83	2383.79	$51,146.07
		✓	✓	✓	✓	↙	✓	✓		372.00
										51,518 07

924 Gilman St. / 1993 Banking EXPENSES

1993 INCOME SUMMARY

# Paid	# Work	# Guest		Door	Security	Bands	House	KickBack	Mmbrshp	DEPOSIT	Misc. Income	TOTAL
994	103	327	JAN	$5,251	$553	$2,405	$2,285	$25	$1,082	$3,382	$218	$3,600
1404	71	239	FEB	$7,366	$396	$3,531	$3,439	$131	$1,166	$4,756	$0	$4,756
1233	68	274	MAR	$6,464	$366	$3,150	$2,978	$0	$1,094	$4,082	$273	$4,355
1187	68	322	APR	$6,243 —	$482	$2,890	$2,851	$100	$1,175	$4,615	$324	$4,940
1667	80	344	MAY	$9,467	$846	$4,695	$3,926	$0	$1,870	$5,796	$1,075	$6,871
786	34	197	JUN	$3,770	$410	$2,058	$1,302	$0	$588	$1,890	$2,396	$4,286
2125	116	461	JUL	$11,811	$538	$5,742	$5,242	$25	$2,031	$7,597	$6	$7,603
1603	122	323	AUG	$8,351	$522	$3,962	$3,867	$10	$1,580	$5,484	$479	$5,963
1192	78	262	SEP	$6,039	$364	$3,233	$2,442	$150	$1,298	$4,207	($200)	$4,007
1566	111	361	OCT	$7,911	$550	$3,775	$3,576	$10	$1,339	$5,005	$550	$5,555
1497	120	384	NOV	$7,722	$377	$3,720	$2,704	$0	$1,515	$4,344	$700	$5,044
1020	64	194	DEC	$5,044	$261	$2,665	$2,118	$0	$984	$3,200	$144	$3,344
16274	1035	3688		$85,439	$5,665	$41,826	$36,730	$451	$15,722	$54,358	$5,964	$60,323
				100.0%	6.6%	49.0%	43.0%	0.5%				
+mbrshp= total income			$101,161									
				100.0%	5.6%	41.3%	36.3%	0.4%	15.5%	53.7%	5.9%	59.6%

1993 INCOME / 924 Gilman St.

Financial Statement - March 1999

Income
Shows

Deathreat	656	
Nothing Cool	106	
Merrick	560	
Babyland	764	
Powerhouse	737	
Haram Scarum	236	
Slow Gherkin	1040	
Plan 9	720	
Rent	50	4869.00

Spent

Rent	3295.00	
Insurance (set-aside)	200.00	
Taxes (set-aside)	300.00	
Promotion	207.60	
Phones	197.61	
Local 114.12 (30 hours)		
Pay 47.52		
Long Dist. 3597		
Supplies	88.44	
Maintenance	140.35	
Equipment	145.63	
Trash	75.00	
Pizza at Clean-up	40.00	
Bank Fee	.50	
Gilman's Payroll Taxes	42.07	
4 Windsheilds	664.00	5396.20

Loss (527.20)

Year Financial Statement - 1999

Income

Shows	95,162	
Membership	17,818	
Rent (Carving Shop, N.A.)	955	
Stoar	6,242	
Misc. (Tax Refund, Reimb.)	395	120,572

Expenses

Rent	39,740	
Security	5,163	
"Contracted" Security (trainees, etc.)	2,716	
Bands	46,177	
Phones	2,052	
Insurance	3,320	
Promotion	1,016	
Supplies	1,790	
Maintenance	747	
Trash Removal	1,116	
Medical Expenses	6,047	
Groundskeeping	1,210	
Equipment	1,423	
Stoar's Purchase of Sodas, Candy, Plugz	4,554	
Sales Tax	591	
Replacement Windsheilds, Signs	1,094	
Payroll Service	529	
Gilman (Employer) Payroll Taxes	670	
Tax Preparation	365	
Street Light Fund - City of Benk.	1,000	
Costco Membership	85	
Bank Fees	146	
PO Box	44	
State Corp. Fee	10	
Business License	613	
Taxes (Fed & State)	1,432	
Meals & Entertainment (Pizza)	65	123,718

Loss 3146

Adjusting for Fed. Tx Refund of $632   2514

FINANCIAL STATEMENT APRIL 2000

INCOME
   SHOWS

FROM ASHES RISE	72	
FALL SILENT	986	
NEW BAND NIGHT	150	
SECOND COMING	628	
STRATFORD MERCENARIES	68	
PLUS ONES	593	
MISERY	744	
EAST BAY DRIFTERS	471	
BABYLAND	888	
BLITZKRIEG	20	4620.00

SPENT

RENT	3395.00	
TAXES (SET ASIDE)	300.00	
INSURANCE (SET ASIDE	200.00	
EQUIPMENT	592.53	
PROMOTION	13.11	
PHONE	295.04	
SUPPLIES	70.96	
REPAIR	420.11	
TRASH DISAPPEARANCE	90.00	
PAYROLL SERVICE	51.45	
GROUNDS	183.70	
MEDICAL COSTS	79.00	
MEALS (BLITZ PIZZA)	60.00	
GILMAN PAYROLL TAXES	108.71	
SECURITY PAYROLL TAXES	74.10	
SECURITY (PAID OUT OF HOUSE CUT)	20.00	5953.71

	SHORT	800.21

PAID OUT OF SET-ASIDE:
INS *200   IRS REFUND   632.00
STATE 800

2002 Financial Statement

Notes

Gilman has no debts. We didn't stiff anyone. We paid our taxes. Now we are ripe to be merged by an esteemed U.S. corporation and looted: fake profits and concealed debts, stiff anyone with less money/legal muscle/campaign contributions, and incorporate in Bermuda.

Gilman was right around the break-even point. We had the knowledge and the wisdom to keep the charges and the expenses in balance. And the gain was set aside in savings for that inevitable day when The Shit Hits The Fan.

Because we keep Gilman going week after week, month after month we were able to:

- Buy all the equipment/services and pay all the taxes/licenses/fees to run Gilman: $32,104.

- Have a permanent community space: rent: $42,140.

- Pay our security workers plus their (and Gilman's) social security, medicare, unemployment insurance obligations: $16,900.

- Have an opportunity for bands to get $71,363.

- Provide the health conscious young people of America with flavored sugar, caffeine, lipids, and ear plugz : $8,129.

Not bad at all. Let's hear it for ourselves.

CHAPTER ELEVEN

THE GILMAN SHOWLIST

DEC '86 – DEC '03

COMPILED BY STEVE LIST

(WITH HELP FROM BRIAN E. '86-'88 AND PAT W. '88-'90)

"WE HAVE A SUCCESSFUL CLUB THAT'S RUN OUTSIDE OF THE MAIN-STREAM. SCORE ONE FOR THE PUNX!"

–DAVE S.

Photo by Susan S.

1986

----

dec 31 wed Impulse Manslaughter, Christ On Parade, Silkworms, AMQA, Soup

1987

----

jan 2 fri Mock, Helios Creed, Justice League, Victim's Family, Rabid Lassie
jan 3 sat Capitol Punishment, Special Forces, Naked Lady Wrestlers, Forethought, Sewer Trout
jan 9 fri Neurosis, Dehumanizers, Caroliner, Ten Tall Men
jan 10 sat Short Dogs Grow, Feederz, Mr. T Experience, Undesirables
jan 16 fri Dwarves, Positive Outlook, Crash n Burn, National Disgrace
jan 17 sat Brain Rust, Detonators, Love Monsters, Nasal Sex
jan 23 fri Isocracy, Whitefronts, Corrupted Morals, Sweet Baby Jesus
jan 24 sat Youth Of Today, M.D.C., Justice League, Lookouts
jan 30 fri Blast, Jello Biafra, Blue Movie, Decline
jan 31 sat Child Support, Fatal Rage
feb 6 fri Dot 3, Moto Still Birth, Sister Double Happiness, A.S.H. (Blind Acceptance)
feb 7 sat Grim, Scared Straight, Masked Assassins, Cabaret Of Chaos
feb 13 fri Fang, PMRC, Peach Mob, Kwikway
feb 14 sat Conditionz, Social Unrest, Boss Hoss, Fake Stone Age
feb 20 fri A State Of Mind, Sweet Baby Jesus, Witnesses, Boneless Ones
feb 21 sat Half Blind, Stikky, Verbal Abuse, So What, Ram, (Gilman Art Show)
feb 22 sun Gilman Art Show
feb 27 fri Indian Bingo, Brave New World, Kwikway, Paranoia
feb 28 sat Leaving Trains, Wimpy Dicks, Double Standard, Vomit Launch
mar 6 fri Dwarves, Soup, Frontline, Insanity Puppets
mar 7 sat Crazed, 7 Seconds, Berrypickers, Capitol Punishment, Jai Jai Noire & The Original Beasts
mar 13 fri Mr. T Experience, FFI, Alter-Natives, Spore, Green Man Warriors
mar 14 sat Mighty Sphincter, Sun City Girls, SBF, Crimpshrine
mar 15 sun S.N.F.U., Short Dogs Grow, Forethought, Honor Role, Corrosion Of Conformity, Social Unrest
          (Benefit No More Censorship)
mar 20 fri Bomb, Angry Red Planet, THC, Condemned Attitude
mar 21 sat Angry Red Planet, Visual Discrimination, Nimbus
mar 27 fri Donner Party, Crimpshrine, Skinyard, Nasal Sex
mar 28 sat Die Kreuzen, Boy Dirt Car, Lookouts, Isocracy
mar 29 sun M.D.C., Beatnigs, Fuck Bubble (Benefit N.B.A.U.)
apr 3 fri Short Dogs Grow, Rabid Lassie, Electric Spaghetti
apr 4 sat Naked Lady Wrestlers, Bulimia Banquet, Lookouts, Dead Sam Club
apr 10 fri Oblivious, BHT
apr 11 sat Half Off, Broadax, Merchants Of The New Bizarre, Anxiety
apr 17 fri Kwikway, NoFX, Proper Shoes, World Of Pooh
apr 18 sat Free Will, Cringer, ASF, Frightwig, Fuck Bubble, Pillsbury HC, Blueberry Jam
apr 24 fri Neurosis, Liberation Crutch, POW, Christ On Parade
apr 25 sat Corrupted Morals, M.D.C., Pollution Circus, Sins Of The Flesh, Subversion
may 1 fri Lethal Gospel, Times 2, Sid Terror & The Undead, films
may 2 sat Blast, No Means No, Mr. T Experience, Primal Scream, Unit Pride
may 8 fri Bwana Devils, Eskimo, Sick To Death
may 9 sat Social Unrest, Sweet Baby Jesus, Angst, I Am The Hamster
may 10 sun Rubella Ballet, Last Stand, Isocracy, Brain Rust
may 15 fri Schrodingers Cat, Gork, Akousma, The Web, Hyena Cabaret
may 16 sat Frightwig, Bulimia Banquet, Didjits, Nation On Fire, Que Sera Sera, Dwarves
may 17 sun M.D.C., Operation Ivy, Stikky, Gang Green
          (Benefit Diet For A Small Planet)
may 22 fri Free Fall, Now, Acid Rain
may 23 sat Forethought, Didjits, Condemned Attitude, Freesinger Band, No Dogs
may 24 sun Composer's Cafeteria
may 29 fri Ophelias, Typhoon, Child Support, Social Club, horror/sci-fi films
may 30 sat Capitol Punishment, Corrupted Morals, Crimpshrine, Assassins Of God, SMA, Social Unrest
may 31 sun Christ On Parade, A State Of Mind, Caroliner, Condemned Attitude, Totentan (Benefit Animal
          Liberation Front)
jun 5 fri Vomit Launch, Half Blind, Raining House, Skin & Bones, Social Youth Chaos, super 8 film "To Die Like Elvis"
jun 6 sat Neurosis, Stand To Correction, Vomitorium
jun 12 fri Martian Garden Party with Near Eastern Dancing, film and slide show
jun 13 sat Lazy Cowgirls, Raunchettes, Mock, Blind Acceptance, Peach Mob
jun 14 sun Corrupted Morals, Crimpshrine, Isocracy, Nasal Sex, Operation Ivy, Rabid Lassie, Sewer Trout, Stikky,
          Sweet Baby Jesus, Soup
jun 19 fri Smegma, National Disgrace, Caroliner Rainbow, baking exhibit
jun 20 sat Asexuals, Dead Silence, Wimpy Dicks, Sewer Trout, Posthumous
jun 21 sun Das Damen, Naked Lady Wrestlers, Lethal Gospel, Oblivious
jun 26 fri Blueberry Jam, Electric Spaghetti, Undesirables (Anti-High School Night)

jun 27 sat NoFX, Subculture, Bloodlake, Complete Disorder, Slambodians

jun 28 sun Special Forces, Positive Outlook, No Use For A Name, Vagrants

jul 3 fri Eskimo, Thinking Fellers Union Local 282, Tammy Bakker's Dog House, Shadow Puppet Theatre

jul 4 sat Mr. T Experience, Crimpshrine, Isocracy, Sweet Baby Jesus, Operation Ivy (Vegan-Carnivore Basketball after show)

jul 5 sun Happy World, Dissension, Dissent, Anxiety

jul 10 fri Electric Peace, Barnacle Choir, Boo Hiss Pffft, Out Of The Blue, super 8 movies

jul 11 sat painting party

jul 12 sun Desecration, Last Option, Opinion Zero, No Dogs, Twisted (Arizona comes to Berkeley)

jul 16 thr films: "Indifference", "Framed", "Combat Not Conform", "Periphery", "Port Arthur Blues", "The Psychosis of Tony Lamberg" (Benefit No more Censorship)

jul 17 fri Yo, Mudwimmin, Santa Clan, "Summer of Lust", "Minature Golf Sex Therapy"

jul 18 sat Half Life, Short Dogs Grow, Terminal Choice, Shattered Youth, F.B.I.

jul 19 sun Adrenalin OD, Feederz, Kwikway, Mr. T Experience, Public Humiliation

jul 24 fri Flag Of Democracy, Eugene Chadbourne, Beatnigs, No Use For A Name

jul 25 sat M.D.C., Life Sentence, Corrupted Morals, Paranoia, Transgressor

jul 26 sun Detonators, Underdog, Plaid Retina, THC

jul 31 fri Victim's Family, Muskrats, The Edge, Witnesses, Doughboys

aug 1 sat Doughboys, Vampire Lezbos, Crash n Burn, Operation Ivy, IGD

aug 2 sun Youth Of Today, The Edge, Neurosis, Stikky

aug 7 fri Government Issue, No Trend, Sons Of Ishmael, Youth Of Today, Rabid Lassie

aug 8 sat No Means No, JC Hopkins, Diddly Squat, Dead Jacksons, Chapter 13

aug 9 sun Typhoon, Jai Jai Noire, Cancer Garden, Poultry Magic, Hand To Hand Combat, Max, poets (Benefit Womens Liberation Front)

aug 12/13 Versailles was Full of Spiders - one act play by the Theatre Des Vampyres

aug 14 sat Treacherous Jaywalkers, Sordid Humor, Versailles was full of Spiders - one act play by the Theatre Des Vampyres

aug 15 sat Adolescents, Lookouts, Bulimia Banquet, Isocracy, Capitalist Casualties

aug 16 sun No Means No, Hell's Kitchen, 3 Legged Dog, Operation Ivy, Bacchus

aug 20 thr films & slides on Nicaragua and other neat stuff

aug 21 fri Haters, Big City Orchestra, Kings House, Ashwin Batish

aug 22 sat Reagan Youth, IGD, UTI, Division, Team Urinals

aug 23 sun Ribzy, Crimpshrine, Gail And The Fudgepackers, Bo, Wig Torture

aug 28 fri Mudwimmin, Systems Collapse, Typhoon

aug 29 sat Capitol Punishment, Social Unrest, P.K.G., Joint Effort, Trap A Poodle

aug 30 sun D.I., Detonators, Dayglo Abortions, Neurosis, Rotting Humans

sep 3 thr Hippy night movies

sep 4 fri Helios Creed, Blayarden, Half Blind, Social Youth Chaos, performance art (Incoherent Night #2)

sep 5 sat Special Forces, Visual Differences, Frank Moore, Surrogate Brains, Last Communion

sep 6 sun Barrelhouse Jazz Band

sep 11 fri Thinking Fellers Union Local 282, Boo Hiss Pffft, Crimpshrine, Isocracy, Operation Ivy, Yeastie Girlz (Benefit Gilman Street)

sep 12 sat Kwikway, Offspring, Que Sera Sera, SBF

sep 13 sun Christ On Parade, Corrupted Morals, Neighborhood Watch, Positive Outlook, Misery

sep 17 thr Black Panther movies

sep 18 fri Naked Lady Wrestlers, Mudwimmin, Wrestling Worms, Rick Starr

sep 19 sat Frightwig, Mr. T Experience, Sweet Baby Jesus, Cringer, Unit Pride

sep 20 sun M.D.C. Dag Nasty, Stikky, Soulside, No Use For A Name, JC Hopkins

sep 25 fri Celebrity Skin, Grandpa's Become A Fungus, Big Time Poetry Theatre, American English

sep 26 sat Capitol Punishment, Flag Of Democracy, Celebrity Skin, Dwarves, Stikky, Decline

sep 27 sun Flag Of Democracy, Mr. T Experience, Soup, Christ On Parade, Neurosis, Crimpshrine (Benefit Sasha's legal fees)

oct 2 fri Primus, Dot 3, Eskimo, Oblivious

oct 3 sat Insolents, Half Off, No One's Ally, Mice At Play, No Warning

oct 4 sun Ogie Yocha, Lookouts, Rabid Lassie, Up-Skank, speaker Duncan Murphy (Benefit Brian Willson)

oct 9 fri Thinking Fellers Union Local 282, She Devils, Crimpshrine, Social Club, Middle Eastern dancing

oct 10 sat Capitol Punishment, Isocracy, Sweet Baby Jesus, Sewer Trout, Poultry Magic

oct 11 sun M.D.C., McGuires, Operation Ivy, As Is, Bitch Fight (Benefit AIDs)

oct 16 fri Negativland, Thinking Fellers Union Local 282, Now, light show by: Brotherhood of Light

oct 17 sat Neurosis, Stikky, Corrupted Morals, Bitch Fight, Slambodians, Vagrants (Benefit Gilman Street)

oct 18 sun Christ On Parade, Beatnigs, Isocracy, Surrogate Brains (Benefit African National Congress)

oct 23 fri Dwarves, Vomit Launch, The Idiot, Weeny Roast, Pesky Indians (Circus of Pain night)

oct 24 sat Aggression, Attitude, Herbicide, Nosebleed (THC), Transgressor

oct 25 sun Special Forces, Mr. T Experience, Sweet Baby Jesus, Bo, Operation Ivy, Pioneers From Hell (Ramones cover night)

oct 30 fri False Prophets, Feederz, Tunnel Creeps, Wig Torture, Crows

oct 31 sat Scream, Weeny Roast, Kwikway, Dead Jacksons, PMRC

nov 1 sun Operation Ivy, Rabid Lassie, Corrupted Morals, Nasal Sex, Stikky, Sweet Baby Jesus, Yeastie Girlz, No Use For A Name, Isocracy

nov 6 fri Club Foot Orchestra, Eskimo
nov 7 sat RKL, Artless, NoFX, Paranoia, Trap A Poodle
nov 8 sun Jai Jai Noire & The Original Beasts, Operaton Ivy, Bo, Radio Strangers, Damnit Sequators
    (Benefit Nicaraguan Medical Aid)
nov 13 fri Christ On Parade, Corrupted Morals, Surrogate Brains, Last Communion
nov 14 sat Pillsbury Hardcore, Lethal Gospel, Public Humiliation, Bo, Blasting Agents
nov 15 sun Sacrilege, Neurosis, Plaid Retina, Pillage Sunday, Wild Breed
nov 20 fri Acid Rain, Invertabrates, Iaocore, Hey Lady
nov 21 sat Social Unrest, Ribzy, Nasal Sex, Chapter 13, Have Nots
nov 22 sun No Use For A Name, Surrogate Brains, Wacs Bias, Action Figure
nov 27 fri Mr. T Experience, No Dogs, Transgressor, Poultry Magic, Uncalled 4, Mk Ultra (Benefit Gilman Street)
nov 28 sat Adolescents, Frontline, Hell's Kitchen, Positive Outlook, Subterranean Psychosis, Defiant Youth
nov 29 sun Frightwig, Vomit Launch, Yeastie Girlz, Bitch Fight, Phantom Creeps (An Evening of Pagan
    Goddess Worship)
dec 4 fri Operation Ivy, Lookouts, Terminators Of Endearment, Kevin Army Band (Benefit Gilman Street)
dec 5 sat Capitalist Casualties, Surrogate Brains, Que Sera Sera, Rotting Humans
dec 6 sun Corrupted Morals, Sewer Trout, Vagrant, Social Disease, Bar Things
dec 11 fri Henry Kaiser - Mark Crawford Band, O Type, Board Of Mackarel
dec 12 sat Lazy Cowgirls, Sweet Baby Jesus, Lifestyle, Gail & The Fudgepackers
dec 13 sun Neurosis, Tunnel Creeps, Empty Offer, The Wanted
dec 18 fri Whipping Boy, Tragic Mulatto, Sandy Duncan's Eye, Pioneers From Hell
dec 19 sun Another Destructive System, Atomic Gods, Team Urinals, Speed Demon
dec 26 fri Schizoid, Poor White Trash, Mass Confusion, No Dogs, Scapegoat Lemonade
dec 27 sat Social Unrest, Christ On Parade, Destroyer, Assolt
dec 31 thr Isocracy, Stikky, Operation Ivy (One Year Anniversary - Benefit Gilman Street)

1988
----

jan 1 fri Isocracy, Naked Lady Wrestlers (Battle of the Big Mouths)
jan 2 sat Final Conflict, Half Off, Neurosis, Subvert, Complete Disorder
jan 8 fri Fungo Mungo, Electric Spaghetti, Nancy Boys, Spent
jan 9 sat Victims Family, Corrupted Morals, Posthumous, Virulence, Coffee & Donuts
jan 10 sun Slapshot, Stikky, Isocracy, Transgressor
jan 15 fri Thinking Fellers Union Local 282, Fuck Bubble, Boo Hiss Pffft
jan 16 sat RKL, Attitude, Neighborhood Watch, FFI, MK Ultra, Amenity
jan 17 sun Dwarves, Idiot, Bo, Wild Breed, Scabs
jan 22 fri 16 Walls, Vagrants, Mice At Play, Kill The Messenger
jan 23 sat Bad Religion, The Web, Dead Jacksons, Weeny Roast, Vincent Van Go Go
jan 24 sun Social Unrest, Christ On Parade, Fuck Bubble, Damnit Sequators, Genital Chowder (Benefit El Salvador)
jan 29 fri Beatnigs, Bomb, Systems Collapse
jan 30 sat Lookouts, Sewer Trout, Nasal Sex, Trap A Poodle, BHT, Earwax (Benefit Gilman Street)
jan 31 sun Manifest Destiny, Identity Crysis, No Use For A Name, Herbicide
feb 5 fri Ribzy, Isocracy, Defiant Youth, Jackson Saints
feb 6 sat Hickoids, Rabid Lassie, Surrogate Brains, Visual Discrimination, Straight Arm, Second Chance
feb 7 sun Primus, Half Blind, Phantom Creeps, I Am The Hamster
feb 12 fri Moto Stillbirth, Capitalist Casualties, Insanity Puppets, Cast Of Thousands (Santa Rosa night)
feb 13 sat Mr. T Experience, Offspring, Stikky, Plaid Retina, Division
feb 14 sun Corrupted Morals, Sweet Baby Jesus, No Dogs, Misery, Social Disease (Benefit Gilman Street)
feb 19 fri Beatnigs (multi media show)
feb 20 sat Aggression, Infest, Reason To Believe, Side Effect, Pitchfork
feb 21 sun Neurosis, Operation Ivy, Vagrants, Unit Pride, Tally Hoe (Benefit Operation Ivy tour)
feb 26 fri Blue Movie, Oblivious, Baldo Rex, Quahog
feb 27 sat Don't No, 647-F, Bitch Fight, Have Nots, Blasting Agents
feb 28 sun Victim's Family, Stickdog, Raining House, Crimpshrine
mar 4 fri Dot 3, Spot 1019, Eskimo, Mice At Play, Fungo Mungo
mar 5 sat Doughboys, Twitch, Tunnel Creeps, Decline, Scapegoat Lemonade, Shake
mar 6 sun record swap
mar 11 fri Stikky, Social Disease, Crash n Burn, Wig Torture, McRad
mar 12 sat Isocracy, Complete Disorder, Frontline, Think Twice
mar 18 fri Yeastie Girlz, Desperate Minds, Juji Kari, M.D.C., Sweet Baby Jesus
mar 19 sat Tyrannicide, Public Interest, Rotting Humans, Criss Cross, Telemarines
mar 25 fri Hitchhikers, Child Support, Bedlam Rovers, Muskrats
mar 26 sat Pissed Happy Children, Jolt, Crimpshrine, Vagrants, Sins Of The Flesh
mar 27 sun Youth Of Today, Insted, No For An Answer, Rabid Lassie, Unit Pride
apr 1 fri Caroliner Rainbow, Freesinger, Steelpole Bathtub, Half Blind, Archipelago
apr 2 sat Mr. T Experience, Frightwing, Scab, Bitch Fight, Sabot
apr 3 sun Corrupted Morals, Positive Straightedge Anarchy, Kamala And The Karnivores, Crimpshrine, Bitch Fight
apr 8 fri Attitude, Neglected, Stikky, Paranoia
apr 9 sat Dead Jacksons, Nations On Fire, Surrogate Brains, Last Communion, Earwax
apr 15 fri Attitude Adjustment, No Use For A Name, Boo Hiss Pffft, Raskul

apr 16 sat Victims Family, Insanity Puppets, Capitalist Casualties, Cast Of Thousands, Accolades
apr 17 sun Acid Rain, Furlongs, Looker There, 501 Spanish Verbs, Room 101
apr 22 fri Ribzy, Nasal Sex, Posthumous, Romper Room Rejects, Happy World
apr 23 sat Anxiety, Tommy Rot, Assolt, Uncalled Four (Benefit Gilman Street)
apr 29 fri Adolescents, Melvins, Bo, Team Urinals, Raskul
apr 30 sat NoFX, Neurosis, Dwarves, Fixtures, Mis-Led
may 6 fri Operation Ivy, Neighborhood Watch, No Reason, No Warning, Kamala And The Karnivores
may 7 sat Feederz, Dwarves, Vomit Launch, The Idiot, Weeny Roast
may 13 fri Dead Silence, Dissent, BHT, Necromancy, FFI
may 14 sat Dead Silence, Dissent, Swollen Boss Toad, Abnormal Growth, Skitzo (Benefit Gilman Street)
may 15 sun Naked Raygun, Mr. T Experience, Steelpole Bathtub, The Scab
may 20 fri Beatnigs, Fugazi, Crimpshrine, Yeastie Girlz
may 21 sat Christ On Parade, Surrogate Brains, Public Humiliation, The Unannounced, Tripwire
may 27 fri Non, Caroliner, Frank Moore, Bringdowns
may 28 sat Pagan Babies, Plaid Retina, Division, Tally Hoe, Tommy Rot
jun 3 fri Screeching Weasel, Bitch Fight, Blasting Agents, Assolt, For Peace
jun 4 sat Corrupted Morals, Breakaway, Operation Ivy, Screeching Weasel, Unit Pride
jun 10 fri Dag Nasty, No Use For A Name, MK Ultra, Peace Test, Vagrants
jun 11 sat SNFU, Neurosis, 647-F, Second Thought, Breakdown
jun 17 fri SDT, The Idiot, Yeastie Girlz, Egor Mazeroski (Prom Night)
jun 18 sat Preachers That Lie, Maximum Albacore Reekage, Social Disease, Nothing's Sacred (Benefit Gilman Street)
jun 24 fri Beatnigs, M.D.C., Operation Ivy, Dead Jacksons, Bo, Paranoia (Benefit Rock Against Racism)
jun 25 sat Capitol Punishment, NoFX, Stikky, Plaid Retina, Raskul
jun 26 sun record swap
jul 1 fri Neurosis, Melvins, Lethal Gospel, Vomitorium, Earwax
jul 2 sat Breakaway, Straightarm, Conditionz, No Reason
jul 4 mon Isocracy, Crimpshrine, Raskul, Lookouts
jul 8 fri Surrogate Brains, Steelpole Bathtub, Nasal Sex, Eyeball
jul 9 sat Special Forces, Malicious Grind, Labelled Victims, Rotting Humans, Tyrannicide
jul 15 fri Eyeball, Pissed Happy Children, DSFA, Dead Sam Club, Shit Howdy
jul 16 sat Crimpshrine, Offspring, Neglected, I Am The Hamster, Zona Roja
jul 17 sun Corrupted Morals, For Peace, Blasting Agents, Tommy Rot, MDL
jul 22 fri Dot 3, Mice, Fungo Mungo, Kooch Bajar
jul 23 sat Kamala And The Karnivores, Swollen Boss Toad, Spent, P.I.N.S. (Benefit Gilman Street)
jul 29 fri Neurosis, SDT, A Priori, Discontent, Nuisance
jul 30 sat Sweet Baby Jesus, Naked Lady Wrestlers, A Priori, Koel Family, BHT
aug 5 fri Surrogate Brains, For Peace, Paranoia, Brain Dead
aug 6 sat Soulside, Swiz, Mr. T Experience, P.E.E., Spent, Nobodie
aug 7 sun Youth Of Today, Underdog, Bold, No For An Answer, Mind Over 4
aug 12 fri Stickdog, Skeleton Moses, Cast Of Thousands, Telemarines, Dismal Void
aug 13 sat Last Option, Reason To Believe, Freewill, Walk Proud, Think Twice
aug 19 fri Lazy Cowgirls, Creamers, Operation Ivy, Dwarves, Bhang Revival
aug 20 sat Victim's Family, Cringer, Moral Crux, Bazooka Joe, Flower Leopards
aug 21 sun Fearless Iranians From Hell, Sinister Sisters Of Satan, S.O.C., Diddly Squat, Ex Pistos, Scrutinize My Brain,
          Bazooka Joe
aug 26 fri Isocracy, M.D.C., Animal Clinic, Los Muertos, S.O.B.
aug 27 sat Capitol Punishment, The Hated, Eyeball, Wimpy Dicks, Complete Disorder
sep 2 fri Flag Of Democracy, Doughboys, Stikky, Quahog, Uncalled 4
sep 3 sat Vagrants, No Use For A Name, Skin Flutes, Crackpot (Benefit Gilman Street)
sep 9 fri no show
sep 10 sat Final Comflict, Neurosis, Apocalypse, Raskul, Internal Conflict
sep 11 sun Savage Republic, Steelpole Bathtub, Autumn Fair (last official show for MRR Crew at Gilman)
sep 12 - nov 3 no shows
nov 4 fri Isocracy, Lookouts, Sewer Trout, Santa Clan, Coffee & Donuts
nov 5 sat Mr. T Experience, Stevie Stiletto, Corrupted Morals, Vagrants
nov 7 mon Sink Manhattan, Pig Farm
nov 11 fri Libido Boyz, Systems Collapse, Tally Hoe, Swollen Boss Toad
nov 12 sat Neurosis, Stikky, Vagrants, Plaid Retina, Skin Flutes
nov 18 fri Crimpshrine, Sweet Baby Jesus, Spent, Think Twice
nov 19 sat Vomit Launch, Ribzy, Naked Lady Wrestlers, Surrogate Brains, Nation On Fire
nov 25 fri Lethal Gospel, Attitude Adjustment, Crash n Burn, Mr. Lucky
nov 26 sat Twitch, Raskul, Sweet Children, Altered Ego
dec 2 fri Sacrilege, Blasting Agents, Sins Of The Flesh, Asbestos Death
dec 3 sat Christ On Parade, Mind Over 4, S.D.T., East Bay Mud
dec 4 sun All, Operaton Ivy, Vagrants, Tally Hoe
dec 9 fri Mx Machine, Skitzo, Eminence, Insecticide, Santa Clan
dec 16 fri Hickoids, Jesus Chysler, Conditionz, Big Drill Car
dec 17 sat Bad Religion, No Use For A Name, Inner Strength, Spent
dec 18 sun play "A Punk Xmas Carol" by the Anti-Thespian Players, Skin Flutes, Blatz
dec 23 fri Operation Ivy, Sharkbait, Unit Pride, Breakaway

dec 30 fri Hell's Kitchen, Sosa, Stevie Stiletto, Neglected, Nasal Sex

1989
----

jan 1 sun Sweet Children, Scrut, My Brain, Tally Ho, Vagrants
jan 6 fri Moto Stillbirth, Insanity, Capitalist Casualties
jan 7 sat Eyeball, Nimbus, Lookouts
jan 12 thr Beatnigs, Hobo, Posse, JBAKC
jan 13 fri R.K.L., Premonition, Big Jed, East Bay Mud
jan 14 sat Fungo Mungo, Dot 3, Conceptions, Bug
jan 20 fri Crimpshrine, Inner Anger, Sharkbait, Cheez Boys, 2nd Thought
jan 27 fri Extinction, Lethal Gospel, Pestilence
jan 28 sat Christ On Parade, Atomic Gods, Complete Disorder, Jimi Jackpot
jan 29 sun Fang, Skinyard, Coffin Break, Kester Pi
feb 4 sat Lifeline, Melvins, No Use For A Name, Samiam, Preachers That Lie
feb 5 sun Surrogate Brains, Mental Pygmies, Pollution Circus, Subject To Change, Blatz, East Bay Mud, Boo Hss Pfft
feb 10 fri Fixtures, Pissed Happy Children, Infest
feb 11 sat Mr. T Experience, Crimpshrine, Sweet Children
feb 12 sun MRR record swap
feb 17 fri Victim's Family, No Use For A Name, Cringer, The Wrong
feb 18 sat No Means No, Scrawl, Vomit Launch, Raw Season
feb 19 sun Lookout band showcase
feb 24 fri Sweet Baby Jesus, Samiam, Short Dogs Grow, Sweet Children, Judy Blooms
feb 25 sat Uniform Choice, Insted, Freewill, Inner Strength, Dwarves
mar 3 fri Soulside, Neighborhood Watch, Samiam, Night Soil Man, Vagrants
mar 4 sat NoFX, Grim, Big Drill Car, Skin Flutes
mar 11 sat Primus, Acid Rain, 501 Spanish Verbs, Crash n Burn
mar 12 sun Christ On Parade, Operation Ivy, Hell's Kitchen, Special Forces, Legion Of Doom (Benefit Contra Costa
         Alternative High School)
mar 18 sat Fidelity Jones, Fire Party, The Offspring, Kamala & The Karnivores
mar 19 sun Flower Leopards, Chemical People, Econochrist, Raskul
mar 24 fri No For An Answer, Hand Stand, Amenity, Chain Of Brotherhood, Naked Lady Wrestlers
mar 25 sat Sabot, Pollution Circus, Christ On Parade, Peter Plate, The High Risk Group (dance), Richard Loranger,
         Hank Hyena (rude films) (Anarchist Conference & Festival)
mar 31 fri Mr. T Experience, No Alternative, Toads, Resurrection, The Original
apr 1 sat Sweet Children, Samiam, Stikky (Benefit Gilman sound)
apr 7 fri Let's Go Bowling, Liquidators, Dance Hall Crashers
apr 8 sat Beatnigs, M.D.C., Eskimo, Weeny Roast
apr 14 fri Victim's Family, Sharkbait, Jawbreaker, East Bay Mud
apr 15 sat Gwar, Operation Ivy, Yeastie Girlz, Popstitutes, Econochrist
apr 21 fri Muskrats, Bedlam Rovers, Ed, Phoenix
apr 22 sat Bad Religion, NoFX, Lethal Gospel, Mr. Lucky, Necromancy
apr 23 sun Samiam, Corrupted Morals, Nothing Sacred, Defective Year, Econochrist, Skin Flutes, Big Big Big
apr 29 sat Neurosis, Hoss Braten, Ex Pistos, Sinister Sisters Of Satan
apr 30 sun House Of Large Sizes, Stickdog, S.D.T., Thinking Fellows Union Local 282, Blow
may 5 fri S.N.F.U. Desperate Minds, Chemical People, Complete Disorder, Gross Negligence & Evil Swineage
may 6 sat Scream, Uniform Choice, Unit Pride, Nation On Fire, Implement (Benefit Rock Against Racism)
may 12 fri Donkey Show, Skeletons, Needs
may 14 sun Slapshot, Stains, Breakaway, Headfirst
may 19 fri Flipper with Mari St. Mary, The Bar-Donkeys, Weasel Contingent, Fuzz Factor
may 20 sat Fugazi, Pitchfork, Crash Worship, Vagrants, Skin Flutes
may 26 fri Tyrranicide, Breakaway, Anxiety, Yellow Snow
may 27 sat 7 Seconds, Bulimia Banqet, Neurosis, Lookouts
may 28 sun Operation Ivy (last show), Lookouts, Green Day, Surrogate Brains, Crimpshrine
jun 2 fri Buffalo Roam, Natives, Midnight Radio, Counting The Sky (Berkeley Free Clinic anniversary)
jun 4 sun Bim Ska La Bim, Let's Go Bowling, Crucial DBC
jun 9 fri Mr. T Experience, Screeching Weasel, Samiam, Square Meal
jun 10 sat Fuck-Ups, No Alternative, Dwarves, Parasites, Gaping Wounds, Dick & Jane
jun 11 sun Snailtrax, Whipping Boy, Pacludacts, Fungus, Rudder (Benefit Palo Alto skatepark)
jun 16 fri Caroliner, The Idiot
jun 17 sat Christ On Parade, Steelpole Bathtub, Jawbreaker, Econochrist, DJ Lebowitz
jun 23 fri N.Y. Citizens, Liquidators, Skankin Pickle
jun 24 sat N.Y. Citizens, Bad Mutha Goose, Fungo Mungo, C.B.M.T.
jun 25 sun All, Sweet Baby Jesus, Wrong, Green Day, Clown
jun 30 fri Angry Samoans, NoFX, Insanity, Elvis B, Vince Neil
jul 2-6 Movement - Artist - Collective "Funk in da' Trunk"
jul 4 tue Isocracy, No Alternative, Boo Hiss Pfft, Monsula, Nuclear Roach
jul 8 sat Poison Idea, Life Sentence, Herbicide, Schizoid
jul 9 sun Wrecking Crew, Corrupted Morals, Some Velvet Sidewalk, Nasal Sex, Inner Struggle
jul 15 sat Hell's Kitchen, Hunger Art, Ugly But, Hotbox 9, Sinister Sisters Of Satan

jul 21 fri Agression, Grim, F.F.I., Preachers That Lie
jul 22 sat Dead Silence, Political Asylum, M.D.C., Yeastie Girls (Anarchist Convention)
jul 28 fri Subvert, Christ On A Crutch, Offspring, Econochrist, Skin Flutes
jul 29 sat Gorilla Biscuits, Swiz, Shitothink, American Standard, Inside Out
jul 30 sun MRR record swap
aug 2 wed Bad Manners, Skankin Pickle
aug 4 fri Toxic Reasons, Libido Boyz, Moral Crux, Neurosis, Serial Killers, Jolt
aug 5 sat Bold, Judge, Super Touch, Upfront
aug 10 thr Uptones, Skeletones, Upbeat
aug 11 fri Uptones, Donkey Show, Skanking Pickle
aug 12 sat Verbal Assault, Underdog, Jawbreaker, Plaid Retina, Amenity
aug 18 fri Sharkbait, Shades Apart, No Empathy, Orifice
aug 19 sat Scout's Honor, Faith Healers, Monsula
aug 25 fri Primus, Dot 3, Harm Farm, Squeeble Squabble
aug 26 sat UK Subs, Lost Generation, No Alternative, Special Forces, Distant Silence
aug 27 sun Midas & The Bridge, Let's Go Bowling, Dance Hall Crashers
sep 1 fri Verbal Abuse, Attitude, Malicious Grind, No Use For A Name, Twelve
sep 2 sat Mannequin Beach, Sick Of It All, Naked Lady Wrestlers, It's Not What You Think, Square Meal
sep 8 fri Secret Society, Liquidators, Dance Hall Crashers, D.J. Ska Dance
sep 9 sat Dwarves, Green Day, Halo Of Flies, Cast Of Thousands, Dick & Jane
sep 15 fri Samiam, Scab Cadillac, Wig Torture, Wild Stares, Stikky
sep 16 sat Blind Illusion, Slambodians, Preachers That Lie
sep 17 sun All Mighty Senator, Amadaffair, Fluid, Squelch
sep 22 fri Corporate Humor, Untamed Youth (Mod Nite)
sep 23 sat Capitol Punishment, Neurosis, Melvins, 647-F, Bhang Revival
sep 29 fri Sweet Baby Jesus, Vagrants, Monsula, Thumper, Crummy Musicians
sep 30 sat Blast, Virulence, No Use For A Name, World Citizen
oct 6 fri Homeless Kids, Kwikway, Econochrist
oct 7 sat N.Y. Citizens, Skeletones, Smoke Stack
oct 13 fri Victim's Family, Mecca Normal
oct 14 sat Detonators, Mr. T Experience
oct 21 sat Bad Religion, NoFX, Grim
oct 27 fri Toasters, Donkey Show (Haloween Bash)
oct 28 sat Sloppy Seconds, G-Whiz
oct 29 sun Christ On Parade (last show)
nov 3 fri Tragic Mulatto
nov 4 sat Insight, Inner Strength (J. Pitts)
nov 10 fri Penelope Houston, Women's Day
nov 11 sat Bad Mutha Goose, Fungo Mungo, Bimskalabim, Crucial DBC
nov 17 fri Hard Ons, Coffin Break
nov 18 sat Dissent, Christ On A Crutch
nov 24 fri Public Humiliation, Skankin Pickle (Wajlemac)
nov 25 sat Angry Samoans, Gargoyles
dec 1 fri Doughboys, Samiam, Econochrist, Fuel
dec 2 sat U.A.F., Blatz, Wrong, Dread, Collateral Damage
dec 8 fri Victim's Family, Corrupted Morals, Monsula, Green Day, Crummy Musicians
dec 9 sat Lifeline, Monsula, Filth, Friendly Dead Kids (Benefit Gilman Street)
dec 15 fri Rabbit Choir, Acid Rain
dec 16 sat Industrial Rainforest
dec 17 sun MRR record swap
dec 23 sat No Use For A Name, Downfall, Grim, M.D.
dec 24 sun Poison Idea, Tyrranicide
dec 29 fri spoken word
dec 30 sat Special Forces, Sinister Sisters Of Satan
dec 31 sun Primus, Mr. Bungle, Fungo Mungo, East Bay Mud

1990
----

jan 5 fri Mr. T. Experience, Offspring, Plaid Retina, Lookouts, Crummy Musicians, Coffee & Doughnuts (Very Small
        Records)
jan 6 sat Blast, Slam And The Mother Fuckers, Sinister Sisters Of Satan, Eulogy
jan 12 fri Victim's Family, Sharkbait, Thinking Fellers Union Local 282, Himalayans, Oceanfire
jan 13 sat Penelope Houston, Flophouse, Bedlam Rovers, Sonya Hunter Trio (Rap Against Racism)
jan 19 fri APG Crew, Beatnigs, Monet Preemo, Lady D, Possee (Rap Against Racism)
jan 20 sat NoFX, Neurosis, 647-F, Morbid Life Society
jan 21 sun Monsula, Vagrants, Anger Means, Filth, Blatz, Krupted Peasant Farmers
jan 26 fri Econochrist, Green Day, Downfall, Dance Hall Crashers
jan 27 sat Beatnigs, Gargoyles, Fixtures, Public Humiliation (Anti Drug War)
jan 28 sun D.I., Bulimia Banquet
feb 2 fri Scared Straight, Samiam

feb 3 sat Blaspheme, Kondomnation, Delinquent Johns, Anger Means (Benefit Slingshot)
feb 4 sun No Means No, Vomit Launch, Gargoyles, Fuel, Blatz
feb 9 fri Sacrilege, Hell's Kitchen, Subversion, Nuclear Roach
feb 10 sat Steel Pole Bathtub, 501 Spanish Verbs, God Bullies, Platypus Scourge
feb 16 fri Insted, Inner Strength, Implement, Rick Starr, Against The Wall
jan 17 sat Smoking Rhythm Prawns, Blast, Squeeble Squabble
feb 23 fri All, Left Insane, Nasal Sex, Krackpot
feb 24 sat Econochrist, Capitol Punishment, No Use For A Name, Slam And The Mother Fuckers
mar 2 fri Mentors, Yeastie Girlz, Slambodians, Misled
mar 4 sun Vandals, Samiam, D.J. Lebowitz, Preachers That Lie, Nightfall
mar 9 fri Penelope Houston, The Movie Stars, Wanna Be Texans, Chinese Water, Rats
mar 10 sat Death Of Samantha, Corrupted Morals, Dwarves, Cringer, Killer Crack
mar 16 fri Neurosis, Mr. T Experience, Samiam, Green Day (Lookout Records)
mar 17 sat Thumper, Kondom Nation, Reaction, Friendly Dead Kids, Drippy Drawers (Benefit Amnesty International)
mar 23 fri Victim's Family, Downfall, Vapor Lock, Scout's Honor
mar 24 sat G-Whiz, Fuel, Monsula, Vagrants, Inside Out, Dread
mar 30 fri Sharkbait, Melvins, A Different Kitchen, Fungus
mar 31 sat Acid Rain, Bluchunks, Harm Farm, Wonderful Broken Thing
apr 1 sun Judge, Boom And The Leigon Of Doom, Against The Wall, Gargoyles
apr 6 fri Cat's Pajamas, No Use For A Name, Fifteen, East Bay Mud, Lung Butter (Rock Against Boredom II)
apr 7 sat Killatar, Slam And The Mother Fuckers, Pirranha, Warlock Pinchers, D.M.Z. (Speed Metal)
apr 8 sun Samiam, Filth, Blatz, Green Day, Capitalist Casualties (Benefit George Hated)
apr 13 sat NoFX, Blister, Naked Lady Wrestlers, Butt Ugly Hillbillies
apr 14 sat M.D.C., APG Crew, Econochrist, Sins Of The Flesh, Stuck Against Stone (Bay Area Anti Racist Allience)
apr 20 sat Bad Religon, Creamers, Mr. T Experience, Lookouts
apr 21 sat Sinister Sisters Of Satan, Boom And The Legion Of Doom, Special Forces, Misled, Abuse (Benefit Big
          Mountain)
apr 27 fri Accused, Lifeline, Stevie Stiletto, Scherzo
apr 28 sat Neurosis, Econochrist, Filth, Blister (Benefit Neurosis)
may 4 fri Haywire, Fuel, Carry Nation, Headfirst, Yuckmouth (Orange County Nite)
may 5 sat L7, Green Day, Starvation Army, Public Humiliation, Voodoo Glow Skulls
may 11 fri Sharkbait, Plaid Retina, Third Rail, 23 More Minutes, Galaxy Chamber
may 12 sat Detonators, No Alternative, Sinister Sisters Of Satan, Filth, Anger Means
may 18 fri Fuck Ups, Dwarves, Corrupted Morals, Blister, Capitalist Casualties, Missing Children
may 19 sat Screamin Sirens, Frightwig, Fixtures, Love Dog, Cantankerous
may 20 sun Fugazi, Offspring, Monsula, Beat Happening, Pez
may 25 fri Green Day, Brent's T.V. And Appliance, Filth, Blatz, Juke (Benefit Cometbus Fanzine)
may 26 sat M.D.C., Ultraman, Big Thing, Cracks in The Sidewalk, The Hated
jun 1 fri Dot 3, Skankin Pickle, Scout's Honor, Less Is More, Drippy Drawers
jun 2 sat Mr. T Experiance, Econochrist, Resist, Elegy
jun 8 fri Grim, Dread, Stain, F.F.I., Five Finger Discount
jun 9 sat Bulimia Banquet, Subvert, Apocalypse, Asbestos Death
jun 15 fri Gargoyles, Eeek?, Dangerhaus, Harsh, Fuck Boyz
jun 16 sat Capitol Punishment, Sam I Am, Alcoholics Unanimous, Basic Black, Pervs
jun 22 fri Econochrist, Mr. Bones, Admiral, Yermom (last show), Team Sheep
jun 23 sat Victim's Family, Sub Society, Wig Torture, Milestone
jun 29 fri Flipper, Anger Means, Hate X9, Anti-Schism, Nuisance
jun 30 sat Helios Creed, Happy World, 501 Spanish Verbs, Skitzoid, The Hated
jul 6 fri Blast, Aisle Nine, Lifeline, Third Rail, Scherzo
jul 7 sat Penelope Houston, Ed Haines, Sundials, Kevin Army's Rummage Sale
jul 13 fri Green Jello (L.A.), White Trash Debutantes, Comrades in Arms, Rick Starr, Killer Crack
jul 14 sat Smokin' Rhythm Prawns, Sprawl, Paul's God, Cringer, Disauradhus, The Hated
jul 20 fri Warlock Pinchers (Denver), Blatz, Filth, Demise (Wisconsin), Ben Weasals new movie "DisgusTeen"
jul 21 sat Big Drill Car, Left Insane, G-Whiz, Big Mistake (CT), Platypus Scourge
jul 27 fri Blast, Offspring, Meat Wagon (San Diego), Slambodians
jul 28 sat Angry Samoans, Yard Trauma, Mummies, Ag's-AK-47
aug 3 fri Doc Dart, Moral Crux, 929, Nation of Ulysses (D.C.)
aug 4 sat M.D.C., Go! (NYC), 23 More Minutes, Bad Trip, Seeds Of Peace, Bob Zee, Power Plagues
aug 10 fri Hoi Polloi, Barbara Manning, Wanna Be Texans, Thornucopia
aug 11 sat Jawbreaker, Samiam, Fuel, Juke, Monsula
aug 17 fri NOFX, No Use For A Name, 647-F, Drowning Roses (Germany)
aug 18 sat Scream (D.C.), Sandy Duncan's Eye, Rude Awakening (NY), Mutly Chix (FL), Jack Acid
aug 24 fri Happy World, Steel Toes, Verbal Abuse
aug 25 sat Fungo Mungo, Voltage, Slambodians, Scout's Honor, Systems Collapse
aug 31 fri Victim's Family, Green Day, Pieces of Lisa, Woodenhorse (FL)
sep 1 sat Econochrist, Grimm Tales, Pollution Circus (Sacramento), The Hated, (benefit for Bay Area Anti Racist
          Alliance and Love and Rage Anarchist newspaper)
sep 2 sun Shelter, Up To Here, Far Sight, Chain Of Strength, Fifteen
sep 7 fri Corrupted Morals, Change of Heart (Toronto), The Dread, Capitalist Casualities, Thumper
sep 8 sat Dwarves, Gargoyles, Christ On A Crutch, Derelicts (WA), Wynona Riders

sep 14 fri Radicts (NY), Threadmill (MN), Chemkill (OR)
sep 15 sat Chumbawumba (UK), Neurosis, Offspring, Radicts, Treehouse (WA), Jello Biafra (sp)
sep 21 fri Skankin' Pickle, Fixtures (L.A.), Voo Doo Glow Skulls, Nuisance
sep 22 sat Green Day, Paul's God, Asbestos Death, Preachers That Lie, Morbid Life Society
sep 28 fri Accused, Boom And The Legion Of Doom, No Alternative, Lifeline, Mufan
sep 29 sat Toxic Reasons, Special Forces, Filth, Collateral Damage, Fitz Of Depression (Olympia), F.F.I.
oct 5 fri Victim's Family, Fuel, Ill Repute (Oxnard), Sow Bellies (OR), Glee (Vancouver)
oct 6 sat E.M.G. (Houston), Insanity Puppets, Monsula, Scherzo, The Unjust (924 Gilman Street Benefit)
oct 12 fri Neurosis, Agnostic Front, Assasins Of God, Dangerhaus, White Trash Debutantes, Wynona Riders
oct 13 sat Capitol Punishment, Econochrist, Mummies, Blatz
oct 19 fri Scratch (ex-Fear members), Third Rail, Happy World, Asbestos Death, Blister
oct 20 sat Public Humiliation (Riverside), Big Satan Ltd. (Washington), Urge, Bonk, Vomit Launch
oct 26 fri Flipper, Green Day, Swinging Teens (Minneapolis), Monsula, Fifteen
nov 3 sat K.P.F., Platypus Scourge, Corrupted Morals, Blatz, Filth, Scherzo, Crummy Musicians, Dread, Asbestos
         Death, Fifteen, The Hated, Emcee D.J. Lebowitz (924 Gilman Anniversary show)
nov 9 fri Econochrist, Holly Rollers (DC), Laughing Hyena (MI), F.F.I., The Dread
nov 10 sat Liquidators, Hepcats (L.A.), Skankin Zippo (Filth), All State Steppers
nov 16 fri Derelicts (WA), Cringer, Hossbruten, Hyper Kowtow (San Diego)
nov 17 sat Acid Rain, Wedge Of Chastity, Invertabrates, Iaocore, (art show)
nov 23 fri All You Can Eat, Tyrranicide, Oops My Pants Fell Down (Wajlemac Zine Silly Fest II)
nov 24 sat Wholes (Las Vegas), Thrill Hammer (OR), Slut Zombies, Steel Toes
nov 30 fri Judy Blooms, Grenvilles, Model Americans, Five Year Plan
dec 1 sat Nausea (NYC), Neurosis, Econochrist, Glycine Max (L.A.), Filth, Asbestos Death
dec 7 fri Shattered Faith, TvTv$ (L.A.), Large Hardware (L.A.), Thinking Fellers Union Local 282, Shit Howdy
dec 8 sat Special Forces, Preachers That Lie, Unjust, Three Legged Dog, Total Fucked
dec 14 fri Smokin Rhythm Prawns, Trash Can School (L.A.), Gargoyles, Scout's Honor, Fuck Boyz
dec 15 sat Mr. T Experience, Samiam, Creamers (L.A.), No Use For A Name
dec 21 fri Dwarves, Plaid Retina, Sawhorse, Juke, Schlong
dec 22 sat Engage (Santa Rosa), Aisle Nine (Bay Area Anti-Racist Action Benefit)
dec 28 fri All Sorts (Aust.), Sprawl (TX), 100 Men (England), Liquidators, Rudiments
dec 29 sat M.D.C., Final Conflict, Undertow (Seattle), Anger Means, Elegy
dec 31 mon Angry Samoans, Green Day, Mummies, The A.G.'s, Blatz

1991
----

jan 4 fri L7 (L.A.), Warlock Pinchers (CO), Libido Boyz (Minn), G-Wiz (AZ), Iowa Beef Experience, Monsula
jan 5 sat Contempt, Unjust, Tungsten, Scherzo (Concord), Pain's Grey (Seattle)
jan 11 fri Econochrist, Born Against (NYC), Downcast (L.A.), The Hated (last show), Grinch
jan 18 fri Aggression (Oxnard), The Mummies, Fastbacks (WA), Hellbillies, Friendly Dead Kids, Johnny Trouble (sp)
jan 19 sat Nip Drivers (L.A.), Cringer, Affirmative Action (N.Y.C.), Bad Samaritans (L.A.), Hedgehog (Santa Cruz)
jan 25 fri Nuisance, The Dread, Paul's God, Aisle Nine, Engage, 976 (Gilman Street Benefit)
jan 26 sat Big Drill Car, Jerme Spew (sp), David McCord (sp), Fifteen, Wendy O'Matic (sp), Nuclear Roach, Spitboy
feb 1 fri Bedlam Rovers, Bob Z, The Peels
feb 2 sat NoFX, Offspring (L.A.), Pennywise (L.A.), Jughead's Revenge (L.A.)
feb 3 sun Offspring (L.A.), Cringer, Monsula, Spitboy
feb 8 fri Victim's Family, Nuisance, Chomphard, Capitalist Casualties, Engage
feb 9 sat Blatz, Scared Straight, Hemi, Blister, Jerme Spew (sp)
feb 15 fri Green Day, Econochrist, No Use For A Name, Saw Horse, Blatz
feb 16 sat Capitol Punishment, Samiam, Special Forces, Hellbillies, Momi Bello
feb 22 fri Gargoyles, Filth, Electric Ferrets (L.A.), Scherzo, Total Fucked (Jessie naked ticket benefit)
mar 1 fri Hoi Polloi, Halfhead Special, A Different Kitchen, Himlayans, Mighty Bushmen (A.C.M.E. Showcase)
mar 2 sat Econochrist, Plaid Retina (Fresno), Nuisance, 23 More Minutes, Schlong
mar 8 fri Gargoyles, Monsula, Das Klown (L.A.), Assasins Of God
mar 9 sat Detonators (Oregon), Mr. T Experience, George Hated (sp), Creamers (L.A.), Glycine Max (L.A.), Corrupted
         Ideals (L.A.)
mar 15 fri Neurosis, Offspring (L.A.), Citizen Fish, Cringer, Lung Butter
mar 16 sat Sharkmeat, Skankin' Pickle (ska), Boom And The Legion Of Doom, Aspirin Feast (Seattle), Good Riddance
         (Santa Cruz)
mar 17 sun Naked Raygun, The Dread, Wynona Riders
mar 22 fri Spitboy (East Bay), Kai Kln (Sacramento), Grimace (Arcata), Junglefish (Santa Barbara), Byproducts
mar 23 sat Fifteen, Nip Drivers (L.A.), Slam Suzanne (Seattle), Grinch
mar 29 fri NoFX, No Use For A Name, Corrupted Morals, The Screw (CO),
mar 30 sat Samiam, Jawbox (D.C.), Mummies, Preachers That Lie (San Jose), Scherzo (Concord)
mar 31 sun No Means No (Canada), Victim's Family, Positive Greed, Hellbillies
apr 5 fri 3-Legged Dog, Downcast, Engage, Shortlived
apr 6 sat Big Drill Car, Ill Repute (Oxnard), X-O Tokins (L.A.), Vicious Midgets
apr 12 fri Verbal Abuse, Econochrist, Filth, Grinch, Spitboy (C.C. Alternative School Benefit)
apr 13 sat Bluchunks, Private Culture, Fishwife, Swallow My Pride, New Order Soul
apr 19 fri Burn Baby Burn, Skunkweed, All You Can Eat, Fuck Shit Up, Captain Krunch (new band showcase)
apr 20 sat Medicine Men, Cardinal Art (L.A.), Malt Horse Drudge, Nuclear Rabbit

apr 21 sun Blast, The Accused, Slambodians, Rites Of Passage
apr 26 fri Popstitutes, Nip Divers, Blatz, Action Figure (Reno), Horny Mormons
apr 27 sat The Dread, Jughead's Revenge, Bad Samaritans (L.A.), The Henchmen
may 3 fri Green Day, That's It, TvTv$ (L.A.), Generator, Pay The Man (L.A.)
may 10 fri Moral Crux (Washington), Rhythm Collision (L.A.), Thrillhammer, Octatractor (Van), Jumpstart (Sacramento)
may 11 sat Jodie Foster's Army, Slam And The Motherfuckers, Boom And The Legion Of Doom, Totally Fucking Lit (WA),
          Mother Load (WA)
may 17 fri Fishwife, Slam Suzanne, Good Riddance
may 18 sat Neurosis, Urge, Blister, Grinch (Women's cancer research center benefit)
may 24 fri Warlock Pinchers, Beat Happening, The Cannanes (Aust.), Motorpsycho
may 25 sat Econochrist, Filth, Dogma Mudista, Spitboy, Total Fucked (Benefit for Econochrist tour and Filth tour)
may 26 sun Flesheaters, Fixtures (L.A.), Paper Tulips (L.A.), Pop Defect (L.A.), Anger Means
may 31 fri Fifteen, Blatz, Engage, Tribe 8, Good Grief
jun 1 sat Monsula, White Trash Debutantes, Tree People, Fitz Of Depression, Dave Diamond
jun 7 fri Spot 1019, Wedge Of Chastity, Malt Horse Druge, Little My, Little Fyodor (CO)
jun 8 sat Vampire Lezbos, Special Forces, Cracks In The Sidewalk, Aisle Nine
jun 9 sun Capitol Punishment, S.A.D. Boyz, Slut Vinyl, The Tomb Stones, The Neanderthals, Sharon Tate, Electric Sex
          Hens, Failure, Nightshift, Paste, Scowl Scurf, Pug Mug (Fresno Punk Fest)
jun 14 fri L7 (L.A.), Gray Matter (D.C.), Offspring (L.A.), Sinister Sisters Of Satan, Spitboy
jun 15 sat One Man Running (Arcata), Stickleback, Alter Ego, Salt Lick, Paxton Quiggly (new band night)
jun 16 sun Glass Eye, Jack Killed Jill, Wynona Riders
jun 21 fri Nation Of Ulysses (WA), Monsula, Angry Son (OK), Bikini Kill, Stand Up
jun 22 sat Green Day, Fifteen, Jack Acid, Insaints, Nocturnal Burrito (Benefit for Punk Picnic on June 30)
jun 28 fri D.I., Blast, Lungfish (D.C.), Jughead's Revenge, Bad Samaritans (L.A.)
jun 29 sat Just Say No (MI), Eight Ball (WA), Last Call (PA), Phantasmorgasm (CO)
jul 5 fri Screeching Weasel, Blatz, Voodoo Glow Skulls, Jerme Spew, Anna Joy, Grimace (Arcata)
jul 6 sat Neurosis, Distant Silence (Fl), Grinch, Hate X9 (Utah), Confrontation (L.A.)
jul 7 sun Improv Music Noise-Jam, Swap Meet, Pot Luck
jul 12 fri Born Against (NYC), Rorschach (NYC), Sleep, Juke, Das Klown (L.A.)
jul 13 sat Final Conflict (L.A.), Generator, George Hated (sp), Billingsgate (Il), Say No More (Il), Smog
jul 19 fri Surrogate Brains, Vagrants, Fabulous Frostbitten Waffles (Blatz), Discontent (Gilman Street Benefit)
jul 20 sat Capitalist Casualties, 23 More Minutes, The Dread, Total Fucked, Drippy Drawers
jul 26 fri Funnel Head, Low
jul 27 sat Monsula, Pheg Camp, Sub Society, House Of Suffering, Hunger Farm (L.A.)
jul 28 sun Didjits, Urge, Chemical People, Good Riddance
aug 2 fri Gargoyles, Sandy Duncan's Eye (L.A.), Neil Smith
aug 3 sat Stabb, Commonwealth (D.C.), Aspirin Feast (WA), Whipped (WA), Elegy
aug 4 sun U.K. Subs, Special Forces, Wynona Riders
aug 9 fri Ill Repute (Oxnard), Filth, Youth Gone Mad (L.A.), Letch Patrol (NY), Platypus Scourge
aug 10 sat Pollution Circus, Resist (OR), Unamused
aug 16 fri Fifteen, Juke, 23 More Minutes, Spitboy, Carlos (food not bombs benefit)
aug 17 sat 411, Mecca Normal (Vancouver), Edgewise (PA), Corrupted Ideals (L.A.), Suckerpunch
aug 23 fri Econochrist, 23 More Minutes, Anger Means, Paxton Quiggly
aug 24 sat Gas Huffer (WA), The Banned (Mont), Downcast (L.A.) Heroin (San Diego), Brain Tourniquet (San Diego)
aug 30 fri Jawbreaker, Samiam, Bhang Revival (Chicago), Hellbillys, Preachers That Lie
aug 31 sat Blister, Urge, Carlos, Peon Me, Phil Steir, Fat Mike (sp) (Schoolhouse Rock Benefit)
sep 1 sun Fugazi (D.C.), Nation Of Ulysses, Vagrants, Tribe 8
sep 7 sat The Fixtures, Media Children, Resist To Exist, Total Chaos
sep 13 fri Thatcher On Acid (UK), Green Day, Cringer, Paxton Quiggly, Morphius (WA)
sep 14 sat F.F.I., Engage, Nuisance, Wynona Riders, Hood House
sep 15 sun Spoken word by Jello Biafra, Bucky Sinister, Saint Stupid, Wendy O'Matic, Anna Joy, Jerme Spew, Andy
          Razor, Krystaur of Blondies, Gene of Idiot Flesh, B-town/O-town Posse, Performance art by members of
          Sharkbait (Schoolhouse Rock Benefit)
sep 20 fri Funnelhead, House Of Pimps, Anal Mucus, Concrete Fondue, The Blamed (new band night)
sep 21 sat Monsula, Radicts (NYC), Scherzo, Rhythm Collision (L.A.), Horace Pinker (AZ)
sep 27 fri Speed Racer, Tyrrannacide, Boom And The Legion Of Doom, That's It, Schleprock
sep 29 sun Alice Donut, Victim's Family, Thatcher On Acid (UK), Blister
oct 4 fri Jawbreaker, Subvert (WA), Cringer, Monsula, Spitboy
oct 5 sat Plaid Retina, Nuisance, Bitchcraft, Schlong
oct 6 sun Coffin Break, Dwarves, Engage, Supersucker (WA), My Name (WA)
oct 11 fri Muff, Fifteen, Wynona Riders, Bedlam Court
oct 12 sat NoFX, Pennywise, No Use For A Name, Grim
oct 18 fri Green Day, Blatz, Jack Acid, Alter Ego, Grimple (New Mexico) (Jack Acid tour Benefit)
oct 19 sat Les Thugs, Jonestown, Samiam, Your Mother
oct 20 sun Green Day, Mr. T Experience, Samiam, Blatz, Scherzo, Lookouts, Monsula, The Vagrants, Wynona Riders
          (Lookout records benefit for 924 Gilman St.) (East Bay Firestorm Day)
oct 25 fri Lithium Milkshake, The Unsound, Corn, Pillhead And The Reds
oct 26 sat Econochrist, Hellbillies, Mermen, Grinch
oct 27 sun record swap
nov 1 fri Bl'ast, Jughead's Revenge, The Insaints, The Giants

nov 2 sat Samiam, Offspring, Scherzo, Triggerman, Transition
nov 8 fri Unjust, The Fiendz (NJ), Fishwife (San Diego), Uncommon Society (Canada)
nov 9 sat Clawhammer, Sleep, Monsula, Cringer (last show), Oswald 5-0, Plutocracy
nov 15 fri Fifteen, Trusty, Treadmill, Horny Mormons, Lung Butter
nov 16 sat Jawbreaker, Alien Beach Head, Tribe 8, Naked Lady Wrestlers
nov 17 sun Pegboy, Nuisance, Mr T Experience, Wynona Riders
nov 22 fri Engage, Pollution Circle, Paxton Quiggly, Insurgent, Nar
nov 23 sat Blatz, Jack Acid, Wynona Riders, Yellow #5, Jerme Spew (sp)
nov 29 fri Lithium Milkshake, Heroin, Undertow, Platypus Scourge
nov 30 sat White Trash Debutantes, Paul's God, Cambridge Riders, Breakdown
dec 6 fri Citizen Fish, Econochrist, Jack Acid, Yellow #5
dec 7 sat Victim's Family, Citizen Fish, Plaid Retina, Schlong, Foreskin 500 (CO)
dec 13 fri Monsula, Spitboy, Engage, Wendy O' Matik (sp), Paxton Quiggly
dec 14 sat Bomb, Grotus, Vomit Launch, Stalin (Japan), Bob Evans (Boston)
dec 21 sat Ill Repute, Motorpsycho, Krupted Peasant Farmerz, Sharon Tate
dec 27 fri Juke, Outspoken, Resurrection, Mouthpiece, Bedlam Court
dec 28 sat Nuisance, Logical Nonsense (New Mexico), Lizards (Sacramento), Fuzzzone (Benicia), 3 Finger Spread
dec 31 tue Disco Till You Puke Dance Party

1992
----

jan 3 fri Warlock Pinchers, Fifteen, Grinch, Assassins Of God, The Blamed
jan 4 sat Monsula, Blatz, Primitive Tribes (AZ)
jan 10 fri D.C. Beggars (Seattle), Hedgehog, Ruination (Seattle), Vicious Midgets, Big Thumbs
jan 11 sat Scherzo, The Dread, Wynona Riders, The B-Sides, Joybus
jan 12 sun My New Tattoo video magazine video screening
jan 17 fri Green Day, White Trash Debutantes, Insaints, Hunger Farm (L.A.), Bitchcraft
jan 18 sat Paxton Quiggly, Schleprock (L.A.), Jumpstart (Sacramento)
jan 24 fri No Use For A Name, Pollution Circus, Litmus Green (L.A.), Disengage, Grimple
jan 25 sat Jeff Dahl & Rikk Agnew, Gargoyles, The Electric Ferrets, Screaming Bloody Mary's, Mind Over Metal
jan 31 fri Ska dance party with D.J. Lulu from KALX, Mellow Fellows
feb 7 fri Neurosis, Plaid Retina, Grinch, Lithium Milkshake, Full Metal Chicken
feb 8 sat Paxton Quiggly, Jack Acid, Rancid, The Aborted
feb 14 fri Green Day, Nuisance, Fifteen, The Overwhelming Colorfast, Strawman
feb 15 sat Born Against, Jawbreaker, 411, Monsula, Scarecrow
feb 21 fri Sleep, Capitalist Casualties, Plutocracy, 976, Discrepancy
feb 22 sat Econochrist, Grimple, Rancid, False Testament, Circus Tents (Gilman Benefit)
feb 23 sun Jawbox, Samiam, Captain Crunch, Five Year Plan (L.A.), Shudder To Think
feb 28 fri Filth, George Hated, Paxton Quiggly, Grimple, The Aborted (Needle Exchange Benefit)
feb 29 sat Bug Lamp (L.A.), Bl'ast, Bad Samaritans (L.A.), Flying Dead Skin
mar 6 fri M.D.C., No Use For A Name, Sekiri (Japan), Gecko
mar 7 sat Spitboy, Bitchcraft, Schlong, Sister Placebo, Grady Sisters
mar 8 sun Cracker Barrel, Juke, Wynona Riders
mar 13 fri NOFX, Tribe 8, Lag Wagon, Rancid
mar 14 sat White Trash Debutantes, Slang, Dangerhaus, Johnny Peabucks & The Swinging Udders, Mike Bonner
mar 15 sun film fest
mar 20 fri Screaming Bloody Mary's, Fuckboys, Schleprock, Political Blister
mar 21 sat Jawbreaker, Christ On A Crutch, J-Church, Good Grief, Jabberjaw (Homemade Records Benefit)
mar 27 fri Nuisance, Savalas (CO), Sparkmarker (Vancouver), Krupted Peasant Farmers, Transition
mar 28 sat Green Day, Creamers, Wynona Riders, Juke
mar 29 sun Olive Lawn, Zipgun, Scherzo, Horny Mormons
apr 3 fri Detonators, Econochrist, D.C. Beggars, Lizards, The Aborted
apr 4 sat Filth, The Tree People (WA), Section Eight, Total Chaos (L.A.), Grimple, Lung Butter
apr 10 fri Monsula, Commonwealth (D.C.), Jumpstart, Hydrant
apr 11 sat Dogma Mundista (L.A.), Entrivista (L.A.), The Officials (L.A.), Rapscallion (WI), Pinhead Gunpowder
apr 17 fri Jonestown (Minneapolis), Trenchmouth (Chicago), Unwound (Olympia), Mol Triffid
apr 24 fri Citizen Fish, Paxton Quiggly, Spitboy, Gr'ups
apr 25 sat Circus Lupus (D.C.), Gas Huffer (WA), Supersuckers (WA), Crain (KY), Backwoods
may 1 fri Nuisance, Strawman, Bitchcraft, Big Ed
may 2 sat Fifteen, Hoodhouse, Scherzo, Corn, Lank, The Lifers (play)
may 3 sun The Lifers (play)
may 8 fri Filth, Econochrist, Jack Acid, Rancid, Shark Attack (Benefit for Fraggle)
may 15 fri Mr. T Experience, Wynona Riders, Some Velvet Sidewalk, Samiam, Sybil
may 16 sat Motherlode, Schlong, Pounded Clown, Seapigs
may 22 fri Spitboy, Downcast, Heroin, Good Grief, Shark Attack, Kent McClard (sp)
may 23 sat Titwrench (San Diego), Grinch, Fu Manchu (L.A.), Sonisary
may 29 fri Neurosis, Grotus, Neutralnation (RI), Bunny Gengis (CO),
may 30 sat Citizen Fish, Paxton Quiggly, Econochrist, False Sacrament, Gag Order, The Gr'ups
jun 5 fri Monsula, Wynona Riders, Monkey Brittle, Doug
jun 6 sat Oswald 5-0 (Eugene), Gnome (Seattle), Jabberjaw, Less Miserables, Mindslam

jun 12 fri Bratmobile (Olympia), Strawman, Heavens To Betsy (Olympia), PreMarital Sex, Circus Tents

jun 13 sat Sleep, The Hated, Juke, The Aborted Wood (George Hated Benefit)

jun 19 fri Jawbreaker, Econochrist, World's Collide (WA), No Escape (NJ), Pen (IL)

jun 20 sat Sluggo, Sharon Tate (Fresno), One Man Running (Humbolt)

jun 21 sun 411, Vz Jjme Duma, Wynona Riders, Triggerman, Jumpstart

jun 26 fri Libido Boys, Bloodline (Minn), Lack Of Social Decency, Jolt, The Aborted

jun 27 sat Green Day, Gargoyles, Yes Ma'am, Tilt

jul 3 fri Naked Aggression, Spitboy, Hellnation (WI), Plutocracy, 976

jul 4 fri Fifteen, Insaints, Schlong, Positive Greed (Benefit for legal defense of David Nadel of Ashkenaz Club)

jul 10 fri Green Day, Farside (L.A.), Schleprock (L.A.), Neil Smith, Jack Knife

jul 11 sat Wild Stares (L.A.), Woodpussy (OK), Meatminder (Seattle), (Benefit for Komotion International)

jul 17 fri Paxton Quiggly, Spitboy, Wooden Horse (FL), Buck-O (New Orleans), Voodoo Glow Skulls (L.A.)

jul 18 sat Deviators (NYC), Meices, Johny Peebucks And The Swingin' Utters, Hoodlum Empire

jul 24 fri Sideshow, 49 Reasons, By Products, Last Pariahs

jul 25 sat Capitol Punishment, Sleep, Natural Cause (WI), Nest Of Fools (Misws), My Name Is Chris

jul 31 fri White Trash Debutantes, Special Forces, Insaints, Nightshift (Benefit for Food Not Bombs)

aug 1 sat Paxton Quiggly (last show), Jack Acid (last show), Clutch (D.C.), 4 Walls Falling, Aborted

aug 7 fri Green Day, The Daves (WA), Dumpt, Vex (CO), Less Miserables

aug 8 sat Model Citizens (Seattle), The Hellbillies, North American Bison, Engage

aug 14 fri Genbaku Onanies (Japan), Officer Down (Seattle), Lockjaw (Canada), Third Leg (Austin)

aug 15 sat Good Grief, Patrick "Hooty" Croy (sp), Lithium Milkshake, Five Year Plan (L.A.), Reach Out (Big Mountain Benefit)

aug 22 sat Rudiments, Rancid, Rice (San Diego), Bumblescrump, Zero Tolerance Task Force

aug 23 sun Nation Of Ulysses (D.C.), Heroin (San Diego), Sluggo, Lung Butter, Bakamono

aug 28 fri Blatz, Tribe 8, Wendy O'Matic (sp), Insaints, False Sacrament, Tiger Trap (Sacramento), Sink You Up - A play by Nosmo Queen Productions (Radical Avant-Garde Garage Extravaganza 92)

aug 29 sat Green Day, Face Value (OH), Jabberjaw, Jerme Spew (sp), The Peels, Fuzzone (noon record swap, acoustic jam) (Radical Avant-Garde Garage Extravaganza 92)

aug 30 sun Steel Pole Bathtub, Neurosis, Plaid Retina, Snair, Bitchcraft, Big Ed (noon art/video/poetry/The Potatomen and more) (Radical Avant-Garde Garage Extravaganza 92)

sep 4 fri Drive Like Jehu (San Diego), Fishwife (San Diego), Nuisance, One Man Running, Navio Forge

sep 5 sat Youth Brigade, The Offspring, Monsula, Scherzo, The Dread

sep 6 sun Final Conflict, Bulemia Banquet, Econochrist, Wynona Riders (Scary Mikes birthday)

sep 11 fri M.D.C., 7-League Boots (RI), The Gr'ups (last show), Placenta Sandwich, Pivot

sep 12 sat Hellbillies, Grimple, Jolt, Tilt

sep 13 sun Neo-Nurd Garage Sale

sep 18 fri The Plagerists, Carde Nada, 3 Stoned Men

sep 25 fri Green Day, Rancid, Oiler, Night Shift, Krupted Peasant Farmerz

sep 26 sat Plaid Retina, Blister, Schlong, False Sacrament, Guano, Raooul

sep 27 sun Chumbawumba (U.K.), Voo Doo Glow Skulls, Letch Patrol (NY), Qore

oct 2 fri Ill Repute, Bad Samaritans, Fuck Boys, Twine, Chorea

oct 3 sat Seaweed (WA), Alien Boyz (Germany), Nimrod (Japan), Bliss (Montreal), One Man Running (Arcata)

oct 9 fri Voice Of Reason, Rhythm Collision, Scherzo, Reach Out

oct 10 fri Bikini Kill, Tribe 8, Wynona Riders, Pansy Division, Pre-Marital Sex, Raooul

oct 16 fri Diesel Queens (first a/a show), Hedge Hog, Pounded Clown, The Blown, Horny Mormons

oct 17 sat Spitboy, Buzzov-en (NC), Sleep, Grimple, Gag Order, Less Miserables

oct 23 fri NOFX, Sandy Duncan's Eye, Plaid Retina, Lag Wagon, Buzzov-en (NC)

oct 31 sat Special Forces (last show), Fifteen, Lung Butter

nov 6 fri Jawbreaker, Fifteen, J-Church, Less Miserables, Ted Hunters

nov 7 sat Green Day, B'last, Tilt, Candle, Salt Lick

nov 8 sun New Tattoo video night

nov 13 fri Naked Aggression, Rancid, Driptank, Fuzzone, Slip

nov 14 sat Samiam, Phleg Camp, Monsula, Waterfront, Sharon Tate

nov 20 fri U.K. Subs, Moral Crux, Metalist, Qore, Never

nov 27 fri Blister, Oiler, Paul's God, Dark Horse Candidate

nov 28 sat Crash Worship, Rig, Flatten Manhattan, Lung Butter

dec 4 fri Spitboy, 2000 Dirty Squatters (U.K.), Christ Driver, Stomp Box, Y-Gricga

dec 5 sat Mr. T Experience, Tilt, Log Jam, Tiger Trap

dec 11 fri D.O.A., Econochrist, Rancid, Itch, Endorphins

dec 12 sat D.I., Bad Samaritans, Hellbillys, The Pells, Guns Of Elvis

dec 13 sun Into Another, Up To Here, Reach Out, Soul Fire, Your Mother (straight edge fest)

dec 19 sat Rocket From The Crypt, Wool, J-Church, Beekeeper

dec 26 sat Green Day, Brent's TV And Appliance (one time reunion), The Ne'er Do Wells, The Potatomen, Earl

1993

----

jan 1 fri Unwound, Spitboy, The Vagrants, Raooul, Bitch Craft

jan 2 sat Assuck (FL), Man Is The Bastard, Crossed Out, Capitalist Casualties, Plutocracy (last show) (Slap a Ham Records Fiestagrande #1)

jan 8 fri Dogma Mundista, Atoxxxico, A-Solucion, Juke, Lid

jan 9 sat Econochrist, The Conditionz, Hell No, Merel, Ted Hunters
jan 15 fri Corrupted Ideals, Schlong/Raooul, False Sacrament, Sponge (CO)
jan 16 sat Tilt, Strawman, Word Salad (NM)
jan 23 sat ST-37 (Austin), Flatten Manhattan, Liquor Ball
jan 29 fri M.D.C., Laceration (WA), Fuck Boyz, Last Round Up (rock against racism)
jan 30 sat The Lizards, Nar, The Seapigs, Bananas, Barbara's Bush (sacramento invaision)
feb 6 sat Grimple, Sludge Plow, Backwash, Less Miserables
feb 12 fri Nuisance, Schlong, Pounded Clown, Sheephead, Glass Babble Radio
feb 13 sat Spitboy, Monsula, Diesel, Reachout, Still Life
feb 19 fri Born Against, Econochrist, Naked Aggression, John Henry West, Aluminum Piranhas
feb 20 sat Johnny Peebucks And The Swingin' Utters, Hellbillies, Krupted Peasant Farmerz, Drippy Drawers
feb 26 fri Sharkbait, Zipgun, Rain Like The Sound Of Trains, Anus The Menace, Salt Lick
feb 27 sat Tesco Vee's Hate Police, Mr. T Experience, Samiam, The Mieces, Lost Ground, Dark Horse Candidate
mar 5 fri J-Church, Schleprock, Butt Trumpet, Scherzo, Bob's Bait Shop
mar 12 fri Plaid Retina, Capitalist Casualties, False Sacrament, The Seapigs, Infestation
mar 19 fri Neurosis, Spitboy, Econochrist, Gag Order, Captain 9's And The Knickerbocker Trio
mar 20 sat Jawbreaker, Voodoo Glow Skulls, Tilt, Pot Valiant, Yah Mos
mar 26 fri Hansen Brothers, Debris Stream, Lithium Milkshake, G-Spot Tornado, Ub-Zub
mar 27 sat Unsane, Slug, Lois, Pansy Division, Spinnanes
apr 2 fri Nuisance, Twine, Navio Forge, Your Mother, Mindslam
apr 3 sat Naked Aggression, Grimple, Insaints, Sharon Tate, Psychiatric Petting Zoo (Reno)
apr 9 fri J-Church, Supertouch (NYC), Monsula, John Henry West
apr 10 sat Screeching Weasel, The Queers, Gr'ups, Nar
apr 16 fri Victims Family, Fitz Of Depression (WA), Lung Butter, Big Ed, Chronic Decay
apr 17 sat Verbal Abuse, Leaving Trains, Snair, Bean, S.O.S.A.
apr 23 fri Tribe 8, Hellbillies, Parasites, Malibu Barbi, State Of Grace
apr 24 sat Bitchcraft, Johnny Peebucks And The Swingin' Utters, Pot Valiant, Earl, Rummage Sale (Gilman benefit)
may 2 sun Jawbreaker, Monsula, Rancid, Fuzzzone, All You Can Eat
may 7 fri Chaos U.K., Grimple, Capitalist Casualties, The Dread, Spazz
may 8 sat Green Day, Motherload (WA), False Sacrament, Schlong, The Locals
may 9 sun Citizen Fish (U.K.), Buzzov-en (NC), Voodoo Glow Skulls, Strawman
may 14 fri Econochrist, Rancid, The Detonators, Agent 86, Lumpin Proletariat (Canada)
may 21 fri Frumpies, Blueprint (TX), Junglefish, Here Kitty Kitty, Bumblescrump
may 22 sat Creamers, Horace Pinker (AZ), Groovie Ghoulies, Seapigs, The Clots
may 28 fri Offspring, Avail (VA), Naked Aggression, Second Coming, Lost Ground
may 30 sun Crash Worship, Ub-Zub, Mental Pigmies
jun 5 sat Natural Cause (Wisconsin), Fixtures, Yah Mos, Circus Tents (Sacramento)
jun 11 fri Worlds Collide, Scherzo (last show), Chicken (WA), Not My Son (WA), Sick And Tired (Detroit)
jun 12 sat Youth Gone Mad (NYC), Rhythm Collision (L.A.), Rudiments, The Underside (D.C.), Total Fucked
jun 19 sat Tilt, Mr. T Experience, Pot Valiant, Havoc And The Rhythm Section, Bumblescrump
jun 25 fri Fifteen, Subterfuge, Brutal Juice (TX), Salt Lick, Alcohol Funnycar
jun 26 sat Rancid, Hydrofist, Furley, Nub, Parasites
jul 2 fri Bratmobile (WA), Spoon (L.A.), Gr'ups, Raooul (last show), Dead And Gone
jul 3 sat Jawbreaker, Beekeeper, Engine Kid, Fuckboyz, Moist (Sacramento)
jul 9 fri Sleep, Spilth, Gag Order, Chino Horde (AR)
jul 10 sat Monsula, Crackerbash (WA), The Shaven (WA), Chino Horde (AR), Here Kitty Kitty
jul 16 fri Rorshach (NY), Psycho (MA), Man Is The Bastard, 3 Finger Spread, Capitalist Casualties, Spazz
jul 17 sat Ranciid, Fifteen, Chicken Head (FL), Parasites
jul 23 fri Naked Aggression, Destroy (MN), John Henry West, Sharon Tate, Dartboard
jul 24 sat Rancid, Face To Face, Johnny Peebucks And The Swingin' Utters, Sideshow (N.E.), 49 Reasons (SC)
jul 30 fri Plaid Retina, Logical Nonsense, Pounded Clown, The Seapigs, Los Huevos, 3 Finger Spread (Very
           Small Records final record release party)
jul 31 sat Drive Like Jehu (San Diego), Pee, Naked Violence (OR), Frog Sandwich, Fat Chick
aug 1 sun Shelter (NY), 108 degrees, Critical Mass, Second Coming
aug 5 thr Antigone (post modern interpretation of Greek classic)
aug 6 fri Unwound, Farside, Undertow, Sparkmarker, Desmortz
aug 7 sat Antigone (post modern interpretation of Greek classic), Huasipungo, Unamused (OR), Los Crudos, John
           Henry West
aug 8 sun Antigone (post modern interpretation of Greek classic)
aug 12 thr Antigone (post modern interpretation of Greek classic)
aug 13 fri Grimple, Malignis Youth (AZ), Schlong, Grief (MA), Iconoclast (NJ)
aug 14 sat Antigone (post modern interpretation of Greek classic), Tribe 8, The Gr'ups, Skinhead Magnet, Submachine,
           Lizards
aug 15 sun Antigone (post modern interpretation of Greek classic)
aug 20 fri J Church, Cupid Car Club, Sticks And Stones, Ego (NY), Junkman Run
aug 21 sat Rancid, Tilt, Oiler, Floodgate, Dog Star
aug 27 fri Dropdead, Crossed Out, A.C., Capitalist Casualties, Spazz
aug 28 sat Samiam, Monsula, Pot Valiant, Sheephead, Hanshan (last show)
sep 3 fri Blair Hess (Olympia), All You Can Eat, Fiddlehead (GA), Bristle (WA)
sep 4 sat Artless, Parasites, Pansy Division, Verticle After (Canada), The Ne'er Do Wells

sep 5 sun Rancid, Artless, Diesel Queens, Bo (benefit for legal fees of Marian Anderson of the Insaints)
sep 10 fri Dr. Know, Oswald 5-0, Elmer's Shotgun
sep 11 sat Huggy Bear (England), Frumpies, Tiger Trap, Clams, Ida
sep 19 sun Offspring, Impatient Youth, Dead And Gone, Dartboard, Terminal Disgust (TX)
sep 25 sun Ill Repute, Bad Samaritans, Johny Peebucks And The Swingin' Utters, Trench, Crutch
oct 1 fri Monsula, Strawman, Indian Summer, "Happy Blood Shed" (perf. art)
oct 8 fri M.D.C., Iowa Beef Experience, Bent
oct 9 sat Spitboy, Man Is The Bastard, Universal Order Of Armageddon (MD), Queen Mab
oct 10 sun Phleg Camp (Canada), Pot Valiant, Pivot, Rug Burn
oct 15 fri Naked Aggression, Total Chaos, Krupted Peasant Farmerz, Nuclear Armed Hogs
oct 16 sat Rancid, The Queers (NH), Parasites, The Rip Offs
oct 22 fri Face To Face (L.A.), Johnny Peebucks And The Swingin' Utters, The Hellbillies, The Seapigs
oct 23 sat Fifteen, L-Sid, Queen Mab, Whole Lot Of Nothing Going Nowhere (critical mass benefit)
oct 29 fri Unwound, J-Church, Everready, Strawman, Car De Nada
oct 30 sat Counter Clock, Room 237, Wise Young Turk, Nondos new band (Mookie's Daughter benefit)
nov 5 fri Voodoo Glow Skulls, Schlong, Pounded Clown, Zoinks (Reno), The Knock-Offs
nov 6 sat Tilt, Rhythm Collision (L.A), Lazy Boy (OR), Dartboard, The Ne'er Do Wells
nov 12 fri Steel Pole Bathtub, Bouncing Souls, The Beyonds (Japan)
nov 13 sat Spitboy, Karp (Olympia), Godheadsilo (ND), Long Hind Legs (Olympia), Kerosene 454
nov 14 sun NoFX, Dartboard
nov 19 fri J.F.A., Hemi, Exploited Fuck Doll, Ice Cream Headache (Thrasher Magazine skaterock show)
nov 20 sat Manumission, State Of The Nation, Indian Summer, Mohinder
nov 26 fri Johnny Peebucks And The Swingin' Utters, Schleprock, Wax, The Tourettes, 12 Eyes, 2nd Story Window
nov 27 sat Solmania (Osaka, Japan), Masonna (Japan), Ub Zub, Trance
dec 4 sat Aztlan Nation, Siren, Pivot, Ground Round, Culture Of Rage, Young Eagle Drum, Aztlan Underground
        (Benefit Int. Indian Treaty Council And American Indian Movement)
dec 5 sun Four Winds Drum and Dancers, Vukani Mawethu, La Pena Chorus, Freedom Song Network, Tivela,
        Floyd Red Crow Westerman (Benefit Int. Indian Treaty Council And American Indian Movement)
dec 10 fri Copass Grinders (Japan), Blood Thirsty Butchers (Japan), Nuclear Armed Hogs, Counter Clock, Queen Mab,
        Numb, Big Lie Department
dec 12 sun Nomeansno, Victim's Family, Plaid Retina
dec 17 fri Fifteen, Manumission, Ted Hunters, Nub
dec 18 sat Ovarian Trolley, Ida, Ed Asner And The Little Bandits, Siren, Fat Chance Belly Dance Group, Sarah
        Jacobson's film "I was a teenage serial killer" (Epicenter Women Outreach Koalition benefit)
dec 26 sun Lag Wagon, Propagandhi (Canada), Face To Face, Dartboard

1994
----

jan 1 sat Tilt, Johny Peebucks And The Swingin' Utters, Safehouse (AZ), Junior Tubs, Temper Tantrum
jan 7 fri Rancid, Avail, Siren, Among The Thugs, Gift Of The Magi
jan 8 sat Man Is The Bastard, Capitalist Casualties, Lack Of Interest, Spazz, Word Salad (Slap-A-Ham Fiesta
        Grande II)
jan 14 fri Jawbreaker, Cop Out (TN), Indian Summer, Tourettes (and Raool), Queen Mab
jan 15 sat Delightful Little Nothings, The Trouble Makers, The Potatomen, Ne'er Do Wells
jan 22 sat Kicking Giant (Oly), Pot Valiant, Tattle Tale (Oly), Pinhead Gunpowder, Here Kitty Kitty
jan 23 sun D.O.A., Seapigs, Dead And Gone, Crutch
jan 28 fri Voodoo Glow Skulls, Schlong, Hellbillies, All You Can Eat, Big Lie Department
feb 4 fri Tilt, Queen Mab, Tourettes, Curbs
feb 11 fri M.D.C., U.X.A. (United Experiments Of America), Corrupted Ideals, Stitches, The Unhappy
feb 12 sat J-Church, Stolen Face, No Empathy, Good Riddance, Slip
feb 18 fri M Is For Murder, Hypochondriacs, Local 101, The Wankin' Teens,
        The Unhappy, Spank Magic, Chumpslap (new band night)
feb 19 sat Fifteen, 8-Bark, K-Pants, Mohinder, Nub
feb 20 sun S.N.F.U., Capitol Punishment, Swingin' Utters, Rug Burn
feb 25 fri Rocket From The Crypt, 68 Comeback, Deadbolt, Napsack
mar 4 fri Jawbreaker, 16 (L.A.), Everready (San Diego), Godheadsilo (Oly), 2nd Story Window
mar 5 sat The Queers, Parasites, Potatomen, Knock-offs, Bananas
mar 11 fri Mudwimmin, Fibulator, Bloodtest, Zero Hour, A Minor Forest (Benefit for Infoshop)
mar 12 sat Schlong, Capitalist Casualties, Counterclock, Trench, Discrepancy
mar 18 fri Spitboy, Heavens To Betsy, Gagorder, Excuse 17, Noise Gate
mar 19 sat Groundwork, Sense Field, Yahmos, Harvest Theory, Among The Thugs,
mar 25 fri Tribe 8, Pansy Division, Mukiliteo Fairies (Olympia), Aunt Fister (Outpunk records showcase)
mar 26 sat Youth Brigade (L.A.), Fifteen, Weed, Garden Variety (NJ), Dartboard
apr 1 fri The Humpers, Swingin' Utters, Bombs For Whitey, Big Ed
apr 2 sat Gus, Screw 32, Mental Pygmies, Sheephead
apr 8 fri Insult To Injury, Zoinks!, Mindslam
apr 9 sat M Blanket (Canada), Indian Summer, Antioch Arrow (SD), Second Story Window, Gage, The Panic
apr 10 sun Neurosis, Grotus, Zero Hour, Gag Order
apr 15 fri Undertow, Outspoken, Second Coming, Torn, Portraits Of Past (East Bay Vegan Benefit) (straight edge fest)
apr 16 sat J-Church, Parasites, Four Point Star, Sourmash

apr 22 fri Ne'er Do Wells, Roger Nusick, Nar, Kerosene 454, Here Kitty Kitty
apr 23 sat God's Guts (Japan), Volume Dealers (Japan), Garlic Boys, Trenchmouth (Chicago), Your Mother
apr 25-29 Art show and performance art
apr 29 fri Naked Aggression, Sick And Tired, 30 Ought Six, The Fanatics, Hypochondriacs
apr 30 sat Spitboy, Mohinder, Sixteen Bullets, Stolenface
may 6 fri Tilt, Strawman, Krupted Peasant Farmerz, Two-Line Filler, Stick Figure
may 7 sat Fixtures (L.A.), Society Gone Mad (L.A.), Dead And Gone, Oppressed Logic, Cup O Grind
may 13 fri Swingin' Utters, The Rudiments, Screw 32, The Tourettes, Tunstin Gat
may 14 sat Rancid, Total Chaos, Hellbillies, Parasites, A.F.I.
may 20 fri Ne'er Do Wells, Huevous Rancheros, Fleabag
may 21 sat Unwound, Pot Valiant, Antioch Arrow, Thumbnail (TN), Lunchpail
may 27 fri M.D.C., Rhythm Pigs, Dartboard, Pop A Wheelie, The Hypochondriacs
may 28 sat Jello Biafra (sp), Jerme Spew (sp)
jun 3 fri All You Can Eat, V.B.F. (TX), Wankin' Teens, Red #9, Shag
jun 4 sat Offspring, Current, Indian Summer, Among The Thugs, Araby
jun 10 fri The Mr. T Experience, Sicko (WA), Lennard Innards (IN), Jara
jun 11 sat Hellbillies, Rudiments, Highway 66, A.F.I., Multi Facet
jun 17 fri Deformed Conscience (CN), Capitalist Casualties, Spazz, Wormhole (PA), The Dread
jun 18 sat Godheadsilo (Olympia), Logical Nonsense, Schlong, Counterclock
jun 24 fri Agent 86, Earl's Family Bombers, Pot Valiant, Mindslam, Screw 32
jun 25 sat Total Chaos, The Rickets (Olympia), Crutch, The Insignificant (DE), The Slackers (AL)
jul 1 fri Floodgate, Dead And Gone, Mohinder, Portraits Of Past (Heart Attack Fanzine Benefit)
jul 2 sat Bikini Kill, Word Salad (NM), Tourettes, Pee Chees, Blunt (FL)
jul 8 fri J-Church, Pitchblender (D.C.), Fat Day (MA), Shit Fits, Therapeutic, Trevor, and two others
jul 9 sat Jerm Flux, Counter Clock, Scared Of Chaka (NM), Punch Buggy
jul 15 fri The Pist (CT), Brutally Familar, Your Mother
jul 16 sat U.X.A., Shot Maker (Canada), Screw 32, Snap-Her, Rejected Motherfuckers
jul 22 fri Spitboy, Policy Of Three, Bleed, Five Year Plan, Jack Kevorkian
jul 23 sat Final Conflict, 16, Blood Thirsty Butchers (Japan), Copass Grinders (Japan), Noisegate
jul 24 sun Heavens To Betsy, Excuse 17, Moist, Ida
jul 29 fri Haggis (ID), Ass Factor 4 (SC), Semi Pro Bowlers, Franklin (PN), Fracture (PN)
jul 30 sat Impetus Inter (Minn.), Hellnation, Capitalist Casualties, Blackfork, Blown Apart Bastards
aug 5 fri Spitboy, Los Crudos, Spazz, Stolen Face, Nuclear Armed Hogs, Ambassador Krill
aug 6 sat Gauge (IL), Lean (DE), Whirleybird (VA), Teeth
aug 7 sun Chaos UK (UK), M.D.C., Swingin' Utters, A.F.I., Toxic Narcotic (NJ)
aug 12 fri Dead Silence (CO), Dead And Gone, Outspoken (L.A.), Chokehold (Canada), Bloodlett (Canada)
aug 13 sat Lifetime, Indian Summer, Snapcase, Jara, The Soulsuckers
aug 14 sun Raw Power (Italy), Rhythm Pigs, The Hellbillies
aug 19 fri Wrongway Right, Apartment 213, 40 Miles Behind, Lapaz, Radioactive Lunch, Therapeutic (new band night)
aug 20 sat Sparkmarker (Canada), Lync (WA), Sharon Tate, Siren, Prozac Memory (MO), Liars and Fingers (play)
aug 21 sun Liars and Fingers (play)
aug 26 fri Tourettes, Creature Did, Multi Facet, Jinx, Erik Core Liars and Fingers (play)
aug 27 sat Naked Aggression, Rye, Bombs For Whitey, Chumpslap, Invalids, Liars and Fingers (play)
sep 2 fri Skankin' Pickle, Voodoo Glow Skulls, Step Ahead
sep 3 sat Tilt, Rudiments, One Man Running, Brain Transplants, Criminal Intentions
sep 9 fri Hellbillies, Screw 32, Wankin' Teens, Crutch, Eightna-Quarter (Punk Rock Prom)
sep 10 sat Spitboy, Universal Order Of Armageddon, A Minor Forest, Harvest Theory, Hypochondriacs
sep 16 fri Bristle (WA), Catfood, Play Ground, Nancyville (Oly), Flake
sep 17 sat Mermen, Driving Wheels, Offense AD, Sheephead
sep 23 fri Shoegazer, Rummage Sale, Parasites, Loose Change (Shredder Records Anniversary)
sep 24 sat Swingin' Utters, Roger Music, Exploding Crustaceans, Oppressed Logic, Grout Villa
sep 30 fri Insult To Injury (Canada), Inner Frog, Tickle, Suggestive Suicide
oct 1 sat Fifteen, The Darts, Wrong Way Right, Randoms, The Need (cop watch benefit)
oct 7 fri Man Is The Bastard, Ruins (Japan), Dirt (England), Final Warning, Hedgehog
oct 8 sat Los Huevos, Walleye, Big Steamy
oct 14 fri Second Coming, Sleeper, Eightna-Quarter, A.L.E., Some Are Evolving
oct 15 sat A.F.I., Screw 32, The Other, Multi Facet, Hellbender, Mental Pygmies
oct 21 fri Trite, Hope Bombs, The Fireflies, Kid Dynamo, Tork (new band night)
oct 22 sat Godheadsilo, Jara, Dartboard, Noisegate, Crack
oct 28 fri Schlong, Sharon Tate, Buttafuoco, Zero Tolerance Task Force, Struggle Buggies
oct 29 sat Sicko (WA), Jinx, Krupted Peasant Farmerz, Dieselboy, John Cougar Concentration Camp
nov 4 fri Dead And Gone, Cars Get Crushed, Second Story Window, Pottersfield, Subincision
nov 5 sat record swap
nov 5 sat Fifteen, Swingin' Utters, The Smears (IN), Harvest Theory, The Product
nov 11 fri Monster Truck Driver, The Process (Ukiah), Cuban Rebel Girl, La Paz, Ibiza
nov 18 fri Screw 32, Red #9, One Spot Fringehead, Chumpslap, Inquisition
nov 19 sat Hellbillies, Fury 66, Crutch, Illiterate, Plaight
nov 20 sun Bikini Kill, Tourettes, Team Dresch, Moist, Kitty Cat Spy Club
nov 25 fri Naked Agression, Multi Facet, 12 Inch Rulers (L.A.), The Darts, Criminal Intentions
nov 26 sat Stitches (L.A.), Fierce Nipples, Good Riddance, Pluto (Canada), The Unhappy (last show)

dec 2 fri Citizen Fish (UK), Spitboy, Swingin' Utters, Nuclear Armed Hogs
dec 3 sat China White (L.A.), Hard Fast Loud, Wrong Way Right, The Need, Riot Gun
dec 9 fri The Nards, Monster Zero, Love Props, Pant Lick Bell, Throttle, Shotwell Coho (new band night)
dec 10 sat Rudiments, The Invalids, Willies, Kid Dynamo, Loose Change
dec 16 fri Screw 32, Blackfork, A.F.I., Dead And Gone (Zafio Records "This is Berkeley, Not West Bay" comp release)
        (ABC NoRio Benefit)
dec 17 sat Nancyville (Oly), Donner Party, Aluminum Piranhas, Brain Transplants, Inner Frog, Botch
dec 23 fri Schlong, Bo, Five Year Plan, The Crumbs (FL) (x-mas sets)
dec 30 fri Unwound, A Minor Forest, The Waydowns, The Neighbors, Ned Kelly

1995
----

jan 6 fri Avail (VA), Spitboy, Screw 32, Jara (L.A.)
jan 7 sat Pee Chees, Cars Get Crushed, Spanakorzo, Spinning Jenny
jan 13 fri M.D.C., Phobia, Copout, Capitalist Casualties, Bludgeon, No-Less (Slap A Ham Records Fiesta Grande)
jan 14 sat Man Is The Bastard, Lack Of Interest, Spazz, Stapled Shut, Evolved To Obliteration (Redwood City), Nuclear
        Armed Hogs (Slap A Ham Records Fiesta Grande)
jan 20 fri Ill Repute, Bad Samaritans, Sharon Tate, Not My Son, Man Bites Dog
jan 21 sat Fifteen, Witticus, Sheephead, Struggle Buggies
jan 27 fri Shoegazer, Nothing Cool, Blow Holes
jan 28 sat Voodoo Glow Skulls, Big Steamy, Enclave, Your Mother, Wooly Mammoth
jan 29 - mar 09 no Shows at 924 Gilman Street (earthquake upgrade)
mar 10 fri Spitboy, Strawman, J-Church, A Minor Forest, Ten Days Later
mar 11 sat Queers, Swingin' Utters, Los Huevos, The Criminals
mar 17 fri Pansy Division, Dead And Gone, The Potatomen, Black Fork, Tantrums
mar 18 sat The Fixtures, Das Klown, Cancer Alley, Strychnine
mar 24 fri Tilt, Mr. T Experience, Good Ridance, Wynona Riders, The Nards
mar 25 sat Fitz Of Depression, Screw 32, Multi-Facet, Behead The Prophett, No Lord Shall Live, Murder City Devils,
        Noggin
mar 31 fri Krupted Peasant Farmerz, Red #9, Roil, The Curbs, Apeface (Farmhouse comp. record release)
apr 1 sat Hellbillies, Schlong, Groovie Ghoulies, Sharon Tate, The Cherries (L.A.)
apr 7 fri Heyokay, Link 80, 9 Days Wonder, Poor Impulse Control, Matewan, Oader Forresion, Adjective Noun
        (new band night)
apr 8 sat Yahmos, Siren, Second Coming, Exhale, Amber Inn
apr 14 fri Wynona Riders, Multi-Facet, Zoinks! (Reno), Dartboard, Nothing Cool
apr 15 sat Final Conflict, Capitalist Casualties, Dead And Gone, Emission, Strychnine
apr 16 sun Black Fork, Nuclear Winter, Area 51, Ned Kelly, 3 Years Down, Multi-Facet, The Criminals, Tether
        (moved from the union hall, Oakland)
apr 21 fri Tilt, A.F.I., Lapaz, Kid Dynamo, He's Dead Jim
apr 22 sat Trusty (D.C), One Spot Fringehead, Harvest Theory
apr 28 fri Excuse 17 (Oly), Solid Gold, Fisticuff's Bluff, The Hundred Holiday, The Original Two
apr 29 sat Fifteen, Fury 66, Wrongway Right, Squat, Therapeutic
may 5 fri Spitboy, Black Fork, U.X.A., Mushface (L.A.) Trench
may 6 sat Spazz, No Less, Muzumuzu Suru
may 12 fri Screw 32, Gus (Van), Multi-Facet, Sheephead, Tantrums
may 13 sat Solid Gold, Second Story Window, Kerosene 454, The V.S.S. (CO), Ned Kelly, 3 Years Down, The Criminals
may 19 fri Total Chaos, Serpico (NY), Sideshow (Nebraska), Riotgun (L.A.), Moist
may 20 sat Schlong, Roger Music, E.D.A. (Japan), Chumpslap, Hypochondriacs, Struggle Buggies
may 26 fri Hellbillies, Wankin' Teens, Mental Pygmies, Donuts (L.A.), Poor Impulse Control
may 27 sat The Mr. T Experience, Parasites, Dr. Badd, Squirtgun, Sparker
jun 2 fri A.F.I., Defiance, Kisses And Hugs (N.Y.), Subincision, The Need
jun 3 sat Wynona Riders, Black Fork, Eight'na Quarter, Operation Ernsty, The Hope Bombs (Black Fork tour benefit)
jun 9 fri Dystopia, Wellington (AZ), Excruciating Terror, Radioactive Lunch, Highway 66 (FL)
jun 10 sat Mudwimin, Bimbo Toolshed, Fibulator, Wretched Ethel, Erik Core, Raggedy Ann
jun 16 fri PeeChees, Cars Get Crushed, The Waydowns, A Minor Forest, Plaight
jun 17 sat Five Year Plan (L.A.), Yah'Mos (Sacramento), Propagandhi (Canada), Contagon (VA), Unconquered (Reno)
jun 18 sun Screw 32, Fury 66 (SC), 3 Years Down, Struggle Buggies
jun 23 fri Swingin' Utters, Hellbillies, Los Rudiments, Scared Of Chaka (NM), Low Rent Souls (OR)
jun 24 sat Bollweevils, The White Kaps, Quadliacha (GA), Levelhead (GA), The Pomeranians, Incurable Complaint
jun 30 fri Big Steamy, Naked Angels (NC), Crutch, Tito, The Force
jul 1 sat Jack Killed Jill, Hogan's Heroes (NJ), Second Coming, Redemption 87
jul 7 fri Parasites, Submission, The Acrylics, Shifter, Loose Change
jul 8 sat Los Crudos (Chicago), Weston (PA), Exhaust, Blackkrown Stadt, Fucko
jul 9 sun Neurosis, Dead and Gone, Multi-Facet, Cancer Alley
jul 14 fri Feast Upon Cactus Thorns (AZ), Chalk (AR), Half-Man (NY), Tinkle Potty, Grain (Ohio)
jul 15 sat The Pist, Brutally Familiar, The Slackers (AL), The Dread, The Criminals
jul 21 fri Fifteen, Frail (PA), Spirit Assembly (PA), Matewan, Bisy Backson
jul 22 sat Avail, Rice, Siren, Gus (FL), Tired From Now On (FL)
jul 28 fri Spitboy, A Minor Forest, Crown Hate Ruin (D.C.), Against All Authority, Bureau Of The Glorious
jul 29 sat John Cougar Concentration Camp (San Diego), Loose Change, Slacker (PA), Gob (Canada), Skidfish (ID)

aug 4 fri Assuck (FL), Man Is The Bastard, Assfort (Japan), Capitalist Casualties, Cancer Alley
aug 5 sat Wynona Riders, Quincy Punx (MN), Helv, Brother Inferior (OK), Attempted Erns (TX)
aug 6 sun Sleater-Kinney, Raggedy Ann (South Bay), Candice Cameron, The Fancies (women in punk show)
aug 11 fri A.F.I., Anti-Flag (PA), Ida, Wet-Nap, The Wobblies
aug 12 sat Unbroken, Impel, Amber Inn, Ig-88, Matewan
aug 18 fri Squirtgun, Whirleybird (VA), Wrong Way Right, Kid Dynamo, Plinko
aug 19 sat Screw 32, Bouncing Souls (NJ), Policy Of 3 (PA), Shotmaker (Canada), Hutch (OR)
aug 25 fri Good Riddance, La Paz (San Lorenzo), Flemmings, Skyscraper, Life After Johnny
aug 26 sat Schlong, Lizards, The Flies, Rick Starr, The Gimps
sep 1 fri Parasites, Cletus (SC), Famous Last Words, Mayhem, Nothing Cool
sep 2 sat Dead And Gone, Act Of Faith (GA), Subincision, Inquisition (Canada), Sake
sep 8 fri Varukers (England), Final Warning (N.Y./U.K.), Black Label, Encrusted, Terminal Disgust (TX)
sep 9 sat Hellbillies, Pansy Division, Your Majesty (D.C.), Les Turds (AL), Jacob Ham
sep 15 fri Naked Aggression, Oppressed Logic, Shove, The Doormats, Enclave
sep 16 sat PeeChees, Cars Get Crushed, Ohio Bluetip (D.C.), Calm, Physics
sep 22 fri Tilt, Hi-Fives, Sheephead, Wankin' Teens, He's Dead Jim
sep 23 sat Black Fork, Teenage Warning (Holland), Multi-Facet, K-Pants, Limp
sep 29 fri Fifteen, All You Can Eat, Gob, Inquisition (VA), Hell Mach 4 (VA)
sep 30 sat A.F.I., Heckle (NJ), Struggle Buggies, Hopebombs, T-61
oct 6 fri Hi-Fives, The Smugglers (Canada), The Need, Your Mother, Link 80
oct 7 sat Dead And Gone, Hose Got Cable (VA), Boy's Life (MO), V.B.F. (TX), Perilisium Cantos, Art Of Murder
oct 13 fri Swingin' Utters, Screw 32, Snap-Her (L.A.), Bo, Vertabrae
oct 14 sat Fifteen, Subincision, Rick Starr, Superhate (L.A.), Fetish
oct 20 fri Trusty (D.C.), Yahmos, No Fraud (FL), Harvest Theory, Rue
oct 21 sat Bus Driver, Tarn, Charity Case, F-Hole, Better Than Your Hand, Utter Bastard, Concubines, Ten Ton Halo
       (new band night)
oct 27 fri Groovie Ghoulies, Chumpslap, Sick Little Monkey (TX), Spinning Jennies, The Gimps
oct 28 sat Multi-Facet (last show), Hot Rod Shopping Cart, Squat, Apeface, Erik Core (I.W.W. Benefit)
nov 3 fri God Is My Co-Pilot, Squirtgun, Cars Get Crushed, Torches To Rome, Skyscraper
nov 4 sat Vktms, Blag Dahlia, Criminals, Loudmouths, Decon (Palm Springs)
nov 10 fri Fifteen, Leftovers, Hellbillies, Bisybackson, Half Empty (Needle Exchange Benefit)
nov 11 sat Bikini Kill, Gala (Tokyo), PeeChees, Emily's Sassy Lime (L.A.)
nov 17 fri The Queers, 3 Out Of 4, Loose Change, The Struggle Buggies, Belligerents
nov 18 sat Link 80, Sake, Mickey And The Big Mouths, Grout, Allegiance To None (Independent Arts Coalition Benefit)
nov 19 sun Lunachicks, Black Fork, Spinning Fish, Wobblies
nov 24 fri Matewan, Calm, Q-Factor, Both Hands Broken, Patient Zero
nov 25 sat Everready, A Minor Forest, 3 Years Down, Portraits Of Past, Malcriada
dec 1 fri Tribe 8, Pansy Division, Wankin' Teens, Stone Fox, Erik Core (International Aids Day Benefit)
dec 2 sat Subincision, Loose Change, Goodfellas, Falling Sickness, Thugs From Mars
dec 8 fri Wynona Riders, Sharon Tate, Original 2, Plinko, Noisegate
dec 9 sat Krupted Peasant Farmerz, The Dread, Red #9, The Barfeeders, Hairy Italians
dec 15 fri Mr. T Experience, Groovie Ghoulies, The Hi-Fives, Bomb Bassets, Aquamen
dec 16 sat Citizen Fish, Hellbillies, Calavera (L.A.), Poor Impulse Control, Barking Spiders
dec 23 sat The Rudiments, Yah Mos, Link 80, Sick Teens (TX), Veronica (TX)
dec 29 fri Media Blitz, Juke, Loose Change, Wet-Nap, Heyokay
dec 30 sat A.F.I., Heckle (NJ), Struggle Buggies, The Force

1996
----

jan 5 fri Phobia, Spazz, Charles Bronson (Illinois), Crom, Noothgrush (Slap-A-Ham's Fiesta Grande #4)
jan 6 sat Capitalist Casualties, Cattlepress (NYC), Dystopia, Lack Of Interest, Gob (Reno), Locust (San Diego),
       Agents of Satan (Slap-A-Ham Fiesta Grande #4)
jan 7 sun Boba Fett Youth, Half Empty, The Criminals, F.Y.P., Wet-Nap (show moved to Gilman from Old Northside
       Theater)
jan 12 fri Young Pioneers (VA), Scared Of Chaka (NM), The Gain (L.A.), Sam's Laff, Girl's Soccer
jan 13 sat Dead And Gone, Blackfork, Sheephead, Tantrums, The Criminals (Zafio Records Showcase/Benefit)
jan 19 fri Subincision, Wynona Riders, Impact, The Hope Bombs, Yellow
jan 20 sat Tilt, White Trash Debutantes, Nails Of Hawaiian (Japan), Noisegate, Box Butchers (San Diego)
jan 26 fri Mishaps, Mighty Blue Balls, Spies Like Us, The Plumbers, Silage, Hank Stram, Feitzer, Rerelith (New Band
       Night)
jan 27 sat Ignite (L.A.), Redemption 87, Both Hands Broken, Torches To Rome, Kublai Khan
feb 2 fri Subincision, Wankin' Teens, Link 80, Wet-Nap, Tinklepotty
feb 3 sat Oppressed Logic, Strychnine, Skavin, The Need, Young And The Useless (Free Radio Berkeley Benefit)
feb 9 fri Abscess, Noothgrush, Pale Existence, Agents Of Satan, E.T.O., Butt
feb 10 sat Good Riddance, Blackfork, Chumpslap, Dog Pound (NJ), Thugs From Mars
feb 16 fri Capitalist Casualties, Oppressed Logic, Subincision, Greed (L.A.), The Young And The Useless (Punker Than
       Puke Benefit)
feb 17 sat Fifteen, The Leftovers, Bisybackson, Fetish
feb 23 fri J-Church, Red #9, 3 Years Down, Oliver, Adjective Noun U.K.
feb 24 sat Link 80, Parasites, Hellbender (NC), Erik Core

mar 1 fri All You Can Eat, Rickets (OR), Death Wish Kidz (WA), The Criminals, Muscle Bitches (Canada), Yanky Wuss (OR)

mar 2 sat A Minor Forest, Torches To Rome, Instant Girl, Leadfoot Broadcast, Super Soldier Serum

mar 8 fri Screw 32, Siren, S.P.S. (Czech Rep.), Curbside

mar 9 sat Cars Get Crushed, The V.S.S., Calm, Uranium 9 Volt, Kublai Khan

mar 10 sun Swingin' Utters, Redemption 87, Poor Impulse Control, The Lowdowns

mar 15 fri Dead And Gone, Blackfork, El Dopa, Art Of Murder, Apeface

mar 16 sat Final Conflict (L.A.), Five Year Plan, Blag Dhalia, Half-Empty, Nothing Cool

mar 22 fri Malcriada, Electrocutes (OR), Therapeutic, Red Scare, Farouke

mar 23 sat Ex-Ignota, Adjective Noun, Patient Zero, Perilisium Cantos, Chuck Norris Is The Hit Man

mar 29 fri Askin For It (formerly Abuncha Fucking Idiots, aka A.F.I.), Groovie Ghoulies, Limp, Tiger Army

apr 5 fri Bouncing Souls (NJ), Ten Foot Pole, The Rudiments, Alien Spy, Triple A

apr 6 sat Hellbillies, Sheephead, Loose Change, The Gimps, Driving Wheels

apr 12 fri Subincision, White Trash Debutantes, No Motive (L.A.), Cards In Spokes (FL), Snap Krackle Drop (AZ)

apr 13 sat Good Riddance, Fury 66, Struggle Buggies, Cavities, Willies

apr 19 fri Eldopa, Noisegate, Cypher In The Snow, Dirt Bike Gang, Erik Core

apr 20 sat The Pist (CT), Jon Cougar Concentration Camp (San Diego), The Dread, Half-Empty, The Tantrums

apr 26 fri Groovie Ghoulies, Pee Chees, Wankin' Teens, Nothing Cool, Stinkaholic

apr 27 sat Funeral Oration (Holland), Red #9, D.B.S. (Canada), Ten Dead Men (Canada), Falling Sickness

may 3 fri Subincision, The Criminals, Link 80, Half-Empty, American Steel (Copwatch Benefit)

may 4 sat Piss Jar, Angry Samoans, Tarn, Barfeeders, Better Than Your Hand

may 10 fri Cell Block, The Lubes, Flat Planet, Tijuana Gasser, Bonafido, The Pures, Cog

may 11 sat A Minor Forest, The V.S.S., 3 Years Down, Skyscraper, Shove

may 17 fri Dead And Gone, Instant Girl, Lost Goat, The Leadfoot Broadcast, Beautiful Ugly

may 18 sat Naked Aggression, Schlong, Jacks (IL), Wet-Nap, Utter Bastards (Punk Prom)

may 24 sat Blackfork, Sake, Grout, Frantics (SC), Dial Panama 7

may 25 sat Redemption 87, Second Coming, Q-Factor, The Promise Ring (WI), Collateral Damage (L.A.)

may 31 fri Struggle Buggies, Spinning Jennies, Four (CO), Brainsick (WA), Toxic Narcotic (MA)

jun 1 sat The Parasites, Boris The Sprinkler (WI), Horace Pinker (AZ), N.R.A., The Jerks, The Lizards

jun 7 fri Propagandhi (Canada), Zero Tolerance Task Force (AZ), Yellow Brick Roadkill (AZ), Mental Pygmies

jun 8 sat Eldopa, Noisegate, Ojo Rojo, Fields Of Shit, Masked Men

jun 14 fri Fifteen (last show ever), Wynona Riders, Siren, Fetish, Vintage 46 (Larkin Street Youth Benefit)

jun 15 sat Suppression, Eucharist (VA), Huasipungo (NY), Inquisition (Canada), Everymen (Canada)

jun 16-21 The Big Movement Artist Collective Annual Gilman Art Show Extravaganza

jun 21 fri Heckle (NJ), Link 80, Oppressed Logic, The Force

jun 22 sat Dirt Bike Gang, Sta-Prest, The Vegas Beat, Sleater-Kinney (Dirtybird Fest)

jun 28 fri Death Wish Kidz, The V.S.S., The Leadfoot Broadcast, Patient Zero, Juhl (CO)

jun 29 sat Hellbillies, Sheephead, Discount (FL), My Pal Trigger (FL), Wimpy Dicks

jul 5 fri Screw 32, Inquisition (VA), Sleepasaurus (NY), Buford (S. Calif.), Busdriver

jul 6 sat Blackfork, Los Canadiens (FL), Submission Hold (Canada), Jasta 14 (CT), In Vain (CT)

jul 12 fri Blanks 77 (NJ), Against All Authority (FL), The Criminals, Detestation (OR)

jul 13 sat Shades Apart (NJ), Spanakorzo (San Diego), Lesser Of Two (FL), Dillinger Four (MN), Wade (ND)

jul 19 fri Vktms, Slacker (PA), The Undecided (Canada), Hope Bombs, Gut Monkeys

jul 20 sat Instant Girl, Calm, Malcriada, Bluebird (L.A.), Enclave

jul 21 sun Seein' Red (Holland), Torches To Rome, Constantine Sankathi (MI), Anasarca (MD), Palatka (FL), Set Vector (OR)

jul 26 fri 924 Gilman DIY Festival

jul 26 fri Groovie Ghoulies, Sawpit (Japan), Struggle Buggies, Your Mother, Wobblies

jul 27 sat 924 Gilman DIY Festival

jul 27 sat Pee Chees, The V.S.S., Trauma (IL), Black Label (Santa Cruz)

jul 28 sun 924 Gilman DIY Festival

aug 2 fri Tilt, Red #9, Big Fella, Psychodrama (NM), Ex Presidents

aug 3 sat Lifetime (NJ), Crumbs (FL), Griver (NC), Clairmel (FL), Dead Man's Choir (WA)

aug 9 fri Man Is The Bastard, Blackfork, The Criminals, Pud (WA), Red Scare

aug 10 sat Mr. T Experience, The Tantrums, Grapefruit (HI), Anti-Flag (PA), D.B.S. (Canada)

aug 16 fri Ninety Nines, Drown In Empathy, God Stomper, Simon Says, The Misanthropists, Sad Boy Sinister, Drag Inferno (new band night)

aug 17 sat Schlong, Roger Music, Sharon Tate, Tinklepotty, Alternative Sections

aug 23 fri PeeChees, Wankin' Teens, Emily's Sassy Lime, Manta Ray (CO), The Vatican

aug 24 sat Avail, Screw 32, Subincision, His Hero Is Gone (TN), Leadfoot Broadcast

aug 30 fri Run For Your Fucking Life (San Diego), Parasites, Sheephead, Cletus, Exhaust (GA), Mean People (OR)

aug 31 sat Redemption 87, Collateral Damage (L.A.), 1134, Built To Last, Rely

sep 6 fri Gauze (Japan), Assfort (Japan), Dead And Gone, Spazz, Eldopa

sep 7 sat Naked Agression, Hellbillies, Couch Of Eureka, Anti-World (OR), Backside

sep 13 fri Piss Jar, Ojo Rojo, Fields Of Shit, Noisegate, Red Scare (ABC No Rio Benefit)

sep 14 sat Link 80, Teenage Warning (Holland), Poor Impulse Control, S.F.B.

sep 20 fri Stitches (L.A.), Goober Patrol (England), The Automatics (OR), Chumpslap, The Bastards

sep 21 sat The V.S.S., Instant Girl, Hell Mach 4 (VA), Dragon Rojo, Hero

sep 27 fri J Church, John Cougar Concentration Camp (San Diego), Hellbender (OR), American Steel, Big Bubba

sep 28 sat The Queers (NH), The Smugglers (Canada), Hellbillies, Adjective Noun, The Need

oct 4 fri Spies Like Us, Alien Spy, Triple A, Abecadarians, Flat Planet
oct 5 sat Sake, Ojo Rojo, Serpico (NY), Apeface, Red Rockets (WA)
oct 11 fri Kerosene 454 (D.C.), Blue Tip (D.C.), Malcriada, Amber Inn, Blue Bird (L.A.)
oct 12 sat Sacto Hoods, Accustomed To Nothing, Pressure Point, Model American
oct 18 fri Young Pioneers (VA), Cars Get Crushed, Instant Girl, The Leadfoot Broadcast, Fun People (Argentina)
oct 19 sat Groovie Ghoulies, Black Fork, Ubzub, Cypher In The Snow, Sad Pygmy (TX)
oct 25 fri The Nuns, The Criminals, Kingpin, 98 Mute, Angry Little Man
oct 26 sat U.S. Bombs, Bonecrusher (Los Angeles), Vintage 46, Puke (West Bay All Ages Club Benefit)
nov 1 fri Hi-Fives, Tantrums, Thorazine (PA), Los Huevos, Bananas
nov 2 sat Dystopia, Damad (GA), Eldopa, Useless I.D. (Israel), Word Salad (NM)
nov 8 fri V.S.S., Malcriada, Mocket (Oly), Starlight Desperation Show, Nexus 6
nov 9 sun Man Is The Bastard, Excruciating Terror, No Less, Benumb, Faggot
nov 10 sun Art Show at 924 Gilman Street
nov 15 fri Hellbillies, Subincisicon, This Bike Is A Pipe Bomb (FL), Shit Bastards, Thugs From Mars
nov 16 sat H2O (NY), Powerhouse, Second Coming, Built To Last, Sacto Hoods
nov 22 fri PeeChees, Couch Of Eureka, Smart Went Crazy (D.C.), Peaceful Meadows (San Diego), Hero
nov 23 sat The Joykiller, Groovie Ghoulies, Good Riddance, Redemption 87, Struggle Buggies (Epicenter Benefit)
nov 29 fri Karp (Oly), Jenny Piccolo, Norman Mayer Group (D.C.), Bunnyfoot Charm
nov 30 sat Citizen Fish, Black Fork, The Fixtures, Ojo Rojo, Wet-Nap
dec 1 sun Subincision, Hope Bombs, Bobby Joe Ebola And The Children McNuggits, Erik Core, Impact, Slackbone,
        Yellow, Macho Gaspacho, Uberkunst, Nexus Junket, My Sunny Disposition, Eggs Erroneous, mc Bob Weirdos
        (Spam compilation cd release)
dec 6 fri Eldopa, Melt Banana (Japan), Rudolph, Apeface, Super Arachnoid Space
dec 7 sat Tribe 8, The Criminals, Loudmouths, Cypher In The Snow, Lost Goat
dec 13 fri Instant Girl (last local show ever), Q Factor, Sharks Kill, Shove, Staple
dec 14 sat The Love Pigs (Japan), Schlong, Fields Of Shit, The Lizards, Masked Men
dec 20 fri A Minor Forest, Cars Get Crushed, Ebony Brown, Saint James Infirmary (Food Not Bombs)
dec 21 sat Dystopia, Noothgrush, Red Scare, Deadbodieseverywhere
dec 27 fri Boy Kicks Girl, Human Beans, Teargas Pinup, Christian Prohibition, The Oozies, Dogfather, Visitor 42
        (New Band Night)
dec 28 sat Heckle (NJ), Loose Change, Fury 66, Pay Neuter (AZ), The Goodfellas

1997
----

jan 3 fri PeeChees, The Drags (N.M.), Submission Hold (Canada), Scared Of Chaka (NM), Ribbon Fix
        (Tenth Anniversary Weekend Show)
jan 4 sat A.F.I., Eldopa, Art Of Murder (Tenth Anniversary Weekend Show)
jan 5 sun Robert (eggplant and drummer), Bo, The Criminals, Human Beans (Gilman workers party)
jan 10 fri Hellnation (KY), Slight Slappers (Japan), Cavity (FL), Spazz, Noothgrush, Utter Bastard (Slap A Ham
        Records Fiesta Grande #5)
jan 11 sat Lack Of Interest, Discordance Axis (NJ), Enemy Soil (VA), Capitalist Casualties, Benumb (Slap A
        Ham Records Fiesta Grande #5)
jan 17 fri The Hellbillys, Link 80, D.B.S. (Canada), I-Farm (NY), 99's
jan 18 sat Dead & Gone, Ojo Rojo, Q Factor, Saint James Infirmary (Prisioners Literature Project Benefit)
jan 24 fri Missing Link, Critical Mass, Slow Gherkin, Monkey, Alvin George And His Fly Right Orchestra
jan 25 sat Parasites, Tantrums, Pinhead Circus (CO), Alien Spy, Smoke Jumpers
jan 26 sun Team Dresch, Pansy Division, Cypher In The Snow, Half Empty, Eye Claudia
jan 31 fri Black Fork, Malcriada, Dragon Rojo, Adjective Noun, American Steel (self defense benefit)
feb 1 sat The Stitches, The Workin' Stiffs, Lil' Bunnies, Lowdowns, Reducers
feb 7 fri Schlong, Your Mother, Wet-Nap, Useless I.D., Dogfather (Benefit Haight Ashbury Free Clinic)
feb 8 sat Angry Samoans, Subincision, Bimbo Toolshed, Sam The Butcher (AZ), The Pants
feb 14 fri Born N Razed, Makarac, Letters To The Lord Himself (Canada), T-Tauri (L.A.), Nexus 6
feb 15 sat F.Y.P., Das Klown, Fields Of Shit, Apeface, Human Beans
feb 21 fri Sake, Ten Days Late (Canada), Bobby Joe Ebola & The Children McNuggets, Human Beans, Dogfather
        (Benefit for Building a Community of Resistance)
feb 22 sat Good Riddance, Lifetime, Struggle Buggies, The Thumbs (Annapolis), The Wrestlers, Jacob Ham
feb 28 fri Exhumed, Grim Skunk (Canada), Tarn, Lickety Split (DC), Godstomper
mar 1 sat The Gaia, Capitalist Casualties, The Dread, Fields Of Shit, Gunpro (Portland)
mar 7 fri Babyland, Molitov Cocktail (NY), Wet-Nap, Magnum, Tinkle Potty
mar 8 sat Black Fork, The Softies, Couch Of Eureka, Original Two, E.F.S., The Clayton Experience
mar 14 fri Hellbillys, Subincision, Eveready (San Diego), Murder City Devils, 3 Out Of 4
mar 15 sat Ignite (L.A.), Second Coming, 1134 (L.A.), Model American, Rely
mar 21 fri Oedipus, Nowhere Fast, Mac Crows, Beyond All Hope, Burnt Sienna, The Neumans (new band night)
mar 22 sat V.S.S., Malcriada (last show ever), Saint James Infirmary, Shaharazad (Bakersfield), Angel Assassins
mar 23 sun Mr. T Experience, Parasites, Squirtgun, Butcher Holler (Oly)
mar 28 fri Eldopa, Fields Of Shit, Young And The Useless, Masked Men, Misanthropists (Frank Depression
        Record Benefit)
mar 29 sat The Wives, Cypher In The Snow, Semi-Sweet, Vegas Beat, Eye Claudia
apr 4 fri Ink & Dagger (PA), Amber Inn (Seattle), Botch (Seattle), Nine Iron Spitfire (Seattle), Harkonan
apr 5 sat Ojo Rojo, Noisegate, Remission (WI), The Enemies

apr 11 fri Screw 32, Saint James Infirmary, Red Scare, Uranium 9 Volt, The Sellouts
apr 12 sat Missing Link, Norman Mayer Group (D.C.), Nothing Cool, Curbside
apr 18 fri Schlong, Eldopa, Pachinko (WI), Strychnine, East Bay Mud
apr 19 sat Trusty (D.C.), Red #9, Transmegetti (N.J.), He's Dead Jim, Toyboat
apr 25 fri Dead & Gone, Black Fork, Lost Goat, Art Of Murder, Rolling Studs (Dead & Gone/Black Fork tour benefit)
apr 26 sat H2O (N.Y.), Redemption 87, Powerhouse, Fury 66 (Santa Cruz), Straight Faced (L.A.), Useless I.D.
apr 27 sun Stratford Mercenaries (England - ex Crass and Dirt), Cypher In The Snow, Lachrymose, The Enemies
may 2 fri Christdriver (WA), Dystopia, Man Is The Bastard, Apeface, Noothgrush
may 3 sat V.S.S., Cars Get Crushed, The Great Unraveling, Blank (MD), Fire Engine Grey
may 4 sun Citizen Fish, The Criminals, American Steel
may 9 fri Subincision (cd release), Fetish, Soda Pop Fuck You, Chemical Imbalance, Problem (N.Y.)
may 10 sat 924 Gilman cleanup
may 16 fri Bouncing Souls (NJ), Hellbillys, Anti-Flag (PA), Pen (Chicago), Boxcar Children (OK)
may 17 sat Spazz, Code 13 (MN), Fall Silent (NV), Benumb, Ringwurm
may 23 fri Redemption 87, Sparkmarker, Three Years Down, Gob (Vancouver), Model American
may 24 sat Naked Aggression, Final Conflict (L.A.), Funeral Oration (Holland), Bastards (Sacramento),
    Misanthropists
may 25 sun 25 Ta Life (N.Y.), Hoods (Sacramento), Powerhouse (moved from Bomb Shelter)
may 30 fri Sleater Kinney (WA), Peechees, Farouke, Angora, Project Hate, Rally 200 (Punk Prom Nite)
may 31 sat Noisegate, Ubzub, Crooked Letter Youth (Miss), Sean Porters Midnight Lazer Beam, Erik Core,
    Moe! Staiano's Moe!kestra!
jun 6 fri Link 80, Powerhouse, Eye Claudia, The Mooches, Mr. Harlequin (Berkeley High School Radio Benefit)
jun 7 sat Siren, Your Mother, Wet-Nap, Alien Spy, Tilt Wheel
jun 13 fri Spinning Jennings, Workin' Stiffs, The Receivers (ex Struggle Buggies), Wallside (MICH), Worker
jun 14 sat Fang, Wag Platy (Japan), Smash Your Face (Japan), The Frantics (SC)
jun 20 fri Avail, The Criminals, Parasites, Smokejumpers, Revolvers (MD)
jun 21 sat Quixote (MI), Violent Nine (CO), Yum Yum Tree (NY)
jun 27 fri Apeface, Cause (WA), Intifada (WA), Clabberhag (WA), Adhesives (WA)
jun 28 sat Against All Authority, Falling Sickness, Assorted Jelly Beans, Eyeliners (N.M.), Decrepit (WA)
jul 4 fri Black Fork, Bisy Backson (WA), Gunpro (OR), Hardship (OR), Ellery Queens
jul 5 sat Groovie Ghoulies, The Crumbs (FL), Operation Cliff Clavin (IN), Fear Without Falling (NC), Homesick (UT)
jul 11 fri Hellbillys, United Blood, Asbestos, My Lai (Chicago), Kid With Man Head (NJ)
jul 12 sat Peechees, The Criminals, Cold Cold Hearts (DC), Monorchid (DC), Smallville
jul 13 sun A Minor Forest, 400 Years (VA), Sleepytime Trio (VA), Fire Engine Grey, Enclave
jul 18 fri Amber Inn, John Dawn Baker, State Route 522 (WA), Drift (Canada), Angel Assassins
jul 19 sat Poison Idea, Electric Frankenstein (NY), Eightna-Quarter, Deface, Zero Bullshit
jul 25 fri Huasipungo (NY), Noisegate, Violent Society (Philly), Profits Of Misery (NY), Choking Victim (NY)
jul 26 sat no show at 924 Gilman street (show cancelled)
aug 1 fri Stitches (L.A.), One Man Army, Willhaven (Sacramento), Bodies (Sonoma), Wednesdays (AL)
aug 2 sat His Hero Is Gone (TN), Brother Inferior(OK), Black Army Jacket (NY), Noothgrush, Luxvanitas (MN)
aug 3 sun Bonfire Madigan, Angora (San Jose), The Midriffs (UT), The Otterpops, Molly Bolt (Oakland), workshops
    (girl convention show)
aug 8 fri Converge (MA), Botch (Seattle), Exhale, Training For Utopia
aug 9 sat Strychnine, The Enemies, Cream Abdul Babar (FL), The Boy Sets Fire (DE), A Sometimes Promise,
    Antiques (TX)
aug 15 fri Babyland, Summerjack (ID), Special Olympics (Canada), Grapefruit (HI), Empire O' Shit
aug 16 sat Vandals, Ojo Rojo, Receivers, Ataris
aug 22 fri Pansy Division, Smokejumpers, Wet-Nap, D.B.S. (Canada), No Fraud (FL)
aug 23 sat F.Y.P., Furious George, Subincision, Orlock (VA), Sinker (N.Y.)
aug 24 sun In My Eyes (Boston), Built To Last, Second Coming, Rely
aug 29 fri Workin' Stiffs, Fury 66, The Force, Showdown 76 (Canada), Belvederes (Canada)
aug 30 sat 3 Years Down, Fire Engine Grey, Waxwing (WA), Fuck You I'm Stealing Home (Canada)
sep 5 fri Powerhouse, Hoods, Turbo AC's (NY), The Tantrums, Zero Bullshit
sep 6 sat Red Scare, Eye Claudia, Christian Prohibition, 976, Conviction
sep 7 sun The Golden Showers (Berlin), The Audience, Swipe (Japan), Fluff Girl
sep 12 fri Black Fork, Rolling Studs, Candy And The Hot Dice (WA), Rumor 39, Knucklehead (WA)
sep 13 sat Hellbillys, Anti-World (OR), Fun People (Argintina), Fetish, Slobber
sep 19 fri B-Sides, 3 Hung Lo, The Moscones, Lucy's Crush, The Void, The Mooks (new band night)
sep 20 sat 1332 (ex. Eldopa), Vktms, Hot Water Music (Gainsville, FL), Ann Barretta (VA)
sep 21 sun Neurosis, Logical Nonsense, Lost Goat, Kiss It Goodby
sep 26 fri Tilt, Karp (WA), Criminals, Young Pioneers (VA), At The Drive In (TX)
sep 27 sat Collateral Damage, Trial (Seattle), No Innocent Victims (S. Barbara), Rely (last show), Model American
oct 3 fri Jenny Piccolo, Dragon Rojo, Saint James Infirmary, Harriet The Spy (OH), Thumbnail (AR)
oct 4 sat Capitalist Casualties, No Less, Benumb, Misanthropists, Godstomper
oct 10 fri Diesel Boy, Limp, Flatus (N.Y.), Loose Change, Jato
oct 11 sat Spanakorzo (San Diego), Short Wave Channel (San Diego), Calabash Case (San Diego), Uranium 9 Volt,
    Shove
oct 17 fri Smugglers (Canada), Peechees, Hi-Fives, Dagobah (England),
oct 18 sat Suspects, Fixtures (L.A.), Das Klown (San Diego), Society Gone Madd (L.A.), No One's Victim
oct 24 fri Corrupted (Japan), Hellchild (Japan), Word Salad (N.M.), Disassociate (N.Y.), Noothgrush

oct 25 sat Sake, Submission Hold (Vancouver), Mocket (WA), Love Is Laughter (WA), Get Hustle (San Diego)
oct 31 fri Missing Link, Mikey of Your Mother, Critical Mass, Roger Music (OR), Jacob Ham
nov 1 sat Black Fork, Lost Goat, Little Princess, The Enemies, Los Rabbis
nov 7 fri Babyland, Nuclear Rabbit, Tongue, Magnum, It's In The Stars
nov 8 sat Dystopia, Phobia, Ojo Rojo, Conviction
nov 14 fri Wet-Nap, D.B.S. (Canada), Dwarf Bitch (NV), Human Beans, 7X
nov 15 sat Man Is The Bastard, Noelle Hanrahan/Prison Radio Project, No Less, Noisegate, Stone Vengeance
nov 21 fri Turmoil (N.Y.), Straight Faced (L.A.), Second Coming, Today Is The Day (TN), Downshift (Hayward)
nov 22 sat The Dread, Fuckface, The Faggz, Los Terribles (CO)
nov 28 fri Swingin' Utters, One Man Army, Union 13, Side Project, Debris
nov 29 sat Subincision, Kirby Grips, Nothing Cool, Astrolloyd, Your Mother
dec 5 fri Hellbillys, Workin' Stiffs, American Steel, Soda Pop Fuck You, The Forgotten
dec 6 sat Stratford Mercenaries (U.K.), Strychnine, Shanti, The Enemies, Character Builder
dec 12 fri Baseball Furys, Cope, Towards An End, The Inadequates, Cardboard Pin-Up, Lost Cause (new band nite)
dec 13 sat Slow Gherkin, The Unsteady (San Diego), The Ziggens (L.A.), K.G.B., Blast Bandits (Fresno)
dec 19 fri Strife (L.A.), Powerhouse, Hoods, Receivers, All Bets Off (Bomb Shelter Benefit)
dec 20 sat Smokejumpers, Luckie Strike, Alien Spy, Bobby Joe Ebola And The Children McNuggets, Poontwang
         (Xmas Show)
dec 21 sun A.F.I., The Criminals, Saint James Infirmary, Fetish
dec 26 fri no show at 924 Gilman Street
dec 27 sat Juke, Eye Claudia, Big Skull Science, Manner Farm (Canada), You Fucking Hippy (Canada)

1998
----
jan 2 fri Senseless Apocalypse (Japan), Man Is The Bastard, Black Army Jacket (N.Y.), Lack Of Interest, Gasp,
         Noothgrush (Slap A Ham Fiesta Grande #6)
jan 3 sat Slight Slappers (Japan), Grief (MA), Capitalist Casualties, Asshole Parade (FL), Phobia, God Stomper
         (Slap A Ham Fiesta Grande #6)
jan 9 fri Hi-Fives, Auntie Christ, Black Fork (last show), The Donnas, Bomb Bassets (Lookout Records'
         10th Anniversary Party)
jan 10 sat Union 13 (L.A.), Fury 66, Limp, Fetish, The Fuses (MD)
jan 16 fri Monkey, Critical Mass, Blind Spot, Adjustments, Flat Planet
jan 17 sat His Hero Is Gone, Saint James Infirmary, Talk Is Poison, Conviction
jan 18 sun Anal Mucus, Adjective Noun, Michael Dean, The Enemies, Ding Dang, Little Tin Frog, 3 Hung Low,
         Captured By Robots, Nme, The Idiots, Avant Gardeners, Bay Bombers, The Secretions (Geekfest 13 - The
         Year of Geek)
jan 23 fri Your Mother, Nuclear Rabbit, The Bar Feeders, 976, Midnight Lazer Beam
jan 24 sat Criminals, U.X.A. (L.A.), Subincision, 3 Years Down, B-Sides
jan 30 fri Workin' Stiffs, Loose Change, Reducers, Burdens
jan 31 sat Creeping Death, Rocket Queens, American Metal, Iron Vegan, Motley Jews, Blizzards Of Schnozz,
         Anal Tap (Metal Madness Show)
feb 1 sun Clean up day
feb 6 fri United Blood, 1332, Ding Dang, The Enemies, Turbo Jurk
feb 7 sat PeeChees, Locust, Sunshine (Czech. Rep.), Starlite Desperation, The Audience
feb 13 fri Hoods (cd release), Downshift, Uranium 9 Volt, Standoff
feb 14 sat Hellbillys, Tantrums, W.hen E.very T.hings N.ot A.ctually P.lanned, The Wrestlers, Drunk & Disorderly
feb 20 fri Strife, Powerhouse, Fury 66, Straight Faced, Built To Last
feb 21 sat Insult (MA), Noothgrush, The Dread, Medication Time
feb 27 fri Saint James Infirmary, Criminals, Cypher In The Snow, Conviction, The Great Divide
feb 28 sat Blanks 77, Randumbs, Forgotten, Burdens
mar 6 fri Slow Gherkin, Siren Six! (MN), The Nobodys (CO), Pinhead Circus (CO), 78 Rpm's
mar 7 sat Wankin' Wayne, Hi-Fives, Johnny Dilks And His Visitacion Valley Boys, The Mutilators (Johny Cash Tribute)
mar 8 sun Ensign (NJ), Second Coming, Indecision (NY), Model Amercian (cd release)
mar 13 fri Moral Crux, Plan 9 (OH), The Force, Goodfellas, Snubnose
mar 14 sat Naked Aggresion, Red #9, Subincision, Eye Claudia, Nowhere Fast
mar 20 fri Romantic Gorilla (Japan), Spazz, Abstain (L.A.), Talk Is Poison, Medication Time
mar 21 sat Workin' Stiffs, Ojo Rojo, Strychnine, The Enemies (East Bay Menace Benefit)
mar 22 sun fixing stuff day
mar 27 fri Tilt (record release), Criminals, American Steel, Loca-Vida, End Of The World
mar 28 sat Good Riddance, The Audience, 90 Pound Wuss (WA), Dragus (L.A.), Its In The Stars
apr 3 fri Defiance (OR), The Dread, Misanthropists (last show), Religious War (OR), Cathy Ames (million punk
         march #2)
apr 4 sat Bluetip, Kerosene 454, Sweet Belly Freak Down, Uranium 9 Volt
apr 10 fri Groovie Ghoulies, Smart Went Crazy (D.C.), Receivers, Devil Bean (AR)
apr 11 sat Unhinged (Belgium), Dystopia, Zed (PA), Noisegate, Noothgrush
apr 17 fri Damad (GA), Word Salad (NM), Lost Goat, Talk Is Poison, Conviction
apr 18 sat Behead The Prophet, No Lords Shall Live, Cypher In The Snow, Men's Recovery Project (VA), Thrones (WA),
         Pants
apr 24 fri 25 Ta' Life (N.Y.), Hoods, Jason Lee (Japan), Towards An End
apr 25 sat Your Mother, Krupted Peasant Farmerz, Erik Core, Useless I.D. (Israel), Gutmonkeys

apr 26 sun Art Show

may 1 fri Workin' Stiffs, One Man Army, Three Years Down, Model American, No One's Victim

may 2 sat No Less, Benumb, Godstomper, Shedwellas, Slobber

may 8 fri Automatics (OR), B-Sides

may 9 sat Submission Hold (Canada), Jenny Piccolo, Noisegate, Poisen Pen, Pawns

may 15 fri Avail (VA), Saint James Infirmary, Ann Berretta (VA), Artemus Pyle

may 16 sat Stitches, No Talents (France), Bobby Teens, Cretins (MA), Bodies

may 22 fri Willhaven (Sac.), And You Will Know Us By The Trail Of The Dead (TX), Nerve Agents, Exhale (Sacramento), Box (Davis)

may 23 sat Fury 66, The Force, Traitors (Chicago), Summerjack (ID), Keener (Canada)

may 29 fri Babyland, Wet-Nap, Eye Claudia, 400 Blows (Canada), Jailbait (Punk Prom)

may 30 sat Subincision, Soda Pop Fuck You, Nuclear Rabit, The Thumbs, Electric Summer (Japan)

may 31 sun K.G.B., Bitesize, The Mooches, Ten Times Fast, Human Beans, Space Man Spiff, Dory Tourette, Stackables, Pop Tards (Free Radio Berkeley Benefit)

jun 5 fri Against All Authority (FL), Criminals, American Steel, Cards In Spokes (FL), Angora

jun 6 sat F.Y.P., Ultra Bid'e (Japan - N.Y.), Frantics (S.C.), 976, Hers Never Existed

jun 12 fri Strychnine, Federal Offense (CO), The Enemies, Booby Hatch (TN), Party Of Helicopters (OH)

jun 13 sat Workin' Stiffs, Speak 714 (L.A.), Flatus (N.Y.), Turbo A.C.'s (NY), U.K.S.

jun 14 sun Tongue, Stranger Death 19, God Hates Computers, Bobby Joe Ebola And The Children McNuggets, Astrolloyd, Luckie Strike, Lung Butter, Defile, Anancastia, Apeface, Medication Time, Lesser Of Two, Majestic 12, Cataract, The Mooches (Geeks Vs. Pirates)

jun 19 fri Magnum, Conviction, Milemarker (S.C.), Waxwing (WA), Kitty Badass (CT)

jun 20 sat Joby (W.A.), Cypher In The Snow, Harum Scarum (OR), What's Her Face (OR), Ample Plexion

jun 26 fri Fall Silent (NV), Unruh (AZ), Fucking Thunder (AZ), Noothgrush, We All Fall Down (UT)

jun 27 sat Wet-Nap, I-Farm (N.Y.), Zero Tolerance Task Force (AL), Project Wyse (Canada), Dogfather

jun 28 sun Meri St. Mary, John Shirley, Richard Cadrey, Jemuel, Daniele Willis, Chicken John, Michael Peppe, Julia Vinograd (Punk Poetry Show) (Benefit Women's Refuge)

jul 3 fri Your Mother, Operation Cliff Clavin (IN), Gob, Rank Review (ID), Bobby Joe Ebola And The Children McNuggets, The C.M.N.

jul 10 fri Seein' Red (Holland), Bread & Circuits, Fun People (Argentina), Yaphet Koto, Former Members Of Alfonsin

jul 11 sat Soda Pop Fuck You, Receivers, Magnum, Mr. Harlequin

jul 17 fri Hellnation (KY), Capitalist Casualties, Ambassador 990 (OH), Sea Of Cortez (AZ), Disassociate (N.Y.)

jul 18 sat Fixtures, Subincision, Larry (WA), Veteran Flashbacks (San Diego), Smocks (ID)

jul 24 fri Buzzoven, Divide n Conquer (France), Season To Risk, Robotinichka (France), Lesser Of Two

jul 25 sat Assuck, Reversal Of Man (FL), From Ashes Rise (TN), Pretentious Assholes (IL), Astrolloyd (Pinole)

jul 26 sun Ensign (N.J.), Eyelid (L.A.), Nerve Agents, Adam Antium (L.A.)

jul 31 fri Los Crudos (Chig.), Mk Ultra (Chig.), My Lai (Chig.), Fields Lay Fallow (PA), Talk Is Poison

aug 1 sat Tilt, Hellbillys, American Steel, All The Answers (Canada), The Gods Hate Kansas

aug 7 fri Cave In (N.Y.), Botch (WA), 18 Visions (San Diego), Jesuit (PA), Ire (Canada)

aug 8 sat Drop Dead, Ruins (Japan), Inflicted, Noothgrush, Murder Takes No Holiday

aug 9 sun cleanup

aug 14 fri Babyland, Wet-Nap, Tres Kids (GA), Quadaliacha, Secretions

aug 15 sat Ten Yard Fight (MA), Straight Faced (cd release), Built To Last (San Diego), Fast Break (CT), All Bets Off

aug 21 fri 88 Finger Louie, Loose Change, 78 Rpms, Punch The Clown, Red Session

aug 22 sat Union 13, Sam The Butcher (AZ), Kill Your Idols (N.Y.), Nerve Agents, Death By Stereo (L.A.)

aug 23 sun Trial, Powerhouse, Model American, Left With Nothing (Seattle)

aug 28 fri Criminals, Plan 9, Red Scare, Pants, Shotwell

aug 29 sat Capitalist Casualties, Short Hate Temper (TX), At The Drive In (TX), Fat Day (MA), Artimus Pyle

sep 4 fri A.F.I., Good Riddance, Fury 66, Towards An End

sep 5 sat Hoods, United Blood, Nuclear Rabbit, Forced Life, Second Coming (Breakout Records Benefit)

sep 11 fri Slow Gherkin (cd release), Wet Nap, Soda Pop Fuck You, The Gods Hate Kansas, Hasselhof

sep 12 sat Phobia, Dystopia, Mark Bruback (sp), Whore House Of Representatives (WA), Subtract To Zero (WI), Defile

sep 18 fri Conviction, Geri Live, Creeps On Candy, Astrolloyd (cheap date night #2)

sep 19 sat F.Y.P., Quincy Punx (MN), Sex Offenders, Moscones

sep 25 fri Jello Biafra (sp), Erik Core

sep 26 sat Babyland (record release), Magnum, God Stomper, D.B.S. (Canada), Mooches

oct 2 fri Fleas And Lice, Toxic Narcotic (Boston), Calloused, Medication Time, Lesser Of Two

oct 3 sat Excruciating Terror, Hoods, Atom & His Package, Bad Acid Trip, Benumb

oct 9 fri Siren Six, 78 Rpm, Pain (GA), Edna's Goldfish (N.Y.)

oct 10 sat Electric Frankenstein, Hellbillys, Receivers, Cheap Dates,

oct 16 fri One Man Army, American Steel, Bodies, Sam The Butcher, No One's Victim

oct 17 sat Powerhouse, Fury 66, Second Coming, Model American

oct 23 fri Christdriver (WA), Grimple, Noisegate, Artimus Pyle, Derailer (KS)

oct 24 sat Wet-Nap, Critical Mass, Your Mother, Ten Times Fast, The Wonder Years

nov 6 fri Butchies, The 3rd Sex, Harum Scarum, Talk Is Poison

nov 7 sat Vae Victus (NV), The Karcus Line

nov 13 fri Spazz, Melt Banana (Japan), Human Thurma (VA), Creeps On Candy, Medication Time

nov 14 sat Phantom Rockers (England), Criminals, Plan 9, Billyclub (TX), B-Sides

nov 20 fri Plan 9, Caverage (WA), Black Cat Music

nov 21 sat Lost Goat, Bongzilla (WI), Noothgrush, Next Of Kin, Sledwreck

nov 22 sun The Gods Hate Kansas, Adjective Noun, Carniseal, Captured By Robots, God Hates Computers, Jailbait, Othello's Revenge, Big Train (Geek Fest #23)

nov 27 fri Apeface, Reina Aveja (Gainsville), The Enemies, Panthro U.K. United 13 (Gainsville), Held Hostage

nov 28 sat Logical Nonsense (N.M.), Grimple, Word Salad, Red Scare, Godstomper

dec 4 fri Hoods, Benumb, Abstain, All Bets Off, Ruido (L.A.)

dec 5 sat Babyland, Los Cincos, Gob (Canada), Midnight Lazer Beam

dec 11 fri Clone (ex 7-Year Bitch), Welcome (WA), The Gods Hate Kansas, The Little Deaths, By A Thread

dec 12 sat Talk Is Poison, Bisy Backson, Hers Never Existed, Deep Throats, Black Cat Music

dec 18 fri Exhumed, Weakling, Black Goat, Scratched, What Happens Next (Epicenter Zone Benefit)

dec 26 sat Aus-Rotten (PA), Resist And Exist, Lesser Of Two

1999
----

jan 1 fri Dystopia, Seized (Canada), Noothgrush, Trailer Hitch, Yankee Wuss

jan 2 sat In My Eyes (MA), Nerve Agents, Kill Me Kate (San Diego), Plan A Project (N.J.)

jan 8 fri Spazz, Gob (Reno), Geri Live

jan 9 sat Criminals, Jailbait, Pezz

jan 15 fri Receivers, American Steel, Bobby Joe Ebola And The Children McNuggets, Black Cat Music, No Comply

jan 23 sat Young Pioneers, Locust, Nervous System (WA)

jan 29 fri Groovie Ghoulies, Pansy Division, Subincision (cd release), Loudmouths, Kablamies (Joel's Birthday)

feb 5 fri Cost, Operation Cliff Clavin, Wonder Years, Los Rabbis, Jocks

feb 6 sat Drunk Horse, Cuts, Red Stars, Richmond Sluts (Benefit Fire Victims)

feb 12 fri Noothgrush, Capitalist Casualites, What Happens Next?, AFU (L.A.)

feb 13 sat Excruciating Terror, 16, Crom, Lana Dagales

feb 19 fri Jim Yoshi Pileup, Midnight Lazer Beam, Casiotone For The Painfully Alone, The Natural World

feb 20 sat Redemption 87, All Bets Off, Model American, Eddie Haskells

feb 26 fri Penelope Houston And The Scavengers, American Steel, Eyeliners (NM), Cuts

mar 5 fri Deathreat (TN), Talk Is Poison (last show), Your Mother, Artimus Pyle, Emo Summer

mar 6 sat Nothing Cool, Songs For Emma, Pussy Gato, Drunk Horse

mar 12 fri Merrick, Scratchabit, 5th Limb, Emo Dance Party '99, Kung Fu Grip, Ostinato (new band night)

mar 13 sat Babyland, Creeps On Candy, 400 Blows (L.A.), Pawns

mar 19 fri Powerhouse, Hoods, Sworn Vengance, Disepticons

mar 20 sat Harum Scarum (OR), Red Scare, Cost, Hers Never Existed, Knockups

mar 21 sun Wonder Years, Bobby Joe Ebola & The Children McNuggets, Scratchabit, Jailbait, Supper, Moscones, 789, Los Rabbis (Geekfest)

mar 26 fri Mu330 (St. Louis), Slow Gherkin (Santa Cruz), Alkaline Trio (Chicago), Chinkees (San Jose) (Asian Man Records Showcase)

mar 27 sat Plan 9 (Misfits Tribute), Nerve Agents, Zed (PA), Facet (CO), Intreped A.A.F.

mar 28 sun cleanup

apr 2 fri Midnight Lazer Beam, Black Cat Music, Bunnyfoot Charm (WA), The Gods Hate Kansas, Streets & Avenues

apr 3 sat Jim Yoshi Pileup, The Most Secret Method (DC), Paper Lantern (L.A.), Court & Spark, The Cave-In

apr 9 fri Defiance, Hellbillys, Riffs (WA), Fracas, Aka Nothing

apr 10 sat Robot Assassins, Jalopaz, Captured By Robots, Pantyraid, Lesser Of Two (Reclaim May Day Benefit)

apr 11 sun Dropkick Murphys, Oxymoron, Ducky Boys, No One's Victim

apr 16 fri Dystopia, Noothgrush, Strong Intention (MO), Twenty-Third Chapter

apr 17 sat American Steel, The Enemies, Slingshot Episode (IN), Bobby Joe Ebola And The Children McNuggets, Fits

apr 24 sat Morgion, High On Fire, Benumb, Mange, Black Goat

apr 25 sun Hers Never Existed, Scratchabit, Mr. Harlequin (last show), Title Fight, Outside-In, Jessica Rabbit, Leisure (Berkeley High School Show Case)

apr 30 fri Ensign, Kill Your Idols, Second Coming, Show Of Hands, D.F.M.

may 1 sat Babyland, Midnight Lazer Beam, 400 Blows, Audry Le

may 2 sun art show

may 7 fri Submission Hold (Vancouver), Creeps On Candy, Manner Farm (Canada), Cost, Sledwreck

may 8 sat Receivers, The Gods Hate Kansas, Cuts, Sam The Butcher (AZ), Merick

may 14 fri Burned Up Bled Dry (AK), Phobia (L.A.), Capitalist Casualties, Geri Live (last show), Godstomper (Slap A Ham 10th Anniversary)

may 15 sat Fuck On The Beach (Japan), Lack Of Interest (L.A.), Spazz, Gasp (L.A.), Kralizec (Reno - last show) (Slap A Ham 10th Anniversary)

may 21 fri Bread And Circuits, Out Hud, Sissys

may 22 sat Abcess, Exhumed, Hail Mary (N.Y.), Ruido, Feces Munchers

may 23 sun Geekfest Benefit Yard Sale, music by Dori Tourette (acoustic), Mick (acoustic), Mucus' Folk Band

may 28 fri The Wunder Years, 78 Rpms, Bobby Joe Ebola And The Children Macnuggits, Flatus (N.J.), Summerjack (ID)

may 29 sat Plan 9, Anti-World (OR), B-Sides (record release), Johnny X & The Groadies (OR), Eddie Haskells

jun 4 fri Red Scare (Oakland), Your Mother, Captured By Robots, Dairy Queens, Yogurt (Geekfest Benefit Show)

jun 5 sat Hellnation, Wisigoth, Smash Your Face, The Heck, Noothgrush

jun 6 sun Cave-In (MA), Isis (MA), Jerme Spew (sp), Time In Malta

jun 11 fri Hellbillys, Oozzies, Larry And The Go-Nowheres (WA), Pig Iron, Three Years Down

jun 12 sat Anti-Flag, Smugglers, Subincision, Pinhead Circus, Sticklers (HI)

jun 13 sun Aus-Rotten, Mark Bruback, Anti Product (N.Y.), Sarah O' Donald, Scratchabit (1999 Primate Freedom Tour)
jun 18 fri The Need (WA), Plus Ones, Lies, Kablamies, Panty Raid (Punk Prom '99)
jun 19 sat Criminals, Blood Brother (WA)
jun 25 fri Phobia, Capitalist Casualties, Axium (Portland), My Lai (Chicago), Kungfu Rick (Chicago)
jun 26 sat Nameless And Faceless, Yaphet Kotto, Keepers Of Tyme, Life's Halt, Soofie Nun Squad (AK),
        Christianne Dugan-Cuadra (spoken)
jun 27 sun Trial (Seattle), Catharsis, Zegota, What Happens Next?, Your Mother
jul 2 fri OxBow, Creeps On Candy, Redscare (TN), Pankration (TN), Kill Sadie, The Kill In Me
jul 3 sat Midnight Lazer Beam, Wunder Years (cd release), Good Night Moon, California Lightning
jul 10 sat The Outside, 90 lb Wuss, Cost, Mercury, Jocks
jul 16 fri Criminals (record release), Plus Ones, Hers Never Existed (record release), Matterhorn
jul 17 sat Coming Correct (N.J.), Dysphoria, All Bets Off, Page 99 (VA), Kill The Man Who Questions
jul 23 fri Second Coming, Fall Silent (ND), Creation Is Crucifixion, Time In Malta, Fleshies
jul 24 sat Rye Coalition, Bratmobile, Black Cat Music, Subtonix, The Kill In Me
jul 31 sat Reversal Of Man (FL), Combat Wounded Veteran (FL), Lesser Of Two, Artemus Pyle, A Death
        Between Seasons (N.Y.)
aug 1 sun Tight Brothers From Way Back When, Bangs, Cuts, Waxwing
aug 6 fri Groovie Ghoulies, Three Years Down, Thee Impossibles, Young Hasselhoffs, Merrick
aug 7 sat Locust (San Diego), Devola (N.Y.), I Robot (N.Y.), Black Cat 13, Anasazi
aug 13 fri Hoods, 97A (N.J.), State Of The Union (WA), Renfield
aug 14 sat Dr. Know (L.A.), Subincision, Medication Time, D.S.F.A. (L.A.), Wormwood (KS)
aug 20 fri Plan 9 (Misfits Tribute), Ding Dang, Bobby Joe Ebola And The Children MacNuggits, Frustraters, Dori
        Tourette And The Skirtheads
aug 21 sat Grimple, Brother Inferior (OK), Che Chapter 127 (Canada), Vendetta Red (WA), Exit Wound
aug 27 fri Trial, Second Coming, Talk Is Poison, Full Speed Ahead (N.Y.C.), Pig Iron
aug 28 sat Melt Banana (Japan), Spazz, Lack Of Interest, Black Queen, Lana Dagales
aug 29 sun Bobby Joe Ebola And The Children MacNuggits, Lucas, Fleshies, 789, Milhouse, Sneaky Greekins,
        Sorry About The Fire, Jocks, The Dillion McKay's, spoken word (Geek Fest)
sep 3 fri D.B.S. (Canada), Cost, The Gods Hate Kansas, The Enemies, Jocks (cd release) (New Disorder Fest)
sep 5 sun Swingin' Utters, Stitches, Phoenix Thunderstone, Enemy You
sep 10 fri Tilt, Plus Ones, Tantrums, Venus Bleeding, Summerjack (ID)
sep 17 fri The Need (WA), Automaticans (L.A.), Me Me America (WA), Wolf Colonel (OR), Panty Raid
sep 18 sat Dystopia, Counterblast (Sweden), Guyana Punchline (N.C.), Godstomper, Noisegate
sep 24 fri Citizen Fish, Mark Bruback (sp), Criminals, Malcontent (OR), Brain Blood Volume
sep 25 sat T.S.O.L., Hellbillys, Mutiny (Aus.), Nerve Agents, Intrepid A.A.F.
oct 1 fri The Suffering, Fourspeed, Shut Up Donny, Monster Squad, Little Birds, Animal Number 54 (new band night)
oct 2 sat Talk Is Poison, High On Fire, Noothgrush, Exit Wound (Oakland)
oct 3 sun In My Eyes (Boston), Bane (Boston), Model American, Staircase
oct 8 fri Powerhouse, The Sick, Bullyrag (AZ), 46 Short (L.A.)
oct 9 sat Strychnine, Toxic Narcotic (Boston), Shoot The Hostages, Murder Takes No Holiday
oct 15 fri At The Drive In, Hers Never Existed, Homeless Wonders (WY), The Kill In Me
oct 16 sat Monkey, Link 80, Thorazine (PA)
oct 22 fri film "Mary Jane's Not A Virgin Anymore"
oct 23 sat Criminals, Enemies, The Curse (OR), Side Sixty Seven, Hillbilly Devil Speak (AZ)
oct 29 fri American Steel (record release), Black Cat Music, The Cost, Yankee Wuss (OR), War Machine (OR),
        Nothing Cool
oct 30 sat Plan 9, Anti-World (Portland), Keno Champ (S.D.), Blue Flesh Velvet
nov 5 fri Yaphet Kotto, Atom And His Package, Your Mother, Sean Na Na (Seattle), Charmless
nov 6 sat Nuclear Rabbit, Bobby Joe Ebola And The Children Mac Nugitts, Roger Nusic (OR), Erik Core, Jocks
nov 12 fri Subincision, Alkaline Trio (Chicago), Crosstops, Kiss The Clown (Orange County), Faded Angels
nov 13 sat High On Fire, Noothgrush, Sour Vein (New Orleans), Lana Dagales
nov 19 fri Dead And Gone, Ink And Dagger, Time In Malta, Bluebird (L.A.), Icarus Line (L.A.)
nov 20 sat Nerve Agents, Tiger Army, Lonely Kings, Dragus (L.A.), Very Be Careful (L.A.)
nov 27 sat Plus Ones, 78 Rpms, Towards An End, Hot Rod Circuit (Conn), Floaters
dec 3 fri The Gods Hate Kansas, Disarm (TN), Downway (Canada), Kill Me Kate (S.D.)
dec 4 sat Capitalist Casualties, Life's Halt (L.A.), No Reply (L.A.), What Happens Next
dec 10 fri Talk Is Poison, The Cost, Severed Head Of State, Scratchabit, Kill In Me
dec 11 sat Babyland, Midnight Lazer Beam, Jim Yoshi Pile Up, Uberkunst
dec 17 fri Good Riddance, Scared Of Chaka (N.M.), Creep Division, Los Rabbis, Little Birds
dec 18 sat Second Coming (record release), Hoods, All Bets Off, Low Life, Vulgar Pigeons

2000
----

jan 7 fri Hellbillys, Three Years Down, Suicide Doors
jan 8 sat Dystopia, Like Flies On Flesh (TX), Shiva (L.A.)
jan 9 sun Your Mother (last show), Schlong, Drippy Drawers, Girls Soccer, Jenny Piccolo
jan 15 sat Creeps On Candy, Hers Never Existed, Honey Suckle Serantina (Canada), Grand American Modified
jan 21 fri Capitalist Casualties, Benumb, Self-Inflicted (L.A.), Progeria (L.A.), Exit Wound
jan 22 sat Morigon, Noothgrush (L.A.), Godstomper, Lana Dagales
jan 28 fri Groovie Ghoulies, Pansy Division, Subincision, Jocks, Bob Weirdos (Joel's birthday bash)

jan 29 sat Hi-Fives, Criminals (last show ever), Tantrums (record release), B-Sides, Dory Tourette And The Skirtheads
feb 4 fri Sangre Amado, Brainboodvolume, Murder Takes No Holiday, Scurvy Dogs, Comatoast (pyrate punx discount night)
feb 11 fri Crow (Tokyo), Talk Is Poison, War Machine (OR), A.F.U. (L.A.), Artimus Pyle
feb 12 sat Strychnine, Smokejumpers, Enemies, All The Answers (Canada), Lacky (TX), Blue Flesh Velvet
feb 13 sun Yaphet Kotto, Time In Malta, Mile Marker, All-Scars (D.C.), Volume 11
feb 18 fri Good For Nothing, Inner Struggle, Growth Of Alliange, Stitch, Killing Independent, Suburbanites (new band night)
feb 19 sat Yogurt, 50 Million, Human Beans, Fleshies, Chita Vajina (Geekfest Benefit)
feb 25 fri Plan 9, Wesley Willis (Chicago), Jerme Spew (spoken word), Bobby Joe Ebola And The Children MacNuggits, Today Is My Super Spaceout Day
feb 26 sat Phobia (L.A.), Gehenna (San Diego), Spider Cunts, (N.Y.), Exhumed
mar 3 fri Alkaline Trio (Chicago), Gods Hate Kansas, Towards An End, Honor System (Chicago), Merrick
mar 5 sun Bobby Joe Ebola And The Children Macnuggits, Dairy Queens, Evan Symons (Canada), Jocks, Mark B. And The Alphabets, Finky Binks, Open mic spoken word event, Heather P., Steph Colhane, Jamie Kennedy, Dory Tourette And The Skirtheads, Enemies, Pilgrims, Fleshies, Off Balance, Armada (Santa Cruz), plus Dean and Mike's happy hour (S.P.A.M. Records Showcase)
mar 10 fri Hellbillys, Venus Bleeding, Model American, Mad At Sam
mar 17 fri Strychnine, Murder Takes No Holiday, Molotov Cocktail (N.Y.), 46 Short (L.A.), The Sissies (IN)
mar 18 sat Nerve Agents, No Reply (L.A.), Carry On (L.A.), Distillers (L.A.), God Hates Computers (OR)
mar 19 sun Locust, Le Shok, Convocation Of, Subpoena The Past
mar 24 fri Moe! Staiano, Vacuum Tree Head, Species Being, Barney, Rumah Shakit
mar 25 sat Iron Vegan, Harum Scarum, Hers Never Existed, Rondelles, Scratchabit
mar 31 fri Noothgrush, Old Grandad, Exitwound, Lana Dagales (Libertatia 2000 Campout Benefit)
apr 1 sat From Ashes Rise (TN), Abstain, Remains Of The Day (L.A.), Dairy Queens
apr 7 fri Fall Silent, Good Clean Fun (D.C.), Life's Halt (L.A.), What Happens Next, Redrum
apr 8 sat 30 Second Fury, Spishak, Shoot The Dog, Iron Ass (new band night)
apr 14 fri Sworn Vengeance, All Bets Off, Contenders For The Crown, Inner Struggle, Threat Assessment
apr 16 sun Stratford Mercenaries (England), 46 Short (L.A.), Scurvy Dogs
apr 21 fri Plus Ones, Divit, Camera Obscura (S.D.), Dory Tourette And Ashly (acoustic), Four Speed
apr 22 sat Misery (MN), Extinction Of Mankind (England), Murder Takes No Holiday
apr 28 fri East Bay Drifters, Tantrums, Thumbs (MD), Smokejumpers
apr 29 sat Babyland, Black Cat Music, Blackie (N.M.), Pale Horse
apr 30 sun Blitzkrieg (U.K.), The Forgotten, Intrepid A.A.F., Society Dog
may 5 fri Code 13 (MN), Abstain (L.A.), United Super Villains (WI), Godstomper, Vulgar Pigeons
may 6 sat Hellbillys, Strychnine, Enemies, Trots (WA), Fracas
may 12 fri Sangre Amado, Bloodhag (WA), Totimoshi, Noise Of Struggle
may 13 sat Nerve Agents, Oozzies, Trust Fund Babies, Hopelifter, Lugosi
may 19 fri Dairy Queens, Phantom Limbs, Off Balance, Pilgrims, Missing Cousins (D.I.Y. Skillshare Conference)
may 20 sat Submission Hold (Canada), Tragedy (OR), Honeysuckle Serontina (Vancouver), Manchurian Candidates (Austin), Vae Victus (Reno) (D.I.Y. Skillshare Conference)
may 26 fri Hoods, Kill Your Idols (N.Y.), Adamantium, In Control
may 27 sat Capitalist Casualties, Despite (WI), Plutocracy, Maneurysm, Neighbors (San Diego), Ruido (L.A.) (Six Weeks Records Showcase)
may 28 sun Record Swap
jun 2 fri Subincision (cd release), Venus Bleeding, Intrepid A.A.F., Homeless Wonders (CO), Ranters
jun 3 sat Dystopia, Scum Brigade (Sweden), Benumb,Tarantula Hawk (S.D.), Contravene (AR)
jun 10 sat Plus Ones, Smokejumpers (last East Bay Show), Allison Williams (OR), Sarah Bishop (MN), Coleman Lindbergh (MN) (Punk Prom)
jun 11 sun Brian Ass, Human Beans, Bobby Joe Ebola And The Children Macnuggits, Pindrum Swing, Blast Rocks (Geek Fest)
jun 16 fri Bane, Calloused, Adamantium, Death By Stereo, Vulgar Pigeons
jun 17 sat Iron Vegan, Noothgrush, Kojak (VA), PCP Roadblock (VA), Hell Hath No Fury (N.M.)
jun 23 fri Time In Malta, Engine Down (D.C.), 7 Days Of Samsara (WI), Grand American Modified, Under A Dying Sun
jun 24 sat Damad (GA), What Happens Next?, Crispus Attucks (D.C.), Brainbloodvolume
jun 30 fri The Cost, Hi-Fives (last show), Bobby Joe Ebola And The Children MacNugitts (cd release - last show), Maurice's Little Bastards (WA), Party Of Helicopters (OH)
jul 1 sat Midnight Lazer Beam, Convocation Of (VA), Merrick, Heart Of Snow
jul 7 fri Dead And Gone, Catheter (CO), Hog (Mexico), Laughing Dog (N.M.), Jeno (CO)
jul 8 sat Dystopia, Scratchabit (Benefit for Nicki Sicki Legal Defense)
jul 14 fri Wolfpack (Sweden), Men's Recovery Project, Axiom (OR), Deface
jul 16 sun Alkaline Trio, Chris Murray, Mu330, Link 80, Lawrence Arms, Honor System, Dan Potthast, Mike Park (Plea for Peace Tour)
jul 21 fri Dory Tourette And The Skirtheads, Blood Brothers (WA), Divit, Panty Raid, Erase Errata
jul 22 sat American Steel, Enemies, Thumbs (MD), I-Farm (N.Y.), Pitch Black
jul 28 fri Plan 9, Loose Change, Debris, The Weakerthans (Canada), Big Link, Potatomen (acoustic)
jul 29 sat Gehenna, Demon System 13 (Sweden), Malefaction, Falling Over Drunk
jul 30 sun Dillinger Escape Plan (N.Y.), Candira (N.Y.), Isis (MA), Cadillac Blindside (MN)
aug 4 fri Hellchild (Japan), Benumb, Yellow Machine Gun (Japan), Spaceboy, Vulgar Pigeons

aug 5 sat The Causey Way, Black Man - White Man - Dead Man (WA), Boy Pussy USA (AR), Monday Mornings

aug 18 fri Raw Power (Italy), Capitalist Casualties, Life's Halt, No Justice, Tongue (L.A.), What Happens Next? (lp release)

aug 19 sat Time In Malta, Run For Your Fucking Life (San Diego), Suicide Party (N.Y./OR), Sangre Amado

aug 25 fri Hoods, 18 Visions, Punishment (PA), New Jersey Bloodline (N.J.), Lowlife

aug 26 sat Tilt, Nerve Agents, Missing 23rd, Turndown, Larry

sep 2 sat Blessing The Hogs, Zegota (N.C.), Kakistocracy (TN), Ludicra, Morbosidad

sep 3 sun El Sobs, Doozers, Feldman And Haim, Pink Swastika, Off Balance, Iron Ass, Finky Binks, Beckett and Friends, Blottos, Gazillions, Riff Randalls, Shoot The Dog (Geekfest)

sep 8 fri Black Cat Music, Summerjack (ID), Useless I.D. (Israel), Jocks, U.V.R.

sep 9 sat Fall Silent, Second Coming, Shitlist (MN), Holier Than Thou, Scholastic Death

sep 15 fri Kill Your Idols (N.Y.), Movielife (N.Y.), Oozzies (record release), Divit, Inner Struggle

sep 16 sat Dystopia, Anticon, Noothgrush, Tarantula Hawk (San Diego), Yeti (TX)

sep 17 sun clean up

sep 22 fri Strong Intention (MD), Berzerk (OR), Bad Acid Trip (L.A.), Bullshit Excuse

sep 23 sat Plan 9, Anti-World (OR), Venus Bleeding, Switchblade Kings, Eights & Aces

sep 29 fri Hellbillys (record release), Subincision, Fracas, Union Of The Dead, Monster Squad

sep 30 sat Yaphet Kotto, Pitch Black, Phantom Limbs, Sangre Amado, the Stolen Lives wall (Benefit October 22nd Coalition to Stop Police Brutality)

oct 6 fri Hammer Of Misfortunes, Amber Asylum, Remains Of The Day (OR), Bent Over Backwards (OR), Gault

oct 7 sat Stitches (L.A.), Goons, Le Shok (L.A.), Three Years Down, Deminer (Chicago)

oct 13 fri Black Cat Music, Drunk Horse, The Pattern, Fun People (Argentina), Derelectrics (N.M.)

oct 20 fri Human Beans, Jocks, Radio Activekids (San Pedro), Unit Breed, Quest For Quintana Roo (cheap date night)

oct 21 sat Throat Oyster, Sabians, Anonymus, The Congested Few, Dead Food, Cliftons (new band night)

oct 27 fri Elliott (KY), Jazz June (PA), Lovelight Shine (S.D.), Killing Independent

oct 28 sat Fron Ashes Rise (TN), Time In Malta, Born Dead Icons (Canada), Le Shok (S.D.), Lesser Of Two

nov 3 fri Slow Gherkin, Tsunami Bomb, Loose Change, Flatus, Homeless Wonders (WY)

nov 4 sat Tiger Army, Union Of The Dead, All Bets Off, Sean Na Na (MN)

nov 5 sun Dayglo Abortions (Victoria), Oppressed Logic, Decry (L.A.), Dekontrol (Canada), South 75 (TN)

nov 10 fri Lord Weird Slough Feg, Cruevo, Mr. Brainoil, Nocturnium, Insidious (Pyrate Discount Nite)

nov 11 sat Melt Banana (Japan), Vas (Japan), The Cost, World Inferno Friendship Society (N.Y.)

nov 17 fri Strychnine, Toxic Narcotic (Boston), Oozzies, Scurvy Dogs, Monster Squad, Insurgent (N.Y.C.), Potatomen

nov 18 sat The Sick, Lonely Kings, Towards An End, Youth Gone Wild, No Regrets (Benefit for Temenos Project - Tyler & Lauren's Birthday)

nov 24 fri Creep Division (N.Y.), F-Minus (L.A.), Amendment 18 (L.A.), Paris Texas (WI), A.K.A. Nothing

nov 25 sat Citizen Fish (U.K.), Time In Malta, Ding Dang, Cream Abdul Babar (FL), Drag-Body (FL)

dec 1 fri Plan 9, Kowalskis (N.Y.), American Heartbreak, Big Bubba (OR), Secretions

dec 2 sat Spazz (last show), Total Fury (Japan), Oath (N.Y.), Iron Lung (NV), Falling Over Drunk

dec 8 fri Link 80, Good Clean Fun (D.C.), The Cost, Kill The Messenger (SF), S.E.E.D. (Santa Rosa) (Benefit Toys for Tots)

dec 9 sat Phobia (L.A.), Grief (MA), 16 (L.A.), Noothgrush, Asunder

dec 15 fri Moe!Kestra!, Monopause, Pendulum, Iron Ass, Spezzarotto

dec 16 sat Yaphet Kotto, Lions Of Judah (S.D.), Blood Brothers (WA), The Shivering (S.B.)

dec 22 fri Dead And Gone, Phantom Limbs, Angel Dust, Justin Bailey, Fleshies

dec 23 sat Hammers Of Misfortune, Dekapitator, Black Goat, Sangre Amado, Black Queen

dec 29 fri Nerve Agents, American Nightmare, Kill Me Kate (S.D.), P.B.R. Street Gang (San Diego), Frisk

dec 30 sat Unseen (MA), F-Minus (L.A.), Intrepid A.A.F., Broken Society, Stockyard Stoics (N.Y.)

dec 31 sun Crucial Section (Japan), What Happens Next?, Sin Orden (Chicago), Scott Baio's Army (Denver), Godstomper

2001
----

jan 5 fri Remnants (Santa Rosa), Clumsy Bears, Eleventeen, Whorange, (new band night)

jan 6 sat Locust (S.D.), Beautiful Skin (N.Y.), National Acrobat, The Pattern, Heart Of Snow

jan 12 fri The Sick, Totimoshi, 7 Days Of Samsara (WI - with a fire Juggler), Vida Blue (IO), Sabians (ex members of Sleep)

jan 13 sat Stitches (L.A.), Tsunami Bomb, Starvations (L.A.), Derelectrics (N.M.), Labrats

jan 19 fri Plus Ones, The P.A.W.N.S., Strike-O-Matics (S.C.), This Bike Is A Pipe Bomb (FL), Bob Weirdos (Joel's Birthday)

jan 20 sat Groovie Ghoulies, Pansy Division, Subincision, Potatomen, Nicky Danger (acoustic), Sidekicks (Joel's Birthday)

jan 26 fri Tragedy (OR), Yaphet Kotto, Vae Victis (NV), Esperanza (L.A.), Under A Dying Sun

jan 27 sat no show

feb 2 fri Nerve Agents, All Bets Off, Three Years Down, Harbinger, Jemuel (spoken word), Blottos (Benefit Gilman Sound System)

feb 3 sat Bobby Joe Ebola And The Children McNuggitts (reunion), Drunk Horse, Eddie Haskells, Breathe In, Fuck Yea!, Avocado (Benefit Gilman Sound System)

feb 9 fri Hellbillys, Divit, Teenage Harlots, Deficient, Arno Corps (Austria)

feb 10 sat Life's Halt (L.A.), Rocket Queen (GnR tribute), Barry Man-O-War, Rosemary's Billygoat, Adversives (ID) feb 16 fri Bananas, Pitch Black, Shotwell, Pirx The Pilot, Rocknrolladventurekids

feb 17 sat Lack Of Interest (L.A.), Neighbors (S.D.), Black Hands (Canada), Iron Lung

feb 18 sun Good Riddance, Missing 23rd, Fire Sermon, Anti-Domestix, Lugosi

mar 2 fri Books Lie (NY), Living Under Lies (OR), Remnants, No Regrets, Fadeaways, LWL (NJ) (Cheap Date Night)

mar 3 sat Dr. Know, The Dread, Hot Box, Anal Mucus

mar 9 fri Dead And Gone, Sworn Vengance, Punishment (Philadelphia), Misdura (N.Y.), This Computer Kills (NV)

mar 10 sat Varukers (UK), 46 Short (L.A.), Scarred For Life (L.A.), Oppressed Logic, Facedown

mar 16 fri Dorry Tourette And The Skirtheads, Kill The Messenger, Lesser Of Two, The P.A.W.N.S.,
        Phoenix Thunderstone, Sugarlips

mar 17 sat Hoods (Sacramento), Benumb, Above The World, Chronic Disorder, Eulogy

mar 23 fri 18 Visions (L.A.), Walls Of Jericho (MI), Time In Malta, Undying (CT), Betray The Species

mar 24 sat Workin' Stiffs, Strychnine, Pitch Black, East Bay Chasers, For The Alliance

mar 30 fri Deathreat (OR), Ahisma (OR), Fuckgodintheface (OR), The Black, Creation Is Crucifixion

mar 31 sat Jocks (last show ever), The Cost, Fleshies, Quest For Quintana Roo, Chu Chi Nut Nut And The
        Pinecone Express, Sacrilegious

apr 6 fri Link 80, Counterfeit (S.D.), 5th Wheel (S.D.), Kung Fu Chicken

apr 7 sat Plus Ones, Evaporators (Canada), The Pattern, Dukes Of Hamburg, The Goblins/Skablins/
        Discoblins /Gothblins (Canada)

apr 13 fri Locust (S.D.), Dead And Gone, Honeysuckle Serontina (Vancouver), Tourettes Lautrec (S.D.),
        Last Great Liar (WA)

apr 14 sat Oozzies, 16 (L.A.), Red Light Sting (Canada), Powers Of Darkness... (Seattle), Antagony

apr 19-22 D.I.Y. Skillshare Conference

apr 20 fri Uberkunst, Blastrocks, Sissies (IN), Pirx The Pilot

apr 21 sat MU330, Slow Gherkin, Lawrence Arms (IL), Big D And The Kids Table, Short Round

apr 27 fri Atom & His Package (PA), Phantom Limbs, Har Mar Superstar (MN), Frisk, Shubunkins

apr 28 sat 7 Seconds, Throwdown (L.A.), Vitamin X (Holland), Over My Dead Body (S.D.), Breaker Breaker

may 4 fri Plan 9, Zodiac Killers, Reverend-B-Dangerous, Dorry Tourette And The Skirtheads, Knockoffs

may 5 sat Shikabane (Tokyo), Phobia (L.A.), Harum Scarum (OR), Vulgar Pigeons, Insidious

may 11 fri Subincision, Fracus, Thrice (L.A.), Next To Nothing (TX), Average Joe

may 12 sat The Sick, Wendy-O-Matic (spoken word), Impaled, Creuvo, Brainoil, Tearing Down Standards
        (Benefit Sparring Club)

may 18 fri Ensign (N.J.), All Bets Off, Playing Enemy (Seattle), Association Area (N.Y.), Blessing The Hogs

may 19 sat Pansy Division, Plus Ones, Dave Hill (World's Greatest Hypnotist), Iron Ass, Blottos (Punk Rock Prom -
        Benefit for India Earthquake Relief)

may 25 fri Controlling Hand (L.A.), Wormwood (WA), Goats Blood (OR), American Waste, Quick To Blame (N.Y.)

may 26 sat Divit, Reflector (Beijing, China), Enemy You, Quest For Quintana Roo, Tragedy Andy

jun 1 fri Alkaline Trio (IL), Hot Rod Circuit (CT), No Motiv (L.A.), Dashboard Confessional (FL), Bluejacket

jun 2 sat El Dopa, Deadbodieseverywhere, Shadow People, Ludicra, Ballast (Canada) (Cannabis Action Network)

jun 8 fri Enemies, Pitch Black Fleshies, Supersift (Canada), Texas Thieves

jun 9 sat Groovie Ghoulies, Influents, Red Planet, Mallrats (Sacramento), Goat Shanty (GA)

jun 10 sun Video night

jun 15 fri Strike Anywhere (VA), Missing 23rd (L.A.), Crispus Attucks (D.C.), Planesmistakenforstars (CO),
        Deadlock Frequency (CO)

jun 16 sat Nerve Agents, American Nightmare (MA), Fields Of Fire (L.A.), Affront (D.C.), Scissorhands

jun 22 fri Hoods (Sacramento), Fall Silent (NV), Clenched Fist (FL), Osiva (N.Y.), Hellcrew

jun 23 sat Hellbillys, Fartz (WA), Tossers (IL) Ruido, Fightbacks (IL)

jun 24 sun American Steel (record release), The Pattern, Agent 51 (L.A.), Parkway Wretch (AZ)

jun 29 fri Barfeeders, Pac-Men (CT), Hell After Dark, AKA Nothing, Maurice's Little Bastards (WA),
        Fuck Yea! Avocado (in bathroom)

jun 30 sat The Cost, Pg. 99 (VA), Majority Rule (VA), 7 Days Of Samsara (WI), Since By Man (WI),
        Creation Is Crucifixion

jul 1 sun Art Show

jul 6 fri Victim's Family, Fleshies, Once For Kicks (WA), Modern Machines (WI), Blottos

jul 7 sat Stitches (L.A.), Real McKenzies (Canada), Spits (WA), Eddie Haskells

jul 13 fri Special Duties (U.K.), Oppressed Logic, Violent Society (PA), Zero Bullshit, Born/Dead

jul 14 sat Lonely Kings, One Time Angels, Stay Gold (WA), Thought Riot, Youth Gone Wild

jul 15 sun Bobbyteens, Los Rabbis, Finky Binks, Off Balance

jul 20 fri Raw Power (Italy), Decry (L.A.), S.M.D. (L.A.), Scurvy Dogs, Blown To Bits

jul 21 sat Babyland (L.A.), 78 Rpms. Derelectrics (N.M.), Man Alive (CO), Philips & Renter

jul 27 fri Throw Down (L.A.), Good Clean Fun (D.C.), Count Me Out (VA), Time Flies (VA), Faded Grey (Las Vegas),
        Lab Rats

jul 28 sat Over My Dead Body (S.D.), Carry On (L.A.), Scissorhands, Black Lung Patriots (TX), Some Still
        Believe (Redding)

aug 3 fri Sworn Vengence, NJ Bloodline (N.J.), Settle The Score (Germany), Existence (Reno), Step (Tahoe)

aug 4 sat Toxic Narcotic (MA), Menstrual Tramps (MI), Emo Summer, Four Letter Words (L.A.), Shitty Wickets (L.A.)

aug 5 sun Talk Is Poison, Time In Malta, self defence class (maybe), Hell After Dark

aug 10 fri Defacto, 90 Day Men (IL), Assembly Of God (OH), Strong Intention (MD), Under A Dying Sun

aug 11 sat Toys That Kill (formerly F.Y.P.), Enemy You, Soophie Nun Squad (AZ), The Insurgent (N.Y.), Debris,
        Clarendon Hills (in store)

aug 12 sun Citizen Fish (U.K.), J-Church, Pirx The Pilot, Eleventeen, Selah (U.K.)

aug 17 fri Blood Brothers (WA), True North (FL), The Cost, Red Light Sting (Canada), Betray The Species
aug 18 sat Dr. Know, The Sick, Society Of Friends (TX), Manchurian Candidates (TX), S.T.F.U.
aug 24 fri Black Cat Music, Pitch Black, The H.S. (Canada), Spitting Teeth (WA)
aug 25 sat Fleshies (record release), Phantom Limbs (record release), Totumoshi, Bible Of The Devil (IL), Finky Binks, Los Rabbis (in store)
aug 31 fri What Happens Next?, They Live (N.Y.), No Time Left (N.Y.), Remains of the Day (OR), Scholastic Death
sep 1 sat Anti-45, Walken, Confidante, Prop 808, Creeps (Santa Cruz), N.C.S. (new band night)
sep 7 fri Carry On (L.A.), Champion (WA), Breaker Breaker, Saturday Supercade (OH), Fields Of Fire (L.A.)
sep 8 sat Quest For Quintana Roo, Lab Rats, Kill The Messenger, Relative (IN), Scissorhands
sep 9 sun movie night
sep 14 fri Groovie Ghoulies, Kevin Seconds, Sidekicks (record release), Secretions (Sacramento), Miso Militia
sep 15 sat Tragedy (OR), Run For Your Fucking Life (San Diego), fire breathing, film "behind The Screams" by Martin Crudo, film "Kamala's Revenge" by Eban Kwik Way, assorted films by Jules Kwik Way, Harum Scarum (OR), Funeral (OR), assorted films by Nick Zedd, film "Brainbox" by Bob Moricz (Punk movie night)
sep 16 sun Green Day, Influents, Thumbs (MD), One Time Angels, Agent 51 (L.A.) (Adeline Showcase)
sep 21 fri Slow Gherkin, 78 Rpms, Enemy You, Wisecracker (Germany)
sep 22 sat Yaphet Koto, Breaking Pangaea (PA), Jason Webley (Seattle), Box the Compass
sep 23 sun Subtonix, Running Ragged (Canada), "The Third Antenna" (documentary film)
sep 28 fri Erase Errata, Intima (OR), Total Shutdown, Ibobuki (WA), Impeller
sep 29 sat Life's Halt (L.A.), Demon System 13 (Sweden), Beware (L.A.), Blown To Bits, S.T.F.U.
sep 30 sun art show
oct 5 fri U.X.A. (L.A.), Subincision, Jonny X & The Groadies (OR), Gary's Agenda (AZ), Eugene
oct 6 sat Tight Brothers From Way Back When (WA), C-Average (WA), Three Years Down, Cherry Valence (FL), Peyote Calamity
oct 7 sun movie night
oct 12 fri One Line Drawing, Funeral Diner, Diefen Baker (Sweden), Til 7 Years Pass Over Him
oct 13 sat Dead And Gone, Cattle Decapitation (S.D.), Vulgar Pigeons, Wormwood (OR), Antagony
oct 19 fri What Happens Next?, Jellyroll Rockheads (Osaka), Ex-Claim (Tokyo), Crucial Attaack (NV), Sharp Knife
oct 20 sat Fleshies, Blast Rocks, Blottos, Gravy Train, Rabid Rat Fondue, Fuck Yea! Avocado (in the bathroom), Onion Flavored Rings (in store) (Benefit S.P.A.M./October 22nd Coalition)
oct 21 sun Throwdown (L.A.), Martyr A.D., Bleeding Through (L.A.), Everytime I Die (L.A.), Fate 13 (N.Y.)
oct 26 fri Influents, Plus Ones, Divit, Summer Jack (L.A.) Bobot Adrenaline (L.A.), Clarendon Hills (in front of Girl's room)
oct 27 sat Babyland (L.A.), Tsunami Bomb, Scissorhands, Dexter Danger (haunted house)
nov 2 fri Mood Frye, Creammasters Of Disaster (Stockton), Relentless, Bottles And Skulls, Lorax, Sociopath (Local Band Night)
nov 3 sat Cruevo, Nigel Peppercock, Impaled, Systemic Infection, Depressor
nov 9 fri Hoods, Punishment (PA), Necktie Party (WA), Confidant(e)
nov 10 sat Sunday's Best (L.A.), Mock Orange (IN), Elizabeth Elmore, Fighting Jacks, Benton Falls
nov 16 fri Oozzies, Pitch Black, Blottos, Miracle Closure (WA), 2:40 (Al Blottos Birthday)
nov 17 sat Limp Wrist (ex Los Crudos), Carry On (L.A.), All Bets Off, Lab Rats, Thought Riot
nov 18 sun Mad Caddies, Monkey, Fabulous Disaster, Over It (VA)
nov 23 fri Stitches (L.A.), Starvations (L.A.), Neon King Kong (San Diego), Kill Devil Hills (IN), Problem
nov 24 sat Tilt, Missing Link, Cry Baby Cry (D.C.), Miso Militia
nov 30 fri Shit List (WA), Atrocious Madness (Portland), Fuerza X (Guatelmala), Catheter (Denver), Sbitch (TX), Voetsek (next to Girls room), Delta Force (in store) (Rampaging Insane Depravity Fest - day 1)
dec 1 sat Yaphet Kotto, Cattle Decapitation, Creation Is Crucifixion, Kalibas & A Death Between Seasons (N.Y.), Lo-Fi Neisans (Japan)
dec 2 sun Dead And Gone, Venus Bleeding, Subtonix, Geoff Trenchard (spoken word), East Bay Chasers, Lesser Of Two (bEASTfest)
dec 7 fri Har Mar Superstar (MN), The Pattern, Blast Rocks, Your Enemies Friends (L.A.), Hate Mail Express
dec 8 sat Scurvy Dogs, Nigel Peppercock, S.T.F.U., Offering To The Sun (Reno) (Pyrate Discount Nite/Pyratepunx)
dec 9 sun Poison The Well (FL), Unearth (MA), Sworn Enemy, Spark Lights The Friction (N.Y.)
dec 14 fri Hot Water Music (FL), American Steel, F-Minus (L.A.), Trial By Fire (D.C.)
dec 15 sat Strung Out (L.A.), Limp, Frisk, Deadlines (OR), Creeps
dec 16 sun Good Riddance, Missing 23rd, Downway (Canada), Audio Crush
dec 21 fri Amber Asylum, Kepi, Bonfire Madigan, Kevin Seconds, Wendy-O-Matik (spoken word), David Dondero (A Solstice Celebration: Plugged and Unplugged)
dec 22 sat Lab Rats, One Time Angels, A Great Divide (OR), Under A Dying Sun, Gabrie's Ratchet
dec 23 sun Over My Dead Body (S.D.), Panic (MA), Breaker Breaker, Some Still Believe (Redding)
dec 28 fri What Happens Next?, Rambo (PA), Lie (Tokyo), Youth Riot (L.A.), Lugosi
dec 29 sat Defiance (OR), Panty Raid, Before The Fall, The P.A.W.N.S. (Chico), drag show, Gruk

2002
----

jan 4 fri Champion (WA), Stay Gold (WA), First Step (N.C.), Knives Out (PA), Damage Done
jan 5 sat Benumb/Vulgar Pigeons, Iron Lung (Reno), B.G. (AK), Crucial Attack (NV), Elephant Man
jan 11 fri Bananas, Numbers, Low Down, Doozers, Iron Ass
jan 12 sat Plan 9, Sick, Hellbillys, Oppressed Logic, Delta Force
jan 18 fri Christian Reich, Dystrophy, Stalker Potential, Lower 48, Thought Crime, No Direction (local band night)

jan 19 sat Capitalist Casualties, Phobia (Orange County), Pig Destroyer (VA), Index (VA), Kalmex And The Riff Merchants

jan 25 fri Brainoil, Creuvo, Scurvy Dogs, Horafrost

jan 26 sat Mile Marker (N.C.), Yaphet Kotto, Pirx The Pilot, Himsa (WA), Confidante

jan 27 sun Bane (MA), Over My Dead Body (San Diego), Striking Distance (N.J.), Breath In

feb 1 fri American Steel, Pitch Black, Fleshies, Blottos, Sexy (on floor) (924 Gilman's 15th Anniversary Weekend)

feb 2 sat Dead & Gone, Black Cat Music, Cost, Frisk (924 Gilman's 15th Anniversary Weekend)

feb 3 sun 924 Gilman Heritage & Archive Swap - Bring records, Tapes, stickers, flyers, photos, etc. Dubbing equipment & copy machines will be on hand (15th Anniversary Weekend)

feb 8 fri Divit, Scissorhands, Rufio (L.A.), Don't Look Down (N.J.), Fenway Park

feb 9 sat Pansy Division, Subincision, Kepi, Rock And Roll Adventure Kids, Fadeaways (Joel's B-Day show)

feb 10 sun Tragedy (Portland), Tragatelo (Los Angeles), Born/Dead

feb 15 fri One Time Angels, Eleventeen, Audio Crush, Counterfeit (S.D.), Bikini Bumps

feb 16 sat Iron Vegan, Nigel Pepercock, Lost Goat, Iron Lung/Delta Force

feb 22 fri Oppressed Logic, Deface, Eddie Haskells, Lick Golden Sky (PN), Throat Oyster

feb 23 sat From Ashes Rise (OR), Artimus Pyle, Brainoil, Down In Flames (N.J.), Dystrophy, Scholastic Death (in store)

feb 24 sun clean up day

mar 1 fri Street To Nowhere, Calamigo, Sociopath, Somsara, Dead In The End, Mistake (Holland) (new band night)

mar 2 sat Funeral Diner, Confidante, Betray The Species, The Cause, Get Get Go (in the Store), The Shivering (Benefits Animal Rights Direct Action Coalition) (5pm meeting)

mar 8 fri Dead & Gone, Drunk Horse, Cost, Scurvy Dogs, Walkie Talkie

mar 9 sat Flipper (cover band), Sick, Lo-Fi Niesans, Stalker Potential, Deficient

mar 15 fri 90 Day Men (IL), One Line Drawing, Division Day, Reputation (is ex-Sarge singer's band - IL), Sloe

mar 16 sat Gilman short film festival with Nick Zedd's "Ecstasy in Entropy", Green Pubes, A Documentary on The Jocks, WTO riot footage from Seattle

mar 22 fri Lonely Kings, Downway (Canada), Gamits (CO), Silent Film Stars (ex-member, Scissorhands)

mar 23 sat Atom & His Package (PA), Plus Ones (record release), Am/Fm (PA), Contender (Denver)

mar 29 fri Toys That Kill, All You Can Eat, Subtonix, Bananas, Sharp Knife (M.R.R. 20th Anniversary Weekend)

mar 30 sat 9 Shocks Terror (OH), What Happens Next?, Phantom Limbs, Curse (OR), Onion Flavored Rings (M.R.R. 20th Anniversary Weekend)

apr 5 fri Frisk, Tantrums, Last Great Liar (WA), Intrepid A.A.F., I Decline (L.A.)

apr 6 sat All Bets Off, Time In Malta, Animosity, Breathe In, For The Crown

apr 7 sun Art Workshop

apr 12 fri Himsa (WA), Bleeding Through (San Diego), Avenged Sevenfold (San Diego), No Direction, Over The Top

apr 13 sat Lab Rats, Enbrace The End, Damage Done, Allegience, Outbreak

Apr 14 Sun "D.I.Y. or Die: How to Survive as an Independent Artist", a film by Michael Dean, featuring: Ian MacKaye (Fugazi), Lydia Lunch, Mike Watt, j Mascis, Jim Rose, Jim Thirlwell (Foetus), Richard Kern, Ron Asheton (Stooges), Madigan Shive (Bonfire Madigan), Dave Brockie (Gwar), Lynn Breedlove (Tribe 8), Keith Knight, plus 2 shorts: "Love and the Monster" and a short movie about The Gits

apr 19 fri Ludicra, S'bitch (TX), Watch Them Die (ex Grimple & Word Salad), Beware (L.A.), Hate Mail Killerz (Fresno), Crimson Baboon (in store) (Urban Guerrilla Zine)

apr 20 sat Vitamin X (Holland), The Sick, All Bets Off, Sharp Knife (record release), Dead In The End (Benefit Scattered Productions)

apr 21 sun Harum Scarum (Portland), Iowaska (U.K.), What Happens Next, Fleshies, Desobediencia Civil (Mexico D.F.), speakers: ASAP (Local RAWA Solidarity Group), Jello Biafra, S.F./Bay Indymedia, Heads Up (Anti-War Collective) (Benefit Women of Afghanistan and SF/Bay Indymedia Center)

apr 26 fri Lawrence Arms (IL), Short Round, Before The Fall, Street To Nowhere

apr 27 sat Pitch Black (record release), Fall Silent (NV - record release), Cause (San Diego), 86'ers (OR), As Is (L.A.)

may 3 fri Hail Marys, Pre-Teens, Tenth Of Always, Caesura, Somsara (Benefit LadyFest S.F.)

may 4 sat Born Dead Icons (Canada), Reagan SS (L.A.), Kontraklasse (L.A.), S.M.D. (L.A.), Voetsek, "New World Border" a film by Jose Palafox

may 10 fri film "Beyond the Mat", "Heavy Metal" (animated), and a short film (movie night)

may 11 sat Four Minute Mile, All About Evil, Dismembers, One's Own Ruin, Eskapo, No Way Out (new band nite)

may 17 fri Bananas, This Bike Is A Pipe Bomb (FL), Shotwell, The Devil Is Electric (FL), Once A Hero (MI), This Is My Fist (in store)

may 18 sat American Steel (last show), The Cost, Red Light Sting (Canada), Moneen (Canada)

may 19 sun Walken, Light The Fuse And Run (VA), Kill The Messenger, Dead In The End

may 24 fri Time In Malta, Thought Crime, Prop 808, Arno Corp, Calamigo (Benefit Sparring Club)

may 25 sat Distillers (L.A.), Fracas, Dory Tourette And The Skirtheads, Creeps, Clarendon Hills

may 31 fri Drowning Man (VT), Time In Malta, Holier Than Thou (L.A.), Crucial Unit (PA), Eiffel (CO)

jun 1 sat Tragedy (Portland), Amdi Petersens Arme (Denmark), Reeds (Israel), Artimus Pyle, Brainoil, Scholastic Death (in store)

jun 7 fri Lab Rats, Scissorhands, Thought Riot, Damage Done

jun 8 sat Blast Rocks, Jason Wembley (WA), Phenomenauts, Kingdom (OR), Lawrence Livermore's Extreme Discomfort (Punk Prom)

jun 14 fri Hellbillys, Narcoleptic Youth (L.A.), Memento Mori (OH), Dead By Dawn (OR), October Allied

jun 15 sat Kill Your Idols (N.Y.), Toxic Narcotic (Boston), Breathe In, Profits (MA), Diehard Youth

jun 16 sun Demented Are Go (U.K.), Hellbillys, Suicide Doors (S.B.)

jun 21 fri Submission Hold (Canada), Anti-Product (PA), Kung Fu Rick (IL), 7 Days Of Samsara (WI), Off Minor (N.Y.), Life Detecting Coffins (N.Y.)

jun 22 sat Ghost (IL), Velvet Teens, Operation Makeout (Canada), Exit (N.Y.), Frentics (Canada)

jun 28 fri Unholy Grave (Japan), Phobia (L.A.), Catheter (CO), Balance Of Terror (N.Y.), Unpersons (GA)

jun 29 sat Page 99 (VA), Epeleptic Terror Attack (Sweden), Majority Rule (VA), Che Chapter 127 (Canada), Def Choice (IL)

jun 30 sun Bleeding Through (L.A.), Every Time I Die (N.Y.), Norma-Jean (N.Y.), Embrace The End

jul 5 fri Plan 9, Lo Fi Neisans, Depressor, Affront (D.C.), Broken Society (Sacramento)

jul 6 sat Comin' Correct (N.Y.), All Bets Off, Final Plan, My Luck, Damage Done

jul 12 fri Funeral Diner, Miracle Closure (L.A.), Strategies For A Hangman (San Diego), Brute Medium (San Diego), Armed With Intelligence (N.Y.), Young Ones (N.Y.)

jul 13 sat Dead And Gone, From Monument To Masses, Charm City Suicides (MD), Science Of Yabra (OR), Gabriel's Ratchet

jul 19 fri Pitch Black (record release), Tear It Up (N.J.), Down In Flames (N.J.), Against Me (FL), Flya (FL), Fusty Lugs (AZ)

jul 20 sat Sick, All Bets Off, S.T.F.U., Enemies Front, Gigantic (Warner Harrison Memorial Show)

jul 21 sun Fartz, Resist And Exist, Elder Wrath (OR), Songs For Emma, John The Baker (Green Anarchy Tour)

jul 26 fri Scurvy Dogs, Midnight (OR), Awakening (OR), Dismembers, Laudanum

jul 27 sat Cathether (CO), Municipal Waste (VA), Holier Than Thou (L.A.), Hate Mail Killers, Voetsek

aug 2 fri Insurgent (N.Y.), Pirx The Pilot, Deconditioned (WA), Blast For Me (OR), Deadfall

aug 3 sat Enemies (cd release), Divit, Fleshies, Blottos (last show), Maneurysm (WI)

aug 4 sun Locust, Lightning Bolt (R.I.), Arab On Radar, Hella (Sacramento)

aug 9 fri Explosion (MA), Damn Personals (Boston), Modern Machines (Milwaukee), Somsara, High Wire Daze (Santa Cruz)

aug 10 sat Dillinger Four (MA), Lawrence Arms (IL), Toys That Kill (San Diego), Arrivals (IL), Attack (Canada)

aug 11 sun Yaphet Kotto, Calvary (Chicago), Omega Cinco (Spain), Shivering, Funeral Diner

aug 16 fri Champion (WA), Stay Gold (WA), Terror (L.A.), Circle Takes The Square (GA), Allegiance

aug 17 sat Benumb (Redwood City), Reagan SS (L.A.), Bombklaas (Mexico), Faces Of Death (In Stoar), Black Market Fetus (L.A.), Skarp (Seattle) (Rampaging Insane Depravity Fest)

aug 18 sun Time In Malta, Dream Is Dead (L.A.), Find Him & Kill Him (San Diego), Cause (San Diego), Time For Living

aug 23 fri For The Crown, Beneath The Ashes, Pains Of Sleep, End Of All, Over The Top

aug 24 sat Phantom Limbs, Dead And Gone, Pitch Black, Fire Fighting For Christ (L.A.), Sticks & Stones (TN)

aug 25 sun Women's Group Meeting

aug 30 fri Lab Rats, Damage Done, First Step (D.C./N.C.), Diehard Youth (L.A.), Impact (L.A.), Some Still Believe

aug 31 sat Plan 9, S.T.F.U., Hit Me Back (L.A.), Dystrophy, Monster Squad

sep 6 fri Gehenna (L.A.), Brainoil, Blown To Bits, Witch Hunt (N.J.), Voetsek

sep 7 sat Hirax (L.A.), Phobia (L.A.), Lack Of Interest (L.A.), Structure Of Lies (AZ), Walken

sep 8 sun Women's Group Meeting

sep 8 sun movie night

sep 13 fri From Ashes Rise (OR), Manifesto Jukebox (Finland), Submachine (PA), This Is My Fist

sep 14 sat Denali (VA), Velvet Teen, Kenji (L.A.), Broken October

sep 20 fri New End Original, Counterfeit (San Diego), Lo Lite (Holland), Attention (AZ)

sep 21 sat Rock 'n' Roll Adventure Kids (12" record release), Jason Webley (WA), Phenomenauts (8 track release), Sidekicks, Triple Niple (dance nite)

sep 22 sun Women's Group Meeting

sep 27 fri Fairweather (VA), Liars Academy (MD), Open Hand (L.A.), Caesura, Code Seven (N.C.)

sep 28 sat From Monument To Masses, Victory At Sea (N.Y.), The Cost, Stalker Potential, Contracepticons

oct 4 fri Hellbillys, Von Steins (L.A.), The Fuse (L.A.), Tread Asphalt Trio (Stitches and Radio Vago cancelled)

oct 5 sat All Bets Off, Benumb, Uphill Battle (San Diego), Animosity, First Blood (WA)

oct 6 sun Yaphet Kotto, Lesser Of Two, Desmade Enorisis, Fleshies (opening) (Benefit for the October 22nd Coalition against Police Brutality)

oct 11 fri Exit Wound, S.T.F.U., Lana Dagales, Elephant Man, Deadfall

oct 12 sat Ludicra, Watch Them Die, Teen Cthulhu (WA), Carol Ann (AZ), All Shall Perish

oct 13 sun film nite

oct 18 fri Influents, Flipsides, Fighting Jacks, Mercy Mile (Redding), Americas (Chico)

oct 19 sat For The Crown, Scissorhands, Ten Grand (IL), Life Long Tragedy, Creeps (Santa Cruz)

oct 25 fri Ladies Art Revival Film Fest: Bonfire Madigan, "I was a Teenage Serial Killer" a film by Sara Jacobson, "She's Real: Worse than Queer" a film by Lucy Thame, "How the Miracle of Masturbation Saved Me from Becoming a Teenage Zombie" a film by Dulcie Clarhson, Hello Guerrilla

oct 26 sat Iron Vegan, Hail Satan, Lord Weird Sloughfeg, Brutalica, Hacksaw To The Throat ($1 off if in non-punk costume)

oct 27 sun Plan 9, Dead Poetic (OH), Man Alive (Israel), Dismembers

nov 1 fri Diehard Youth (L.A.), My Luck (OH), Blue Monday (Canada), Miracle Mile (L.A.), Treason

nov 2 sat Dystopia, Ludicra, Brainoil, Anubis Rising (L.A.)

nov 3 sun Epoxies (OR), Phenomenauts, Triggers (OR), This Bike Is A Pipe Bomb (FL)

nov 8 fri Capitalist Casualties, Futures (Osaka, Japan), Out Cold (MA), Born/Dead, Stivs (OR)

nov 9 sat Benumb, Abigail (Japan), Blown To Bits, Bullet Train Mafia (N.M.), Morbosidad

nov 15 fri Subincision (cd release), Fracas, Last Great Liar (WA), Eskapo, Contracepticons

nov 16 sat Thought Riot, Scattered Fall, Never Again, Outbreak

nov 17 sun movie night

nov 22 fri Pretty Girls Make Graves (WA), J.R. Ewing (Norway), Hint Hint (WA)

nov 23 sat Embrace The End, Damage Done (record release), Scissorhands, For The Crown, Allegiance nov 29 fri Sharp Knife, Trial By Fire (D.C.), City Of Caterpillar (VA), Before The Fall, Stalker Potential

nov 30 fri In Control (L.A.), All Bets Off, Terror (L.A.), Animosity, First Blood

dec 1 sun swapmeet & heritage exchange

dec 6 fri Exit Wound, Reagan S.S. (L.A.), Desolation, video WHN? - Life's Halt Tour Documentary, John The Baker (Documentary), Chronicles Of Lemur Mutation (Claymation by Greg Brainoil) (punk movie night)

dec 7 sat Lab Rats, Enemies, Dismembers (last show), Sexy, Duckbutters (Benefit S.P.A.M. Records) (5pm membership meeting)

dec 8 sun Bleeding Through (L.A.), Champion (WA), Embrace Today (N.J.), Jim Jones Brigade

dec 14 sat Tragedy (OR), Born/Dead, This Is My Fist, Dead Fall, Allergic To Bullshit (Benefit M.R.R. Radio)

dec 15 sun Counterfeit, Stereotype Rider (AZ), Benton Falls, Time Spent Driving

dec 20 fri Bananas, This Bike Is A Pipe Bomb (FL), Clarendon Hills, Feldmans

dec 21 sat Exhumed, Nunslaughter (OH), Capitalist Casualties, Noctuary (L.A.), All Shall Perish

dec 27 fri Yaphet Kotto, Off Minor (N.Y.), Confidante, The Bunny (Davis), Heart Cross Love (Benefit DIY Skillshare)

dec 28 sat Blown To Bits, Akimbo (WA), Fracas, Hellshock (OR) (Benefit People Under No King Zine)

dec 29 sun movie night "Hong Kong Sundays #1" two films in Cantonese with English subtitles

2003
----

jan 3 fri Tear It Up (N.J.), Brutal Fight (WA), Last Days Of Torment (U.K.), Time For Living, Treason

jan 4 sat Striking Distance (D.C.), Diehard Youth (L.A.), Damage Done, Desperate Measures (D.C.), Far From Breaking (TX)

jan 5 sun For The Crown, Modern Life Is War (Iowa), Rosary (WA), Allegiance

jan 10 fri Holding On (MN), In Control (L.A.), Scott Baio's Army (CO), Five Day Messiah (CO), Self Defense (CT)

jan 11 sat Lost Film Fest (with Scott Beibin), films: "Hot and Bothered: Feminist Pornography" (with Becky Goldberg), "Straight Outta Hunters Point" (with Kevin Epps)

jan 11 sat All Or Nothing (L.A.), Love Songs, Copy & Destroy zine tour with Urban Hermitt, Alex Wierk, Joe Biel

jan 12 sun clean up day

jan 17 fri Under A Dying Sun, Librarians, A Light In The Attic, Pteradactyl, Second Opinion

jan 18 sat Pains Of Sleep, Animosity, Embrace The End, All Shall Perish, Clearing Autumn Skies, Something Must Die (Local Hardcore Night)

jan 24 fri Tribe 8, Gravy Train, Drag Dancers, Vega Lee's Apocalipstick, Confidante (What A Drag! Show)

jan 25 sat Groovie Ghoulies, Subincision, Man Planet, Maurice's Little Bastards (WA), This Is My Fist!, Spring Break (Joel's B-Day)

jan 26 sun Mirah (WA), film "Stand Up & Be Vocal": interviews with Queer Punks, Flim Feminist, Bonfire Madigan, Haggard (L.A.), Kingdom

jan 31 fri Kung Fu Rick (IL), Breakfast (Japan), Crucial Unit (PA), Guyana Punchline (S.C.), Lack Of Interest (L.A.), Artimus Pyle (Super Sabado Gigante Fest)

feb 1 sat Shank (Glasgow), Municipal Waste (VA), Kylesa (GA), Holier Than Thou, Reagan SS (L.A.), Burn Your Bridges (L.A.) (Super Sabado Gigante Fest)

feb 7 fri Funeral Diner, Betray The Species, Beneath The Ashes, Confidante

feb 8 sat Babyland (L.A.), Brainoil, Midnight Laser Beam, Follow The Bastards (OR), Beehive Collective, Vanishing

feb 9 sun Hong Kong Sunday #2

feb 14 fri From Ashes Rise (OR), Born/Dead, Call The Police (OR), Bacteria (OR), Democracy Is A Lynch Mob

feb 15 sat Thought Riot, Staring Back (Goleta), Agent 51, Choke (Canada), Don Cikuto (Spain)

feb 21 fri Phenomenauts, Rock N' Roll Adventure Kids, Teenage Harlots, 8 Track Mind, Tronn (Benefit Berkeley Liberation Radio 94.1FM)

feb 22 sat All Bets Off, Scissorhands, For The Crown, Walken, Time For Living (Benefit Nick Traina Foundation)

feb 28 fri Phantom Limbs, Offering To The Sun, Neptune (MA), Experimental Dental School, Swann Danger

mar 1 sat Divit, Plus Ones, Elevenleen, Lonely Kings, Unfinished Symphony

mar 2 sun Mile Marker (N.C.), From Monument To Masses, Cost, Kerbloki (N.C.), Vaux (CO)

mar 7 fri Ted Leo & The Pharmacists (N.J.), Pattern, Fourth Rotor (IL), This Is My Fist!

mar 8 sat Damage Done, First Blood, Diehard Youth (L.A.), Comeback Kid (Canada), Time For Living, Love Songs

mar 14 fri Atom And His Package (PA), Dominatrix (Brazil), Sixty Stories (Canada), Haggard (L.A.), Sky Flakes

mar 15 sat Fleshies, Sharp Knife, Rock N Roll Adventure Kids, Panty Raid, Jewdriver (Benefit Fleshies tour)

mar 16 sun Hong Kong Sunday #3 movie night, a Chow Yun Fat Film

mar 21 fri Alliegance, To See You Broken (Seattle), Life Long Tragedy, Stars Are Falling (Sacramento)

mar 22 sat Influents, Reputation (IL), Insurgent (N.Y.), Escape Engine, Perfect Hate Letter

mar 23 sun Pretty Girls Make Graves (WA), Hint Hint (WA), Cobra High (WA), Scheme

mar 28 fri Weak Leads, Crop Knox, Kung Fu Chicken, Draw Blank, Beneath My Dreams, Social Drones (local band night)

mar 29 sat Toys That Kill (San Diego), Arrivals (IL), Hang On The Box (Beijing), Clarendon Hills, La Plebe

apr 4 fri Feederz, Born/Dead, Brainoil, Scurvy Dogs, Funeral Shock (UGZ B-day)

apr 5 sat Funeral Diner, Deconditioned (WA), An Arrow In Flight (San Diego), End On End (L.A.), Takaru

apr 6 sun art show

apr 11 fri Bananas, This Is My Fist!, Operation Make Out (Canada), Pirx The Pilot, Abi Yo Yo's, Hit Me Back

apr 12 sat Contracepticons, Scissorhands, Stalker Potenitial, Megan March, Gally 99 vs. Teen Girl Squad (Gilman workers show)

apr 13 sun Butchies (N.C.), Cost, Gynopunks (a film), Free Verse (WA)

apr 18 fri Groovie Ghoulies, Apers (Holland), Librarians, Mallrats, Mind (OR)

apr 19 sat Plan-9, Lo Fi Neisans, Punk Rock Orchestra, Find Him And Kill Him (San Diego), Doppleganger

apr 25 fri Holy Molar (San Diego), Ex-Models (N.Y.), What Life Makes Us, Cold Shoulder (L.A.), City To City
apr 26 sat Xiu Xiu, El Guapo (D.C.), Paper Chase (TX), Yellow Press, Cartographer (Ben from Replicator)
apr 27 sun Allegiance, Embrace Today (MA), Blue Monday (Canada), Lightsout
may 2 fri For The Crown, Playing Enemy (WA), For All It's Worth, Xwhere The MarkX, Blessing The Hogs
may 3 sat S.T.F.U., Born/Dead, Dead Fall, Dead By Dawn (OR), Stockholm Syndrome, Abandon (Benefit
         Born/Dead tour)
may 9 fri Small Brown Bike (MI), Pitch Black, Choke (Canada), Scattered Fall, Charlevoix (MI)
may 10 sat Against Me (FL), Pansy Division, Fifth Hour Hero (Canada), Jason Webley (WA), Panty Raid (Punk Prom)
may 16 fri Ludicra, Insidious, Vanishing, Skarp (WA), Desolation
may 17 sat Lungfish (D.C.), Yaphet Kotto, Shivering, Enablers, Once A Hero (MI)
may 23 fri Thought Riot, Scissorhands, Stalker Potential, D.O.R.K. (CO), Beneath My Dreams
may 24 sat Planes Mistaken For Stars (CO), Lo-Fi Neisans, Black Eyes (D.C.), Love Me Destroyer (CO), Mach
         Tiver (Canada)
may 30 fri Monster Squad, Whiskey Sunday, La Plebe', Sainte Catherines (Canada), 30 Years War (Benefit Punk
         Priest, S.F.)
may 31 sat Influents, This Is My Fist!, Clarendon Hills, Specs, Hit Self Destruct (Benefit for Prisoners Literature Project)
jun 6 fri Himsa (WA), Beneath The Ashes, Answer (WA), With Passion, Harms
jun 7 sat Hellbillys, Iron Lung (NV), Profits (MA), Facedowninshit (OR), Case Of Emergency
jun 13 fri Inspect Her Gadget, Spag, Second Opinion, Solamente, Resilience, Peels (Local Band Night)
jun 14 sat Phenomenauts, D.S.B. (Japan), Assault (Japan), From Ashes Rise (OR), Black Lung Patriots (TX)
jun 20 fri Virus 9 (OR), Enemies, Frisk, Endless Struggle (TX), Contracepticons
jun 21 sat Under A Dying Sun, Light The Fuse And Run (VA), Transistor Transistor (N.H.), November Group (WA),
         Angry For Life
jun 27 fri Missing 23rd, Breathe In, Members Of The Yellow Press (WI), Clampdown (WI), Filthy Vagrants (L.A.)
jun 28 sat Babyland (L.A.), Replicator, Brillant Red Lights, 8-Bit (L.A.)
jul 4 fri S.T.F.U., Crucial Unit (PA), Dead Fall, Death From Above (Canada), Strung Up
jul 5 sat Cost (last show), From Monument To Masses, Red Light Sting (Canada), 1905 (D.C.), Cinema Eye (Canada)
jul 11 fri Shotwell, Grabass Charlestons (FL), Billy Reese Peters (FL), Tiltwheel (San Diego), Before The Fall
jul 12 sat Subincision, Link (Japan), Effection, Mona Reels (WA), Librarians
jul 18 fri Majority Rule (VA), Del Cielo (MD), Dear Diary I Seem To Be Dead, Promis, Takaru
jul 19 sat Born/Dead, Conga Fury (Japan), Chainsaw (Japan), Voetsek, Case Of Emergency, Doppelganger
jul 25 fri What Happens Next?, Cut The Shit (MA), Artimus Pyle, Rites (MA), Funeral Shock
jul 26 sat Scorpion Death Rock (Japan), Clarendon Hills, Latterman (N.Y.), Speakeasy (MA), Weak Leads
aug 1 fri Beneath the Ashes, To See You Broken (WA), Enemies, Diskords (OR), Secret Janet
aug 2 sat Plan 9, Penis Flytrap, Proud Flesh, Free Verse (WA), Pox
aug 3 sun For The Crown, In Control (Oxnard), Modern Life Is War (L.A.), Dragnet
aug 8 fri Locust (San Diego), Erase Errata, Hella, Rah Brahs, My Name Is Rar Rar (IL)
aug 9 sat Strike Anywhere (VA), From Ashes Rise (OR), They Live (N.Y.), Robot Has Werewolf Hand (N.Y.),
         Disaster (N.Y.), Stalker Potential
aug 15 fri Ludicra, Brainoil, Wormwood (WA), Fall Of The Bastards (OR), In The Wake Of The Plague
aug 16 sat Annihilation Time (L.A.), Iron Lung (NV), Gatecrashers (N.J.), Out Of Vogue (L.A.), Takaru
aug 17 sun Desperate Measures (D.C.), Lights Out, With Or Without You, These Days
aug 22 fri Cast Of Thousands, Short Round, Mud, Our Turn, Jenny Choi
aug 23 sat Thought Riot, Scattered Fall, Love Songs, Kadena (N.Y.), Eskapo
aug 29 fri Allegiance, Answer (Canada), Cross The Line, Physical Challenge, Lahar
aug 30 sat Pitch Black, Scurvy Dogs, Deadfall, Desolation, Look Back And Laugh
sep 5 fri Phenomenauts, La Plebe, Third Grade Teacher (L.A.), Them Apples, Here Kitty Kitty
sep 6 sat Benumb, Blown To Bits, All Shall Perish, Doppelganger, Brutal Death, A Sleeping Irony (Benefit
         Destructive Youth)
sep 12 fri Tommy Lasorda, Before The Fall, Peels, Sleepover
sep 13 sat John Brady's Illegitimate Children, Midnightmare, Giant Haystacks, S.C.A., Consign (local band night)
sep 19 fri Municipal Waste (VA), Capitalist Casualties, Caustic Christ (PA), Voetsek, Agents Of Satan, Strung Up
sep 20 sat Influents, Clarendon Hills, Enemies, Eskaped (OR), Rabid Rad Fondue
sep 26 fri Phantom Limbs, 400 Blows (L.A.), Scurvy Bastards, Nakatomi Plaza (N.Y.), Marathon (N.Y.)
sep 27 sat Over My Dead Body (San Diego), In Control (Oxnard), Control (N.Y.), Stand Up And Fight (L.A.), Our Turn
sep 28 sun tape/heritage exchange
oct 3 fri Fleshies, Toys That Kill (San Pedro), Killer Dream (San Pedro), Swing Ding Amigos, Civil Dysentery,
         Tommy Lasoda, Little Army
oct 4 sat Champion (Seattle), For The Crown (last show), Damage Done (last show), Allegiance, Lights Out
oct 5 sun Structure Of Lies, Brutal Death, All Shall Perish, Hacksaw To The Throat
oct 10 fri Dwarves, Frisk, This Is My Fist!, Scattered Fall
oct 11 sat Hammers Of Misfortune, Bread And Water (TX), Garuda, Abandon, A Sleeping Irony
oct 17 fri All Bets Off, Powerhouse, Life Long Tragedy, Love Hope And Fear
oct 18 sat Cripple Bastards (Italy), Phobia (L.A.), La Fraction (France), Born Dead Icons (Canada), Depressor
oct 24 fri Lovemakers, Boyskout, Ned
oct 25 sat Yaphet Kotto, Lick Golden Sky (PA), Hot Cross (N.Y.), Anodyne (N.Y.), 30 Years War
oct 31 fri Babyland (L.A.), Plan 9, John The Baker And The Malnourished, Ashtray
nov 1 sat Deadfall, Brain Failure (China), Hang On The Box (China), Love Songs, Systema Brutale
nov 7 fri Time For Living, Physical Challenge (OR), Tarkaru, Wear The Mark
nov 8 sat Thought Riot, F-Minus (L.A.), Afront (D.C.), Go It Alone (Canada)

nov 14 fri Fabulous Disaster, Pin Up Motel, Butcher & Smear, Whore U (Benefit Femina Potens Artist Co-Op)
nov 15 sat Bananas, I Farm (N.Y.), Stivs (OR), Mermaid-Unicorn, Problem
nov 21 fri Holier Than Thou, Voetsek, Knife Fight, Strung Up, Covered In Scars, Rabid
nov 22 sat Mike Park, Clarendon Hills, Pete The Genius, Skyflakes, Charmin (food drive Benefit for N. Korean Famine Relief)
nov 28 fri S.T.F.U., Lewd, Words That Burn (WI), Cropknox, Eskapo
nov 29 sat Embrace The End, Animosity, 30 Year War, Romance Of Crime, Killing The Dream
nov 30 sun Oranges Band (MD), Scissorhands
dec 5 fri Grand Unified Theory, Forget The Joneses, Apples, Static Thought, Underminded
dec 6 sat Yaphet Kotto, Burmese, The Yellow Press, Bottled O.G. (Matt Davis Memorial Benefit)
dec 7 sun Total Fury (Japan), Find Him And Kill Him (San Diego), Deadfall, Our Turn, Cross The Line
dec 12 fri Toys That Kill (L.A.), From Ashes Rise, Frisk, Love Songs
dec 13 sat Phantom Limbs, Nigel Peppercock, Annihilation Time, Funeral Shock, Case Of Emergency (Benefit P.U.N.K. Zine)
dec 19 fri Brainoil, Street Trash (L.A.), Bury The Living (TN), Slit Wrists (L.A.), Friday Night Youth Service (WA)
dec 20 sat Plan 9, Ashtray, Tabaltix, Live Ammo, Brutal Death (Benefit Plan 9)
dec 27 sat Phenomenauts, Soviettes (MN), Stellas (OK), (No) Apologies Project (L.A.), Skyflakes

Photo this page by Lauren L., photo next page by Emilie V.